Outlook® 2003 Bible

Outlook® 2003 Bible

Rob Tidrow, et al.

WILEY

Wiley Publishing, Inc.

Outlook® 2003 Bible

Published by
Wiley Publishing, Inc.
10475 Crosspoint Boulevard
Indianapolis, IN 46256
www.wiley.com

Copyright © 2004 by Wiley Publishing, Inc., Indianapolis, Indiana

Published by Wiley Publishing, Inc., Indianapolis, Indiana

Published simultaneously in Canada

ISBN: 0-7645-3973-6

Manufactured in the United States of America

10 9 8 7 6 5 4 3 2

1O/QY/RQ/QT/IN

For general information on our other products and services or to obtain technical support, please contact our Customer Care Department within the U.S. at (800) 762-2974, outside the U.S. at (317) 572-3993 or fax (317) 572-4002.

Wiley also publishes its books in a variety of electronic formats. Some content that appears in print may not be available in electronic books.

Library of Congress Cataloging-in-Publication Data: 2003101886

WILEY is a trademark of Wiley Publishing, Inc.

This book is dedicated to my wonderful wife, Tammy, and my two fantastic sons, Adam and Wesley. Thank you for your patience and understanding. Let's go to the beach!

Rob Tidrow

Preface

Welcome to Microsoft Outlook 2003 Bible — your complete guide to Outlook 2003! Microsoft Outlook is a great multipurpose program that has many useful features. Despite this fact, Outlook often suffers from an image problem. Most people know that it handles e-mail messages, but that's for the only way they use it. Outlook has so much more to offer.

By taking an in-depth look at Outlook 2003, this book is intended to open many doors for you. What you'll find may surprise you, because Outlook handles so many tasks other than e-mail. After you learn what you can do with the program, you'll wonder why it took you so long to start doing things the easy and efficient way.

Although the book begins with basic functions and simple tasks, you'll find that the book gradually teaches higher-level tasks at a comfortable pace. After you reach the later sections of the book, you'll find yourself designing complex workgroup solutions. However, don't feel you have to read this book from cover to cover to gain from its content. Perhaps you are only interested in learning certain aspects of Outlook 2003. That's okay; each chapter stands on its own.

To drive home the point and help you understand the methodologies behind the tasks, this book provides you with in-depth examples of how Outlook 2003 solves problems. The examples demonstrate the same methodologies utilized in the real world, and can easily be adapted to suit your specific needs. As a result, you learn to identify areas in your day-to-day business that Outlook 2003 can help simplify.

Is This Book for You?

Because Microsoft Outlook 2003 Bible covers virtually every aspect of Outlook 2003, this book is intended to help beginning, intermediate, and advanced users. If you're an advanced user interested in developing custom applications using Outlook 2003, you will mostly be interested in the later sections of the book. Even if you're an experienced Outlook 2003 user, however, you may want to start at the beginning of the book because there are many new features in Outlook 2003 that did not exist in previous versions.

So, is this book for you?

Yes, if you don't know how to use e-mail

If your company just implemented an e-mail system, or if you want to send e-mail over the Internet from your home computer, this book provides you everything you need to know to get up and running. After you've mastered the e-mail, you'll be geared up to learn other Outlook 2003 features that can help you work more efficiently.

Yes, if you know how to use Outlook but don't feel you're using it to its full potential

Although it's easy to use after you know what you're doing, Outlook 2003 is a complex application. Most Outlook users only utilize a small portion of the capabilities this program has to offer. This book provides real-world examples of how Outlook 2003 can be applied to your day-to-day activities to enable you to work more efficiently. After you understand the intent behind the functionality, you can use Outlook to its fullest potential.

Yes, if you want to develop custom applications using VBScript, Outlook forms, COM add-ins, and Web integration

Custom Outlook forms and VBScript have traditionally been the foundation for custom application development within Microsoft Outlook; however, Outlook 2003 has expanded custom application development to include COM add-ins, Web integration, and collaboration within other Office 2000 applications. The details behind the extended capabilities of Outlook 2003 custom application development are explained in Parts V and VI.

What You'll Find in This Book

Part I, Getting Started with Microsoft Outlook 2003, provides you with an in-depth look at the features of Outlook. You learn about each of the major areas of the program, what's new in the latest versions, and how to install and configure Outlook so that it works the best for your needs.

Part II, Mastering E-mail, takes you from the basics of e-mail into both intermediate and advanced topics. You learn how to create, send, and receive e-mail messages, including messages that have attachments. You see how to make your e-mail messages stand out, and how to have Outlook automatically process certain messages for you. You learn how to create and use distribution lists so that e-mailing a group is just as easy as e-mailing one person.

Part III, Information Manager, teaches you about Outlook's little known but extremely useful features. You learn about contact management, scheduling, to-do lists, document activity tracking, and electronic sticky notes. You also learn how you can use the Outlook Newsreader to access tens of thousands of Internet newsgroups so you can view a vast array of information that you won't find anywhere else.

Part IV, Getting the Most out of Outlook 2003, shows you how to customize Outlook so that it works for you the way you want it to. These chapters also show you how to share Outlook information with other people and how to use Outlook with other programs.

Part V, Managing Outlook Users, helps you manage Outlook for multiple users, with a focus on Exchange Server. This part covers roaming users, provides virus protection and spam filtering, implements change control with group policy, and provides security and backup for Outlook data.

Part VI, Basics of Microsoft Outlook 2003, is the first of two parts focused on developing custom applications using Outlook 2003 and its related technologies. After getting a general overview of the different types of applications you can create with Outlook, you learn the elements of a simple Outlook form and how to create one. You also learn the specifics behind each of the various form controls and how to use them, and know what custom fields are and when they are appropriate.

Part VII, Advanced Messaging Development, covers advanced application development tasks within Outlook 2003 and its related technologies. These chapters describe how to incorporate Exchange folders into your applications effectively, provide an introduction to collaborative messaging, and introduce the Outlook 2003 Object Model. You also learn how to incorporate COM add-ins into Outlook 2003, what Collaborative Data Objects and Exchange Routing Objects are, and when they are appropriate to use.

Part VIII, Advanced Outlook Administration, covers ways in which the business user or system administrator can benefit from Outlook's extended features, including the Microsoft Outlook Business Manager and Outlook Web Access feature. With the Outlook Business Manager, for example, readers learn how to manage business-related contact information and track sales opportunities. This part also covers ways in which advanced users or system administrators can optimize the Outlook installations.

The Appendix at the end of the book describes the contents of the CD-ROM and how to use it.

Conventions Used in This Book

Microsoft Outlook 2003 Bible is designed to be easy to use and informative, so several conventions are used to help you understand what you're reading. For example, when you need to make a series of selections from a menu, the commands appear like this:

File ➪ Open

This tells you that you need to open the File menu and then choose the Open option from that menu.

When you need to type something exactly as shown in the text, the text that you should enter is presented in bold. Here's an example:

Type these exact words

Several icons are also placed in the margins to alert you to special information. These icons include the following:

 Notes highlight something of particular interest about the current topic or expand on the subject at hand.

 These icons clue you in to hot tips, or show you faster, better ways of doing things.

 If a process holds some risk of losing data, irrevocably altering a document, or annoying the heck out of you, this icon will warn you about it.

 This icon points you to another section of the book where additional information on the current topic can be found.

The entire Microsoft Outlook 2003 Bible team hopes you enjoy this book. We feel it's your best source of up-to-date information about Microsoft Outlook.

Acknowledgments

A project as large as Microsoft Outlook 2003 Bible is the result of much hard work by many different people. We'd like to thank everyone personally, but that's just not possible because so many people contributed in one way or another. Here are some of the people who helped make this book possible:

Sharon Nash, our development editor, was instrumental in helping us produce a quality piece of work we can all be proud of. Her expertise helped kick it up a notch and add those finishing touches that made all the difference. Excellent work!

Without Julia Kelly and William Lefkovics' technical expertise, readers would not be able to obtain the superior level of understanding they can expect. Great job!

We also want to thank Susan Hobbs, our copy editor, whose efforts helped improve our writing and contributed to the overall quality of the book.

Finally, without the coordination and logistical efforts of Sharon Cox, our acquisitions editor, we would have been lost. Andy was also great source for good advice. Thanks a lot!

Contents at a Glance

Preface ix
Acknowledgments xiii

Part I: Getting Started with Microsoft Outlook 2003 1
Chapter 1: Outlook 2003 in a Nutshell 3
Chapter 2: Installing Outlook 2003 23
Chatper 3: A Guided Tour of Outlook 2003 57
Chapter 4: Configuring Outlook 2003 85

Part II: Mastering E-mail 113
Chapter 5: E-mail Basics 115
Chapter 6: Message Options and Attachments 131
Chapter 7: Advanced E-mail Concepts 159
Chapter 8: Processing Messages Automatically 173

Part III: Information Manager 191
Chapter 9: Managing Your Contacts 193
Chapter 10: Managing Your Calendar 223
Chapter 11: Scheduling Your Time 249
Chapter 12: Tracking Tasks 265
Chapter 13: Keeping Your Journal 285
Chapter 14: Taking Notes 301
Chapter 15: Organizing Information with Categories 317
Chapter 16: Using Outlook Newsreader 333

Part IV: Getting the Most Out of Outlook 2003 355
Chapter 17: Customizing Outlook 2003 357
Chapter 18: Using Folders Effectively 385
Chapter 19: Integrating with Other Applications 407
Chapter 20: Delegating Tasks to an Assistant 427
Chapter 21: Using Windows SharePoint Services 439

Part V: Managing Outlook Users 463

Chapter 22: Supporting Roaming Users 465
Chapter 23: Managing Security and Performance 487
Chapter 24: Controlling Outlook (and Office) with Group and System Policies . . . 501
Chapter 25: Backing Up and Recovering User Data 515
Chapter 26: Managing Exchange Server for Outlook Users 533

Part VI: Basics of Microsoft Outlook 2003 559

Chapter 27: Outlook 2003 Application Types 561
Chapter 28: Creating a Simple Outlook Form 579
Chapter 29: Controls in Outlook Forms 591
Chapter 30: Utilizing Custom Fields 609
Chapter 31: Adding Functionality to Outlook Forms 621

Part VII: Advanced Messaging Development 635

Chapter 32: Working with Application Folders 637
Chapter 33: Collaborative Messaging Basics 655
Chapter 34: Using the Outlook 2003 Object Model 665

Part VIII: Advanced Outlook Administration 675

Chapter 35: Using Business Contact Manager 677
Chapter 36: Using Outlook Web Access 703
Chapter 37: Optimizing Outlook Installations 723

Appendix: What's on the CD-ROM 737

Index 745
End-User License Agreement 785

Contents

Preface ix

Acknowledgments xiii

Part I: Getting Started with Microsoft Outlook 2003   1

Chapter 1: Outlook 2003 in a Nutshell 3
Easy Messaging 3
    What is messaging? 4
    Integrating with forms 4
Increased Productivity 5
    Sharing information 6
    Getting organized 7
    Integrating with other applications 11
Collaboration 12
    What is a collaborative solution? 12
    Business solutions 14
Outlook Development Capabilities 15
What's New in Outlook 2003? 17
    Search folders 17
    Navigation Pane 19
    Reading Pane 19
    Quick flagging 20
    Block Web beacons (external content) 20
    Signatures, encryption, and security 21
    Network/Offline improvements 21
    Windows SharePoint Services and critical event notification . . . 21
    Calendar and Contact sharing and access 22
    Instant messaging 22
    Other changes 22
Summary 22

Chapter 2: Installing Outlook 2003 23
Understanding Deployment Options 23
Standalone and One-by-One Installations 24
    Running Setup 26
Changing, Repairing, or Removing an Office Installation 28
    Updating Office 29

Wide-Scale Outlook Deployment 30
    Deploying with SMS and DECM (group policy) 30
    Deploying Office with group policy 31
Automated and Unattended Setup 49
    Using Setup switches and custom INI files 50
Creating and Migrating Office Profiles 54
Summary 55

Chapter 3: A Guided Tour of Outlook 2003 . . . . **57**

Understanding the Outlook Interface 58
    Changing the view 60
Using Outlook Today 67
Working with Outlook Folders 69
    Using the Navigation Pane 70
    Using the Folder List 72
    Using the Calendar 73
    Using Contacts 74
    Using the Inbox 75
    Using the Outbox 76
    Using the Deleted Items folder 77
    Using the Drafts folder 78
    Using the Sent Items folder 78
Using E-mail 78
Creating Tasks 80
Keeping an Outlook Journal 81
Taking Notes 82
Summary 83

Chapter 4: Configuring Outlook 2003 . . . . **85**

Configuring E-mail Accounts 85
    Using the E-mail Accounts Wizard 86
    Configuring Exchange Server accounts 87
    Configuring POP3 and IMAP accounts 94
    Configuring HTTP accounts 99
    Adding Data Files 100
Creating and Managing Outlook Profiles 102
    Creating an Outlook profile 103
    Copying a profile 104
    Switching between profiles 105
Configuring Message Delivery Options 105
Setting Your E-mail Options 106
    Setting the e-mail preferences 106
    Setting the mail format options 109
Summary 111

Part II: Mastering E-mail   113

Chapter 5: E-mail Basics 115

Composing a Message 115
  Starting a new message 116
  Addressing your message 116
  Entering a subject 120
  Entering the message text 121
Sending a Message 122
  Sending a message immediately 122
  Setting message options for individual messages 123
Reading a Message 124
Replying to a Message 126
  Choosing the type of reply 126
  Composing and sending your reply 126
Managing the Mail Folders 127
Summary 130

Chapter 6: Message Options and Attachments 131

Using Message Format Options 131
  Sending messages as plain text 131
  Sending messages as rich text 133
  Sending messages as HTML 135
  Sending messages as Office documents 136
Using Advanced Message Options 138
  Flagging a message 139
  Setting message importance and sensitivity 139
  Creating an auto signature 140
  Using business cards 144
  Using stationery 147
Attaching Files 148
  Attaching files while composing a message 149
  Sending a file while using Microsoft Office 150
Organizing and Sharing Messages 152
  Organizing e-mail with personal folders 152
  Creating a folder 152
Using Outlook with Exchange Server 154
  Using Cached Exchange Mode 154
  Voting 154
  Recalling sent messages 156
Summary 158

Chapter 7: Advanced E-mail Concepts 159

Digitally Signing and Encrypting Messages 159
  Sending a digitally signed message 161
  Encrypting messages 163

Using Distribution Lists 164
    Creating a distribution list 164
    Using a distribution list 166
Using Remote Mail 167
    Connecting and downloading headers 168
    Marking items for action 170
Summary 171

Chapter 8: Processing Messages Automatically **173**

Securing Against HTML Content 173
    Blocking external HTML content 174
    Configuring security zones 175
Using Rules 176
    Using the Rules Wizard 176
    Responding automatically to messages 183
    Importing, exporting, and backing up rules 184
    Filtering junk and adult content mail 185
Using the Out of Office Assistant 187
Summary 190

Part III: Information Manager   191

Chapter 9: Managing Your Contacts **193**

An Overview of Contacts 193
    What are contacts? 194
    What are the new Outlook contact features? 195
Viewing Your Contacts 195
    Understanding the General tab 196
    Understanding the Activities tab 204
    Understanding the Certificates tab 205
    Understanding the All Fields tab 206
Creating Contacts 208
    Importing contacts 208
    Creating contacts manually 211
    Creating contacts while viewing an e-mail message 212
Using Contacts 213
    Composing an e-mail message from contacts 213
    Searching contacts 215
    Viewing address maps 218
    Using the AutoDialer to make a phone call 219
Summary 221

Chapter 10: Managing Your Calendar **223**

Understanding the Outlook Calendar 223
    How is the Outlook Calendar useful? 225
    Understanding the new Calendar features 225

Viewing the Calendar 226
    Accessing different Calendar views 226
    Understanding Calendar view types 227
    Customizing Calendar views 237
Sharing Your Calendar with Others 243
Saving Your Calendar as a Web Page 246
Summary 248

Chapter 11: Scheduling Your Time 249

Understanding Scheduling 249
Creating an Appointment 250
Creating a Meeting 255
    Beginning a new meeting 256
    Specifying recurring activities 261
Integrating with NetMeeting, Windows Media Services,
    and Microsoft Exchange Conferencing 262
Summary 264

Chapter 12: Tracking Tasks 265

Understanding Tasks 265
Creating a Task 268
Setting Task Options 270
Assigning Tasks to People 273
Creating Recurring Tasks 275
Using the TaskPad 279
Summary 284

Chapter 13: Keeping Your Journal 285

Understanding the Journal 285
Viewing the Journal 287
    Using the By Type view format 288
    Using the By Contact view format 289
    Using the By Category view format 290
    Using the Entry List view format 292
    Using the Last Seven Days view format 293
    Using the Phone Calls view format 294
Controlling Journal Data 295
    Limiting Journal data 296
    Adding Journal entries manually 297
Sharing Journal Information 299
Summary 299

Chapter 14: Taking Notes 301

Understanding Notes 301
Creating and Editing Notes 303
Using Note Options 305
    Specifying a color 305
    Specifying a category 306

Specifying a contact 307
Specifying Note default options 309
Specifying timestamp options 310
Viewing Your Notes 311
Using the Icon views 311
Using the Notes List view 311
Using the Last Seven Days view 313
Using the By Category view 314
Using the By Color view 315
Summary 316

Chapter 15: Organizing Information with Categories **317**
Understanding Categories and the Master Category List 317
Personalizing Your Category List 319
Assigning Categories to Outlook Items 320
Managing Categories 322
Organizing Data and Views with Categories 323
Printing Category Items 325
Sharing Categories 327
Summary 331

Chapter 16: Using Outlook Newsreader **333**
What Is a Newsgroup? 333
Preparing to Use Newsgroups 335
Setting up newsgroups 335
Subscribing to newsgroups 338
Viewing Newsgroup Messages 341
Viewing messages 341
Filtering messages 343
Following message threads 349
Viewing the new messages 351
Posting to Newsgroups 352
Summary 354

Part IV: Getting the Most Out of Outlook 2003   **355**

Chapter 17: Customizing Outlook 2003 . . . . **357**
Customizing Outlook 357
Customizing Outlook Today 358
Customizing the menus 362
Customizing the toolbars 363
Customizing the Navigation Pane 365
Controlling security 366
Organizing Your Outlook Folders 368
What is the Organize feature? 368
Using the Organize feature 369

Integrating with the Web 374
Showing and Hiding the TaskPad 377
Adding Holidays To Your Calendar 381
Adding Macros for Repetitive Tasks 382
Summary 383

Chapter 18: Using Folders Effectively **385**

Understanding Folders 385
    Why use Outlook folders? 386
    Understanding folder types 387
    Understanding folder categories 387
Creating Folders 388
    Adding new folders 388
    Customizing your new folders 390
    Creating additional Personal Folders 393
Managing Items within the Folders 397
    Moving items 397
    Saving items as text files 399
Sharing Folders 400
    Sharing Personal Folders 400
Using the Deleted Items Folder 402
    Deleting items 402
    Purging deleted items 404
Summary 406

Chapter 19: Integrating with Other Applications **407**

Integrating Outlook with Office 407
Creating a Mail Merge 410
    Getting names from contacts 411
Sending an E-mail from an Application 415
Importing and Exporting Data 418
    Importing information into Outlook 419
    Exporting information from Outlook 422
    Saving Outlook messages 424
Summary 425

Chapter 20: Delegating Tasks to an Assistant **427**

Understanding Delegation 427
Assigning Delegates 428
Granting Folder Access 431
Acting as an Assistant 433
Send E-mail on Behalf of Someone Else 435
Manage Another Person's Calendar 436
Summary 438

Chapter 21: Using Windows SharePoint Services 439

Understanding Windows SharePoint Services 439
Setting up an WSS Site 440
   Installing WSS prerequisites 441
   Installing WSS 442
   Managing users and site groups 443
   Adding a user 444
   Removing users and changing site group
     membership for existing users 447
   Advanced user and site group membership management 448
Viewing Data in the WSS Site 452
   Viewing documents 453
   Viewing discussion boards 456
   Viewing lists 457
Adding Data to an WSS Site 459
   Adding documents 459
   Adding to discussions 460
   Adding to lists 460
Summary 461

Part V: Managing Outlook Users   463

Chapter 22: Supporting Roaming Users 465

What Are Roaming Users? 465
Folder Redirection and PST Location 472
   Redirecting the .pst file 473
Applying Group Policies 476
Roaming With Different Versions of Outlook 477
   Roaming with Personal Folders (.pst) files and
     Personal Address Books (.pab) 477
Roaming Issues for Exchange Server Users 481
Creating and Migrating Office Profiles 482
   Creating a .prf file using the Custom Installation Wizard 482
Summary 485

Chapter 23: Managing Security and Performance 487

Managing Virus Settings and Attachment Blocking 488
   Macro virus security 491
Backing Up and Restoring User Certificates 493
Blocking Spam 494
   Rules and filters 495
Summary 500

Chapter 24: Controlling Outlook (and Office) with Group and System Policies 501

Understanding Group Policies 502
    Creating a Group Policy Object 503
Adding Office Administrative Templates for Group Policy 505
    Adding an Office Administrative Template 506
Deploying Outlook Group Policies 508
Understanding System Policies 509
Adding Office Administrative Templates for System Policies 510
Deploying Outlook System Policies 512
Summary 513

Chapter 25: Backing Up and Recovering User Data 515

Backing Up and Restoring PSTs 515
    Quick and easy PST file backup 516
    Exporting Personal Folders file data 518
    Importing PST file data 519
Exchange Server Mailbox Backup and Restore 519
    Backing up data on a Microsoft Exchange Server 519
Backing Up Rules and Other Data 522
Setting Retention Policies 524
Configuring and Using Automatic Archival 525
    What is the Archive? 525
    Using AutoArchive 526
    AutoArchiving for individual folders 528
Summary 531

Chapter 26: Managing Exchange Server for Outlook Users 533

Managing Mailboxes 534
    Adding a mailbox automatically 534
    Adding, removing, and moving mailboxes manually 536
    Configuring global mailbox options 538
    Configuring mailbox-specific options 541
Creating External Addresses
    (Mail-Enabled Contacts) 547
Distribution Groups with Exchange 550
    Creating a group 550
    Adding group members 552
    Delegating send on behalf permission to a group 553
Configuring Exchange Instant Messaging 554
    Instant Messaging configuration 555
    Creating an Instant Messaging virtual server 555
    Enabling Instant Messaging for user accounts 557
Summary 558

Part VI: Basics of Microsoft Outlook 2003 — 559

Chapter 27: Outlook 2003 Application Types 561

Outlook 2003 Client Applications 561
    Outlook 2003 Forms Designer 562
    Message forms 563
    Post forms 567
    More built-in forms 569
Outlook 2003 Office Applications 571
Outlook 2003 Web Applications 572
    Building your own Outlook Today page 572
Summary 577

Chapter 28: Creating a Simple Outlook Form 579

Accessing the Outlook Forms Designer 579
    Choosing a form 580
Manipulating the Form in the Design Window 581
Adding Controls with the Toolbox 583
Using the Properties Window 585
Adding Fields to the Form 586
Introduction to the Script Editor 588
    Using VBScript with a command button 588
Publishing the Form 589
Summary 590

Chapter 29: Controls in Outlook Forms 591

Labels 591
Text Boxes 594
Frames 595
Option Buttons 596
Check Boxes 597
Combo Boxes 598
List Boxes 599
Multiple Pages 600
Tab Strips 602
Image Controls 602
Spin Buttons 603
Command Buttons 604
Toggle Buttons 606
Summary 607

Chapter 30: Utilizing Custom Fields 609

Custom Form Fields 609
    Planning your custom fields 609
    Creating custom fields 611

Working with Fields 613
    Working with shared fields 613
    Using combination fields 615
    Using formula fields 617
    Validating user input 618
    Specifying default values for fields 619
Summary 620

Chapter 31: Adding Functionality to Outlook Forms 621

Compose versus Read: Changing Form Appearance 621
    Switching between Compose and Read Mode 622
Adding Form Pages 623
Using Form Properties 624
    Version control 625
    Icons and Word templates 625
    Linking a form to a contact 626
    Protecting your form 626
    Including form definition 627
    Limiting to a response 627
Modifying Behavior with the Actions Page 627
Changing the Tab Order 629
Testing Design-Time Form Applications 630
Installation and Deployment of OFD Applications 631
    Publishing a form 631
    Publishing to Public Folders 632
    Publishing to a Personal Folder file 632
Summary 633

Part VII: Advanced Messaging Development   635

Chapter 32: Working with Application Folders 637

Application Folder Types 637
    Discussion folders 637
    Tracking folders 640
    Built-in module folders 644
Managing Folder Properties 645
    Specifying a default form 645
    Defining permissions 646
    Using rules 647
Using Views 647
    Customizing versus defining a view 648
    Manipulating field headings 649
    Grouping information 650
    Sorting and filtering 650
    Other view settings 651
Summary 653

Chapter 33: Collaborative Messaging Basics 655

Understanding the Lingo 655
   Collaboration 655
   Collaborative solution 656
   Collaborative messaging 657
   Workflow applications 658
   Messaging application programming interface 660
Outlook 2003 Custom Forms 661
E-form Basics 662
Summary 662

Chapter 34: Using the Outlook 2003 Object Model 665

Understanding an Object Model 665
   Component Object Model (COM) 666
Outlook 2003 Application Object Model 667
   Methods versus properties 668
Using the OFD Script Editor 669
   Event handlers 669
   Object Browser 670
Debugging Your Code 671
   Break mode 672
   Setting break points 673
Summary 674

Part VIII: Advanced Outlook Administration   675

Chapter 35: Using Business Contact Manager 677

What is the Business
   Contact Manager? 677
Installing Business Contact Manager 679
Adding a New Account 680
   Filling out the Account form 680
   Importing an account 682
   Viewing Business Contact Manager Accounts 684
Managing Business Contact Information 686
   Filling out the Business Contact form 686
   Moving a contact from the Outlook Contacts folder 688
   Importing a business contact 688
Exporting Business Contact Manager data 689
   Exporting Business Contact Manager Accounts 689
   Exporting Business Contact Manager Contacts 691
Tracking Sales Opportunities 692
Adding Business Notes to a Record History 694

Adding Phone Logs to a Record History 696
Linking an Item to a Record 697
    Linking an item to a Business Contact record 697
    Linking an item to an Account record 699
    Linking an item to an Opportunity record 700
Working with Other Office 2003 Application 701
Summary 702

Chapter 36: Using Outlook Web Access 703

What is Outlook Web Access? 703
Preparing To Use Outlook Web Access 704
Using Outlook Web Access 705
Performing Outlook Tasks in OWA 707
    Using e-mail in OWA 708
    Using the Outlook Calendar in OWA 712
    Using the Contacts feature in OWA 716
    Working with reminders in OWA 718
    Working with Public Folders 719
Managing OWA 720
Logging Off OWA 721
Summary 722

Chapter 37: Optimizing Outlook Installations 723

Improving Outlook Performance 723
    Work offline 724
    Prompt for connection type 725
    Optimize rules 727
    Disable the Reading pane 730
    Compact Your OST file 731
Securing Outlook 733
Summary 736

Appendix: What's on the CD-ROM 737

Index 745

End-User License Agreement 785

Getting Started with Microsoft Outlook 2003

◆ ◆ ◆ ◆

In This Part

Chapter 1
Outlook 2003 in a Nutshell

Chapter 2
Installing Outlook 2003

Chapter 3
A Guided Tour of Outlook 2003

Chapter 4
Configuring Outlook 2003

◆ ◆ ◆ ◆

Outlook 2003 in a Nutshell

Microsoft performed a usability study during the Outlook 2002 beta. This study determined that most Office users spend at least 60 percent of their time in Outlook, and much of that time working with e-mail. If you were to ask a cross-section of Outlook users how they use the program, it would be a safe bet that most of them would immediately mention e-mail. Some users would probably also talk about using Outlook to keep track of their calendar and maybe their contacts, but that would likely be about all most people would think about. Very few people actually use Outlook as effectively as they could, in part because they don't know how much Outlook can do for them.

You don't have to use all the features of Outlook any more than you have to eat every type of food you might find at a buffet dinner. On the other hand, you'll probably find that knowing all the different things that are available may stimulate your appetite, so you'll want to try some new things. So maybe that's the way you should approach this chapter — as a "sampler tray" that whets your appetite about what Outlook can do for you.

Easy Messaging

You would not be alone if all you thought about doing with Outlook was sending and receiving e-mail messages. Messaging is really at the heart of Outlook, even though only using Outlook for e-mail would be similar to visiting a family gathering and ignoring all the relatives because you were only interested in seeing your grandma's dog.

What is messaging?

In Outlook, messaging is synonymous with e-mail — electronic mail. E-mail has changed the way people communicate in a number of fundamental ways. Some of these changes include the following:

✦ Messages can be delivered almost instantly nearly anywhere in the world. Although this has been possible for voice messages sent over telephone lines for some time, e-mail encompasses additional types of messages such as document attachments. (It's also much cheaper than long-distance calls.)

✦ Sending an e-mail message is generally much less expensive than other methods. You can, for example, send the entire text of a 500-page book over the Internet without paying a special delivery charge. Compare that to the cost of sending a 500-page printed document via an overnight air express service!

✦ Time zones are far less important when you can send a message, and the recipient can read it at his or her convenience. As a result, it may be far easier to collaborate on a project with someone half-way around the world than it used to be to collaborate with someone two time zones away.

✦ It's almost as easy to send a photo or a fully formatted document as it is to send a plain text message because messages can easily include attachments. This makes it far more likely that the sender and the recipient both understand the message in the same way.

E-mail has truly made the world a bit easier to reach, and has brought about many changes in the way people communicate on a daily basis.

Integrating with forms

Outlook forms are a method of standardizing the way you send and receive information. You use Outlook forms when you create and store contact information and when you create a new message. Forms make interacting with your computer far easier because forms are a visual method of presenting information.

You aren't limited to the standard forms Outlook provides for its purposes. As detailed in the latter chapters of this book, you can create your own forms for use with Outlook. You might, for example, create a form that members of your workgroup could use to report on their progress or to report problems with a project.

Outlook forms can effectively connect any other computer in the world into your Outlook information database. If you e-mail a message that contains the proper form, the information the recipient enters into the form can be automatically e-mailed back to your computer and used on your system. If you need this type of integration, read all about forms later in this book.

You can also use templates, which are nothing more than Outlook items (messages, contacts, and so on) saved to disk, to simplify repetitive tasks. For example, you might create a template to submit a monthly progress report or expense reimbursement report. You can use templates for non-messages items, as well. You might use a contact template to create multiple contacts with the same company information, for example. Or, you might use an appointment template to create appointments with the subject, label, and other properties already set. Whatever the case, you'll find more information about templates in Chapter 17.

Increased Productivity

Everyone has certainly heard the old saying, "time is money." In today's busy world, that old saying is probably even truer than ever. There just isn't enough time for everything you need to accomplish — unless you can get some good help, that is. Outlook can provide lots of that help so you can be more productive and get more done in the time you have available.

Outlook has many different ways to help you increase your productivity, including providing a common collection of contacts to use for e-mail, phone calls, and letters, as well as the ability to easily locate information associated with specific projects or contacts. You aren't likely to use all of them, but using even some of them can be effective. Figure 1-1 shows the Calendar folder with the Contacts folder opened in a second window.

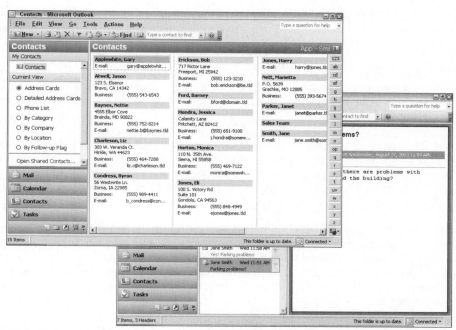

Figure 1-1: Use Outlook to help organize your life so you can be more productive.

Sharing information

Virtually no one works in actual isolation. Even if you were to go off to the top of a mountain to sit in a cave for the rest of your life, you'd still need to communicate with others once in a while—even if that meant creating a fire and sending out smoke signals. Fortunately for those of us with far more normal lives, Outlook is designed to make sharing information simple and straightforward. Outlook isn't likely to make your eyes water as much as smoke signals would, either!

Outlook offers several ways for you to share information. Here are a few possibilities for sharing information through Outlook:

✦ You can send information to other people in the form of e-mail messages. This is by far the simplest method, and will serve the needs of many users.

✦ You can use Outlook to schedule meetings—either online or face-to-face meetings—as the need arises. Meetings are an obvious method of sharing information, of course, but you may never have thought of using Outlook for this type of scheduling. To be effective, each of the meeting participants must keep his or her personal schedule in Outlook.

✦ You can publish information in public folders on an Exchange Server, which allows others to access the information. If you've been given the necessary permissions in a particular public folder, you can create additional folders and control the actions that others can take within the folder (create items, read them, and so on). Users across the Internet can also access the items in public folders if the folders are configured as publicly available newsgroups by the Exchange Server administrator. Figure 1-2 shows a public folder opened in Outlook.

Tip   An Exchange Server administrator can also set up newsfeeds to pull public newsgroup messages to public folders, where they can be read and replied to by Outlook users from within Outlook. For more information on working with newsgroups, see Chapter 16.

✦ Exchange Server users can grant other users various levels of access to their Outlook folders. For example, you might set up a shared Contacts folder to enable everyone in your Sales department to access customer addresses. Unfortunately, it isn't practical to share a set of personal folders, but it can be done. Chapter 18 explains how.

With only a few exceptions, e-mail messages being the most notable, you'll have a difficult time sharing most Outlook information with anyone who doesn't also use Outlook. The items on your Calendar, for example, aren't readily usable for scheduling unless everyone in your workgroup is using Outlook. Some types of information, such as your contacts, can be shared indirectly by exporting the information to another format.

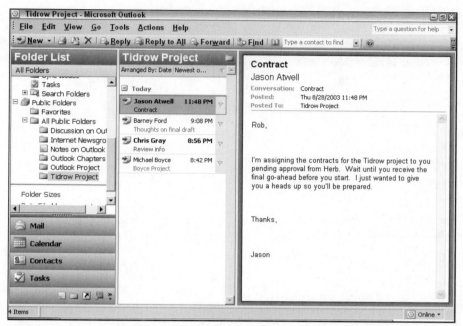

Figure 1-2: Use public folders to publish information for view and use by others.

Getting organized

People have different definitions of what it means to be organized. For some people, it's enough that they're able to get up and get to work on time. Other people take organization to the extreme and aren't happy unless each pair of socks in their underwear drawer is lined up according to a color chart. Outlook's organization features are intended for people who fit somewhere between these two extremes.

Several of Outlook's capabilities may help you get organized. Depending on your personal definition of what it means to be organized, you many find some or all of these capabilities useful.

Keeping track of your schedule

Figure 1-3 shows the Outlook feature that probably comes to mind first when you're thinking about organization. The Outlook Calendar enables you to plan your schedule, plan for meetings, and even block out times when you don't want to be disturbed.

The Outlook Calendar may look somewhat like the paper calendar that may already sit on your desk, but the Outlook Calendar can do things no paper calendar ever could. It's easy to forget to look on your desk calendar to see what might be scheduled for that week when you're planning a vacation, but the Outlook Calendar won't allow you to "accidentally" be gone when you have that dental appointment.

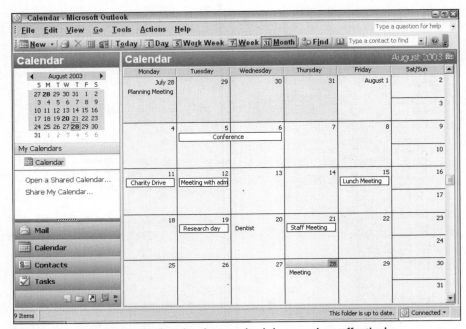

Figure 1-3: Use the Outlook Calendar to schedule your time effectively.

In addition to notifying you about scheduling conflicts, the Outlook Calendar can also provide both visible and audible reminders of important events. With a little planning, you could even have Outlook greet you on your special day by playing Happy Birthday when you check your schedule.

Staying in contact

If you've ever tried to rely on one of those little pocket organizer books to keep track of your address list, you'll quickly come to appreciate the Outlook Contacts list. Gone are the problems of running out of space simply because you know too many people with a last name such as Smith or of virtually illegible entries that are the result of making too many corrections.

The Outlook Contacts list can store far more than the obvious e-mail addresses. As Figure 1-4 shows, the Outlook Contacts list has room for additional information such as mailing addresses, phone numbers, business information, and quite a bit more. If you need to keep track of information about someone, the Outlook Contacts list can likely accommodate your needs.

Tip   If you want to share contact information with people who may not be using Outlook, you might want to send the information as a vCard — an Internet standard for creating and sharing virtual business cards. (More on vCards in Chapter 9.)

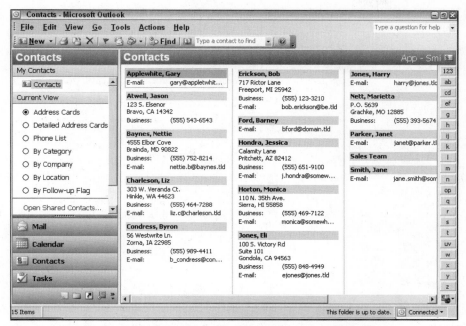

Figure 1-4: Use the Outlook Contacts list to organize your address list.

Getting even more organized with the Journal

Outlook doesn't stop at organizing your schedule and your address book. Outlook also keeps track of how you use your computer. You may not realize it, but each time you work on a Microsoft Office document, Outlook can make a note about the document in the Journal, a special Outlook folder. There is an automatic record of not only when you opened each document but also how long you worked on it.

As Figure 1-5 shows, the Outlook Journal automatically tracks information about e-mail messages in addition to Access, Excel, PowerPoint, and Word documents. You can add your own categories such as phone calls to the Journal, too.

Entries in the Outlook Journal are organized by date, so you can scroll to any particular date, click the plus sign (+) in front of the entry type, and see which items are recorded in the Journal for that date. If you want more details about an item, all you need to do is double-click the item to view the Journal entry.

Tip   The Outlook Journal can be a valuable tool for tracking the time you spent working on a project — especially if you need to bill for projects based on time.

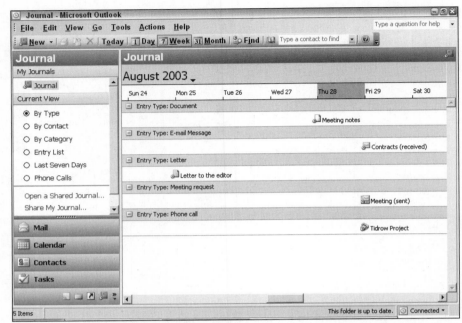

Figure 1-5: The Outlook Journal automatically keeps track of your Office documents.

Using the Tasks folder

The Tasks list, contained in the Tasks folder, is another important Outlook organizational tool. The Tasks list is useful for organizing those projects you need to complete but which don't fit neatly on a calendar. For example, Figure 1-6 shows a Tasks list that includes a number of items. Some items have a specific due date; others simply need to be done at some point in time. What sets all of these items apart from standard Calendar entries is that tasks are generally somewhat difficult to schedule. It's easy, for example, to schedule a business trip because your flight will leave at a specified time whether you're there or not. It's much harder to schedule something such as finishing a manuscript because it's difficult to foresee any problems that might delay the completion. In addition, the task of finishing a manuscript is one that you could finish early; there's no penalty for being ahead of schedule for most task-type items.

Tip   Be sure to clean out old completed tasks from time to time so that it's easier to see what's left to be done. Select a completed task and click the Delete button to remove the task from the list.

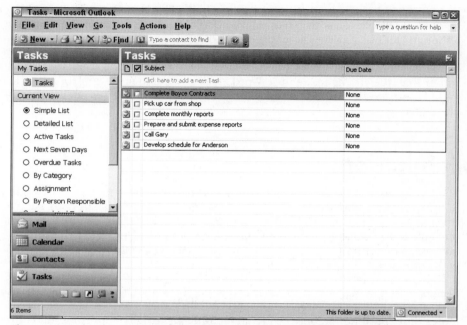

Figure 1-6: Use the Outlook Tasks list to plan items that don't easily fit a calendar-dictated schedule.

Integrating with other applications

Increasing your productivity using Outlook isn't limited to the various tasks you can perform within Outlook itself. Much of the information that you create or store in Outlook is also useful in other applications. You might, for example, want to create a form letter in Word and then use your Outlook Contacts list to address those letters. Sure, you could just create a second address book, but why do all that extra work when Outlook already has just what you need? Besides, do you really want to try to keep two different address lists up to date?

One productive way to integrate Outlook with other applications is a slight variation on the old form letter process. You've probably used mail merge to create form letters, but did you realize that you could use mail merge to create a series of e-mail messages, too? If you've ever considered changing to a different Internet service provider (ISP) but decided that notifying all your contacts about your new e-mail address was just too much of a hassle, why not use Outlook and Word together to create an e-mail notification of your new e-mail address? That way, each message recipient will receive his or her personalized copy of your address change and will be far less likely to ignore the message.

Even if you never use mail merge, you'll probably find that Outlook has a certain amount of integration with the other Microsoft Office applications. For example, although Outlook has a rudimentary text editor that you could use to create e-mail messages, it's likely that you'll never actually use this simple editor. It's far more probable that when you click the New Message button, Outlook will start Word rather than the simple text editor. Word gives you much more control over the format of messages in addition to providing easy access to features such as spell checking.

Collaboration

Many projects can be successfully completed only through the efforts of a number of different people all working together towards a common goal. A book such as this one is a good example. It covers a range of topics that are simply too broad for one author to complete in a reasonable amount of time. Only by having a team of authors and editors working in collaboration can a project of this size be completed within a reasonable amount of time.

Collaboration works only if all the members of a team are working together. Those team members may be spread thousands of miles apart, or they may be office mates, but coordination between team members is usually important. An editor can only begin work after an author has begun submitting pieces of the manuscript. If the authoring team decided to hold all their chapters until the last minute, the editorial team would be hard pressed to complete their work on time. Likewise, if people on a project team all decided to work independently without regard to anyone else's schedule, it would be extremely difficult to finish any project on deadline. Fortunately, Outlook offers solutions that can help solve these problems.

What is a collaborative solution?

A collaborative solution to a problem is only possible when team members agree to work together. A simple example of this is seen in a project planning meeting. It's difficult to hold a successful project planning meeting unless everyone agrees to attend the meeting at the scheduled time.

Even if you can get everyone to agree that they need to work together, it can still be a lot of work trying to coordinate everyone's schedule. Outlook can make this part of a project somewhat easier by helping you schedule meetings at times when everyone will be available. Figure 1-7 shows how you might use Outlook to begin this process.

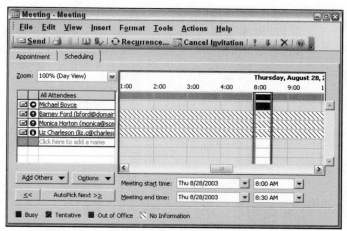

Figure 1-7: Use the Outlook meeting request to schedule a meeting that will fit into the team members' schedules.

As Figure 1-7 shows, you begin the process by setting up a meeting request. You can include as many details as necessary and determine where you'll hold your meeting. Online meetings require a bit of extra coordination to make certain that everyone uses the correct software and server location, which Outlook enables you to specify (see the example in Figure 1-7).

Tip It's a good idea to plan a dry run before an important online meeting. Inevitably, at least one of the attendees will need to install and configure their online meeting software before they can connect, and this can easily disrupt your entire meeting if it has to be done at the last minute.

After you've used Outlook to request a meeting, it's time to finalize the schedule and attendance list. If all the people you've invited to the meeting are using Outlook, it's much easier to coordinate this event because you'll be able to check on their availability and even automatically log their responses to the meeting request. Figure 1-8 shows an example of an in-progress meeting request. One attendee has indicated he'll attend, and another has declined.

The advantage to scheduling meetings with other users in Outlook is that you can view at a glance their availability for the meeting and easily adjust the meeting date or time to accommodate everyone.

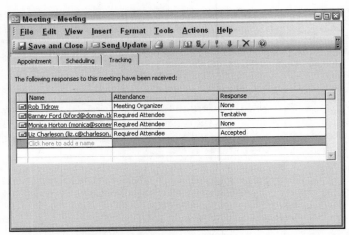

Figure 1-8: Check the responses to your meeting request using the Tracking tab.

Business solutions

Business, of course, is about more than just scheduling meetings. There are plenty of business solutions that don't involve meetings, but can use Outlook to help people work together. A common example might be to use public folders to keep everyone informed of important new developments or to share information about a new project.

Another less obvious example would be to use specialized forms to enable people to make standardized requests. Imagine that your company used special letterhead paper, but didn't want branch offices to maintain too large a supply because rapid growth was resulting in frequent changes. You might create an Outlook form that enables each branch to easily request letterhead paper on an as-needed basis so that they wouldn't be tempted to hoard too large a supply of possibly outdated materials.

The last half of this book concentrates on many different custom business solutions that use Outlook. You'll find more ideas there about what you can do to make Outlook an important part of your organization's collaborative efforts.

Outlook Development Capabilities

Unlike many of the other Microsoft Office applications, Outlook doesn't give you the ability to record a macro for playback; however, Outlook does offer extensive programming ability, both for macros and full-blown applications.

Developing for Outlook can be as simple as automating a common task through a macro or creating a custom form to obtain information from others, or as complex as creating a custom application that ties together Outlook and other applications to perform a specific function.

As the latter chapters of this book cover in detail, Outlook 2003 includes a Visual Basic editor (Figure 1-9) that you can use to create macros or more complex applications. The editor provides an integrated development environment that offers a code editor, form-layout tools, extensive Help documentation and samples, and several other features to make Outlook development a snap, even for beginners. The editor also provides a good selection of debugging features to help you troubleshoot problems with your programs.

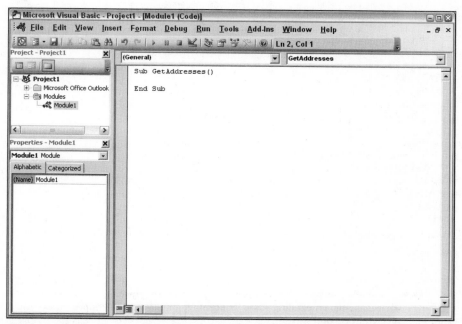

Figure 1-9: Use the Visual Basic editor to create Outlook macros and more complex custom programs.

The Forms editor (Figure 1-10) makes it easy to customize existing Outlook forms or create new ones. You don't need to be a rocket scientist to customize a form in Outlook. Even inexperienced users can do it, thanks to the tools provided in the Forms editor.

Although you'll find the Visual Basic editor a good solution for developing applications for Outlook and the other Office applications, you're not limited to it as your only development tool. You can use many other tools such as Microsoft's Visual Studio .NET to create custom programs that take advantage of and integrate with the Office application suite. You're also not limited to Visual Basic. Visual Studio, for example, offers several language choices including C++ and C#. Figure 1-11 shows the Visual Studio .NET development environment.

Whatever your development needs, you'll find that Office provides a relatively rich programming interface that enables you to take advantage of Office's capabilities without developing a lot of custom code. In fact, I suspect you'll discover that you can accomplish many programming and automation tasks with very little code.

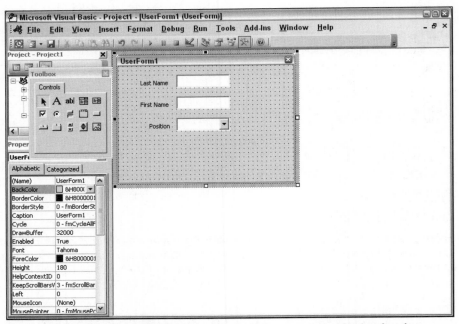

Figure 1-10: Modifying an existing form or creating a new one is simple when you work with a form in design mode.

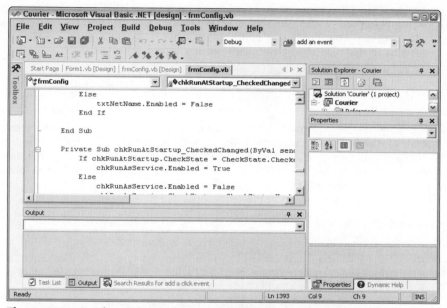

Figure 1-11: An alternative to the integrated Office Visual Basic editor is Visual Studio .NET, the latest development platform from Microsoft.

What's New in Outlook 2003?

Although Microsoft has initially downplayed this release of Office, there are some significant changes in the interface and in its feature set. This section focuses on the major features that are either changed or new in Outlook 2003.

Search folders

Search folders are virtual folders you create by specifying filter conditions, and these new folders are handy for organizing and displaying Outlook information. Outlook includes three search folders by default, and these three folders search all of the Inbox folders and subfolders and show the results in a single list:

✦ **For Follow Up.** This search folder shows all messages that are flagged for follow up, which helps you quickly scan through the messages you've flagged for further action.

✦ **Large Mail.** This folder shows messages larger than 100KB, and it is handy when you need to trim the size of your mailbox or just need to locate a particular message that you know is relatively large. You can change the size criteria for this folder or create other ones with different criteria.

✦ **Unread Mail.** This folder shows all of your unread messages, and is a great help when you have lots of messages in your Inbox and want to view only those that are marked as unread.

You can easily create your own search folders to browse or organize your messages and other Outlook items in ways that make the most sense and offer the most benefit to the way you use Outlook. You can even include items from multiple Outlook folders in a search folder, which helps you consolidate data from different folders into a single view. Figure 1-12 shows the Unread Mail search folder.

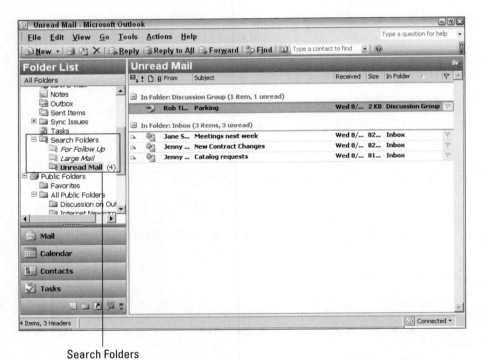

Search Folders

Figure 1-12: Search folders are powerful tools for organizing and displaying Outlook items.

Navigation Pane

The Navigation Pane has experienced a major facelift, incorporating the features formerly found in the Navigation Pane with the folder list. Combining the folder list and the Navigation Pane simplifies the Outlook interface, and provides more room for displaying the Outlook folders and items. Figure 1-13 shows the Navigation pane at the left of the Outlook interface.

Reading Pane

The Reading Pane (Figure 1-14) has also seen a facelift that makes it more useable. It now has a paper-like appearance and can be located either at the right or bottom of the Outlook window. The changes enable the Reading Pane to show much more information, and Microsoft has added the ability for users to respond to meeting requests and use voting buttons in the Reading Pane without having to open the items.

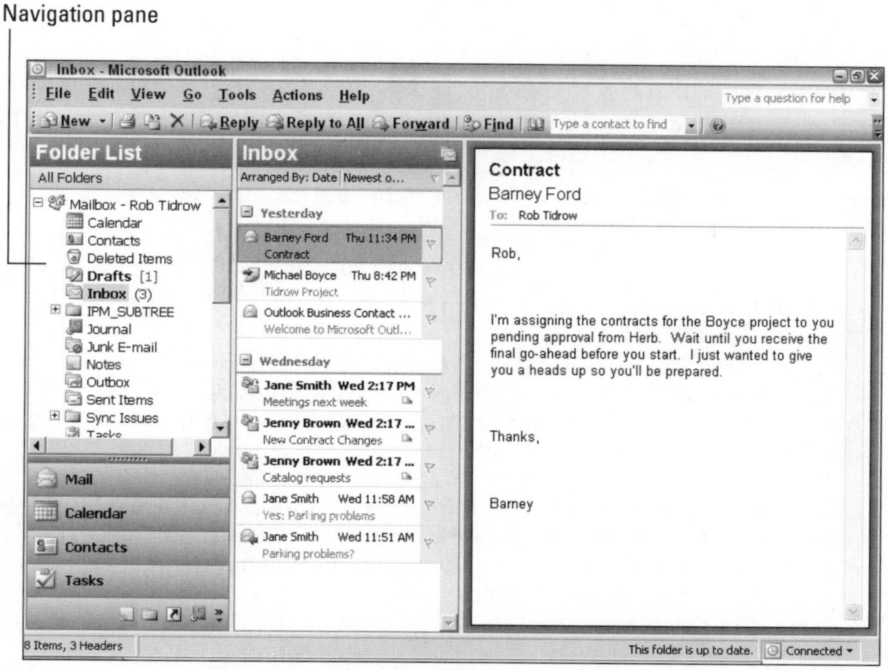

Navigation pane

Figure 1-13: The new Navigation Pane combines the features of the old Navigation Pane and the folder list to simplify the Outlook interface.

Reading Pane

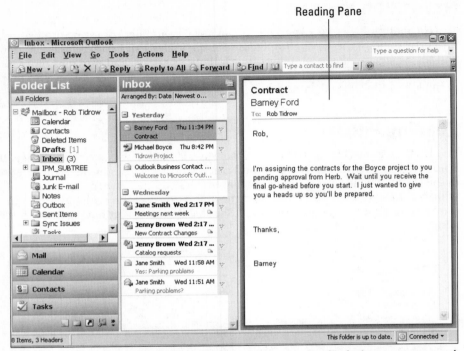

Figure 1-14: The Reading Pane offers more real estate for displaying messages and other items, and greater flexibility.

Quick flagging

Previous versions of Outlook allowed you to flag an item for follow-up, and added a red flag icon beside flagged items. Outlook 2003 gives you six flag colors to use to help you organize flagged items. You can also flag an item with just a couple of mouse clicks.

The flag color is stored as a unique property, so Outlook recognizes the different colors of flags. This means you can, for example, create a search folder that shows all red-flagged or blue-flagged items. These multiple flag types are therefore useful for sorting and organizing messages.

Block Web beacons (external content)

Spammers have become much craftier about separating the wheat from the chaff — good e-mail addresses from bad. One technique they use is to add links to external content in HTML-based messages so that when a user previews or reads the message, the external content is retrieved. The spammer can then gather the IP address of the client along with other information to help them determine which addresses are good. These loaded messages are called *Web beacons*. To help reduce spam and block these Web beacons, Outlook by default blocks external content in HTML-based messages.

Signatures, encryption, and security

If you use e-mail signatures — text or other data added to each outgoing e-mail — you might find another new Outlook feature handy. Outlook now lets you specify separate signatures for each e-mail account. When you send a message from a specific account, Outlook uses the signature assigned to that account. This gives you flexibility in message signing.

Outlook 2003 also offers improvements in digital signature verification and simplified security use. You now have the ability to easily add a digital signature or encrypt a message even if you use Word as your e-mail editor. Chapter 7 offers detailed information about digital signatures and message encryption.

Network/Offline improvements

Outlook 2003 includes a new service mode called Cached Exchange Mode. Users with Exchange Server mailboxes can cache a copy of their Exchange Server mailbox on the local computer, which improves performance for offline use and slow/unavailable connections. Outlook 2003 also does a much better job of detecting and adjusting to connection changes, moving from online to offline status as needed and adjusting to network changes such as moving from a LAN to a dial-up connection.

Windows SharePoint Services and critical event notification

Office 11 includes several features that enable it to integrate well with Microsoft Windows SharePoint Services (WSS), a superset of FrontPage Server Extensions that facilitate collaboration. An WSS Web site is used by a group or team to provide and share information about a project, meeting, or other event. For example, a team might use an WSS site to coordinate a major meeting, posting the agenda and other supporting documents on the site for comment and review by all.

Outlook 2003 lets you use e-mail rules to generate alerts when items are added or modified on an WSS site. For example, you can receive a notification when the agenda is changed, meeting times are updated, or new documents are added to the site. These notifications can appear in an alert window, be routed to a special alerts folder, or even be forwarded to a mobile phone, pager, or other e-mail address.

Cross-Reference WSS is a complex product that offers excellent collaboration capabilities for Office users. You'll find a detailed description of WSS and how to put it to work in Chapter 21.

You can take advantage of the critical event notification feature in Outlook 2003 even if you don't use WSS. For example, you can configure Outlook to display an alert when you receive new e-mail messages.

Calendar and Contact sharing and access

Outlook 2003 takes advantage of some new features to make it easier for users to work with multiple calendars. For example, maybe you use one calendar for your business events and meetings and a second for your personal items or for a special project. You can view these two calendars side by side, which is handy for planning and coordinating your schedule. This capability also makes it easier to work with another user's calendar in addition to your own when scheduling meetings and other events. WSS users can view other team members' calendars, as well.

Outlook 2003 also provides better offline access to calendar and contact information. It caches locally your Exchange Server contacts as well as WSS contacts so you can use them when you're offline.

Instant messaging

Instant messaging (IM) now pervades Outlook and other Office applications. You can start an IM session easily any time you see a contact displayed in the application. For example, you can click on a sender's address in an e-mail to start a chat session. This feature is available in Outlook 2002, but has been expanded in Outlook 2003.

Other changes

Outlook 2003 offers many other changes in addition to the ones I've already mentioned. For example, you now have better control over views and more options for organizing various types of Outlook items. We'll cover all of these new features throughout the rest of the book.

Summary

This chapter provided a quick sampling of some of the tasks you can accomplish with Outlook. You probably weren't aware just how versatile and adaptable Outlook could be, especially if you thought Outlook was only another e-mail program. But because this chapter is just a quick sampler, we hope you'll read on and learn much more about this powerful application called Outlook.

The next chapter provides a guided tour of Outlook, where you learn some of the basics of using Outlook for yourself.

✦   ✦   ✦

Installing Outlook 2003

◆   ◆   ◆   ◆

In This Chapter

Outlook installation options

Changing your settings

Adding additional features

◆   ◆   ◆   ◆

Microsoft made a significant change to Outlook 2002 that carries over to Outlook 2003: the switch from a handful of operating modes to a single, unified mode. Similar to Outlook 2002, Outlook 2003 does not offer Corporate Workgroup or Internet Mail Only modes. Instead, all e-mail services can coexist in a single profile with a unified mode. This simplifies Outlook installation because you no longer need to choose your operating mode; therefore, there are relatively few options involved when installing Outlook 2003. There are, however, some different approaches you can take depending on how you want to deploy Outlook, such as for a handful of users or for a large group. In this chapter I'll examine the options and methods you have for installing Outlook.

If you're performing an upgrade over a previous version of Outlook, you will not have much to do to get the software installed because Setup will simply install over your existing copy. Whether you upgrade or install new, however, there are many configuration issues and settings to consider so you can set up Outlook the way you want it. This chapter covers installation and set up issues, while Chapter 4 covers configuration tasks.

Understanding Deployment Options

One feature that is new in Outlook 2003 is Cached Exchange Mode (CEM). This mode is an extension of previous Outlook versions' use of an offline store, or OST file. CEM uses the same OST as Outlook would normally use if you set up the Exchange Server account for non-cached behavior, but automates the connection state management and synchronization process for you. Outlook works from the locally cached copy of the mailbox, and updates the cache when a connection to the server is available.

Choosing between CEM and non-cached mode isn't really a setup consideration because it doesn't come into play for the actual Outlook installation; however, part of the installation routine includes (optionally) setting up an e-mail account, so it's a consideration if you take that additional step during installation. For that reason, I'll focus on CEM in Chapter 5.

When it comes time to deploy Outlook, your primary consideration is how many computers are involved. The installation process for single, at-the-PC installations is almost a no-brainer. I'll run through it in the next section. Installation becomes more complicated when you need to deploy Outlook to many users. There are several tools to do that, including group policy, Microsoft SMS, and several third-party solutions. I take a look at some of these, as well as related issues, in the section, "Wide-Scale Outlook Deployment."

Tip Outlook offers several features that you can install or not, regardless of the type of installation you perform. See the "Standalone and One-by-One Installations" section for a discussion of the Outlook features you can add or remove during Office installation. The section, "Wide-Scale Outlook Deployment," explains how to control which of these options is installed during automated and push deployments.

Standalone and One-by-One Installations

It's likely that at some point you will need to perform a single-instance installation of Microsoft Office or Outlook. The process isn't difficult, particularly if you focus specifically on Outlook. There are lots of features, however, that you can choose to add or not add depending on how you intend to use Outlook. The following list describes the components included with Outlook and which ones are added when you install Outlook using the Typical Setup option (explained in more detail later in this chapter):

✦ **Help.** This is the Help documentation for Outlook and is installed with the Typical option.

✦ **Importers and Exporters.** These components enable Outlook to import data from other applications such as Act 3.0, ODBC, Lotus Organizer, Schedule Plus, and others. They also provide Outlook with the capability to export data to other applications and common data file formats (such as text files). The Typical option adds the PAB (Personal Address Book) converter; all others are added on first use.

✦ **Stationary.** These HTML templates enable you to add backgrounds, fonts, and other embellishments to your e-mail. The stationary is installed on first use with the Typical option.

✦ **Junk E-mail.** These components help filter out spam and adult-content messages. The Typical option adds this component.

✦ **Address Book Control.** This component enables you to select addresses and some Web site URLs from the Outlook Address Book. This is installed with the Typical option.

✦ **Visual Basic Scripting Support.** This component provides Visual Basic script debugging for custom forms and is installed with the Typical option.

✦ **Collaboration Data Objects.** This component installs the desktop version of the Microsoft Exchange Server Object Programming Library, which enables you to develop applications that interact with Exchange Server and Exchange Server mailboxes. This component is not installed with the Typical option but requires a Custom installation.

✦ **Schedule Plus.** This component adds Schedule Plus compatibility to Outlook 2003. Schedule Plus is the scheduling mechanism used in earlier versions of Windows Messaging. It is installed on first use with the Typical option.

✦ **Outlook Template Files.** These templates provide common forms for messaging, contacts, and other Outlook items. It is installed on first use with the Typical option.

✦ **Outlook Messaging Components.** This branch (set of components) contains the Outlook Mail Application Programming Interface (MAPI) Service Provider group, which contains services that support the Outlook Address Book, Microsoft Exchange Server, Microsoft Lightweight Directory Access Protocol (LDAP) Directory service, and Personal Folders. All of the components in this branch are added with a Typical installation.

Many of these components are required for even the most basic installation of Outlook 2003. For example, you need Personal Folders to store your Outlook data unless you are only using Exchange Server for your mail. Exchange Server is a separate server application that provides e-mail and other communication services. Other components are optional; you don't need the Microsoft Exchange Server provider, for example, if you don't have any mail accounts hosted by Exchange Server, or you access them through another mechanism such as Outlook Web Access or the Internet Message Access Protocol (IMAP) protocol. Outlook Web Access is a component of Exchange Server that enables users to access their mailboxes from a Web browser such as Internet Explorer. IMAP is a standard Internet protocol that supports remote access to a mail server.

As the next section explains, you can pick and choose the components you want Setup to install, or you can let Setup choose components for you based on some common installation options.

Running Setup

Similar to most applications that come on a CD, Microsoft Office will automatically launch Setup when you insert the CD unless you have turned off auto-insert notification for the CD. If Setup doesn't launch when you insert the CD or double-click it in My Computer, open My Computer, open the CD drive where the Office 11 CD is located, and double-click Setup.exe. You can also right-click the CD drive in My Computer, and choose AutoPlay from the context menu.

The Setup Wizard prompts for several items and options, the first of which is the 25-character product key. The key consists of five groups of letters and numbers, and is included on the back of the CD case or on the Certificate of Authenticity that you should have received with the software or with your PC. If you have neither the CD nor a certificate, you need to contact the company that sold you the computer and obtain both; otherwise, your software isn't legally licensed.

Setup then prompts for your name, initials, and organization. Office uses your initials in Word to indicate document authorship and in certain other applications for similar purposes.

After you accept the End-User License Agreement (EULA), Setup offers four common installation options, shown in Figure 2-1. The previous section identified the components that Setup installs if you choose the Typical installation option. This option installs the components required by most users.

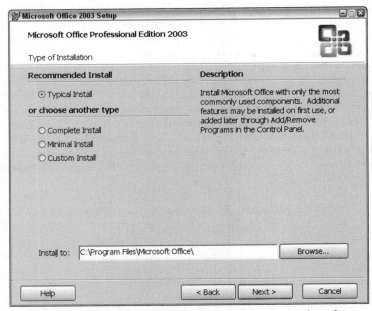

Figure 2-1: You can choose between four common options for installing Microsoft Office.

The Minimal option is useful if you don't have a lot of space on the installation hard disk, but even with this option Setup needs over 110MB to install Office. The Complete option installs all components on the hard disk. The Custom option enables you to choose which applications to install (Figure 2-2).

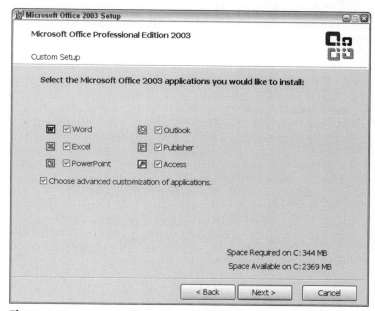

Figure 2-2: You can select which Office applications to install.

If you want to further customize the installation and choose which components for each application are installed, select the option Choose advanced customization of applications from the Custom Setup page shown in Figure 2-2. When you click Next, Setup displays a page that allows you to select which components it will install (Figure 2-3).

Click the plus sign beside a branch to expand it and then click the down arrow on the disk icon beside each component to choose one of the following four options:

✦ **Run from My Computer.** Installs on the computer those components listed for a Typical installation, and installs all other subcomponents on first use.

✦ **Run all from My Computer.** Installs all subcomponents on the computer.

✦ **Installed on first use.** Installs the component the first time you attempt to use the component (called just-in-time (JIT) installation).

✦ **Not available.** The component is not installed on the computer; Setup will not perform a just-in-time installation if you attempt to use the feature.

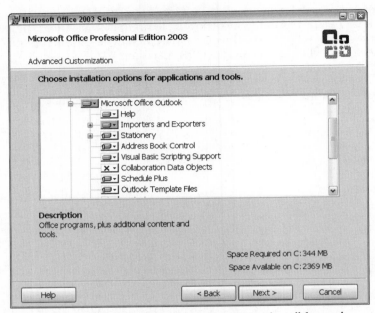

Figure 2-3: Select the components you want to install for each application.

After you select the components to install, click Next and then click Install to begin the actual installation process.

Changing, Repairing, or Removing an Office Installation

As explained in the previous section, you can configure Outlook for just-in-time installation of certain features or even an entire Office application. If you select the option Installed on first use, Setup adds the component the first time you attempt to use it. You can also add components by running Setup again after Office is already installed.

When you run Setup after Office is installed, Setup offers three options as shown in Figure 2-4:

✦ **Add or Remove Features.** Choose this option if you want to add or remove components from Outlook or other Office applications. Setup presents the page shown in Figure 2-3, which enables you to choose the components to be installed on your computer.

✦ **Reinstall or Repair.** Setup offers additional options when you click Next. Select the Reinstall Office option if you want to restore the Office installation to its originally installed state (removes or adds components as needed). Choose the Detect and Repair errors in my Office installation option to have Setup fix your Office installation. Setup recopies files as needed and performs other tasks, such as rebuilding the Office registry entries. Select the Restore my Start Menu Shortcuts option to have Setup recreate the Office application shortcuts on the Start menu.

✦ **Uninstall.** Select this option to remove Office from your computer.

Updating Office

As it does for every product, Microsoft frequently offers updates for Office. Previously these updates were distributed at the Office Update Site, but Microsoft has integrated product updates into the Office Web site at `http://office. microsoft.com`. At the main page, click the Product Updates link to access the latest Service Pack for Office and other updates. You'll also find many other resources such as additional templates, clip art, and other items at the Web site.

If you need to update Office on multiple computers, or if you prefer to install updates manually, point your Web browser to the Office Download Center. You'll find a link to the Download Center on the Product Updates page. The Download Center lets you search for updates, add-ins and extras, and converters and viewers for use with Office.

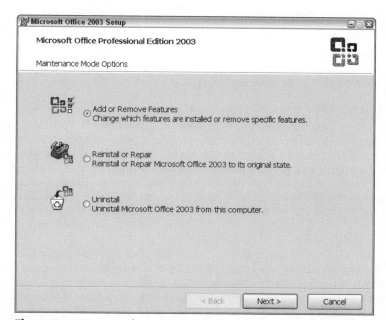

Figure 2-4: You can change, reinstall, repair, or uninstall an Office installation.

Wide-Scale Outlook Deployment

Just running Setup from the CD is the easiest way to install Microsoft Office and Outlook on a single computer or a handful of computers. As the number of computers goes up, so does the amount of time required for installation. Installing one at a time on five computers might be practical, but installing on 200 computers individually is not.

Deploying with SMS and DECM (group policy)

Microsoft offers two main ways to deploy Microsoft Office and other applications to a large number of computers across an enterprise. System Management Server (SMS) is a full-featured deployment suite that not only allows you to deploy Office, but operating systems, updates, patches, and so on. In addition, SMS provides update tracking, system management, and much more.

SMS is a complex product that would require a book of its own to explain adequately, so we'll focus here on telling you where to find more information about it. The home page for SMS is located at www.microsoft.com/smserver/default.asp. There you'll find technical documentation, a downloadable evaluation copy, and other resources to help you determine if SMS is the best deployment solution for you.

Tip   SMS offers the advantage over Remote Installation Services (RIS) (explained later in this section) of being able to deploy operating systems other than Windows 2000 or later. RIS can only deploy Windows 2000, Windows XP, or Windows .NET Server.

Another option you have for automated application deployment is IntelliMirror, a collection of technologies built into Windows 2000 Server and Windows .NET Server. IntelliMirror is also referred to as Directory-Enabled Client Management (DECM).

DECM relies on group policy support in Windows 2000, Windows XP, and Windows .NET Server to automate the installation process. Group policies apply to a user's computer when it starts up, and others apply when the user logs on. These group policies define the user's working environment as well as actions and tasks the user can take within the operating system and specified applications. Group policy therefore enables administrators to apply *change control* (the ability to restrict changes) over the user and the computer, limiting and restricting the actions the user can perform.

To deploy an application with group policy, you first define the software package at the group policy level at which you want the policy applied. For example, you can apply group policy at the local, site, domain, and organizational unit (OU) level within the user's domain. The most common approach is to create OUs to deploy applications because the OUs can mirror the users' job responsibilities. For example, let's say you need to deploy one set of Office applications for people in the Sales department and a different set for those in the Engineering department. You would create a Sales OU and an Engineering OU, and apply policies at each OU as needed to define which applications are installed.

You can deploy applications in either of two ways through group policy. Applications that you *assign* appear to the user as if they are already installed, showing up, for example, in the user's Start menu. When the user attempts to use an application, Setup performs a just-in-time installation if the application or component is not already installed.

When you *publish* an application, the application appears to the user in the Add or Remove Programs applet in the Control Panel. The user can then select which applications they want to install. I'll explain in more detail later in this section how you can organize published applications into groups to help users identify the applications they need or should have.

Assigning applications provides the least interaction with the user to install applications. When used in combination with Remote Installation Services (RIS), which lets you deploy the user's operating system automatically, and user folder redirection, DECM-based application deployment offers outstanding disaster recovery. Let's assume you've taken the trouble to set up RIS, assigned applications through group policy, and redirected the users' document and other data folders to a network server. Monday morning, a user discovers that his computer has died. You hand him a new computer with a blank hard disk and tell him to connect it to the network, plug it in, and turn it on.

The user does so. The computer boots and RIS installs the user's operating system. After the computer reboots, Windows prompts the user to log on. He does so, and the group policy you've defined for him in the Active Directory deploys his applications so they appear in his Start menu. When he clicks on Outlook in the Start menu, for example, Setup installs Outlook for him. He then starts Word (which installs automatically), opens My Documents, and finds all of his documents waiting for him because you've redirected his My Documents folder to a network server through group policy. The end result is that, as an administrator, all you've done to get the poor soul back up and running is handed him a new computer or installed a new hard disk. Group policy and RIS have done all the disaster recovery, and in only an hour or so. Of course, you have to set up the framework ahead of time, but that isn't as difficult as it might seem.

 Note   Because this book focuses on Microsoft Outlook rather than Windows, I don't cover RIS or how to deploy the operating system automatically. Instead, the following section explains how to deploy Office using group policy.

Deploying Office with group policy

Deploying Office with group policy requires a bit of preparation, including creating an administrative share in addition to defining group policies. You start by adding the application package to a server. The package is the file or set of files that contains the application.

Adding the package

The first step in deploying an application through group policy is to install the application files on a server accessible to the users under the scope of the policy. If you don't already have a share assigned, create a share on a network server and then set permission to allow users read access to the share and its contents.

Next, run `Setup /a` to install the administrative share in the network share. The `/a` switch directs Setup to create an administrative share. Setup starts an Administrative Installation wizard, the first page of which is shown in Figure 2-5. Specify the folder on the server in which you want to install the administrative share, enter the installation key, and click Next. After presenting the EULA for you to accept, Setup begins the installation process. The end result of all this fun is a folder containing the files necessary to install Microsoft Office 11.

Creating transforms

After you create the administrative share, you can create transform files that will provide for a customized Office installation. You can create these files manually, and you could also hike the Sahara without a hat. Neither is a good idea. Instead, use the Custom Installation Wizard included with the Microsoft Office 11 Resource Kit to create a transform file.

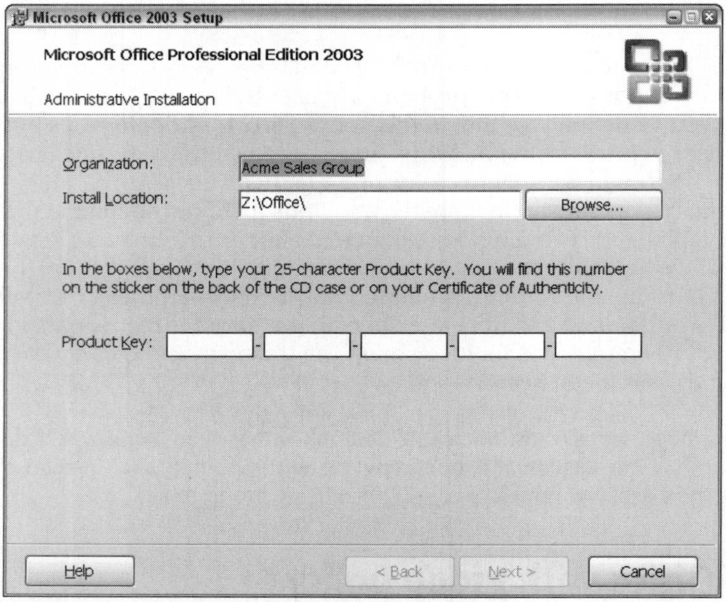

Figure 2-5: Specify the location for the administrative share and the installation key.

The wizard prompts you for the information you want Setup to use during installation and creates the transform file for you. When the user's group policy is applied and Windows installs the application, the transform files determine how the installation takes place.

The wizard first asks for the path to the Microsoft Installer (MSI) file for the application as shown in Figure 2-6. Point it to the `Pro.msi` file in the root of the administrative share; then click Next.

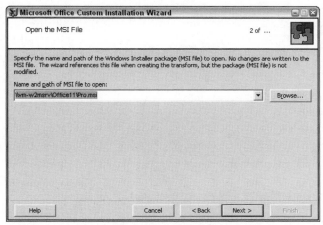

Figure 2-6: Specify the path to the Pro.msi file in the administrative share.

The wizard next prompts you for the name of an existing MST (transform) file to modify or to create a new MST file. In this example, select Create a new MST file and then click Next. Specify the name for the file, specify the root of the administrative share as the path (Figure 2-7), and click Next.

As you move through the wizard, it prompts you for several items of information, such as folder for installation, organization name, and much more. In addition, the wizard asks how you want to handle installation tasks such as which previous versions to remove (Figure 2-8). If you choose the Default Setup behavior option, Setup uses a predetermined set of criteria to remove previous versions of Office. Click the Remove option and review its default settings to understand how Setup behaves if you choose the Default Setup behavior option.

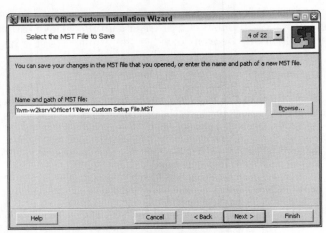

Figure 2-7: Place the new MST file in the root of the Office 11 administrative share.

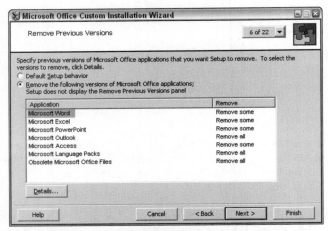

Figure 2-8: You can control which previous versions Setup will remove during installation.

As you do for an attended Setup, you specify which components you want Setup to install for Office (Figure 2-9). Go through the list of components and set each one to one of the following states.

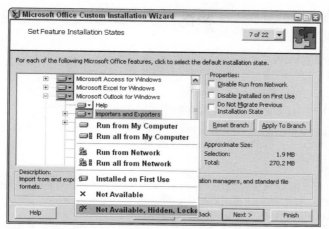

Figure 2-9: Choose the components to be installed.

✦ **Run from My Computer.** Setup installs the selected component on the user's local computer.

✦ **Run all from My Computer.** Setup installs the selected component and all child components on the user's local computer.

✦ **Run from Network.** Setup installs the component so it runs from the network installation share rather than the local computer.

✦ **Run all from Network.** Setup installs the component and all child components so they run from the network installation share rather than the local computer.

✦ **Installed on First Use.** Setup configures the application for just-in-time installation but doesn't actually install the files on the user's computer. Setup installs the application or component when the user attempts to run it from the Start menu, shortcut, or document/application association.

✦ **Not Available.** The application or component is not installed, nor is it advertised on the user's computer as being installed (as are components that are installed on first use). The user receives an error message if he attempts to use a component that is not available, and is directed to re-run Setup to add it.

✦ **Not Available, Hidden, Locked.** Select this option to prevent the component or application from being installed on the user's computer as long as Office 11 is installed. This option effectively disables the component. You can run the wizard again to change the state when you're ready to deploy the application.

There are three options on the Set Feature Installation States page of the wizard that give you additional control over components:

✦ **Disable Run from Network.** This option, when enabled, removes the Run from Network option from the application state drop-down list.

✦ **Disable Installed on First Use.** This option, when enabled, removes the Installed on First Use option from the application state drop-down list.

✦ **Do Not Migrate Previous Installation State.** This option determines whether Setup uses the previously installed version's component state to install components.

This last option was added in Office XP. Previously, Setup would use the installed state of the existing version to determine if it should install a component. Setup used the same installation state for the upgrade. For example, if a component was previously installed as Run from Network, Setup would add the component during the upgrade as Run from Network. The Do Not Migrate Previous Installation State option, if enabled, directs Setup to ignore the installation state for previous version components and use the settings defined in the transform file to determine whether to install components.

The Customize Default Application Settings page (Figure 2-9) lets you specify how Setup handles the users' existing application settings. Choose the Do not customize option if you don't want Setup to change application settings during installation. Select the option Get settings from an existing settings profile to specify the name of a file you've previously created with the Profile Wizard, which is also included with the Office 11 Resource Kit. The Profile Wizard is described later in this chapter.

If you enable the Migrate user settings option, Setup migrates the users' settings from their existing Office applications to the new Office 11 versions. In cases where there are new features or features are replaced, the Office 11 default settings are used instead for those features.

Even if you direct Setup to use the default settings, you still have the ability to specify which settings, if any, Setup should change. The Change Office User Settings page (Figure 2-10) lets you set options for each Office application. Expand the branch, locate the setting you want to change, and double-click that setting. The wizard displays a dialog box in which you set the option. The contents of the dialog box vary according to the option being set. Figure 2-11 shows an example.

Next, use the Add/Remove Files page to add files to the installation process or remove files from the user's computer. For example, if you have custom template files, you can deploy those to the user's computer during installation. When you select a file to add, you also specify the target folder to which the file should be copied. The File Destination Path dialog box, from which you choose the target folder, includes several profile-defined locations. These include several folders in the user's Application Data folder, My Documents, and so on.

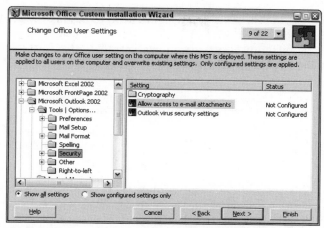

Figure 2-10: Use the Change Office User Settings page to view and configure Office user settings.

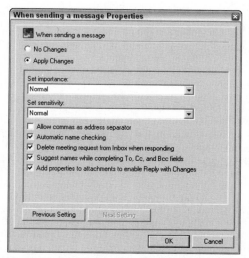

Figure 2-11: The properties you can set for an option vary from one option to another.

The Add/Remove Registry Entries page lets you add custom registry keys and values during Office installation in addition to those automatically created by Setup. For example, you might deploy a custom Master Category List by creating the necessary registry values that define it.

Use the Add, Modify, or Remove Shortcuts page (Figure 2-12) to modify the shortcuts created during installation or remove existing shortcuts. For example, you might not want the Office application shortcuts added directly to the Start menu. You can use the Not Installed tab to remove them.

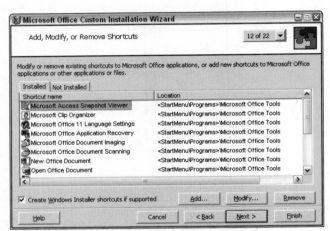

Figure 2-12: You can control the shortcuts Setup adds or removes during installation.

The Identify Additional Servers page lets you specify other administrative installation shares for Office. You can create additional shares on other servers manually or use the file replication technologies built into Windows 2000 and .NET Server to copy the shares. Specifying additional shares ensures that a share is available for installation and when the user runs a component that is configured to run from the network.

You should spend some time with the Specify Office Security Settings page (Figure 2-13) to control the actions users can take that affect system and application security. The Trust Settings group of options determines sources that are trusted for add-on features. You can also configure security settings for each application to control macro security level and whether Office trusts add-ins and templates.

 Macro security is explained in Chapter 17.

You can use the Add Installations and Run Programs page of the wizard to identify other applications to deploy along with Office 11. For example, you might use a custom Office application for customer management, and you can deploy that right along with Office. You can specify a Microsoft Installer package (MSI, MST, or MSP file) or other executable such as an EXE file. You can also run scripts, and even display a document if needed through this page.

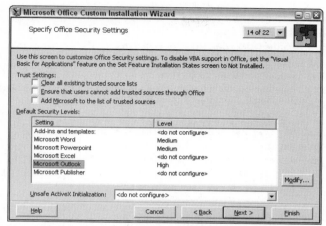

Figure 2-13: Configure security-related settings on the Specify Office Security Settings page.

Use the Outlook: Customize Default Profile page (Figure 2-14) to control how Setup creates or updates Outlook profiles during installation. The Use existing profile option, if enabled, causes Setup to prompt users to create a profile the first time they run Outlook. If the user already has an Outlook profile, Setup uses that profile instead.

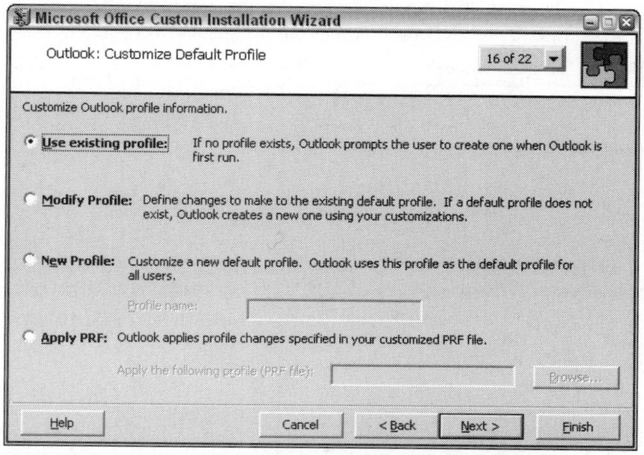

Figure 2-14: Control Outlook profile creation with the Outlook: Customize Default Profile page.

Use the Modify Profile option to modify the user's existing profile with settings that you specify through additional wizard pages. If no profile exists on the user's computer, Setup creates a new profile with the settings you specify.

The New Profile option lets you force all users to receive a new profile, even if they already have one on their computer. Setup uses the settings you specify in the wizard pages that follow to create the profile during installation.

The option Apply PRF enables you to specify an existing Outlook profile (PRF) file. You create the PRF file through the Custom Installation Wizard using the Modify Profile or New Profile options. On the last of the pages that prompt you for information about the Outlook profile, the wizard provides an Export Profile Settings button that you can click to export the Outlook profile settings to a PRF file.

The next three wizard pages prompt you for information about the Outlook profile to create or modify on the user's computer. Naturally, we'll focus a little more attention on these pages.

The wizard prompts you for Exchange Server settings. If you don't use Exchange Server, you can choose the option not to configure an Exchange Server account; otherwise, specify the user name for the account and the Exchange Server name, as shown in Figure 2-15. Use %UserName% in the User Name field rather than an explicit user name to have the profile created with the user's account name. If necessary, you can also include the user's domain, such as mydomain\%UserName%. If you're modifying an existing profile, you can choose the Overwrite existing Exchange settings option to have Outlook modify the user's existing Exchange Server settings in the profile.

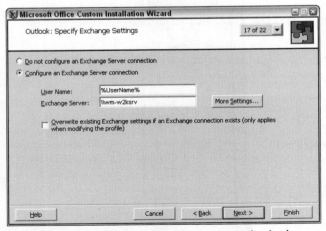

Figure 2-15: Specify Exchange Server properties in the Outlook: Specify Exchange Settings page.

Tip You can specify the IP address, fully-qualified domain name, or NetBIOS name for the Exchange Server.

Click More Settings to open the dialog box shown in Figure 2-16. Here you can enable offline use, specify that the account use a locally cached copy of the Exchange Server mailbox, and the directory path to store the Offline Address Book (OAB).

The Outlook: Add Accounts page (Figure 2-16) enables you to add other POP3, IMAP, or HTTP e-mail accounts to the user profile. For example, if all of your users have POP3 accounts on your local mail server or they have Hotmail accounts, you add them on this page. You can also add personal folder (PST) files, the Outlook Address Book (OAB), Internet Directory Service (LDAP), and Personal Address Book (PAB) to the profile.

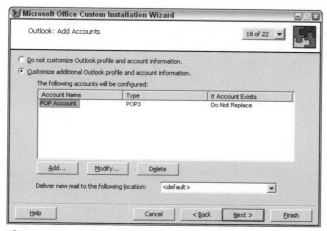

Figure 2-16: Use the Outlook: Add Accounts page to add other e-mail accounts, address books, and directory services.

Select the option Customize additional Outlook profile and account information; then click Add to display the Add Account dialog box, which lists the types of items you can add. Select the item and then click Next. The wizard presents you with additional pages that you use to specify the account settings. The settings vary depending on the type of item you are adding. These settings are essentially the same as those you would specify if creating an account within Outlook. Rather than specify a user name, however, you will typically use %username% to have Outlook use the user's logon name for the mailbox account name.

The next page, Outlook: Remove Accounts and Export Settings, enables you to remove existing account types if you're modifying an existing profile. Because they are no longer supported by Outlook 2003, Lotus cc:Mail and Microsoft Mail are included on this page as account types you can remove. You can also click Export

Profile Settings to export the settings to a PRF file. You should export the settings in case you want to import and modify them later.

Use the Outlook: Customize Default Settings page to set options that control how Setup handles certain default settings. You can direct Setup to migrate the user's Personal Address Book to the Outlook Address Book and specify the default e-mail editor and mail format.

Finally, use the Modify Setup Properties page (Figure 2-17) to modify values used by Setup during installation. You can also add and remove values, although you can't remove any of the default values; you can only remove those you've added yourself.

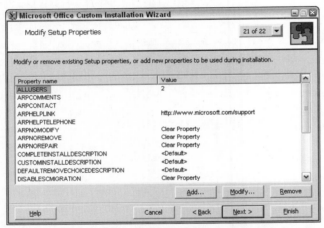

Figure 2-17: Modify, add, or remove values used by Setup during installation.

When you click Finish, the wizard creates the MST file in the location you specified at the beginning of the wizard. You can use the MST with group policy to control Setup, or you can use the file with Setup from a command line. The following section explains how to publish and assign applications with group policy. See the section "Automated and Unattended Setup" later in this chapter for more details on using a transform file from the Setup command line.

Defining group policy

As explained previously, you can apply group policy at the local, site, domain, or OU levels. Group policy application is cumulative and hierarchical. For example, the user's local policy is applied first, followed by site, domain, and OU levels. Policies defined at a higher level typically override those at a lower level. So, if a policy applies at the domain level but is applied differently at the OU level, the OU policy will take precedence.

The next step in deploying applications with group policy is to decide the level at which you will apply the policy. If everyone in your organization needs an application, define it at the site or domain level. Define application policies at the OU level if you need more control over who receives what application. I'll assume you want to deploy at the OU level in this section, but the process is the same for the domain level. The only difference is which group policy object (GPO) you edit.

Open the Active Directory Users and Groups console on the server where you will define the policy. Expand the domain and then locate the OU of which the user is a member and at which you want to define the application. Right-click the OU, and choose Properties. Click the Group Policy tab (Figure 2-18).

Tip   The Active Directory Users and Groups console is an administrative tool installed on Windows 2000 and .NET Server domain controllers.

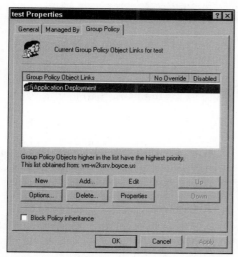

Figure 2-18: The Group Policy tab shows all GPOs currently linked to the selected container.

If there are no GPOs, or if you prefer to apply software policies through a different GPO, click New to add one. Alternatively, select an existing GPO and then click Edit to open the Group Policy editor (Figure 2-19).

You can define software policies either at the computer or user level. In this situation I'm assuming you want to assign at the user level, so expand the User Configuration\Software Settings branch. Right-click Software Installation, and choose New ➪ Package. In the Open dialog box, enter the Uniform Naming Convention (UNC) path to the folder where the Office 2003 administrative share is located; then select the Pro.msi file, and click Open.

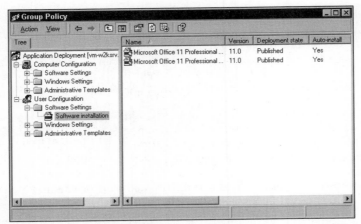

Figure 2-19: Use the Group Policy editor to define group policies, including those for Outlook and other Office applications.

The Group Policy editor next offers options in the Deploy Software dialog box:

✦ **Published.** Select this option if you want the application to appear in the user's Add or Remove Programs applet as available for installation.

✦ **Assigned.** Select this option if you want Office to appear as if it is already installed (appears on the Start menu, for example).

✦ **Advanced published or assigned.** Select this option if you want to configure additional properties for the package before the policy object is created. You can modify these properties after the fact if you use either of the previous two options.

If you choose the last option or you double-click a package after you create it, the editor displays the property sheet shown in Figure 2-20.

The General tab displays the product information for the package, and enables you to change the name for the package. The Deployment tab offers the following options:

✦ **Deployment type.** Choose either publishing or assigning the application.

✦ **Auto-install this application by file extension activation.** Allow Setup to install applications when a user attempts to use a document associated with the application. For example, Setup will install Word if the user tries to open a document (.doc) file.

✦ **Uninstall this application when it falls out of the scope of management.** Remove the application from users' computers when the GPO no longer applies.

✦ **Do not display this package in the Add/Remove Programs control panel.**
Hide the application from the users' Add or Remove Programs applet.

✦ **Installation user interface options.** Choose the Basic option to display only
basic progress information to the user during installation; choose the
Maximum option to have Setup show all progress dialog boxes.

✦ **Advanced.** Click this button to access the following two options:

• **Ignore language when deploying this package.** Deploy the package even
if it uses a different language from that in use on the user's computer.

• **Remove previous installs of this product for users** if the product was
not installed by group policy-based Software Installation. If the previous
installations of the product were installed manually on the user's computer, such as from local CD, remove the previous installation. This
option enables you to migrate your users to group policy-based installation for better change control and management.

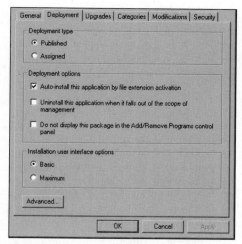

Figure 2-20: Use the package's property
sheet to modify its properties.

The Upgrades tab enables you to specify one or more existing packages that the
current package will upgrade. You select the package from the current GPO or from
a different GPO. You also specify whether the current package upgrades the older
package in place, or Setup should remove the old package first and then install the
current one. You can also specify that the current package is a required upgrade for
the existing one(s).

Use the Categories tab to specify in which categories the package will appear in the user's Add or Remove Programs applet. You can only assign categories through the Categories tab; you can't create them. See the section "Setting global package properties" later in this chapter for detailed instructions on how to create and manage categories.

The Modifications tab (Figure 2-21) enables you to assign transforms (MST files) for the package. If you open the properties of an existing package, however, you'll find that all the controls are unavailable, preventing you from assigning any MST files. You can only assign transforms when you create the package; you can't do it afterward.

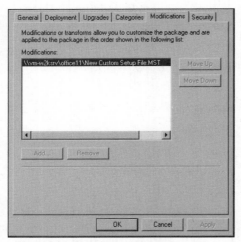

Figure 2-21: Use the Modifications tab to assign transforms to the package.

If you choose the Advanced Published or Assigned option when you create the package, the controls in the Modifications tab are available. If you've already created a package and need to apply one or more transforms to it, you can take one of three approaches:

✦ **Change the original package to Published and assign a new package.**
Right-click the existing package and then choose Publish (unless it is already published). Create a new assigned package that includes the transform. The assigned package will take precedence over the published package. The new package should use the same product code as the original.

✦ **Deploy an upgrade.** Create an upgrade package for the original package and include the transforms in the upgrade. The Upgrade should use a different product code from the original.

✦ **Create a new package and remove the old one.** Choose the option Advanced Published or Assigned when you create a new package, either published or assigned, and include the desired transforms. After you deploy this second package, remove the original package from the GPO.

You can add multiple transform files to a package using the Move Up and Move Down buttons to arrange the transforms in the correct order. Keep in mind that you can't change the modifications after you click OK to create the package. If the transforms are not in the correct order and the GPO gets applied to users and the package gets installed, you will have to redeploy the application to those users. So make sure the transforms are ordered properly before you click OK.

You can use the Security tab to control the permissions that users have for the package. One of the primary reasons to change security settings is to prevent a particular package from applying to a user or group that is under the scope of the GPO. To prevent a user or group from having the package deployed or assigned, modify the permissions and deny that user or group Read permission for the package.

Changing the deployment method

You can change a package's deployment method after creating it. For example, you might publish a package to test it and then decide to assign it when you're ready for full deployment. Alternatively, maybe you need to add transforms to the package and want to change an assigned package to published. Whatever the case, right-click the package and then choose the desired deployment method from the context menu.

Setting global package properties

The Software Installation node offers some general properties you can set to control the way group policy deploys the applications within its scope. Right-click the Software Installation node and then choose Properties to display the property sheet shown in Figure 2-22.

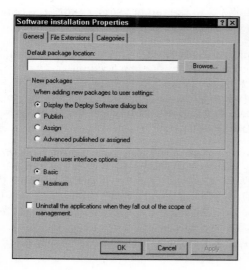

Figure 2-22: You can specify the default behavior for new packages with this property sheet.

Use the General tab to specify the default location you want the editor to look for packages. This will save you time when you're hunting for the MSI file for a new package. The New Packages group on the General tab lets you set the default behavior when creating new packages:

✦ **Display the Deploy Software dialog box.** The editor prompts you to choose one of the following three options.

- **Publish.** Packages are published by default.

- **Assign.** Packages are assigned by default.

- **Advanced publish or assign.** The editor displays the properties for the package to enable you to modify them before creating the policy object.

The File Extensions tab is the place to go to control which applications Windows uses to open a document. Select a file extension from the drop-down list to add it to the list; then use the Up and Down buttons to change its precedence. Move the application to the top of the list to make Windows use that application for the selected file type.

Use the Categories tab to create and manage the application categories that you want to appear in the user's Add or Remove Programs applet in the Control Panel. Click Add, specify a category name, and click OK. Select a category and then click Modify if you want to change it, or click Remove to remove it. Keep in mind that you don't actually assign categories here to application packages — you only create the categories. You assign the categories when you create or modify a package's properties.

Testing and deploying the package

After you create the transforms and create the deployment policy, you're ready to test it. I recommend that you first publish a package for testing, and after you've worked out the bugs, you can apply the GPO to the target users, change the deployment method to assigned, or both.

To test the package, add a test account to the OU or domain where you've defined the package. On a test workstation, log on with that domain account and verify that the application appears in the Add or Remove Programs applet (published) or appears on your Start menu (assigned). Run through the installation process to check for bugs, particularly in the creation of Outlook profile settings. If all looks good you're ready to deploy the policy to your users.

One other technique you might find handy when developing and testing packages for deployment is to use a non-production OU to develop the policies and then migrate the GPO to the production OUs or domains where they will be applied. For example, create an OU named DeployTest and then add a test account to it. Modify the properties for the OU to create the GPO, and add the application packages as needed.

After you've completed the development and tested the applications, you can assign the GPO to other OUs and domains. For example, open the properties for a production domain and then click the Group Policy tab. Click Add to open the Add a Group Policy Object Link dialog box (Figure 2-23) and then open the test OU. Select the applicable policy object(s), and click OK to link them to the production OU or domain.

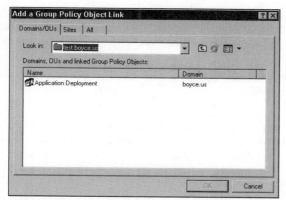

Figure 2-23: You can easily link GPOs to multiple domains or OUs.

Controlling Office applications with group policy

In the previous sections, I've explained how to deploy applications with group policy. While the deployment package lets you control the applications that a user receives, it does not control what the user can do with the application once he has it installed. You can use group and system policies to apply change control and restrictions on Office applications. I cover this in detail in Chapter 24.

Automated and Unattended Setup

In addition to using group policy to deploy Office and Outlook, you can create and use Setup scripts that automate the installation process. You can employ this method with logon scripts or manual installation methods to automate Setup.

A Setup information (INI) file is a text file that contains settings that control how Setup installs an application. You can create this text file manually, but that would be worse than coding an entire Web site manually in Notepad. There are people who enjoy that sort of thing, but you probably have other ways to occupy your time.

The method I recommend for creating customized Setup INI files is to use the Setup INI Customization Wizard included with the Microsoft Office 11 Resource Kit. As with the Custom Installation Wizard, the Setup INI Customization Wizard steps you through the process of specifying settings and provides a custom INI as the result of your input.

When you run the wizard, it prompts you for the administrative installation share and the existing INI file that you want to customize. As you progress through the wizard, it asks for a considerable amount of information about the installation, including the following:

✦ **Logging and default display mode.** These settings control how Setup writes to the setup logs during installation and the amount of progress information Setup displays to the user. The display setting can be overridden by specific package settings.

✦ **Location and inclusion of MSI and EXE files.** The wizard searches the installation share for applicable files, and allows you to select the ones to be installed.

✦ **Installation sequence.** When Setup is installing multiple packages, you can specify the order in which they are installed. For example, you would probably have Setup install Office before installing the Office Web Components. You can also specify for each package the default display mode and any transform to apply during installation of the package.

✦ **Custom Installer properties.** You can specify your own set of Microsoft Installer properties to further control the installation.

At the completion of the wizard, click Save As to save the resulting INI file to disk. You can then use the file as I explain in the next section.

Using Setup switches and custom INI files

Setup supports a handful of command-line switches to help control the Office installation process, including specification of a custom INI file. This section of the chapter explores each switch.

/a [*msifile*]

Use this switch to create an administrative share point from which users can install the software. You must specify the path to the MSI file if it is not in the same folder as Setup.exe.

/checkupdates

Specify this option if you want Setup to check Microsoft's Web site for program updates during the installation process.

/f[*options*] *msifile*

Use this option to force a repair of an application in the specified package. Table 2-1 lists the options and their functions.

Table 2-1
Options for the /f Setup.exe switch

Option	Description
a	Reinstall all files regardless of checksum or version
c	Reinstall file if it is missing or corrupt
d	Reinstall file if it is missing or a different version
e	Reinstall file if it is missing or an older or equal version exists
m	Rewrite the HKEY_LOCAL_MACHINE registry entries
o	Reinstall file if it is missing or an older version exists
p	Reinstall file only if it is missing (disregard existing versions)
s	Reinstall all application shortcuts, overwriting existing shortcuts
u	Rewrite the HKEY_CURRENT_USER registry entries
v	Copy the package from the original source and cache it on the local computer

The Detect and Repair command in an application's Help menu is synonymous with running `Setup.exe /focums`. Selecting the Repair option when you re-run Setup is synonymous with running `Setup.exe /fecums`.

/i [msifile]

This option directs Setup to install applications using the specified MSI file. This is the default behavior for Setup. Specify the full path to the MSI file if it is not located in the same folder as Setup.exe.

/joption [msifile] [/t mstfile]

The /j switch directs Setup to advertise the application for installation on the local computer and configure it for install-on-first-use. In effect, this is the same as assigning the package through group policy. The applications within the scope of the package appear in the user's Start menu. When they click an application or attempt to open an associated document, Setup performs a just-in-time installation of the product.

You can advertise the application either to the current user only or to all users on the computer. Use the m option to advertise to all users or the **u** option to advertise only to the current user. The following example would advertise Office to all users from Pro.msi and apply the Custom.mst transform file:

```
Setup.exe /jm Pro.msi /t Custom.mst
```

You can also use the /l, /q, and /settings command-line switches in combination with the /j switch. These additional switches are explained later in this section.

/l[options] logfile

Use the /l switch to specify the type of logging you want Setup to perform during installation. There are several options you can use with this switch, shown in Table 2-2.

Table 2-2
Logging Options for Setup.exe

Option	Description
a	Start of action notification
c	Log initial UI parameters
e	Log error messages
i	Log information-only messages
m	Log out-of-memory messages
o	Log out-of-disk-space messages
p	Include property table list in form property=value
r	Log action-specific information
u	Log user request messages
v	Verbose mode; include debug messages
w	Include warning messages
*	Turn on all logging options except v
+	Append to existing log file

Use the *logfile* parameter to specify the path and file name of the log file.

/nocache

This switch directs Setup to not install the Source Engine file, Ose.exe, and to not cache the installation files locally when Office is installed from the CD. Setup does not create a local cache if the user installs from an administrative share point.

/nocheckupdates

Do not check the Microsoft Web site for Office updates during installation.

/noreboot

This switch prevents Setup from restarting the computer at completion of the installation process, or from displaying the restart message upon completion. This switch causes Setup to pass the property REBOOT=ReallySuppress to each package in the installation set except the last one.

/p [*mstfile*]

Apply the patch specified by *mstfile* to an existing installation of Office.

/q[*options*]

The /q switch specifies the user interface level for Setup. You can use the options in Table 2-3 to control the interface.

<table>
<tr><td colspan="2" align="center">Table 2-3
User Interface Levels</td></tr>
<tr><td>*Option*</td><td>*Description*</td></tr>
<tr><td>b</td><td>This basic option displays only simple progress indicators and error messages.</td></tr>
<tr><td>f</td><td>This full option displays all dialog boxes and messages and is the default behavior without the /q switch.</td></tr>
<tr><td>n</td><td>Do not display a user interface; synonymous with /q and no additional options.</td></tr>
<tr><td>r</td><td>This option displays all progress indicators and error messages but does not collect user information.</td></tr>
<tr><td>-</td><td>Suppress all modal dialog boxes; used with b, f, n, or r.</td></tr>
<tr><td>+</td><td>Add completion message to the n or b option.</td></tr>
</table>

/settings *file*

Use a custom Setup INI file in place of Setup.ini. If the INI file is not located in the folder with Setup.exe, you must specify the path to the INI file. This is the switch that allows you to use the custom INI file you created with the Setup INI Customization Wizard that was discussed at the beginning of this section.

/x [*msifile*]

Direct Setup to remove the application contained in the package specified by *msifile*. Specify the path to the MSI file if it is not in the same folder as Setup.exe.

property=value

Use this Setup parameter to pass additional installation properties to Setup. See the Setup.htm file on the Office CD for a description of the allowed property values.

Creating and Migrating Office Profiles

The Microsoft Office Resource Kit includes a couple of utilities you can use to create Office profiles that are stored in OPF files. The main purpose of an OPF is to store a group of application settings that you can use to configure a user's Office installation after Setup. You can also use an OPF to migrate user settings between computers. The OPF is a snapshot of the registry values and related settings files that comprise the user's Office environment.

Tip   Office also includes a Save My Settings Wizard, which performs the same function as the Profile Wizard.

The Save My Settings Wizard and Profile Wizard both create a snapshot of the current Office installation on the local computer, so your first step in using the wizard is to install Office and configure each application. When you run the wizard, it gives you the option of creating a profile or restoring an existing profile (Figure 2-24).

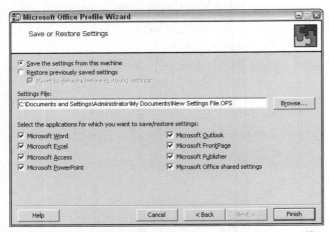

Figure 2-24: Use the Office Profile Wizard to save an Office configuration to a file.

As Figure 2-24 indicates, you can select the applications you want included in the profile. Specify the path to the OPS file and then click Finish to create the OPF. To apply the settings to the user's computer, install Office, run the Profile Wizard, and choose the option Restore previously saved settings.

Summary

This chapter explained the options that are available when you install Outlook and showed you how to add the options and services you need. You also learned how to make certain that items are installed when it is convenient for you — not necessarily when they would otherwise be installed.

You have a handful of methods available for deploying Office across an enterprise. One method I particularly like is group policy, but you can also use SMS and any of several third-party deployment applications. When used in combination with RIS, group policy deployment offers an excellent method for disaster recovery as well as wide-scale system rollout.

If group policy isn't practical for you, consider using a customized INI file to automate the installation process. You can launch Setup with a custom INI file from a logon script, or use similar methods to deploy Office to your users.

The next chapter takes you on a guided tour of Outlook's interface and basic features so you can get up to speed with its more advanced features.

✦   ✦   ✦

A Guided Tour of Outlook 2003

◆ ◆ ◆ ◆

In This Chapter

Understanding the
Outlook window

Using Outlook Today

Understanding
Outlook folders

Using e-mail

Creating tasks

Keeping a journal

Taking notes

◆ ◆ ◆ ◆

Any program with as many features and capabilities as
Outlook can seem confusing at first glance. There are
menus, toolbars, icons, status lines, links you can click, and
many other bits and pieces that may seem designed specifically to make it difficult to know where to begin. Of course,
those same screen elements are all there to help you use
Outlook, but that doesn't make it any easier when you're trying to get started. This chapter is intended to help remove
some of the confusion you may be feeling if you don't feel
quite at home with Outlook.

Similar to Outlook 2000 and later, Outlook 2003 — indeed all of
Office 11 — installs program features as you need them. This
is called just-in-time (JIT) installation. You may well discover
that as you attempt to access certain Outlook features, you
are prompted to insert your Outlook Program CD. If you are
asked to insert the CD, you'll have to wait a few minutes while
a new feature is installed. You may find this to be a bit of a
nuisance, but remember that after a feature is installed, you
won't have to install it again in the future. Waiting to install
program features until they are first used is intended to minimize the amount of disk space that is used by Office 11, but it
does add some complication to using the programs. Always
be sure to keep your Office 11 CDs handy so that you'll be
able to install program options as needed.

**Cross-
Reference**

See Chapter 2 for a discussion of how to install Office, and
ensure that all applications and components are installed
to your local computer during Setup, which eliminates the
need for a just-in-time installation.

Understanding the Outlook Interface

Figure 3-1 shows how the Outlook window may appear when you first open the program. Your copy of Outlook may not look exactly the same as shown in the figure, but for now you can ignore minor differences. Outlook can take on many different appearances depending on how you have configured the view.

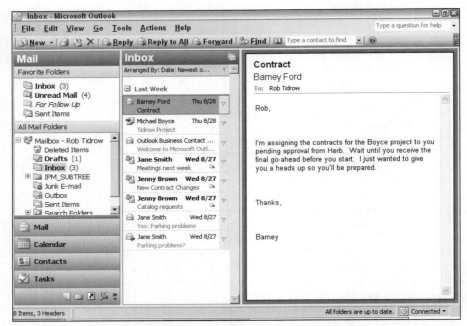

Figure 3-1: The Outlook window has many different elements you can use to get the most out of the program.

To use Outlook effectively you should have an understanding of how each of the elements in the Outlook window functions. Here's a brief explanation of the major items shown in Figure 3-1:

✦ The title bar shows more than just the name of the program. The title bar changes to show the name of the open folder as you open different Outlook folders. This is especially handy if you hide the Folder List because a quick glance at the title bar can confirm that you have opened the correct folder.

✦ The menu bar provides access to all the Outlook commands. The Outlook menu bar is always available because, unlike the toolbars, the menu bar cannot be hidden.

✦ The toolbars consist of buttons you can click to perform actions within Outlook, such as the Send/Receive button that sends and receives e-mail. Outlook has several toolbars that you can choose using the View ➪ Toolbars command. As you open different folders, the Outlook toolbars change so that an appropriate set of tools will be displayed. If you like, you can move the toolbars by dragging them to a different location, you can hide the toolbars if you prefer to use menu commands for everything, or you can customize the toolbars to include different sets of tools.

✦ The Navigation Pane, formerly known as the Outlook Bar, provides one-click access to Outlook folders as well as to the folders on your computer or network. You can add new shortcut icons to the Navigation Pane, remove existing icons, or rename the icons as you please. You can learn more about the Navigation Pane in "Using the Navigation Pane" later in this chapter.

Tip   Numbers in parentheses next to folders in the Folder List indicate the number of new items in each folder.

✦ The Folder List also enables you to access your Outlook folders, as well as the folders on your computer and those available on your network. Because the Navigation Pane and the Folder List provide virtually the same access to Outlook's features, most people choose to display either the Navigation Pane or the Folder List by making selections on the View menu. There are, however, a few functions that can only be done through the Folder List and not through the Navigation Pane.

Tip   Folders whose names appear bold in the Folder List contain items awaiting action, such as unread mail.

✦ The Folder Contents pane displays the contents of the currently selected folder. The view of this pane changes considerably as you select different folders, and you also have the option to customize the view of almost any folder.

✦ The Preview pane, also called the Reading pane, functions as a preview pane for e-mail. You can move the Reading pane from the right to the bottom edge of the folder pane, or remove it altogether. The Reading pane adds additional functions in Outlook 2003, including the ability to respond to meeting requests and to use voting buttons without opening the message. Throughout the book we'll continue to refer to the Reading pane as the Preview pane.

✦ The status line provides a quick summary of the contents of the selected folder, although no summary is shown when the Outlook Today folder is selected. If you select one of the mail folders, the status line tells you both the total number of items and the number of unread items. The right edge of the status line displays information about Outlook's connection status, the synchronization state of the current folder, and overall synchronization status. This is particularly useful when you're working with cached Exchange Server mode, which caches a copy of your Exchange Server mailbox on your local computer.

Because Outlook is so customizable, there are often several ways to accomplish the same task. You can browse your Outlook folders by clicking either an Navigation Pane shortcut icon, or by selecting the folder in the Folder List. Alternatively, you can select Go on the menu bar and then choose the folder. You can check for new e-mail by clicking the Send/Receive button or by selecting Tools ➪ Send/Receive and selecting the account you want to check. In many cases, you'll have access to additional options if you select a menu command rather than simply clicking a button or an icon, but the default action executed by the toolbar buttons is generally the one desired by most users.

You can create more room for the Folder Contents pane by toggling off either the Navigation Pane or the Preview pane. There's no harm in displaying both of them, but you'll probably find the Outlook window a bit crowded unless you choose one or the other, or move the Preview pane to the bottom of the Folder Contents pane.

Changing the view

It almost seems as though each Outlook user could make his or her copy of Outlook appear completely different from everyone else's copy. There are almost unlimited possible combinations of view settings that enable you to customize the appearance of Outlook. And if that doesn't seem like quite enough for you, remember that each Outlook folder can have its own view settings!

Note   Do you not appreciate the way Outlook displays menus yet? If you'd rather see all the commands that are available immediately rather than only the most recently used commands, select Tools ➪ Customize and then click the Options tab in the Customize dialog box that appears. Select the Always show full menus check box, and click the Close button. You'll now be able to see the complete menus all the time, without delay.

In addition to choosing to display the Navigation Pane, the Folder List, or both, you can choose which toolbars you'd like to see. The Outlook toolbars change automatically as you display different types of folders, but you'll probably find that there are times when one or more of the optional toolbars has just what you need. Figure 3-2 shows the three different toolbars that you can display when one of the mail folders — such as Inbox — is selected.

To choose which toolbars are displayed, select View ➪ Toolbars and then the toolbar you want to display. In Figure 3-2, the toolbars were dragged into three rows (excluding the menu bar) to make it easier to differentiate between each of the toolbars. You can also drag the toolbars to other positions, such as docking them at the left, right, or bottom of the Outlook window. In some cases, more than one toolbar can fit into a single row. You can make a toolbar into a floating toolbar rather than one that is docked at the top of the Outlook window by dragging the toolbar down below the toolbar area.

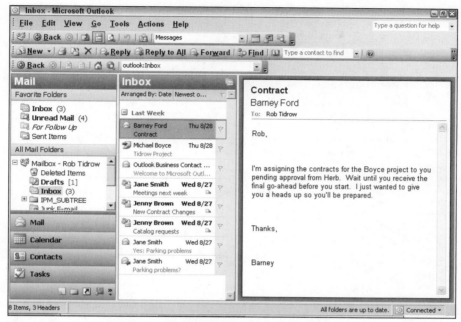

Figure 3-2: Outlook has several different toolbars you can use.

You can drag docked toolbars by moving the mouse pointer over the vertical bar at the left side of the toolbar. When the mouse pointer changes to a four-headed arrow, hold down the left mouse button and then drag the toolbar to the new location. Release the left mouse button when the toolbar is in the position where you'd like to drop it. Drag floating toolbars by their title bars.

Tip   Choose View ➪ Toolbars ➪ Customize to add or remove buttons from the toolbars. This is often a better choice than displaying several toolbars at the same time because your customized toolbar can include only the buttons you need without using as much screen space as multiple toolbars would.

In addition to selecting which toolbars are displayed, you can also decide how you'd like the folder contents pane to appear. Each type of Outlook folder has its own unique set of viewing options, and the following sections explain the possibilities by folder type.

Selecting Calendar views

The Outlook Calendar keeps track of your schedule so that you don't miss important meetings or other appointments. You can view the Calendar folder a number of different ways to suit your individual needs. As Figure 3-3 shows, the default view looks similar to a calendar pad you might have on your desk.

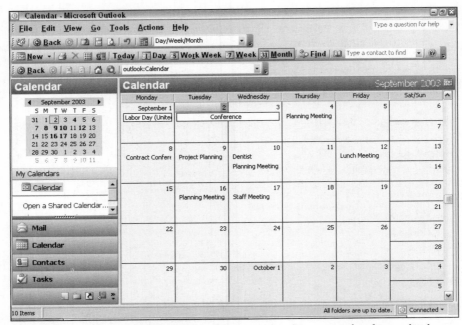

Figure 3-3: Choose the Outlook Calendar view that fits your style of organization.

If you choose View ➪ Day, Work Week, Week, or Month, you can view a single day, the work week, the entire week, or the entire month at one time. You'll likely find that the number of appointments you track may well dictate which view is most convenient.

Tip   You may find it easier to work on your schedule if you temporarily hide the Navigation Pane while you are viewing the calendar folder. You can easily move to another folder using the Go menu.

Selecting Contacts views

The Outlook Contacts folder helps you keep track of addresses, phone numbers, e-mail addresses, and all sorts of other useful information about the people with whom you deal. Not surprisingly, you can choose many different ways to view your Contacts list, too. Figure 3-4 shows the Contacts list using the default Address Card view. Notice that the menu changes when you display different types of Outlook folders.

Some entries in the Contacts folder might use the format *last name, first name*, whereas others use the format *first name last name*. Because different entries appear in different formats, the address list may not be sorted quite the way you would expect. Would you look for Jim Boyce under the letter J or the letter B? One way to correct this problem would be to use the View ➪ Arrange By ➪ Current View ➪ Customize Current View command and then click the Fields button to display the Show Fields dialog box, as shown in Figure 3-5. Select a different field, such as Last Name, rather than the default of File As for the top entry in the Show these fields in this order list box to change the sort order. You'll probably want to use First Name as the second entry in the list box, and remove File As from the list.

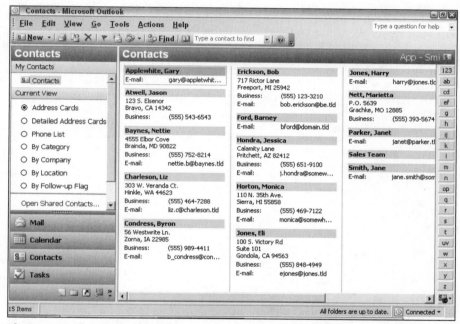

Figure 3-4: Choose the Outlook Contacts list view that works best for you.

Figure 3-5: Correct sorting problems in the Contacts list by customizing the view.

Selecting mail folder views

Several different Outlook folders fall into the category of mail folders. Typically these include the Deleted Items, Drafts, Inbox, Outbox, and Sent Items folders. If you add additional folders of your own, you may have more mail folders.

Mail folders are generally used to hold e-mail messages and faxes, either incoming or outgoing. Each mail folder can be configured to display its contents differently. You might, for example, want to view your Inbox messages sorted by date received and with a preview of the first few lines of unread messages. You might prefer to sort Sent Items according to the name of the recipient so that you can more easily see to whom you've sent messages. Figure 3-6 shows the View ✪ Arrange By options you can choose for mail folders.

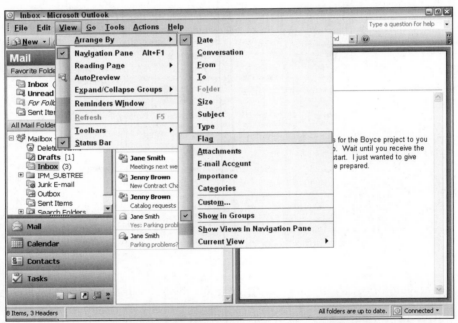

Figure 3-6: You can choose different view options for each different mail folder.

Notice that the mail folder View menu includes a Reading pane submenu. If you select this option, you can choose to turn off the Preview pane, place the Preview pane at the right of the folder pane, or below the folder pane. The folder pane shows the folder contents, and the lower pane displays the contents of the currently selected message. If you choose this option, you'll probably want to turn off AutoPreview, which, if enabled, causes Outlook to display the first few lines of a message under the message header. The Preview pane shows as much of the message as will fit in the pane, so using AutoPreview in concert with the Preview pane is generally a waste of desktop real estate.

Selecting Journal views

The Outlook Journal helps you track your time by automatically making a note of when and how long you work on Office documents (Figure 3-7). You can also add other items to your Journal manually. You have several useful options for viewing the Journal entries.

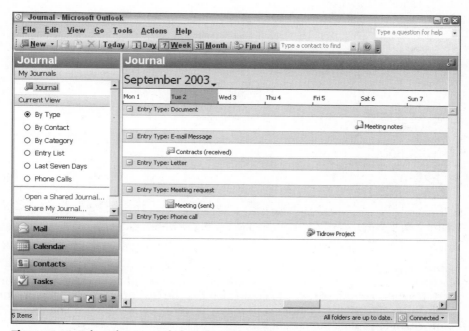

Figure 3-7: Select the Journal view that shows the entries in a style most useful to your way of working.

If you need to track the time you've spent on several different projects, you may find the By Contact view more useful. This view enables you to easily determine how much time you spent working with each client so you can bill for your time.

Selecting Notes views

The Outlook Notes folder (Figure 3-8) holds notes that you create as reminders to yourself. They're essentially the electronic equivalent of those pesky paper sticky notes that people often use to jot down a quick phone number, remind themselves to take out the garbage, or to set up a lunch appointment.

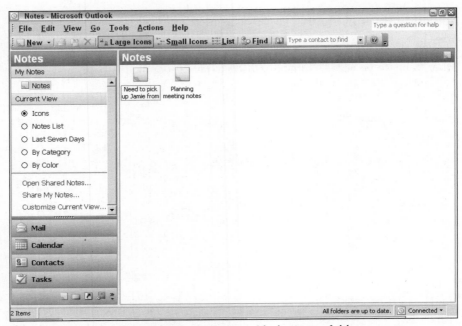

Figure 3-8: Keep track of other information with the Notes folder.

Similar to paper sticky notes, Outlook notes can be different colors. If you use a lot of notes, you may want to choose the By Color view and then use different colors of notes for different purposes. You could also use the By Category view to sort the notes, but using different colors is probably faster because you can change a note's color with a few quick mouse clicks.

Selecting Task views

The Outlook Tasks folder (Figure 3-9) helps you track things you need to do that you can't easily fit on a calendar schedule. Tasks may or may not have a specified due date. Figure 3-9 shows the Tasks view options.

Even though Outlook allows you to set up tasks without specifying a due date, it's usually best to try to assign due dates. You can then use a task view that shows when tasks are overdue or are due during the next week. Of course, you may want to assign your own priorities to the tasks and use a view that reflects their importance in your organizational scheme.

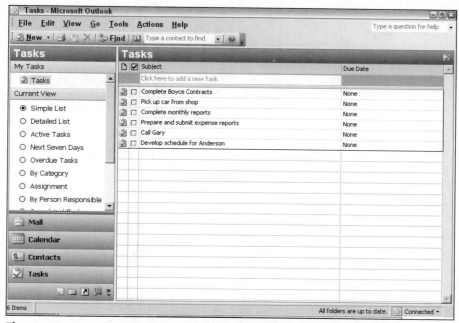

Figure 3-9: Organize your tasks to help you complete them on time.

Using Outlook Today

Outlook Today is a special folder that summarizes all your active Outlook items. Its main benefit is that you don't have to hunt around to make certain you keep track of everything yourself. Figure 3-10 shows the Outlook Today folder. It's difficult to miss any active item when all of them are listed in one place like this. In the All Mail Folders list in the Navigation Pane, click the top-most branch of your mailbox, such as Mailbox - *<name>*, where *<name>* is the name of your Exchange Server mailbox, or the root of your Personal Folders.

The items shown in Outlook Today are linked to their source. This means that you can check off a completed task in Outlook Today, and it will also appear as completed in the Tasks list. Or you can click the Inbox link in Outlook Today to open the Inbox so you can view your new messages.

The Outlook Today calendar section is especially useful because all your upcoming appointments are summarized so you can easily see what's on your schedule. By default, the Outlook Today calendar section shows your appointments for the next five days, but you can easily adjust this to show the number of days you prefer.

It's quite easy to customize Outlook Today. Click the Customize Outlook Today button that's usually near the upper right corner of the Outlook Today folder contents pane to display the customization options as shown in Figure 3-11.

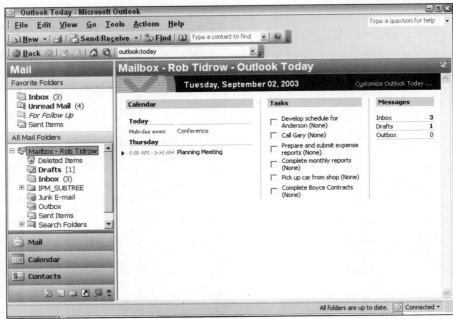

Figure 3-10: The Outlook Today folder organizes all your active items in one place.

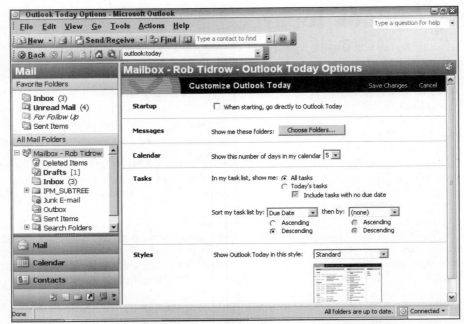

Figure 3-11: Make Outlook Today work your way by customizing the folder.

You have several useful options for customizing the Outlook Today folder:

✦ Remove the check from the check box in the Startup section if you would rather have Outlook open the same folder that was open when you last closed Outlook. If you remove this check, you can still open Outlook Today by clicking the Outlook Today folder in the Folder List, or by clicking the mailbox in the Navigation Pane.

✦ Use the Choose Folders button to select which folders are included in the Messages section of Outlook Today. The number of unread items in the selected folders will appear in the Messages section.

✦ Use the list box in the Calendar section to select the number of days of appointments you'd like to see in Outlook Today. You can choose between one and seven days of appointments, and you may want to adjust this number according to how full your appointment schedule is normally.

✦ Use the options in the Tasks section to determine which tasks you want to see in Outlook Today and how you'd like them sorted. If you've assigned due dates to each of your tasks, Outlook Today can help you organize your tasks by showing you which ones are due soon and which ones you can delay for a bit longer.

✦ Select a style from the list box in the Styles section to display Outlook Today using a different appearance. Styles are simply a matter of personal preference, but you may find that one of the available styles makes your organization of messages, appointments, and tasks a bit easier.

When you're done customizing the Outlook Today options, click the Save Changes button to apply the changes and view your new version of Outlook Today. You can return to the customization options any time to choose new settings.

Working with Outlook Folders

The Outlook Folder List may give you the impression that Outlook folders are similar to any other folders on your computer. While you're working inside Outlook, you can certainly act as though this is true. You can easily rename or add new folders, and, within certain limitations, you can move folder contents from one folder to another.

Outlook folders are unlike ordinary folders in a number of important ways, however, and you must keep these differences in mind as you use Outlook. Outlook folders can only be accessed from within Outlook. You cannot browse your Outlook folders using Windows Explorer. Also, each type of Outlook folder is restricted in the types of items it can hold. You can't, for example, store mail messages in the Calendar folder, nor can you store anything except mail messages in mail folders.

Tip   Although you can only store mail messages in mail folders, that doesn't prevent you from storing other types of objects such as attachments to mail messages. You can create a new mail message and then add your attachments. If you close the message before it is sent, you can save a copy in the Drafts folder and move the message to any other mail folder later.

Using the Navigation Pane

The Navigation Pane has several groups of shortcut icons that you can click for quick access to your folders. Just choose the folder you want to view, click the icon, and the folder's contents will be displayed in the folder contents pane.

The Navigation Pane is considerably changed in Outlook 2003 from previous versions. The bottom part of the Navigation Pane is called the Button Bar, and includes buttons that let you quickly select a folder. When you click a button, the top portion of the Navigation Pane changes to reflect the selected folder. For example, click the Mail button, and the top portion of the Navigation Pane shows two lists: Favorite Folders and All Mail Folders. Click Calendar, and the top portion of the Navigation Pane shows the Date Navigator (a small monthly calendar). Regardless of the selected folder, you can resize the Button Bar portion of the Navigation Pane; just drag the horizontal bar with the dots on it (at the top of the Mail icon). Icons come or go from the list depending on the space available.

As you'd probably expect, the Navigation Pane is customizable, and you customize it through the bottom button of the Navigation Pane. This button displays icons for those Outlook folder icons that do not fit on the Navigation Pane, an icon that shows or hides your shortcuts, and a button that opens a context menu you can use to customize the Navigation Pane (Figure 3-12).

The first two options on the menu let you resize the Button Bar. You can accomplish the same thing by dragging the top border of the Button Bar, as I've already explained. Clicking Navigation Pane Options opens the Navigation Pane Options dialog box shown in Figure 3-13.

You can add or remove items from the Navigation Pane through the Navigation Pane Options dialog box. You can also change the display order by moving items up or down in the list with the Move Up and Move Down buttons.

 Tip   Click Reset to reset the Navigation Pane back to its default settings.

The last menu item on the context menu lets you quickly add or remove icons from the Navigation Pane. Click Add or Remove Buttons and then select an item to either turn on or turn off display of its icon on the Navigation Pane.

Most of the time, you'll probably want to keep the Navigation Pane open. Sometimes, however, you'll need all the space you can get for an Outlook folder. You can turn on or off display of the Navigation Pane by choosing View ➪ Navigation Pane.

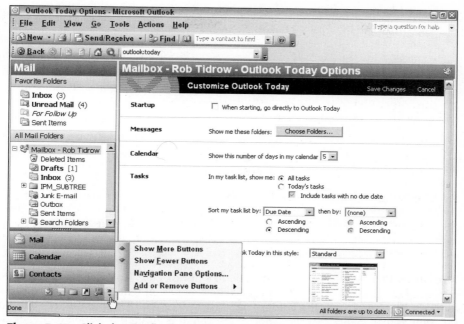

Figure 3-12: Click the Configure Buttons icon to select the type of customization you want to perform.

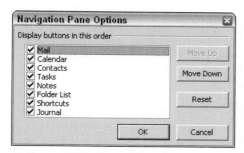

Figure 3-13: Use the Navigation Pane Options dialog box to add or remove Navigation Pane items.

You can also right-click any of the shortcut icons or other items on the Navigation Pane to view a menu of options for the selected icon. Right-clicking a button on the Navigation Pane gives you the option of opening the selected folder in a new window or opening the Navigation Pane Options dialog box. Right-clicking other types of items in the Navigation Pane give different results, depending on the selected item. For example, right-click a folder in the Folder List, and Outlook 2003 presents a context menu with several choices for setting folder properties, copying items, creating a new folder, and much more.

Tip

This chapter just touches on the Outlook interface, so I'll cover all of the advanced tasks you can perform from a folder's context menu in other chapters.

Using the Folder List

The Folder List serves almost the same purpose as the Navigation Pane. You can use the Folder List to browse your folders, rename folders, add or delete folders, and move folders within the folder tree. Figure 3-14 shows a typical Folder List.

Tip

Drag the right edge of the Folder List to the right or left to adjust its width. If the Folder List is too narrow, a scroll bar appears at the bottom, and you may need to use the scroll bar to see the entire folder tree.

You can add new folders to the Folder List by right-clicking an existing folder and then choosing New Folder, or by selecting File ➪ New ➪ Folder and then choosing the location for the folder. Folders that contain other folders are indicated by a small box where they connect to the folder tree. Click the minus or plus sign beside a folder to collapse or expand it, respectively.

The Folder List behaves a bit differently in Outlook 2003 from previous versions, primarily because of its new location in the Navigation Pane rather than to the right of the Navigation Pane. The Folder List shows all of your Outlook folders, including the Sync Issues, Search Folders, and Public Folders branches. When you click the Mail button to work with your mailbox, the Navigation Pane shows a Folder List, but this is a subset of the entire Folder List and shows only your mail folders.

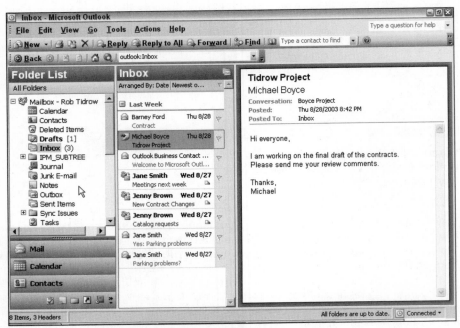

Figure 3-14: Use the Folder List to browse your folders.

Likewise, when you open the Calendar, Contacts folder, or other Outlook folder, Outlook includes a list of all folders of that type. For example, create additional calendar folders and Outlook includes those in the Navigation Pane list. You can set the properties for a folder, create subfolders, and perform other actions with the folder by right-clicking the folder and choosing a command from its context menu.

Using the Calendar

The Outlook Calendar is used to keep track of your schedule. If you have appointments, events, or regular meetings that you need to track, the Outlook Calendar is an excellent choice for doing so. This is especially true if you're already using Outlook as your e-mail program because you'll likely have Outlook running all the time anyway.

Figure 3-15 shows the whole month view of the Calendar. You can click and drag in the Date Navigator to select the range of days that are displayed.

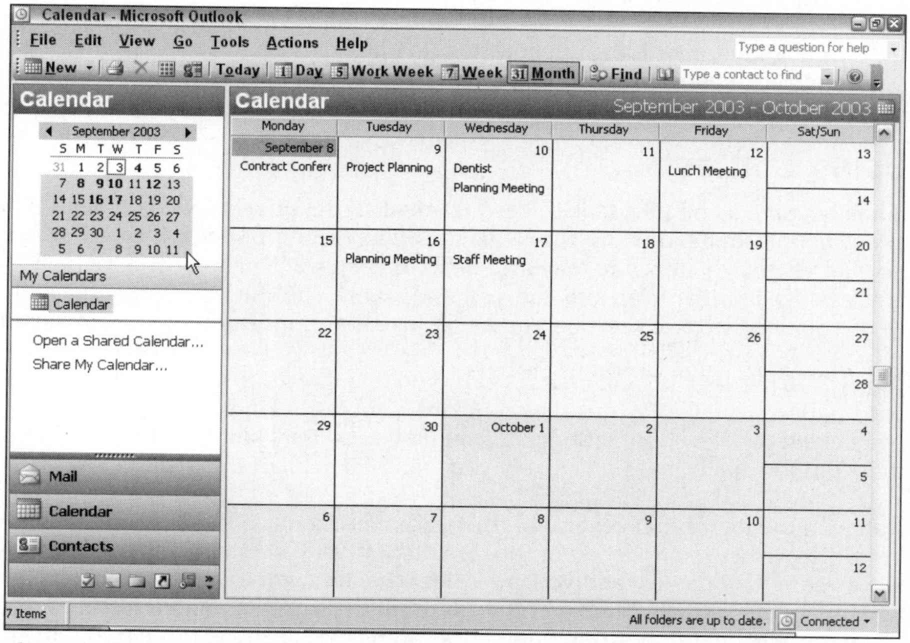

Figure 3-15: Use the Calendar to track your appointments and schedule your time.

When you first open the Calendar, the current date will automatically be selected. Selecting another day is easy, but the method you use depends on the view you've selected. In the month view, you use the scroll bar at the right edge of the Calendar to move through the months. In all Calendar views you can use the Date Navigator — a small calendar with forward and back arrows on either side of the month name — to select a day or month. In any view, you can click a specific date to view the schedule for the date.

If you'd prefer that all the days (not just weekdays) have equal-sized blocks on the Calendar, select View ➪ Arrange By ➪ Current View ➪ Customize Current View and then click the Other Settings button in the Customize View dialog box. Remove the check from the Compress weekend days check box, and click OK twice to close the dialog boxes. Saturday and Sunday will then be displayed just the same as the other days of the week.

To add an appointment to your Calendar, click the time period for which you'd like to add the appointment and start typing to create a new appointment. If you need to do more than just specify a name, double-click in the time period where you want the appointment to open a new Event dialog box. Enter the details in the Event dialog box and then click the Save and Close button to add the item. You may need to adjust the start and end times, especially if you're using the month view, because it may be difficult to double-click the correct time period. You can also drag an appointment to a different time period after it's on your schedule.

 Tip   Double-click an existing calendar item to open its dialog box and add, change, or remove properties.

Using Contacts

It has become a complex task to keep track of all the information you need to know about people. Instead of the simple name, address, and phone number that you needed years ago, now you may also need to keep track of someone's e-mail address, fax number, Web site address, and so on. The Outlook Contacts list is just what you need to make certain you never lose that important information again.

Figure 3-16 shows a typical contact card you may create to keep track of all this information. You display this dialog box by double-clicking an existing contact, or by clicking the New Contact button. You may need only some of the information that Outlook can track, so it's likely you won't fill in all of the fields.

Notice in the figure that several of the text boxes (such as Business and Home) have a down arrow to the left of the text box. When you click the down arrow, you'll see a list of field names, and you can select the field you want from the list. When you do so, the list box name will change to reflect the field you've selected, and you can enter information for that field. For example, you can set three different e-mail addresses for each contact simply by selecting a different e-mail field from the drop-down list. In addition, you can click the button beside a text box to open a dialog box in which you enter extended information, or choose from a list the type of item you want to add.

 Tip   Be certain you click Save and Close if you've made any changes.

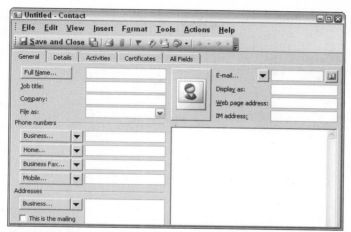

Figure 3-16: Use the Contacts list to track information about people.

Using the Inbox

The Inbox is the place where Outlook stores all your incoming messages. When someone sends you an e-mail message or a fax, the Inbox is the place to look. Figure 3-17 shows the Inbox with the Preview pane turned off.

Messages that you have not yet read are shown in bold to distinguish them from messages that you have read. Double-click a message to open it so you can read it (assuming the Preview pane isn't displayed). If the message includes an attachment, such as a document file, you'll see a paperclip icon to the left of the From column.

Note   Items that appear in your Inbox can stay in the Inbox almost indefinitely unless you choose to move or delete them. You have several options for dealing with old messages. In addition to just leaving them where they are, you can move them to another folder, delete them, or export them for use in other programs. In Chapters 17 and 18, you'll learn more about managing the items in your Outlook folders. See Chapter 26 for an explanation of how to set retention policies for Exchange Server users.

Although Outlook initially places all your incoming messages into the Inbox, you may want certain types of messages placed in other locations. If you're working on an important project, you may want all the messages relating to that project placed in a special folder. Or you may find that someone constantly sends you e-mail that you'd just as soon not bother with and would rather have their messages automatically deleted. Outlook allows you to create rules for handling specified messages.

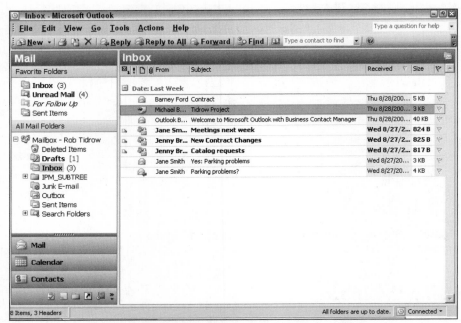

Figure 3-17: The Inbox stores all your incoming messages.

Cross-Reference   Chapter 8 covers the Rules Wizard that you can use to customize the way Outlook handles incoming messages.

As Figure 3-17 shows, Outlook organizes your Inbox by date. You can click on any of the column headings to sort the Inbox based on that column. For example, click Subject to sort the Inbox based on the message subject. Click the column heading again to reverse the sort order.

Using the Outbox

The Outbox is the folder where Outlook places all your outgoing messages until they can be sent to the mail server. Depending on just how you have Outlook configured, messages may sit in the Outbox for a few minutes or until you click the Send/Receive button, or they might remain in the Outbox for only a few seconds, in effect being sent immediately.

E-mail doesn't have an Unsend button, but the Outbox is about the closest you'll come to this function. As long as an item remains in the Outbox, you can cancel the message; but after a message has left the Outbox, you should assume that it's on the way to the recipient and can't be stopped (some mail servers may offer the option to cancel a message after you send it, but your timing would have to be absolutely perfect to accomplish this).

Note   If you forgot to print out a copy of a message before you clicked the Send button, open the message in the Outbox and then print it. Click Send to place the message back in the Outbox message queue. Don't use the right-click Print command for items in the Outbox because this can prevent Outlook from sending the message unless you remember to open the message and click Send. You can also print the message from the Sent Items folder if you have Outlook configure to retain a copy of your messages.

Exchange Server is one mail server that does offer a readily accessible unsend feature for Outlook users. You can recall a sent message from another Exchange Server user if the user has not already read the message. See Chapter 6 to learn how to recall messages and use other Exchange Server features in Outlook.

Using the Deleted Items folder

All Outlook items you delete from any of the Outlook folders end up in the Deleted Items folder. This gives you a second chance in case you deleted the item in error.

Similar to any other Outlook folder, the Deleted Items folder can quickly fill up with items you no longer need. You'll eventually find that Outlook seems to be running a bit slower than normal as it loads all the items in each of the folders. One way to prevent this from becoming a problem is to empty the Deleted Items folder. There are several methods you can use to empty this folder:

✦ Right-click the Deleted Items folder and choose Empty "Deleted Items" Folder from the pop-up menu. This method is effective but it is not selective; all items in the folder are deleted.

✦ Open the Deleted Items folder and select the items you want to delete. You can hold down Shift as you click to select a range of items, or hold down Ctrl as you click to select noncontiguous items. After the items are selected, click the Delete button on the toolbar and then confirm the deletion.

✦ Select Tools ⇨ Options, and click the Other tab. Place a check in the Empty the Deleted Items folder upon exiting check box and click OK. Your Deleted Items folder will then be emptied automatically whenever you exit from Outlook.

Although it's important to delete items you no longer need and to empty the Deleted Items folder on a regular basis, these steps won't prevent your Outlook Personal Folders file from continuing to grow and eat up your disk space. There's one extra step that's necessary to regain the space that was used by those old items if you're using a set of personal folders (PST file). Select File ⇨ Data File Management to open the Outlook Data Files dialog box. Select the PST, and click Settings. Click Compact Now to compact the folders and reclaim wasted space. Click OK and then click Close to return to Outlook.

Using the Drafts folder

The Drafts folder could also be called the works-in-progress folder. If you begin to create a message in Outlook but then decide to cancel the message before sending it, Outlook offers to save a copy of the message in the Drafts folder. Messages that you save in the Drafts folder are simply stored in that folder until you decide to delete them, send them, or open them for additional editing.

If you decide that you may need to revise a message before sending it, save that message in the Drafts folder by choosing File ➪ Save. You won't have to start the message over from the beginning, and you won't have to worry that you've sent a message that's incomplete or incorrect.

Using the Sent Items folder

The Sent Items folder holds copies of each message that you've sent. You can check this folder to make certain that you actually did send a message to someone. You can also go to this folder if you need to resend a message that someone had problems receiving. Simply open the message and choose Actions ➪ Resend This Message. You can also select the message and then click the Forward button to open the message editor so you can address the message to someone else.

Similar to any of the other Outlook mail folders, the Sent Items folder can easily become loaded with hundreds of old messages that you've sent out. Unlike some of the other mail folders, however, you may forget to clean out your Sent Items folder on a regular schedule. You can configure the Sent Items folder to automatically empty itself of old items. In the Navigation Pane, right-click the Sent Items icon and choose Properties. Click the AutoArchive tab and select the Archive This Folder Using These Settings option, and then click the Permanently Delete Old Items option. Use the Clean Out Items Older Than boxes to set how long items should remain before being deleted.

 Cross-Reference   See Chapter 18 for a complete discussion of AutoArchive and other methods and features you can use to manage the items in your Outlook folders.

Using E-mail

E-mail is usually the first thing that comes to mind when someone talks about Outlook. In fact, many people never even take advantage of all of the power of Outlook and simply use the e-mail features without ever bothering to learn about any of the other things that Outlook can do.

It's easy to create and send messages using Outlook. Figure 3-18 shows a message that has been created but not yet sent.

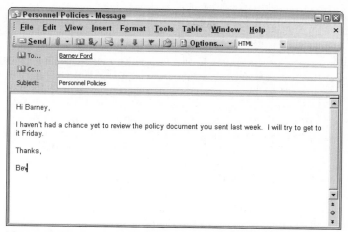

Figure 3-18: You can quickly create and send e-mail using Outlook.

To create and send a simple e-mail message, follow these steps:

1. Select File ➪ New ➪ Mail Message, or click the New Mail Message button on the toolbar to open the message editor.

2. Enter the e-mail addresses in the boxes next to the To: and Cc: buttons. If the e-mail addresses are in your Contacts list, you can click the To: or Cc: buttons and select the addresses from your list.

3. Type a short message description on the subject line.

4. Type your message in the message body area.

5. Click the Send button to place the message in the Outbox.

6. If Outlook is not configured to automatically check for new messages, click the Send/Receive button to send the message to your mail server.

If you want to include an attachment such as a document file or a scanned photo with your message, click the Insert File button on the message editor toolbar before you send the message. The Insert File button is the button that looks like a paper-clip. Choose the file and then click Insert to attach it to your message.

Reading your e-mail messages is even easier than creating and sending messages. Open the Inbox folder, and double-click the message if you want to read it in a separate window; or simply click on the message header if you want to read it in the Preview pane, assuming the Preview pane is open. You may want to click the Maximize button to view more of the message at one time if you're reading them in the message window rather than the Preview pane.

Tip   Click the Print button to print a copy of the message. Outlook will include the message date and time on the printout.

By default, Outlook displays your messages in the order they were received, with the newest messages at the top. If you have a lot of messages in your Inbox, you may find it's somewhat difficult to locate a particular message — especially if you don't remember exactly when the message was received. You can quickly sort the messages by clicking any of the column headers. For example, click the From column header to sort your messages according to who sent the message. Click the same column header a second time to sort the messages in reverse order.

Cross-Reference   The chapters in Part II show you much more about using e-mail in Outlook.

Creating Tasks

The Outlook Tasks list is a handy way to keep track of those jobs you need to do. There are, of course, many types of tasks and different priority levels for those tasks. Packing for a trip or finishing a book manuscript are examples of tasks that typically have firm due dates. Cleaning up your office is more likely to be a task without a due date — unless you're expecting important clients, of course! Creating and tracking the status of tasks in Outlook is easy.

To create a simple task item, follow these steps:

1. Open the Tasks folder.
2. Click the subject line where you see the words "Click here to add a new Task."
3. Type a brief description of the task.
4. Optionally, click the Due Date box and enter a date when the task must be completed.
5. Press Enter to finish.

Figure 3-19 shows a Task that includes several items. Notice that some of the items are checked off to indicate that they have been completed. When you complete a task, click the check box to show that it has been completed. You can also click the Delete button to remove a selected task from the list.

Cross-Reference   See Chapter 12 to learn more about creating tasks.

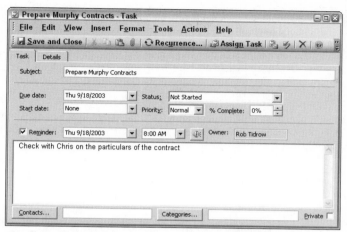

Figure 3-19: Keep track of the tasks you need to complete using the Tasks folder.

Keeping an Outlook Journal

If you ever need to track the time you spend on specific projects, you'll probably really appreciate the Outlook Journal. The Journal automatically tracks the time you spend working on Office documents, and you can easily use it to track other activities, too. Figure 3-20 shows an example of how you might use the Journal to log the time spent on phone calls discussing a project.

The Journal uses a scrolling timeline to display the Journal entries. To view the entries in a category, click the plus sign (+) to the left of the entry type and then scroll to the date you'd like to view. Outlook shows the subject in the timeline. To view more details, double-click an item in the timeline. You can also double-click the timeline to create a new entry, as shown in the figure. For manually created entries, you can enter the duration yourself or use the timer by clicking the Start Timer button. When you finish modifying a Journal entry, click the Save and Close button to save your changes.

Chapter 13 shows you much more about using the Outlook Journal to track the time that you spend on particular tasks.

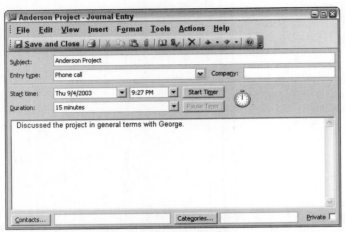

Figure 3-20: Use the Journal to track the time you spend on projects.

Taking Notes

Is your monitor covered with a bunch of sticky notes? Do you jot down reminders and then discover that you've misplaced the one you really need? The Outlook Notes folder can help. Figure 3-21 shows how you can use Outlook's sticky notes to create reminders that won't get lost.

The notes you create in Outlook can't get lost because they're always in one place — the Notes folder. You can use different colors or separate your notes into categories if you need a bit more organization. You can even send notes to someone else.

 Cross-Reference   You can learn much more about notes in Chapter 14.

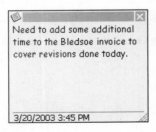

Figure 3-21: Use Notes to remind yourself about events, tasks, or other bits of information that don't fit the way you use your other Outlook folders.

Summary

This chapter provided you a quick guided tour of Outlook 2003. You learned about the various parts of the Outlook screen and how you can modify the appearance of almost anything in Outlook. You also had a look at the different folders and learned how to use them, as well as how to compose and send an e-mail message. Finally, you learned about some of the things you can do with Outlook.

The next chapter explains how to add e-mail accounts, data files, and otherwise configure Outlook so you can start using it to manage your information and schedule.

✦　　✦　　✦

Configuring Outlook 2003

✦   ✦   ✦   ✦

In This Chapter

Configuring e-mail accounts

Adding data files

Creating and managing Outlook profiles

Configuring message delivery options

✦   ✦   ✦   ✦

Similar to most applications, Outlook configures itself automatically using a host of settings based on specific assumptions that Microsoft has made about how you will use Outlook. Although those assumptions are based on usability research, there is no guarantee those default settings will suit your needs or preferences. What's more, you'll need to set up your own e-mail accounts because, all privacy jokes aside, Microsoft can't possibly know what accounts you use.

It isn't difficult to set up an account, a profile, and a new file in which to store your Outlook data. In this chapter you learn how to perform each of these tasks as well as configure Outlook to function the way you want. Some of these tasks include adding other data storage files to your profile, creating additional profiles, and defining the way Outlook delivers messages.

Configuring E-mail Accounts

Although you could use Outlook solely for tasks other than e-mail, it's likely that you'll want to use Outlook for at least one e-mail account. Before you can send or receive e-mail with Outlook, you must set up the account.

Outlook 2000 offered two modes — Internet Mail Only (IMO) and Corporate Workgroup (CW) — that were designed for two different uses. IMO was targeted at non-Exchange Server users, and CW was targeted primarily to Exchange Server users. These two modes made it difficult to manage multiple account types.

In Outlook 2002, Microsoft did away with these two modes, and introduced a single unified mode that enabled Outlook users to work with multiple account types in a single profile. This capability carries over to Outlook 2003, making it easy, for example, to work with an Exchange Server account, a POP3 account, and a Hotmail account, all in one profile.

The following sections explain how to add accounts to an existing profile. For information on adding profiles, see "Creating and Managing Outlook Profiles" later in this chapter.

Using the E-mail Accounts Wizard

Outlook provides a wizard to help you add e-mail accounts to a profile. This section explains how to use the wizard; the following sections explain how to configure specific types of e-mail accounts.

Follow these steps to launch the E-mail Accounts Wizard:

1. Close Outlook, right-click the Outlook icon on the desktop (or in the Start menu), and then choose Properties, or open the Mail applet from the Control Panel. Either action opens the Mail Setup—Outlook dialog box.

2. In the Mail Setup—Outlook dialog box, click E-mail Accounts to start the wizard.

3. To add a new account, choose the Add a New E-mail Account option. You can choose the type of account to add to the existing profile (Figure 4-1). To modify an existing account, choose View or Change Existing E-mail Accounts; then click Next.

Tip   You can add or modify accounts with Outlook running. Choose Tools ➪ E-mail Accounts to open the wizard.

At this point in the wizard, you can choose the type of account to add or select an existing account to modify (Figure 4-2). The following sections explain how to configure specific types of accounts.

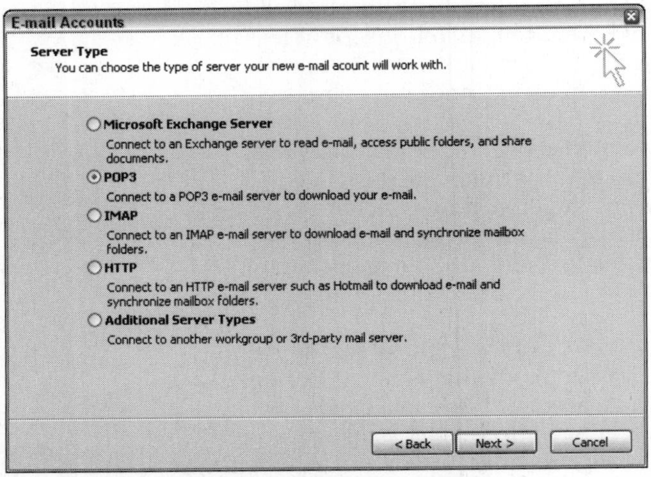

E-mail Accounts

Server Type
You can choose the type of server your new e-mail account will work with.

○ **Microsoft Exchange Server**
Connect to an Exchange server to read e-mail, access public folders, and share documents.

⊙ **POP3**
Connect to a POP3 e-mail server to download your e-mail.

○ **IMAP**
Connect to an IMAP e-mail server to download e-mail and synchronize mailbox folders.

○ **HTTP**
Connect to an HTTP e-mail server such as Hotmail to download e-mail and synchronize mailbox folders.

○ **Additional Server Types**
Connect to another workgroup or 3rd-party mail server.

[< Back] [Next >]   [Cancel]

Figure 4-1: Choose the type of account to add to the existing profile.

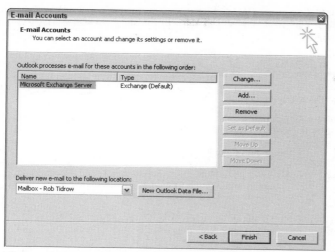

Figure 4-2: You can modify existing accounts with the wizard.

Configuring Exchange Server accounts

It's relatively easy to set up an Exchange Server account in Outlook because you need to specify only a handful of settings, such as the server name and the account name. You don't have to worry about the e-mail address or other settings as you do with a POP or IMAP account because these settings are configured at the server by the Exchange Server administrator.

1. Run the E-mail Accounts Wizard as explained in the previous section.

2. From the Server Type page of the wizard, choose Microsoft Exchange Server and then click Next.

3. In the Exchange Server Settings page (Figure 4-3), enter the server name or IP address in the Microsoft Exchange Server field.

4. In the User Name field, type the mailbox name or the account alias (this is often the logon account name).

5. Choose the Use Local Copy of Mailbox option if you want to work with Exchange Server in cached local mode (explained later in the section, "Setting advanced options").

Tip You can enter the NetBIOS name for the server in the Microsoft Exchange Server field, or specify the Fully Qualified Domain Name (FQDN) for the server.

At this point you can click Next and then click Finish to add the account with default settings. In many cases, however, you will need to configure some additional settings. You can do this when adding the account, or change the settings afterward. On the Exchange Server Settings Wizard page, click More Settings to open the

Microsoft Exchange Server property sheet shown in Figure 4-4. The following sections explain the options available in this property sheet.

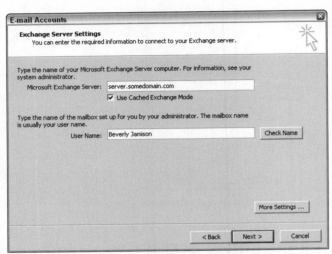

Figure 4-3: Set the server and account name on the Exchange Server Settings page.

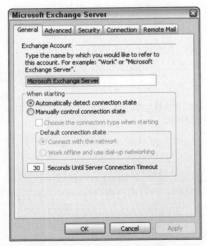

Figure 4-4: Use the General page to configure connection settings.

Setting general properties

The General page controls basic settings and the connection state for the account. The following list summarizes the options:

Exchange Account. Specify the name by which you want the account to appear in the profile's account list. By default, the name is Microsoft Exchange Server.

Automatically Detect Connection State. Let Outlook choose the connection state automatically. Choose this option if you never disconnect your computer from the network, or if you simply want Outlook to detect the connection state by itself.

Manually Control Connection State. This option enables you to control whether Outlook uses the Exchange Server mailbox or the locally cached copy, rather than allow Outlook to control the connection state. If you do not choose the option Choose the Connection Type When Starting, Outlook automatically uses the connection method specified by the Default Connection State options.

Choose the Connection Type When Starting. Select this option to have Outlook prompt you at startup to select the type of connection method to use.

Connect with the Network. Use this option to have Outlook connect to the server through the local area network, whether through a hardwired connection or existing dial-up.

Work Offline and Use Dial-Up Networking. Have Outlook dial a specified dial-up connection to connect to the Exchange Server.

Seconds Until Server Connection Timeout. Set the amount of time Outlook will wait for responses from the Exchange Server before timing out. Increase the value if you are working over a slow link, such as a dial-up connection, that frequently causes Outlook to timeout and disconnect.

Setting advanced options

The Advanced page (Figure 4-5) enables you to open one or more other mailboxes along with your own. For example, an assistant for a small group of users might open the mailboxes of those other users to manage their schedules or handle mail processing. Or, perhaps you want to keep your mail in separate mailboxes for different purposes. Whatever the case, you can click Add to specify a mailbox name, and add it to the list of mailboxes that Outlook will open at startup.

Tip   You can also open a single folder from another user's mailbox by choosing File ⇨ Open ⇨ Other User's Folder. With either method, you must either own the mailbox or have been given delegate access to it.

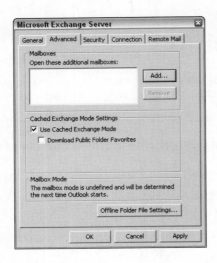

Figure 4-5: Use the Advanced page to configure mailbox settings.

The settings under the Cached Exchange Mode Settings group let you specify how Outlook downloads messages from the mailbox, and whether it uses a local cached copy of the mailbox or works only from the server:

Used Cached Exchange Mode. Select this option to direct Outlook to create a local copy of the mailbox on your computer.

Download Public Folder Favorites. This option directs Outlook to download the Public Folders to the local cache.

Setting the offline store location

Outlook uses an offline store (OST) file to store the offline mailbox cache. You can use an OST whether or not you work in cached mode. When you use an OST without CEM, Outlook functions just as it did in previous versions with an OST file. Synchronization doesn't take place until you perform a send/receive for the Exchange Server account, either manually or at a scheduled send/receive. Outlook uses the OST only if it can't connect to the Exchange Server.

With CEM, Outlook defaults to using the OST and handles synchronization automatically based on the settings you provided in the Mailbox Settings group on the Advanced property page. The main distinction between the two, therefore, is that with CEM, Outlook always uses the OST and handles synchronization for you.

When you enable CEM, Outlook automatically creates an OST to contain the offline cache. You can't directly change the location of the OST, which you might want to do if you're running low on disk space where the OST resides. You can, however, disable offline storage and then re-enable it to change the location. Follow these steps to accomplish the change:

1. Close Outlook, and start the E-mail Accounts Wizard from the Mail applet in the Control Panel.

2. Click E-mail Accounts; then choose View or Change Existing E-mail Accounts, and click Next.

3. Select the Exchange Server account, and click Change.

4. Clear the Use Local Cached Exchange Mode option, and click Next; then click Finish.

5. Repeat steps 2 and 3.

6. Click More Settings and then click the Advanced tab.

7. Click Offline Folder File Settings, click Browse, and specify a new path and location for the OST; then click Open.

8. Click OK and then click Yes when prompted to create the new OST (assuming you specified a new one and not an existing one).

9. Click Next and then Finish; then Close.

When you start Outlook, it will use the new OST and will synchronize it accordingly.

If you want to use Outlook with an OST file but without CEM, you can follow the previous steps 1 through 8 to create a new OST file. Uncheck Use Cached Exchange Mode on the Advanced Tab and close the account properties. Keep in mind that you must manually perform a synchronization, or use a scheduled send/receive to synchronize the OST before Outlook can use it.

See Chapter 6 for a detailed discussion of Cached Exchange Mode and how to configure and use it.

Configuring security settings

You can configure a small number of security settings for an Exchange Server account on the Security page of the account's properties (Figure 4-6).

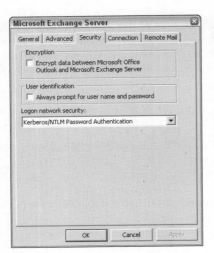

Figure 4-6: Use the Security page to enable encryption and specify authentication settings.

Following is an explanation of these settings:

Encrypt data between Microsoft Office Outlook and Microsoft Exchange Server. Use this option to enable encryption to secure transmission between the client and server computers.

Always Prompt for User Name and Password. Select this option to require Outlook to prompt you for your account and password, rather than caching it and logging on automatically. You should use this option if you leave your computer unattended or share a computer with others.

Logon Network Security. Choose the authentication method required by your server. Use Password Authentication (NTLM) if your Exchange Server is running on Windows NT or you need to use NTLM when accessing a Windows 2000 or Windows 2003 Server. Choose Kerberos if your Exchange Server supports Kerberos-based authentication. Kerberos is the default authentication mechanism for Windows 2000 and Windows 2003 Server platforms.

Note The Distributed Password Authentication (DPA) option available in Outlook 2002 is not included with Outlook 2003.

Configuring connection settings

Use the Connection page of the Exchange Server's additional settings (Figure 4-7) to tell Outlook how to connect to the Exchange Server. Choose an option based on the following list:

Connect Using My Local Area Network. Select this option if you connect through a LAN, or want to use a dial-up connection that is already dialed and connected.

Connect Using My Phone Line. Select this option to use a specific dial-up connection to the Internet or server's network. Use the Modem group of controls on the page to select the dial-up connection and set its properties.

Connect Using Internet Explorer's or a 3rd Party Dialer. Select this option to use the dialer configured in Internet Explorer, or to use a third-party dialer included with other network client software.

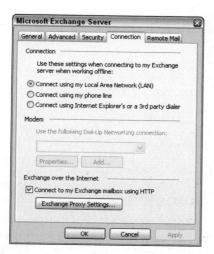

Figure 4-7: Use the Connection page to specify how Outlook connects to the Exchange Server.

The option Connect to my Exchange Mailbox Using HTTP lets you connect to the server across the LAN or Internet using the HTTP protocol. This connection method enables you to connect to an Exchange Server sitting behind a firewall that blocks traffic other than HTTP (port 80). It's also a handy mechanism for remote users who need to access an Exchange Server across the Internet but don't want to use Outlook Web Access (OWA) or when OWA isn't supported on the server.

Click Exchange Proxy Settings to open the Exchange Proxy Settings dialog box (Figure 4-8), which enables you to specify proxy settings for the connection to the server. These settings are self-explanatory.

Configuring Remote Mail settings

You can use the Remote Mail page to configure general options for using Remote Mail with the Exchange Server account. Remote Mail enables you to retrieve headers only and/or retrieve only those messages that fit the filter criteria you specify. See Chapter 7 for detailed discussion of using Remote Mail features for all types of e-mail accounts.

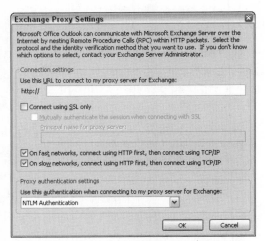

Figure 4-8: Use the Exchange Proxy Settings dialog box to configure proxy settings for the connection.

Configuring POP3 and IMAP accounts

Post Office Protocol 3 (POP3) has long been the primary protocol used by Internet mail servers. POP3 is gradually being replaced by Internet Mail Access Protocol (IMAP), and by HTTP-based mail, such as that used by Hotmail and Yahoo!. Both POP3 and IMAP are standards-based, public protocols supported by a wide variety of mail servers. Most Internet Service Providers (ISPs) that offer mail accounts support both POP3 and IMAP.

POP3 is primarily an offline protocol, which means you download the messages from the server and work with them locally. IMAP, by contrast, is primarily an online protocol. You work with your IMAP folders and messages from the server. The fact that the messages remain on the server simplifies the synchronization problems (such as having messages scattered on different computers) you would otherwise face if you needed to access the same POP3 account from more than one computer. Another useful benefit to IMAP is the capability it gives you to selectively process messages and attachments without downloading them from the server; however, you can gain most of these advantages for all account types by using Outlook's Remote Mail features.

Tip   IMAP offers better security than POP3 because it uses a challenge-response mechanism to authenticate the user, rather than passing the password across the network as plain text.

If your server supports both POP3 and IMAP, I recommend using IMAP. The configuration process is essentially the same for each.

1. Start the E-mail Accounts Wizard from the Mail applet in the Control Panel and then click E-mail Accounts. Alternatively, choose Tools ⇨ E-mail Accounts in Outlook.

2. Choose Add a New E-mail Account and then click Next.

3. Choose POP3 if adding a POP3 account, or IMAP if adding an IMAP account; then click Next.

4. On the Internet E-mail Settings page (Figure 4-9), specify settings according to the following list:

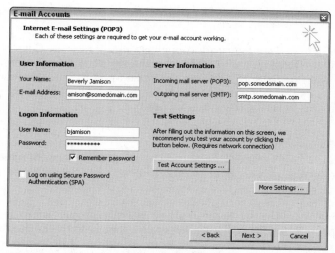

Figure 4-9: Use the Internet E-mail Settings page to configure basic account properties for POP3 and IMAP accounts.

Your Name. Specify your name as you want it to appear in the From field of messages that others receive from you through this account.

E-mail Address. Enter the e-mail address for the account in the form *account@domain*, such as jim@boyce.us.

Incoming Mail Server. Specify the IP address or DNS name of the server where your mailbox is located.

Outgoing Mail Server. Specify the IP address or DNS name of the SMTP server that this account should use for sending outgoing mail. The outgoing and incoming servers need not be the same, and in the case of large ISPs such as CompuServe, are often different.

User Name. Enter the name of your mailbox or logon name on the server. Typically, this is the first part of your e-mail address. Do not include the *@domain* portion of the address.

Password. Specify the password associated with the account you entered in the User Name field.

Remember Password. Select this option to have Outlook cache the password. Clear the option if you want Outlook to prompt you for the password each time it connects to the server. Clearing this option provides better security and prevents others from retrieving your mail when you are away from the computer.

Log On Using Secure Password Authentication (SPA). Select this option if the mail server requires SPA for authentication. Most mail servers do not.

 Tip   You can click Test Account Settings when creating a POP3 account to send a test message through a specified outgoing mail server and attempt a logon to the incoming mail server. This helps you verify your settings before you finish creating the account.

In most situations you can click Next and then Finish at this point to create the account; however, you can configure additional settings, if needed. Click More Settings to display the Internet E-mail Settings property sheet. The General, Outgoing Server, and Connection pages are the same for POP3 and IMAP accounts. Most of the options on the Advanced page are the same, with a few exceptions. The following sections describe the available options.

General settings

Use the Mail Account field on the General page to specify the account name as you want it to appear in Outlook's list of accounts. You can add a company or organization name in the Organization field. These settings are optional.

Use the Reply E-mail field to specify the reply to message property for the account. By default, the account uses the e-mail address you specify in the E-mail Address field for the account as the reply address. In some situations, however, you might want these to be different. For example, you might want replies sent to a discussion list rather than to your own mail address.

Outgoing server settings

Use the settings on the Outgoing Server page to enable authentication for your SMTP server. You can use the same authentication credentials as for the incoming server, or specify a different account and password. You can also configure the account to use Secure Password Authentication (SPA) for the outgoing server, if required.

POP3 accounts have an additional setting on this page: Log on to incoming mail server before sending mail. Enable if your account is serviced by the same server for incoming and outgoing mail, and requires that you authenticate to send messages.

Connection settings

Use the Connection page to specify how Outlook should connect to the server(s) to send and receive messages. Use the LAN option if you connect through a network, or want to use whatever dial-up connection is already established at the time you perform a send/receive. The option Connect via modem when Outlook is offline, if enabled, causes Outlook to dial the connection specified by the Modem options when Outlook detects that the server is offline. Check your operating system's Help documentation if you need help configuring a dial-up account.

Advanced settings

The Advanced page differs slightly between POP3 and IMAP accounts. Figure 4-10 shows the POP3 version.

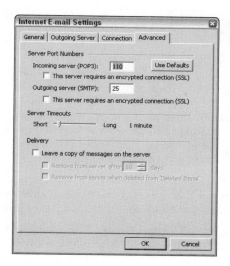

Figure 4-10: The Advanced page for POP3 accounts.

Figure 4-11 shows the IMAP version.

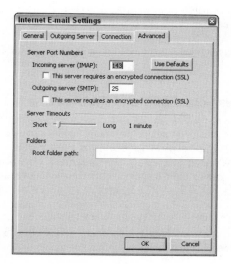

Figure 4-11: The Advanced page for IMAP accounts.

The Incoming and Outgoing server options specify the ports on which the mail servers are configured to respond to incoming and outgoing mail requests, respectively. (In this usage, incoming means mail coming from the server to you, and outgoing means mail going from your computer to the server.) The default port for POP3 is 110 and is 143 for IMAP. The default SMTP port is 25. For both POP3 and IMAP, you can select the SSL connection if the server requires SSL for added security.

Use the Server Timeouts slider to set the amount of time that Outlook will wait for the server to respond to requests before timing out. Increase the timeout if you are working over a slow connection or with a busy server that tends to time out your sessions before they complete.

POP3 delivery

A POP3 account's properties include a Delivery group of options that determine how Outlook handles the messages on the server. These options are:

Leave a Copy of Messages on the Server. Download a copy of the message from the server, but don't delete the original from the server. Use this option when you want to be able to retrieve the messages from other computers, or when you are troubleshooting and don't want Outlook to remove the messages from the server.

Remove from Server After *n* Days. Select this option to have downloaded messages removed from the server after the specified number of days has elapsed.

Remove from Server When Deleted from 'Deleted Items'. Select this option to have Outlook remove the messages from the server when they are removed from the Deleted Items folder, either manually by you or automatically by Outlook.

IMAP folders

The Advanced page for an IMAP account contains only one setting that is different from those for a POP3 account. The Root Folder Path specifies the path to the folder in your mailbox that you want to use as the root folder for the mailbox. Leave this field blank if you're not sure of the folder path, and Outlook will use the default root for the account on the server.

Understanding where Outlook stores your POP3 and IMAP messages

When you add a POP3 account and you already have a default mail store configured for the profile such as an Exchange Server mailbox, set of personal folders, or PST file, Outlook uses that default mail store as the delivery location for your POP3 mail. The other folders in the default store serve to contain the Calendar, Contacts, and other non-mail folders. If there are no other existing accounts, Outlook creates a PST to contain the message store. It uses this same PST to store the nonmail items, as well.

When you create an IMAP account, Outlook automatically creates a PST to contain the IMAP account's folders. It does this even if you already have a message store for another account. Each IMAP account you add gets its own PST. Outlook also creates a PST to contain your nonmail Outlook folders.

Configuring HTTP accounts

Similar to Outlook 2002, Outlook 2003 supports HTTP-based e-mail accounts for MSN and Hotmail. Follow these steps to configure an HTTP account:

1. Start the E-mail Accounts Wizard from the Mail applet in the Control Panel, and click E-mail Accounts. Alternatively choose Tools ➪ E-mail Accounts in Outlook.

2. Choose Add a New E-mail Account and then click Next.

3. Choose HTTP, and click Next.

4. On the Internet E-mail Settings page (Figure 4-12), specify settings according to the following list:

> **Your Name.** Specify your name as you want it to appear in the From field of messages that others receive from you through this account.

> **E-mail Address.** Enter the e-mail address for the account in the form *account@domain*, such as jimboyce999@hotmail.com.

> **HTTP Mail Service Provider.** Select either Hotmail or MSN, depending on your account type. You can select Other if you have the URL of an HTTP mail server compatible with Outlook.

> **Server URL.** This field is read-only for Hotmail and MSN accounts. Enter the URL for your mail server if you selected Other from the HTTP Mail Service Provider drop-down list.

> **User Name.** Enter the name of your mailbox or logon name on the server. Outlook creates this field automatically if you choose the MSN or Hotmail server options based on your e-mail address.

> **Password.** Specify the password associated with the account you entered in the User Name field.

> **Remember Password.** Select this option to have Outlook cache the password. Clear the option if you want Outlook to prompt you for the password each time it connects to the server. Clearing this option provides better security and prevents others from retrieving your mail when you are away from the computer.

> **Log On Using Secure Password Authentication (SPA).** Select this option if the mail server requires SPA for authentication. Most mail servers do not.

As with other types of accounts, you can click More Settings to set a handful of other options. These are the same as those on the General and Connection pages specified in the sections, "General settings" and "Connection settings," earlier in this chapter.

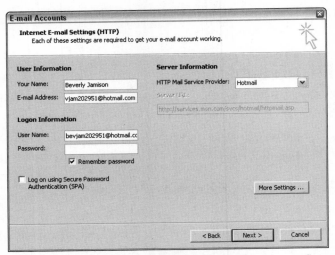

Figure 4-12: Use the Internet E-mail Settings page to configure basic account properties for POP3 and IMAP accounts.

Adding Data Files

The previous section explained how to add e-mail accounts to an Outlook profile. When you add a POP3 account with no existing Exchange Server account, Outlook creates a personal folder file (PST) for you to store your messages. If this is the only account, Outlook also stores your nonmail items (Calendar and so on) in the PST.

When you add an IMAP account to a profile, Outlook creates a PST specifically for the IMAP account. It does not, however, store your nonmail items in the IMAP PST. Instead, Outlook creates a separate PST to store those items.

Although Outlook automatically creates PSTs as needed when you add accounts, you might want to add your own PSTs to a profile. For example, perhaps you use an Exchange Server account for your primary Outlook store, but want a set of personal folders to serve as an archive; or perhaps you have an Exchange Server account and are adding a POP3 account. Outlook will, by default, deliver your POP3 messages to the Exchange Server mailbox, but you can create a rule that moves them to the PST after they come in. See Chapter 8 to learn more about rules and how to create them.

Follow these steps to add a set of personal folders to your profile:

1. If Outlook is not running, right-click the Outlook icon and then choose Properties, or open the Mail applet from the Control Panel. Click Data Files to open the Outlook Data Files dialog box (Figure 4-13). If Outlook is running, choose File ➪ Data File Management.

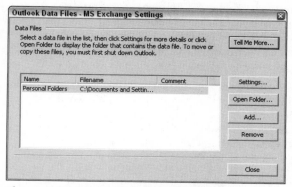

Figure 4-13: The Outlook Data Files dialog box.

2. Click Add to display the New Outlook Data File dialog box (Figure 4-14). Choose one of the following options:

Microsoft Outlook 97-2002 Personal Folders File (.pst). Choose this option to create a PST that is compatible with other Outlook versions. Use this type of PST if you need to share a PST between different versions of Outlook.

Microsoft Outlook Personal Folders File (.pst). Choose this option to create a PST that is not compatible with previous Outlook versions, but which supports a larger PST file size and multilingual Unicode data.

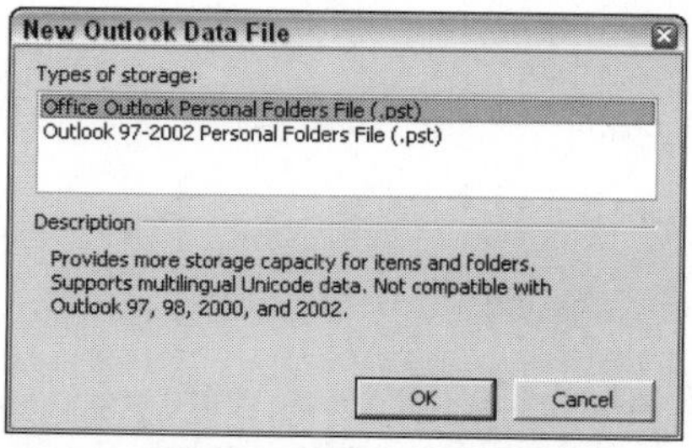

Figure 4-14: The New Outlook Data File dialog box.

3. Outlook displays the Create or Open Outlook Data File dialog box, which is similar to the standard Outlook Open or Save dialog box. Choose a location and file name for the PST, and click OK.

4. In the Personal Folders dialog box (Figure 4-15), enter settings according to the following list:

Name. Specify the name for the PST as you want it to appear in the Outlook folder list. Using a unique name will help you identify the set of folders more easily.

Encryption Setting. Choose No Encryption if you don't want to use encryption for the PST. Choose Compressible Encryption to use encryption that also allows the PST to be compressed to conserve disk space (this is the default). Choose Best Encryption to provide extra security at the expense of losing compression capability for the PST.

Password. Enter and confirm an optional password to protect the PST, and choose the Save This Password in Your Password List to have Outlook cache the PST password in your password cache. Use this option if you are concerned that others might be able to access your computer and view the items in the personal folders.

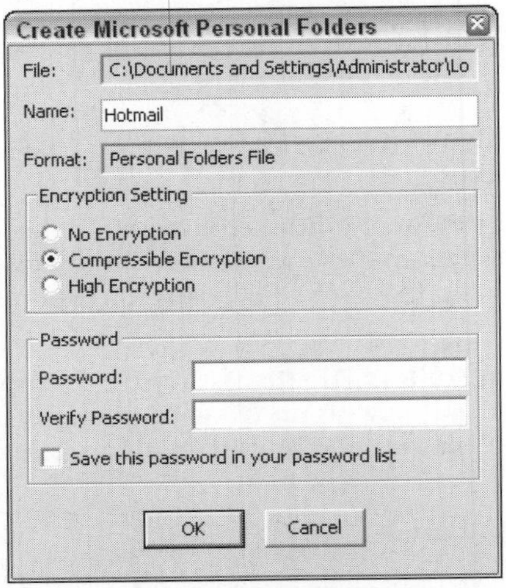

Figure 4-15: The Create Microsoft Personal Folders dialog box.

5. Click OK to create the PST; then click Close.

After you add a PST, it appears in the folder list under its own branch. The branch name comes from the Name field you specify when you create the PST.

See Chapter 18 to learn how to use PSTs to store messages and other Outlook items. See Chapter 8 to learn how to create rules to move messages to and from PSTs.

Creating and Managing Outlook Profiles

An Outlook *profile* stores a set of accounts and their associated settings such as the data files associated with the profile. In most cases you will have only one profile that contains all of the accounts that you use. In a few situations, however, you might need to create additional profiles on a computer. For example, even though

Outlook can handle multiple e-mail accounts in one profile, you might prefer to keep your work account separate from your personal accounts. Or, maybe two users work with the same computer and each need their own profiles.

You can configure Outlook to use a particular profile by default, or you can configure it to prompt you to choose a profile when Outlook starts. Use the former when you work from the same profile most of the time, and use the latter when you need to change profiles frequently.

Keep in mind that Outlook profiles have nothing to do with the other kinds of profiles you will find on a typical Windows computer, including hardware profiles, user profiles, or even Office settings profiles. These are discussed in Chapter 2. Outlook profiles store the accounts and related settings for Outlook only, not for any other application or system.

Outlook profiles store specific types of information, including the following:

Services. This includes data file properties and settings for each of the e-mail accounts in the profile. Services can also include address books, LDAP directory service settings, and third-party services such as one that delivers faxes to your Inbox.

Delivery Settings. An Outlook profile stores settings that determine where it should deliver new incoming messages.

Address Settings. The profile stores settings that determine which address book Outlook uses by default and the address book order it uses to validate e-mail addresses.

When you run Outlook for the first time, it steps you through the process of adding a profile and creating an e-mail account for the profile. The following section explains how to create a new profile.

Creating an Outlook profile

You can add to or modify the contents of a profile in Outlook, but you can't create a profile. Instead, you must use the following steps:

1. Open the Mail applet in the Control Panel, or right-click the Outlook icon and then choose Properties to open the Mail Setup dialog box.

2. In the Mail Setup dialog box (Figure 4-16), click Show Profiles to display the Mail dialog box (Figure 4-17).

3. Click Add to display the New Profile dialog box, enter a name for the profile, and click OK.

Two options on the Mail dialog box control how Outlook handles multiple profiles:

Prompt for a Profile to be Used. Select this option to have Outlook display a dialog box when the application starts from which you choose the profile to use.

Always Use This Profile. Select this option if you want Outlook to use a particular profile automatically. Select the desired profile from the drop-down list.

4. The E-mail Accounts Wizard launches automatically. Use the wizard to add accounts, address books, or directory services to the profile. When you complete the wizard, you'll be returned to the Mail dialog box. Create any other profiles as needed, and set the default profile as explained next; then click OK.

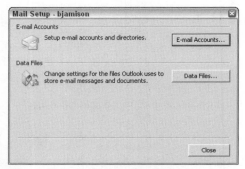

Figure 4-16: Use the Mail Setup dialog box to access the profiles stored in the user's profile.

Figure 4-17: The Mail dialog box shows all existing profiles within the user's system profile.

Copying a profile

In some cases you might want to use the settings from an existing profile but make certain changes, such as create two profiles that include a common e-mail account but which each have a unique secondary account. If that's the case, you can copy the existing profile and then modify the copy. To do so, open the Mail dialog box as explained in the previous section; then click Copy. Specify a name for the new profile, and click OK. You can then modify the newly copied profile as needed.

Switching between profiles

If you maintain multiple Outlook profiles, it's likely that sooner or later you will need to switch to a different profile. If you switch frequently, the best approach is to configure Outlook to prompt you to select a profile when Outlook starts. The section "Creating an Outlook profile" earlier in this chapter explained how to do that.

There is no mechanism in Outlook to change profiles dynamically. You must exit Outlook and, unless you've configured Outlook to prompt you for a profile at startup, change the default profile before starting Outlook again. Here are the steps to take:

1. Open the Mail applet from the Control Panel and click Show Profiles to open the Mail dialog box.
2. Select Always Use This Profile and then select the required profile from the list.
3. Click OK, and start Outlook to use the new profile.

Configuring Message Delivery Options

When an Outlook profile contains more than one e-mail account, Outlook prioritizes them and uses the one with the highest priority as the one through which it sends e-mail by default. For example, if you have an Exchange Server as well as a POP3 account in a profile, and the Exchange Server account is at the top of the account list, Outlook will send new messages through the Exchange Server account.

You can choose an account when you compose a message, and Outlook will send the message through that account. To use a specific account, start a new message, click the Accounts button in the toolbar, and select the account. Compose the message and then click Send. Outlook will send it through the specified account.

 Note   The Accounts button doesn't appear unless you have at least two accounts set up.

You can easily change the account order so that Outlook uses a different account by default for outgoing messages:

1. In Outlook, choose Tools ➪ E-mail Accounts.
2. Choose View or Change Existing E-mail Accounts and then click Next.
3. Select an account in the list, and click Move Up or Move Down to adjust the account list. Set the desired account at the top of the list.

Setting the account order does more than just set the account Outlook uses by default for outgoing messages — it also changes the order in which Outlook processes accounts. Outlook performs sends and receives for multiple accounts in the order they are listed. Moving an account up in the list means it will be processed before those below it.

One other change you might want to make for the profile is to specify the account to which incoming mail is delivered. For example, imagine you have a POP3 account and an Exchange Server account. In most cases you'll likely want to leave the Exchange Server as the location for incoming mail; however, you might decide to deliver mail to the POP3 account, which uses a local PST, because of network considerations or other reasons.

Here are the steps needed to specify the incoming mail store:

1. In Outlook, choose Tools ➪ E-mail Accounts.
2. Choose View or Change Existing E-mail Accounts and then click Next.
3. In the E-mail Accounts dialog box (Figure 4-2), choose the mail store from the Deliver New E-mail to the Following Location drop-down list.
4. Click Finish.

Setting Your E-mail Options

After you have the Internet e-mail service properly configured, you can set your e-mail options. There are lots of these options, some more critical than others. In the following sections, you have the opportunity to take a look at these settings so that you can learn how the e-mail options affect you and your use of Outlook. Some of these settings will also be covered in more detail in Part II of this book.

Setting the e-mail preferences

The e-mail preference settings affect the appearance and handling of your e-mail messages — from what happens to messages you send to how replies are handled.

To set your e-mail options, follow these steps:

1. Select Tools ➪ Options to display the Options dialog box. Click the Preferences tab if necessary to bring it to the front.
2. Click the E-mail Options button to display the E-mail Options dialog box, shown in Figure 4-18.
3. Select an action from the After moving or deleting an open item drop-down list box. This specifies what you want to do when you close a message.
4. Select Close original message on reply or forward so that you won't return to a message you've replied to or forwarded. If you don't select this check box, you'll need to close the original message yourself.

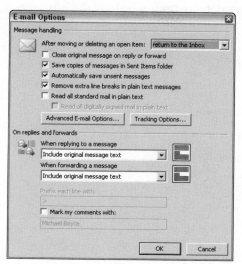

Figure 4-18: Choose the basic e-mail options in this dialog box.

5. Select Save copies of messages in Sent Items folder to always save a copy of any messages you send. If you don't select this option, there will be no record that you've sent messages, except in the Journal if those contacts have been selected for recording in the Journal. Be sure to clean out the Sent Items folder occasionally if you've selected this option. See the previous chapter for more information on cleaning out the Sent Items folder.

6. Select Automatically save unsent messages to place copies of messages you've begun but not yet sent in the Drafts folder.

7. Select Remove extra line breaks in plain text messages to have Outlook remove extra line breaks in plain text messages, which compresses the message somewhat and can make them easier to read.

8. Select Read all standard mail in plain text to have Outlook remove formatting in messages.

9. Use the On replies and forwards options to specify how you want to handle the original text of a message that you reply to or forward. You can only choose a line prefix for the original message if you select the Prefix each line with option. It's become an Internet e-mail custom to prefix the original message lines with a greater-than symbol (>), but you can use the options you prefer.

Tip Some of these e-mail option settings are codependent; others are mutually exclusive. For example, you will not be able to use a character to prefix the lines of the original messages when replying to messages if you also choose to include and indent the original message.

9. Click the Advanced E-mail Options button to display the Advanced E-mail Options dialog box, shown in Figure 4-19.

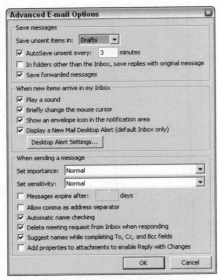

Figure 4-19: Choose the advanced e-mail options in this dialog box.

10. Choose the options you prefer from this dialog box. These options are generally self explanatory. Use the following list as a guide:

Save messages. These options control whether Outlook saves unsent messages, saves replies along with an original message, and saves forwarded messages in the Sent Items folder.

When new items arrive in my Inbox. Use these options to specify the actions that Outlook takes when new messages arrive.

When sending a message. These options set the default sensitivity and importance for new messages and the options that Outlook makes available when you create a new message. In addition, the Add properties to attachments to enable Reply with Changes option, if enabled, makes it possible for recipients of messages with attachments to make changes to the attached document and then reply back to the sender with those changes.

Note   Although you can set the importance and sensitivity level for messages, these settings generally accomplish very little in the real world. Mail recipients can choose to observe or ignore both of these settings with impunity, which is one of the reasons that they are seldom used.

11. Click OK to close the Advanced E-mail Options dialog box.

12. Click the Tracking Options button to display the Tracking Options dialog box, shown in Figure 4-20.

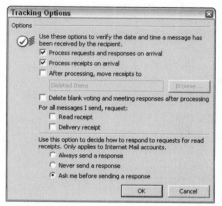

Figure 4-20: Set tracking options in this dialog box.

13. Choose the tracking options you prefer. Be aware of the differences between the two receipt request options:

- A read receipt is a message that tells you the recipient has actually opened your message.

- A delivery receipt is a message that simply tells you your message was delivered. The message recipient may choose to ignore all your messages, even if they are delivered, so a delivery receipt won't confirm that your message was actually read.

14. Choose how you want to respond to read receipt requests.

Tip

Notice that because you can turn off responses to read receipts, a sender can never be certain that you've actually opened a message. It's relatively difficult to block the sending of delivery receipts, so both types of receipt requests do serve a useful function when it's important to know that your message arrived at its destination.

15. Click OK to close the Tracking Options dialog box.

16. Click OK to close the E-mail Options dialog box.

Setting the mail format options

The mail format options affect the default appearance of outgoing e-mail messages that you create. These options are covered extensively in Chapter 6, but Figure 4-21 shows the Mail Format tab of the Options dialog box so you can get a feel for all the available mail options.

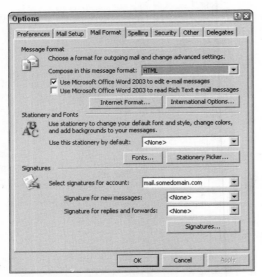

Figure 4-21: The Mail Format page

The Mail Format page contains three option groups:

Message Format. These options enable you to specify either Word or Outlook as your default mail editor, the default message format for new messages, and whether Outlook uses Word or Outlook to read rich text messages. Click Internet Format to specify how Outlook handles HTML- and rich text-based messages, as well as plain text messages. You can also specify that Outlook use the UUENCODE format to encode attachments for plain text messages.

Stationery and Fonts. Use this group of options to specify a default *stationery*, which is a background and other elements that create a custom look for your messages. Click Fonts to specify the fonts that Outlook uses for composing new messages, replies, and forwarded messages, as well as other font-related settings.

Signature. Use this group to specify an optional signature (block of data, usually text) to include at the bottom of each outgoing message. Note that your mail server might also append notifications to your outgoing messages automatically.

As mentioned above, these options are covered in more detail in Chapter 6.

Summary

Before you can use Outlook to send and receive e-mail, you must add at least one e-mail account to your profile. This chapter explained how to add the various types of e-mail accounts supported by Outlook. The chapter also explained the function of personal folder (PST) files and how to add them. Personal folder files store Outlook items and enable you to organize your Outlook items, for example keeping old items in a set of archive folders.

This chapter also explained a variety of options you can configure in Outlook that control the way Outlook handles e-mail, both for incoming and outgoing messages. Finally, the chapter explained the purpose of Outlook profiles, how to create them, and how to use them effectively.

✦   ✦   ✦

Mastering
E-mail

◆ ◆ ◆ ◆

In This Part

Chapter 5
E-mail Basics

Chapter 6
Message Options
and Attachments

Chapter 7
Advanced E-mail
Concepts

Chapter 8
Processing Messages
Automatically

◆ ◆ ◆ ◆

E-mail Basics

CHAPTER

5

♦ ♦ ♦ ♦

In This Chapter

Composing a
message

Sending a message

Reading a message

Replying to a
message

Managing the mail
folders

♦ ♦ ♦ ♦

If Outlook did nothing other than enable you to efficiently send and receive e-mail messages, it would still likely be one of the most often-used programs on your PC. For many different reasons, e-mail has become one of the most prevalent forms of communications in the modern world. There is no other method of sending messages that has quite the combination of speed, convenience, and low cost that e-mail offers.

This chapter shows you the basics of using Outlook to send and receive e-mail. Along the way, you learn a number of handy little tricks that will make common e-mail tasks just a bit easier. In no time at all, you'll be completely comfortable with using Outlook's e-mail features to manage all your e-mail messages.

Composing a Message

Composing an e-mail message isn't much different from writing a letter to someone. Sure, your e-mail message is likely to be delivered a lot faster than a letter that you mail, but you're still using the written word to communicate your thoughts in either case.

If you aren't much of a letter writer, you may discover that composing your first e-mail messages is a bit harder than you thought it might be. This may be especially true if you're the type of person who uses a lot of gestures or vocal inflections to help convey much of the meaning when you're talking to someone. Sometimes it can be difficult to find the right words to explain just how you feel about a subject. If this happens to you, don't worry—using e-mail will become a lot easier as time goes along and you have more experience with this communications medium.

Tip   It's best to keep your e-mail messages short and to the point. No one wants to read "War and Peace" in an e-mail message. Keeping a message short and to the point makes it more likely that your message will be read and responded to more quickly than a lengthy one.

Starting a new message

Outlook offers you a number of ways to begin composing a new e-mail message. You can select File ➪ New ➪ Mail Message to open the message editor. There are other ways, as well, which work when you have an e-mail folder open in Outlook:

✦ Select Actions ➪ New Mail Message.

✦ Press Ctrl+N.

✦ Select Actions ➪ New Mail Message Using and then select an option from the list of choices.

✦ Click the New Mail Message button at the left side of the Outlook toolbar when a mail folder is open.

Tip The default for the New button changes function depending on what folder is currently open. Hold the mouse pointer over the button for a few seconds to verify which type of new object will be created.

Unless you choose the Actions ➪ New Mail Message Using command and then select from one of the choices on the menu, Outlook will open the message editor using the default message format that you selected when you configured Outlook. If you'd prefer to set a different default message format, see Chapter 4 for information on configuring Outlook.

Addressing your message

The new message window has several different places for you to enter information, as you can see in Figure 5-1. To begin your message, you'll most often start by adding the addresses that are used to deliver your message. Each of the address text boxes has a labeled button to the left of the text box that identifies the address field. Here's an explanation of those text boxes:

✦ The From text box can be used to enter an e-mail address that identifies the sender. This text box is rarely used because Outlook automatically enters your return e-mail address when sending messages. You may want to use this text box if you need to send a message but want replies to be routed to a different e-mail address instead of your own. You can display this text box by selecting View ➪ From Field.

✦ The To text box is used to specify the e-mail addresses for the primary message recipients. You must always specify this address.

✦ The Cc — carbon copy — text box is used to specify the e-mail addresses for secondary message recipients. Use the Cc text box for people who need to be aware of a message, but who aren't expected to respond to the message.

✦ The Bcc — blind carbon copy — text box is used to specify the e-mail addresses for message recipients to whom you are sending a copy of the message without informing the primary and secondary message recipients. For example, if you need to send copies of certain messages to your attorney without letting the other message recipients know that copies were being sent to the attorney, you would enter the attorney's e-mail address into the Bcc text box. You can display this text box by selecting View ➪ Bcc Field.

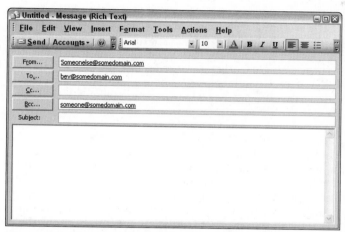

Figure 5-1: The new message form.

You need to address e-mail messages properly for your messages to be delivered. This is really no different from any type of message. If you drop a letter that is addressed simply to "John Smith" in the mailbox, it's likely your letter won't be delivered. On the other hand, a letter addressed to "John Smith, 1 Dirt Road, Virginia City, NV 89440" has a pretty good chance of being delivered — assuming, of course, that the address is a real address.

E-mail addresses use a standard format that allows e-mail messages to be routed to the intended recipient. This format is *name@mailserver*. For our friend John Smith, this might be something like johns@vcnv.net, where *johns* is John's e-mail account name and *vcnv.net* is the name of John's mail server. Here are a few rules about e-mail addresses that you should know:

✦ The account name and the mail server name are always separated by an at sign (@).

✦ Spaces are not allowed in e-mail addresses.

✦ E-mail addresses are not generally case-sensitive. JohnS@VcNv.net and johns@vcnv.net should be equivalent in most cases.

✦ If you have even one character incorrect in an e-mail address, your message will not go to the intended recipient; however, it may end up in someone else's inbox if his or her e-mail address happens to match the address you entered incorrectly.

If you address an e-mail message incorrectly (and the address you entered did not match someone else's e-mail address), the mail server will usually bounce your message back to you. This generally happens fairly quickly, but some mail servers can take several days to bounce messages. If a message bounces back to you, it might be accompanied by an automatic message from the mail system administrator informing you that the message was undeliverable and that no message transport was available for the intended recipient. These messages are called Non-Delivery Receipts (NDRs). If this happens, check the e-mail address carefully, correct any errors, and resend the message. Unfortunately, you'll also see this same automatic message returned on correctly addressed messages if your ISP has incorrectly configured the IP addresses on its mail server. If e-mail addresses that you've used successfully in the past suddenly stop working, you may need to call your ISP for assistance.

You can enter e-mail addresses into the address text boxes several different ways. You can, of course, simply type the address into the appropriate text box. This may be the best choice for an address you won't use again and don't want to add to your address book. If you already have someone's e-mail address in your Contacts list, you can also simply type that person's name into the text box. When you send the message, Outlook will verify the e-mail addresses and replace the name with the correct e-mail address. You can request that Outlook immediately check the names by clicking the Check Names button. As Figure 5-2 shows, Outlook will ask you to help verify any entries that it cannot positively identify (or ask you to select the e-mail address or fax number).

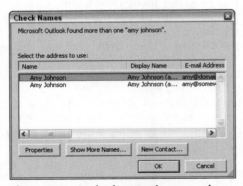

Figure 5-2: Outlook sometimes needs a little help identifying addresses.

If Outlook displays the Check Names dialog box, as shown in Figure 5-2, you have several options:

✦ Select the correct entry from the list and then click OK.

✦ Verify that you've selected the correct entry by using the Properties button to view the selected contact record.

✦ Select the New Contact button and then click OK to create a new contact record.

✦ Click the Show More Names button to select the correct recipient from your contact list.

If Outlook can identify the message recipient without any extra help, it will replace the name you entered with an underlined link that indicates a correct e-mail address. You can verify that the correct recipient was selected by double-clicking the underlined link to display the contact record, as shown in Figure 5-3.

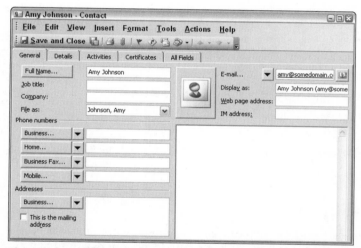

Figure 5-3: Verify that the correct recipient is selected by opening the contact record.

If you prefer clicking to typing, Outlook offers another method of addressing your e-mail messages that is fast, easy, and unlikely to result in an incorrect e-mail address. In place of typing anything in the address text boxes, click the appropriate button and then select the names from a list. In Figure 5-4, for example, clicking the To button displayed the Select Names dialog box. Double-clicking on a name adds the name to the To box in the dialog box, and clicking OK adds the name to the To text box at the top of the message.

While the Select Names dialog box is open, you can select additional names and add them to any of the address fields by clicking the appropriate button. If the desired recipient isn't already in the list, click Advanced ➪ New to create a new address entry. Verify that you've selected the correct recipient by clicking Advanced ➪ Properties. If you have more than one address list, such as a list in Contacts and another in a separate Outlook address book, use the drop-down Show Names from the list box to select the correct address list.

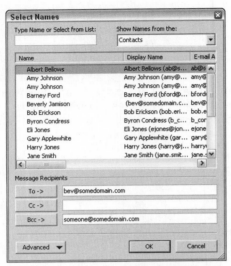

Figure 5-4: The Select Names dialog box.

Tip   You can quickly verify a recipient by right-clicking the recipient's entry and select-ing Properties.

Entering a subject

After you've addressed your e-mail message, you should enter a brief description of the message in the subject text box. Adding a subject is optional, but highly recom-mended. When you look at the messages in your Inbox, it's easy to see why the sub-ject line is so important. The Inbox typically displays several pieces of information about each message, but the two items that stand out are the name of the sender and the subject. A catchy subject line can be the difference between your message getting immediate attention and one that sits around until the recipient finds some spare time.

There is, of course, more to devising a good subject line than simply coming up with something that catches the eye. Sure, you want the recipient to read your message, but you probably want the recipient to be able to associate messages with the actual message topic, too. Remember that the recipient may well receive hundreds of e-mail messages, and it's important for them to be able to locate specific messages based on the topic. An example of this might be e-mail messages you send to your lawyer. You would probably want to include a reference to a specific case in the sub-ject line. That way the lawyer would be able to quickly see which of your messages concerned your lawsuit against the apple grower who sold you an apple that contained a worm, and which of your messages were related to redoing your will.

Note

Many people use filters or rules to automatically delete junk or adult-content e-mail messages. You could accidentally cause your messages to be seen as fitting into one of these categories by trying to be too sensational in creating your message subject lines or including certain words or phrases in the body of a message. You may want to refer to Chapter 8 to learn more about the Outlook Rules Wizard so you can see how to avoid this problem when sending your messages.

Entering the message text

Entering the text of your message is your chance to express your thoughts and make your point. Unfortunately, it also can turn into a chance to embarrass yourself if you're not careful.

Just because e-mail messages are quick and cheap to send doesn't mean that you should throw all of your good sense out the window when you create a new message. If you wouldn't think of allowing misspellings, poor grammar, or foul language to appear in a letter that you were writing to someone, why would you lower your standards and allow them into your e-mail messages? Because e-mail messages are so immediate, people sometimes allow their emotions to rule the day. They may send out an e-mail that is poorly written, or contains derogatory statements that they would never use in a face-to-face conversation. The term for this type of boorish message is a flame. The result of a flame is seldom the desired one. Frequently flames result in flame wars in which both sides trade insults endlessly — certainly not a productive use of anyone's time!

Certain conventions are often used in the text of e-mail messages. One example is the use of several acronyms — such as BTW for "by the way" — that slightly reduce the amount of typing in creating a message. Another common convention is the use of emoticons — sets of characters used to express an emotion — such as "<G>" for "big grin." It's generally best to limit the use of acronyms and emoticons in any message — especially in any business-related correspondence, which you hope to be taken seriously.

In reality, creating the text of an e-mail message is no different from writing a letter. In some cases, a casual style makes sense; in others, it's important to put on a more formal appearance. Only you can decide what is appropriate in your messages.

Figure 5-5 shows a completed e-mail message that is ready to be sent. The recipient's e-mail address has been added, a descriptive subject line was entered, and the text in the body of the message has been completed.

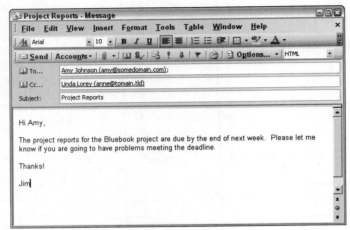

Figure 5-5: The e-mail message has an address, subject, and message body so it is now ready to send.

Sending a Message

After you've created your message and are ready to send it, you have a couple of questions to consider. Should the message go out immediately? Do you want replies sent to someone else? Do you need to know if the message was delivered? In most cases the answer is simple — no special handling is needed. Outlook does give you several options that you can use in those instances where special handling is required. In the following sections, you learn how to use those options — and how to simply ignore them and send the message on its way.

Sending a message immediately

When you finish creating an e-mail message, you'll likely just want to send it immediately. In most cases, all you need to do is just click the Send button to place the message in the Outbox. If you have Outlook configured to automatically check for new e-mail messages at regular intervals, your message will probably sit in the Outbox for a short time until Outlook next logs onto the mail server.

Note   To send any outgoing messages immediately, click the Send/Receive button. Outlook will immediately log onto the mail server to send the messages from the Outbox and download any new messages into the Inbox.

Remember that you can only cancel or edit messages that you've sent while they're still in the Outbox. After a message leaves the Outbox, you might as well consider it delivered. The one exception to this is if you use an Exchange Server. You can cancel a message that has left your Outbox if that message is still sitting at the Exchange

Server waiting for the recipient to collect his or her mail. Still, the best time to cancel any e-mail message is before you send it! See the section "Recalling Sent Messages" in Chapter 6 for details on recalling a message with Exchange Server.

Setting message options for individual messages

For those times when your messages require special handling, Outlook offers a number of very useful options. For example, you could delay a message telling your boss that you have absconded with the company bank account until the day after you leave on your flight to Fiji. Or you could prepare your new product announcement ahead of time, but have Outlook hold the messages until the date of the official announcement.

To set the message options, follow these steps:

1. In the message form, click the Options button (or select View ➪ Options) to display the Message Options dialog box, shown in Figure 5-6.

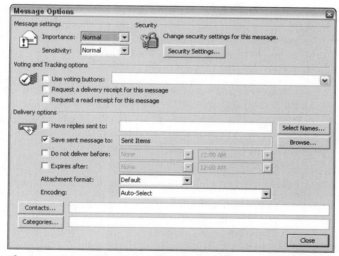

Figure 5-6: Use the Message Options button to control how your message is sent.

2. Select Use voting buttons if you want to attach reply buttons to your message so that the recipients can easily send a reply. This option applies only if you are using an Exchange Server.

3. Select the Request a delivery receipt for this message check box to automatically receive a message informing you that your message was delivered. Remember: Just because a recipient receives your message does not guarantee that they will read the message.

4. Select the Request a read receipt for this message check box to automatically receive a message informing you that your message was read. Unfortunately, there are several factors that can prevent you from receiving this confirmation message. As you learned in Chapter 4, you can configure Outlook so that it does not send read receipts for messages you receive. In addition, some mail systems automatically reject these requests.

5. Select the Have replies sent to check box to have any replies sent to someone else. You might use this option, for example, if you are sending out a survey and want your assistant to tally the results. You can use the Select Names button to choose the reply recipient.

6. Select the Save sent message to check box to keep a copy of the message in the Sent Items folder. You can also click the Browse button to select a different Outlook folder for saving the message copy. Clear this option if you don't want this message saved.

7. Select the Do not deliver before check box and then select a date from the drop-down list box to delay sending the message until a specified date. Outlook will hold the message until the date you select.

8. Select the Expires after check box and then select a date from the drop-down list box to make the message unavailable if it is not delivered by a specific date. This option may not work with all mail servers. You might use this option to send out a message that tells recipients that you'll be on vacation for the next week, but to delete the message if it isn't delivered before you return.

9. Click the Contacts button to link this message to specific contacts. This will add a link in their contact cards so you can easily refer to this message when viewing those cards. This option is handy if you aren't sending the message to the contact, but perhaps want to send a message about the contact to someone else. That way you'll be able to find easily all messages relating to the contact.

10. Click the Categories button to link this message to specific categories of messages. This, too, is intended to make it easier for you to find related messages.

11. Click the Close button to close the dialog box. You will still need to send your message after you've set the message options.

The remaining message options are discussed in Chapter 6.

Reading a Message

Almost everyone likes to get mail — at least the kind that doesn't come in those window envelopes! Reading your e-mail messages is usually fun, too, especially because most bills still come as regular mail rather than as e-mail.

By default, Outlook places all new messages into the Inbox folder. As Figure 5-7 shows, messages that you have not yet read are distinguished from the messages you have read by being displayed in bold type. In addition, the default settings display a brief preview of the text of unread messages.

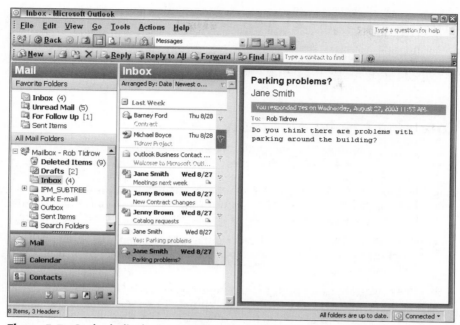

Figure 5-7: Outlook displays unread messages in bold type.

Tip Select Edit ➪ Mark as Read or Edit ➪ Mark as Unread to change the status of messages in your Inbox. Because unread messages are bold, making a message "unread" can help you prioritize your pile of e-mail messages.

In addition to displaying unread items in bold, Outlook indicates the number of unread items in the folder list, in the Navigation Pane, and in the Outlook Today window.

The easiest way to read a message is to double-click the message. This works whether the message has been read or not.

Tip To sort your messages in a different order, click the column header of the column you want to use to control the sort. Click again to sort in reverse order.

After you've opened your message, click the Print button on the toolbar if you would like a printed copy of it. Outlook will include the message header so you can see who sent the message and the subject. The printout will also include the date and time when the message was sent. To print just part of the message, highlight the portion you want to print and then select File ➪ Print. In the Print dialog box, click the Selection option before you click OK. Outlook will then print just the portion of the message that you've highlighted. (This option may not always be available.)

Tip To copy some or all of a message to the Clipboard, highlight the part of the message you want to copy, right-click the selection, and choose Copy.

Replying to a Message

Replying to an e-mail message that you've received is very simple. You just click a button, add your response, and send off your reply. There are, of course, a few things to consider when sending a reply, and they are discussed in this section.

Choosing the type of reply

You've probably noticed that the Outlook toolbar has three buttons that you can use when replying to a message. Each of these buttons has a slightly different purpose:

- ✦ The Reply to Sender button opens the message editor, adds the sender to the To address box, adds RE: in front of the message subject, and places the insertion point at the beginning of the message so you can type a reply.

- ✦ The Reply to All button functions similarly to the Reply to Sender button except that all the original message recipients — except you — are added to the To or Cc address boxes.

- ✦ The Forward button opens the message editor, adds "Fwd:" in front of the message subject, and places the insertion point at the beginning of the message so you can type a message. You must manually select the message recipient.

Regardless of whom Outlook adds to the address boxes, you can add additional recipients or delete recipients as you please. You can even add a Bcc recipient if you don't want to advertise the fact that you're sending a copy of the message to someone.

Composing and sending your reply

Composing and sending a reply is a virtually identical process to that of creating a new e-mail message from scratch. As Figure 5-8 shows, a message reply generally does have one important difference from an original message — the original message usually appears in the body of the reply below the reply text that you add. This makes it easier for everyone to keep track of the complete message thread.

Note   Although there's no rule that says you must include the original message text in your reply, leaving out the original message can lead to confusion. Suppose, for example, that someone sends you five messages during a day, and you reply to each one with a simple yes or no. Unless the original sender knows for certain which message you are replying to, it's very likely that at least one of your responses will be misinterpreted.

As you learned in Chapter 4, you have several options for how the original message text is included in your reply. Many people prefer to use the convention of prefixing each reply line with a greater-than symbol (>). This convention has both good and bad points. On the good side, it's easy to follow the message stream because each time someone replies to a message another greater-than symbol is added to the beginning of each line. This convention also makes it easier to include responses within the original message text because new lines won't be prefixed with the greater-than symbol. On the bad side, prefixing the original lines with greater-than symbols often results in hard-to-read text composed of a mixture of long and short lines, which is caused by the line length limit setting that breaks lines over a certain length.

After you've composed your reply, click the Send button to send the message. Outlook adds a small curved arrow to the Inbox icon for messages after you send a reply or if you forward the message. The direction of the arrow is different for replies and forwards. The reply arrow points left and the forward arrow points right.

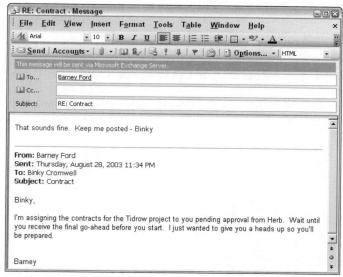

Figure 5-8: The original message is normally included below your reply.

Managing the Mail Folders

The Outlook mail folders handle all your incoming and outgoing messages. Although the mail folders may look similar to normal folders that appear in Windows Explorer, Outlook's mail folders are quite different from those types of folders. Here are some of the important differences:

✦ Mail folders don't exist as actual separate folders on your hard disk. Rather, they are contained within a special database-type file in the Outlook Personal Folders file or as objects in your Exchange Server mailbox.

✦ Mail folders can hold messages that include multiple attachments.

✦ The items in your mail folders continue to use disk space even after they've been deleted. You must compact the mail folders from time to time to recover this lost space.

✦ You can easily move items directly between Outlook mail folders and Windows Explorer folders. Simply drag the message from the Outlook mail folder to the desired file folder or the desktop.

✦ You cannot move entire Outlook folders between Outlook and Windows Explorer.

Outlook periodically archives old items that are in your mail folders. This removes those items from the mail folders and stores them in a file that Outlook can open if you need to refer back to an old message. The archive file is normally named Archive.pst and can usually be found in the Local Settings\Application Data\ Microsoft\Outlook folder of the user's profile.

Outlook automatically creates a standard set of mail folders, but you are not limited to just those folders. As Figure 5-9 shows, you can create new folders as needed to help you better organize your messages. Creating, renaming, copying, moving, or deleting Outlook folders is just as easy as working with Windows Explorer folders. Right-click the folder to display the context menu; then make your selection.

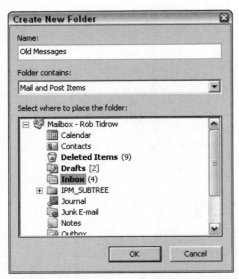

Figure 5-9: You can easily create new folders to organize your mail.

Tip   Each folder can have its own view settings. Use the commands on the View menu to set the view for each folder.

When you first start Outlook, five different mail folders are created by default:

✦ The Inbox holds all of your incoming messages. Unread messages appear in bold type to alert you to the messages you haven't viewed yet. Double-click a message to open it.

✦ The Drafts folder holds copies of messages that you started but have not yet sent. If you begin composing a new message but click the Close button rather than the Send button, Outlook will ask you if you want to save a copy in the Drafts folder. You can reopen messages that are in the Drafts folder for further editing before you send them.

✦ The Outbox folder holds messages that you have sent but which have not yet been delivered to the mail server. Generally speaking, the Outbox provides your last chance to successfully recall a message to prevent its delivery.

✦ The Sent Items folder holds copies of messages that you have sent. Items appear in the Sent Items folder after they are removed from the Outbox.

✦ The Deleted Items folder holds those items that you have deleted from another folder.

An important part of managing your Outlook folders and the items they contain is getting rid of unnecessary clutter. You may not realize it, but the Deleted Items folder can continue to hold onto old items long after they are of no use. Figure 5-10 shows how you can control this excess more carefully by making certain the Deleted Items folder is emptied periodically. Select Tools ➪ Options to display the Options dialog box. Click the Other tab and then make certain you select the Empty the Deleted Items folder upon exiting check box. You may not want to select this option if you would rather exert more direct control over the Deleted Items folder — but you'll have to remember to manually empty the Deleted Items folder yourself occasionally.

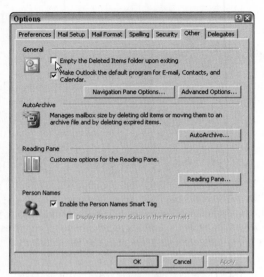

Figure 5-10: Choose the option Empty the Deleted Items folder upon exiting to empty the Deleted Items folder automatically whenever you close Outlook.

Summary

In this chapter, you learned the basics of using e-mail in Outlook. The chapter didn't assume that you were already a seasoned e-mail user but rather showed you everything that a beginning e-mail user would want to know to get started. You learned how to compose and send messages, how to read your messages, and how to reply to messages. Finally, the chapter covered the subject of managing your mail folders.

The next chapter builds on the topics covered in this chapter. You'll see how you can get a bit more creative and make your messages look a little fancier. You'll also learn how to include files with messages as well as how to use features such as an automatic signature. You'll also see a bit more about how you can use mail folders to effectively organize your e-mail messages.

✦   ✦   ✦

Message Options and Attachments

In This Chapter

Using message
format options

Using advanced
message options

Using file attachments

Organizing your
e-mail

Using Exchange
Server-specific
features in Outlook

In the very early days of e-mail messages, people were satisfied with the idea that it was possible to send a simple text message from one computer to another. Everyone understood that an e-mail message was different from something such as a formal business letter. Fancy formatting and attachments simply weren't a part of the e-mail game — plain old text was all there was.

Today the picture is quite different. E-mail messages are no longer limited to looking plain and boring. If you want to create an e-mail message that really stands out, Outlook gives you plenty of fancy options. If you want to send a file along with your message, that's easy to do. In many ways, e-mail messages have gone well beyond the capabilities of most other types of communications to combine style, immediacy, and utility into a medium that has transformed the way people communicate. In this chapter, you learn how you can use these capabilities in creating your Outlook e-mail messages.

Using Message Format Options

Outlook 2003 supports three major e-mail message formats. Each of these formats varies in the level of message formatting options they allow and also in the ability of message recipients to successfully read the message and view the formatting that you have applied. In the following sections, you learn about the Outlook e-mail message formats.

Sending messages as plain text

The simplest e-mail message format is plain text. Messages sent in plain text format do not include any character formatting, background images, or other elements to make the message look fancy. Plain text messages can include attachments — files that are transmitted along with the message.

As detailed in Chapter 4, Outlook enables you to set a default message format that will be used whenever you select File ⇨ New ⇨ Mail Message or Actions ⇨ New Mail Message, or when you click the New Mail Message button. You can override the default by selecting Actions ⇨ New Mail Message Using ⇨ Plain Text to begin creating a new message in the plain text format. As Figure 6-1 shows, you can also choose Format ⇨ Plain Text to change a message's format.

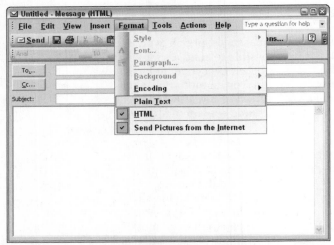

Figure 6-1: Override the default message format by selecting the format for an individual message.

The plain text message format may not be very exciting, but it does offer one major advantage over any other message format — plain text messages can be successfully received and read using any e-mail client software. It doesn't matter if the recipient has the fanciest graphical workstation or the simplest character-based Braille terminal device — plain text messages can always get through.

Note   Although plain text messages can include file attachments, there's no guarantee that your intended recipients will be able to open and use those attachments. If you must be absolutely certain that your message will be delivered, it's safest to use the plain text format with no attachments.

Figure 6-2 shows a simple e-mail message that is being created in plain text format. Notice that although the Formatting toolbar is displayed, all the toolbar controls are inactive. No character formatting, not even something as simple as making text bold or italic, can be used in plain text format.

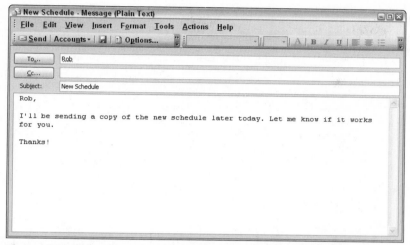

Figure 6-2: Plain text message format is the one universal format anyone can read.

Outlook provides one character format setting for plain text messages. Because different languages use different sets of characters, you may need to choose a different character set to correctly create messages in foreign languages. Outlook provides many character set options. You can choose an option by selecting Format ⇨ Encoding and then selecting the character set, as shown in Figure 6-3. This menu shows only Auto-Select if you have configured Outlook to automatically choose the character set. To change this option, choose Tools ⇨ Options in the main Outlook window, click the Mail Format tab, and click International Options. Select or clear the option Auto-Select Encoding for Outgoing Messages as desired.

Note   If you receive an e-mail message or need to send an e-mail message in a language that you do not understand, you may be able to use software to translate the message for you. For example, EasyTranslator from Transparent Language can automatically translate e-mail messages between English and German, French, Spanish, Italian, and Portuguese. For more information, visit the Transparent Language Web site at www.transparent.com. At the Web site, you'll also learn about additional products, such as 101 Languages of the World, which can help you learn to read and speak the world's major languages quickly. You can also do limited translations online at http://babelfish.altavista.com.

Sending messages as rich text

Rich text format (RTF) was originally created as a word processing document format. Early word processing software used many different and incompatible methods of specifying character formatting. If you created a document in a version of WordPerfect, for example, you wouldn't be able to share that document with someone who was using Microsoft Word or WordStar. Nor could those people share their document files with you.

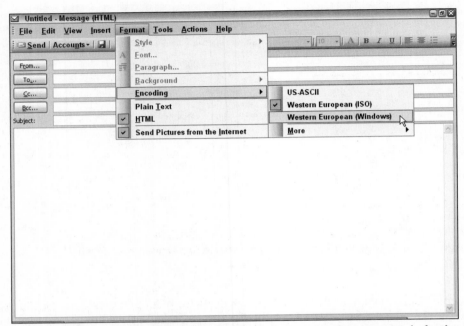

Figure 6-3: You may need to select the correct character set for messages in foreign languages.

Eventually, document format translators became a standard part of most word processing programs, but these had several problems. You had to know the format of a document before you could successfully translate it. Also, the translators typically left quite a bit of room for improvement. Word processor developers simply didn't have much incentive to produce translators that were very good — if translating document formats was too much trouble, maybe users would decide to stick with one brand of word processor.

Rich text format was intended as a type of universal document format. If you created an RTF document in one word processor and then opened the document in a different word processor, the document would look the same — in theory, that is. The reality was usually somewhat less than full fidelity. The reason for this was simple — RTF is one of those "standards" that everyone sees in their own way. Microsoft's definition of RTF might include a few enhancements that are slightly different from WordPerfect's RTF enhancements. The result is that while RTF started out as a good idea, using the RTF message format may not always be a good idea.

If rich text is so troublesome, you may be wondering why anyone would ever use that format for messages. The simple answer is this: Rich text message format does offer several features that simply aren't available in any other message format. The following shows some character formatting options that you'll find only in rich text message format:

Font sizes. A full range of font sizes is available in rich text. Plain text format does not include any font size information, and HyperText Markup Language (HTML) format offers a limited range of choices.

Multiple text alignments. A rich text message can easily include different text alignment for each line of text. HTML also offers this capability.

Flush left bullets. When you create a bulleted list in a rich text message, the bullets can appear flush with the left margin rather than indented. In HTML format, bullets are always indented.

Figure 6-4 shows a message being created in rich text format. Notice that the Formatting toolbar is active and has been used to apply a number of different character formatting options to the message.

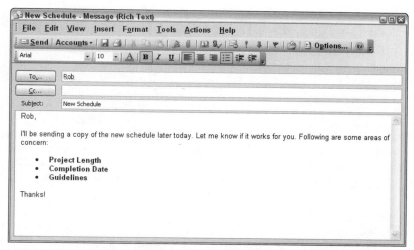

Figure 6-4: Rich text format includes many character formatting options.

Sending messages as HTML

Because the rich text message format can be rather troublesome, Microsoft added a new message format in Outlook 2000 and has expanded this format in Outlook 2002 and 2003. The additional rich format is HTML — the same document format that is used to create Web pages. HTML-based messages offer one major advantage over rich text messages — virtually everyone can successfully view HTML documents. If you can view Web pages, you can view HTML messages.

HTML was originally designed as a page layout language that was intended to make it easy to link different documents on the World Wide Web. The original language specification has been extended considerably, but HTML-based documents still don't have all the capabilities that you would find in a native word processor format document. For example, if you are creating a document in Word, you have the ability to select virtually any font size for your text. When you're creating an HTML document, Outlook gives you seven different font size choices.

These minor hassles aside, HTML is a good choice for the message format of your Outlook e-mail messages. The nearly universal ability for anyone to read HTML messages would by itself be a good reason to use this message format. Figure 6-5 shows an HTML-based message with examples of some of the elements you can use in this type of message.

Figure 6-6 demonstrates how easy it is to read HTML messages. In this case, the same message that was shown in Figure 6-5 has been opened in Internet Explorer to help illustrate that it really is an HTML message. If you compare the two figures, you can see that all of the character formatting that was placed in the message when it was created in Outlook is still visible when the message is opened in Internet Explorer.

Sending messages as Office documents

Outlook enables you to create and send messages that are really Office documents. This means that the recipient will be able to open and work with the document. In the "Attaching Files" section later in this chapter, you learn how to use Outlook to send these types of messages. Sometimes, though, you may want to use one of the Office applications to create a message without actually sending a file that the recipient can manipulate. For example, you may want to use Excel to create a budget worksheet to show your managers how the company is doing, but you don't want anyone playing around with the formulas to make their division look better than the rest of the company. Figure 6-7 shows how to begin this process by selecting Actions ⇨ New Mail Message Using ⇨ Microsoft Office ⇨ Microsoft Excel Worksheet.

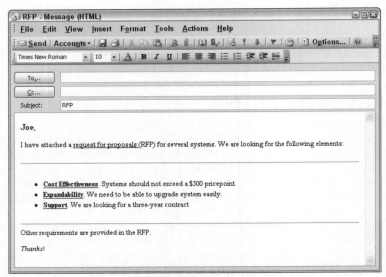

Figure 6-5: HTML format ensures that almost anyone can read the message and see the formatting.

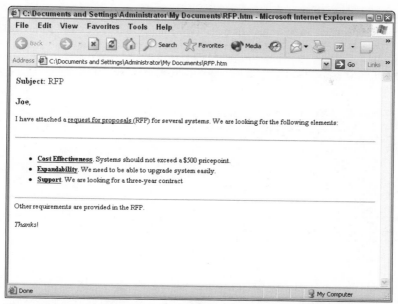

Figure 6-6: An HTML message can be opened and viewed in an ordinary Web browser.

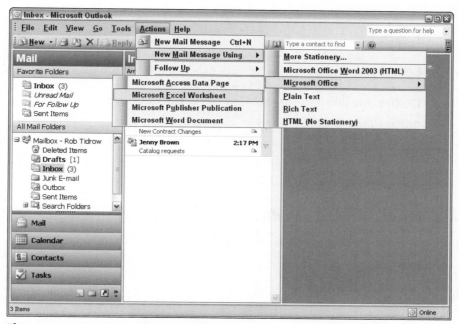

Figure 6-7: You can use different Office applications to create and send mail messages.

The options shown in the Actions ➪ New Mail Message Using ➪ Microsoft Office menu will vary according to which Office applications you have installed on your system. As Figure 6-8 shows, you can create your message as though it were a standard document — an Excel worksheet, in this example. You can use any formulas, text formatting, and so on that you like to create the message.

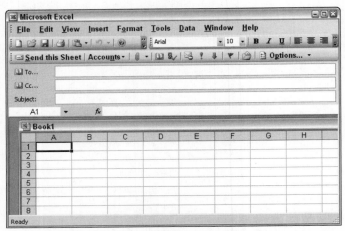

Figure 6-8: Create your message as if it were a standard Office document.

When you click the Send this Sheet button to send the message, something you may not quite expect will happen. Your message will be sent, but it won't be sent as an actual Office document; rather, the message will be converted into an HTML document for sending. The recipient will be able to view your message complete with any formatting, but any formulas that you used won't be a part of the document.

Tip If the recipient will need to manipulate the document rather than simply read your message, be sure to send the document as a file attachment rather than as an HTML message.

Using Advanced Message Options

Outlook offers you several advanced message options that you can use to personalize your messages. In the following sections, you learn how to use these options to make your messages stand out a bit from ordinary e-mail messages.

Flagging a message

Flagging a message means that you're marking the message for special treatment. You might use a flag to indicate that the message recipient is expected to reply to the message no later than a specific date. You might use the No Response Necessary flag to inform a message recipient that they don't need to send any reply, or the Do Not Forward flag to ask the recipient to refrain from forwarding your message.

You can flag outgoing messages before you send them, or incoming messages that you've received. Figure 6-9 shows how you can choose a message flag while you're creating a message. Click the Follow Up button on the toolbar to display the Flag for Follow Up dialog box, shown in the figure. Choose the type of flag in the drop-down Flag to list box. If you want to add a due date, choose a date using the Due by list box.

Figure 6-9: Choose the type of message flag you want to attach.

Note   Recipients can choose to ignore message flags if they want. You shouldn't depend on message flags to make certain a recipient will actually follow up as you'd like. It may be more effective to simply send the recipient a reminder as necessary — especially if you're not certain that the recipient is using Outlook for their e-mail messages.

Notice that you can use the Flag Type drop-down list to choose one of six flag colors for incoming messages. This new Office 2003 feature gives you more flexibility in assigning flags, which ultimately means better ability to organize and track your messages.

Setting message importance and sensitivity

In addition to flagging a message for follow up, you can set indicators of the message's importance and sensitivity. Similar to the follow up flag, these settings are mostly advisory in nature — the recipient can simply ignore these settings if he or she prefers.

To change the importance and sensitivity settings for a message, click the Options button to display the Message Options dialog box, shown in Figure 6-10. You can also use the Importance High and Importance Low buttons to quickly make one of those two importance settings.

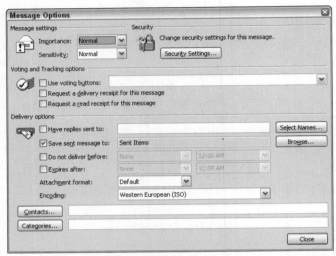

Figure 6-10: Choose the message importance and sensitivity settings in the Message Options dialog box.

Outlook messages can be labeled as low, normal, or high in importance. They can also be labeled as Normal, Personal, Private, or Confidential in regards to sensitivity. No matter which of these settings you choose, your messages probably won't receive any special handling from the mail system — you'll have to depend on the recipient to follow your wishes in handling the message. However, these settings can be useful for helping you sort messages.

Note   Messages labeled as Private can't be edited by the recipient

Creating an auto signature

A signature is a tagline that Outlook adds to your outgoing messages. Your signature can include information such as your mailing address, phone number, job title, or any other bits and pieces that you want to include with each message. After you create a signature and tell Outlook to use it, that same information will automatically be included with your messages so that you won't have to type it in every time you create a new message.

Note   Make certain you only include information in your signature that you want everyone to see. If you don't want every e-mail recipient to know your home address, don't include that information in your signature (or create a second, optional signature with different information).

To create a signature, follow these steps:

1. Select Tools ➯ Options to display the Options dialog box. After you have created a signature, you'll use this dialog box to select a default signature to use with each new e-mail message.

2. Click the Mail Format tab, shown in Figure 6-11.

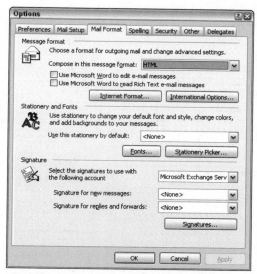

Figure 6-11: Use the Mail Format tab to set up your signature.

3. Click the Signatures button to display the Create Signature dialog box, shown in Figure 6-12. If you have any existing signatures, they will be listed in the Signature list box, and a preview of the selected signature will be shown in the Preview box.

4. Click the New button to begin creating a new signature. This will display the Create New Signature dialog box.

5. Type a descriptive name for your signature in the Enter a name for your new signature text box, shown in Figure 6-13. This name should be descriptive enough so that you'll easily be able to identify which signature you are selecting when you later choose a default signature. The name you enter here won't appear in your e-mail messages. It's simply to help you identify a particular signature.

Figure 6-12: Use the Create Signature dialog box to preview any existing signatures.

Figure 6-13: Enter a descriptive name so you'll be able to easily choose a signature later.

6. Choose one of the radio buttons to specify whether you want to begin a totally new signature or if you'd rather base it upon an existing signature or other file. For now choose the Start with a blank signature radio button.

7. Click Next to continue.

8. Type the signature text as shown in Figure 6-14.

Figure 6-14: Enter the text that you want included with each of your e-mail messages.

9. To change the font options for the signature, click the Font button to display the Font dialog box. Remember, though, that any font selections you choose will have no effect if you create a plain text message or if the message recipient is unable to read the formatting.

10. Click the OK button to close the Font dialog box after you've made any changes to the font settings.

11. Click the Paragraph button to display the Paragraph dialog box. In this dialog box, you can select the alignment options for the signature and you can choose to display the signature as a list of bulleted items.

12. Click the OK button to close the Paragraph dialog box after you've made any changes to the paragraph settings.

13. If you want to clear out any existing text and start over, click the Clear button.

14. If you want to use Word to create your signature, click the Advanced Edit button. Do this if you want to use the spell checker to make certain you haven't made any typos.

15. Click the Finish button to return to the Edit Signature dialog box.

16. Click the OK button to return to the Options dialog box. Your new signature will appear in the Signature for New Messages list box.

17. Click OK to confirm your selection and return to Outlook.

When you have specified a default signature, Outlook automatically appends the signature to new messages that you create. Figure 6-15 shows how Outlook adds the signature automatically when you choose one of the new message options.

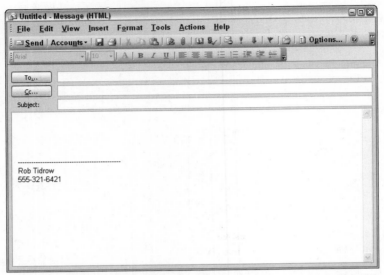

Figure 6-15: After you specify a signature, Outlook automatically adds that signature to all new messages.

If you like, you can edit the signature that Outlook has added to the new blank message. Creating a signature can save you considerable time when you send e-mail messages because you don't have to retype the same information for each new message.

Tip   Keep your signature short. It's generally considered poor form to use signature files that are longer than five or six lines.

If you decide to create and use signatures in Outlook, keep in mind that your e-mail server might also append a notification block to your outgoing e-mail. Many companies have turned to adding disclaimers or other text to messages. Make sure to consider these company disclaimers when deciding what text, if any, to include as your own signature block.

Finally, if you want to turn off signatures, choose Tools ➪ Options, and click the Mail Format tab. Select None from the Signature for new messages drop-down list. Or, choose a different signature, if desired.

Using business cards

Outlook enables you to exchange contact information in the form of electronic business cards known as vCards. A vCard file is a standard way of exchanging such information over the Internet. Just as a printed business card provides a convenient method of passing along information, vCards make it easy to ensure your message recipients have accurate information about how they may contact you. They are also useful for sharing contacts with others, because you can forward your contacts as vCards using e-mail.

Outlook uses records in the Contacts folder to create vCards. If you want to create a vCard file to send along with your messages, you'll have to start by first creating a Contact record for yourself. If you've never created a Contact record, refer to Chapter 9 for more information about this process.

To create a vCard file from an existing Contact record, follow these steps:

1. Open the Outlook Contacts folder.

2. Double-click the Contact record you want to use to open the record.

3. Select File ⇨ Export to vCard file.

4. As shown in Figure 6-16, specify a name for the file in the File Name text box. You will normally want to use the same name as the Contact record name, but you can use a more descriptive name if necessary so that you can more easily identify the vCard file.

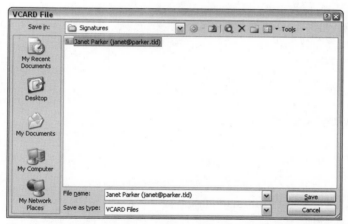

Figure 6-16: Save your vCard file to send it along with messages.

5. Click the Save button to save the file.

6. Click the Close button to close the Contact record.

To attach a vCard file to your messages, you include the vCard as part of your signature. To modify your signature file to include a vCard, follow these steps:

1. Select Tools ⇨ Options to open the Options dialog box.

2. Click the Mail Format tab to view the mail format options.

3. Click the Signatures button to display the Create Signature dialog box.

4. Choose the signature file you wish to modify.

5. Click Edit to open the Edit Signature dialog box.

6. Choose the vCard file from the Attach this business card (vCard) to this signature drop-down list box, as shown in Figure 6-17.

   If you haven't already created a vCard file, as shown earlier, you can also create a new vCard file by using the New vCard from Contact button to create the vCard file now.

Figure 6-17: Select the vCard you want to include with your signature.

7. Click OK to close the Edit Signature dialog box.

8. Click OK to close the Create Signature dialog box.

9. Click OK to close the Options dialog box.

Note   You can send a vCard without using a signature. Just open the contact form and choose Actions ⇨ Forward as vCard to open a new mail message with the vCard attached.

Although vCards are a convenient method of distributing your contact information, you probably won't want to automatically include a vCard with each new message. Not only will this increase the size of your messages, but it's also likely to annoy message recipients who receive multiple copies of the same vCard each time they receive one of your messages. It might be better to create a separate signature that includes your vCard file and then select that signature for use with specific messages rather than as your default signature.

Using stationery

Stationery is a background image that you can use to give your e-mail messages background colors and images, special fonts, and other formatting options. Whether using stationery truly adds to the quality of e-mail messages is open to personal interpretation. Some people enjoy the often interesting visual effects, whereas others find that stationery can make messages more difficult to read—especially if the sender isn't careful to select contrasting background and text colors!

Note Stationery may look pretty, but it increases the file size of your e-mail messages and takes longer for you to upload them and for recipients to download them.

To create a new message using stationery, follow these steps:

1. Select Actions ➪ New Mail Message Using ➪ More Stationery to open the Select a Stationery dialog box, shown in Figure 6-18.

Figure 6-18: Select the stationery you want to use.

2. Scroll down through the stationery choices until you find the stationery that appeals to you.

   You might find several stationery choices that display the message Stationery not installed yet. It will be installed when you compose mail. If you want to choose one of these options, you will need to have your Outlook 2003 CD-ROM available so that your selection can be copied to your hard disk.

3. If the choices shown in the Select a Stationery dialog box don't quite fit your needs, you can click the Get More Stationery button to visit the Microsoft Office Web site. There you'll find additional stationery options that you can download.

4. Click the OK button to close the dialog box and begin creating a new message using your selected stationery. Figure 6-19 shows an example of using stationery.

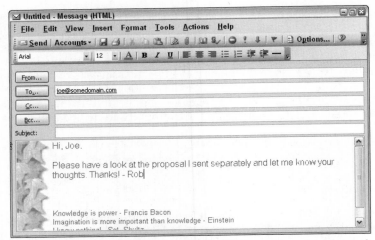

Figure 6-19: The stationery you select will appear as a background image in your message.

Make certain the text of your message stands out, especially if the stationery you choose uses a dark background. It may be necessary to change the text color and size to make sure your message is readable.

Attaching Files

As fancy as a rich text or HTML message may appear, all the e-mail message enhancements discussed so far in this chapter have really done little other than improve the appearance of the message text. Changing the font or adding a background image doesn't increase the functionality of your messages. For that, you need something more practical.

Attaching a file to a message enables the message to carry a lot more than a simple text note. Rather than trying to describe the view out your office window, you could attach a digital image that shows the view. In place of telling someone where they could find the latest version of a shareware program, you could attach a copy of the program file so that the message recipient would be sure to get the correct program. Instead of sending a complex word processing document through the mail on a disk, you could attach the document file to a message to deliver the file immediately. These are just some of the ways that file attachments can make your e-mail messages more effective.

A few mail systems will not accept e-mail messages that include attachments. But even those that do accept message attachments often limit the overall size of messages. Because of the way messages must be encoded for sending over the Internet, these message size limitations generally prevent you from sending a message that is more than about two-thirds the stated message size limit. Therefore, if someone's mail system rejects messages over 2MB in size, you probably won't be able to successfully send messages that exceed about 1.3MB. Whenever you need to send a relatively large attachment, consider using a product such as WinZip to compress the attachment.

Attaching files while composing a message

When you send a file attachment along with a message, the recipient receives a single e-mail message that consists of both your message text and the file that you attached. Each file attachment is, however, kept separate from the text and from any other attachments. This enables the recipient to open or save the attachment just as if you handed them a disk containing the file.

Although plain text e-mail messages pose no threat to your system, files that are attached to a message could be dangerous. If you aren't completely sure of the source of e-mail file attachments, it's best not to open those attachments. You may also want to save any attachments in a special folder and then use a virus scanner to check for computer viruses before opening the files. Many virus scanners work in conjunction with Outlook to scan messages as they arrive in your Inbox so you don't have to scan them manually.

To include file attachments with an e-mail message, follow these steps:

1. Open a new message by clicking the New Mail Message button (or by using any of the other Outlook new mail message options).

2. Address and compose your message as you would any other message.

3. Select Insert ➪ File, or click the Insert File button.

Selecting Insert ➪ Item will enable you to attach another message or other Outlook item to your new message.

4. As shown in Figure 6-20, choose the file you want to attach. You may need to search in the Look in list box to locate the correct folder.

5. Click the Insert button to insert the file into your message.

You can also drag and drop file attachments quickly from Windows Explorer (or the Desktop) onto your message window.

You can attach more than one file to the same message, although you should remember that file attachments may greatly increase the overall size of the message. It's often more prudent to send several smaller messages rather than one huge message. That way you'll have far less to resend if a mail delivery problem occurs.

Outlook shows the attachment size next to the attachment name in the message form. Get in the habit of checking the attachment size before sending a message.

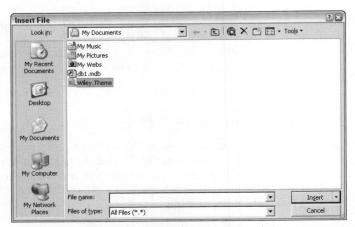

Figure 6-20: Choose the file you want to attach to your message.

Sending an e-mail message that includes an attachment is no different from sending any other e-mail message. When you click the Send button, Outlook places the message in your Outbox until the next time you connect to the mail server. If the attachments are large, it will take quite a bit longer for the message to be sent to the mail server, especially if you use a slow connection like a modem.

Tip You can insert a document as text in a message, which is useful when you need to send someone the contents of a text file but want the text included in the body of the message. Use the same steps you use to insert a file, but in the Insert File dialog box, click the arrow beside the Insert button and choose Insert as Text.

Sending a file while using Microsoft Office

If you're working on a document in one of the Microsoft Office applications, there's no need to switch to Outlook simply because you want to send the document file to someone else. All the Office applications enable you to send the current file as either a message attachment or as the body of the message itself.

In most cases, you'll probably want to send Office documents as file attachments rather than as the message body. Sending the document as a file attachment enables the recipient to open and use the document in the correct Office application. Sending the document as the message body enables the recipient to open and view the message even if he or she does not have Microsoft Office installed on his or her system, but it does not allow the recipient to use the document as if it were the original file. To better understand the differences, consider the case of a complex Excel worksheet that includes numerous formulas along with the data. If you send the worksheet as an attachment, the formulas remain active in the document, and the recipient can add new data and can see the recalculated results. If you send the worksheet as the message body, all the results are static, so any changes the recipient makes won't change the results. On the other hand, the recipient won't need a copy of Excel to view the results, either.

To send an Office document from within an application, follow these steps:

1. Open the document within the application that you used to create the file.

2. Select File ⇨ Send To ⇨ Mail Recipient, as shown in Figure 6-21.

   You may see additional choices on the File ⇨ Send To menu. In the figure, the additional choices provide methods of sending the file as an attachment, routing the file to one or more recipients so several people can collaborate on a project, or sending the file to an Exchange Server folder so that it is available to everyone who has been granted access to the folder. Choose Mail Recipient to send the document within the body of the message; choose Mail Recipient as Attachment to send the document as an attachment.

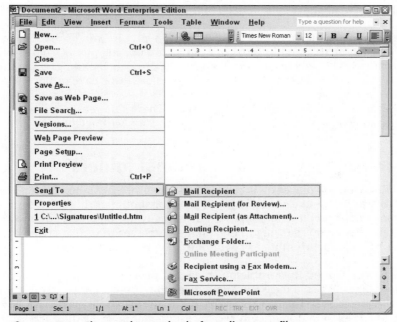

Figure 6-21: Choose the method of sending your file.

3. Address your message as you would any other e-mail message. You may also wish to include a brief message so that the recipient understands the purpose of the file you are sending.

4. Click the Send button to place the message in the Outbox.

Messages you send from within an Office application are really no different from messages that you create and send from within Outlook itself. The message recipient will not be able to tell whether you created the message in Outlook and then added an attachment, or if you started in one of the other Office applications and used the File ➪ Send To command. Therefore, you should choose whichever option is most convenient for you.

Organizing and Sharing Messages

A little organization can go a long way towards making life a lot easier. If your telephone book weren't organized so that the records were in alphabetical order, you probably wouldn't find the book too useful for looking up phone numbers, would you? If the addresses on your street were assigned randomly without being organized into ascending order, making deliveries to your neighborhood would be pretty hard, too. You can probably think of many more examples where a bit of organization really helps out in daily life.

Organizing your e-mail messages can help out a lot, too. You probably don't just place everything that comes into your office into one big pile. It's more likely that you organize the chaos by separating different projects into different folders. That way it's easier to find everything that relates to the Prior Lake project — you don't have to sift through everything from the Lake Tahoe and Lake Hiawatha projects and check out each piece of paper each time. There's no reason you can't apply this same reasoning to your e-mail message organization within Outlook.

Organizing e-mail with personal folders

By default, Outlook places all incoming messages into the Inbox folder. This may work okay at first, but eventually you'll probably find that this causes one little problem — you can't find messages quite as easily as you'd like. Even worse is the likelihood that if you're trying to find all the messages that relate to a particular project you'll inadvertently pass over one or more critical messages.

The easy way around this problem is to create new folders that you use to organize your messages. When a message about a specific project arrives, you can simply move the message to the project folder. In Chapter 8, you'll even learn how you can instruct Outlook to automatically move certain messages as they arrive.

Creating a folder

Creating new folders is easy. If you've used Windows Explorer to create new folders on your computer, you'll find that creating Outlook folders is similar.

To create a new Outlook folder, follow these steps:

1. Right-click a folder in your Outlook folder list (in the Navigation Pane). It's best to right-click the folder that you want as the parent of the new folder, but this is not absolutely necessary.

2. Select New Folder from the context menu to display the Create New Folder dialog box (Figure 6-22).

3. Select the location for the new folder from the Select where to place the folder list box. The folder you select will be the parent of the new folder.

4. Select the type of folder content from the Folder contains list box. Normally, you'll want to choose Mail Items in this list box because you'll probably be storing messages in the new folder.

5. Enter a name for the folder in the Name text box.

Figure 6-22: Enter the information for the new folder in the Create New Folder dialog box.

6. Click OK to create the new folder.

You can manually move items to your new folder either by right-clicking the item and choosing Move to Folder from the context menu or by dragging and dropping selected items. Messages will retain the same read or unread status when they are moved between folders. If you move messages that you have not yet read, Outlook will show the destination folder in bold. In addition, the number of unread items in each folder is shown just to the right of the folder name in the folder list.

Using Outlook with Exchange Server

Outlook offers many useful features for composing, reading, and sending e-mail. Some of its best features, however, are available only when Outlook is used as a Microsoft Exchange Server client. This section of the chapter explains how to take advantage of these Exchange Server-specific features.

Using Cached Exchange Mode

Outlook 2003 introduces a new mode called Cached Exchange Mode (CEM) in which Outlook uses a locally cached copy of your Exchange Server mailbox as its main data store. In other words, Outlook copies your entire Exchange Server mailbox to your local computer and works from that local copy. Outlook automatically handles synchronization between the local cache and the mailbox on the server. You no longer need to worry about how and when Outlook synchronizes the online and offline copies of its data.

CEM uses an Offline Store (OST) file to store the local cache. Outlook can also use an OST when you don't use CEM; the OST is the mechanism that Outlook uses to provide offline access to a server when it is unavailable. For example, the server might go offline for maintenance, or you might disconnect your computer from the network. The difference between using an OST for offline access and using CEM is that CEM fully automates the synchronization between your mailbox and the OST. Just using an OST without CEM requires that you perform a synchronization, either manually or by configuring a scheduled synchronization.

Follow these steps to configure an Exchange Server account to use CEM:

1. Open Outlook and choose Tools ⇨ E-mail Accounts.
2. Choose View or Change Existing E-mail Accounts and then click Next.
3. Select the Exchange Server account, and click Change.
4. On the Exchange Server Settings dialog box (Figure 6-23), select the option Use Local Copy of Mailbox.
5. Click Next; then click Finish.

You don't need to worry about performing a synchronization to synch the mailbox and OST; Outlook will do that for you automatically. Monitor the Outlook status bar for synchronization messages. See Chapter 4 for a complete discussion of configuring Exchange Server accounts, including specifying the location of the OST.

Voting

Exchange Server supports *voting*, which enables users to vote on a topic by clicking a button in a message form. You compose the message with text explaining the reason for the vote, set voting options for the message, and send it. When the recipients receive the message they can vote as they want. You can then tally the votes from the recipient group. Voting is a handy way to solicit input on proposals and other issues.

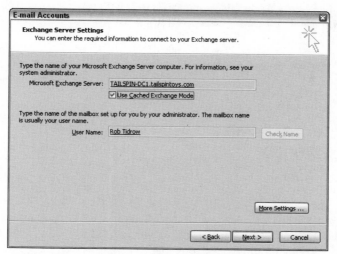

Figure 6-23: Enable CEM on the properties for the Exchange Server account.

Sending a message for voting

It's easy to send a message for voting. Just follow these steps:

1. Open Outlook and then start the new message.

2. Click Options in the message toolbar.

3. In the Message Options dialog box (Figure 6-24), select the Use Voting Buttons option.

4. Select a set of voting buttons from the drop-down list, or click in the list and then type your own choices, separate by semicolons.

5. Click Close.

6. Finish the message by adding message text, subject, and so on; then click Send to send the message.

Voting

When you receive a message about which you need to vote, the message header indicates that there are voting options. When you open the message, the message form shows the voting buttons between the toolbar and the message header, as shown in Figure 6-24. Click one of the buttons to cast your vote.

When you click the button, Outlook displays a simple dialog box with two options:

Send the Response Now. Choose this option to send the message immediately.

Edit the Response Before Sending. Choose this option if you need to edit the body of your reply.

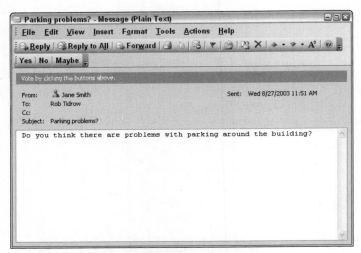

Figure 6-24: Click a voting button to cast your vote.

If you choose the former option, Outlook sends your reply with the cast vote but doesn't close the message window. Click the Close button in the form's title bar to close the message. If you choose the latter option, Outlook opens a message form in which you can enter reply text. Add the text and then click Send.

Essentially, what the voting buttons do is add the vote option to the subject line of the reply. For example, if you receive a message with the subject, "Vote on Project Aurora," and you click No, your reply goes back with the subject, "No: Vote on Project Aurora."

Tallying votes

When you send out a message for voting and receive replies, those replies come back as regular messages. Their subject lines, however, include the sender's vote, as explained in the previous section. You can view the results of the vote through any one of the replies. Follow these steps to do so:

1. In Outlook, double-click one of the replies.

2. In the message form, click the Infobar and choose View Voting Responses, then click the Tracking tab to display the form shown in Figure 6-25.

3. View individual votes within the body of the tracking form and the vote totals in the message just below the Tracking tab.

Recalling sent messages

When you send a message to another user on your Exchange Server, have the ability to *recall* the message if the recipient hasn't read it yet. When you recall a message, Exchange Server removes the message from the recipient's mailbox as if it had not been sent. This is a useful feature, particularly if you accidentally send a message before you finish composing it or change your mind about what you included in the message.

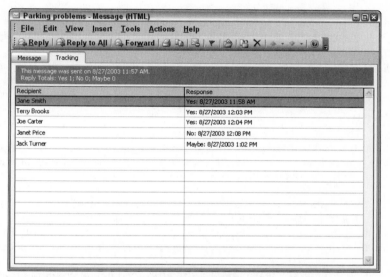

Figure 6-25: Use the Tracking tab to tally and monitor votes.

Recalling a message is easy when you follow these steps:

1. Open the Sent Items folder, and double-click the message.

2. Choose Action ➪ Recall This Message to open the Recall This Message dialog box shown in Figure 6-26.

3. Select from the following options:

> **Delete Unread Copies of this Message.** Delete the message from the recipient's mailbox without replacing it with a different message.

> **Delete Unread Copies and Replace with a New Message.** Delete the message from the recipient's mailbox, and display a new message form to create a replacement message.

> **Tell Me if Recall Succeeds or Fails for Each Recipient.** Have Exchange Server notify you if the recall succeeds or fails.

Figure 6-26: The Recall This Message dialog box

Summary

In this chapter, you learned e-mail techniques that go beyond the basics of e-mail messages. You learned to use the message format options, how to send file attachments with your messages, and how to organize your e-mail.

This chapter also explored how to use advanced message features, such as adding signatures to a message and sending documents as e-mail right from the document's application. Some additional advanced features covered include the ability to vote and tabulate votes, and to recall sent messages with Exchange Server accounts.

In the next chapter, you'll learn about more advanced e-mail concepts that can really make Outlook work for you.

✦   ✦   ✦

Advanced E-mail Concepts

In This Chapter

Using certificates for signed and encrypted messages

Using distribution lists

Using remote mail

◆   ◆   ◆   ◆

As powerful and easy to use as Outlook e-mail already seems, there are a number of advanced tools that we have not yet covered. For example, if you have a need for tight security, you can obtain and use a digital identification certificate. You can set up a distribution list to easily send messages to a specified group of people. For those times when you may only want to retrieve certain messages and leave all others on the server, you can use Remote Mail. This last feature can also be useful when your mailbox contains a message with a large attachment, or a corrupted message, either of which can cause problems downloading your messages. With Remote Mail, you can delete the message without downloading it.

Digitally Signing and Encrypting Messages

Certificates — or digital IDs — are a form of digital identification that you can use to send and receive secure e-mail messages. When you obtain and use a digital ID, message recipients can verify messages that they receive with your name on them are actually from you. In addition, if someone sends you their digital ID, you can send securely encrypted messages that only your intended recipient will be able to read.

Tip

128-bit encryption is commonly used when high security is a requirement. Each extra bit of encryption doubles the effort required to break a message's encryption, so if you really need to be certain that your messages are secure, you will definitely want to select the highest available encryption level. As of this writing, the United States prohibits the export of truly secure forms of encryption to certain countries proscribed by the United States Department of Commerce. Most of the European Union, however, is allowed for high encryption export. For more information about encryption as regards to U.S. export, see www.bxa. doc.gov/Encryption/Default.htm.

To obtain a digital ID, follow these steps:

1. Select Tools ⇨ Options to display the Options dialog box.
2. Click the Security tab, shown in Figure 7-1.

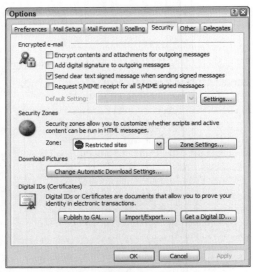

Figure 7-1: Use the Security tab to obtain a digital ID and set up secure e-mail.

3. Click the Get a Digital ID button to connect to the Internet and then choose a certificate authority.

4. Follow the instructions you see on your screen for supplying the necessary information and obtaining your certificate. The exact procedures will vary according to which of the certificate authorities you select.

5. After the certificate has been sent to your computer, you can install the certificate and begin using it. Generally, the certificate authority will provide a link on its Web page that automatically installs the certificate for you. So, you need to do nothing other than complete the request process to install the certificate.

Note

Generally, personal identification certificates suitable for e-mail authentication are not free, but the cost is minimal. If you have a Windows 2000 or 2003 Server in your network, you can install Certificate Services on the server and configure it as a Certification Authority, or CA. This CA can then issue certificates for a variety of purposes, including e-mail authentication and encryption. However, unless the recipient adds the server's certificate to his list of trusted CAs, he'll receive a warning about the possible validity of the certificate. If this occurs, the recipient can direct Outlook, when prompted, to explicitly trust your certificate, which will avoid the warning in the future.

After your certificate has been issued, you should again open the Security tab of the Options dialog box. Click the Settings button in the Encrypted option group to display the Change Security Settings dialog box. Enter a descriptive name for your security settings, and click the Choose button next to the type of security you want to use. For example, if you want to use a digital signature to positively identify your e-mail messages, click the Choose button next to the Signing Certificate text box. Figure 7-2 shows the Change Security Settings dialog box after a typical certificate has been obtained and installed.

Figure 7-2: Set up your secure e-mail options after your certificate has been issued.

Note If you use more than one PC, you can share the same certificate between those systems. Use the Import/Export Digital ID button on the Security tab of the Options dialog box to export the certificate to a password-protected file that you can later import to your other computer. Choose Export your Digital ID to a file, enter a file name in the Filename field, enter a password in the Password and Confirm fields, and click OK.

To use message encryption, you will need to know the message recipient's digital ID. To send your digital ID so that someone can send you an encrypted message, make certain the Add digital signature to outgoing messages checkbox on the Security tab of the Options dialog box is selected. You must exchange messages that include digital IDs before you can send encrypted messages.

Sending a digitally signed message

After you have the appropriate certificate installed on your computer as explained in the previous section, you can start using it to *digitally sign* outgoing messages. Adding a digital signature to a message enables the recipient to confirm that the message really came from you and not from someone pretending to be you. What's more, sending a digital signature to another person enables that person to send you encrypted messages; his or her e-mail client uses your unique digital signature to encrypt the message, and Outlook on your computer uses it to decrypt the message.

Tip   Digitally signing a message is not in any way the same as adding a signature block to a message. You don't actually see a digital signature.

Follow these steps to add a digital signature to an outgoing message:

1. Open Outlook and start a new message.

2. Address the message, add a subject, and message body; then click Options on the message form's toolbar to open the Message Options dialog box (Figure 7-3).

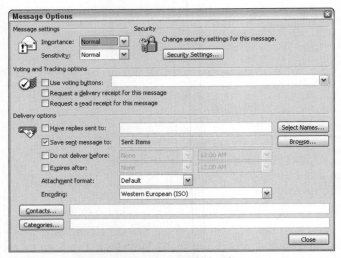

Figure 7-3: The Message Options dialog box.

3. Click Security Settings to open the Security Properties dialog box (Figure 7-4).

4. Select the option Add Digital Signature to This Message.

5. If you have multiple certificates installed and need to choose a specific one, select the corresponding security settings from the Security Settings drop-down list.

6. Click OK and then click Close.

7. Send the message.

Tip   Outlook displays an icon with a small red ribbon in the message header to indicate that the message is digitally signed.

Figure 7-4: The Security Properties dialog box.

The Security Settings dialog box contains two settings related to digital signing:

Send This Message as Clear Text Signed. Outlook will send a clear text copy of the message for any recipients who don't have S/MIME-capable e-mail applications. You can clear this option if you don't want these recipients to be able to read the message.

Request Secure Receipt for This Message. Request a secure receipt from the recipient to verify that the recipient has validated your digital signature. You will receive a receipt if the recipient's e-mail application validates your digital signature.

Encrypting messages

In situations where you need to ensure that others can't read your messages if they get misdirected, you can encrypt the message. Before you can send someone an encrypted message, they must send you a digitally signed message. Outlook uses this digital signature to encrypt the message. When the recipient receives the message, their e-mail client (such as Outlook) decrypts the message using their copy of the certificate.

After you receive the digitally signed message from the recipient, follow these steps to send an encrypted message:

1. In Outlook, start a new message and fill in the address, subject, text, and other fields as needed.

2. Click Options on the message form to open the Message Options dialog box (Figure 7-3).

3. Click Security Settings to open the Security Properties dialog box (Figure 7-4).

4. Select the option Encrypt Message Contents and Attachments.

5. Click OK and then click Close.

6. Send the message.

You don't have to do anything special to read an encrypted message, although they do not display in the Reading Pane. You must open the message to view the message.

Tip   Encrypted messages display a small blue lock icon on top of an envelope in the message header in Outlook.

Using Distribution Lists

If you ever work on projects that include a number of different people, you'll easily be able to appreciate the purpose of distribution lists. A distribution list is a group of people that you specify as the recipients of certain messages or meeting requests. What sets a distribution list apart from simply choosing the recipients when you send the message is that you create and name a distribution list in advance; then you select the distribution list rather than the individuals when you address the message.

Have you ever prepared a message that you wanted to send to a number of different people, and later discovered that you forgot to address the message to one of the intended recipients? That is something that is easy to do, especially if there are a large number of people who should be receiving the message. A distribution list is the easy answer to eliminating that problem.

Tip   Outlook normally treats a distribution list as if it were a single address. In a few instances, however, it becomes necessary to split out the individuals within the list and work with individual addresses. For example, if you want to check the availability of potential meeting participants who are part of a distribution list, Outlook must break down the distribution list into its individual members. After Outlook breaks down a distribution list in this manner, all further processing of the meeting request (or any other type of message) must be done on an individual basis. You can no longer work with the single distribution address.

Creating a distribution list

You can create multiple distribution lists that serve different purposes. If necessary, some of the same people may show up in more than one of your lists. You might, for example, create a distribution list that includes all the department managers, another that includes the inside sales staff, another for the customer service department, and so on. In addition to these individual lists, you might have another distribution list that includes all of the employees. When you send out an important message, you could simply choose the correct distribution list to make certain that the correct group would receive the message.

Tip   You can't specify some addresses for the To field and others for the Cc or Bcc fields in a distribution list. Instead, create separate distribution lists for each field. You can also save a blank message with the appropriate addresses already entered in each field and then use that message any time you need to send a message to that group of people.

To create a distribution list, follow these steps:

1. Select File ⇨ New ⇨ Distribution List. You can also click the down arrow at the right edge of the New button, and select Distribution List from the drop-down menu.

2. Enter a descriptive name for the distribution list in the Name text box.

3. Click the Select Members button to display the Select Members dialog box.

4. Select each member from the list, and click the Members button to add them to the distribution list, as shown in Figure 7-5.

Figure 7-5: Select the members of your distribution list.

5. Click OK to close the Select Members dialog box. The Distribution List dialog box should now look similar to Figure 7-6.

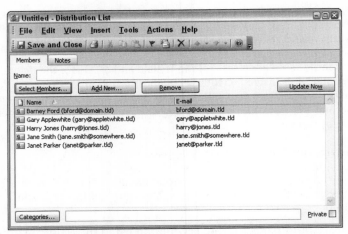

Figure 7-6: You can continue to modify your distribution list after you have added members.

6. If you need to add addresses for additional distribution list members, open the distribution list from the Contacts folder, click the Add New button, and then enter the required information in the Add New Member dialog box. You might use this option to add new distribution list members who you did not want to add to your contacts list.

7. If you need to remove someone from the list, select the name in the list and click the Remove button. Outlook does not ask for confirmation before deleting the selected entry.

8. Click the Categories button if you want to assign this distribution list to an Outlook category. You might want to use this option to help organize your contacts.

9. If you want to add notes about the distribution list, click the Notes tab and enter your comments there.

10. Click the Save and Close button to save your distribution list and close the dialog box.

Note   If the e-mail address of a distribution list member changes, you do not need to change the distribution list. Instead, simply change the e-mail address in the person's contact item. The new address will be used automatically the next time you use any distribution list of which that person is a member.

Using a distribution list

A distribution list makes it easy to send messages to a group of people, and it all but eliminates the problem of forgetting to include someone in the message distribution. You simply choose the correct distribution list, and all members of that list are automatically included.

To use a distribution list to address a new message, follow these steps:

1. Begin a new message as you normally would — by clicking the New Mail Message button, for example.

2. Click the To button to open the Select Names dialog box.

3. Select the distribution list (shown in bold) and then click the To button, as shown in Figure 7-7. You can add additional message recipients, if necessary.

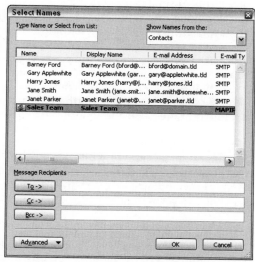

Figure 7-7: Select a distribution list to include all its members as message recipients.

4. Click OK to close the Select Names dialog box.

5. Complete your message and click the Send button.

Tip

When you send a message using a distribution list, Outlook expands the list and shows each recipient's address in the message header. If some of the message recipients do not wish their e-mail addresses to be known to the other message recipients, it would be better to send the message to those recipients privately or to use the Bcc address box for their e-mail addresses. Outlook does not provide a method of suppressing the recipient list directly.

Using Remote Mail

Outlook normally handles e-mail messages in a rather straightforward manner. Whenever Outlook connects to the mail server, any messages that are in your

Outbox are sent to the mail server, and any incoming messages are downloaded and then usually deleted from the mail server. This routine ensures that your mail server is not overloaded with old messages that you have already downloaded, and that there will be room for new messages as they arrive.

Note   Exchange Server, IMAP, and HTTP accounts maintain messages on the server until you delete them. You can also configure a POP3 account to leave a copy of messages on the server.

There may be times, however, when this normal routine doesn't quite meet your needs. Suppose, for example, that you must take a business trip while you are waiting for an important e-mail message from one of your customers. You need to respond to that message as quickly as possible, so you take along your laptop computer so that you can log in and check your messages on the road. Because you'll have to dial a long-distance number to access your ISP, you'd rather not bother downloading the 50 other messages that may arrive in your mailbox in addition to the one important message. Those messages can wait until you return home. How can you download the one important message and ignore those others?

Here's another scenario: You normally work from a broadband connection at the office, but have to use a dial-up connection at home or while on a trip. You sometimes receive messages with large attachments and don't want to download those while you use a dial-up. Or, perhaps you've received a corrupted message that is preventing Outlook from downloading the remaining messages in your mailbox.

The answer to all of these problems is to use Remote Mail — a set of Outlook tools that enable you to find out what messages are available and then send and receive just the ones you want. Remote Mail connects to the mail server, downloads the message headers — the information about the sender and subject of each message, and then disconnects so that you can make your decisions about which messages to retrieve offline. After you have marked the messages you want to retrieve, you can reconnect to the mail server and download just those messages you marked, leaving the remaining messages on the server for later retrieval.

Tip   You can use Remote Mail over a network or broadband connection; you're not limited to using it for dial-up connections. For example, you might need to delete a corrupted message from your mailbox on a local server, and Remote Mail enables you to do that.

Connecting and downloading headers

Using Remote Mail is a little different from using the normal Outlook mail services. When you use Remote Mail, you connect, download the message headers, mark the messages you want to retrieve, and then connect again to download the actual messages. You can work with Remote Mail using Outlook's menus, but it's usually a bit easier to display the Remote Mail toolbar while you're working with Remote Mail.

To use Remote Mail, follow these steps:

1. Open your Inbox and select Tools ⇨ Send/Receive ⇨ Account Only where Account is the account from which you want to download headers, and select Download Inbox Headers.

Note

You need to select an account only if you want to download from an account that stores its messages in a different folder. If you have only one account, or just want to download headers from the current folder, the command is Download Headers in This Folder.

2. Outlook downloads the headers and displays them in the Inbox. Messages whose headers only have been downloaded have a slightly different icon from those already downloaded. Figure 7-8 shows three downloaded headers at the top of the Inbox list.

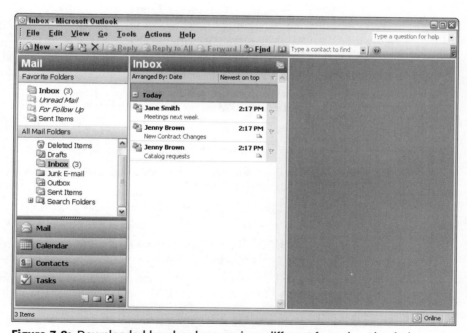

Figure 7-8: Downloaded headers have an icon different from downloaded messages.

Marking items for action

After you have downloaded the message headers, you can decide what you want to do about each of the messages. You use the Remote Mail tools to mark message headers to indicate the desired action.

To mark and process the message headers, follow these steps:

1. Double-click the item you want to retrieve to display the Remote Item Header dialog box, shown in Figure 7-9.

Figure 7-9: Choose how you want to handle the messages that Remote Mail found on the server.

Tip   You can also right-click a message header and then choose Mark to Download Message(s), Mark to Download Message Copy, or Delete to specify the action for Remote Mail.

2. Select the action you want Remote Mail to perform on the selected item:

   • Select Mark to Download This Message to retrieve the message and delete it from the mail server.

   • Select Mark to Download This Message and Leave a Copy on the Server to retrieve the message and leave the original on the mail server.

   • Select Mark to Delete This Message from the Server to delete the message from the mail server without retrieving it.

   • Select Unmark This Header Item to remove any marks you've added to the item. This will leave the item on the mail server.

3. Click OK; then repeat steps 1 and 2 for any other messages you want to process.

4. Choose Tools ➪ Send/Receive ➪ Work with Headers ➪ Process Marked Headers to start processing the messages as marked.

After you have downloaded the messages that you marked to retrieve, those messages will appear in your Inbox just as they would if you had clicked the Send/Receive button. Outlook will remove the message headers that you marked and replace them with the actual messages.

If you work with Remote Mail often, you'll no doubt get tired of digging through the Tools menu to get to the Remote Mail commands. If that's the case, consider creating your own custom toolbar that contains the Remote Mail commands. See Chapter 17 for more information on customizing Outlook.

Summary

This chapter has covered a lot of ground. You saw how to make your messages secure by using digital IDs to verify your identity and encrypt messages. You also learned how to create and use distribution lists. Finally, you learned how to use Remote Mail to manage your e-mail messages when it might not be convenient to use the shotgun approach.

The next chapter covers topics that will help you gain even more control over your messages. Chapter 8 covers Outlook rules that enable you to automatically process messages when they come in or when you send them. You can use rules to filter out unwanted messages, move messages to other folders when they arrive, and perform many other actions.

✦　　✦　　✦

Processing Messages Automatically

◆   ◆   ◆   ◆

In This Chapter

Using rules to filter
your e-mail

Backing up rules and
moving them
between computers

Using auto-
responders

Filtering out junk mail
and adult content

Using the Out of
Office Assistant with
Exchange Server

◆   ◆   ◆   ◆

You are probably inundated with e-mail messages each
day. The flood of e-mail only continues to get worse,
even though many states are finally starting to take action to
try to stem the flood from spammers. Even solicited mail can
become a burden unless you know how to process it automatically, moving it to specific folders or handling it in other ways
when it arrives.

Note The term *spam* refers to unsolicited and unwanted e-mail.
A *spammer* is a person or entity that sends out spam.

Outlook provides an excellent set of features that enable you to
process messages automatically, both when they arrive in your
Inbox and when you send messages out. You can use these
rules to move messages to specific folders, generate automatic
responses, filter out unwanted messages, and much more. In
this chapter you will learn how to put Outlook's rules to work
for you, how to back them up and restore them if needed, and
how to use the Out of Office Assistant to manage your messages in your Exchange Server mailbox when you are out.

Securing Against HTML Content

Junk mail — or spam, as it is generally called — can be a
major headache for anyone who has an e-mail account.
Although most spam includes instructions on how to unsubscribe to the list that generated it, unsubscribing often yields
questionable results. Some spammers simply ignore your
requests, while others use the request to validate your e-mail
address so they can continue sending to you. However, others
have gone to a more indirect but more effective method,
explained next.

Blocking external HTML content

Many spammers are now using more advanced methods to validate addresses, such as sending HTML-based messages that contain embedded external links. When you open the message, your e-mail application attempts to retrieve the external content, and server-side software then identifies your e-mail address as valid. These embedded URLs are often called *Web beacons*.

Outlook 2003 helps reduce spam by blocking external content in HTML messages. This is the default configuration, but if needed, you can configure Outlook to allow external content:

1. In Outlook, choose Tools ➪ Options and then click the Security tab.

2. Click Change Automatic Download Settings in the Download Pictures group to open the Automatic Download Settings dialog box (Figure 8-1).

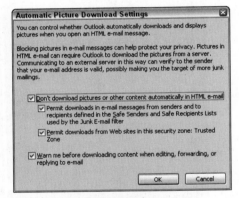

Figure 8-1: The External Content Settings dialog box.

3. Choose options based on the following list:

   Don't download pictures or other content automatically in HTML e-mail. Select this option to block Web beacons; clear the option to allow Outlook to retrieve external content.

   Permit downloads in e-mail messages from senders and to recipients defined in the Safe Senders and Safe Recipients Lists used by the Junk E-mail filter. Allow Outlook to retrieve external content if the message is sent to a recipient in the Safe recipients list or received from a sender in the Safe Senders list.

   Except if the external content comes from a Web site in these security zone: Trusted Zone. Allow Outlook to retrieve external content only if the target site is listed in the Trusted Zone or Intranet Zone. You define the sites that belong in this zone through Internet Explorer's security settings.

Warn me before downloading blocked content when editing, forwarding, or replying to e-mail. Have Outlook prompt you that a message contains external content when you edit, forward, or reply to the message.

Configuring security zones

Outlook uses the security zones you define in Internet Explorer to decide not only how to handle messages with external content, but also how to handle messages that contain scripts. By default, Outlook uses the Restricted Sites zone for handling messages. The default settings for this zone prevents HTML messages from accomplishing potentially dangerous or harmful tasks such as running scripts, downloading unsigned ActiveX controls, and scripting Java applets. Regardless of the zone you select, however, Outlook always deactivates ActiveX controls and does not run scripts. Even so, there might be other settings that you want to configure for the security zone. Keep in mind that changing the settings affects Internet Explorer as well as Outlook.

Tip   Outlook does not take into account any domains you might add to a particular zone. It uses the settings for the zone, but ignores the domains. For example, if you add sites to the Trusted Sites zone but configure Outlook to use the Restricted Sites zone, it will use the settings defined for the Restricted Sites zone even if you receive a message from a domain in the Trusted Sites zone.

To change zone settings, in Outlook choose Tools ➪ Options and then click the Security tab. Choose from the Zone drop-down list the zone you want Outlook to use for processing HTML-based messages. Click the Zones Settings button if you want to change zone settings, click OK at the warning message, and configure settings in the resulting Security dialog box (Figure 8-2).

Figure 8-2: The Security dialog box.

Select one of the four zones and click Custom Level to open the Security Settings dialog box. Configure settings as needed and then click OK. Change other zones as needed, click OK on the Security dialog box to close it, and return to Outlook.

Note The default settings for Outlook generally provide good protection against unwanted content and malicious code. For that reason, you should modify the security settings only if you have a very specific reason to do so. For that reason, and because these settings are more applicable to Internet Explorer than to Outlook, this chapter doesn't cover zone settings in detail.

Using Rules

Rules are sets of instructions that you create to tell Outlook how to handle certain types of messages. Rules are sometimes called filters, and they are often used to screen out unwanted messages. You can set up your own rules to give special handling to important messages and to send junk mail directly to the Deleted Items folder without it ever appearing in your Inbox.

You can set up rules for handling both incoming and outgoing e-mail messages. Most of the time, you'll only concern yourself with incoming messages. Still, it's nice to know that you can automate both if necessary, and there are some important uses for outgoing rules. For example, you might want to keep a copy of outgoing messages to certain people in a folder other than Sent Items to make these messages easier to locate. For example, you could create a folder for several of your most important clients, and store sent messages for those people in their respective folders.

Although it's really quite easy to set up rules, Outlook has a few rules that have been set up and are ready to use immediately. In the following sections, you learn first about setting up rules of your own and then about how you can use the junk e-mail lists that are built into Outlook.

Using the Rules Wizard

Outlook provides a Rules Wizard to help you set up your own rules for handling e-mail messages. This Rules Wizard steps you through the entire process so that creating or modifying rules is really simple and straightforward.

Creating a rule

To use the Rules Wizard to set up an e-mail message-handling rule, follow these steps:

1. Select Tools ⇨ Rules and Alerts. This will display the Rules and Alerts dialog box (Figure 8-3).

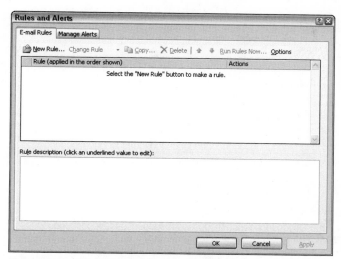

Figure 8-3: The Rules and Alerts dialog box.

2. Click the New Rule button to start the Rules Wizard, and begin creating a new rule. You can start from a blank rule or use one of several rule templates to create the rule, as explained in the next step.

3. Select a rule template from the Step 1 box, as shown in Figure 8-4. As you select different types of rules, the Step 2 box provides a brief description of the rule. If you choose the option Start from a Blank Rule, you can instead choose Check Messages When They Arrive or Check Messages After Sending to create a rule that processes messages either when they arrive or when you send them, respectively.

Tip

Choosing a rule template simply predefines certain rule properties. You can then modify these properties to customize the rule as needed. If you choose to start from a blank rule, you must manually select all rule properties. The general process is the same regardless of which method you choose.

4. Click Next to continue.

5. Scroll through the Which condition(s) do you want to check? list box, and choose the items that you want to apply to this rule. You can specify multiple conditions.

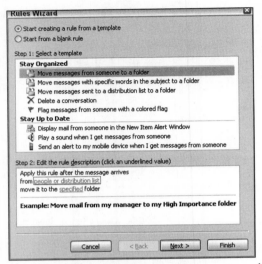

Figure 8-4: Use the Rules Wizard to create and modify Outlook message rules.

Keep in mind that all the conditions that you choose must be met before the rule will be applied. If you were to choose both the where my name is in the To box and the where my name is in the Cc box conditions, for example, the rule would apply only if your name were in both the To and the Cc boxes. The more conditions you specify, the less likely it is that any message will meet the full set of conditions. It's generally better to set as few conditions as possible — you can always go back later and add additional conditions if you discover that the rule is too broad.

6. After you have applied all the necessary conditions to the rule, click each of the underlined items in the Rule description list box in turn. This will enable you to edit the item, as shown in Figure 8-5.

7. The choices you must make will vary depending on the type of value you are editing. When you have selected all the items for the selected value, click OK to continue.

8. If there are additional underlined items, click each in turn and choose the values. When you have completed your selections, the Rules Wizard dialog box should look something like Figure 8-6, with no remaining underlined items that need to be specified.

Figure 8-5: Click the underlined values to replace each with specific condition criteria.

Figure 8-6: Make certain that you have specified the values for all underlined items before continuing.

9. Click the Next button to continue.

10. Choose any additional actions for this rule from the What do you want to do with the message? list box, as shown in Figure 8-7.

Figure 8-7: Add any additional actions for the rule.

11. Notice that specifying additional actions generally adds additional underlined items to the Rule description list box. Click the new underlined items to edit them as you did for the rule conditions. Click OK when you are done specifying the actions.

12. Click the Next button in the wizard to continue.

13. If necessary, select any exceptions to the rule using the options in the Are There Any Exceptions list box. If you add exceptions, you may need to edit additional underlined items that appear in the rule description list box.

14. Click the Next button to continue.

15. Enter a descriptive name in the Specify a name for this rule text box (Figure 8-8). The name you enter should clearly identify the rule — especially if you plan to specify a number of rules in the future.

16. If you want to apply the new rule to existing messages, select the Run this rule now on messages already in "Inbox" check box. Selecting this option is a good way to check the operation of your new rule.

17. Make certain the Turn on this rule check box is selected. You can deselect this checkbox if you don't want the rule to apply immediately, but you'll have to remember to apply the rule later.

Figure 8-8: Set final options for the rule.

18. Select the option Create this rule on all accounts option if you want to apply the rule to all of your e-mail accounts. This option is available only if you have multiple accounts.

19. Click the Finish button to complete the creation of your new rule.

20. Click OK to close the Rules Wizard dialog box.

Controlling rule processing order

If you set up a number of rules for handling your messages, you may discover that some of those rules conflict with each other. As an example, consider what would happen if you set up a rule that displayed a special message telling you that an important message had arrived whenever someone marked their message as important. In addition, suppose you decided that you wanted to forward all incoming messages from a particular person to an assistant without reading them yourself. If the sender marked all messages as important, which rule would apply? The answer is simple — Outlook applies rules starting at the top of the list of rules as they appear in the Rules Wizard dialog box. To change the order in which the rules are applied, you can use the Move Up and Move Down buttons in the Rules and Alerts dialog box.

Keep in mind that more than one rule can apply to the same message. If the rule notifying you of important messages appears before the rule forwarding the message, both rules would likely be triggered by messages sent by that person. If you move the forwarding rule up above the important message notification rule, then the message would be forwarded before the important message notification rule could be applied.

Running rules manually

In most cases, your rules will fire automatically when messages arrive or depart. In a few cases, however, you might need to run rules manually, such as when you create a new rule and want to apply it to messages already in the Inbox. The Rules and Alerts dialog box enables you to do just that.

1. Create the rule as explained in the previous section.

2. In the Rules and Alerts dialog box, click Run Rules Now to display the Run Rules Now dialog box (Figure 8-9).

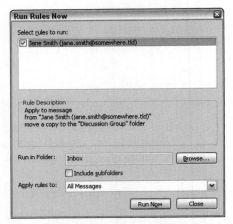

Figure 8-9: The Rules and Alerts dialog box.

3. Place a check by each rule you want to run; then click Browse to select the folder in which to run the rules.

4. Choose the Include Subfolders option if you want to run the rules on subfolders of the specified folder.

5. Select from the Apply Rules To drop-down list the types of messages to which you want to apply the rules.

6. Click Run Now to run the rules on the specified folders and messages.

7. Click Close when finished.

Modifying and copying rules

It's likely that you will at some point need to change a rule to fine-tune its behavior or adjust to changes in the way you receive or send messages. You can easily modify any custom rule through the Rules and Alerts dialog box. Simply select the rule and then click Change Rule to display a menu of actions you can assign to the rule. Choose Edit All Rule Settings if you want to make step-by-step changes to a rule.

The Rules and Alerts dialog box also enables you to copy rules between locations. For example, you might have two mail servers, each of which enables you to define rules. When you create a rule, it is assigned to a particular location. To copy it to another, open the Rules and Alerts dialog box, select the rule, and click Copy in the toolbar to open a simple dialog box in which you select the target server from a drop-down list. Select the server and then click OK.

Responding automatically to messages

One reason to use rules is to process messages when they arrive, deleting or moving them as needed; however, one very useful purpose for rules is to create automatic replies, or *auto-responders*, for incoming messages that fit certain conditions. For example, perhaps you have a product for which you want to provide information to your clients. You can create a message that contains information about the product and then send that message any time someone sends a message requesting the information.

You can use a couple of methods to generate the reply. You can set up a special e-mail address in your mail server that points to your mailbox, and when you receive a message for that address, have Outlook send the appropriate reply. For example, the person might send a message to productinfo@yourdomain.tld. A rule you define in Outlook checks the messages as they come in; when it finds one addressed to that address, it replies with the information.

Another method is to have people send their message with certain identifying text in the subject. For example, any messages with "Product Info" in the subject field of the incoming message could trigger the rule.

Setting up an automatic response is fairly easy:

1. Open Outlook and start a new message.
2. Enter the Subject field, but leave the address fields blank.
3. Add the desired information in the body of the message and then choose File ➪ Save As.
4. Choose Outlook Template from the Save As Type dialog box.
5. In the Save As dialog box, enter a name for the message, such as Product Info. Choose the path for the file and then click Save. Close the message form.

 Tip You can place the message anywhere you want, but using the default location will help you quickly locate the message in the future if you need to edit it.

6. Choose Tools ⇨ Rules and Alerts.

7. Click New Rule to start the Rules Wizard, choose Start from a Blank Rule, and click Next.

8. Set the condition you want to match (such as With Specific Words in the Subject or Body), specify the words or other criteria in the bottom pane of the dialog box, and click Next.

9. Select the action Reply Using a Specific Template, click the underlined A Specific Template link, and select the Outlook template created in step 5. Click Open.

10. Click Next, set exceptions as needed, and click Finish.

11. Click OK to close the Rules and Alerts dialog box.

Which condition or method you use to identify incoming messages depends in part on your mail server. If you set up an account specifically for the auto-responder, you can use a condition that identifies the message by its account or address. If you can't create a separate account, the best option is to use the Subject field as the condition trigger.

Note   Unless you are using Exchange Server, which supports server-side rules that can continue to function even when Outlook is not running, you must leave Outlook running to process incoming messages. You must also configure Outlook to process messages automatically and set the scheduled time for send/receive.

Importing, exporting, and backing up rules

Outlook 2003, similar to Outlook 2002, stores rules in the PST if you use a PST as your message store, or stores them in your Exchange Server mailbox. If you have created several rules, it's a good idea to back them up so you don't have to recreate them from scratch if something happens to your mail store. What's more, you can move rules from one computer to another, such as when you get a new computer or you want to share your rules with someone else.

Back up rules to a file

You simply export your rules to a file whenever you want to back them up or copy them to another computer:

1. In Outlook, choose Tools ⇨ Rules and Alerts.

2. Click Options in the Rules and Alerts dialog box to open the Options dialog box shown in Figure 8-10.

3. Click Export Rules to open the Save Exported Rules As dialog box.

4. Enter a file name, choose a path for the file, and click Save. Outlook saves the file with a RWZ file extension.

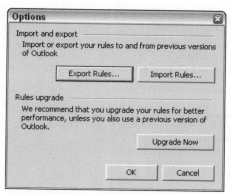

Figure 8-10: The Options dialog box

Import rules from a file

When you need to import rules from another computer or another profile, you can do so easily. After you export the rules to a file as explained in the previous section, follow these steps to import the rules:

1. In Outlook, choose Tools ➪ Rules and Alerts.
2. Click the Options button to open the Options dialog box.
3. Click Import Rules, locate and select the rule file, and click Open.
4. Click OK to close the Options dialog box, and verify that the rules now appear in the Rules and Alerts dialog box; then click OK to close the Rules and Alerts dialog box.

Filtering junk and adult content mail

Because junk e-mail is such a common problem, Outlook already has rules in place to handle junk mail. These rules are already in place, but you might need to adjust them to suit your needs.

Outlook actually defines two classes of junk e-mail messages — junk messages and adult content messages. In both cases, those classes of messages are defined by keywords and other factors that Outlook looks for in the messages.

Because no simple keyword search can be 100% effective, Outlook can also maintain lists of people who send junk or adult content e-mail messages. By adding someone to one of these lists, you are telling Outlook to apply the junk or adult content e-mail message rules to all messages that you receive from that person — whether those messages include the keywords or not.

To modify the junk mail settings, follow these steps:

1. Select Tools ➪ Options, and click the Preferences tab.

2. Click Junk E-mail to open the Junk E-mail Options dialog box, as shown in Figure 8-11.

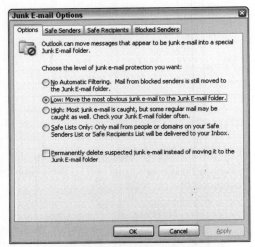

Figure 8-11: Use the Junk E-mail Options dialog box to configure junk e-mail filters.

3. Select one of the four options to set the level of protection. Each option is explained on the dialog box.

4. Click the Safe Senders tab and select the option Also trust e-mail from my Contacts if you want Outlook to accept e-mail from senders in your Contacts folder regardless of the message content, subject, or other message properties.

5. Click Add and enter the e-mail address of a sender whose messages you don't want Outlook to treat as junk mail. You do not need to add the address if the contact is already in your Contacts folder and you enabled the option in step 4 to allow messages from your contacts.

6. Click OK.

Tip   To add someone to the junk or adult content e-mail message lists, select a message from that person and then choose Actions ➪ Junk E-mail ➪ Add Sender To Blocked Senders List. You can also add addresses to this list from the Blocked Senders tab of the Junk E-mail Options dialog box.

After you have specifically added someone to the junk e-mail message lists, all messages they send to you will be handled according to the rules you have specified. To remove someone from the list, follow these steps:

1. Choose Tools ⇨ Options and click Junk E-Mail on the Preferences tab.

2. Click the Blocked Senders tab (see Figure 8-12).

3. Click the address and click Remove.

4. Click OK.

Figure 8-12: Edit the junk senders list to add or remove people from the list.

All messages from someone that you add to the junk or adult content e-mail message lists will be treated the same regardless of their content. If someone only occasionally sends you offensive or unwanted messages, you may find that it is more effective to use the Rules Wizard to create a special filter that applies to messages from that person.

Using the Out of Office Assistant

Exchange Server users have one additional means for automatically processing messages: the Out of Office Assistant. This handy tool helps you automatically responds to messages when you are out of the office. For example, you might want to have each sender receive a reply similar to the following when they send you a message:

Thanks for your message. I am out of the office until Monday of next week. I will respond to your message when I return.

The main reason to use the Out of Office Assistant rather than create a rule in the Rules Wizard is that the Assistant keeps track of the senders to which it has already sent an out-of-office reply. That means that senders only receive one copy of the automatic reply, rather than a reply for each message they send you. You can't accomplish this through the Rules Wizard.

Setting up the Out of Office Assistant isn't difficult. Follow these steps:

1. In Outlook, choose Tools ⇨ Out of Office Assistant to open the Out of Office Assistant dialog box (Figure 8-13).

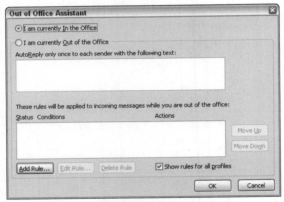

Figure 8-13: The Out of Office Assistant dialog box

2. Click in the field AutoReply only once to each sender with the following text: then type the text you want sent automatically when you are out of the office.

3. When you are satisfied with the reply text and ready to turn on the assistant, choose I am currently Out of the Office, and click OK.

The Out of Office Assistant is a server-side mechanism that continues to fire even when Outlook is not running; therefore, you can close Outlook, shut down your computer, and the Exchange Server will still generate automatic replies to incoming messages. When you get back in the office and are ready to turn off the Out of Office Assistant, open Outlook, choose Tools ⇨ Out of Office Assistant, select I am currently In the Office, and click OK.

Tip   Turning off the Out of Office Assistant clears the sent list that Exchange Server maintains to keep track of the people to whom it has sent out-of-office replies.

When you define the general reply and turn on the assistant without taking any other action, Exchange Server sends the out-of-office reply to all senders alike, but only the first time they send a message. You can create custom rules to provide additional processing, if needed. For example, you might want all messages from a particular sender or group of people to be forwarded to your assistant for handling, or to an external e-mail account to enable you to process it yourself.

Follow these steps to create custom Out-of-Office Assistant rules:

1. Choose Tools ⇨ Out of Office Assistant.

2. In the Out of Office Assistant dialog box, click Add Rule to open the Edit Rule dialog box shown in Figure 8-14.

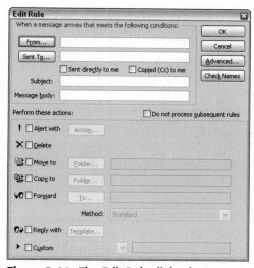

Figure 8-14: The Edit Rule dialog box

3. Use the condition controls to specify the condition that identifies the message, just as you do for rules created with the Rules Wizard.

4. Use the controls under the Perform these actions group to specify what you want Exchange Server to do with the items.

5. Click OK to save the rule. Outlook automatically names the rule and it appears in the Out of Office Assistant dialog box, as shown in Figure 8-15.

6. Repeat steps 2 through 5 to create other rules as needed and then click OK to close the Out of Office Assistant dialog box.

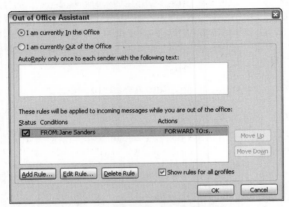

Figure 8-15: A custom rule added to the Out of Office Assistant

Summary

Rules are a very important feature of Outlook that enable you to gain quite a bit of control over your messages. For example, you can use rules to automatically move messages from certain people to special folders to help you identify them quickly. Rules also are an important means for helping you recognize and respond to important messages when they arrive.

Outlook 2003 incorporates some major changes to the junk e-mail filter found in previous editions. Outlook's Junk E-mail Options dialog box helps you identify messages from certain senders as junk mail so those messages are routed automatically to the Junk E-mail folder. With just a little bit of configuration, it's a good bet that the junk filter in Outlook will be able to do a very good job of separating the good messages from the junk.

Finally, this chapter explained how to use the Out-of-Office Assistant, a component of Exchange Server that enables your mailbox to automatically respond to messages when you are out of the office.

✦   ✦   ✦

Information Manager

P A R T

◆ ◆ ◆ ◆

In This Part

Chapter 9
Managing Your
Contacts

Chapter 10
Managing Your
Calendar

Chapter 11
Scheduling Your Time

Chapter 12
Tracking Tasks

Chapter 13
Keeping Your Journal

Chapter 14
Taking Notes

Chapter 15
Organizing
Information with
Categories

Chapter 16
Using Outlook
Newsreader

◆ ◆ ◆ ◆

Managing Your Contacts

◆ ◆ ◆ ◆

In This Chapter

An overview of contacts

Viewing your contacts

Creating contacts

Using contacts

◆ ◆ ◆ ◆

If you have used Outlook primarily as an e-mail program, you have missed much of what makes Outlook so useful and powerful. Outlook is also a great manager of contacts — Outlook can help you keep track of all of those addresses, phone numbers, Web sites, and various other bits of information that you need constantly. Using Outlook to keep a record of all that information beats easily the old "write it on the back of the business card" method that passes for organization on far too many desktops.

Using Outlook to track your contacts doesn't have to be an all-or-nothing affair. If you have a tattered old address book, there's no reason you can't continue to use it while you gradually add people to your Outlook Contacts list. You can even start by just adding e-mail addresses as you send and receive messages. Of course, to get the full benefit of Outlook's contact management capabilities, you'll want to begin storing your contact information in Outlook as soon as possible. This chapter shows you how to use the Outlook Contacts list — after you see how easy and useful this is, you can proceed at your own pace.

An Overview of Contacts

People often think of contacts in a business context, but there's no reason why your definition has to be that narrow. In addition to business contacts, you probably keep in touch with both family and friends, and maintaining address and phone number changes for them is just as much a chore as for your business associates. In fact, you likely keep track of more information about family and friends than you do for business contacts. Who can remember all those birthdays and anniversaries without making a mistake?

Outlook has the capability to work with the older Windows Address Book (also called Personal Address Book) in addition to the Contacts list that is built into Outlook. The Contacts list has many more capabilities for managing your contacts than do the Address Books, so only the Contacts list are covered in this chapter. You may want to use the Import and Export command on the File menu to import your old Address Book into the Outlook Contacts list before continuing with this chapter.

Outlook also enables you to create multiple Contacts lists so that you can have one for business contacts, another for personal contacts, and yet another you can share with other people. In addition, if you connect to a network that uses Microsoft Exchange as its e-mail server, you can download the company's contact list that is stored on the Exchange server.

What are contacts?

Just what are contacts, anyway? In the context of Outlook, contacts are essentially the records that you keep about people. Figure 9-1 shows a typical Outlook contact card that records some of the types of information that you might keep handy.

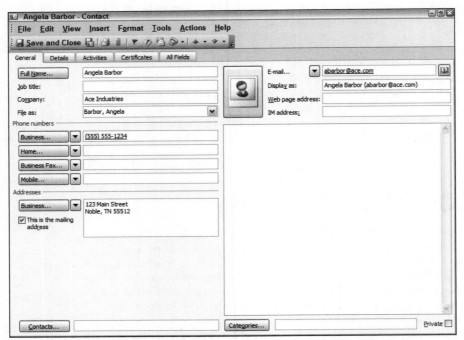

Figure 9-1: A typical Outlook contact includes a number of pieces of useful information about someone.

If you have trouble thinking of a contact as the information that you know about someone, it might be a little easier to think about how Windows deals with objects. Almost everything you see in a Windows program can be considered an object. A simple text box is an example of an object that you've dealt with numerous times. That simple object — the text box — has properties that define the object. A text box might have a font property that describes the font used to display information in the text box. It might also have other properties such as size, color, and so on. You aren't normally aware of those properties, but the information that makes up those properties is what makes the object useful. The same applies to your contacts — the information you know about someone such as his or her name, phone number, e-mail address, and so on is how you define that person. If you don't have any information about someone, you have no way to define that person. With Outlook 2003, you can also add a picture of a contact, helping you to identify and remember a contact visually.

What are the new Outlook contact features?

With each new version, Outlook has added a number of features that make the program more powerful and easier to use. To get the most out of the contact-related features in this latest version of Outlook, it will be handy to have a quick look at what's new. Here's a brief synopsis of what's new about managing your contacts in Outlook:

✦ Instant Messaging (IM) information can be stored with a contact so you can quickly request an online meeting with a contact without having to remember the contact's IM address.

✦ You can display a picture of your contacts on the contacts page. This makes it much easier to remember contacts and what they look like. If it's a contact you've never met but have plans to meet him or her in the future, you can print the picture along with the contact information to take with you to the meeting.

Although each of these new or enhanced features is contact related, some of them really add most of their utility to other areas of using Outlook. For example, Instant Messaging is discussed in some detail in Chapter 26.

Viewing Your Contacts

The Outlook Contacts folder enables you to easily create, view, or modify your contacts. As Figure 9-2 shows, you have several options for viewing the Contacts folder. The default view — Address Cards — represents a good compromise between showing just enough information to be useful and showing so much information that you are constantly scrolling in an attempt to locate people.

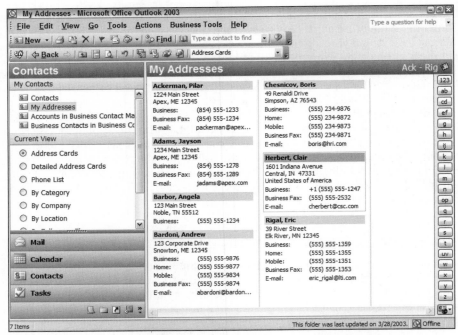

Figure 9-2: The Contacts folder provides easy access to all your contacts.

Regardless of the view you select for the Contacts folder, Outlook uses a standard form to display the detailed information about each of your contacts. In the following sections, you learn how to use each part of the Contact form to manage this information.

Understanding the General tab

The Contact form has a number of parts — too many to view on a single screen. In these sections, you learn about the elements of the General tab of the Contact form, shown in Figure 9-3. To display this tab, double-click one of the entries in your Contacts folder. The General tab is displayed by default.

Name options

The first piece of information that you're likely to enter about any of your contacts is his or her name. Contact records would, after all, be useless without including the person's name.

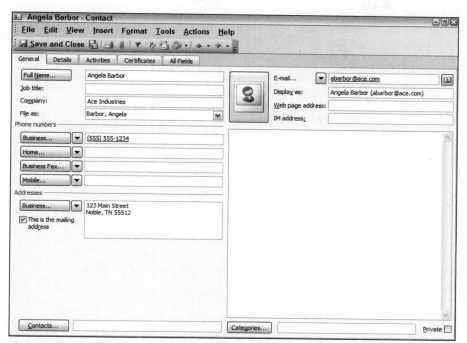

Figure 9-3: Use the General tab of the Contact form to record basic information about your contacts.

Outlook uses the information that you type in the Full Name and Company text boxes to create the range of entries that are available in the File as list box. As Figure 9-4 shows, you have several options from which to select after you have entered both a name and a company for the contact.

If you don't enter a company name, the File as list box will show only two choices — last name, first name, or first name and then last name.

Tip Choose the same File as format for all your contacts; otherwise, some entries may be filed according to the first name and others may be filed by last name. If you enter a company name in the Full Name field, however, such as if you want to list a company from which you order supplies and that company has two names, select the option that lists the company name first name first. For example, if you add Amex Premium to your list of contacts, select Amex Premium from the File as list; do not select Premium, Amex. That way you can see the company name alphabetically in your list of contacts, which is the natural way to look up company names.

Another possibility is to type your own File as name. For instance, type AAA in front of a name to place it at the top of the contacts list. You also can type Rev., Fr., or Dr. if you want to display a contact by his or her professional name.

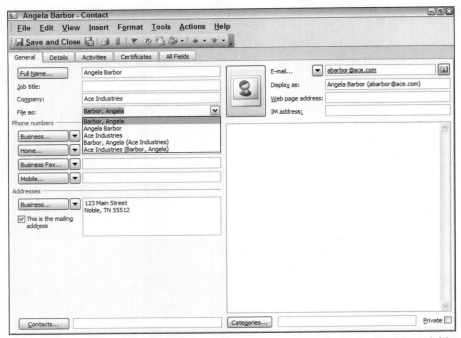

Figure 9-4: Select how you would like this contact to appear in your Contacts folder.

You can enter the contact's name by simply typing it in the Full Name text box, or by clicking the Full Name button and then using the separate text boxes in the Check Full Name dialog box. The only advantage to using the Check Full Name dialog box is that this dialog box has drop-down list boxes for title and suffix. Unless you assign an unusual title or suffix to someone's name, Outlook should have little trouble understanding most names you might enter in the Full Name text box.

The entries in the Job Title and Company text boxes are optional, but Outlook will use them if they are available. For example, if you send a fax and include a cover page, Outlook will use these entries to help identify the intended fax recipient on the cover page.

Phone number options

Below the name area in the Contact form are some interesting text boxes. The four phone number text boxes are actually multipurpose text boxes. As Figure 9-5 shows, each of these text boxes can hold information from a variety of different fields.

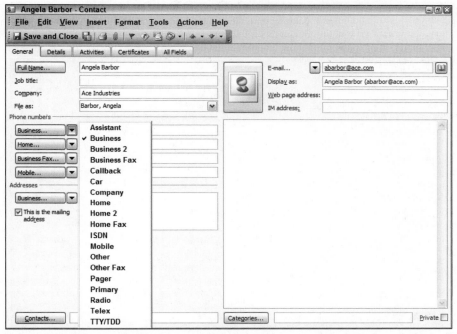

Figure 9-5: Select the type of phone number for each field by clicking the down arrow button to the left of the text box.

Although only four phone number text boxes are displayed at one time, you can actually enter as many of the different types of numbers as necessary. Simply click the down arrow to select a different field to be displayed and then enter the associated number. Outlook will store as many of the different numbers as you enter. To view the number that is stored in a field, choose to display that field in one of the text boxes.

Address options

The Address text box is used to hold the contact's addresses. As Figure 9-6 shows, Outlook has a provision for storing three different addresses for each contact — Business, Home, and Other.

You can also click the Address button to display the Check Address dialog box if you would rather use separate text boxes for each element of the address. You may want to use this dialog box to create address entries for foreign addresses because the dialog box includes a Country/Region list box.

Figure 9-6: Select the type of address by clicking the down arrow button to the left of the Address text box.

 Note   The Check Address dialog box displays if you enter an incomplete address, such as one line from an address without a state, Zip code, and the like. If you do not want this dialog box to appear like this again, deselect the Show this again when address is incomplete or unclear option on the Check Address dialog box; then click OK.

If you enter more than one address for a contact, be sure that you select one of the addresses as the mailing address by clicking the This is the mailing address check box. Only one address should be designated as the mailing address, but you may need to include a shipping address as the Other entry if the shipping and mailing addresses are not the same.

 Tip   The address you select as the designated mailing address will be used as the default address when you perform mail merges in Microsoft Word.

Add Picture button

With Outlook 2003, you can include a photograph of contacts on their contact pages. To do this, scan or save a picture of your contact on your computer. Make sure the photo is in one of the following file formats:

✦ BMP

✦ EMF

✦ ICO

✦ ICON

✦ JPG/JPEG

✦ GIF

Click the Add Contact Picture button and then select your picture in the Add Contact Picture dialog box. Click OK to close the dialog box and to add the picture to your contact page.

E-mail address options

Just as people often have a number of different telephone numbers, multiple e-mail addresses are also becoming fairly common. The e-mail text box accommodates this reality by being linked to three different e-mail address fields — just as the address and phone number text boxes link to multiple fields. You can click the down arrow to the left of the e-mail text box to choose which of the e-mail address fields is displayed in the text box.

To the right of the e-mail address text box is a button that displays the Select Name dialog box. If you click this button, you can choose the contact's name from the list of names in your Contacts folder. Although this may sound useful at first glance (for example, you would think you could select the contact's e-mail address from the Select Name dialog box), this option essentially offers what would be known as a circular reference in a spreadsheet. If your Contacts list already has an e-mail listing for this contact, it would likely be shown in the e-mail address text box of the Contact form, so there would be no need to select it from the list. If you haven't already entered an e-mail address for this contact, it's also unlikely that you would be able to select the nonexistent entry from the list. The one time this is useful is if your company has a Contacts list you download to be used offline. You might add a person's name to your personal contact list and then use the Select Name dialog box to select his or her e-mail address so you don't have to type in the address manually.

More option on the General tab

The remaining elements of the General tab of the Contact form enable you to enter further useful information about the contact. Here's a brief look at these elements:

✦ The Display as text box shows how you want the Outlook to display a contact's information in the To: line when creating an e-mail message to him or her.

✦ The Web page address text box enables you to enter the URL of a Web site that you want to associate with this contact. Although this address would most commonly be the contact's Web site, you may also choose to display a different Web site address. For example, you might choose an address such as www.wiley.com so that you could easily locate the latest books from your favorite computer book author.

✦ The IM address text box lets you enter the Instant Messenger address for a contact. That way you do not have to remember the IM address when you want to contact that person via IM.

✦ The notes text box is really a multi-use area. You can enter notes about the contact, or you can show links to Calendar-related events for this contact. You might use this area to remind yourself about the contact's food preferences so that you could select the correct type of restaurant when inviting the contact out for a business lunch.

✦ The Contacts notes area enables you to link this contact with other contacts, such as the contact's assistant, so you would know whom to call if you couldn't reach the contact in an emergency.

✦ The Contacts notes area also includes a shortcut icon if you set up the contact's birthday or anniversary on the Details tab. You can double-click the icon to display the calendar event for that contact. To insert shortcuts to other items, select Insert ⇨ Item to display the Insert Item dialog box. Select Calendar (or whichever folder stores the item you want to insert) and then choose the item in the lower part of the dialog box. Click OK to display that item's shortcut icon in the General text box area.

✦ The Categories text box enables you to classify your contacts into groups so it is easier to locate specific types of contacts. If you combine business contacts with family and friends in your Outlook Contacts folder, you could use categories to help you organize these different groups.

✦ The Private check box makes it possible to hide this contact record from others if you share your Contacts folder. For example, you might want to use this if you've been in touch with a management recruiter who has been trying to find a better job for you.

Understanding the Details tab

The Details tab of the Contact form provides additional text boxes that you can use to add more detailed information about a contact. Figure 9-7 shows the Details tab.

You should be able to figure out the function of most of the text boxes on the Details tab simply by reading the label on the text box. You may, however, need a little clarification of the items associated with Microsoft NetMeeting settings and the Internet Free-Busy information.

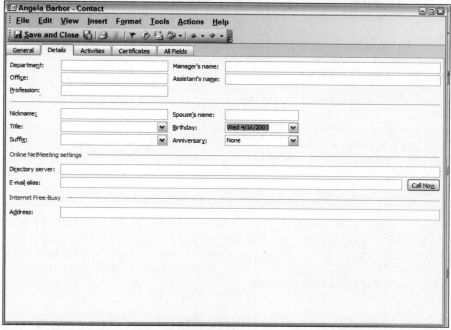

Figure 9-7: Use the Details tab to enter additional information about a contact.

NetMeeting is an application that enables you to hold online meetings with one or more people via the Internet. A NetMeeting meeting may consist of several elements including the following:

✦ Text-based chat, which enables participants to type their comments for all the other participants to see.

✦ A whiteboard, which enables participants to illustrate points using an electronic slate on which you can draw simple images.

✦ Application sharing, which enables all participants to view and use a program that may only be installed on one of the participant's computers.

✦ Audio conferencing, which enables the participants to discuss subjects as if they were participating in a telephone conference call.

✦ Video conferencing, which enables the participants to see each other.

Of course, which of those elements are available depends on a number of factors. Video cameras are necessary to enable the video conferencing features, and fast access to the Internet is necessary to make any of the features really usable.

Attempting to use a high-bandwidth feature such as video conferencing over slow dial-up connections would likely be nothing more than an exercise in futility!

To use NetMeeting, each of the participants must connect to the same directory server. This is a computer on the Internet that provides the link between each of the meeting participants. Because there are many different NetMeeting servers, it is important that all meeting participants coordinate so that they use the same server. You use the Directory server text box to specify which server the contact uses.

After you are connected to a directory server, you must specify a name that the other participants can recognize so that you will all be able to join the same meeting. You use the E-mail alias text box to specify the name for the contact so that NetMeeting can locate the meeting participants.

Clicking the Call Now button connects you to the specified NetMeeting server and attempts to locate the contact on that server.

The Internet Free-Busy item is a feature that enables Outlook users to share their Outlook Calendars with others over the Internet using the Microsoft Office Free/Busy Feature. If a contact has a site at which he or she shares calendar information, list that site's address here.

Understanding the Activities tab

The Activities tab of the Contact form shows all outstanding Outlook items that are related to the selected contact. These may include items such as Journal entries, contact records, open documents, e-mail messages, notes, phone calls, or upcoming activities. Figure 9-8 shows the Activities tab.

The Activities tab is one place where you'll really start to appreciate just how useful and powerful Outlook's contact management features really are. Not only can you see a listing of all the open items for the contact, but you can easily open any of those items by double-clicking the item. You don't have to hunt through your Calendar, Tasks list, Inbox, Drafts folder, and so on to see what might need to be done. All you need to do is open the Contact form and have a quick look at the Activities tab. You can select which types of items should appear by making a selection from the Show drop-down list box.

Tip   You can quickly sort the items on the Activities tab by clicking a column heading.

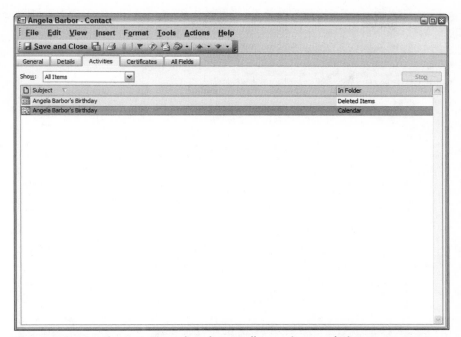

Figure 9-8: Use the Activities tab to locate all open items relating to a contact.

Understanding the Certificates tab

The next tab of the Contact form is the Certificates tab. Figure 9-9 shows the Certificates tab.

Certificates are digital IDs that can be used to positively identify someone when they send an e-mail message. Certificates can also be used to encrypt messages so that only the intended recipient can read the message.

Tip   You must have someone's digital ID to send them an encrypted message. The easiest way to obtain someone's digital ID is for them to send you a digitally signed message.

It's important to remember that certificates generally have a limited life span. When a certificate expires, it can no longer be relied upon as a valid identification. If you have obtained more than one certificate for someone, you may have to remove obsolete certificates from the list on the Certificates tab, or you may have to select one of the certificates to set as the default certificate. You can click the Properties button to view the information about a selected certificate — that way, you can check to see whether the certificate is still valid.

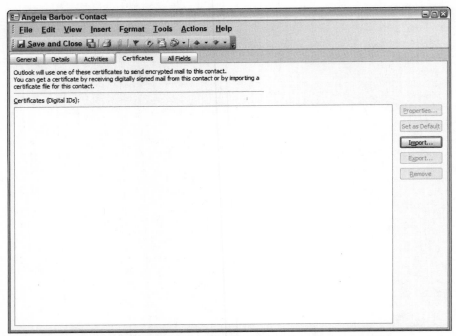

Figure 9-9: Use the Certificates tab to manage digital IDs for a contact.

Most certificate authorities provide personal certificates at no charge. To learn more about obtaining your own digital identification, see Chapter 7.

Understanding the All Fields tab

Outlook can track an incredible amount of information about your contacts. Using standard database terminology, each of your contacts is one record, and each piece of information about that contact is stored in a field. The Outlook Contacts database has far too many fields to completely display all of that information on any tab of the Contact form. That's why the Contact form includes the All Fields tab — so that you can see whatever information you want about a contact. Figure 9-10 shows the All Fields tab of the Contact form.

Rather than simply attempting to show every field on the All Fields tab, Outlook enables you to select the types of fields you would like to see from the Select from list box. In the figure, Frequently-used fields was selected to show the most common fields that are in the database. No matter which set of fields you choose to display, the fields will be listed in alphabetical order sorted by the name of the field.

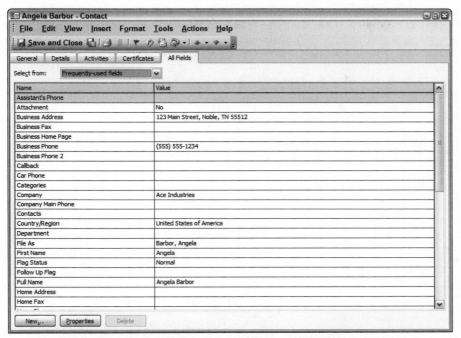

Figure 9-10: Use the All Fields tab to view all information for a contact.

The All Fields tab is also the location where you have the opportunity to create new fields or to modify the properties of some existing fields. You cannot generally modify fields that are standard Outlook fields, but you can change certain properties for fields that you created earlier. To add a new field, click the New button to display the New Field dialog box, shown in Figure 9-11. To modify a field that you had created earlier, you would click the Properties button to display the Field Properties dialog box—which is identical to the New Field dialog box except for the dialog box title.

After you have entered a name for the new field, you can select a field type and format. Different field types have different available formats, so choose the type first. You should choose a field type that is compatible with the type of data that you intend to store in the field. For example, if you wanted to add a Date Hired field, you would choose Date/Time. Click the OK button to finish creating the new field.

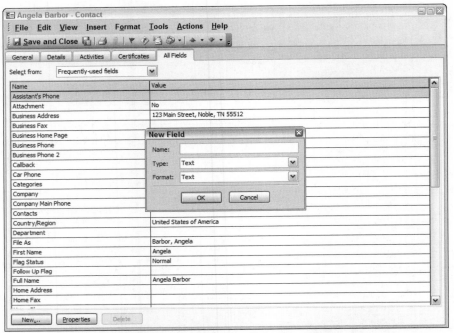

Figure 9-11: Use the New Field dialog box to add your own fields to the Outlook Contact database.

Creating Contacts

Your Outlook Contacts list is only useful after you've added people to the list. Creating contacts is easy, and Outlook provides several different methods to make the task even easier. In the following sections, you learn how to use several of these methods.

Importing contacts

The easiest way to create your Contacts list is to not create the list at all. Instead of creating a list from scratch, you may be able to import a list that exists in a different format.

Outlook can import contact information in several different formats. If you were using another program that included contact information when you installed Outlook, you were probably given the option to import that information during the installation process. If you decided not to import the information at that time, or if you now have new data that you could import, you can choose to import that information at any time you like.

Note   If someone sends you vCard files, you can use Outlook's import capabilities to add the vCard information easily to your Contacts list.

To import data into your Outlook Contacts list, follow these steps:

1. Select File ⇨ Import and Export to display the Import and Export Wizard, shown in Figure 9-12. If you have the Microsoft Business Contact Manager feature installed, you will need to select File ⇨ Import and Export ⇨ Outlook.

Figure 9-12: Use the Import and Export Wizard to quickly import existing data into your Outlook Contacts list.

2. Choose the type of information you want to import. It's a good idea to scroll through the list to see if one of the choices mentions the source program in the description. Choosing the correct type of import greatly increases the chances of success.

3. Click Next to continue.

4. Depending on the type of import you selected, you will next need to select the source program. You may also need to choose the types of information that you want to import, as shown in Figure 9-13.

5. Click Next to continue.

6. You may have additional choices to select, as shown in Figure 9-14.

   If you have a choice for the destination, choose the Outlook Contacts Folder option button. The Outlook Contacts folder has additional capabilities that are not available in the Personal Address Book.

Figure 9-13: Select the source program and any import options.

Choose how Outlook should handle duplicates. You may want to base your choice on which database contains the most recent information. If you choose to import duplicate records, you should check for duplicates immediately after performing the import and correct any errors that you find.

Figure 9-14: Select the file to import and the duplicate import options.

7. Click Finish to complete the task.

You can repeat the import process as often as necessary. If you have contact data from several sources, you can use Outlook to consolidate all of the information in one central location by importing from each source in turn.

Note   If you are importing data from several sources, be especially careful with your choice of duplicate handling options. Keeping track of duplicate records that exist in many different locations can be difficult. Keep all of your contact information in Outlook to prevent future confusion over which records are correct.

Creating contacts manually

You probably won't be lucky enough to be able to import all the contacts that you'll need to track in your Contacts list. Indeed, you'll probably end up creating a large number of contact records yourself. Fortunately, this is a simple process that won't take much time at all.

To begin creating a new contact record, follow these steps:

1. Open the Contacts folder.

2. Click the New Contact button to open a new Contact form, as shown in Figure 9-15. Alternatively you can select File ➪ New ➪ Contact or Actions ➪ New Contact to open this form. If you have a contact created from one company and want to create another contact for the same company, select Actions ➪ New Contact from Same Company. This opens a new contact, but has the company-related information already filled in.

3. Enter as much or as little information as you need for the new contact. At a minimum, you must enter the contact's name or company, but all other information is optional.

4. Click the Save and Close button to save the information on the new contact and close the Contact form.

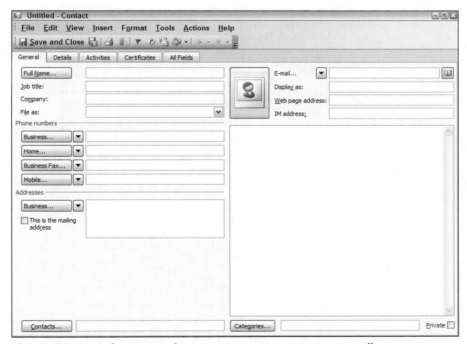

Figure 9-15: Use the Contact form to create a new contact manually.

Note   Remember that Contact form text boxes that show a down arrow to their right are multipurpose fields. You can select a different field to display in the text box by clicking the down arrow and then choosing a field name from the list.

After you have created contact records, you can easily reopen those records for editing. Double-click a contact in the Contacts folder to open the Contact form so you can edit the selected record.

Creating contacts while viewing an e-mail message

If you receive an e-mail message from someone who isn't already in your Contacts list, you can easily add him or her to the list with just a few clicks of your mouse. This ensures that you can later send that person a message and be certain of having the correct e-mail address.

Note   You can add any person who is shown in a message header to your Contacts list the same way you add the sender. This includes anyone in the To, Cc, or Bcc address boxes.

As Figure 9-16 shows, the quickest method of adding to your Contacts list someone who is listed in an e-mail message header is to right-click th name and then choose Add to Outlook Contacts.

Figure 9-16: Right-click a name and choose Add to Outlook Contacts.

When you select Add to Outlook Contacts, Outlook opens the Contact form so that you can add additional information if necessary. When you right-click a name, if it turns out that the contact you are trying to add is a duplicate, Outlook displays the Look Up Outlook Contact option on the context menu, shown in Figure 9-17. This way you do not fill Outlook with duplicate contact information.

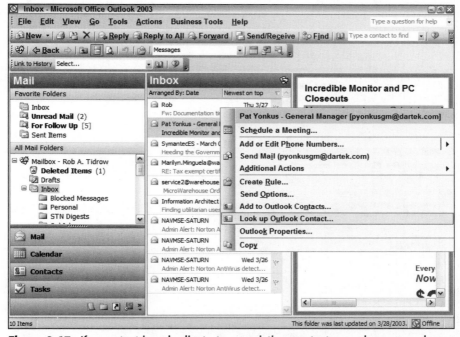

Figure 9-17: If a contact is a duplicate to an existing contact record, you can choose the Look up Outlook Contact command.

Using Contacts

After you have a fairly complete Contacts list, you'll begin to appreciate how useful this list can be. You may even start to wonder why you took so long to begin tracking your addresses in such an efficient way. (Chapter 19 describes how your Outlook Contacts list can be even more useful by providing information that can be used in other applications such as the programs in Microsoft Office.)

Composing an e-mail message from contacts

The most obvious use of your Contacts list is probably for making certain that the e-mail address is correct when you compose and send a new e-mail message. Entering e-mail addresses manually can be a real exercise in frustration — especially because mail servers don't tolerate any errors. If you mistype a single character in an e-mail address, your message won't be delivered — or, perhaps worse, it will be sent to the wrong person!

Outlook helps you use your Contacts list records to correctly address e-mail messages in several ways. As Figure 9-18 shows, when the Contacts folder is open, the Outlook toolbar includes a New Message to Contact button. If you click this button, Outlook opens the New Message form with the selected contact already added to the To text box.

Although the New Message to Contact button is convenient if you are working in the Contacts folder, you probably won't begin most new e-mail messages from the Contacts folder. It's more likely that you'll click the New Mail Message button and be greeted by an empty New Message form. If so, you can still use the entries in your Contacts list to quickly and accurately address the message.

Figure 9-18: Click the New Message to Contact button to begin a new e-mail message to the selected contact.

Each address text box on the New Message form has an identifying button to the left of the text box. If you click this button, Outlook displays the Select Names dialog box, shown in Figure 9-19. Double-click a name to add it to the appropriate address box in the Select Names dialog box. You can also click the To, Cc, or Bcc button to add the selected address to an address box. Click OK to close the Select Names dialog box and return to the New Message form with the names added to the correct address boxes.

Searching contacts

As your Contacts list grows, you may find that it is more difficult to locate specific information than you would like. This can be especially true if you aren't consistent in choosing the same File as format for each record. Outlook has the potential to use five different File as formats. In addition, you may need to find information that is somewhat hidden — such as which of your contacts are located in Nevada.

There are several different ways to search for information in your Outlook Contacts folder. The following sections show you these methods.

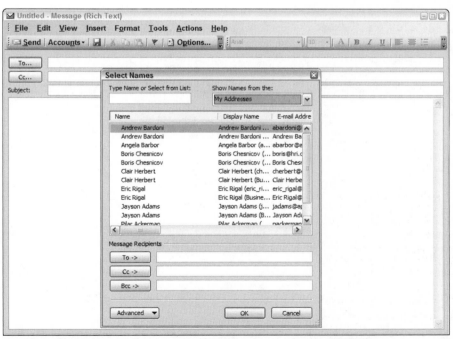

Figure 9-19: Use the Select Names dialog box to add addresses from your Contacts list to new messages.

Using QuickFind

The fastest way to locate a contact is to use the QuickFind feature. As Figure 9-20 shows, you can find people using this method even if you are only sure about part of their name.

To use the QuickFind feature, enter as much of the contact's name as you're sure of in the Find a Contact text box and press Enter. This text box appears on the Outlook toolbar regardless of which Outlook folder is currently open. If Outlook can positively identify the contact based on the name you typed, it opens the associated Contact form for that contact. If your entry was somewhat ambiguous, Outlook may not be able to positively identify the contact. If this is the case, Outlook displays the Choose Contact dialog box so you can select the correct contact from the short list that is displayed.

Using Find

If you need to locate a contact using information other than the contact's name, you'll need to use something a bit more advanced than the QuickFind feature. The Find tool searches the name, company, address, and category fields to locate contacts.

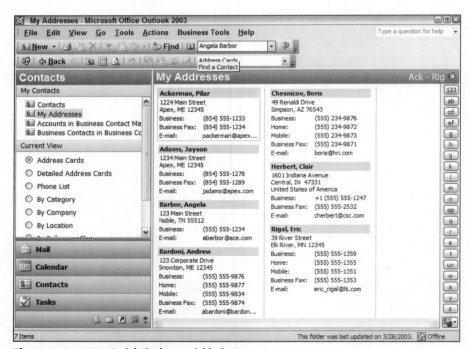

Figure 9-20: Use QuickFind to quickly locate contacts.

To use the Find tool, follow these steps:

1. Begin by clicking the Find button on the Standard toolbar. This displays the Find bar.

2. Enter the search phrase in the Look for text box.

3. Click the Find Now button to search for matching records. As Figure 9-21 shows, Outlook hides any contact records that do not match the specified search criteria.

4. Click Clear or the Find bar close button to again display all your contact records.

Using Advanced Find

Sometimes even the Find tool isn't specific enough. That's when you need to try the Advanced Find tool so that you can specify a broad range of selection criteria. This tool enables you to specify a search that is extremely specific. Not only can you search for a single word or phrase, but you can combine several criteria. If you want to search for all contacts who work in law firms in Nevada or California, you can use Advanced Find to locate them. If you want to find all contact records that were created during the past month, Advanced Find will help you do that, too. Figure 9-22 shows the Microsoft Office Outlook advanced find dialog box that you can display by selecting Tools ⇨ Find ⇨ Advanced Find.

Figure 9-21: Use Find to locate contacts using the name, company, address, and category fields.

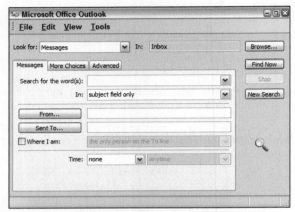

Figure 9-22: Use Advanced Find to locate contacts using any criteria you need.

Tip   Use Advanced Find to locate contact records that were modified when you imported information from another source. That way you won't have to manually search all the records to see if any records were incorrectly updated.

Be cautious in specifying the criteria for an advanced find. Use as few qualifiers as possible. Remember that each additional condition you specify makes it that much more difficult for any of the contact records to satisfy all the conditions. You could easily create a set of conditions that exclude all contact records — even the ones you are trying to locate.

Viewing address maps

Outlook incorporates one very handy feature that may be a surprise to you. For contacts located within the United States, Outlook can connect to the Microsoft Expedia Web site and display a map that shows where the contact is located. You can even obtain directions for driving to the contact's location!

If you click the Display Map of Address button while you have a contact open, as shown in Figure 9-23, Outlook attempts to connect to the Microsoft Expedia Web site and displays a map with the contact's address designated by a map pin. You may need to confirm that you want to connect to the Internet if you aren't already connected when you click the button.

Note   While you are viewing the map, you can use the zoom in and zoom out controls located next to the map to change the level of detail that is displayed.

If the Expedia Web site is unable to positively identify the address, you will be given the option to select from other address possibilities that appear to be similar to the specified address. You may be able to determine that one of these is the correct address — especially if you can see that your contact record contains an obvious misspelling.

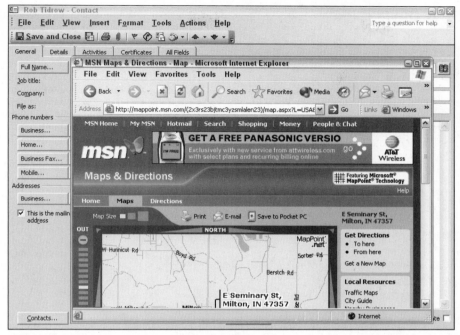

Figure 9-23: Click the Display Map of Address button to view a map of the contact's location.

Using the AutoDialer to make a phone call

Outlook has another feature that is intended to make working with your contacts just a little easier. The program includes a built-in AutoDialer to dial a phone number using your computer's modem. Not only that, but you can have Outlook keep track of phone calls by recording the date, time, and duration in the Outlook Journal.

Note

Using the Outlook AutoDialer requires that your modem share the same telephone line that you use for voice calls. You may find this quite inconvenient because you will not be able to make a voice call and use the modem at the same time. Because you can use more than one modem with your computer, you may find that this provides an excellent way to use an old modem that is too slow to be practical for Internet access. You can connect the old modem to your voice line and designate it as your AutoDialer modem. No matter how slow the old modem is, it will be plenty fast enough if all it has to do is dial phone numbers for your voice calls.

Figure 9-24 shows the drop-down menu that appears when you click the down arrow to the right of the AutoDialer button. This button appears on the Outlook toolbar whenever the Contacts folder or a Contact form is open. If you simply click the AutoDialer button, Outlook dials the number that is at the top of the drop-down menu. You can also display the AutoDialer menu by selecting Actions ➪ Call Contact and selecting the number you want to dial from the submenu.

Figure 9-24: Click the down arrow by the AutoDialer button to view the AutoDialer menu.

If you need to track your telephone calls — perhaps for billing purposes — you can use Outlook to automatically log calls made using the AutoDialer. Outlook logs calls using the Outlook Journal, which is covered in detail in Chapter 13.

To log calls you make using the AutoDialer, follow these steps:

1. Click the down arrow next to the AutoDialer button (or select Actions ⇨ Call Contact) to display the AutoDialer menu.

2. Select New Call to open the New Call dialog box.

3. Select the contact to call in the Contact text box, as shown in Figure 9-25. If no contacts are listed in the Contact box, enter the contact name in the box.

4. Select the Create new Journal Entry when starting new call check box. This causes Outlook to create an entry in the Journal when the call begins.

5. Click Start Call to dial the contact and begin the call log.

6. Click End Call to stop the call log and record the ending time of the call.

Outlook can only record the date, time, and duration of your phone calls. If you need to add additional notes to the call log, you'll need to open the call log and add your notes manually. See Chapter 13 for more information on using the Outlook Journal.

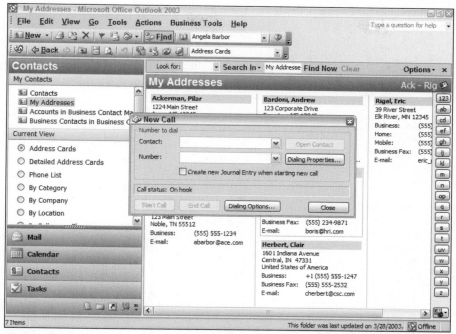

Figure 9-25: Use the New Call dialog box to log calls you make using the AutoDialer.

You can also set up the Outlook AutoDialer to include a list of phone numbers in the Speed Dialer. Click the Dialing Options button and add the numbers to the Speed Dial list. You can then choose the numbers you've added from the AutoDialer menu. You can have up to eight numbers listed in the Speed Dial list.

Summary

Outlook is a powerful contact manager. In this chapter, you learned how to use Outlook's Contacts list to create, view, and manage all those addresses, phone numbers, and personal details that you need to track. You also learned that Outlook enables you to do advanced tasks such as locate the precise location of your contacts automatically by using the Microsoft Expedia Web site.

The next chapter shows you how to use Outlook's Calendar to manage your time, schedule your activities, and coordinate your schedule with others.

✦   ✦   ✦

Managing Your Calendar

In This Chapter

An overview of the Outlook Calendar

Viewing the Calendar

Sharing your Calendar with others

Saving your Calendar as a Web page

It would be almost impossible to live in today's world and not have a calendar. How else would you keep track of when jobs need to be done, when bills need to be paid, and when you get to go on vacation? What about planning that big family reunion that's a year and a half away? The Outlook Calendar can help you do all these tasks and much more. Unlike paper calendars, the Outlook Calendar never goes out of date or needs a refill.

In this chapter, you learn how to use the Outlook Calendar as your daily calendar as well as how you can share the Outlook Calendar so that group planning becomes much easier. You also learn how to save an Outlook Calendar as a Web page so that it can be shared on the Internet.

Understanding the Outlook Calendar

You've probably seen many different calendars in dozens of different formats. But have you ever considered what a calendar really is? We use calendars to represent the passage of time and to allow ourselves to plan for events that will occur on specific dates. We need calendars for these purposes because calculating dates is so complex.

Consider for a moment the facts that you think you know about time. A day is equal to 24 hours, a week is 7 days, a month is usually about 30 days, and a year is typically 365 days. In reality, only one of these is an exact figure. Days are exactly 24 hours long, months can be anywhere from 28 to 31 days, and we have leap years almost every fourth year to adjust the length of the year. All these adjustments are necessary because we expect certain events to line up neatly with our calendar. If we just settled on a fixed calendar, we'd eventually find that winter was beginning in June this year, and we'd need to find a totally different method of planning for seasonal events.

Publishers have made a big business out of producing paper calendars. You can't just reuse last year's calendar, so most people get new calendars each year. That's one reason why an electronic calendar such as Outlook's Calendar is so useful — it doesn't need to be replaced on New Year's Day. Figure 10-1 shows the Outlook Calendar.

Note   As you read this chapter, you'll encounter these terms: appointment, meeting, and event. Appointments are activities you plan that do not involve inviting other people (or reserving resources, if you use Exchange Server). Meetings are appointments that involve inviting other people (or reserving resources). Events are activities that last a full day or longer. Reserving resources is when you want to reserve a conference room or other company resource (audio/visual device, for example) for your meeting.

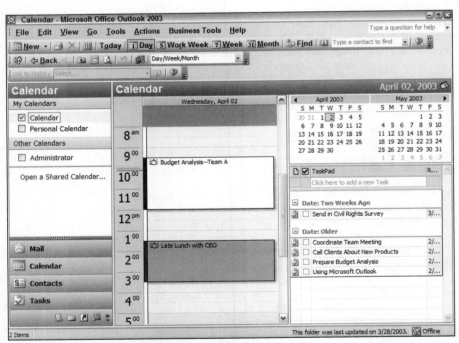

Figure 10-1: The Outlook Calendar never goes out of date.

How is the Outlook Calendar useful?

Any calendar is useful for keeping track of what day it is. The Outlook Calendar does this, of course, but it can also do a lot more for you. Here are just a few of the ways you may find the Outlook Calendar pretty useful:

✦ If you add someone's birthday to your Outlook Calendar as a recurring event, their birthday will appear on the same date every year. If you're not good at remembering birthdays, the Outlook Calendar can make you look as though you're a truly thoughtful person — although you still have to buy the birthday cards yourself.

✦ If you have a bill that is due on the same date each month, the Outlook Calendar can remind you when to get out the checkbook.

✦ If you are the events planner for an organization, you can use the Outlook Calendar to track events so that two events don't conflict. You can also publish the event schedule on your Web site so members can check for last minute updates.

✦ If you want to plan an around-the-world trip next year, you can easily view next year's dates on the Outlook Calendar. If you were using a paper calendar, you might have some difficulty obtaining printed calendars that show dates far enough in advance.

✦ If you work an unusual schedule, you can customize Outlook's Calendar view to show your schedule and even print out weekly planner sheets to match your needs.

As you use the Outlook Calendar, you'll find even more ways that you can use it to make your life a little easier.

Understanding the new Calendar features

Outlook 2003 has several new or enhanced features that make the Outlook Calendar more useful than it was in earlier versions. Here are some of the important improvements:

✦ You can view multiple calendars side by side, enabling you to view several calendar folders at once.

✦ Shared calendars lets you view other users' calendars, as well as share your calendar with others in your workgroup or over the Internet using the Microsoft Office Internet Free/Busy Service feature. Appointments and meetings can be set up more efficiently — just look for open times on another person's shared Calendar and invite him or her to your event.

✦ Show or hide alternative calendar options such as the lunar calendar, zodiac signs, and Rokuyou markers.

Viewing the Calendar

The Outlook Calendar can look like many different types of calendars. You'll probably find that different views are useful for different purposes. You may be surprised to learn that the Outlook Calendar can also look nothing like any calendar you've ever seen in the past. For example, you can view your calendars by events regardless of the dates on which they fall. Or you can view items by category, such as Holidays, Business, and so on. These unique views make it much easier to perform certain tasks and understand just what is in the Calendar.

Accessing different Calendar views

Choosing the Outlook Calendar view can be a little confusing because you choose the Outlook Calendar views in two different places, depending on just what you want to accomplish.

To choose the actual Calendar view, use the View ➪ Arrange By ➪ Current View menu shown in Figure 10-2. This menu enables you to select the types of views you would normally associate with a Calendar as well as some of the unique Outlook Calendar views that focus more directly on what is on your Calendar.

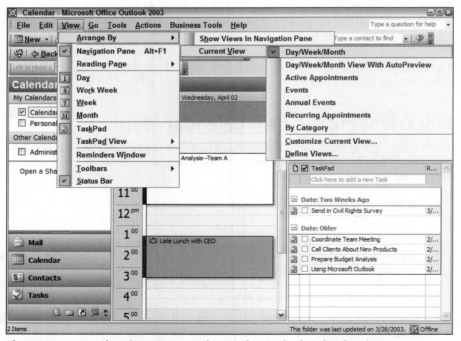

Figure 10-2: Use the View menu to change the Outlook Calendar view.

To choose a variation on the Day/Week/Month view, use the time period buttons on the Outlook toolbar, as shown in Figure 10-3. These variations display the types of Calendar views normally associated with calendars.

Understanding Calendar view types

Because Outlook has so many different ways to display the Calendar, it's important to understand how the views differ and why you may want to use some of them. In the following sections, you see each of the views and learn why each view is useful.

Day view

The Day view displays a detailed schedule for one day, as shown in the example in Figure 10-4. In this view, you can easily see which time periods during the day are scheduled and which are free. You can view other times of the day by scrolling up or down using the scroll bar. Click the Day button on the Standard toolbar to change to Day view, or use the View ⇨ Day menu.

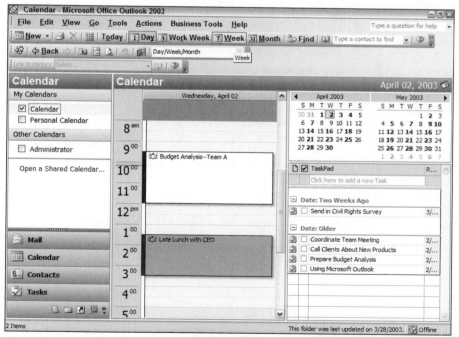

Figure 10-3: Use the time period buttons to vary the Outlook Calendar Day/Week/Month view.

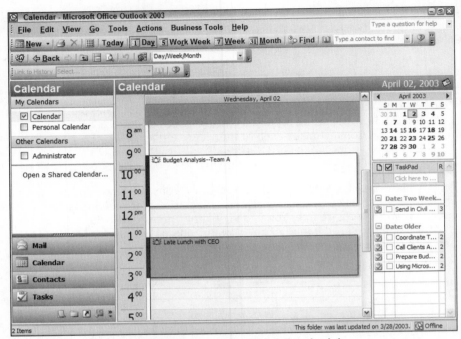

Figure 10-4: Use the Day view to see a detailed daily schedule.

Outlook shows regular business hours shaded a different color than non-business hours. For example, the hours from 8:00 AM to 5:00 PM are shaded a light yellow, while the other hours in the day are shown as a slightly darker shade of yellow.

When you display the Day view, Outlook shows the current date by default. You can view a different day by clicking a date in the monthly calendars shown in the upper right section of the Calendar view. To display a date in a month that is not currently shown, click the arrows that are just above the monthly calendars. The left arrow displays earlier months, and the right arrow displays later months.

Tip   You can always return quickly to the current date by clicking the Today button on the Standard toolbar.

See "Customizing Calendar views" later in this chapter for more information on setting the start and end times for the workday.

Work Week view

The Work Week view is similar to the Day view, except that Outlook attempts to show the schedule for Monday through Friday on one screen, as shown in Figure 10-5. This view is handy when you need to plan events for your entire work week; however, because each day has such a narrow slot available, it's difficult to view the details of any event. Click the Work Week button on the Standard toolbar to display the Work Week view.

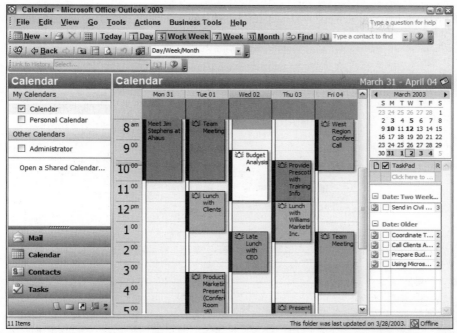

Figure 10-5: Use the Work Week view to see a detailed work week schedule.

Navigation in the Work Week view is similar to navigating in the Day view. The only real difference is that you can choose a particular day of the week by clicking in the appropriate column. If you choose a different date in one of the small calendars, Outlook will show you the workdays for the week you select.

See "Customizing Calendar views" later in this chapter for more information on setting your workdays. For example, you can set Outlook so it displays Friday through Sunday if you work the weekend shift.

Week view

The Week view displays the entire week, starting with Monday and ending with Sunday, as shown in Figure 10-6. Unlike the Work Week view, the Week view does not attempt to show a detailed schedule for each day. It simply lists the scheduled events for each day. Click the Week button on the Standard toolbar to display the Week view.

You can customize Outlook so it shows a different starting day, such as Wednesday, and ends on Tuesday.

To view a different week, you can use the scroll bar to change the display one week at a time. Alternatively, you can click to the left of a week in one of the small calendar displays to go directly to that week.

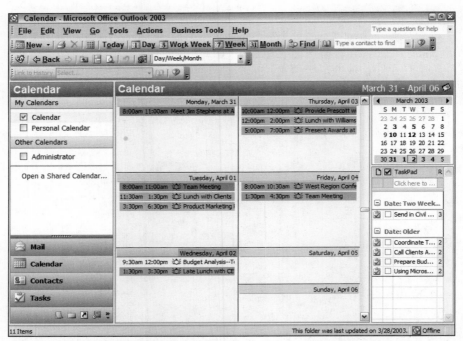

Figure 10-6: Use the Week view to see an events schedule for the week.

By default, Outlook condenses the blocks used to display both Saturday and Sunday. As you'll learn in "Customizing Calendar views" later in this chapter, you can set Outlook to give each day the same size block.

Month view

The Month view is the Outlook Calendar view that looks the most like a traditional calendar. As Figure 10-7 shows, the Month view enables you to easily see anything that is on your schedule for the entire month. If you want to see more of your monthly calendar, turn off the small calendar and TaskPad by deselecting View ⇨ Taskpad. Click the Month button on the Standard toolbar to display the Month view.

You can use the scroll bar to view different dates. If you want to view a date that is more than a few months off, however, it is easier to use the Go To Date dialog box. Select Go ⇨ Go To ⇨ Go to Date to display the Go To Date dialog box and then enter a date in the Date box. Click OK to display that date.

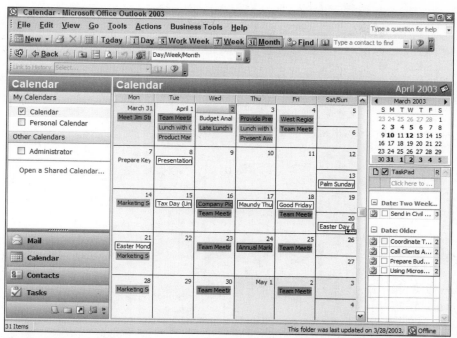

Figure 10-7: Use the Month view to see an events schedule for the entire month.

Tip   Press Ctrl+G to quickly display the Go To Date dialog box.

AutoPreview view

On Outlook's View ➪ Arrange By ➪ Current View menu, you'll find both Day/Week/Month and Day/Week/Month View With AutoPreview listed as options. These two choices are identical except that the second displays the first line of an appointment description when you hover the mouse over the item, as shown in Figure 10-8.

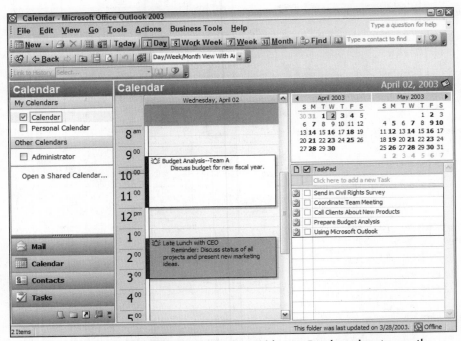

Figure 10-8: Use the Day/Week/Month View With AutoPreview view to see the first line of an appointment description.

You can select any of the standard day, work week, week, or month choices when you choose the Day/Week/Month View With AutoPreview view Navigation is identical whether you choose AutoPreview or Day/Week/Month. Choosing the Day/Week/Month View With AutoPreview view does make it slightly easier to find specific appointments because you don't have to open the appointments to see a brief description of them.

Active Appointments view

The Active Appointments view shows your appointments, events, and meetings starting with today's date as shown in Figure 10-9. You display this view by selecting View ➪ Arrange By ➪ Current View ➪ Active Appointments.

The Active Appointments view separates your appointments and meetings by how often they recur. That enables you to easily see which appointments happen on an ongoing basis and which ones are set for a single time.

You may have numerous appointments in each recurrence category. To make it a little easier to concentrate on specific categories, click the small box that appears just to the left of the word Recurrence. If this box shows a minus sign, the category is fully expanded. If it shows a plus sign, the category is collapsed to provide more room to view the remaining categories.

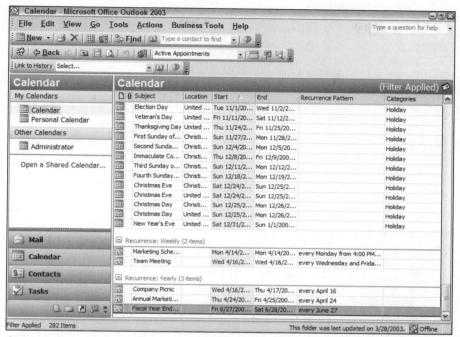

Figure 10-9: Use the Active Appointments view to see your upcoming meetings, events, and appointments.

Events view

The Events view shows the current year events that are on a schedule, as shown in Figure 10-10. You display this view by selecting View ➪ Arrange By ➪ Current View ➪ Events.

Your events list is also separated into recurrence categories, but unlike the active appointments list, the events list includes current year events that have already passed. Items that might be included on your events list include vacations, trade shows, and business trips that last a full day or longer.

Tip   To change an event into an appointment or meeting, remove the check from the All day event check box in the Event form.

Annual Events view

The Annual Events view displays the yearly events that are on your schedule, as shown in Figure 10-11. You display this view by selecting View ➪ Arrange By ➪ Current View ➪ Annual Events.

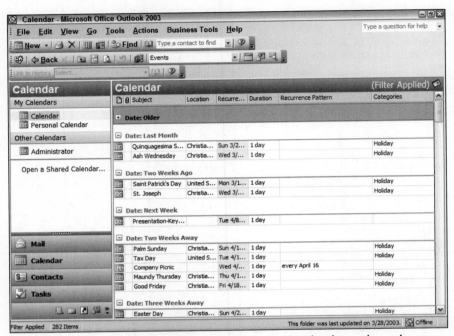

Figure 10-10: Use the Events view to see your activities that last a day or longer.

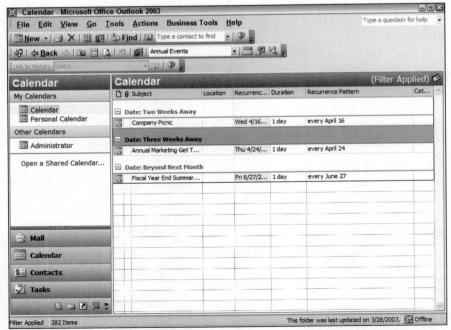

Figure 10-11: Use the Annual Events view to see the activities that happen each year.

Annual events include birthdays, anniversaries, life insurance payments, and anything else that you might need to remember each year. If you've ever forgotten an important date such as your spouse's birthday, the Annual Events view can be just the feature that keeps you out of hot water in the future!

Recurring Appointments view

The Recurring Appointments view displays the ongoing appointments that are on a schedule, as shown in Figure 10-12. You display this view by selecting View ➪ Arrange By ➪ Current View ➪ Recurring Appointments.

You probably have a number of recurring appointments, even if you've never quite thought of them that way. For example, if you belong to a club that meets every month, you probably block out the meeting time mentally, even if you don't show it on your calendar. There's no reason why you shouldn't include such events on your Outlook Calendar so you won't inadvertently schedule something else for the same time. Remember that you can always choose to ignore items that are shown on your Outlook Calendar; however, if you haven't included something, it's likely you'll eventually schedule something else for the same time.

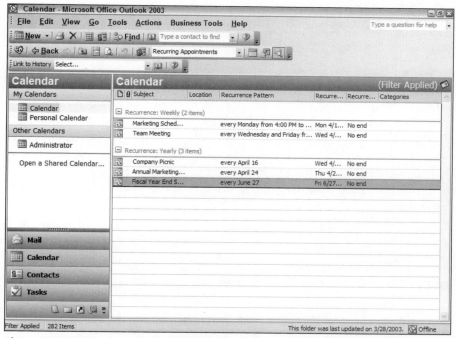

Figure 10-12: Use the Recurring Appointments view to see the activities that occur on a regular basis.

By Category view

The By Category view shows the items on your schedule broken down by category, as shown in Figure 10-13. You display this view by selecting View ⇨ Arrange By ⇨ Current View ⇨ By Category.

You can use categories to organize almost everything in Outlook. Categories make it much easier to separate items into groups so that you can determine their importance. For example, if you need to make time in your schedule to accommodate an important customer, you may decide that certain categories of activities are more expendable than others. (In Chapter 11, you learn more about creating appointments and assigning categories.)

Note   If none of the predefined categories fit your needs, you can create your own categories to classify Outlook items.

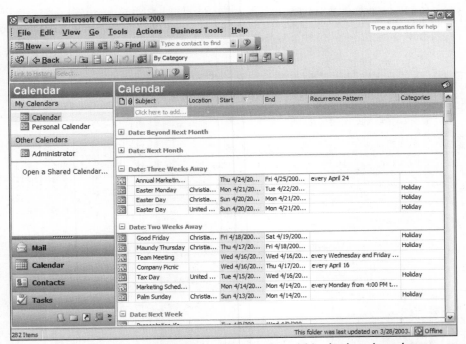

Figure 10-13: Use the By Category view to see your activities broken down by category.

Customizing Calendar views

As you use the Outlook Calendar, you may discover that certain things simply annoy you. For example, weekends may be very important to you, so you may not like the way Outlook condenses the display of Saturdays and Sundays. Or perhaps your workday starts at an earlier hour than the 8 A.M. start time that Outlook shows. Fortunately, it's easy to change these as well as a number of other Outlook Calendar settings.

You can choose to customize a single Outlook Calendar view, or you can open a dialog box that allows you to work with any of the views. In the following steps, you learn how to work with any view.

To customize Outlook's Calendar views, follow these steps. If you only want to modify the current view, select View ➪ Arrange By ➪ Current View ➪ Customize Current View and then skip to step 5.

1. Make certain the Outlook Calendar folder is open.

2. Select View ➪ Arrange By ➪ Current View ➪ Define Views to open the Custom View Organizer dialog box, shown in Figure 10-14.

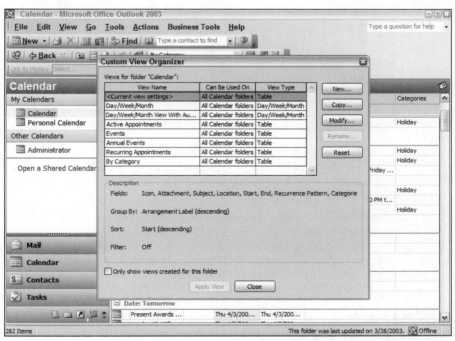

Figure 10-14: Use the Custom View Organizer dialog box to select the views to modify.

3. Select the view that you want to customize. As you select different views, the Description box will show the current settings for the selected view.

4. Click the Modify button to open the Customize View dialog box, shown in Figure 10-15. Depending on the view that you have selected to modify, some of the options in the View Summary dialog box may be unavailable.

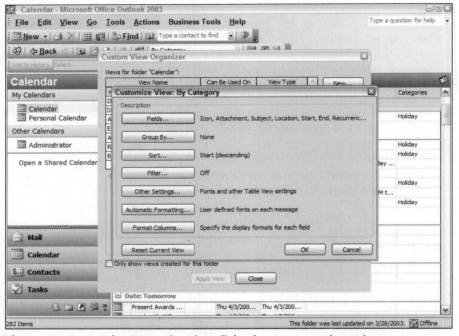

Figure 10-15: Use the Customize View dialog box to customize a view.

5. Click the Fields button to display the Show Fields dialog box (or the Date/Time Fields dialog box, if choosing to modify a Day/Week/Month view), shown in Figure 10-16.

6. Choose the fields that you want to include in the view and then click Add. You may want to add certain fields that will help you better understand the activities that are shown in the view, or remove fields that you don't use so you can present a cleaner display. To remove a field, select it in the Show these fields in this order list and then click Remove.

7. Click OK to close the dialog box when you have completed your changes.

8. Click the Group By button to display the Group By dialog box.

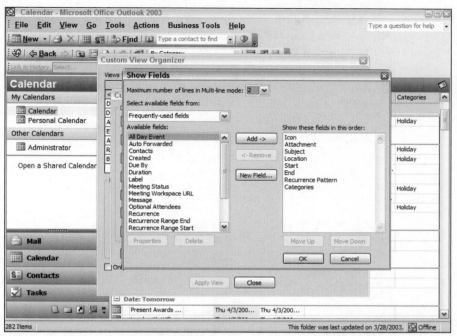

Figure 10-16: Use the Show Fields dialog boxes to choose which fields are shown in the view.

9. Deselect the Automatically group according to arrangement to show the other options on the dialog box. Choose the fields that you want to use for grouping the activities that are shown in the view.

10. Select Ascending or Descending to choose the sort order for the selected field.

11. Choose the Expand/collapse defaults setting you prefer. You may want to choose As last viewed so that Outlook will remember how the view appeared when you last closed the view.

12. Click OK to close the dialog box when you have completed your changes.

13. Click the Sort button to display the Sort dialog box.

14. Choose the sort order settings you prefer. Sort order settings differ from the Group By settings in that Outlook does not separate sorted items into categorized groups. It just sorts the information in ascending or descending order.

15. Click OK to close the dialog box when you have completed your changes.

16. Click the Filter button to display the Filter dialog box, shown in Figure 10-17.

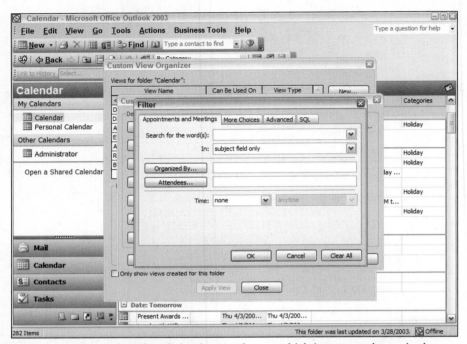

Figure 10-17: Use the Filter dialog box to choose which items are shown in the view.

17. Select the settings that will display the activities you want to see in this view. For example, you may want to view only those activities that will start within the next seven days if your calendar of events is extremely full.

18. Click OK to close the dialog box when you have completed your changes.

19. Click the Other Settings button to display the Other Settings dialog box.

20. Choose the settings you prefer. If you are modifying one of the Day/Week/Month views, you can choose the settings for condensing weekends as well as the start and end times for the work day.

21. Click OK to close the dialog box when you have completed your changes.

22. Click the Automatic Formatting button to display the Automatic Formatting dialog box, shown in Figure 10-18. In this figure, three rules have been added to this view.

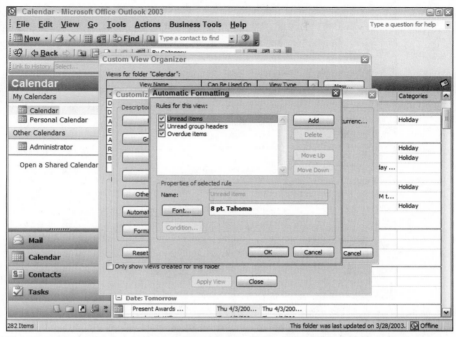

Figure 10-18: Use the Automatic Formatting dialog box to choose how you want Outlook to display items in this view.

23. Click the Add button, and type a name for your new rule. Choose the settings you prefer. For example, you may want to change the font for overdue items to a larger size in a brightly contrasting color so that those items draw your immediate attention. Click the Condition button to format all items that meet a specific criterion, such as all items that have file attachments. Click OK to return to the Automatic Formatting dialog box.

24. Click OK to close the dialog box when you have completed your changes.

25. Click Format Columns to display the Format Columns dialog box, shown in Figure 10-19.

Note   You can format columns in views that are in table formats, not in the Day/Week/Month formats.

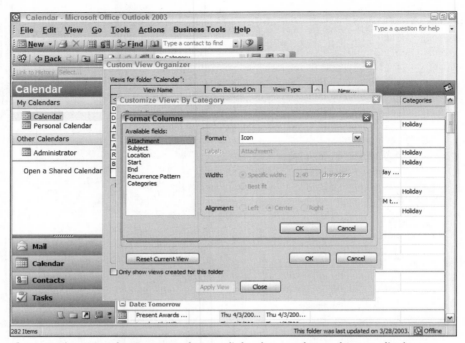

Figure 10-19: Use the Format Columns dialog box to choose how to display columns in your Outlook window.

26. Choose the settings you prefer. For example, you can change the label for the Received field to Date Received or a similar label that helps you understand the contents of the column.

27. Click OK to close the dialog box when you have completed your changes.

28. Click OK to close the Customize View dialog box.

29. Click Apply View to apply the changes you just made.

30. Choose another view to modify, or click the Close button to close the Custom View Organizer dialog box.

Rather than modifying an existing view, you may want to experiment by copying a view and then making your changes to the copy. You'll be able to create a custom view without losing the original.

Note   If your changes have made a real mess out of a view, select the view in the Custom View Organizer dialog box and then click the Reset button to revert to the original settings.

Sharing Your Calendar with Others

It's likely that you have a number of reasons to share a calendar with other people. If you work as part of a project team, it's important that the team members have access to the project schedule so that everyone knows when tasks are due. If you are an officer in an organization, you may want to be able to share committee schedules with the other officers so everyone knows when meetings are scheduled. If you are organizing a large family reunion, you may want an easy way to keep everyone informed of the activities that you're planning. These are just a few of the countless reasons why you may want to share your Outlook Calendar.

Previous versions of Outlook required that you and everyone with whom you wanted to share an Outlook Calendar be connected to an Exchange Server. This was a rather severe limitation that made the feature useless for the vast majority of Outlook users. With the release of Outlook 2000, Outlook enabled everyone to share their Outlook Calendar using Net Folders. Rather than requiring that you have access to an Exchange Server, Outlook enabled you to share your Outlook Calendar over the Internet.

With Outlook 2003, you can share your Outlook Calendar using Microsoft's free Microsoft Office Internet Free/Busy Service on the Internet. Net Folders are no longer available in Outlook 2003. To use the Microsoft Office Internet Free/Busy Service, you must acquire a Microsoft .NET Passport account, which is free as well. You may already have an account if you have a Hotmail or MSN.com e-mail address. After you have a .NET Passport, you can use it to log in to any site on the Internet that uses the .NET Passport sign-in button. The following steps show how to set up an account so you can use start sharing your Outlook Calendar over the Internet.

You also can use other Internet or intranet locations to share your Outlook Calendar. For example, if you are in an organization that uses Microsoft Exchange to handle your e-mail, you can set up your Calendar to display your free and busy times so others in your organization can see them.

Note   Because Microsoft Office Internet Free/Busy Service shares unencrypted information over the Internet, there could be security issues if you are dealing with sensitive or confidential information. You may want to create a separate folder under the Outlook Calendar folder for the items you intend to share. You could then share the separate folder rather than your complete Calendar folder.

To share your Outlook Calendar using Microsoft Office Internet Free/Busy Service on the Internet, follow these steps:

1. Select Tools ➪ Options ➪ Calendar Options.

2. Click Free/Busy Options to display the Free/Busy Options dialog box, shown in Figure 10-20.

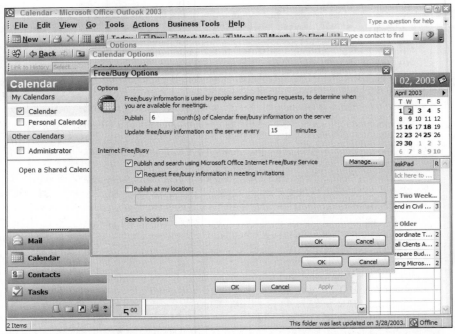

Figure 10-20: Use the Free/Busy Options dialog box to set up your Calendar to be shared over the Internet.

3. Set the Update free/busy information on the server every *X* minutes to the number of minutes you want to share your Calendar information. For example, to share your information every hour, change the setting to 60 minutes. Remember, if you have a dial-up connection, Outlook will need to connect to the Internet every hour to update your changes. You may want to use the maximum setting of 99 minutes to delay the updates if this poses a problem for you.

4. Select Publish, search using Microsoft Office Internet Free/Busy Service, and click Manage. Internet Explorer launches and connects to the Microsoft Office Internet Free/Busy Service Web site. If you have a .NET Passport, sign in using your e-mail address and password. Click Sign In and then skip to step 8; otherwise, go to step 5 to acquire a .NET Passport.

5. Click Get one now to display the Microsoft Office Internet Free/Busy Registration page.

6. Fill out the form using an e-mail address you want to share with others, such as Hotmail, Yahoo! Mail, or other e-mail address you have.

7. Select Share my e-mail address at the bottom of the form and then click I Agree. .NET Passport will send you an e-mail confirming your registration and enclose instructions on how to finish the registration process.

8. When logged in using your .NET Passport, you are sent to the Terms of use page. Click Yes I agree to indicate you agree to use Microsoft Internet Explorer 5 or above when accessing the Microsoft Office Internet Free/Busy feature.

9. On the Enable Outlook to work with the service Web page, click the Click here link to automatically enable Outlook to work with the Microsoft Office Internet Free/Busy feature. This installs an ActiveX control on your computer. You may be prompted for the Office 11 CD.

10. After the control installs, click Continue on the Enable Outlook to work with the service Web page to display the Authorize access and invite nonmembers to join Web page.

11. In the Authorize additional users list, type the e-mail addresses of those people with whom you want to share your calendar. Separate each person's address with a semicolon, but no spaces.

12. In the Message to nonmembers list, type the e-mail addresses of those people you want to share your calendar. The Microsoft Office Internet Free/Busy site will e-mail these users that they are invited to access your shared calendar.

13. Click OK. A page listing members authorized to view your shared calendar displays.

14. Switch back to Outlook, and click OK on the Free/Busy Options dialog box.

15. Click OK and then OK again to close the other dialog boxes.

To manually refresh free/busy information, follow these steps:

1. Connect to the Internet.

2. Select Tools ➪ Send/Receive ➪ Free/Busy Information to display the Sign In with Microsoft .NET Passport dialog box, as shown in Figure 10-21.

3. Click OK to log in and send your free/busy information to the Microsoft Office Internet Free/Busy Service Web site.

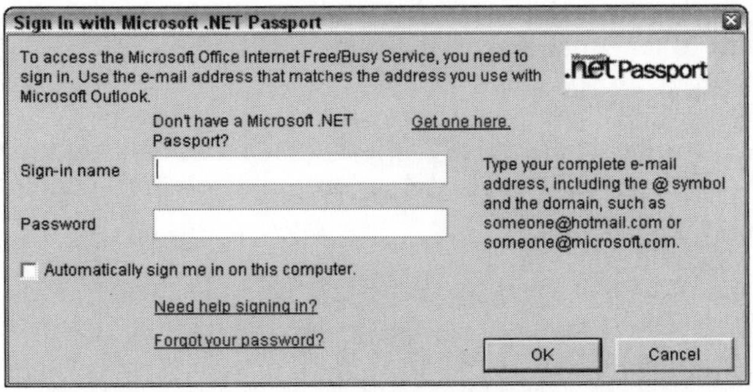

Figure 10-21: Sign in to the Microsoft Office Internet Free/Busy Service using this dialog box.

When you share your Outlook Calendar using the Microsoft Office Internet Free/Busy Service, Outlook sends out subscription requests to the people whom you've selected to share the Calendar. After they accept the request, their response is returned to Outlook, and periodic synchronization requests are sent out to their computer. Outlook uses those synchronization requests to update the remote Calendar folders, and to update your shared Calendar folder if you've assigned anyone permission to make changes.

Cross-Reference   To learn more about editing and opening a shared Calendar, see Chapter 20.

Saving Your Calendar as a Web Page

Outlook provides another way to share your Outlook Calendar — as a Web page. Saving your Outlook Calendar as a Web page means that you can share that Calendar with anyone who has a Web browser. You could, for example, use the Outlook Calendar to create a monthly event calendar for an organization and then display that calendar on your group's Web site. The members would be able to easily view the upcoming schedule just by visiting the Web site.

To save your Outlook Calendar as a Web page, follow these steps:

1. Open the Outlook Calendar folder.

2. Select File ➪ Save as Web Page to display the Save as Web Page dialog box, shown in Figure 10-22.

3. Select the starting and ending dates.

4. Make certain the Include appointment details check box is selected if you want the Web page to include information about your listed events.

5. Select the Use background graphic check box if you want to include an image behind the calendar. You can use the Browse button to locate the image file you want to use. Adding a background image will increase the size of your Web page you create. Take this into account if you need to send your Calendar as an attachment to an e-mail over a modem connection.

6. Enter a title for the calendar.

7. Specify a name for the calendar file. The file name must be a legitimate HTML file name, such as calendar.htm. Spaces are not allowed in the names.

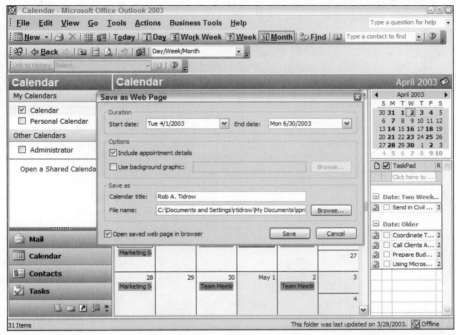

Figure 10-22: Use the Save as Web Page dialog box to save your Outlook Calendar in HTML format.

8. Select Open saved Web page in browser to automatically launch Internet Explorer with your saved Outlook Calendar Web page after you complete step 9.

9. Click Save to save the file. If you haven't used this feature before, you may need your Outlook 2003 CD-ROM to install the Save as Web Page feature. Figure 10-23 shows how the calendar appears when it is opened in Internet Explorer.

Notice in the figure that when your Outlook Calendar is saved as a Web page, visitors can view the event details in the Appointment and Event Details section, as well as the calendar. If you had not selected the Include appointment details check box, visitors would be limited to those details that could be shown in the calendar itself. Also, if you choose to include a background graphic, it is best to use a light-colored one. Visitors may otherwise have a difficult time viewing the text on the calendar.

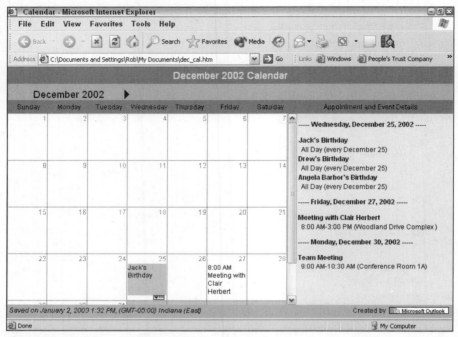

Figure 10-23: After you have saved your Outlook Calendar as a Web page, it can be opened in any Web browser.

Note   If you select the Private check box on a calendar item (look at the lower right corner of a Calendar item dialog box when you are creating a new item or editing one), the item will not appear when the Calendar is published to an online or network server.

Summary

This chapter has provided you with a comprehensive overview of the Outlook Calendar. You've learned about using the various options for viewing the Calendar, sharing your Calendar with others, and saving your Calendar as a Web page.

The next chapter continues the coverage of the Outlook Calendar by showing you how to use the Calendar for scheduling your time. You'll learn how to create appointments, schedule meetings, and set up Outlook to remind you of important events.

✦   ✦   ✦

Scheduling Your Time

◆   ◆   ◆   ◆

In This Chapter

Understanding
scheduling

Creating an
appointment

Creating a meeting

Integrating with
NetMeeting and
NetShow

◆   ◆   ◆   ◆

T he Outlook Calendar is adept at replacing the paper
calendar that you might have hanging on your wall, but
it's even more useful after you start using it for scheduling.
Scheduling isn't just something that is used by busy executives. If you've ever had to look at your calendar to make certain that you would be free for dinner on a certain night, or
tried to plan for a vacation so that you could attend a special
event, you've used scheduling. If you've ever had to rearrange
your schedule so that you could make an appointment for a
haircut, you've used scheduling.

In this chapter, you learn how to use the Outlook Calendar
to schedule your appointments and meetings. You also learn
how to use both NetMeeting and the NetShow services with
the meetings that you schedule in Outlook. Maybe even more
importantly, you learn how Outlook can remind you of events
so you'll never again forget that important birthday or
anniversary!

Understanding Scheduling

When you use Outlook to schedule your time, you create
events that appear on the Outlook Calendar. Outlook uses the
term *appointment* to denote events that last less than a full
day and don't require scheduling anyone else's time. *Meetings*
are similar to appointments except that they do require coordinating your schedule with someone else's schedule. Events
are set up using the same New Appointment dialog box and
are activities that last 24 hours or longer.

Note   If you use Exchange Server, Outlook can also schedule
resources such as meeting rooms or video equipment, just
as it schedules meetings. Because scheduling a resource is
no different than scheduling meeting participants, you can
use the same techniques to schedule a resource as you
use to schedule meeting participants.

Scheduling is merely the task of allocating available time. Time is something that everyone measures the same way, so it's quite possible to schedule a meeting for 10 a.m. Monday and expect that everyone will know when they are to arrive at the meeting. Of course, just because everyone agrees on a schedule is no guarantee that they'll be there on time, but that's one problem that Outlook can't solve.

There are many ways to use Outlook's scheduling capabilities to help manage your time. Here are a few ideas:

✦ If you belong to an organization that holds meetings on a regular basis, you may want to include those meetings on your Outlook Calendar so that you'll always make certain to reserve the time to attend.

✦ If you need to meet with several important clients, you may want to figure out a schedule that allows you to minimize your time away from the office by keeping your travel time to a minimum. You can use the Outlook Calendar to see which days you would be able to visit with more than one client on the same day.

✦ If you're working with a team on a project, you could use Outlook to plan a meeting by automatically finding the next available free block of time for the meeting on everyone's Outlook Calendar.

✦ If you're planning a vacation, you can allocate the time on your Outlook Calendar so that no one schedules an important meeting that you must attend during the time you're planning on being away.

✦ You can add events such as birthdays and anniversaries to your Outlook Calendar and then set Outlook to remind you well in advance so that you can buy a gift or card.

No matter what types of events and activities you need to schedule, the Outlook Calendar can help make scheduling your time a lot easier and more efficient. You'll soon find that using Outlook to manage your schedule can be an improvement over trying to manage your schedule manually.

Creating an Appointment

To begin scheduling your time, you can start by creating appointments. Appointments are the easiest activity to schedule because they don't require that you coordinate your schedule with anyone else's schedule — at least not in Outlook. Most appointments, of course, do involve other people, but you aren't responsible for making sure they have free time in *their* schedule for the appointment.

To create a new appointment in Outlook, follow these steps:

1. Open the Outlook Calendar folder.

2. Select the day of the appointment in the calendar. This step is actually optional, but may save you some time because you won't have to choose the date after you open the Appointment form.

3. Select File ➪ New Appointment (or click the New Appointment button) to open a blank Appointment form, as shown in Figure 11-1.

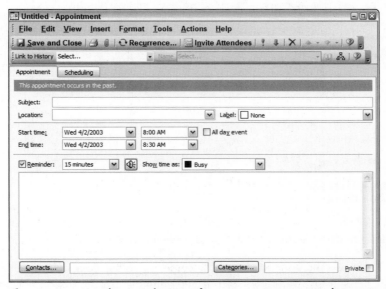

Figure 11-1: Use the Appointment form to create new appointments.

4. Enter a brief description of the appointment in the Subject text box. Only the first part of this description will show in the Outlook Calendar, so don't use this space to write the "great American novel."

5. If necessary, enter the appointment location in the Location text box.

6. Select the date and time of the appointment. If this is an all day event, such as a birthday or anniversary, select the All day event check box rather than a time. This places an event label at the top of the day on which the event occurs. It does not block out times in the day calendar.

7. If you would like to be reminded in advance, select the Reminder check box and then choose how far in advance you'd like to be reminded of this appointment. For example, to be reminded of the event 24 hours in advance, select 1 day from the drop-down list.

8. To choose a sound file that is played when the reminder pops up, click the Reminder Sound button to display the Reminder Sound dialog box, shown in Figure 11-2.

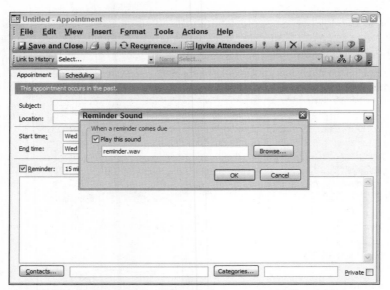

Figure 11-2: Choose a sound file to play as a reminder of this appointment.

9. Click the Browse button if you want to select a different sound file.

Note

You can use the Windows Sound Recorder to record your own reminders that Outlook can play to remind you of appointments. Or, to disable a sound altogether, deselect the Play this sound option on the Reminder Sound dialog box.

10. Click OK to close the Reminder Sound dialog box.

11. Add any special notes you want in the text box in the middle of the Appointment form.

12. Click Save and Close to close the form and save the new appointment. The new appointment will appear on your Outlook Calendar, as shown in Figure 11-3.

To edit an existing appointment, double-click the appointment to again open the Appointment form. Always remember to click Save and Close to save any changes when you close the form.

If you need to change the time of an appointment, you can reopen the Appointment form and adjust the time settings. Another way to adjust the time is to drag the start or end time as shown in Figure 11-4. You can drag to adjust the time in half-hour increments — unless you specify a different time interval (as discussed in Chapter 10).

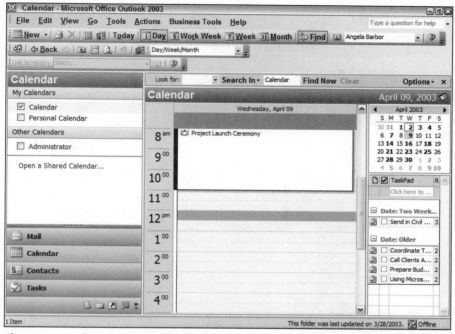

Figure 11-3: Choose the date of the appointment to view the appointment on your schedule.

A neat feature of Outlook is the Autodate feature. When you need to enter a date, you can enter a description of the date, such as one month from today, and Outlook selects that date for you. As an example, select Go ➪ Go to Date. In the Go To Date dialog box, type **next friday** and then click OK. Outlook jumps to next Friday on your calendar. You can then see what activities are set up on that Friday, delete or modify activities there, or create a new activity for that date. Some other phrases to use are as follows:

✦ 3 days

✦ thirty days

✦ one month

✦ this Friday

✦ January 3

✦ Fourth of April

✦ Christmas

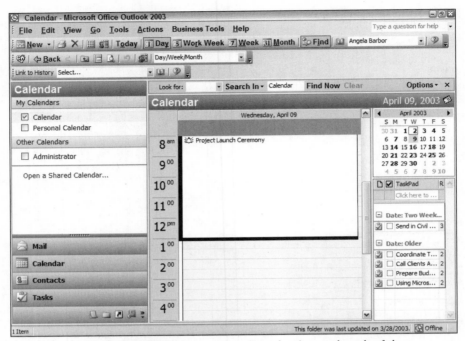

Figure 11-4: Drag the start or end time to adjust the time or length of the appointment.

If you need to move an appointment to a different date, there's no need to start over. You can simply choose a different date in the Appointment form, or you can drag the appointment to a new date, as shown in Figure 11-5. In this case, the appointment was dragged from Monday, February 8th to Friday, February 12th. You'll need to change to Week or Month view to drag an appointment to a new date. Or you can drag the activity from the Day view to a new date on the small calendar on the Navigation Pane.

You can also designate that an appointment is a recurring one. See "Specifying recurring activities" later in this chapter for more information on this subject.

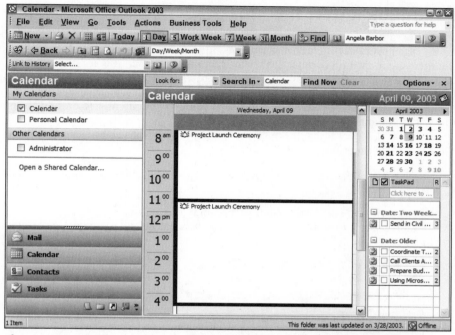

Figure 11-5: Drag an appointment to a new date to move the appointment.

Creating a Meeting

Creating a meeting in Outlook isn't much different than creating a new appointment. There is, of course, the complication of coordinating the schedules for the meeting participants, but Outlook automates most of that process. When you set up a meeting, Outlook can automatically check the availability of participants who use Outlook to schedule their time. You don't have to spend time calling to find out when people will be available because Outlook will find a time for you. The only catch is that the other participants must have e-mail to which you can send and receive meeting request messages with the participants.

In the following sections, you learn how to use Outlook to set up a meeting. Because meetings are similar to appointments in so many ways, we'll concentrate primarily on those settings that are unique to creating a meeting.

Beginning a new meeting

Setting up a new meeting is slightly more complicated than setting up an appointment. One complicating factor is that because meetings involve multiple people, the meeting location is considerably more important than it is for an ordinary appointment. If you set up an appointment to visit your dentist, it's probably clear that the appointment will take place in the dentist's office. With a meeting, however, things may not be quite so clear and you'll want to specify all the details so that there is no chance of confusion.

To start a new meeting, follow these steps:

1. Select File ➪ New ➪ Meeting Request to display the Meeting form, as shown in Figure 11-6.

   Notice that the selected meeting time may conflict with other items on the Calendar. If this is the case with your new meeting, we resolve this conflict later.

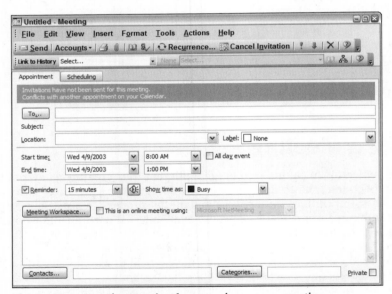

Figure 11-6: Use the Meeting form to plan a new meeting.

2. Enter the meeting description in the Subject text box.

3. Choose a location for the meeting. Later, you will learn how to plan an online meeting.

4. Click the Scheduling tab, as shown in Figure 11-7. You could wait with this step until you have designated the other meeting attendees, but if you already know that there is a conflict with your schedule, you may as well correct that conflict first.

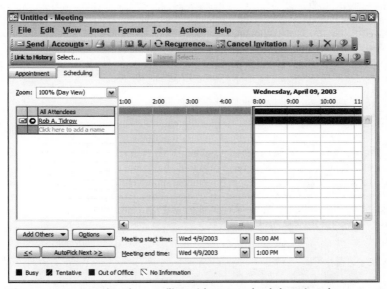

Figure 11-7: Resolve the conflict with your schedule using the Scheduling tab.

5. Click the AutoPick Next>> button to have Outlook choose the next open time slot for the meeting. Alternatively, you can click the << button to schedule the meeting for an earlier time slot. Figure 11-8 shows that Outlook found an available time by setting the meeting for two hours later than the originally scheduled time.

6. Click the Appointment tab to continue setting up the meeting.

7. Click the To button to display the Select Attendees and Resources dialog box. Notice that your name will already be listed in the Required box. This indicates that you are one of the people who is vital to the success of the meeting.

8. Add the additional attendees to the appropriate boxes. If you are using Exchange Server, you may also be able to reserve resources such as meeting rooms if those resources have their own schedules available on the server. Figure 11-9 shows the completed entries.

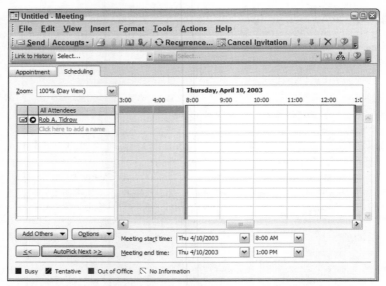

Figure 11-8: Click the AutoPick Next>> button to find the next available time for the meeting.

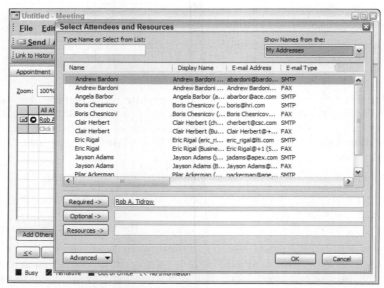

Figure 11-9: Select the people you want to invite to the meeting.

9. Click OK to close the Select Attendees and Resources dialog box and return to the Meeting form.

10. Click the Send button to send the meeting requests.

After you click the Send button, Outlook will send an e-mail message to each attendee inviting them to the meeting. If the attendees are using Outlook to manage their schedules, Outlook will also check their schedules to see if the proposed meeting time seems to be available. If the meeting conflicts with some of the schedules, Outlook can suggest an alternative time that may work better just as it did in moving the meeting time so that it would not conflict with your schedule.

Viewing attendee availability

After the meeting requests have been sent out and the responses returned, you can check on the status of the attendees. You can also manually set the status for attendees who responded in person or with a phone call rather than through e-mail.

To view or update the availability of the meeting attendees, follow these steps:

1. Double-click the meeting in the Outlook Calendar to open the meeting's form.

2. Click the Tracking tab.

3. Click in the Response box to set the attendee's status, as shown in Figure 11-10. Responses include None, Accepted, Declined, and Tentative.

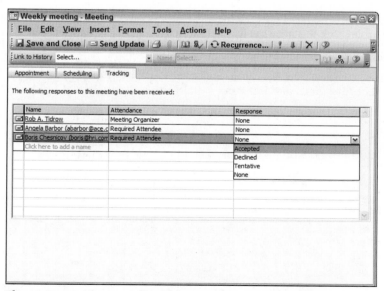

Figure 11-10: View or set attendee status on the Tracking tab.

4. Click in the Attendance box to change an attendee from required to optional, or to a resource if the selected object is a room or other resource. You cannot change the setting for the meeting organizer (which in this case is you).

5. If you need to adjust the meeting schedule, click the Appointment tab.

6. Use the << or the AutoPick New>> button on the Scheduling tab to select a new time that fits everyone's schedule. For example, if you have access to other schedules via a Microsoft Exchange Server, the other attendees free/busy times will be available in real time.

7. If you changed the meeting time, click the Send Update button to send a message to the attendees informing them that the meeting schedule has changed.

8. Click the Save and Close button to save any changes that you made and then close the Meeting form.

Adding additional attendees

Planning a meeting can take some carefully coordinated efforts. It is often necessary to make certain that a few people can attend before you invite the rest of the crowd. This may be the case if you are planning a meeting and want to be sure your speakers can be there first. There isn't much point in inviting everyone to hear a speaker if you are not positive the speaker can attend!

If you need to invite additional attendees after you've set up a meeting, follow these steps:

1. Double-click the meeting in the Outlook Calendar to reopen the Meeting form.

2. Click the Scheduling tab.

3. Click the Add Others button, and select Add from Address Book to open the Select Attendees and Resources dialog box, shown in Figure 11-11.

4. Add any additional people to the lists.

5. Click OK.

6. Click the Send Update button to send out the new invitations.

Note   If you plan on inviting people to a meeting in two stages, make certain that you invite all the required attendees the first time. Optional attendees can be invited later without adversely affecting the meeting.

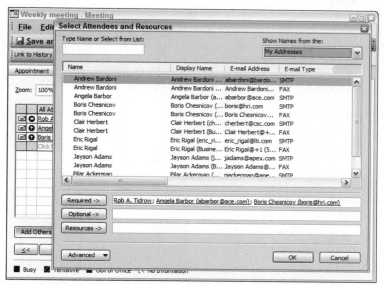

Figure 11-11: Add additional meeting attendees as necessary.

Specifying recurring activities

A recurring activity is one that takes place two or more times. Some recurring activities have a limited duration, whereas others may go on indefinitely. Recurring activities can include meetings, appointments, and events. (Note that Outlook refers to recurring events as recurring appointments.) A good example of a recurring meeting would be the Executive Committee meeting for an organization. This type of meeting might be held on the same day each month — such as the second Friday of each month.

You can change the status of any appointment or meeting into that of a recurring one. To set up the recurrence schedule, follow these steps:

1. Double-click the meeting or appointment in the Outlook Calendar.

2. Click the Recurrence button to display the Appointment Recurrence dialog box, shown in Figure 11-12.

3. Set the appointment time options.

4. Choose the appropriate recurrence pattern options. Note that the dialog box will display different options depending on which of the Daily, Weekly, Monthly, or Yearly radio buttons you select. If you choose Monthly or Yearly, you can choose either a specific date — such as the 12th day of the month — or a specific day — such as the second Friday.

Figure 11-12: Set the recurrence options using this dialog box.

5. Choose the range of recurrence options. You can set a starting date and the duration. For example, you can set the meeting to go on indefinitely by choosing the No end date option button.

6. Click OK to close the Appointment Recurrence dialog box.

7. Click Save and Close to close the Meeting form, and save your changes.

If you've set a meeting reminder, Outlook will remind you before each occurrence of the recurring meeting.

Note   To change a meeting back into a single meeting, open the Appointment Recurrence dialog box and then click the Remove Recurrence button.

Integrating with NetMeeting, Windows Media Services, and Microsoft Exchange Conferencing

It's becoming more and more common for people to work together even though they are physically many miles apart. The Internet has made it possible to communicate with people almost anywhere in the world. Outlook can leverage these facts by enabling you to schedule and hold online meetings using Microsoft NetMeeting, Windows Media Services, or Microsoft Exchange Conferencing.

NetMeeting is an online collaboration service that enables users to conference via audio, video, chat, whiteboard, and application sharing. Windows Media Services providea method of delivering streaming audio and video presentations over the Internet. NetMeeting is a conferencing solution in that it allows two-way interaction. Windows Media Services are intended as a one-way content delivery solution—similar to a TV broadcast. Microsoft Exchange Conferencing enables meetings to be conducted online on a local area network or intranet using a Microsoft Exchange server to handle the conferencing.

To set up an online meeting using NetMeeting, Windows Media Services, or Microsoft Exchange Conferencing follow these steps:

1. Open the Meeting form for the online meeting. This can be an existing meeting or a new meeting.

2. On the Appointment tab, select the This is an online meeting using: check box. Outlook will add an additional section to the Meeting form for the online meeting details, as shown in Figure 11-13.

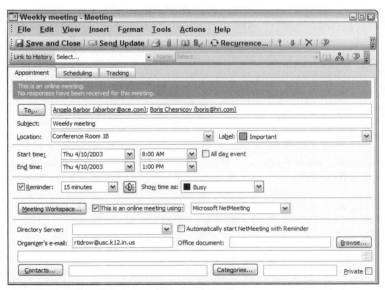

Figure 11-13: Set the online meeting options.

3. Select Microsoft NetMeeting, Windows Media Services, or Microsoft Exchange Conferencing as appropriate for your meeting.

4. If you select Microsoft NetMeeting, specify the directory server that you want to use. Each attendee must use the same directory server. If you are using Windows Media Services, specify the event address. For Microsoft Exchange

Conferencing, specify an appropriate password to log on to the Exchange server. Contact your Media Services administrator or Exchange Server administrator if you do not have the directory server, event address, or password information.

5. To have Outlook start NetMeeting (or Windows Media Services), select the Automatically start NetMeeting (or Windows Media) with Reminder check box.

6. For NetMeetings, if you want the meeting to begin with a document shown on the attendees' screens, enter the filename in the Office document text box.

7. Click the Send Update button to send out e-mail updates to the attendees. If you are creating a new meeting, click the Send button.

Because NetMeeting requires considerable bandwidth for acceptable performance, you probably won't want to use advanced features such as video conferencing if you connect to the Internet via a modem. An ISDN connection is really the minimum speed connection that will allow NetMeeting to work very well.

Summary

In this chapter, you learned how to use the Outlook Calendar to manage your schedule. You learned how to create appointments and how to schedule meetings. You saw how Outlook can automatically take over the task of finding available time slots that will fit into everyone's schedule. Finally, you saw how you could set up an online meeting so that people in remote locations can attend a meeting without traveling hundreds or thousands of miles.

The next chapter shows you how to use the Outlook task list to help you keep track of your to-do items.

✦   ✦   ✦

Tracking Tasks

I f you keep a formal list of tasks that you need to accomplish, you likely have your own informal to-do list. It may be something as uncomplicated as just remembering that you need to clean out your garage sometime, but everyone has things they need to do. Perhaps more important are those often overlooked, work-related tasks you need to accomplish weekly or monthly. For example, you may be responsible for updating the company's Web site to include current information about your product team. A little reminder each time this is due would be helpful, not to mention it may save you from forgetting to do it and losing your job.

The Outlook Tasks list is intended to help bring more organization into the chaos of trying to keep track of those tasks that you need to accomplish. You may not feel that you need anything quite as formal as the Outlook Tasks list, but how many times have you forgotten to do something important? Wouldn't it have been handy to have a gentle reminder so you could be just a bit more efficient at completing your chores?

This chapter will show you how to make the Outlook Tasks list an important yet unobtrusive part of your daily routines. You see how organizing your to-do list can make life a little easier by ensuring you do those things that are important to you.

Understanding Tasks

Chapter 11 demonstrated how to schedule appointments and meetings. At first glance, you might think that tasks could also be scheduled on your Outlook Calendar. There is, however, an important difference between tasks and those items that you schedule — tasks can be difficult to schedule.

Consider this example. Suppose you have a garage and a new car. Your garage is too full of junk to leave room for parking your car. You know that winter is coming in a few months, and

♦   ♦   ♦   ♦

In This Chapter

Understanding tasks

Creating a task

Setting task options

Assigning the task

Creating recurring tasks

♦   ♦   ♦   ♦

you'd like to be able to have your car in the garage during the winter. To do this, you'll have to spend a day cleaning out the garage. You could just schedule a garage cleaning day, but what if it turns out that the day you picked several weeks in advance was just too nice to spend inside your filthy garage? Wouldn't it make more sense to simply place the garage cleaning on a list of chores and set a specific date when you wanted to be done with the job? That way you would have a constant but gentle reminder of the task, but you could do it when the mood struck you.

Tasks don't all require a specific due date. The garage-cleaning task had a due date because you knew that you wanted it done before the bad weather arrived. Other tasks don't have that kind of urgency. Taking out the trash is an example of a task that needs to be done, but doesn't require setting of a specific date — when the trash can is full it needs to go out, no matter how long it has been since it last went out. The Outlook Tasks list can easily handle both types of tasks — those with a due date and those without one.

Figure 12-1 shows the Outlook Tasks list with several examples of both open-ended tasks (those that show "None" as the due date) and those with specific due dates.

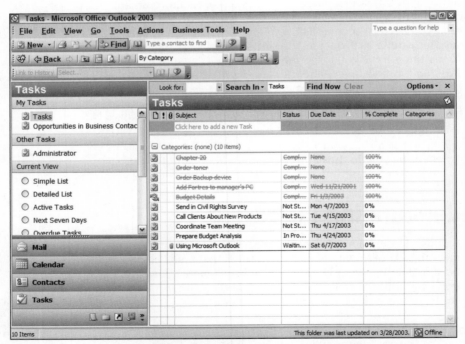

Figure 12-1: Use the Tasks list to help keep track of your to-do list.

The Outlook Tasks list can take on several different appearances. If you display the Outlook Calendar in Day, Work Week, Month, or Week view, the Tasks list shows up in the form of the TaskPad—a condensed view of the Tasks list. If you click the Outlook Today toolbar, a list of tasks appears, along with a synopsis of your appointments and a total of your active message. As Figure 12-2 shows, you also have quite a few options available on the View ➪ Arrange By ➪ Current View menu for viewing your Tasks list in the manner that is most useful to you. To display the Taskpad, choose View ➪ Taskpad. The calendar folder should be open when you do this.

Tip   Click a column heading in the Tasks list to sort the tasks.

Figure 12-2: Choose the view options that make the Tasks list most useful for your purposes.

Creating a Task

It's easy to add a new task to your Tasks list. In most cases, you can create a new task directly in the Tasks list without even opening the Task form. In fact, depending on how extensively you use the Tasks list, you may find that the simplest method completely serves your needs.

To create a new task in the Tasks list, follow these steps:

1. Open the Tasks Folder.

2. Click at the top of the Tasks list where you see the words Click here to add a new task.

3. Type the subject of the task, as shown in Figure 12-3.

4. If you need to set a due date, click the Due Date box and then click the down arrow at the right edge of the box to display a calendar, as shown in Figure 12-4. You can also use Outlook's AutoDate feature. Simply type in a date, such as Aug 11 and press Enter. Outlook changes this to your specified date format, such as Mon 8/11/2003.

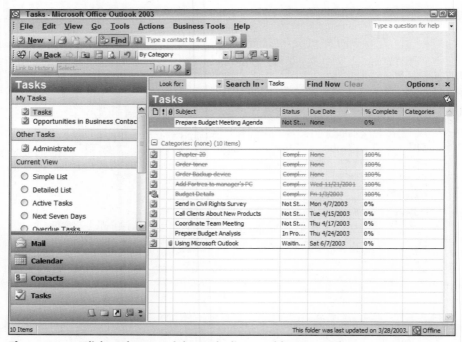

Figure 12-3: Click at the top of the Tasks list to add a new task.

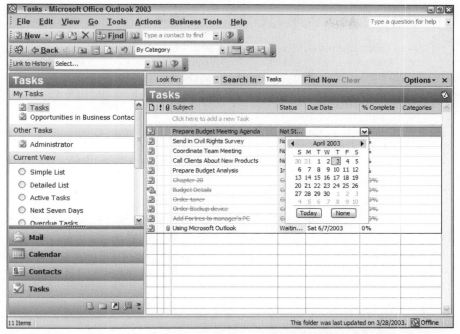

Figure 12-4: Click the down arrow to display a calendar so that you can select a due date.

5. Click a date in the calendar to select the date. If necessary, you can display different months using the right and left arrows at the top of the calendar.

6. Press Enter to add the new task to your Tasks list.

After a task appears in your Tasks list, there's nothing that's quite as satisfying as seeing the task completed. You've probably noticed that the second column of the Tasks list includes a check box in front of each task. To mark a task as completed, you click in the task's check box. Outlook shows completed tasks in a lighter color and with a line drawn through the task subject.

Note Outlook leaves completed tasks in your Tasks list. This enables you to reopen a task by removing the check from the completed check box. But leaving completed tasks in the Tasks list also makes it harder to see which tasks remain to be done. When tasks are truly completed, you can remove them from the Tasks list by right-clicking the completed tasks and selecting Delete.

Setting Task Options

Some tasks are more complicated than others. Although you may be able to handle most tasks by simply using the Tasks list, others are best handled by opening the Task form so you can access the complete range of task options. You don't have to use all the available options, of course. Still, it's handy to know which options are available so that you have an idea how they may be useful to you.

To open the Task form and set the various options, follow these steps:

1. Open the Tasks folder, if it is not already open.

2. Double-click a task to display the Task form for that task.

3. To choose a due date or a start date for the task, click the down arrow at the right of the appropriate text box, as shown in Figure 12-5. You may want to specify a start date for those tasks that cannot be started before a specific date. For example, in most cases you could not begin filing your income tax return before the end of January. At the same time, it would be easy to figure out that the due date for that task would probably be April 15.

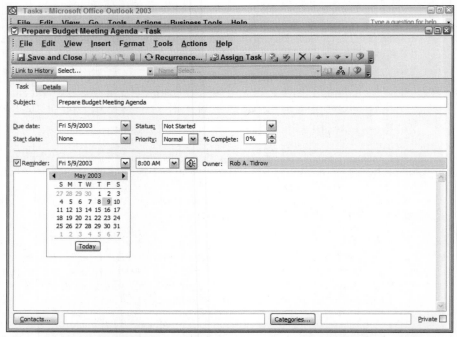

Figure 12-5: Use the Due date and Start date text boxes to specify dates for the task.

4. Click the down arrow at the right of the Status list box, as shown in Figure 12-6, to choose a description of the task's status. Because the Status box is a list box, you must choose one of the options that is shown in the list.

5. Choose Low, Normal, or High in the Priority list box. Setting the task priority is a good way to help you organize your tasks. In most cases, you'll want to complete high-priority tasks first, and leave low-priority tasks for last.

Tip

To view priority levels of your tasks, you must display the Priority field. To do this after setting task options, right-click the TaskPad title bar and then choose Customize Current View. Click the Fields button, and double-click Priority. Click OK and then OK again.

6. Use the up and down arrows next to the % Complete spin box to indicate how much of the task you've completed. This is especially useful for tasks that will require several work sessions to complete or for tasks where you'll need to report on your progress from time to time.

7. If you want Outlook to give you a reminder that the task is due, make certain the Reminder check box is selected.

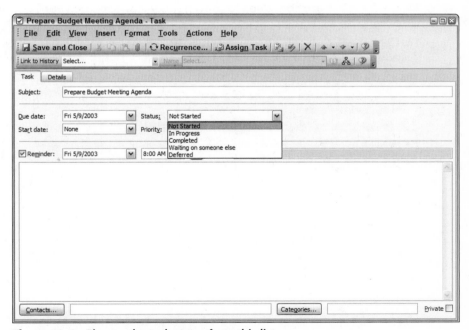

Figure 12-6: Choose the task status from this list.

8. Choose a date and time that you want to be reminded of the task. By default, Outlook issues reminders at the beginning of the work day, which is generally 8:00 A.M. unless you have specified different working hours. To see how to change Outlook's working hours, see Chapter 17 for customizing Outlook.

9. Click the Reminder Sound button to display the Reminder Sound dialog box. You can use this dialog box to select the sound that Outlook plays to remind you that the task is due. Don't forget that you can record your own reminder sounds using the Windows Sound Recorder. Also, to disable the sound reminder, deselect Play this sound on the Reminder Sound dialog box.

10. Enter any notes about the task in the large text box in the middle of the Task form. You can include anything you find useful here. For example, if you'll need some special supplies to complete this task, you might want to include a shopping list of those supplies.

11. If you need to link this task to someone in your Contacts list, click the Contacts button and choose that contact.

12. You can also click the Categories button to assign a category to the task. Outlook can then sort the tasks according to their assigned categories.

13. Click the Private check box to prevent people who share your Tasks list from seeing this task. Private tasks are only visible in your local Tasks list.

14. Click the Details tab, shown in Figure 12-7. You'll use this tab to add some additional information about the task.

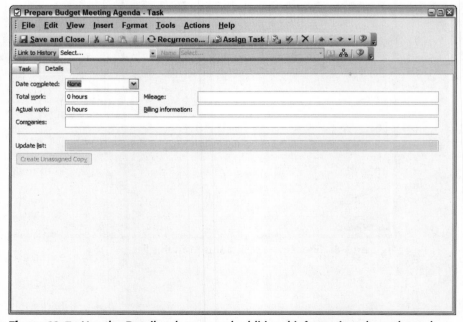

Figure 12-7: Use the Details tab to record additional information about the task.

15. If the task has been completed, the date is automatically entered in the Date completed text box. Change this date if necessary.

16. Use the Total work text box to indicate the length of time you expect the task to require.

17. Use the Actual work text box to indicate the amount of time you have spent on the task. This information might be important for billing purposes.

18. Add any further information necessary in the remaining text boxes.

19. Click the Save and Close button to save your changes, and close the Task form.

To print the details of an open task, select File ➪ Print from the Task form menu. This will enable you to print all of the information that you've entered for the task. This might be handy if the task details include special instructions or something like a necessary materials listing.

 Tip   To print the details of a task in the Tasks list, right-click the task and then choose Print.

If you need to further edit an existing task, remember that you can easily open a task anywhere you see the task. This includes the Tasks folder, the TaskPad if turned on, and in the Outlook Today folder. In fact, because the tasks that are shown in the Outlook Today folder are actually links, simply clicking a task in the Outlook Today folder opens the Task form.

Assigning Tasks to People

One of the nicest things about being in charge is that sometimes you can assign a task to someone else. You may still be responsible for seeing that the job is completed satisfactorily, but someone else will be doing the actual work. In this section, you'll learn how to use the Outlook Tasks list to help you delegate your workload.

You can assign items on your Outlook Tasks list to another person. You might put this feature to good use if you are chairing a committee and need to make certain that a number of items central to the committee's success are completed in a timely manner. By creating the tasks in your copy of Outlook and then assigning those tasks to the committee members, you can track the progress and make certain that you are informed as each task is completed.

To assign a task on your Tasks list to someone else, follow these steps:

1. Open the Task form for the task you want to assign, as shown in Figure 12-8.

2. Click the Assign Task button on the toolbar to begin assigning the task, as shown in Figure 12-9.

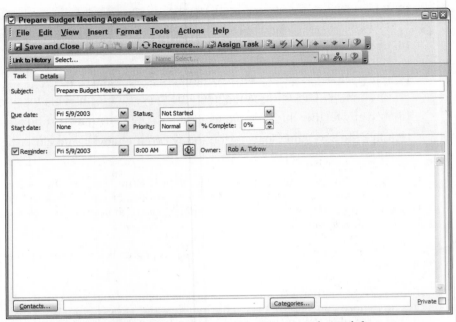

Figure 12-8: To assign a task to someone else, first open the Task form.

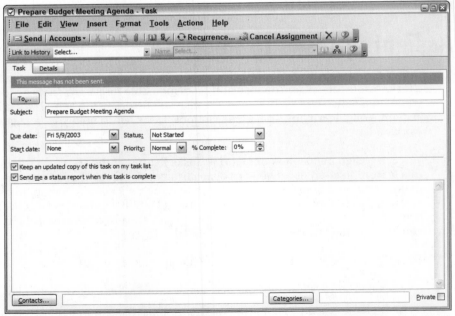

Figure 12-9: Outlook e-mails the task assignment to the person that you specify.

3. Click the To button to display the Select Task Recipient dialog box.

4. Select the person who will be assigned the task.

5. Click the To button.

6. Click OK to close the Select Task Recipient dialog box.

7. To keep a copy of the task in your Tasks list, make certain that the Keep an updated copy of this task on my task list check box is selected.

8. Make certain that the Send me a status report when this task is complete check box is selected so that you will be informed when the task is finished.

9. Click the Send button to send out an e-mail message requesting that the recipient accept the task assignment.

The person who receives the task assignment request can accept the assignment, decline the assignment, or assign the task to someone else. You will receive that response in an e-mail message.

Note   Accepting an assignment request means that you become the owner of the task. Only the task owner can make changes to a task. The person who assigned a task may receive updates regarding the task's status, but they can no longer modify the task.

Creating Recurring Tasks

Some tasks are recurring—you just can't get rid of them no matter how hard you try. For example, your dog probably needs a bath several times a year and your office trash container keeps getting refilled. You probably have other tasks that are recurring, too.

You can specify that a task in your Outlook Tasks list is a recurring task. When you do, Outlook will continue to remind you of the task for as long as you like.

To set a task as a recurring task, follow these steps:

1. Open the task that you want to set as a recurring task.

2. Click the Recurrence button to display the Task Recurrence dialog box, shown in Figure 12-10.

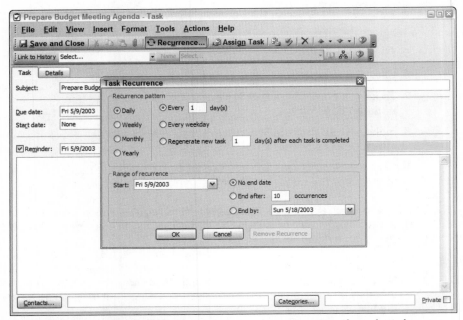

Figure 12-10: Use the Daily button to set a recurrence pattern based on days.

3. Select the daily recurrence pattern options to suit your needs:
   - If you want reminders for this task every so often, select the Every *x* day(s) radio button.
   - If you want reminders for this task every day, select the Every weekday radio button.
   - If you want Outlook to create a new task a specified number of days after this task is completed, select the Regenerate new task *x* day(s) after each task is completed radio button.

4. To set the recurrence pattern based on a weekly option, click the Weekly button, as shown in Figure 12-11.

5. Select the weekly recurrence pattern options to suit your needs:
   - If you want reminders for this task every so often, select the Recur every *x* week(s) on radio button and then choose the days when you want the reminders.
   - If you want Outlook to create a new task a specified number of weeks after this task is completed, select the Regenerate new task *x* week(s) after each task is completed radio button.

6. To set the recurrence pattern based on a monthly option, click the Monthly button, as shown in Figure 12-12.

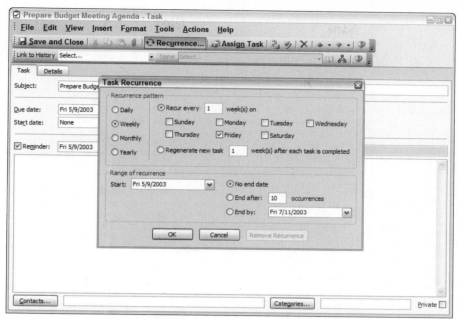

Figure 12-11: Use the Weekly button to set a recurrence pattern based on weeks.

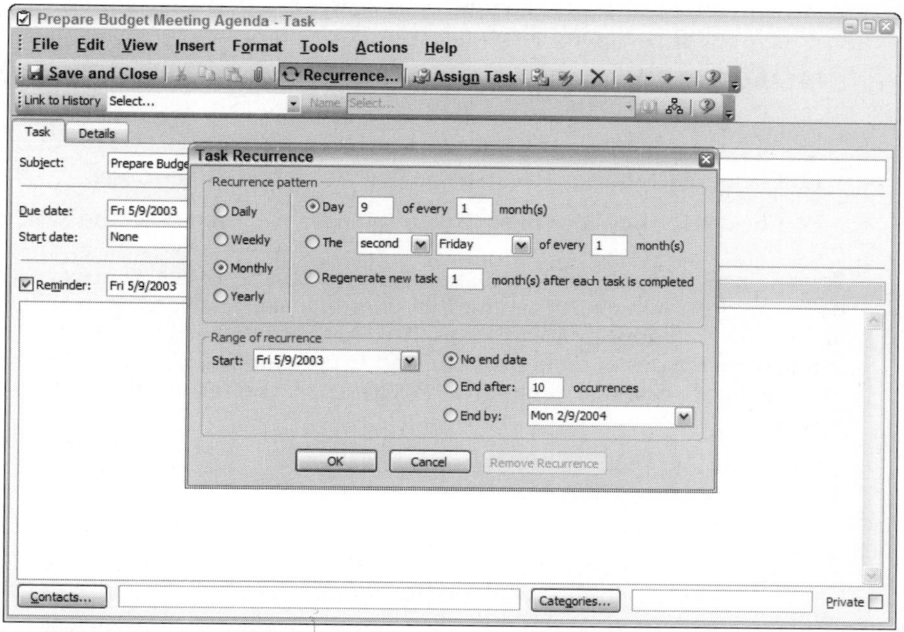

Figure 12-12: Use the Monthly button to set a recurrence pattern based on months.

7. Select the monthly recurrence pattern options to suit your needs:

- If you want reminders for this task every so often, select the Day *x* of every *x* month(s) radio button and then choose the days when you want the reminders.

- If you want reminders for this task on specific days each month, select the *x* (ordinal) *x* (day of the week) of every *x* month(s) radio button and then choose the days when you want the reminders.

- If you want Outlook to create a new task a specified number of months after this task is completed, select the Regenerate new task *x* month(s) after each task is completed radio button.

8. To set the recurrence pattern based on a yearly option, click the Yearly button, as shown in Figure 12-13.

9. Select the yearly recurrence pattern options to suit your needs:

- If you want reminders for this task every so often, select the Every *x* (month) *x* (date) radio button and then choose the dates when you want the reminders.

- If you want reminders for this task on specific days each month, select the *x* (ordinal) *x* (day of the week) of *x* (Month) radio button and then choose the days when you want the reminders.

- If you want Outlook to create a new task a specified number of years after this task is completed, select the Regenerate new task *x* year(s) after each task is completed radio button.

10. After you have set the recurrence pattern options, use the options in the lower section of the Task Recurrence dialog box to specify how long the task should repeat.

11. Click the OK button to close the Task Recurrence dialog box.

12. Click Save and Close to save your changes and then close the Task form.

You can use recurring tasks for a number of useful purposes. One example might be to provide yourself a reminder that your life insurance premium is due every six months, or that your property taxes are due the first of each quarter. Rather than leaving these types of reminders constantly on your Tasks list, you can use one of the regenerate new task options to have Outlook create a new task when the time is right.

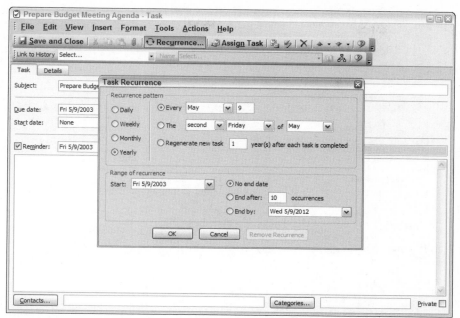

Figure 12-13: Use the Yearly button to set a recurrence pattern based on years.

Using the TaskPad

The Outlook TaskPad is a condensed version your Tasks folder. It shows small versions of monthly calendars and a list of your tasks. To display the TaskPad, perform the following steps:

1. Click the Calendar icon in the Navigation Pane.

2. Choose View ➪ TaskPad. The TaskPad appears on the right side of the Outlook screen as shown in Figure 12-14.

In the TaskPad, you click the Complete checkbox when you finish a task, double-click a task to open it, and select a task and press Delete to remove it.

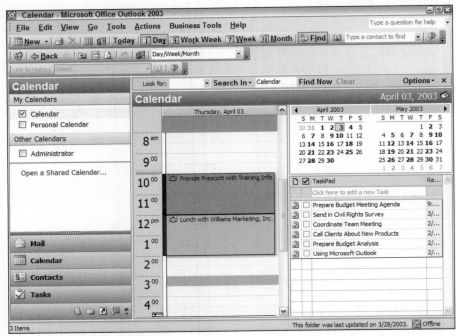

Figure 12-14: The TaskPad

You also can customize the look of the TaskPad, as follows:

1. Right-click a blank line inside the TaskPad.

2. Click TaskPad Settings to see four submenu commands you can select (see Figure 12-15).

3. Select Show Fields to display the Show Fields dialog box as shown in Figure 12-16. Use this dialog box to double-click the fields you want to show on the TaskPad. Click OK when finished.

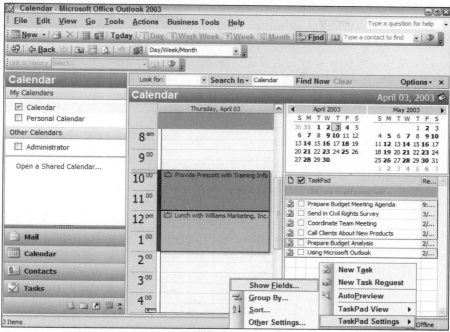

Figure 12-15: Four submenu commands

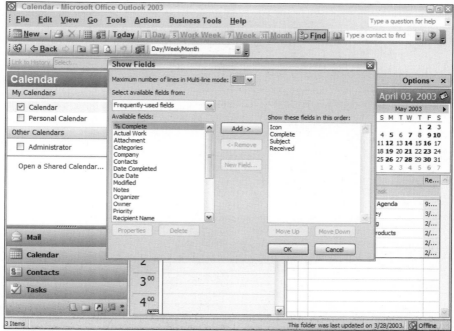

Figure 12-16: The Show Fields dialog box

4. Select Group By from the TaskPad Settings submenu to display the Group By dialog box (see Figure 12-17). Use this dialog box to customize the way in which the TaskPad groups your tasks. Click OK when finished.

5. Select Sort By from the TaskPad Settings submenu to display the Sort By dialog box (see Figure 12-18). Use this dialog box to set the sorting order of your TaskPad. Click OK when finished.

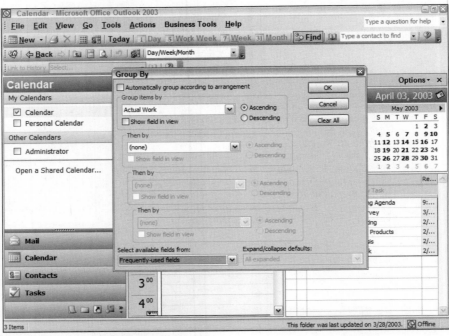

Figure 12-17: The Group By dialog box

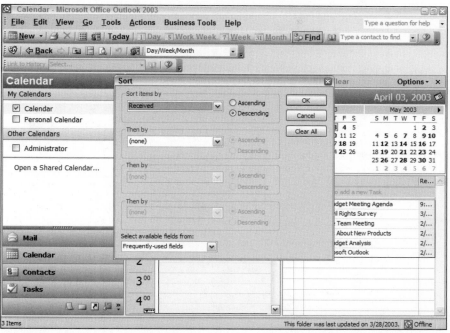

Figure 12-18: The Sort By dialog box

6. Select Other Settings from the TaskPad Settings submenu to display the Other Settings dialog box (see Figure 12-19). Use this dialog box to customize the way the TaskPad looks, including changing font styles, font sizes, and grid line properties. Click OK when finished.

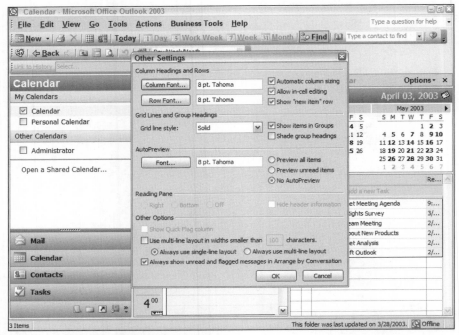

Figure 12-19: The Other Settings dialog box

Summary

Doing tasks may sometimes be boring, but at least remembering what you need to do is one task that you can assign to Outlook. In this chapter, you learned about handling tasks in Outlook and how to set task options. You learned how you can use Outlook to assign tasks to other people and how to set a task as recurring.

In the next chapter, you'll learn about the Outlook Journal. You'll see how you can use Outlook to track the time that you spend working on projects and how the Journal can help you be better organized.

✦   ✦   ✦

Keeping Your Journal

◆ ◆ ◆ ◆

In This Chapter

Understanding
the Journal

Viewing the Journal

Controlling Journal
data

Sharing Journal
information

◆ ◆ ◆ ◆

If you ever need to keep track of the time you spend working on projects, you'll appreciate how the Outlook Journal can keep an automatic record of the documents you create and use. If you need to know how long you worked on that specific project, the Outlook Journal can tell you. If you need to track the time you spend on the telephone supporting certain customers, the Outlook Journal can tell you that, too.

In this chapter, you learn not only how to use the Outlook Journal's automatic tracking features, but also how you can add your own manual Journal entries. You see how you can use the Outlook Journal to view your work record several different ways so that you can make the most of the information that the Outlook Journal has recorded.

Understanding the Journal

You might do well to think of the Outlook Journal as being similar to a diary. Just as you might use a diary to keep track of things that you've done, the Outlook Journal keeps track of some of the things that you do on your PC. When you work on a Word document, for example, Outlook notes the date and time that you open and close the file. If you later open the same document file, Outlook updates the record by adding a new entry to show the new date, time, and duration.

After you activate the Journal, it can automatically track the usage data for Access, Excel, PowerPoint, or Word documents. In addition, the Outlook Journal tracks a number of the activities that you perform within Outlook itself, such as sending e-mail and meeting requests. To get the full benefit of the Outlook Journal's automatic document tracking features, you must use Microsoft Office applications. Outlook Journal does not automatically track documents you create using most other programs, but you can easily create your own manual Journal entries.

Figure 13-1 shows one example of how the Outlook Journal tracks certain activities. In this figure, the Journal items are viewed by Entry List.

Entries in the Outlook Journal are more than just a log of your activities. Each Journal entry includes a number of details about the activity, as shown in Figure 13-2. The Journal shows multiple entries for Wed 26, including an e-mail message about ordering networking connectors. To view a Journal entry, double-click the entry in the Outlook Journal event log.

Although the Outlook Journal can automatically track many different types of activities, it doesn't create Journal entries for everything you do on your PC. You might need to create Journal entries yourself if you want to keep a log of your activities. In some cases, Outlook can provide assistance with beginning a Journal entry, but you'll have to handle some of the details yourself. For example, if you use the Outlook AutoDialer to call one of your contacts, Outlook can create a Journal entry that begins when you click the Dial button. But because Outlook has no way to determine when you complete the call, you'll have to stop the timer yourself. The Journal entry will then include the call duration as well as the information from the Contacts list.

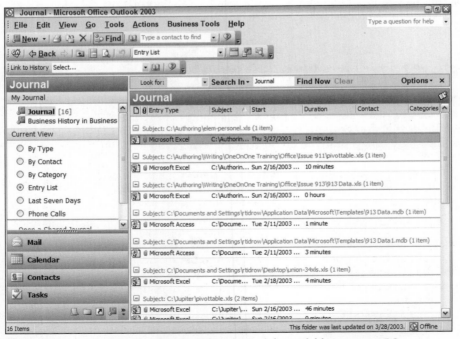

Figure 13-1: The Outlook Journal tracks many of the activities on your PC.

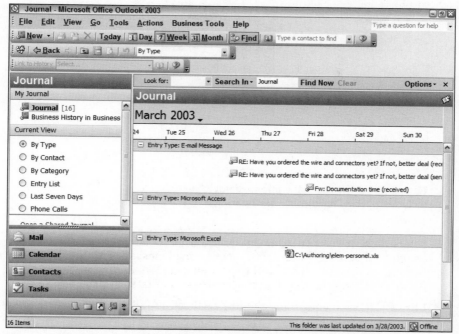

Figure 13-2: Journal entries show timelines regarding the logged event.

Note

Because Journal entries contain links to your documents rather than copies of the actual documents, the Journal entries may reference documents that no longer exist on your system. The Outlook Journal does not have any way to record that files have been deleted, moved, or renamed.

Viewing the Journal

Because the Outlook Journal creates a record of your activities, the information that it contains is displayed in several formats that are considerably different from the formats used in the other types of Outlook folders. In the following sections, you get a chance to see each of the Outlook Journal display formats and learn why you might want to view the Outlook Journal in that ormat.

To turn on the Journal, do the following steps:

1. Choose Go ⇨ Journal. If a window appears asking if you want turn on the Journal, click Yes. The Journal Options dialog box displays, as shown in Figure 13-3.

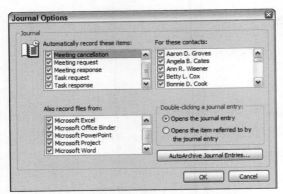

Figure 13-3: The Journal Options dialog box includes options for turning on the Journal.

2. Select those items you want Outlook Journal to automatically record. For example, if you want Journal to record e-mail messages, select E-mail Message from the Automatically record these items list. To learn more about these options, see the section "Limiting Journal data" later in this chapter.

3. Click OK to save your Journal entry settings.

Using the By Type view format

The default Outlook Journal view is the By Type format, shown in Figure 13-4. In this type of view, the Journal entries are arranged in a timeline and are grouped by the document type. To select the By Type view, select View ➪ Arrange By ➪ Current View ➪ By Type. Another way to change the view is to select a view in the Current View section of the Navigation Pane.

Each entry type is indicated by a title bar that shows the Journal entry type — Microsoft Word, for example. The left edge of the title bar includes a small box that you can click to expand or contract the type. A plus sign (+) in the box means that the type is collapsed, whereas a minus sign (–) indicates that the type is expanded. You may need to use the vertical scrollbar to see all of the Journal entry types.

When you expand a type, you can view any Journal entries for that type in the area just below the type's title bar. Outlook expands the Journal entry area just enough to display the entries, but you may be a little surprised to discover that no entries appear when you expand a type. The reason for this is that Outlook displays the entries as a timeline. If no entries for the selected type were created recently, you may need to use the horizontal scrollbar to find the most recent entries.

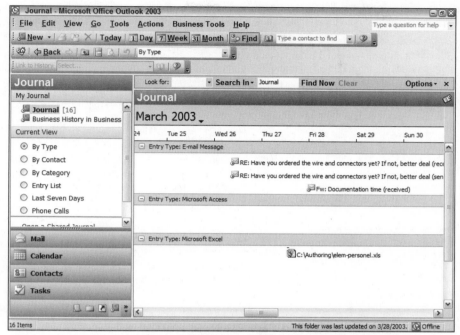

Figure 13-4: The By Type view shows entries grouped by the application that was used.

The By Type view is most useful if you want to find out which documents you worked on during a specific period. This view is not particularly useful for locating documents based on any other criteria. You wouldn't use the By Type view to locate all documents relating to a particular contact, for example.

Using the By Contact view format

The next Outlook Journal view is the By Contact format, shown in Figure 13-5. In this type of view, the Journal entries are also arranged in a timeline and are grouped by the contact. To select the By Contact view, select View ➪ Current View ➪ By Contact.

Each entry type is indicated by a title bar that shows the contact name. Click the small box to expand or contract the type. You may also need to use the vertical scrollbar.

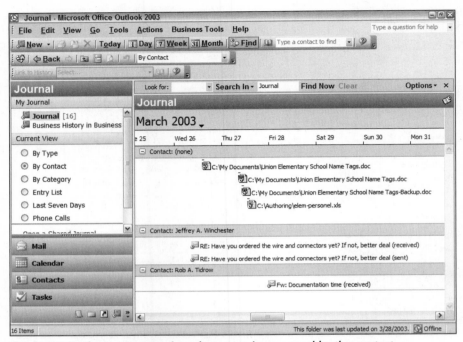

Figure 13-5: The By Contact view shows entries grouped by the contact.

The By Contact view makes it easy to find all documents and e-mail messages related to a specific contact. Any type of document, whether it is an Excel worksheet or an e-mail message, can appear in the list.

To make the By Contact view truly useful, you may need to open the Category (none) category and then assign the existing Journal entries to specific contacts. To do so, double-click the Journal entry to open it, click the Contacts button, choose the contacts you want to link to the entry, and click Save and Close to update the Journal entry.

Using the By Category view format

The next Outlook Journal view is the By Category format, shown in Figure 13-6. In this type of view, the Journal entries are also arranged in a timeline and are organized by the category that you assigned. To select the By Category view, select View ➪ Arrange By ➪ Current View ➪ By Category.

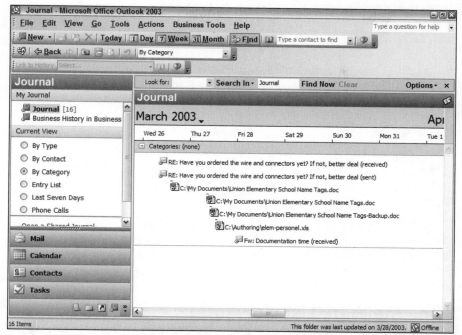

Figure 13-6: The By Category view shows entries grouped using the categories you selected.

The By Category view can be handy, especially if you create categories that break down the Journal entries by project. This view can also be almost useless unless you take the time to click the Categories button when you create documents. By default, Outlook doesn't assign any categories, so the usefulness of this view is totally dependent on your assigning the categories yourself.

You can assign categories using the existing categories, or you can create your own categories. As Figure 13-7 shows, you can click the Categories button at the bottom of the Journal Entry form to display the Categories dialog box. (You'll find the Categories button at the bottom of many types of Outlook forms.) You can choose from the list of available categories, or click the Master Category List button to display the Master Category List dialog box so that you can create your own categories. One handy way to use these options would be to create categories for each project, such as an Outlook Bible category. That would enable you to assign the project's category to all documents relating to that project, and would make it easy to locate everything relating to the project. For more information on assigning categories, see Chapter 15.

Figure 13-7: Create the categories you need to organize your projects.

Using the Entry List view format

The next Outlook Journal view may turn out to be the most useful of all. The Entry List view dispenses with the timeline view and instead displays all the Journal entries, as shown in Figure 13-8. To select the Entry List view, select View ⇨ Arrange By ⇨ Current View ⇨ Entry List.

Because the Entry List view does not use the timeline to display the entries, it's much easier to view the list of entries — you don't have to use the horizontal scroll-bar to locate the items. By default, this view is sorted in descending order based on the start date, but you can quickly sort the list using any of the columns. Simply click a column heading to sort the list based on the entries in the selected column. Click a second time to reverse the sort order.

The paperclip icon in the second column of the Entry List view indicates that an entry has a file associated with the entry, such as a Word document attached to an incoming e-mail message. If there is no paperclip icon, the entry is a log of an activity that occurred within Outlook — such as an e-mail message.

Because the Entry List view makes it easy to see all the Journal entries, you'll find this view is helpful if you want to open Journal entries so that you can assign them to specific contacts or categories. Double-click an entry to open its Journal Entry form so that you can make any necessary changes. Click Save and Close to save your changes and return to the Outlook Journal.

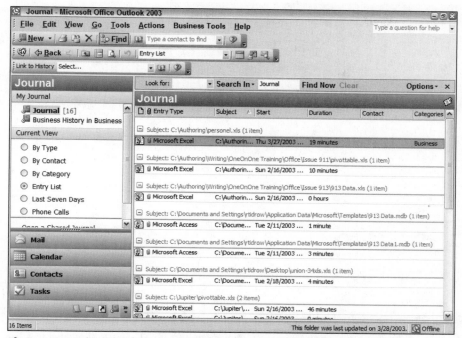

Figure 13-8: The Entry List view shows all Journal entries in a list.

Using the Last Seven Days view format

The Last Seven Days view looks similar to the Entry List view — it shows items started during the previous seven days. Figure 13-9 shows the Last Seven Days view. To select the Last Seven Days view, select View ➪ Arrange By ➪ Current View ➪ Last Seven Days.

The Last Seven Days view is useful when you need to locate items you've worked on recently — especially if you can't quite remember the filename.

Note

You can use the View ➪ Arrange By ➪ Current View ➪ Customize Current View command to customize the Last Seven Days view to specify a different time period, such as the past month. See Chapter 10 for details on customizing views.

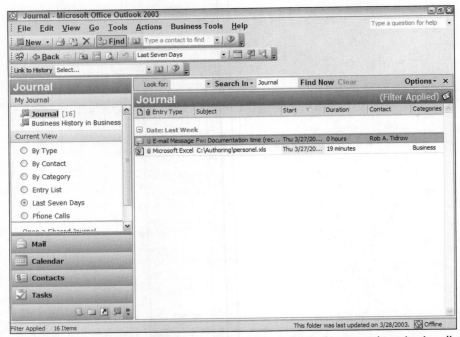

Figure 13-9: The Last Seven Days view shows the last week's Journal entries in a list.

Using the Phone Calls view format

The final Outlook Journal view is the Phone Calls view as shown in Figure 13-10. This view singles out those Journal entries for phone calls. To select the Phone Calls view, select View ➪ Arrange By ➪ Current View ➪ Phone Calls.

Outlook will only create Journal entries for phone calls automatically if you use the Outlook AutoDialer to begin the call. You'll have to specify the duration yourself by entering the appropriate time in the phone call Journal entry. You can do so by actually entering a time, or by clicking the Stop Call button. If you don't use the AutoDialer to place calls, you can still record phone calls in Journal. Select the Phone Calls view and right-click in the Journal window. Choose New Journal Entry and make sure Phone Call is selected from the Entry Type list. Enter a subject in the Subject line. Finally fill in the Start time and Duration options and click Save and Close.

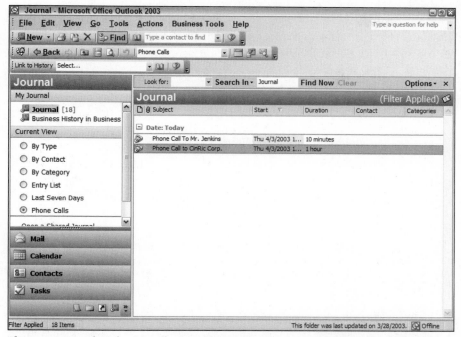

Figure 13-10: The Phone Calls view shows the Journal entries for all your logged phone calls.

Tracking your phone calls in the Outlook Journal may be more useful than you imagine. If you bill for your time, you can use the phone call Journal entries to keep track of the time you spend on billable calls. But even if you don't bill for your time, you'll find that phone call Journal entries make it easier to recall what was said in the conversation.

Note   Remember to link your phone call Journal entries to the appropriate contacts so that it will be easier to find all entries relating to specific contacts.

Controlling Journal Data

The Outlook Journal records a lot of information automatically, but these automatic settings may not completely suit your needs. In the following sections, you learn how to control which types of information the Outlook Journal tracks. You also learn how to create your own entries for items that aren't tracked automatically.

Limiting Journal data

You can easily control which information the Outlook Journal records so that the logs more closely meet your needs.

To select which items the Outlook Journal tracks, follow these steps:

1. Select Tools ➪ Options to display the Options dialog box.

2. Click the Journal Options button on the Preferences tab to display the Journal Options dialog box, shown in Figure 13-11.

3. Select the Outlook events that you want to record from the Automatically record these items box.

4. Select the Microsoft Office documents you want to track in the Also record files from box.

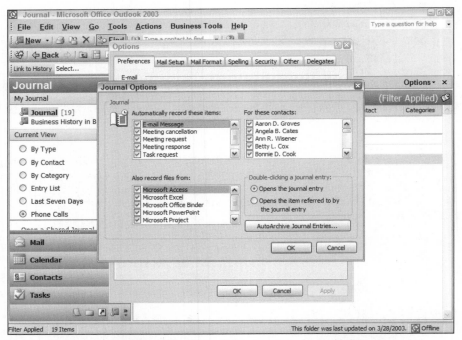

Figure 13-11: Use the Journal Options dialog box to select which items are recorded automatically.

5. Select the contacts you want to track in the For these contacts box. You can choose, for example, to track e-mail messages from certain contacts and ignore those from other contacts.

6. Choose the action that you want to occur when you double-click a Journal entry in the Outlook Journal. It's usually best to open the Journal entry rather than the document; otherwise, it will be more difficult to edit the information in the Journal entry. You can always open the items referenced in a Journal entry from within the Journal entry itself. Alternatively, you can simply open the referenced item using its native application, such as open a Word document from Word, a worksheet in Excel, and so on.

7. If you want to change the way Outlook handles old Journal entries, click the AutoArchive Journal Entries button and then select the settings you prefer.

8. Click OK to close the Journal Options dialog box.

9. Click OK to close the Options dialog box.

Note   Journal entries work even if Outlook is not currently running when you create or edit a document you've set up in the Journal Options dialog box.

If you change the Outlook Journal options, be sure to select all the items that you want to record. If you add a check to any of the check boxes in the Journal Options dialog box, Outlook will stop using the default settings and only record those items that you specifically selected.

Adding Journal entries manually

If you occasionally use programs that don't create automatic Journal entries, you may still want to keep a record of the fact that you've worked on a project. This would be especially true if you need to track the time you've spent for billing purposes, but you may want to keep these records simply to help keep things organized. Fortunately, you'll find that creating your own Journal entries manually is a simple process.

To create Journal entries manually, follow these steps:

1. Select File ⇨ New ⇨ Journal Entry to display a blank Journal Entry form, as shown in Figure 13-12.

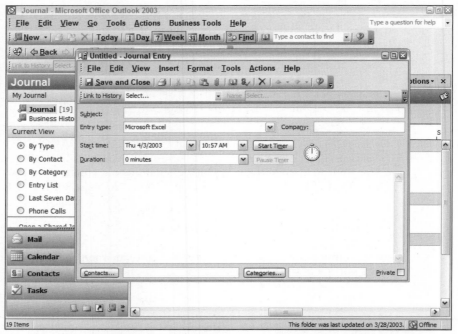

Figure 13-12: Use the Journal Entry form to create your own Journal entries manually.

2. Enter a descriptive subject for this Journal entry.

3. Choose the type of entry.

4. If necessary, enter a company name.

5. To link this Journal entry to a contact, use the Contacts button and then choose the contact.

6. To assign a category, use the Categories button and then choose a category.

7. To link this Journal entry to a file, drag and drop the file into the note area. You'll probably find that Windows Explorer is the easiest tool to use for dragging and dropping a file. Alternatively, choose Insert ➪ File and then select the file to insert. Finish by choosing the Insert button on the Insert File dialog box.

8. Specify a starting date, time, and duration.

9. Alternatively, click the Start Timer button to begin logging the time you spend.

10. Click the Pause Time button to stop logging the time. Click the Start Timer button again to resume working on the item. If you do not want to pause the timer and simply want to end working on the item, see step 11.

11. Click the Save and Close button to save your Journal entry.

You can later reopen your new Journal entry the same way you open any other Journal entry. If you did not change the default double-click setting, you can simply double-click a Journal entry to open it. Regardless of the double-click setting, you can always open a Journal entry by right-clicking it and choosing Open from the pop-up menu.

Tip   If you can't remember which entry type you chose for a manual Journal entry, select View ➪ Arrange By ➪ Current View, and choose Entry List or Last Seven Days as appropriate.

Sharing Journal Information

Because the Outlook Journal keeps track of activities using a timeline, you may find that the Outlook Journal is one of the most useful of Outlook's folders to share. If you are working on a project with several people, a shared Outlook Journal may be just the thing that you need to make certain everyone is on track.

Cross-Reference   See Chapter 18 for details on how to share your Outlook Journal.

Shared folders may not always include the latest updates from every subscriber. You may want to adjust the update frequency if it is important that the subscribers have the most current information available. You can make this adjustment by right-clicking the shared folder, selecting Properties from the pop-up menu, and choosing options on the Sharing tab.

Summary

The Outlook Journal is a handy tool for tracking activities and documents on your PC. In this chapter, you learned how to use the Outlook Journal to automatically track many of these things, and how to create manual Journal entries when necessary. You learned how to change the way the Outlook Journal displays items so that you can more easily find what you need. Finally, you learned that you can easily share your Outlook Journal with others.

The next chapter shows you how to use Outlook's Notes. If you've ever used those little paper sticky notes to remind yourself about something, you'll appreciate the fact that Outlook Notes can fill in quite nicely — and they don't get buried on your desktop or end up filling your trashcan.

✦   ✦   ✦

Taking Notes

Notes are probably the Outlook feature that people use the least. In some ways, that's a little hard to understand, especially when you realize that almost everyone has those sticky paper notes all over his or her desk. Outlook Notes can easily replace those paper sticky notes, and they won't get buried under all the other paper on the top your desk.

In this chapter, you learn how to use Outlook Notes. You have a chance to see if using Notes can help make your desk just a bit less cluttered and your life just a bit more organized.

Understanding Notes

If you've ever written yourself a reminder on one of those little paper sticky notes, you're already familiar with the concept behind Outlook Notes. They're perfect for all that immediate information that you need to jot down, such as a phone number, a name, an address, the title of a book someone just told you about, or whatever you need to jog your memory.

Outlook Notes have several advantages over those paper sticky notes:

✦ Paper sticky notes are easily lost, especially if there's a lot of paperwork covering your desk. Outlook Notes, on the other hand, are easy to find. If they're closed, you'll find them in the Outlook Notes folder. If they're open, they appear on your computer screen—even if Outlook is minimized.

◆ ◆ ◆ ◆

In This Chapter

Understanding Notes

Creating and editing Notes

Using Note options

Viewing your Notes

◆ ◆ ◆ ◆

✦ Paper sticky notes have a limited amount of space for you to write your note, but Outlook Notes can expand to hold as much text as you need.

✦ Paper sticky notes can be hard to read, especially if you have sloppy writing. Outlook Notes are always easy to read — the text is just as clear as any other text on your monitor.

✦ Paper sticky notes must be refilled when the pad runs out, but Outlook Notes are always available in a free, endless supply.

Figure 14-1 shows a typical Outlook Note.

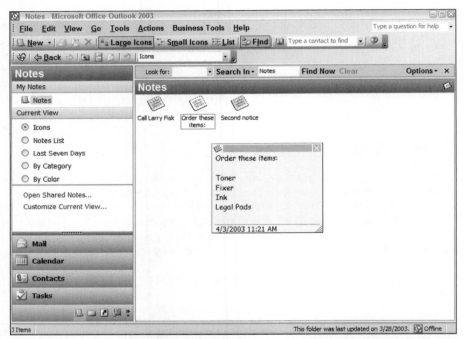

Figure 14-1: Use Outlook Notes in place of those paper sticky notes that are easily lost on your desktop.

Creating and Editing Notes

Paper sticky notes wouldn't be nearly as popular if they weren't so convenient to use. You just grab the pad, jot a quick note, and stick it someplace where you'll find it when you need it. Outlook Notes are just about as easy to create as those paper sticky notes. Outlook Notes are even better than a paper sticky note if you need to edit what's on the note—you don't have to throw away the old note and start over because you ran out of space!

To create a new Outlook Note, follow these steps:

1. If necessary, open Outlook.

2. If you intend to create several Notes, open the Notes Folder. This is optional, but if the Notes Folder is open, you can click the New Note button to begin a new Note without wading through Outlook's menus.

3. Select File ➪ New ➪ Note to display a new, blank Note, as shown in Figure 14-2. Alternatively, you can simply double-click an empty area on the Notes window to display a new, blank Note.

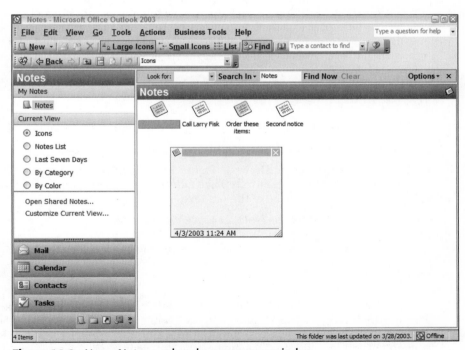

Figure 14-2: Use a Note as a handy onscreen reminder.

4. Type the text of your Note.

5. Click the Close button if you want to close the Note; otherwise, you can click outside the Note to leave the Note open on your screen.

6. Click the Note icon on the Windows taskbar to view open Notes that are covered by other windows.

Tip Right-click in an open Note to display a pop-up menu you can use to cut or copy text from the Note and place it in the Windows Clipboard, or to paste text from the Windows Clipboard into the Note.

Windows treats open Notes almost as though they were separate programs. You can view the text of an open Note even if the Outlook window is minimized. Any open Notes are closed when you close Outlook, however, and if you click the Show Desktop toolbar button on the Windows Quick Launch toolbar, the open Note minimizes to the taskbar.

Note You can drag a note out of Outlook onto the desktop, and it will be completely functional even when Outlook is closed.

The same thing that makes paper sticky notes so convenient — their small size — also makes them hard to edit; they don't have much room for corrections. Unless you write your notes in pencil, making corrections on a paper sticky note usually means crossing out the incorrect information and then trying to find room for the replacement text. Often this means starting over with a new paper sticky note.

Editing an Outlook Note couldn't be easier. Here's how to edit an existing Outlook Note:

1. Open the Outlook Notes folder.

2. Double-click the Note you want to edit.

3. Type the new text, as shown in Figure 14-3. If you want to replace existing text, select the text you want to replace before you begin typing so that your new text will take the place of the old text.

4. You can now close the Note, or leave it open.

Tip If a Note is already open, click within the Note to begin editing the Note.

You may have noticed that the only type of Note content that has been mentioned is text. The reason for this is quite simple — Notes can't hold anything except text. If you were to copy any non-text item to the Windows Clipboard, you wouldn't be able to paste it into a Note. This means that you cannot, for example, place a picture within a Note.

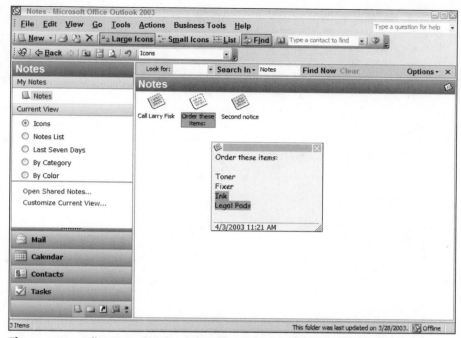

Figure 14-3: Edit a Note by simply opening it and typing your text.

Using Note Options

Because Outlook Notes are so simple, they don't offer a lot of options. There are a few small changes that you can make, however, and they are discussed in the following sections.

Specifying a color

You can use five different colors for your Notes. Whether you choose colors for simple aesthetic reasons or to specify different types of notes is up to you. Outlook treats all Notes equally, regardless of the color.

To choose a color for a Note, follow these steps:

1. Open the Note.

2. Click the Note icon in the upper left corner of the Note.

3. Select Color, as shown in Figure 14-4, and choose the color for the Note.

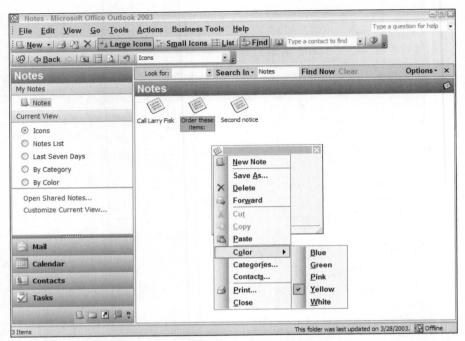

Figure 14-4: You can choose from five colors for your Notes.

You also can right-click a Note in the Notes folder, and choose Color and the color of choice.

As you'll see in the section "Specifying Note default options," you can also choose a default color for your Notes.

Specifying a category

You can assign categories to your Notes if you want to organize them. This will enable you to view your Notes by category—which may be especially useful if you create a large number of Notes.

To assign a category to a Note, follow these steps:

1. Open the Note.
2. Click the Note icon in the upper left corner of the Note.
3. Select Categories to display the Categories dialog box, shown in Figure 14-5.

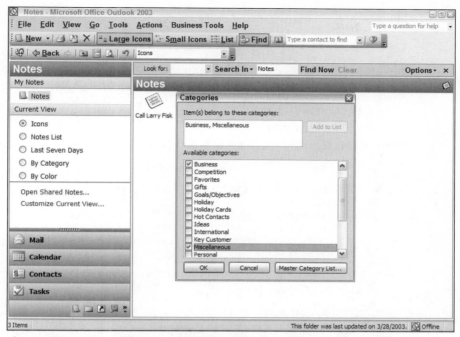

Figure 14-5: You can choose categories for your Notes.

4. Add a check to each category that you want to assign to this Note.

5. Click OK to close the Categories dialog box.

You also can right-click a Note in the Notes folder and then choose Categories to display the Categories dialog box.

Note

Remember that you can click the Master Category List button to create your own custom categories.

Specifying a contact

You can also link a Note to a contact. Anything that you link to a contact will be accessible from that Contact form. You might find this feature handy if you need to create a Note that you want open on your desktop because a Note takes up far less room than the Contact form.

To link a Note to a contact, follow these steps:

1. Open the Note.
2. Click the Note icon in the upper left corner of the Note.
3. Select Contacts to display the Contacts for Note dialog box.
4. Click the Contacts button to display the Select Contacts dialog box, shown in Figure 14-6.
5. Select the contacts you want to link to this Note.
6. Click OK to close the Select Contacts dialog box.
7. Click Close to close the Contacts for Note dialog box.

Note   You can assign several contacts to the same Note if necessary.

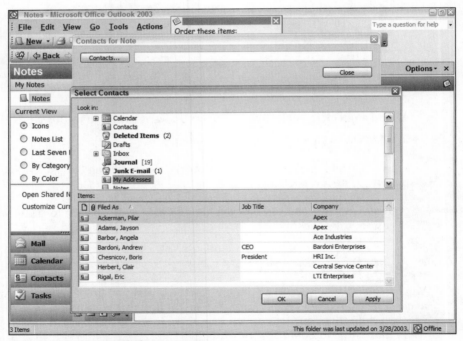

Figure 14-6: You can link your Notes to contacts.

Specifying Note default options

If you use Outlook Notes often, you may decide that you would like your Notes to look just a bit different. For example, if you usually create very short Notes, you may want to choose a smaller default size so that you don't have to drag the Note borders to minimize the space that they occupy on your desktop.

To set the defaults for all new Notes, follow these steps:

1. Select Tools ⇨ Options to display the Options dialog box.

2. Click the Note Options button on the Preferences tab to display the Notes Options dialog box, shown in Figure 14-7.

3. Select the default color from the drop-down Color list box.

4. Select the default size for your Notes from the drop-down Size list box. Don't forget that you can resize a Note no matter what default size is chosen.

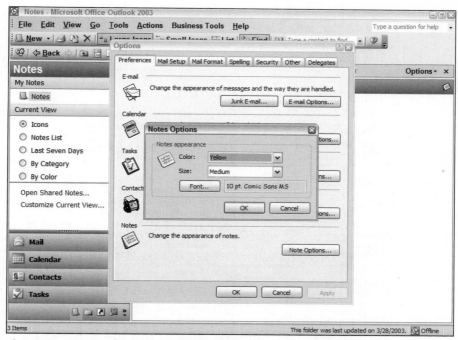

Figure 14-7: Choose the Note default settings you prefer.

5. Click the Font button if you want to change the font settings. If you like, you can easily choose different fonts, sizes, attributes, and colors. Ten point Comic Sans is the default font style. When you change the font for one Note, the font of your existing Notes change as well.

6. Click OK to close the Notes Options dialog box.

7. Click OK to close the Options dialog box.

Specifying timestamp options

Outlook normally adds the date and time that a Note was created to the bottom of each Note. In most cases, you'll probably appreciate having this reminder of the age of the Note, but if you don't want the date and time shown, you can deselect this option. Unlike most Note options, however, this option is well hidden.

To control the display of the date and time on your Notes, follow these steps:

1. Select Tools ➪ Options to display the Options dialog box.

2. Click the Other tab.

3. Click the Advanced Options button to display the Advanced Options dialog box, shown in Figure 14-8.

Figure 14-8: Use the Advanced Options dialog box to control the display of the date and time on Notes.

4. To hide the date and time display, remove the check from the When viewing Notes, show time and date check box.

5. Click OK to close the Advanced Options dialog box.

6. Click OK to close the Options dialog box.

If you change the setting for the time and date display, Outlook will use the new setting for all Notes — new or old. If you later choose to redisplay the time and date, Outlook will remember the dates and times for your existing Notes.

Viewing Your Notes

If you create a lot of Notes, you'll eventually find that you need a little organization to keep track of them. Outlook provides this organization in the form of different views of the Notes Folder. In the following sections, you learn how these different views may be useful to you.

Using the Icon views

There are actually three different views that you can display using the View ➪ Arrange By ➪ Current View ➪ Icons command. When you choose this command, Outlook adds three buttons to the toolbar. The Large Icons button displays each Note using a large Note icon and the first few words of the Note. The Small Icons button displays your Notes using a small Note icon followed by the text of the Note, as shown in Figure 14-9. The List button displays your Notes almost identically to the way they are displayed using the Small Icons button. The difference between these two views is that Small Icons can be moved around at random, while icons shown in List view are fixed in columns and cannot be moved.

Because the Small Icons view displays the largest number of your Notes onscreen at one time, you may want to use this view if you need to locate a particular Note — especially if you haven't used categories or colors to organize your Notes.

Using the Notes List view

The Notes List view looks similar to the Small Icons view except that more of the Note text is displayed on the screen and the List view is a table view. Figure 14-10 shows the Notes List view. To display this view, select View ➪ Arrange By ➪ Current View ➪ Notes List.

Because the Notes List view shows more of the Note text onscreen, you may find this view particularly useful in helping jog your memory as you try to locate a specific Note. Of course, you'll also have to scroll more using this view because each Note takes up so much more of your screen space. Because each Note uses the first line of the Note as its title, consider making the first line as short and to the point as possible. This way you can quickly find the Note you need without reading long passages of your Notes.

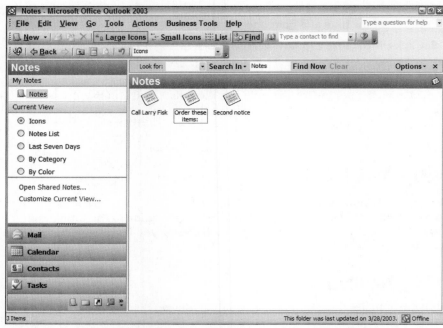

Figure 14-9: The Icon views display your Notes in alphabetical order.

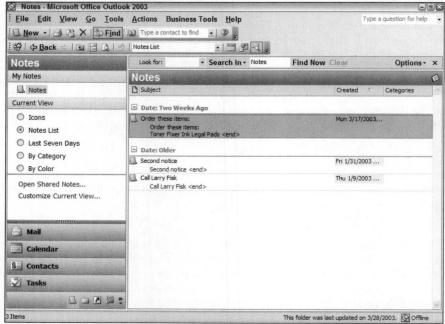

Figure 14-10: The Notes List view displays your Notes showing much of their text.

Using the Last Seven Days view

The Last Seven Days view is virtually identical to the Notes List view, except that the view will only include those Notes created in the past week. Figure 14-11 shows the Last Seven Days view. To display this view, select View ➪ Arrange By ➪ Current View ➪ Last Seven Days.

Note   As Figure 14-11 shows, Outlook displays the default Note that Outlook creates to explain Notes, even though this Note is clearly more than a week old. You can delete this Note if you want.

You'll find the Last Seven Days view very useful if you create a lot of Notes and need to find one of your more recent ones. You probably won't want to use this view as your default view, however, because you'll quickly lose track of important Notes once they have been around for over a week.

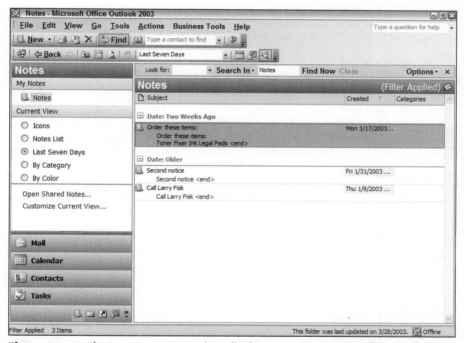

Figure 14-11: The Last Seven Days view displays your Notes created during the past week.

Using the By Category view

The By Category view organizes your Notes by the categories you assign to them. Figure 14-12 shows the By Category view. To display this view, select View ➪ Arrange By ➪ Current View ➪ By Category.

Note   If you open a Note and assign a category to the Note, Outlook does not apply the change until you close the Note. If you've opened a Note in the By Category view and then assigned a category to the Note, Outlook won't update the view until you close the Note.

In the By Category view, Outlook displays a title bar for each category that you have assigned to a Note. At the left edge of the title bar, you'll see a small box with a plus sign (+) or a minus sign (–). You can click the plus sign to expand the category display or the minus sign to collapse the category.

Using categories to organize your Notes can be an excellent way to make certain you can find related Notes. Because you can create your own categories, you can easily organize your Notes by project.

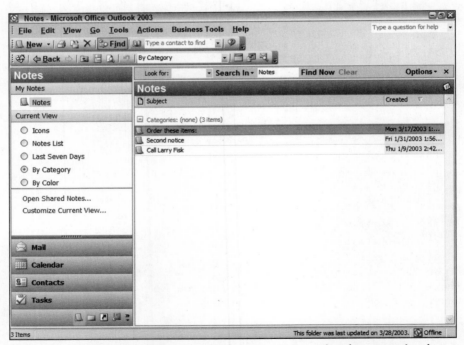

Figure 14-12: The By Category view displays your Notes using the categories that you assign.

Using the By Color view

The final Outlook Notes view is the By Color view, shown in Figure 14-13. In this view, your Notes are grouped using the five available Note colors. To display this view, select View ➪ Arrange By ➪ Current View ➪ By Color.

Similar to the By Category view, Outlook displays a title bar with a small box at the left edge for each color that you have assigned to a Note. You can click the plus sign to expand the color display or the minus sign to collapse the color.

With only five colors available, the By Color view offers far fewer organizational options than the By Category view. Still, if you only need a few Note groups, organizing them by color does offer one large advantage — the different colors are easy to see in any view or even when a Note is simply open on the Windows desktop.

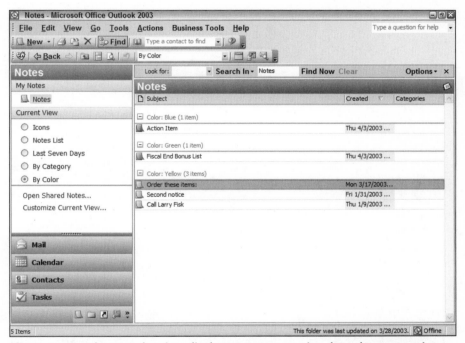

Figure 14-13: The By Color view displays your Notes using the colors you assign.

Summary

Outlook's Notes can be handy. As a replacement for those paper sticky notes, Outlook Notes offer several advantages. In this chapter, you learned how to create and edit Notes, how to use the available options, and how to use the Note views to help you organize your Notes.

In the next chapter, you learn how to use Outlook's Categories to help you organize your Outlook items.

✦　　✦　　✦

Organizing Information with Categories

✦ ✦ ✦ ✦

In This Chapter

Understanding categories and the Master Category List

Personalizing your category list

Assigning categories to Outlook items

Managing and sharing categories

Organizing data and views with categories

Using Entry Types

✦ ✦ ✦ ✦

Outlook is a tool that not only stores information, but also helps you locate and manage your information. With Outlook Categories, you can group related items together to help you complete a task or quickly access information. Categories can also be assigned to e-mail messages, tasks, contacts, and notes. In this chapter you learn how to use Outlook's Categories to make finding key information easier and faster.

Categories can be used to help you search for items using Outlook's Advanced Find feature. Let's say you add meetings to your Calendar, and assign categories called Business and Strategies to these meetings. You can use Advanced Find to search for all the items that have these categories. You also can use Outlook's Current View setting to display your Calendar items by Category, giving you a quick view of all your categorized events.

Understanding Categories and the Master Category List

Outlook Categories can be used to classify your information. For example, categories can be used to classify the types of meetings you have planned. A meeting with a client can be classified using the Business category, Key Customer category, or Suppliers category, depending on the situation. In addition, you can assign the meeting multiple categories to help you group this item with other related items.

Another feature of Outlook Categories is its Master Category List. This list enables you to manage the categories Outlook sets up by default, as well as allows you create your own categories. That means you can create categories called Sales Meeting, Athletic Events, or Kids Stuff, if you want. You can also delete some of the built-in categories to suit your personal and business needs.

To view the categories available in Outlook, perform the following steps:

1. Click an Outlook icon, such as the Calendar icon in the Navigation Pane.

2. Double-click a meeting or appointment in your calendar. If you do not have one listed, create one now. For example, to create an appointment, select File ⇨ New ⇨ Appointment and then complete the Appointment dialog box.

3. At the bottom of the appointment or meeting window, click the Categories button. The Categories dialog box displays, as shown in Figure 15-1.

Figure 15-1: Select categories for your meetings, appointments, and other Outlook items using the Categories dialog box.

When you have the Categories dialog box open, you can select one or multiple categories, deselect categories you've previously selected, or click the Master Category List to open the Master Category List dialog box, as shown in Figure 15-2.

Figure 15-2: The Master Category List provides you with options to create or delete Outlook Categories.

Personalizing Your Category List

When you want to personalize your category list, you simply create a new category name in the Master Category List, as follows:

1. Display the Categories dialog box, as shown in Figure 15-1.

2. Click the Master Category List button to display the Master Category List dialog box, as shown in Figure 15-2.

3. Type a new category name in the New category field.

4. Click the Add button.

5. Enter additional categories, if you want to add more categories.

6. Click OK. The Categories dialog box displays, including your new category.

Another way to add a category is to perform the following steps:

1. Display the Categories dialog box, as shown in Figure 15-1.

2. Type a new category name in the Item(s) belong to these categories field.

3. Click the Add to List button. The category is added to the Available categories list.

4. Click OK.

Assigning Categories to Outlook Items

To make categories useful, you must assign them to your Outlook items. For example, when you set up a meeting with someone, take a few moments to assign a category or multiple categories to the meeting item so your future searches on that item are more efficient. In addition, if you use the View ➪ Arrange By ➪ Current View ➪ By Category view, you can see all your Calendar events organized by categories. This is helpful when you want to see all your Business items, Personal items, and so on.

To assign categories to Outlook items, perform the following steps:

1. Use the Outlook Shortcut Bar to select the type of item you want to categorize. For example, to assign a category to a task, click the Task icon.

2. Select an item.

3. Choose Edit ➪ Categories, as shown in Figure 15-3, to display the Categories dialog box.

Figure 15-3: Use the Edit ➪ Categories command to assign Categories to an item, such as a Task.

4. Select the categories you want to assign to this item.

5. Click OK.

The categories are assigned to the item you selected. To see which categories are assigned to your Task, double-click the task and then look at the bottom of the window next to the Categories button, as shown in Figure 15-4.

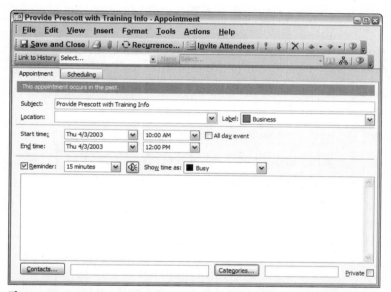

Figure 15-4: You can see your category assignments by looking in the Categories field.

If you already have an item opened, such as a contact, use the following steps to assign categories to the item:

1. Click the Categories button, as shown in Figure 15-5, to display the Categories dialog box.

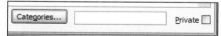

Figure 15-5: Click the Categories button to open the Categories dialog box.

2. Select the categories you want to assign to the item.

    3. Click OK.

    4. Click Save and Close.

Managing Categories

Categories can be added to or deleted from the Master Category List. When you remove a category from the Master Category List, the category listing will still remain if you applied the category to an item. For instance, if you apply a category called "Sales Meeting" to an appointment with Eric Rigals and then delete the Sales Meeting category from the Master Category List, Sales Meeting will still be a category for the Eric Rigals' appointment. Outlook also lets you reset the Master Category List to include only those default categories set up when you initially installed Outlook.

To delete a category, perform the following procedure:

    1. Display the Categories dialog box, as shown in Figure 15-1.

    2. Click the Master Category List button to display the Master Category List dialog box, as shown in Figure 15-2.

    3. Select the category you want to delete.

    4. Click the Delete button.

    5. Click the OK button.

When you delete a category, you do not have an opportunity to undelete it. If you delete one by mistake, simply add a new category and name it the same as the one you mistakenly deleted.

To reset the Master Category List to its original list, perform the following procedure:

    1. Open the Master Category List.

    2. Click the Reset button. A message telling you the list will be reset appears, as shown in Figure 15-6. Custom categories already applied to items will remain with those items. You just won't see them listed in the Master Category List.

Figure 15-6: Click OK to reset your Master Category List to the original list.

3. Click OK.

4. Click OK to close the Categories dialog box.

One important note to keep in mind about categories and the Master Category List is that all categories assigned to your Outlook items are not necessarily displayed in the Master Category List. This list shows only those categories you specifically place in the list. Other categories, which you may assign to an item or that another user may assign to an item you receive from him or her, may not show up in your Master Category List. For example, let's say you receive an e-mail message from Bob about an invoice he sent you last month. Before he sent you the message, Bob assigned a category called "Invoice Prompts" to the message. This is a category he uses frequently and has customized Outlook to include as a Master Category List item. When you receive the message from Bob, the Invoice Prompts category is still assigned to the message, but you probably don't have this same category in your Master Category List. However, when you perform a search or display items using the By Category view option, you will see Invoice Prompts as a category.

Organizing Data and Views with Categories

When you assign Outlook items to categories, you have the option of viewing data using the By Category view. The By Category view is helpful when you want to view Outlook items by which category they are assigned. When you use this view, items assigned multiple categories appear under each of the category headings. For example, if you assign Business and Key Customer to a meeting called Customer Appreciation Get Together, Outlook displays the meeting twice — once under the Business category heading, and another time under the Key Customer category heading.

To view Calendar items with the By Category view, use the following steps:

1. Click the Calendar icon on the Navigation Pane to display your calendar.

2. Choose View ⇨ Arrange By ⇨ Current View ⇨ By Category to display your items by category, as shown in Figure 15-7. You can also click the Current View box in the toolbar and select By Category.

Figure 15-7: Use By Category to get a quick view of your Outlook items' assigned categories.

A gray box is located to the left of each Categories heading. If all the items for a category are displayed, this is called the expanded view and the gray box will have a minus sign in it. Click the minus sign to collapse the view and change the minus sign to a plus sign. Simply click the plus sign to expand the list again. This is handy when your list of items is several screens long and you want to view just a category or two at a time.

Although you can view items using the By Category view without categories assigned, the view is not very helpful because all your items will appear under a listing called "none."

When you have your items in the By Category view, you can quickly assign different or more categories to individual or multiple items. To assign categories to multiple items, follow these steps:

1. Select multiple items. Hold down the Shift key and click items to select a range of items. Alternatively, hold down the Ctrl key to select noncontiguous items.

2. Right-click to open a context-sensitive menu, and choose Categories, as shown in Figure 15-8.

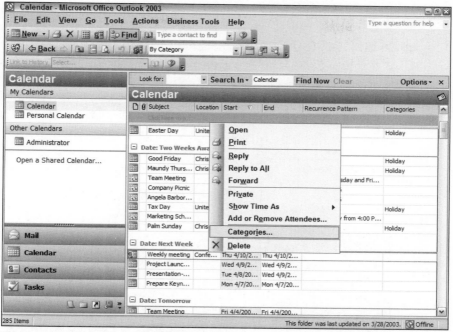

Figure 15-8: The Categories dialog box

3. Select the categories for the items.

4. Click OK.

Printing Category Items

Outlook provides two print styles for printing your items from the By Category view: Table Style and Memo Style. Table Style prints all the information onscreen, such as the Subject, Location, Start, End, Recurrence Pattern, and Categories fields. You can choose to print all the rows, or just selected rows. Memo Style prints selected items on a single page.

To print your items in Memo Style, perform the following steps:

1. Open an Outlook item, such as your Calendar items, in the By Category view.

2. Select the items you want to print, as shown in Figure 15-9.

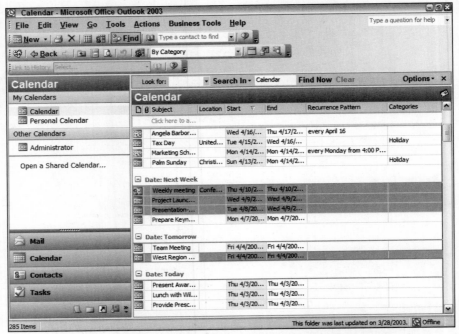

Figure 15-9: You can select multiple items to print with the Memo Style print option.

3. Choose File ➪ Print to display the Print dialog box as shown in Figure 15-10.

4. Select Memo Style.

5. If you want to print file attachments associated with an item, such as a Word document attached to an e-mail, select the Print attached files options.

6. Click OK.

Each item is printed on a separate page with all the information associated with that item.

To print items in Table Style, perform the following steps:

1. Open your Calendar items in the By Category view.

2. Adjust the columns in the view so the information you want to print is displayed.

3. Choose File ➪ Print to display the Print dialog box.

4. Select Table Style.

5. Click OK.

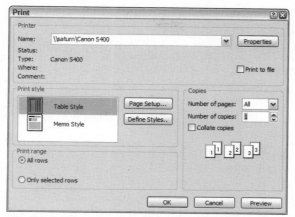

Figure 15-10: Use the Table Style or Memo Style print styles to print your items from the By Category view.

Tip   If you want to print only specific rows, select the rows and then choose File ➪ Print. In the Print dialog box select Only selected rows and then click OK.

Outlook prints the view just as it shows onscreen.

Sharing Categories

If you work in a workgroup, team, or other organized group, you may want to have a common set of categories from which you can all choose. To do this, you must share your Outlook Categories with the other users in your team or group. There are two ways to do this: an advanced method that requires you to use the Microsoft Windows Registry to output the categories, or use Outlook e-mail to collect the categories you want to share and then send your team members the e-mail. Using Outlook e-mail is much easier to perform, and does not require you to edit the Registry.

To share categories using e-mail, perform the following steps:

1. Start Outlook and create a new mail message, as shown in Figure 15-11.

2. Click the Options button on the toolbar to display the Message Options dialog box, as shown in Figure 15-12.

3. Click the Categories button to display the Categories dialog box.

4. Select the categories you want to share. You do not have to share categories that are common to all Outlook installations, such as Business, Competition, and so on.

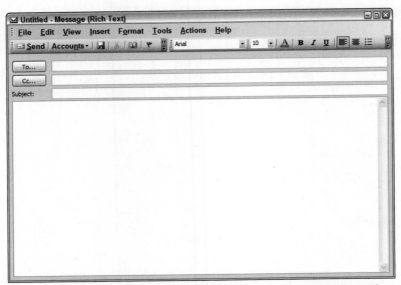

Figure 15-11: Start a new mail message to share your categories with other users.

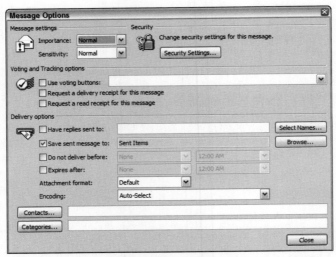

Figure 15-12: Use the Message Options dialog box to select the Categories you want to share.

5. Click OK.

6. Click Close to close the Message Options dialog box.

7. Address the message to your recipients, and add a subject to the message.

8. In the message body, explain to the recipients that the message includes categories you would like to share with them. Also include how they should save the categories to their system.

9. Send the message.

Upon receipt, the user needs to open the message, and Outlook automatically adds the categories to the user's list, as shown in Figure 15-13. They can choose Edit ⇨ Categories to see the Categories dialog box.

Figure 15-13: The shared custom categories appear in the Categories dialog box.

If you want to share the categories using the Registry, perform the following steps. When you use this method, the recipient's entire Master Categories List (MCL) is overwritten by yours. Any customized categories the recipient has made to their MCL will be lost.

Note Be advised that working in the Registry can be detrimental to your computer and Windows. One wrong edit or deletion can result in Windows not working correctly. Do these steps only if you are an experienced Windows user and have worked with the Registry before. Be sure to back up the Registry files before doing these steps.

1. Choose Start ➪ Run and then type REGEDIT.

2. Press Enter or click OK to start the Registry Editor.

3. Locate the following Registry subkey, as shown in Figure 15-14:

   ```
   HKEY_CURRENT_USER\Software\Microsoft\Office\11.0\Outlook\
   Categories
   ```

4. Click the Categories folder.

5. Choose Registry ➪ Export Registry File (or File ➪ Export if using Windows XP).

6. Select a location to store the file and type a name for the exported file, such as Categories, as shown in Figure 15-15.

7. Click Save.

8. Open a new e-mail message, address the message, and attach the Categories.reg file to message.

9. Send the message and attached file.

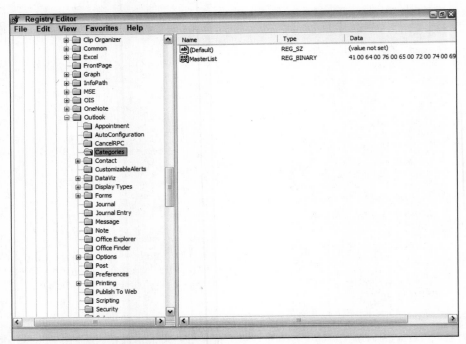

Figure 15-14: Locate this Registry subkey.

Figure 15-15: Select a location and file name for the exported Categories Registry information.

When the recipients receive the message, instruct them to save the attached .reg file to their hard disk and then to double-click the file. This automatically imports the categories into their Master Category List.

Summary

This chapter showed you how to create, manage, and share Outlook Categories. It also showed you how to print your Outlook items when viewing them using the By Category view. Finally, you were shown two ways to share your categories with other users.

In the next chapter, you learn how to use Outlook to view newsgroups on the Internet. You see also how you can use Outlook to search through the thousands of newsgroups to find topics of interest.

✦   ✦   ✦

Using Outlook Newsreader

◆ ◆ ◆ ◆

In This Chapter

Understanding newsgroups

Preparing to use newsgroups

Viewing newsgroup messages

Posting to newsgroups

◆ ◆ ◆ ◆

Outlook is a tool that manages information. In this chapter, you learn about using a newsreader tool called Microsoft Outlook Newsreader to manage information that you can find in newsgroups on the Internet. You may not even realize that this vast source of information exists, but even if you do, you probably aren't aware that you can use Outlook Newsreader to access it.

Those familiar with Microsoft's free newsreader and e-mail message program, Outlook Express, will see lots of similarities between it and Outlook Newsreader. In fact, they are identical products, except for the title bars.

What Is a Newsgroup?

Newsgroups are a part of the Internet, but you may not even be aware they exist. They are places where people get together online to share all sorts of information. In most newsgroups, people post questions and comments, and other people join in with an answer, another question, or a comment. You can often learn a substantial amount just by looking at the messages in a newsgroup, even if you don't post any messages yourself.

Note
Newsgroups contain a wide range of information, although not all of the information posted in newsgroups is necessarily accurate. (This applies to the Web as a whole, by the way.) While most people who post messages in newsgroups are probably trying to provide useful information, it's likely that you'll also encounter people who get their kicks by intentionally misleading people whenever possible. You must be the ultimate judge of the accuracy of the information that you receive from newsgroups. If possible, try to verify important information using a different source before relying on possibly suspect advice from someone in a newsgroup.

Tens of thousands of newsgroups exist on the Internet. No one can give an accurate count of the newsgroups because the number is constantly changing. You'll find that there are several newsgroups devoted to almost any subject that might interest you. Each newsgroup has its own unique flavor that results from the blend of characters that frequent the newsgroup. If you don't care for one newsgroup, you can probably find a different one that better suits your needs.

Unfortunately, newsgroups also have some unpleasant aspects:

✦ Most newsgroups that are not moderated — meaning that there is someone in charge who monitors the messages that are posted — seem to be heavily infested with ads for get-rich-quick schemes and pornography.

✦ Insults, commonly known as flames, are a common form of communication in many newsgroups. Some people seem to feel that the anonymous nature of the Internet makes it perfectly acceptable to be an absolute bore. These people often use language in newsgroups that they would never use in normal conversation. Unfortunately, there isn't a whole lot you can do except to ignore the flames and hope that the bozos will eventually grow up.

✦ Allowing your e-mail address to appear in newsgroups is almost like asking to have your Inbox swamped with spam — junk e-mail messages. Many junk mailers use special programs that search through newsgroup postings looking for e-mail addresses. The garbage they send out typically has nothing to do with the newsgroup subject; they're just hoping that a few of the hundreds of thousands of junk e-mail messages they send out will produce a positive response.

Tip One way to prevent at least some of the junk e-mail messages from reaching your Inbox is to set up and use a separate online e-mail account when you need to post messages in newsgroups. For example, you can get a free online e-mail account from Microsoft by going to www.hotmail.com or by clicking the Hotmail link that appears on the Microsoft Web site. Other free e-mail accounts are available from AOL, Yahoo!, Infoseek, Lycos, and a host of others.

With all the negative things that I've said about newsgroups, you may be wondering why anyone would ever bother visiting them. There are several reasons why you may find newsgroups useful:

✦ Newsgroups are often the best source of information you can find about a subject. For example, a manufacturer's tech support department may deny that a piece of hardware or software has any problems. You've probably heard "you're the only person who's reported that problem" just a few too many times. In a newsgroup, you may find the solution to the problem that the manufacturer says doesn't exist.

✦ Newsgroups can be great places to see what people are thinking about a subject. Where else can you see the thoughts and opinions of people from around the globe so quickly and without government intervention or censorship?

✦ Newsgroups may provide the only source of information about certain subjects. If you want to know where you can find a front axle for a 1939 Ford 9N tractor or how to prepare lutefisk, you'll probably have better luck in the newsgroups than just about anywhere else.

✦ A newsgroup may be the only place where you can find other people who are interested in many obscure subjects. Because newsgroups tend to draw people with deep interest in their subjects, you'll probably find the real experts if you frequent the right newsgroups.

Preparing to Use Newsgroups

Although newsgroup messages bear some resemblance to the e-mail messages that appear in your Outlook Inbox, there are a number of important differences between the two types of messages. Newsgroup messages aren't generally sent to your e-mail address; rather, those messages are posted to a message board so that anyone can read the messages and any replies. Also, the sheer volume of newsgroup messages means that you have to deal with those messages differently than you deal with your e-mail messages.

Instead of downloading all the newsgroup messages to your computer, you first download the list of available newsgroups. Next, pick the newsgroups that look interesting and download a group of message headers from that group. Finally, select individual messages that you want to read and download those messages. Although this may sound like a cumbersome set of steps, it's the only practical method of dealing with the gigabytes of newsgroup messages. Even the fastest modem would never be able to download every newsgroup message — new messages are always being posted faster than you would be able to download them.

Setting up newsgroups

The first time you access newsgroups, you'll need to download the entire list of newsgroup names. Depending on the speed of your connection, this process could take as long as 15 minutes. After the first time you have downloaded the newsgroup list, you won't need to download the whole list again, so future newsgroup access will be much faster than the first time you connect.

You can use Outlook Express Newsgroup Reader to provide you with access to the newsgroups. You won't really notice too much difference except that you'll have a second program running alongside Outlook.

Just as you must specify which mail server Outlook should access to send and receive e-mail messages, you'll need to specify which news server to access for newsgroups. Your ISP will provide this information. The server you want will be called either the news server or the NNTP serve.

To start Outlook Newsreader, add a toolbar button to Outlook, as shown in the following steps:

1. Choose View ➪ Toolbars ➪ Customize.

2. On the Commands tab, click Go in the Categories list and then News in the Commands list as shown in Figure 16-1.

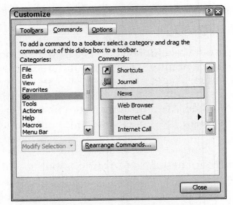

Figure 16-1: Drag and drop the News command on an Outlook toolbar to allow you to quickly launch Microsoft Outlook Newsreader.

3. Drag News to one of the Outlook toolbars and release.

4. Click the News icon to start Outlook Newsreader, as shown in Figure 16-2.

5. You should be prompted to connect to the Internet. Connect to the Internet. If already on the Internet, simply go to step 6.

6. Click the Set up a Newsgroups account link in the right pane of the Newsreader to display the Internet Connection Wizard as shown in Figure 16-3.

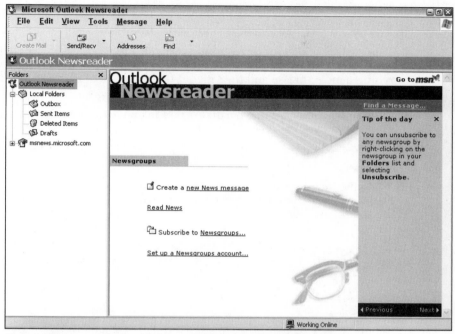

Figure 16-2: Use the Outlook Newsreader to access newsgroups.

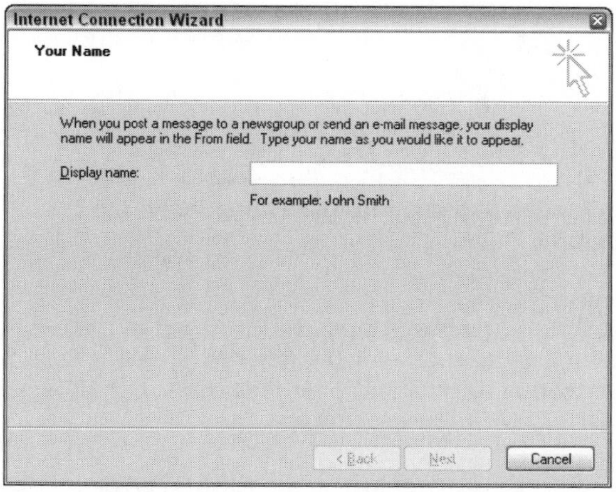

Figure 16-3: Use the Internet Connection Wizard to set up a newsgroup account.

7. Type your name in the Display Name box. Click Next.

8. Type an Internet e-mail address for you. Click Next.

9. Type the name of your newsgroup server, or use a public server such as `msnews.microsoft.com`. If you need to log on to your server, click My server requires me to log on and then fill out the subsequent username and password boxes after you click Next. Click Next now.

10. Click Finish. You are shown a dialog box asking if you want to download newsgroups from your server.

11. Click Yes to continue. If this is your first time accessing the news server, you will have to wait while the newsgroup names are downloaded.

12. When the Newsgroup Subscriptions dialog box is displayed, as shown in Figure 16-4, wait until your modem indicator lights in the System Tray stop flashing and the newsgroup names are displayed. You are then ready to continue.

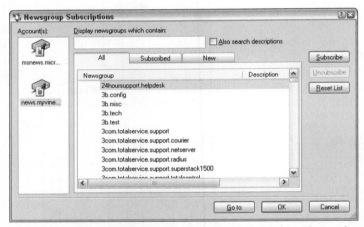

Figure 16-4: The Newsgroup Subscriptions dialog box shows the list of available newsgroups.

At this point, you can subscribe to newsgroups, as described in the next section, or skip ahead to the following section on viewing newsgroup messages. You don't have to subscribe to newsgroups to read and post messages, but subscribing may make it easier to access your favorite newsgroups.

Subscribing to newsgroups

Subscribing to newsgroups offers you one big advantage — you don't have to search through the thousands of available newsgroups to find your favorites. When you subscribe to a newsgroup, that newsgroup appears on your folder list in the Outlook Newsreader. You can then go directly to that newsgroup by selecting it from the folder list.

To subscribe to a newsgroup, follow these steps:

1. Select the newsgroup that interests you in the Newsgroup Subscriptions dialog box, shown in Figure 16-5. To help narrow the range of choices available to you, click in the Display newsgroups which contain box and then type a keyword for the type of newsgroup to which you would like to subscribe.

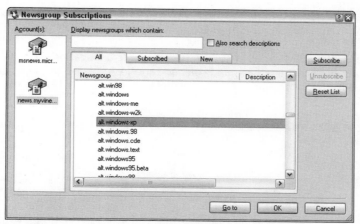

Figure 16-5: Choose the newsgroups to which you wish to subscribe.

2. Click the Subscribe button to add the newsgroup to your subscriptions.

3. Click the Subscribed tab to view the list of newsgroups to which you've subscribed, as shown in Figure 16-6.

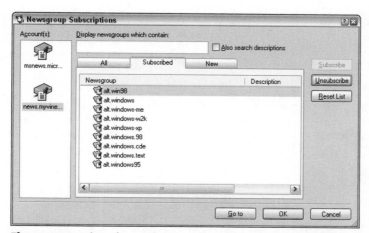

Figure 16-6: View the newsgroups to which you have subscribed on the Subscribed tab.

4. If you want to subscribe to additional newsgroups, return to the All tab and repeat steps 1 and 2.

5. If you want to remove a newsgroup from your subscription list, select the newsgroup on the Subscribed tab and then click the Unsubscribe button.

6. Click the OK button to close the Newsgroup Subscriptions dialog box. Your subscribed newsgroups will appear in the folder list, as shown in Figure 16-7.

After you've subscribed to a newsgroup, you can view the messages contained in that newsgroup by selecting the newsgroup in the Outlook Newsreader folder list.

Note   Subscribing to a newsgroup is not like subscribing to a magazine. Newsgroup subscriptions don't cost anything, and you can cancel your subscriptions at any time. No message is sent to anyone indicating that you've subscribed to the newsgroup.

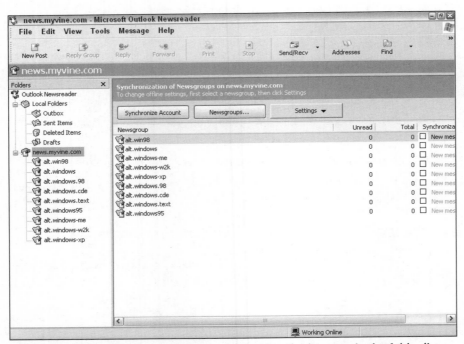

Figure 16-7: Newsgroups to which you have subscribed appear in the folder list for easy access.

Viewing Newsgroup Messages

The method you use to view newsgroup messages varies depending on whether you've subscribed to the newsgroup. If you've subscribed to a newsgroup, you can simply select the newsgroup in the folder list. Viewing messages in nonsubscribed newsgroups is only slightly more complicated, as you see in the following section.

Viewing messages

To view the messages in newsgroups to which you've subscribed, select the news-group in the Outlook Newsreader folder list, shown in Figure 16-8. Click the message you want to read in the upper pane, and the message text will appear in the lower pane. You can also show the viewing pane to the right of the message header pane by choosing View ➪ Layout and selecting Beside messages in the Window Layout Properties dialog box. Click OK.

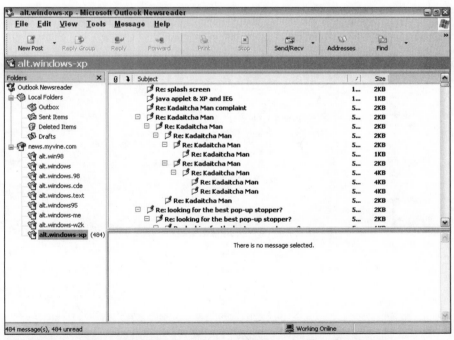

Figure 16-8: Select a subscribed newsgroup to view the list of messages.

Notice the list of messages includes a column at the far right that indicates the size of the message. Some messages, especially those that include attachments, can be quite large. If you select a very large message, the Outlook Newsreader may seem to freeze for a few minutes while the message is downloaded. Watch the modem indicators in the System Tray to see all of the activity that is occurring.

To view the message in any newsgroup, even those to which you are not subscribed, follow these steps:

1. Click the Newsgroups button on the Toolbar to display the Newsgroup Subscriptions dialog box.

2. If necessary, confirm that you wish to connect.

3. Select the newsgroup, as shown in Figure 16-9. Or click a subscribed to newsgroup in the Folders pane.

4. Click the Go to button to download the message headers for the newsgroup.

5. Select a message to download and read the message.

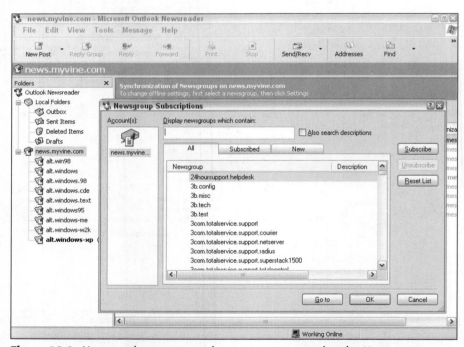

Figure 16-9: You can view messages in any newsgroup using the Newsgroup Subscriptions dialog box.

If you have downloaded the message headers for a newsgroup but haven't subscribed to the newsgroup, you'll see a message similar to the one in Figure 16-10 when you select a different folder in the Outlook Newsreader Folder list. You can choose to subscribe to the newsgroup by selecting Yes. Select No if the newsgroup turns out to be one that doesn't interest you enough to return to it.

Figure 16-10: You can quickly subscribe to a newsgroup after you've had a look at the messages.

Filtering messages

One of the biggest problems you're likely to encounter in newsgroups is that many — if not most — newsgroup messages don't really apply to the newsgroup topic. You may find messages that are promoting get-rich-quick schemes, advertisements for Web sites offering pornographic content, bogus stock market advice, and many other off-topic messages. Because of this, it may be difficult to sort through and find the message that you really want to read.

The Outlook Newsreader provides you with several ways to filter newsgroup messages. You can create a quick filter that simply deletes messages from specified people. You can also create a more complex filter that processes newsgroup messages based on content.

Note   No rule that you can create for filtering newsgroup messages can possibly be 100 percent effective in blocking every message that you might find offensive. You must also use a little common sense and realize that if you are truly offended by the messages that appear in certain newsgroups, you may be better off avoiding those newsgroups entirely. This also applies to rules that you might create to prevent family members from seeing certain types of messages — ultimately you must take personal responsibility for what you or your family views on the Internet. The Internet was never intended as a children's playground.

To create a rule for filtering newsgroup messages, follow these steps:

1. Select Tools ➪ Message Rules ➪ News to open the New News Rule dialog box, shown in Figure 16-11.

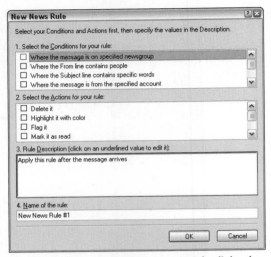

Figure 16-11: Use the New News Rule dialog box to create rules for filtering newsgroup messages.

2. In the Select the Conditions for your rule box, select the conditions that you want to trigger this rule. You can select more than one condition, but remember that messages must meet every condition before the filter will apply. It may be better to create additional rules that use narrow sets of conditions than to try to create a multiple-condition rule that may fail if one condition cannot be met.

3. In the Select the Actions for your rule box, select the actions you want to occur when a message meets the filtering conditions. In most cases, a single action will be adequate.

4. After you have added all the conditions and actions, click each of the underlined values in the Rule Description box to edit the value, as shown in Figure 16-12.

5. Click OK to close the dialog box that you use to specify the values. The name of this dialog box may vary according to the type of value you are entering.

6. Continue replacing each of the underlined values until you have completed the rule. Depending on the complexity of your rule, you may have several values to replace.

7. Type a descriptive name for the rule in the Name of the rule text box. It's probably not a good idea to accept the default name, because you'll want to be able to locate specific rules if you later decide they need modifications.

8. Click OK to close the New News Rule dialog box and display the Message Rules dialog box, shown in Figure 16-13.

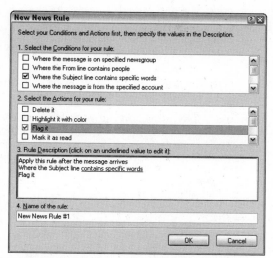

Figure 16-12: Edit the underlined values to specify the filter values.

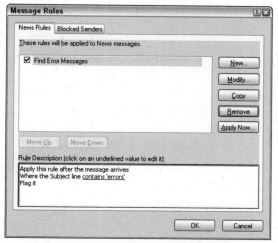

Figure 16-13: Use the Message Rules dialog box to apply your rules.

9. If you have more than one rule defined, you can use the Move Up and Move Down buttons to change the order in which the rules are applied. The order in which rules are applied can be very important. Rules nearer to the top of the list are applied before those lower on the list. Make certain that the rules appear in order of most important to least important.

10. To temporarily disable a rule without removing it, remove the check from the check box to the left of the rule name.

11. To add an additional rule, click the New button and repeat the steps for creating a new rule.

12. To modify an existing rule, select the rule and click the Modify button. Again, follow the same steps you used to create a new rule.

13. Click the Apply Now button to display the Apply News Rules Now dialog box, shown in Figure 16-14. You'll use this dialog box to select rules that you want to apply immediately to specified folders.

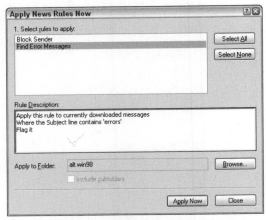

Figure 16-14: Use the Apply News Rules Now dialog box to specify where to apply your rules.

14. Select the rules that you want to apply.

15. Select the newsgroup folder that you want to filter by clicking the Browse button and then choosing the folder.

16. Click OK to return to the Apply News Rules Now dialog box.

17. Click Apply Now to filter the messages in the specified folder using the selected rules.

18. Click OK to confirm that the rules were applied.

19. If you want to filter additional newsgroup folders, use the Browse button and the Apply Now button to apply the rules to those folders.

20. Select Close to close the Apply News Rules Now dialog box.

21. Click OK to close the Message Rules dialog box.

Rules that you create to filter newsgroup messages will apply to future messages that you download from the newsgroups. Unless you use the Apply News Rules Now dialog box, your rules will not be applied to existing messages. When you remove a filter, the messages that are currently stored in the newsgroup server will be available to you. Old, deleted messages will no longer be available to you.

You can also create a quick rule to block messages from a specific sender. This will place the sender on the blocked senders list, and prevent any future messages from that sender from reaching you.

To add someone to the blocked senders list, follow these steps:

1. Open a newsgroup folder that contains a message from the sender you want to block.

2. Select a message from that sender.

3. Select Message ⇨ Block Sender to display the Outlook Express window shown in Figure 16-15. Outlook Express automatically adds the selected sender to the blocked senders list.

Figure 16-15: You can block messages from specific e-mail addresses.

4. Click Yes to remove all messages from the sender from the current newsgroup, or click No to have the sender's messages blocked the next time he or she posts a message to the newsgroup.

The blocked senders list applies only to future messages. Any existing messages that you have downloaded already will not be filtered.

Note Use the blocked senders list to avoid receiving messages from people who have decided to engage in a flame war with you. Flame wars are heated discussions between newsgroup members ("posters"). The best way to deal with people who are attempting to incite you is to simply ignore them. Sending a heated reply generally succeeds only in escalating the conflict.

If you create rules for filtering the newsgroup messages, it's a good idea to test those rules by using the Apply News Rules Now dialog box. It's also a good idea to keep your rules as simple as possible. Rules that are too restrictive can prevent you from seeing important messages that just happen to fit the filter. It's usually better to allow a few items you don't want to slip by your rules than to miss things simply because your rules are too extreme.

You also can remove a sender from your blocked senders list. You may want to do this after a period of time to let the sender cool off or change his posting habits. When you remove the sender from the blocked sender list, Outlook Express will begin to download messages from that sender again.

To remove a sender from your list of blocked senders, follow these steps:

1. Select Tools ⇨ Message Rules ⇨ Blocked Senders List to display the Blocked Senders tab of the Message Rules dialog box, as shown in Figure 16-16.

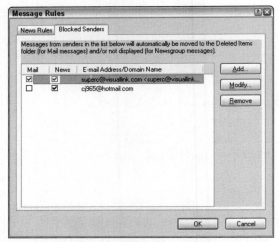

Figure 16-16: You can remove a sender's name from the Blocked Senders List.

2. Select a sender from the list.

3. Click Remove.

4. Click Yes when asked if you are sure you want to remove the selected sender.

5. Click OK to close the Message Rules dialog box.

Following message threads

Very few newsgroup messages are useful by themselves. What makes newsgroup messages useful and interesting are the answers, comments, and questions posted in response to the original message. This group of related messages is known as a message thread. By following a message thread, you can find out much more about the subject than you would from any single message.

Figure 16-17 shows a typical newsgroup with a number of different messages that you can read. Notice some messages include a small box at the left edge of the Subject column. This box indicates that the message is a thread, and that there are replies to the message. If the box contains a plus sign (+), as do several in the figure, you can click the box to expand the list of replies. If the box contains a minus sign (–), the message thread has been expanded so that you can see the replies.

You can view a newsgroup message by selecting it from the list of messages. Viewing a message thread works the same way — you simply select the message that you wish to view. The difference between threaded and nonthreaded messages is minor. As Figure 16-17 shows, messages are normally sorted by the date they were sent. This default sort order would, however, make it very hard for you to follow a message thread. That's why newsgroup messages use message threads — to make it easier for you to see replies.

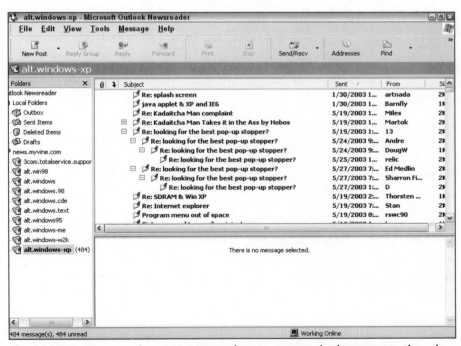

Figure 16-17: You can view messages and any responses in the message thread.

Although it is easy to see the related messages in an existing message thread, you'll probably see many interesting newsgroup messages that have not yet generated a full range of responses. For example, suppose you visit a newsgroup and discover that someone has just posted a very interesting question. You want to know what responses the question generates. You could simply visit the newsgroup regularly and search for the original question to see if there are any replies, but you would have to remember each of the questions that interested you so that you could do your search. Fortunately, the Outlook Newsreader provides a better way to keep track of an ongoing conversation.

As Figure 16-18 shows, you can have the Outlook Newsreader watch for new messages in a message thread. Simply select the message that you want to track and then select Message ⇨ Watch Conversation. The Outlook Newsreader colors the message heading in red to indicate that the message is being watched for you. It also adds a new column to the left and shows a pair of eyeglasses indicating those threads you want to keep an eye on. When new messages arrive in the thread, you'll be notified so that you can read those responses.

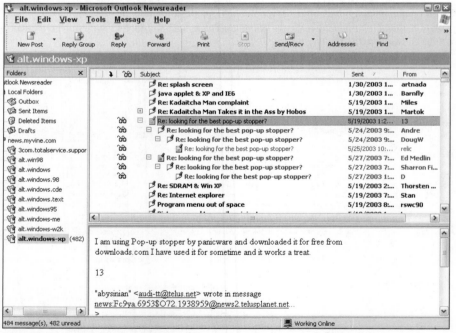

Figure 16-18: You can watch messages to see when responses appear in the message thread.

Viewing the new messages

If you've found an interesting newsgroup, you probably want to update the message headers for that newsgroup often enough so that you can see what new messages have been posted. You can, of course, view the current message headers in any newsgroup by choosing the newsgroup in the Newsgroup Subscriptions dialog box and then clicking the Go to button. If you haven't subscribed to a newsgroup, that is the only way to update the messages for the newsgroup. If you have subscribed to a newsgroup, there's an easier way to update the messages. You can have the Outlook Newsreader synchronize — update — newsgroups to which you've subscribed.

To synchronize the messages for your subscribed newsgroups, follow these steps:

1. Click the news server folder in the Outlook Newsreader folder list.

2. To change the synchronization settings for a newsgroup, select the newsgroup and then click the Settings button, as shown in Figure 16-19. The All Messages option is used when you want to download every message in a newsgroup. Use this setting the first time you synchronize with a newsgroup. The New Messages Only option is used when you want to get only messages new to the group since you last synchronized with it. The Message Headers option is used to download just the header information for each message.

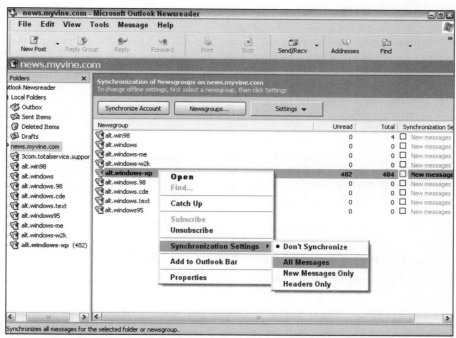

Figure 16-19: Choose the settings for updating your newsgroup subscriptions.

3. Choose the method for updating the messages for this newsgroup.

4. Click the Synchronize Account button to update each of your newsgroup subscriptions according to your selected settings. If you aren't currently connected to the Internet, you may have to respond to prompts to connect. After each newsgroup is synchronized, you can click on it in the left pane to view its messages.

Subscribing to newsgroups and then synchronizing the messages in those newsgroups is one of the best ways to keep track of new messages that may interest you. When you add in the ability to watch certain conversations, you can be ensured of knowing about what's new in your favorite newsgroups.

Posting to Newsgroups

Eventually, you'll decide that simply reading the messages in your favorite newsgroups is interesting, but that it would be even more fun to add your own messages. Adding a message to a newsgroup is known as posting a message to the newsgroup. Posting newsgroup messages isn't much different from creating and sending e-mail messages, except that the message recipient is the newsgroup rather than an individual.

Different newsgroups have different customs. As a newcomer—newbie—to a newsgroup, it's always a good idea to hang around for a while to learn those customs before you blindly post a message that the newsgroup regulars view as stupid or lazy. For example, if you barge in and post a message such as, "I don't have the time to read the old messages so can someone tell me in detail how I should set up my computer to make my software and hardware work correctly," don't expect a friendly response. The people who visit newsgroups and offer their help to others are generally nice people, but they don't have to be nice to you—especially if you act like a world-class boor!

Posting a new message and replying to an existing message are virtually the same. When you post a new message, you need to come up with a descriptive subject line that will make people want to read your message, but otherwise there's no important difference between a new posting and a response.

To post a new message, follow these steps:

1. Open the newsgroup where you want to post the message.

2. If you are replying to a message, select the message for which you want to post your reply.

3. Click the Reply Group button to post a reply or the New Post button to begin a new message subject. Figure 16-20 shows the New Message form that appears when you click the New Post button.

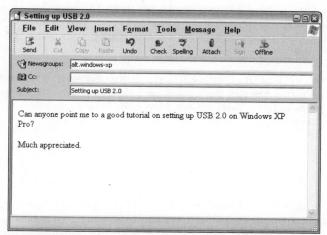

Figure 16-20: Posting newsgroup messages is very similar to creating and sending e-mail.

4. If this is a new message, enter a subject line. Try to be as brief and descriptive as possible. Remember that many people will only see the first few words of the subject line.

Note

Although the New Message form does allow you to specify more than one newsgroup for posting your message, such cross-posting is generally frowned upon. If you can't take the time to locate the correct newsgroup for your posting and simply try the shotgun approach, you won't be welcomed in most newsgroups.

5. Enter the text of your message. If you are replying to an earlier message, it is common to include enough of the text of the previous message so that people can understand your response without opening the earlier post.

6. Click the Spelling button to check your spelling after you've finished typing your message.

7. If you want to include a file attachment, click the Attach button and then choose the file.

8. If you want to use a digital ID so that people who read the message can be sure it was you who sent the message, click the Sign button and then choose the digital certificate you wish to use. See Chapter 8 for more information on using certificates.

9. When you are done creating the message, click the Send button.

10. You may have to click the Send/Recv button to post the message. If you are working offline — that is, not connected to the Internet — you will need to connect to post your message.

Although you may see a quick response to new postings if a newsgroup is particularly active, it's more likely that you'll have to wait a day or two in most newsgroups. While you're waiting, you may want to search for existing postings that address the same or a similar subject.

Note   Be careful about the type of information that you post in newsgroups. Remember that there is no guarantee that the people who read newsgroup messages have your best interests at heart. Posting your address or phone number is never considered to be a wise idea.

Summary

Newsgroups can be an interesting and useful part of the Internet. The Outlook Newsreader makes it possible for you to read and post your own messages to those newsgroups. In this chapter, you learned how to use the Outlook Newsreader to access the tens of thousands of newsgroups, and how to subscribe to your favorite newsgroups.

The next chapter shows you how to make Outlook work more effectively for you by customizing the program to meet your needs.

✦   ✦   ✦

Getting the Most Out of Outlook 2003

P A R T

IV

◆ ◆ ◆ ◆

In This Part

Chapter 17
Customizing Outlook
2003

Chapter 18
Using Folders
Effectively

Chapter 19
Integrating with
Other Applications

Chapter 20
Delegating Tasks to
an Assistant

Chapter 21
Using Windows
SharePoint Services

◆ ◆ ◆ ◆

Customizing Outlook 2003

In This Chapter

Customizing Outlook

Organizing your
Outlook folders

Using Web
integration

By now, you've probably used Outlook enough to discover that there are a number of little things about the program that you would change if you could: customizing views, changing message formats, and setting the types of holidays you want displayed. In this chapter, you learn how to make many of those changes and customize Outlook so that it suits your needs a bit better.

In addition to changing the appearance of Outlook, some changes that you can make may have more fundamental effects on your use of Outlook. In this chapter, you see how you can make some of these types of changes, such as taking charge of the security settings so that you won't have to worry about an e-mail macro virus damaging your computer.

Customizing Outlook

Most of the changes you can make to Outlook primarily affect Outlook's appearance. That is, even if you change the number of days of calendar events that are displayed in the Outlook Today folder, Outlook won't really work any differently than with the default settings. It's true that you'll see a different number of days in the display, but Outlook will still remember all the events that are outside the display range. As a result, you don't have to be afraid to experiment. If you don't care for the results, you can always return Outlook to its original settings.

Some of the Outlook customizations that you see in the following sections have been briefly touched on in earlier chapters. Here, however, you learn more about the changes that you can make that more directly affect how you use Outlook — especially now that you likely have more experience with the program.

Customizing Outlook Today

It's likely that the first thing you see when you open Outlook is the Outlook Today folder. You'll want to know about the various options that are available for customizing Outlook Today so that it shows just what is most useful to you.

To begin customizing Outlook Today, open the View menu, as shown in Figure 17-1. This provides you with access to several interesting options:

✦ Navigation Pane is a toggle that controls the display of the Navigation Pane. The Navigation Pane provides point-and-click access to your folders using icons to represent the folders. As detailed later in the section "Customizing the Navigation Pane," you can add your own shortcuts to the Navigation Pane.

✦ The Toolbars option enables you to decide which of the Outlook toolbars are displayed. As discussed in the section "Customizing the toolbars," you can modify the toolbars to include the tools you prefer, including these toolbars: Standard, Advanced, and Web. You also have the choice of creating your own toolbar, called My Toolbar.

✦ The Customize option on the Toolbars menu lets you modify or create your own toolbars. This is the same Customize dialog box you had in Outlook 2002, but includes an option on the Commands tab that enables you to rearrange commands on individual menu bars or toolbars.

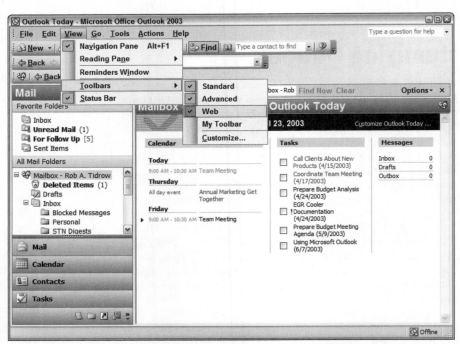

Figure 17-1: Use the View menu to access Outlook Today options.

✦ The Status Bar option is a toggle that controls the display of the status bar at the bottom of the Outlook window. Removing the status bar provides slightly more room to display the items in the window and may be useful if your screen is quite small, you have a large number of items that show in your Outlook Today folder, or you run Outlook at less than full-screen. Remember, though, that the status bar performs several useful functions. The status bar provides information about the current folder and the status of actions that Outlook performs. One piece of information that is helpful is the Online message that appears on the status bar. This lets you know if Outlook is currently connected to a network connection, such as a local area network or the Internet.

In addition to the options that appear on the View menu, you can click the Customize Outlook Today button to display the Customize Outlook Today window, as shown in Figure 17-2. The Customize Outlook Today button appears on the right side of the Outlook Today window, above the section for Messages. The Customize Outlook Today window enables you to change the way the Outlook Today folder displays information you have stored in the other Outlook folders.

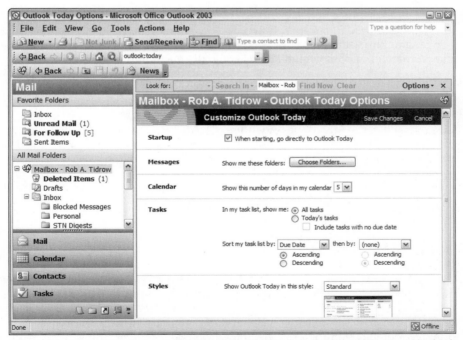

Figure 17-2: Use the Customize Outlook Today window to change the way Outlook Today displays information.

On the Customize Outlook Today window, you can select if you want Outlook to open with the Outlook Today folder opened. This is helpful if you want to get a quick overview of your day from one screen, including any tasks and calendar items you need to be aware of for the day. In addition, you can see the number of messages you have unread in the Inbox, how many e-mail drafts you have saved, and how many messages you have in the Outbox. Simply click one of these folders to display its contents. If you prefer to have a different Outlook folder active when you open Outlook, deselect the When starting, go directly to Outlook Today check box. If you deselect this option, Outlook will remember which Outlook folder was active when you last closed Outlook, and reopen the same folder the next time you start Outlook. Click the Save Changes button to close the Customize Outlook Today form and return to Outlook Today.

By default, the Inbox, Drafts, and Outbox folders are the only ones that show on the Outlook Today screen. You can, however, change this by clicking the Choose Folders button next to Show me these folders. This displays the Select Folder dialog box from which you can select additional folders to show, or deselect folders you no longer want to see. Click OK to close this dialog box and save your settings.

Outlook Today shows five days of events, meetings, and appointments that are stored in your Calendar folder; however, you can increase or decrease this number by changing the value in the Show this number of days in my calendar box. The minimum number of days that show is one; the maximum number of days you can display is seven.

Outlook Today is set to show all of your tasks; however, you can set the In my task list, show me option to Today's tasks to see only those tasks that are due today. In addition, select the Include tasks with no due dates if you want to see tasks that do not have due dates, but are still not completed. Along with setting which tasks to display, you also can sort them by the following criteria:

- ✦ Importance
- ✦ Due Date
- ✦ Creation Time
- ✦ Start Date

Use the Sort my task list by drop-down lists to select how your tasks are sorted. Use the Ascending and Descending radio buttons to set the sort order.

Finally, the Styles option lets you select different styles of your Outlook Today folder. By default, Outlook uses the Standard style; however, you can choose Standard (two columns), Standard (one column), Summer, or Winter styles.

Note   If you choose the Winter style from the Show Outlook Today in this style drop-down list and then click Save Changes, the Customize Outlook Today button appears at the lower right corner of the Outlook Today screen.

Click the Save Changes button to save your changes and return to the Outlook Today folder view.

If you would rather choose a folder to open by default other than Outlook Today, you'll have to dig a little deeper into Outlook's options. To explicitly specify the default Outlook folder, follow these steps:

1. Select Tools ⇨ Options to display the Options dialog box.

2. Click the Other tab.

3. Click the Advanced Options button.

4. Click the Browse button at the right of the Startup in this folder list box to display the Select Folder dialog box, shown in Figure 17-3. Choose the folder you want from the list.

5. Click OK to close the Advanced Options dialog box.

6. Click OK to close the Options dialog box.

7. Select File ⇨ Exit to close Outlook.

8. Restart Outlook.

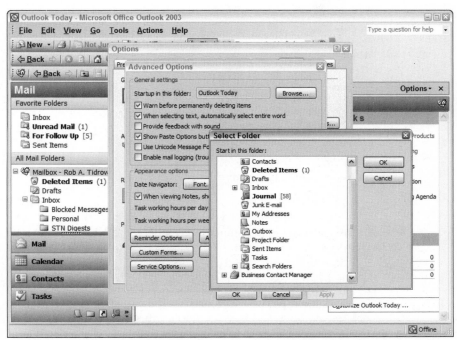

Figure 17-3: You can choose which folder Outlook starts up by default.

Customizing the menus

Outlook 2003 shares a feature with the other applications in Office 2003 that you may find either quite useful or totally annoying. When you open an Outlook menu, only some of the menu's commands appear on the menu. After a short delay, the remaining menu items will appear; but while you're waiting, it's easy to become confused and move on to another menu, thinking that you may have opened the wrong menu. To further complicate matters, commands that you seldom use are moved off the main menus to make way for commands you use more often.

If you find these constantly changing menus confusing, the following steps show you how to change this behavior.

Note   Changing these menu settings affects all Office programs, not just Outlook.

1. Select Tools ➪ Customize to display the Customize dialog box. Choose the Options tab, shown in Figure 17-4.

Figure 17-4: Control those constantly changing menus.

2. To display the full menus immediately, check the Always show full menus check box.

3. If you decide to keep the short menus, deselect Always show full menus (if you selected it in step 2) and then choose Show full menus after a short delay.

4. If you decide to keep the short menus, you can click the Reset menu and toolbar usage data button to have Outlook return to the original set of menu options. Because Outlook will otherwise show only those commands that you've used recently, this button resets the menus to the way they appeared when you first installed Outlook, but it does retain any customized menus or customizations done to Outlook toolbars.

5. To animate the menus, select one of the animation options in the Menu animations list box. This causes the menus to display in an animated manner instead of simply dropping down like normal.

6. Click Close to close the Customize dialog box.

 Note   It's a good idea to display full menus so other users will not be confused by the missing commands on the Outlook menus.

Customizing the toolbars

Outlook's menus aren't the only parts of the user interface that can change automatically. As you use the toolbars, tools that you use the least can often move off the toolbar to make room for other buttons that you use more often. Needless to say, this can be somewhat confusing, too.

Outlook has several toolbars that can be displayed depending on the folder you view. You can choose to display additional toolbars by selecting View ➪ Toolbars and then choosing the toolbars you want to see. Although this changes the selection of toolbars, it does not change the way Outlook adds and removes toolbar buttons automatically.

You can choose additional tools to add to the toolbars by clicking the Toolbar Options arrow that appears at the right side of each toolbar and then clicking the Add or Remove Buttons option. This displays the Add or Remove buttons option list, as shown in Figure 17-5, so that you can choose which buttons to display.

Any of the buttons that have a check to the left of the button name in the list of buttons will appear on the toolbar. You can add buttons by placing a check in front of their names. You can also choose Reset Toolbar to return the toolbar to the default settings.

In addition to changing the tools that are shown on the toolbars, you can change the toolbar locations. There is a vertical column of dots at the left edge of each toolbar that acts as a handle so you can drag the toolbar to a new location. Although you cannot place a toolbar and the Outlook menu on the same row, you can place multiple toolbars onto the same row.

 Note   To maximize the space in the Outlook window without removing important functionality, you can drag a toolbar down to create a floating toolbar. You can even dock a toolbar along the left edge of the Outlook window.

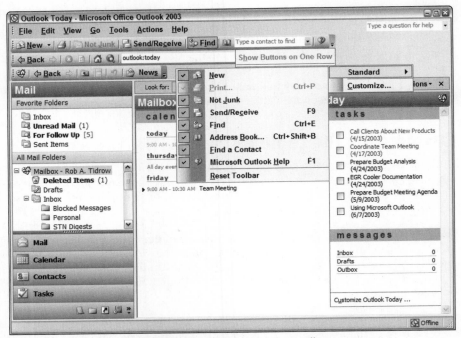

Figure 17-5: Choose the buttons that appear on the toolbars.

If none of the Outlook toolbars has the mix of tools that you need, you can create your own toolbars. To create a custom toolbar, follow these steps:

1. Select View ➪ Toolbars ➪ Customize ➪ Toolbars tab to display the Customize dialog box, shown in Figure 17-6.

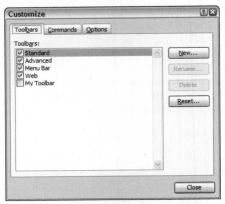

Figure 17-6: Create your own toolbars.

2. Click the New button.

3. Enter a name for your toolbar.

4. Click OK to return to the Customize dialog box.

5. Drag tools from any of the toolbars onto your toolbar. Hold down Ctrl as you drag to copy a tool button rather than move it. This way you can have the same button on multiple toolbars (in case you turn one off later). You also can click the Commands tab and drag tools from the Commands list to your new toolbar.

6. Click Close to close the Customize dialog box.

7. Drag your toolbar to dock it in the desired location, or simply leave it floating anywhere onscreen.

Note   Although you can create your own toolbars to completely replace Outlook's toolbars, remember that your toolbars won't automatically adjust for different types of Outlook folders. It's usually best to create custom toolbars that complement rather than replace Outlook's toolbars.

Customizing the Navigation Pane

With Outlook 2003, the Navigation Pane and Folder List view have been combined on the left side of the screen to give you more real estate on the right side of the screen to display the contents of your folders. To display the Navigation Pane, choose the View menu and select Navigation Pane.

You can click the Button Bar at the bottom of the Navigation Pane to display Outlook folders such as Mail, Calendar, and so on. Above the Button Bar, the Navigation Pane also shows views of your open folder. For example, when you display the Contacts folder, Current View options are available to let you display your contacts by different views such as Address Card, Phone List, and so on.

You can customize the Current View area by clicking the Customize Current View link (you may need to scroll down the view pane to see this link). This is also available with the Mail, Contacts, Tasks, and Journal folders. When you click this link, the Customize View: *<name of current view>* dialog box opens where you can set up different views of your information. Part III shows how to set your own views.

To modify the icons that show on the Button Bar, click the Configure buttons down-arrow at the bottom of the Button Bar. This shows a context menu with an option called Navigation Pane Options. Click it to display the Navigation Pane Options dialog box and then select the buttons you want to display on the Button Bar. You can move them up or down on the Button Bar to reorder them by clicking Move Up or Move Down. Click OK to save your settings.

You can also change the size of the Button Bar icons. Figure 17-7 shows the pop-up menu that appears when you click the Configure buttons drop-down arrow on the Navigation Pane. Click Show More Buttons to decrease the size of each Button Bar icon. Click Show Fewer Buttons to increase the size of the Button Bar icons. You also can drag the top border of the button bar up or down to resize the buttons.

Controlling security

One part of customizing Outlook that generally gets little attention is the area of security. You may not realize that a potential security threat even exists; however, even e-mail messages that you receive could cause problems if you aren't careful.

Computer viruses are programs intended to harm your data or computer components. Oh, it's true that many computer viruses don't do a lot of immediate damage, but by the simple fact of taking up space on your computer, even the most benign viruses are harmful. The first computer viruses were executable programs. For a long time, most people assumed that data files such as documents and e-mail messages couldn't contain viruses. Unfortunately, that's no longer true.

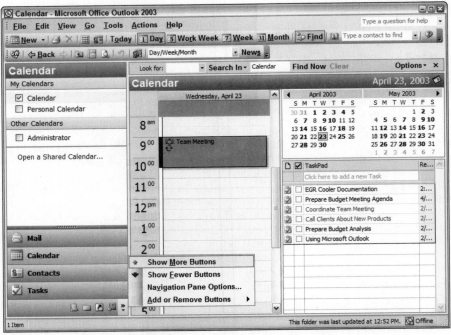

Figure 17-7: You can change the size of the Button Bar icons.

The problem with data files is that they're often more than just data files. Many programs use a macro language that enables the user to include some automation in their documents. In Office 2003, that macro language is Visual Basic for Applications (VBA). Programs that are written in VBA are part of a document, so documents can now be just as destructive as ordinary programs. If a document contains macros that are executed by the application that opens the document, the macro program within the document runs similarly to any other program on your computer.

Because Outlook uses VBA for automation, it's possible for someone to send you an e-mail message that includes VBA code that could be destructive when it runs on your system. To counteract this, you should take control of the Outlook security settings and make certain macros contained in e-mail messages cannot run without your approval. That way, you'll be able to prevent e-mail message macro viruses from harming your computer.

To set the Outlook security level, follow these steps:

1. Select Tools ➪ Macro ➪ Security to display the Security dialog box, shown in Figure 17-8.

2. Choose the security level you prefer. Unless you really like to live dangerously, do not select Low.

Figure 17-8: Make certain that you decide which macros to run on your system.

3. Click the Trusted Publishers tab to display the list of certificates that are available on your system, shown in Figure 17-9. If you have someone's digital ID but do not want to assume that the e-mail they send will be safe, select them from the list and then click Remove.

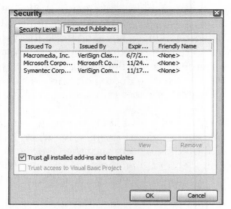

Figure 17-9: Set up your Trusted Publishers using this tab.

   4. Click OK to close the Security dialog box.

Note   No matter which security level you choose, macros from anyone who appears on your Trusted Publishers list will run automatically. If you want the highest level of protection against potential problems, remove everyone from the Trusted Publishers list.

Organizing Your Outlook Folders

If you use Outlook frequently, you probably have a huge amount of information stored in your Outlook folders. Of course, just having a lot of information isn't very useful — you also need to be able to find the information that you need. One of the best ways to make certain information is accessible is to organize that information. In the following sections, you learn about one of the ways that Outlook can help you organize the information in your Outlook folders.

What is the Organize feature?

The Organize feature can be started by choosing Tools | Organize. It displays a small window just above the folder contents pane. In the Organize window, you'll find tools that can help you organize the items in your Outlook folders using several different options.

The organizational options that are available in Outlook include the following:

   Categories. This option enables you to place selected items into existing categories such as business, hot contacts, key customer, and so on. You also have the option to create new categories on the spot. You can later view the items that you've placed in each category, making it easy to find specific types of records based on their assigned category.

Colors. This option enables you to make specific messages stand out by using a contrasting color. You might, for example, have Outlook show all messages that come from your boss in green, and all messages from a special customer in red.

Folders. This option enables you to move selected items to a specific folder. It also enables you to create a rule that moves new messages from certain people into a special folder. This option is useful if you want all e-mail messages from specific customers to automatically be moved to folders that you have created for each customer. Such a setup would help you keep track of all messages from those customers because you wouldn't have to search through your mail folders — you could look directly in the customer-specific folder.

Views. This option enables you to quickly change the view of the current folder. You might, for example, want to use a view such as Flagged for Next Seven Days to quickly see which items you need to deal with immediately before you take off on a suddenly arranged business trip.

Using the Organize feature

Each Outlook folder displays the Organize option on the Tools menu. Selecting the Organize tool displays the Organize pane just above the folder contents pane. Even so, you'll find that the type of Outlook folder that is displayed will control which of the Organize options are available. Table 17-1 shows the Organize options available for each of Outlook's standard folders. New folders that you create will display the same set of options as the folder that is closest to the type of your new folder.

Table 17-1
Organize Options in Outlook Folders

Folder	Options
Calendar	Categories, Views
Contacts	Folders, Categories, Views
Deleted Items	Folders, Colors, Views
Drafts	Folders, Colors, Views
Inbox	Folders, Colors, Views
Outbox	Folders, Colors, Views
Sent Items	Colors, Folders, Views
Journal	Categories, Views
Notes	Folders, Views
Tasks	Folders, Categories, Views

The following sections will show you a little about each of the organizational options.

Using categories to organize

When you use categories to organize your folders, you select the items that you want to assign to specific categories and then choose the category. Figure 17-10 shows the Using Categories option for the Calendar folder.

To use this option, follow these steps:

1. Open the folder you want to organize.

2. Choose Tools ➪ Organize.

3. Select Using Categories.

4. Select the items that you want to assign to a category, such as a meeting or appointment.

5. Either select an existing category from the drop-down list box and click the Add button, or enter a new category name in the text box and click Create.

6. Repeat steps 4 and 5 as necessary until you have finished assigning items to categories.

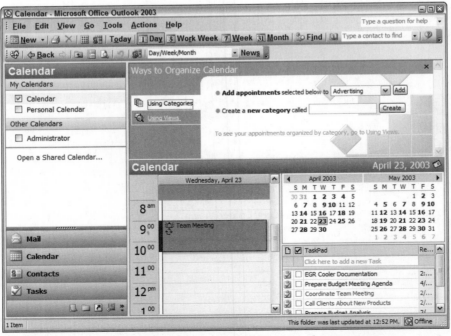

Figure 17-10: Use categories to organize items into logical groups.

Using colors to organize

When you use colors to organize your folders, you specify that messages to or from specific people should be highlighted in a color that you select. You can also specify that messages that were sent only to you are highlighted in color. Figure 17-11 shows the Using Colors option for the Deleted Items folder.

To use this option, follow these steps:

1. Open the folder you want to organize.

2. Choose Tools | Organize.

3. Select Using Colors.

4. Select either from or sent to in the first list box.

5. Specify the name in the second box. The easiest method of doing this is to select a message from the person that you want.

6. Select the color from the drop-down list box.

7. Click the Apply Color button to color all the matching messages as you have specified.

8. To color messages that were addressed only to you, choose a color in the lower drop-down color list box and then click the Turn on button.

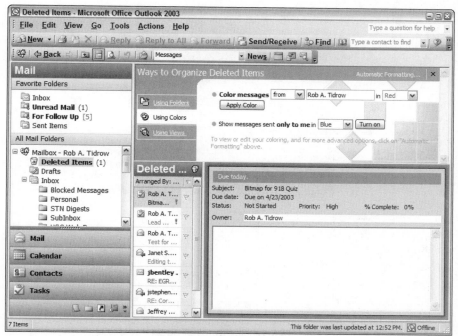

Figure 17-11: Use colors to make specific messages stand out.

Using folders to organize

When you use the Using Folders option to organize your folders, you move items to specific folders. You can also create a rule that automatically moves new items to a specific folder. Figure 17-12 shows the Using Folders option for the Inbox folder.

To use this option, follow these steps:

1. Open the folder you want to organize.

2. Choose Tools | Organize.

3. Select Using Folders.

4. Select items that you want to move or that you want to use as an example for a new rule.

5. To move the selected items immediately, select the destination folder from the upper drop-down list box and then click Move.

6. To create a new rule, select either from or sent to from the middle drop-down list box.

7. Select the destination folder from the lower drop-down list box.

8. Click the Create button to create the new rule.

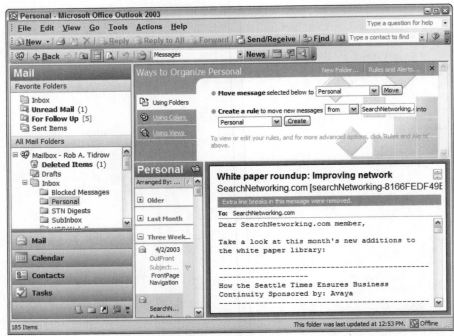

Figure 17-12: Use folders to move specific items to special folders.

Note If you want to create a new rule and move existing items, create the new rule first so that you can use an existing item as a sample. After you have created the new rule, you can move the existing items.

Using Junk E-Mail to organize

Outlook handles junk e-mail in a much more sophisticated manner now than in previous versions of Outlook. In fact Outlook will automatically identify some messages as "junk" mail if the sender of the message is known to be a junk mail (known as *spam* in e-mail lingo) deliverer. To see junk e-mail settings in Outlook, choose Actions ➪ Junk E-Mail ➪ Junk E-Mail Options. Figure 17-13 shows the Junk E-Mail Options dialog box.

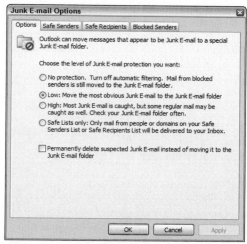

Figure 17-13: Use the Junk E-mail option to move or color junk and adult content messages.

On the Options tab, select the level of protection you want Outlook to use for your messages. For instance, the default setting of Low will flag and move the most obvious junk mail to the Junk E-Mail folder. You can also opt to have junk deleted instead of stored in the Junk E-Mail folder. You can also set up trusted senders and recipients on the Safe Senders and Safe Recipients tabs. This way Outlook knows who you receive mail from that you trust, and who you send mail to that should be trusted (such as if you get a reply back from that person).

Using views to organize

When you use views to organize your folders, you change the way the items in the folder are displayed. Figure 17-14 shows the Using Views option for the Tasks folder.

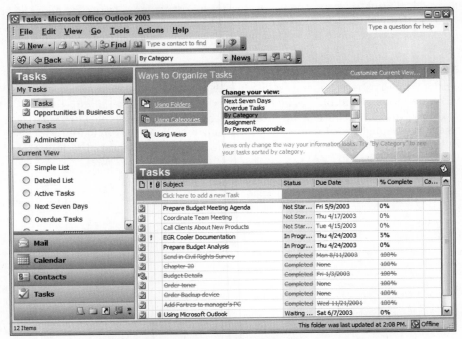

Figure 17-14: Use views to see the items in a different way.

To use this option, follow these steps:

1. Open the folder you want to organize.

2. Choose Tools ❘ Organize.

3. Select Using Views.

4. Select the view you want to try.

Using different views doesn't change any of the items in your folders, but you may want to try the Using Views option after you've used one of the other options to see what effect the other options had.

Integrating with the Web

As the Internet has become more a part of everyday life, we've come to expect that using the Internet should be an easy task. In this latest version of Outlook, you can use the Internet in many ways that greatly simplify many of the actions you do, such as visiting Web sites and sending Web pages with e-mail messages.

If you select View ➪ Toolbars ➪ Web to display the Web toolbar, you can enter a Web page address and visit a Web site without ever leaving Outlook. Figure 17-15 shows a popular Web site as viewed in Outlook.

Figure 17-15: Use the Web toolbar to visit Web sites from within Outlook.

While you're viewing a Web page, you can easily send that Web page to someone as part of an e-mail message. Simply select Actions ⇨ Send Web Page by E-mail, as shown in Figure 17-16. You can even do this after you've gone offline as long as you visited the Web page during the current session—if Outlook can still show the Web page without reconnecting to the Internet, you can send the page.

If you visit the same Web site often, you can add a shortcut to the Web site to your Favorites folder. Right-click the Web page, and choose Add to Favorites. Click OK to save the page address as one of your favorites.

You can also assign a Web page as the home page for an Outlook folder. To do so, follow these steps:

1. Right-click a folder in the Navigation Pane.

2. Choose Properties from the context menu to display the Properties dialog box for that folder.

3. Choose the Home Page tab.

4. Type the address of the Web page in the Address line, as shown in Figure 17-17.

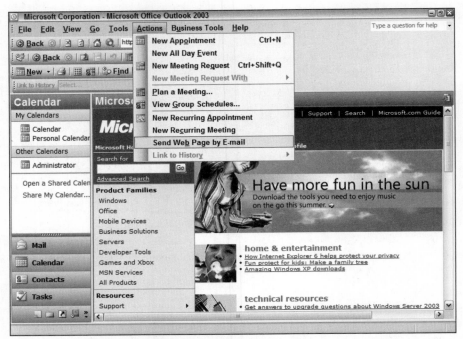

Figure 17-16: You can easily send a Web page via e-mail.

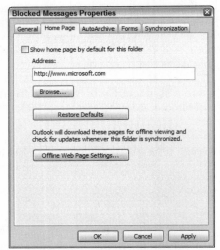

Figure 17-17: Assign a Web page to a folder using this tab

5. If you want this folder to display the Web page by default (each time you open this folder), select Show home page by default for this folder.

6. Click OK.

Tip

If you have a Web-based e-mail servers you like to access via a Web browser, use Outlook's Web feature to do this. Create a new folder and assign the e-mail server's Web page to it. Select the Show home page by default for this folder option. The Web page appears each time you open this folder, letting you access your Web-based e-mail.

Showing and Hiding the TaskPad

You can display the TaskPad when viewing the Calendar folder. The TaskPad is an Outlook pane that displays on the right side of the screen and includes your list of tasks and small monthly calendars, shown in Figure 17-18. If you are in Day view, you can click a date in the small calendars to see that day's calendar items. Today's date is shown with a red box around it. If you are in the Work Week view, clicking a day jumps you to the week that the day is in. This gives you a full view of the work week. If you are in the Week view, clicking a single day changes your view to Day view and jumps you to that day; however, if you click to the left of a week (to the left of a Sunday if your week is set up Sunday – Saturday, for instance), the entire week view is shown.

Figure 17-18: Use the TaskPad to see your tasks and small calendars.

The TaskPad can be turned on or off while in the Calendar folder by choosing View ➪ TaskPad. This toggles off the TaskPad if it's on, or toggles it on if it's off.

To change TaskPad properties, use the following steps:

1. Choose View ➪ TaskPad to turn on the TaskPad.

2. To set which tasks are displayed, choose View ➪ TaskPad View and then select one of the following options (see Figure 17-19).

   - All Tasks shows every task in your Tasks folder.

   - Today's Tasks shows just the tasks due today.

   - Active Tasks for Selected Days shows tasks for days you've selected on the calendars. You can select multiple days by holding down the Ctrl key while you select days.

   - Overdue Tasks lets you see those tasks that are overdue.

   - Tasks Completed on Selected Days shows tasks you completed on the days you've selected on the calendars.

   - Include Tasks With No Due Date shows all tasks that do not have a specific due date. These tasks show up in all other TaskPad views except for the Tasks Completed on Selected Days view.

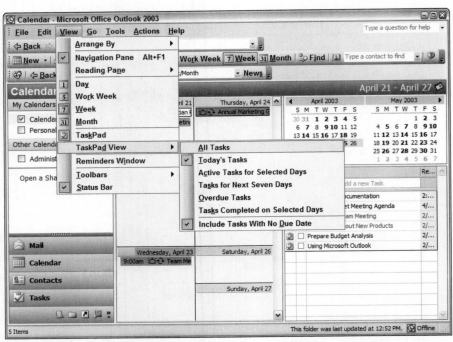

Figure 17-19: Choose TaskPad Views from this menu.

3. To set other TaskPad options, right-click next to the word TaskPad in the TaskPad pane to display a context menu of options, shown in Figure 17-20.

4. Select the options you want to display TaskPad items the way you want to view them. For example, select Sort Descending to see your tasks sorted in descending order.

5. To format the columns that appear in the TaskPad, select Format Columns from the context menu displaying the Format Columns dialog box, shown in Figure 17-21.

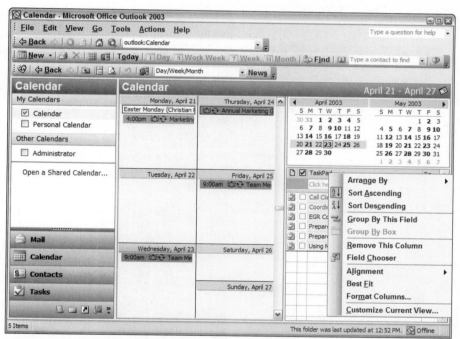

Figure 17-20: Use the options on the TaskPad pane to change the way the TaskPad looks.

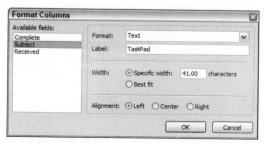

Figure 17-21: Use the Format Columns dialog box to change the columns in the TaskPad.

6. Select a field in the Available Fields list and change its settings. For example, for the Complete field, you can change only its Format property. For the Subject and Received fields, you can select Format, Label (if you want different names than TaskPad or Received to show, for example), how wide the Subject field is, and its text alignment.

7. Click OK after making your changes.

The TaskPad includes other options from which to choose if you right-click a blank task line, shown in Figure 17-22. Here you can select to create a New Task or New Task Request, turn on AutoPreview of your tasks, set TaskPad views, and select other TaskPad settings.

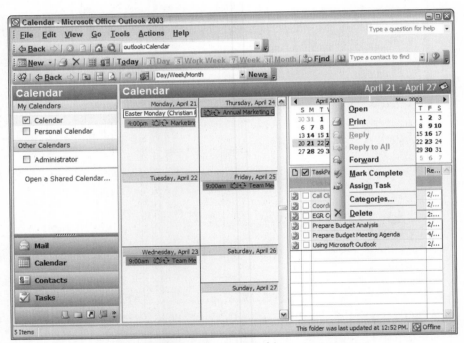

Figure 17-22: Set other TaskPad options using this context menu.

Adding Holidays To Your Calendar

Another important feature of Outlook is its capability to display holidays in the Calendar folder. This way, you can remember all those special times of the year when you need to send out greeting cards, prepare for vacations, or just be aware of these times. Outlook includes several types of holidays based on locations and religious beliefs.

To set holidays in Outlook, perform these steps:

1. Choose Tools ⇨ Options and then click the Calendar Options button on the Preferences dialog box.

2. Click the Add Holidays button to display the Add Holidays to Calendar dialog box, shown in Figure 17-23.

Figure 17-23: Add holidays to your calendar using this dialog box.

3. Select the locations or religious holidays you want shown in Calendar.

4. Click OK. Outlook adds the holidays to your calendar.

5. Click OK when this is finished.

6. Click OK to close the Calendar Options dialog box.

7. Click OK to close the Options dialog box.

8. Any holidays that have passed will display reminders. Click Dismiss All if you do not want reminders displayed. Click Yes if asked if you are sure you want to dismiss all these reminders.

Note   Holidays appear as all-day events in your Calendar folder.

Adding Macros for Repetitive Tasks

Outlook includes a macros feature that enables you to set up macros that perform repetitive tasks so you don't have to. To create a macro, perform the following steps:

1. Choose Tools ➪ Macro ➪ Macros to display the Macros dialog box shown in Figure 17-24.

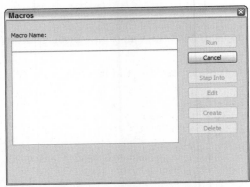

Figure 17-24: The Macros dialog box includes options for creating, running, deleting, and editing your macros.

2. Type a name for the new macro, making sure it's descriptive and only one word.

3. Click Create to show the Microsoft Visual Basic editor, shown in Figure 17-25.

4. Enter your macro code.

5. Choose File ➪ Close and Return to Microsoft Outlook.

Note   The topic of creating actual Outlook macros is beyond the scope of this book. Refer to Outlook Help for more information, or visit `http://www.microsoft.com/office/outlook/`.

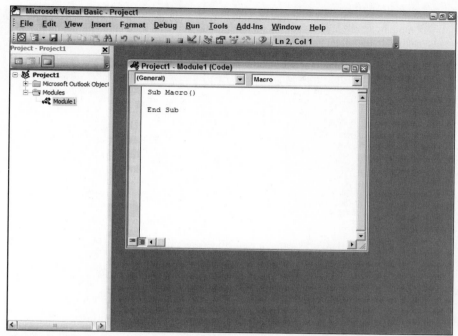

Figure 17-25: Use the Visual Basic editor to create your Outlook macros.

Summary

Customizing Outlook is the best way to make certain Outlook works the way that best suits you. In this chapter, you learned how to customize Outlook, how to use the Organize feature to make working with Outlook items a bit easier, how to manage the Taskbar, and how to use Outlook with the Internet.

In the next chapter, you learn how to use folders in Outlook more effectively.

✦   ✦   ✦

Using Folders Effectively

CHAPTER 18

In This Chapter

Understanding folders

Creating folders

Managing items within the folders

Using the Deleted Items folder

Anyone who has used Windows has certainly been exposed to the concept of folders, so Outlook's folder system shouldn't seem too foreign. Outlook uses folders to organize the different types of information that you can track in the program, but the information in Outlook is somewhat different than the information you store in your Windows Explorer folders. Outlook's folders have some differences from other types of folders, too.

In this chapter, you learn how to use Outlook's folders effectively. You learn about the different types of folders, and how you can manage and share the information contained in those folders. You also learn how to ensure Outlook makes the best use of the space it needs for your information storage needs.

Understanding Folders

If you truly want to understand Outlook's folders, it's good to start with some of the basics. That way you'll have a better understanding of what you can and cannot do with Outlook folders and their contents.

✦ Each type of Outlook folder is intended to hold specific types of items. In most cases, you must store Outlook items such as Calendar events and e-mail messages in the proper type of folder.

✦ Outlook folders are more closely related to an Access database than to almost anything else on your system. A single file, normally called Outlook.pst, contains all the Outlook folders and the items that those folders contain. This file is usually encrypted and can only be opened using Outlook.

✦ When you delete items from your Outlook folders, Outlook does not automatically recover the space that those items were using. As detailed in the section "Using the Deleted Items Folder" later in this chapter, you must explicitly tell Outlook to recover that lost space if you don't want your Outlook.pst file to waste space on your hard disk.

✦ You can share Outlook folders, but only with people who are also using Outlook. In some cases, you can share certain information with non-Outlook users, but that sharing is limited to sending the information via an e-mail message.

Why use Outlook folders?

Outlook's folders store all of the information that you keep within Outlook. But even more than simply storing information, Outlook's folders help you organize that information logically. You don't, for example, have to look through the Inbox folder to find a copy of an e-mail message that you've sent to someone. Messages that you've sent are moved to the Sent Items folder.

You are not limited to the folders that Outlook creates by default when you install it. As Figure 18-1 shows, you can create your own Outlook folders to organize your Outlook items to suit your needs.

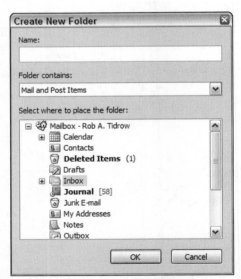

Figure 18-1: Create Outlook folders to organize your information.

Tip Drag the right side of the Navigation Pane to expand the pane so that you don't need to use the horizontal scrollbar to view the entire folder tree.

Understanding folder types

You can create and use several types of Outlook folders. Each of these different types of Outlook folders can also contain several categories of folders with each category being the type of information that you can store within those folders.

Here are the main types of folders that you can use with Outlook:

✦ Personal Folders are the most common type of Outlook folder. Personal Folders are those folders located completely on your computer, not on a remote computer such as a Microsoft Exchange Server. Personal Folders are also personal—they aren't generally shared with other people.

✦ An offline folder is a type of folder that enables you to use information from a Microsoft Exchange Server, even if you are not currently connected to the server. You can work with the information in an offline folder and then synchronize that information later with the information on the Exchange Server. Offline folders are similar to Personal Folders except that they synchronize the information between your local system and the Exchange Server. Offline folders are available only if you connect to an Exchange Server and have the extension .OST.

✦ Public folders enable you to share information with other people who are also connected to your Exchange Server. Public folders provide similar functionality to net folders except that Public folders are usually considered more secure because only those people who have access to your Exchange Server can access your Public folders.

Understanding folder categories

Each type of Outlook folder can contain several categories of folders. The folder category is based on the type of information that you want to store in the folder. You've seen each of these folder categories in earlier chapters, but the following list provides a quick review of them:

✦ Calendar folders contain schedule items such as appointments and meetings.

✦ Contacts folders contain information on people such as e-mail and mailing addresses.

✦ Journal folders contain information on activities that you've performed on your computer such as the length of time that you worked on specific documents.

✦ Mail folders contain incoming or outgoing messages such as e-mail and faxes.

✦ Notes folders contain reminders that you create for yourself. The items in these folders are often compared to paper sticky notes. See Chapter 14 for more information about Outlook Notes.

✦ Tasks folders contain information on your to-do list.

Creating Folders

You can create new Outlook folders to suit your needs. If, for example, you are starting a new project and expect the project to generate many messages, you may want to create one or more folders specifically for the messages relating to that project. In most cases, you'll probably create your new folders within your Outlook Personal Folders list. You likely don't need the extra complication of having multiple sets of Personal Folder files, but in the following sections, you learn about some special circumstances that may make extra Personal Folder files worth the effort.

Adding new folders

You can add folders wherever you like in the Outlook folder tree. In most cases, you'll probably want to keep related items together, but there's no reason that you can't place your folders where they make the most sense to you.

One strategy is to place new folders under existing folders that hold the same type of information. In this case, you may place folders for incoming messages under the Inbox folder, and move messages from the Inbox to the appropriate folders as they arrive.

You may also consider an alternative way to organize your new folders. Rather than creating new folders under the existing Outlook folders, you may want to create a project folder that is on the same level as Outlook folders, such as the Inbox. You could then create subfolders under the project folder for project-related messages, Calendar items, Notes, and so on. In this model, you would find it easy to organize the items for a project because they would all be in folders under the project folder.

Finally, you might even consider using a completely separate Personal Folder file for each project. Although this is by far the most complicated way to organize your Outlook items, it does offer some advantages. A separate Personal Folder file is easy to open and close as needed, is perfect when you want to be able to separately archive everything relating to specific projects, and can easily be transferred between different computers if necessary.

Regardless of the organizational strategy that you choose, creating new Outlook folders is quick and easy. To create new folders, follow these steps:

1. In the Navigation Pane, right-click the folder that you want as the parent for the new folder. Although you can start in any folder, choosing the parent folder reduces the chance that you'll accidentally place the folder in the wrong location.

2. Select New Folder, as shown in Figure 18-2.

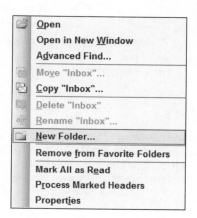

Figure 18-2: Select New Folder from the pop-up menu to create a new folder.

3. In the Name text box, enter a descriptive name for the folder. (Remember, names that are too long can be difficult to view in the Navigation Pane.)

4. Click the down arrow next to the Folder contains list box and then choose the type of items that you will place in this folder, as shown in Figure 18-3. If this is the main project folder (top-level folder) that will later contain additional sub-folders for the project-related items, you can choose any item type because you may not be storing anything in this main folder.

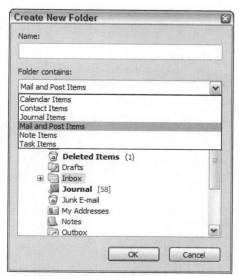

Figure 18-3: Select the type of item you'll store in the folder.

5. If you did not select the correct location for the new folder, choose the location in the folder tree that is displayed in the Select where to place the Navigation Pane box (this list box is hidden behind the drop-down list in Figure 18-3).

6. Click OK to close the Create New Folder dialog box and create the new folder.

If you need to create additional folders, repeat the same steps.

Customizing your new folders

You can customize your new folders in a variety of ways. You learn how to do this using the example from the previous section where you created a new folder in which to store messages pertaining to a project. You can customize other types of folders in a similar way, whether they are folders that store Notes, Tasks, Calendar, or Journal items.

In the example, if you are creating a main project folder, you'll probably want separate subfolders for messages that you receive and messages that you send. This is not, however, something that Outlook requires. If you choose to keep both messages that you receive and messages that you send in the same folder, you will be able to tell which messages were ones that you sent by looking at the From column. Your name will appear in the From column for messages that you sent.

Of course, knowing that you sent a message is important, but you probably would like to know to whom the message was sent. For that, you'll need to customize your new folder so that it better serves the dual purpose of a folder for both sent and received items.

To customize the folder to show additional information, follow these steps:

1. Open the folder that you want to modify.

2. Right-click the column headings in the folder contents pane.

3. Choose Custom from the pop-up menu, as shown in Figure 18-4, to display the Customize View: Messages dialog box.

4. Click the Fields button.

5. Double-click the fields you want to display on your new folder. For example, double-click the Follow Up Flag field in the Available fields list so that it appears in the Show these fields in this order list.

6. To rearrange your fields, drag the field from its current position up or down in the list to where you want it. Figure 18-5 shows an example of moving the Follow Up Flag field up to the second spot.

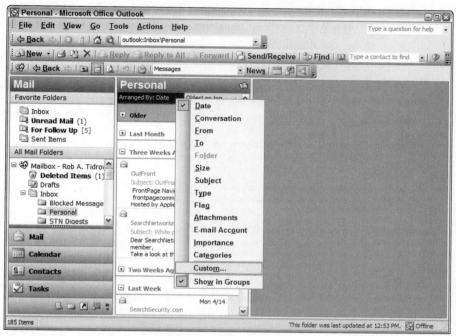

Figure 18-4: Select Custom from the pop-up menu.

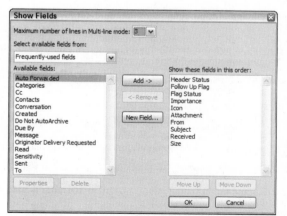

Figure 18-5: You can add and rearrange fields using the Show Fields dialog box.

7. Add any additional fields that will be useful in this folder view.

8. To remove fields you don't need, double-click them in the right list, or select them and click the Remove button.

9. Click the OK button to close the Show Fields dialog box.

10. Click the OK button to close the Customize View: Messages dialog box.

11. If necessary, drag the right edge of a field's column heading to adjust the width so that you can view the information in the column. You can adjust the width to fit the widest entry by double-clicking the right column border.

Figure 18-6 shows the new folder with the added Follow Up Flag field. In this case, other columns were adjusted to show the entire heading of the Follow Up Flag column.

You can also use the options available on the View ⇨ Arrange By ⇨ Current View menu to further customize your new folder. For example, if you select Format Columns, you can choose the display format for the columns in the view, and you can select the format, label, width, and alignment of each column. Figure 18-7 shows the Format Columns dialog box.

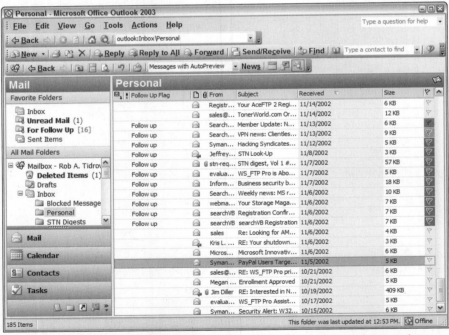

Figure 18-6: The added field showing between the Importance and Icon columns.

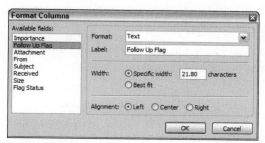

Figure 18-7: You can format column properties using the Format Columns dialog box.

Creating additional Personal Folders

You already know that Outlook uses a Personal Folder file to store Outlook's information on your computer. You may not realize that you can create additional Personal Folder files, and that you can have more than one Personal Folder file open at the same time.

Note   When creating and opening Personal Folder files, Outlook 2003 refers to them as Outlook Data Files; however, the file name extension is still .pst (as in earlier Outlook versions) and the file type is still known as Personal Folder files.

Why would you want to do this? One very good reason for having multiple Personal Folder files is that this is one of the easiest ways to move items between copies of Outlook on two different computers. Suppose, for example, that you use both a desktop and a laptop computer. You normally use Outlook on your desktop system to manage all your e-mail messages, but when you go on a business trip, you take your laptop system so that you can send and receive messages on the road. When you get back to the office, you have some important e-mail messages on the laptop system that you would like to move to your desktop computer. A separate Personal Folder file that you share between the laptop and desktop system is a simple and efficient way to handle this task.

Another reason for having multiple Personal Folder files is so that you can organize multiple projects more easily. You can create a separate Personal Folder file for a project and then keep all the project-related items in that file.

Note   Outlook's Personal Folder files aren't intended for multiple user access. If you have a Personal Folder file open on one computer, you should close the file before you can open it on a different computer. You might otherwise encounter problems if both computers attempt to modify the file contents.

Creating a new Personal Folder file is easy, but there are certainly a few potential pitfalls. If you want to share a Personal Folder file between two computers, you'll probably want to place that file in a location that's just a bit easier to find than the default location. The default folder may be a good and safe location for your mail Personal Folder file, but it's not exactly the first place you would think of looking if you couldn't remember the entire pathname.

Note   Outlook places your default personal folder in your user settings folder. For example, for the user name Jane Doe, the folder path would look similar to this: `C:\Documents and Settings\Jane Doe\Local Settings\Application Data\Microsoft\Outlook`.

To create a new Personal Folder file, follow these steps:

1. Select File ➪ New ➪ Outlook Data File to display the New Outlook Data File dialog box, shown in Figure 18-8.

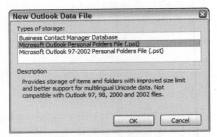

Figure 18-8: Create a new Personal Folder file to make organizing and sharing Outlook data a bit easier.

2. Choose Microsoft Outlook Personal Folders File (.pst). Use the other option if you have earlier versions of Outlook and want to share items between those versions and Outlook 2003.

3. Click OK.

4. Choose the location for the new file. You may want to click the My Documents button because this is a folder that is generally easy to locate on any Windows-based PC.

5. Enter a descriptive name in the File name text box. If you are creating multiple Personal Folder files, be sure to use a name that will enable you to quickly identify a specific Personal Folder file when you want to open the file.

6. Click the OK button to display the Create Microsoft Personal Folders dialog box, shown in Figure 18-9.

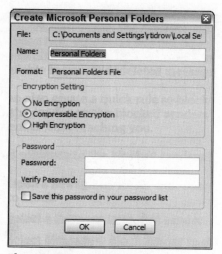

Figure 18-9: Control the access to your new Personal Folder file.

7. Type a name for the new Personal Folder file in the Name text box. This is the name that will appear in the Outlook Navigation Pane. It's a good idea to make this name unique so you can easily identify the new folders.

8. Choose a level of encryption for this file. In most cases, you can accept the default because this makes the file unreadable by programs other than Outlook, but also allows the file to be compressed so that it uses less disk space. You cannot change the type of encryption after a Personal Folder file has been created. If you need to use a specific type of encryption, be sure to select it while you are creating the file.

9. Enter a password in both password text boxes if you want to limit access to those who know the password.

10. Select the Save this password in your password list check box if you want your system to remember the password so that you don't need to enter it. It's usually best not to select this option if you truly need password security.

11. Click OK to close the dialog box and apply your settings. Figure 18-10 shows the new Personal Folder file named Virginia City Project opened in the Navigation Pane.

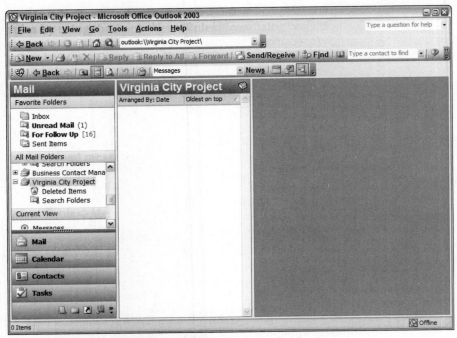

Figure 18-10: Your new Personal Folder file is ready to use.

You'll have to create your own folders for your new Personal Folders file as needed. You can drag and drop folders and their contents between different Personal Folder files, or you can create new folders as described in the "Adding new folders" section earlier in this chapter.

When you no longer need to use a Personal Folder file, you can close the file by right-clicking the file and then choosing the Close option from the pop-up menu, as shown in Figure 18-11.

To open a Personal Folder file, select File ⇨ Open ⇨ Outlook Data File and then select the .PST file from the Open Outlook Data File dialog box. You can easily open a file that is located on your network as long as you have access to the folder where the Personal Folder file is located. You must have full access to the folder if you want to make any changes in the file.

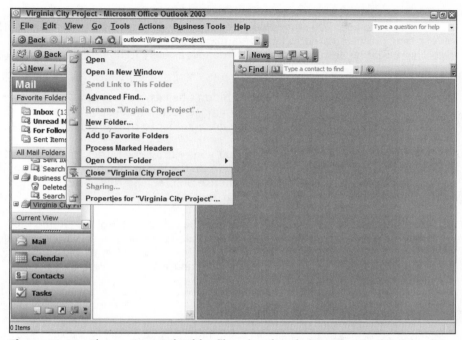

Figure 18-11: Close a Personal Folder file using the Close option on the right-click menu.

Managing Items within the Folders

It's probably a reasonable guess that most Outlook users don't really manage the items in their folders too well. If you take a look at your Inbox, it may contain hundreds of e-mail messages that you've received. Your Sent Items folder is likely just about as bad. Finding any particular item in all of that chaos can be the equivalent of trying to find a needle in a haystack—far too difficult when a little organization can help so much.

Moving items

In Chapter 8, you learned how to use the Rules Wizard to set up rules for handling messages. You saw that you could create a rule that automatically placed messages from someone into a specific folder. Now that you know how to create new folders and, more importantly, new Personal Folder files, you can see how those rules could be very effective in helping you automate the management of projects within Outlook.

You don't, however, have to use rules to move items in Outlook. You'll probably find that it's often easier to do some tasks manually. Moving existing messages to new folders that you've created to help organize your Outlook items is one of those tasks that could be automated, but is often just as easy to do in a few minutes using your mouse.

Moving items within Outlook's folders couldn't be easier. As Figure 18-12 shows, you can drag and drop items using your mouse. Here, the e-mail message titled "WeatherNet" is being dragged from the Inbox folder to the Personal folder.

If you want to make a copy of an item that you're dragging rather than moving the item, hold down the Ctrl key while you release the left mouse button. Holding down the Ctrl key adds a plus sign (+) to the mouse pointer, and this indicates that the selected object will be copied rather than moved.

 Tip

You can move or copy multiple objects at the same time. Hold down the Ctrl key while you select individual items or the Shift key while you select a contiguous range of items. Release the key and then drag the selection to the new location using the Ctrl key just before releasing the mouse button to copy items instead of moving them.

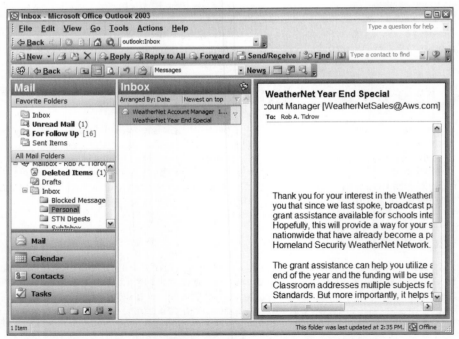

Figure 18-12: Drag and drop works the same in Outlook as it does in Windows Explorer.

If you have many folders, or if you just can't quite get the hang of dragging and dropping, Outlook provides an alternative method for moving selected items. Right-click items that you've selected, and choose Move to Folder from the pop-up menu to display the Move Items dialog box, shown in Figure 18-13. Choose the destination folder and then click OK to move the items.

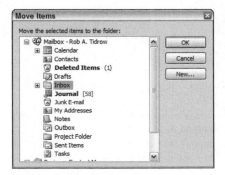

Figure 18-13: You can also move items using the Move Items dialog box.

You can also use the Cut, Copy, and Paste commands on the Edit menu to move and copy items. These commands work the same within Outlook as they do within other Windows applications, but there is one potential problem you need to watch out for. If you copy an item from an Outlook folder and then try to paste it into a Windows Explorer folder, you may be surprised by the result. Rather than creating the readable copy of a message that you might expect, you'll create a file that is listed in Windows Explorer as an Outlook Item. Unfortunately, this Outlook Item will only be readable within Outlook. The next section shows you how to create a file that contains the message text in a format that can be read by many different programs.

Saving items as text files

To save the text of a message in a text file so that the text will be readable in other programs, you have a couple of options. You can open the message in Outlook, select the text, copy the text to the Clipboard, switch to the other application, and then paste the text into your new document. Alternatively, you can save the message as a text file directly from Outlook.

To save an Outlook message as a text file, follow these steps:

1. Select the message that you want to save as a text file.

2. Select File ➪ Save As to display the Save As dialog box, shown in Figure 18-14.

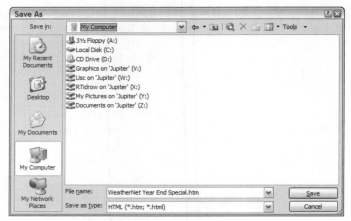

Figure 18-14: You can save Outlook messages as text files for use in other programs.

3. Choose the location for saving the file.

4. Enter a name for the file; Outlook will automatically add the .htm file extension.

5. Click the Save button.

Saving a message as a text file offers an advantage over copying the text using the Clipboard. When you save a message as a text file, Outlook includes the message header in the text file so that you can see who sent the message, when it was sent, to whom the message was sent, and the subject line.

Sharing Folders

Sharing Outlook folders is an excellent way to exchange information. When you share Outlook folders, everyone has access to the latest information. You don't have to remember to send out individual messages to the people who are sharing the folder — they automatically receive any new information that appears in the shared folder.

Sharing Personal Folders

Each Outlook user has a set of Personal folders. These folders are the ones that appear in your Outlook Navigation Pane under the title Personal Folders. As you learned earlier in the section "Creating additional Personal Folders," you can create new Personal Folder files as needed.

Personal Folder files are intended to be just that — personal. These files aren't meant for multiuser access, so sharing your Personal Folders isn't a simple case of allowing someone else access to your files. In fact, if you open the same set of Personal Folder files on two different PCs at the same time, you're likely to see an error message on one or both of the PCs eventually. You may even need to close Outlook and restart your computer to resolve the problem.

Even though you shouldn't try to open the same set of Personal folders on two computers at the same time, there's no reason why you can't open the same Personal Folder file on two different computers at different times. You may want to do this to synchronize items between Outlook on your desktop system and Outlook on your laptop system.

To open a Personal Folder file that is located on another computer on your network, follow these steps:

1. Select File ➪ Open ➪ Outlook Data File to display the Open Outlook Data File dialog box.

2. Click the down arrow next to the Look in list box, shown in Figure 18-15.

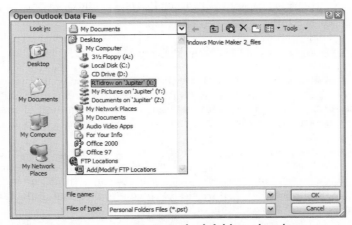

Figure 18-15: You can open Outlook folders elsewhere on your network.

3. Choose the location of the remote file. If you aren't sure of the correct location, you may want to click the Tools button and use the Find command to locate the .pst files on your network.

4. Select the Personal Folder file you want to open, as shown in Figure 18-16.

5. Click OK to open the file.

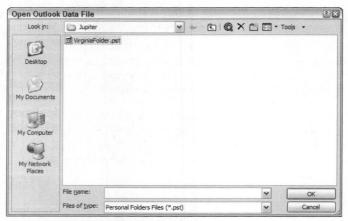

Figure 18-16: Select the file that you want to open.

Note

If you are opening a Personal Folder file that is on another computer, make certain the same file is not open at the same time on both computers. The best way to do this is to close Outlook on the remote system while you work with the file on your computer. Close the file as soon as possible to avoid conflicts.

Using the Deleted Items Folder

An important part of using your folders effectively is to make certain that you do a little housecleaning from time to time. Each item that you store in your Outlook folders takes some room. Although most items take a very small amount of space, eventually you may build up hundreds or thousands of things in your Outlook folders.

Even if you aren't concerned about the amount of disk space that is used by your Outlook data, you should probably be concerned about the amount of time that you spend searching for important messages. If your Inbox has a thousand messages, you might take a bit longer than you would like trying to find that important message that your boss sent you a couple of weeks ago.

The Deleted Items folder is similar to the Recycle Bin on your Windows desktop. When you delete items from other Outlook folders, those items are moved to the Deleted Items folder as a means of giving you a second chance. If you discover that you've deleted something in error, you can recover it from the Deleted Items folder — as long as you haven't already emptied the Deleted Items folder.

Deleting items

You probably have many old messages that you no longer need. Perhaps you have exchanged a series of messages with someone, and each time one of you replied to the earlier message, you included the earlier message text in your response. You could easily delete the earlier messages and keep the final one. You might have received several dozen e-mail messages touting some get-rich-quick scheme — why would you want to keep them?

In most cases, deleting old messages is simple. You select the messages that you want to delete and then click the Delete button on the Outlook toolbar. The selected messages are quickly moved to the Deleted Items folder where you can deal with them later.

Sometimes, though, you may want to delete only part of a message. Suppose you're working on a project and someone sends you an important project-related message that includes a large file attachment. You probably save the attachment for use on your computer, so keeping the attachment with the message effectively doubles the space that is used on your hard disk. You could just delete the entire message, but you can recover that lost space without removing the message — only the unneeded attachment.

Here's how you can remove the file attachment and keep the message:

1. Double-click the message to open it.

2. Right-click the attachment and then choose Remove, as shown in Figure 18-17. Some types of attachments will show a slightly different pop-up menu than the one shown in the figure. If you don't see Remove on the menu, choose Clear or Cut.

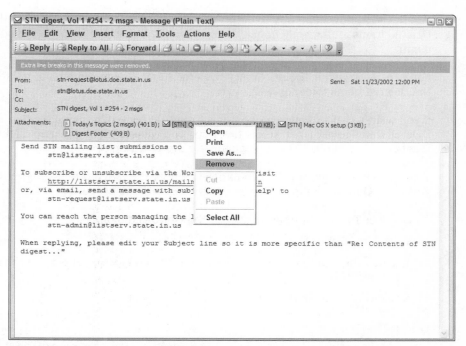

Figure 18-17: Remove attachments that you've saved to save disk space.

3. Click the Close button. Outlook will display a message similar to the one shown in Figure 18-18.

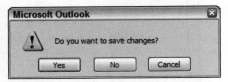

Figure 18-18: Save your changes to eliminate the attachment.

4. Click Yes to save your changes and close the now much smaller message.

Note   When you remove an attachment from a message, Outlook does not place the attachment in the Deleted Items folder. Make certain you have saved the attachment or that you do not need the attachment before removing it from a message.

Purging deleted items

Moving items to the Deleted Items folder cleans up your other Outlook folders, but it does not eliminate the wasted space that is used by those items. You need to empty the Deleted Items folder to truly eliminate the items that you've deleted.

Figure 18-19 shows one way to empty the Deleted Items folder. Right-click the Deleted Items folder, and choose Empty "Deleted Items" Folder from the pop-up menu.

You can also use the Tools ⇨ Empty "Deleted Items" Folder command to clear out the Deleted Items folder.

If you want to selectively remove items from the Deleted Items folder, first open the Deleted Items folder; then select the items you want to eliminate, and click the Delete button. Choose Yes to permanently delete the selected items.

You can also tell Outlook to automatically empty the Deleted Items folder whenever you close Outlook. Follow these steps to automate the process:

1. Select Tools ⇨ Options to display the Options dialog box.

2. Click the Other tab.

3. Select the Empty the Deleted Items folder upon exiting check box, as shown in Figure 18-20.

4. Click OK to close the dialog box.

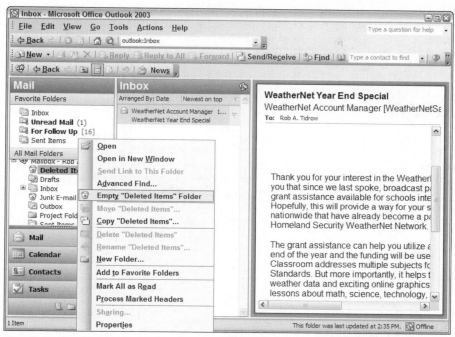

Figure 18-19: Empty the Deleted Items folder to finally remove the items you deleted earlier.

Figure 18-20: Automatically empty the Deleted Items folder whenever you close Outlook.

If you choose to automatically empty the Deleted Items folder when you close Outlook, you'll be asked to confirm that you want to do so when you exit from Outlook. Even so, this is a good way to make certain that your Deleted Items folder doesn't fill up with useless old messages that you no longer need.

Summary

Using your Outlook folders effectively is a good way to help you organize your Outlook data. In this chapter, you learned how Outlook's folders work, how to create folders, and how to manage the items in your folders. You learned several ways to share Outlook folders. Finally, you learned how to eliminate wasted space by using the Deleted Items folder to recover space that Outlook wouldn't recover on its own.

✦   ✦   ✦

Integrating with Other Applications

In This Chapter

Integrating Outlook with Office

Creating a mail merge

Sending an e-mail from an application

Importing and exporting data

Computers are wonderful and complex tools. Unlike a simple tool such as a hammer, a computer is intended to handle many very different tasks. This versatility is the result of the broad range of software that is available for modern computers.

In all likelihood, your copy of Outlook came as a part of Microsoft Office. But even if it did not, you probably have software that provides word processing functions, other software that manages database information, and software that handles calculations. You probably have many other applications on your computer, too. All these different pieces of software may seem totally independent of each other, but as you learn in this chapter, you may want to use some of them to complement each other. You might, for example, want to use the contact information that you have in Outlook to help you create perfectly addressed letters using your word processor. You might also want to send a spreadsheet file that you're working on as an e-mail message. These are just a few of the benefits you can gain from integrating Outlook with some of the other applications on your computer.

Integrating Outlook with Office

As you would probably expect, Outlook works very well with the other applications that are a part of Microsoft Office. If you want to use your Outlook Contacts list to create a mail merge in Microsoft, you'll find a command right on the Outlook menu to begin the process (Tools ➪ Mail Merge). In fact, if you want to share information between applications, Outlook is ready both to provide information to other programs and to use information that is provided by other programs.

Much of this two-way data sharing can be thought of as common to many different programs. It's often quite easy to share data between programs provided by different software manufacturers. You don't have to use Word, Excel, or Access to share information with Outlook. Of course, because Microsoft would like you to use their products, they've made it just a bit easier to share information between the programs of Microsoft Office than with other programs.

One way to share information between programs is to use linking or embedding to place an object from one program into a document in another program. Linking places a link in your document so that changes in the original object are reflected in your document. Embedding places a static copy of the object into your document. Linking offers the advantage of smaller document size and always up-to-date content, but embedding offers the advantage of having everything combined into a single package.

You might include a chart from an Excel worksheet in an e-mail message to show your team members how expenses have really increased over the past year. Or you might use a Microsoft Visio image to illustrate an important point about how your new building proposal will fit in with the existing structures in the neighborhood.

Here's a quick example of how you might place an Excel chart into an e-mail message:

1. Create the chart in an Excel worksheet.

2. Select the object that you want to use in your e-mail message. In this case, select the chart of monthly expense.

3. Select Edit ➪ Copy to copy the object to the Office Clipboard.

4. Switch back to Outlook. If the taskbar is visible, you can click the Outlook icon on the taskbar, or you can use Alt+Tab to switch between applications.

5. Click the Mail Button Bar icon and then click the New Mail Message button to display a new Message form.

6. Choose Format ➪ Rich Text.

7. Enter the addresses and subject line.

8. Type your message.

9. Select Edit ➪ Paste Special to display the Paste Special dialog box, shown in Figure 19-1. You could simply choose Edit ➪ Paste, but this won't enable you to choose the link option.

Note   A link option sends only a link, not actual data.

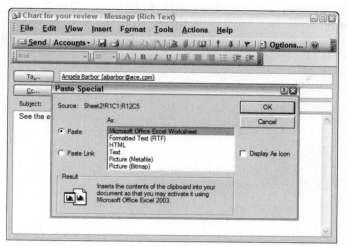

Figure 19-1: You can insert objects into your documents using different options.

10. Choose Paste to embed the object.

11. After you have selected how you want to paste the object, you may be able to select the object type. Generally the types shown at the top of the list will remain the closest to the object's original appearance.

12. Click OK to paste the object as shown in Figure 19-2.

13. Click Send to send the e-mail message.

Note   Don't use plain text as the message format if you want to place objects into the message. You can only paste text into a plain text message.

As you use Outlook and the other applications on your computer, it's a good idea to think about how you might share information between different applications. Don't make the all too common mistake of thinking that information can only be used in documents created in the application where the data resides. As you see in other examples in this chapter, you can almost always find a way to reuse data without going through the work of reentering it in a new program.

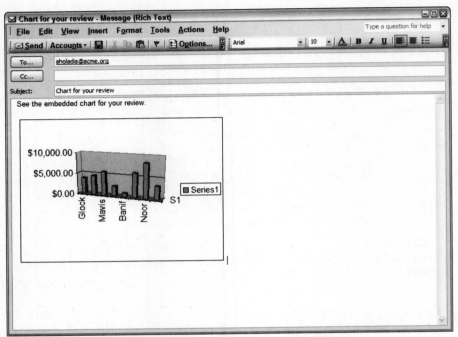

Figure 19-2: Inserted objects become a part of your document.

Creating a Mail Merge

A mail merge is the process of creating form letters, mailing labels, envelopes, or a catalog from a set of related information. There are several ways to create a mail merge document. You can either use your Outlook Contacts list to create these documents, or you can create them from lists of information that you have in other applications.

Choosing the source for your data can affect what you can do with mail merge:

✦ If you have all the names and addresses in Contacts, Outlook will be the easiest program to use because you won't have to export the information to another application.

✦ Outlook, however, doesn't offer some advanced capabilities that you'll find in other Office programs. If you need to do things like automatically separating the mail merge documents into individual zip codes to take advantage of special mailing rates, you may want to use Excel or Access to do the mail merge.

✦ If you need to produce a very large set of mail merge documents, such as thousands of form letters, you may want to use Access. This would be especially true if you have a huge database and need to be able to select a subset of the records for a particular need.

Getting names from contacts

If you already have the names that you want to use for your mail merge in your Outlook Contacts folder, creating a mail merge directly from Outlook is a simple process. Before you begin, however, you should put a little thought into what information the mail merge will use.

When you perform a mail merge, Outlook provides you with two options. You can create a mail merge using only the selected records, or you can create one from all the contact records that are shown in the current view. Unless you have applied a filter to the current view, Outlook includes all your contact records in the view. Although you may want to create a form letter to send to each of your contacts, it's more likely that you'll want to use a subset of the contact records. Suppose, for example, that you have assigned categories to each of your contacts. If you want to send a form letter to your relatives, you could create a view that shows only those contacts in the family category. You can learn more about filtering your contacts in Chapter 9.

To create a mail merge using records in your Contacts list, follow these steps:

1. Open the Contacts folder.

2. If you want to use a subset of the records in the mail merge, do one of the following:

   • Open a view that filters the records so that only the subset of records is shown.

   • Select the records that you want to use. Hold down Ctrl as you select each record to add it to the selection.

3. Select Tools ⇨ Mail Merge to display the Mail Merge Contacts dialog box, shown in Figure 19-3.

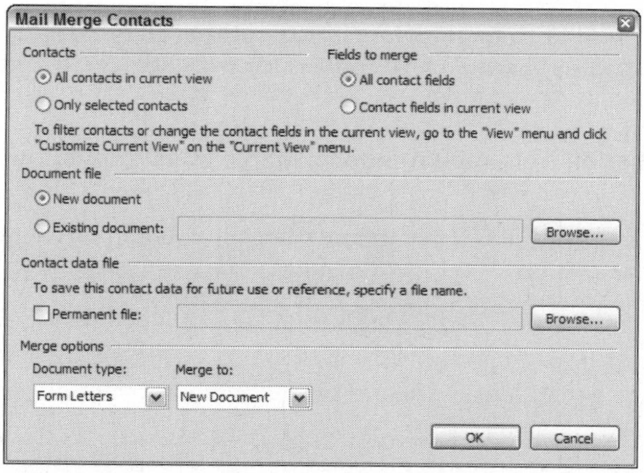

Figure 19-3: Use the Mail Merge Contacts dialog box to produce a mail merge from contact records.

4. Select which records to merge:

   • Choose All contacts in current view if you have applied a filter to select a subset of records or if you want to use all your contacts.

   • Choose Only selected contacts if you selected the subset of records manually before beginning the mail merge.

5. Select which fields to include:

   • Choose All contact fields if you want the mail merge to include all of the contact information.

   • Choose Contact fields in current view if you want the mail merge to include only those fields that are displayed in the current view.

6. Choose whether you want to create a new document or use an existing one. To use an existing document, you can locate the document via the Browse button.

7. Select the Permanent file check box and specify a filename if you want to save the mail merge data for future use. You might want to choose this option to provide a permanent record of the contacts that you used for this mail merge. Normally, though, you'll want to perform a new mail merge each time you need the information so that you don't accidentally use outdated information.

8. Select the type of mail merge document from the drop-down Document type list box, shown in Figure 19-4:

   • Form letters are documents that include merged information along with additional text that you specify.

   • Mailing labels are documents that contain multiple labels on each sheet. These are generally printed on peel-off label stock in standard sizes.

   • Envelopes are similar to mailing labels, except that the addresses are printed directly on standard-size envelopes.

   • Catalogs are similar to mailing labels, except that they are usually printed on plain paper and are intended for uses such as membership lists.

9. Choose the destination from the drop-down Merge to list box, shown in Figure 19-5:

   • New Document produces a document file that you can further edit as needed before printing.

   • Printer sends the merged document directly to the default system printer.

   • E-mail creates e-mail messages and places them in your Outbox.

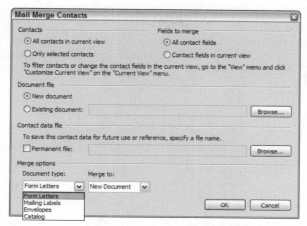

Figure 19-4: Choose the document type appropriate for your needs.

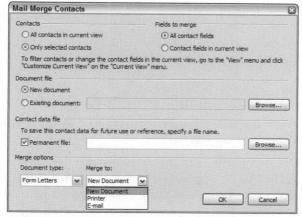

Figure 19-5: Choose the correct destination for the merged documents.

10. If your current view includes any distribution lists, they will not be incorporated in the mail merge. Click OK to confirm the message regarding this if it appears.

11. After Word opens, click the Insert Merge Field button to display the Insert Merge Field dialog box as shown in Figure 19-6. Double-click to add fields to the document. If you need to add spaces between fields, click Close, add a space, and reopen the Insert Merge Field dialog box.

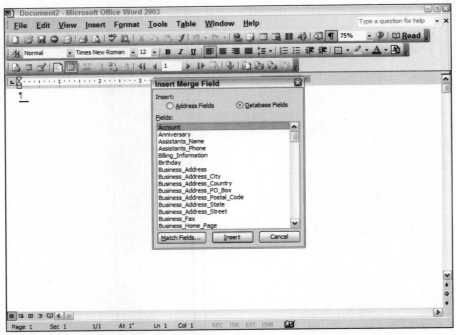

Figure 19-6: Add merge fields to your document.

12. Enter any additional text as necessary to complete your document.

13. Click the Merge to New Document button to display the Merge to New Document dialog box, shown in Figure 19-7.

Figure 19-7: Select the number of records you want to use in your merge.

14. Click All, Current Record, or specify the range of contacts you want included in the mail merge.

15. Click OK to complete your mail merge. Figure 19-8 shows an example of a completed form letter with the contact information substituted for the merge fields. If you chose to merge to the printer, fax, or e-mail, the completed mail merge documents will be directed to the correct destination rather than to documents.

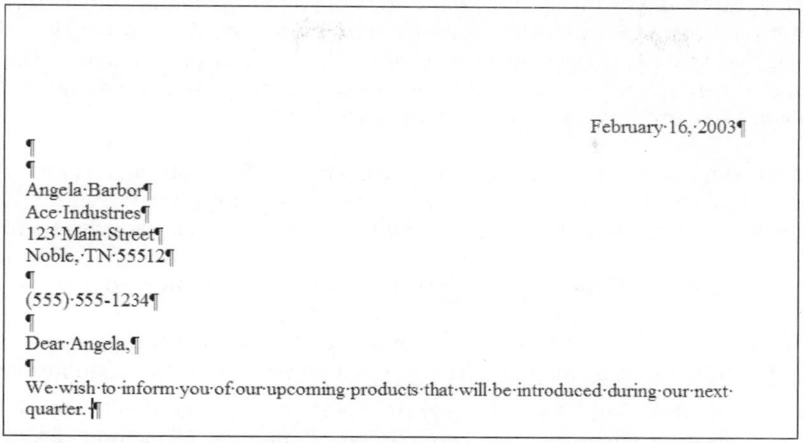

February·16,·2003¶
¶
¶
Angela·Barbor¶
Ace·Industries¶
123·Main·Street¶
Noble,·TN·55512¶
¶
(555)·555-1234¶
¶
Dear·Angela,¶
¶
We·wish·to·inform·you·of·our·upcoming·products·that·will·be·introduced·during·our·next·
quarter.·¶

Figure 19-8: Your completed mail merge replaces the merge fields with the information from your Contacts list.

16. Print and save your mail merge documents as necessary.

> **Note**
>
> Mail merge documents often contain nasty surprises such as missing or misplaced information. It's a good idea to practice using mail merge in advance to make certain that your mail merge works as you expect. In addition, it's always a good idea to take a quick look through the merged documents before you print and mail them. You may find that you need to do some additional tune-up of the master mail merge document before it is really ready to produce the documents that you want.

Sending an E-mail from an Application

Outlook's messaging capabilities make it easy for you to open Outlook and create a new e-mail message. Although this is certainly not a difficult task, switching between applications can be a distraction — especially if you're deep into a project and discover something important that you need to send out immediately. You've probably experienced this; you're working on a spreadsheet or a report and decide that you should send off a copy to someone else. So you switch over to Outlook and click the New Mail Message button, address the message, and begin to type your message. You then click the Insert File button and realize that you can't remember the correct filename. And even if you can remember the name of the file that you want to send, you aren't absolutely certain that you saved your latest revisions to the file. You switch back to the original program, click the Save button, note the filename, and switch back to your e-mail message. You complete the message and send it off, but you're frustrated by all the time that you've wasted.

Even if you've never thought about it before, you're probably starting to realize that it might be just a bit easier if you could send a document as an e-mail message without all that switching back and forth. Not only would it be less distracting to your train of thought, but you wouldn't have to try to remember the name of the file that you want to send, nor just exactly where you saved it.

You can send an e-mail message directly from any Office application as well as from many other Windows programs. The process is similar in most applications, so the following example shows you how to send an Excel worksheet from within Excel.

To send a document directly from an application, follow these steps:

1. Open the document that you want to send. In some programs, you must name the document by saving it before you can send it as an e-mail message.

2. Select File ➪ Send To to display the Send To menu, shown in Figure 19-9. Different applications may have different sets of options on the Send To menu, but most will include a Mail Recipient option.

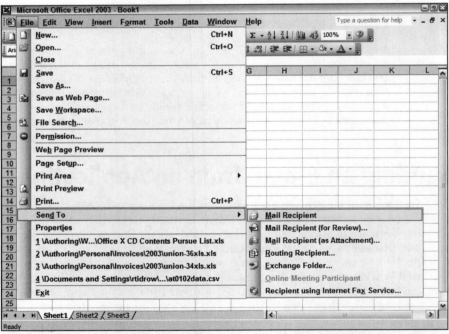

Figure 19-9: You can send a document from within the application that created it.

3. Choose the option you prefer:

- Mail Recipient generally sends the document as a file attachment, but in Office 2003 applications, you can choose to send the document as an HTML page.

- Mail Recipient (for Review) specifies that you want to send this file out for others to insert comments for review.

- Mail Recipient (as Attachment) specifies that you wish to send the document as a file attachment to a text message.

- Routing Recipient sends the file to a specified group of people and returns it to you when everyone has finished adding changes.

- Exchange Folder sends the file to an Exchange Server folder, where it will be available to all authorized users of that folder.

- Online Meeting Participant sends the file to someone who is participating with you in an online meeting using NetMeeting.

- Fax Service enables you to send the document as a fax using a fax driver or fax service (such as via the Internet).

4. If you selected Mail Recipient in an Office 2003 application, you'll next see a message similar to the one shown in Figure 19-10. Choose the format that best suits your needs and then click OK.

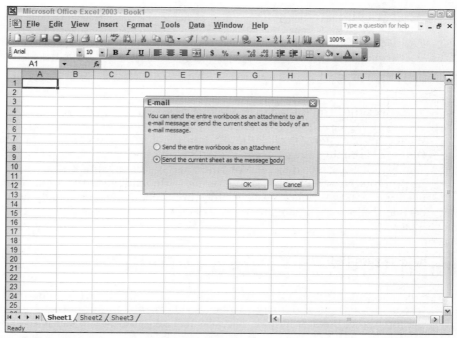

Figure 19-10: Choose the proper document format.

5. Select the message recipients.

6. Enter any additional text and set any message options as necessary. Figure 19-11 shows the message ready to send.

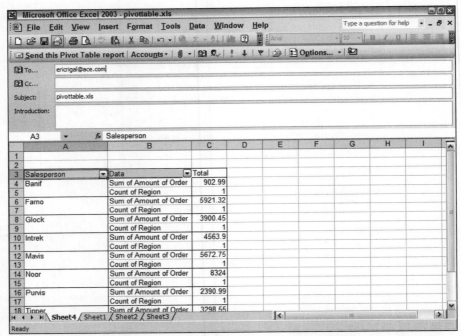

Figure 19-11: Complete the message just as you would if you were sending it from Outlook.

7. Click the Send button to send your message.

What happens after you click the Send button may depend on several factors. If Outlook is running, the message should be sent to your Outbox. If Outlook is not running, the message may be sent immediately using Outlook Express, or you may be prompted to select a messaging profile—depending on the application that you used to create the e-mail message. To prevent confusion, it's usually best to make certain Outlook is running before you decide to send an e-mail message.

Importing and Exporting Data

Your computer is probably worth a fraction of what the data it contains is worth to you. If you think about all the time and effort that you've put into entering information into various programs, documents, and databases, it's easy to see how valuable that information may be. As important as that data may be, it's not useful if you can't use the information the way you need to.

Outlook handles many different types of data. You may have several sources of data that you would like to use in Outlook, and you may have a number of places where your Outlook data might also be useful. The key to making all of this data more useful is to import and export the information so that you can use it where you need it.

Note

Outlook can import more types of data than it can export. If you need to use data from another program in Outlook, or use Outlook data in another program, you may encounter situations where neither program seems to support the other's format. If so, look for another format that both programs support such as dBase, comma-separated values, or even tab-separated values. If you cannot find a common format, you may be able to use Word, Excel, or Access to handle the format conversion.

Importing information into Outlook

There are several types of information that you may want to import into Outlook. Typically, though, these fall into a few categories:

- ✦ Contact information such as e-mail addresses
- ✦ vCard electronic business cards
- ✦ iCalendar scheduling information
- ✦ Messages stored in Personal Folder files
- ✦ Internet mail account settings, such as from other e-mail programs (Eudora Pro for example)
- ✦ Internet mail and addresses, such as from Eudora Pro

To import data into Outlook, follow these steps:

1. Select File ➪ Import and Export to display the Import and Export Wizard, shown in Figure 19-12. If you have the Microsoft Outlook Business Contact Manager installed, you will need to select File ➪ Import and Export ➪ Outlook.

2. Select the type of information that you want to import. If you aren't sure which option to choose, select each option and read the description in the lower part of the dialog box.

3. Click Next to continue.

4. Choose the type of file you wish to import, as shown in Figure 19-13. The choices will vary according to your selection in step 2.

5. Click Next to continue.

6. Select the name of the file that you want to import, as shown in Figure 19-14.

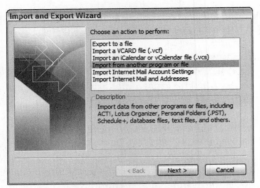

Figure 19-12: Use the Import and Export Wizard to bring data into Outlook.

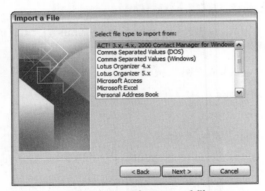

Figure 19-13: Choose the type of file you want to import.

Figure 19-14: Specify the name of file you want to import.

7. Choose any options for the import. These will vary according to the type of file that you are importing, but the options shown in Figure 19-14 are typical when you are importing contact information.

8. Click Next to continue.

9. If you are importing from a Personal Folder file, choose which folders you want to import, as shown in Figure 19-15. If you are importing data from other types of sources, you probably won't have to make this selection.

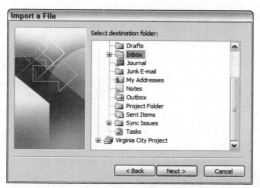

Figure 19-15: Choose which folder information to import and where to place that information.

10. If you want to set up custom field mappings, click the Map Custom Fields button to display the Map Custom Fields dialog box, shown in Figure 19-16. Drag values from the left list to the right list to map the fields as necessary.

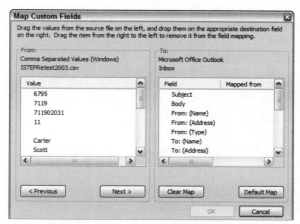

Figure 19-16: Set up field mappings to make sure your imported data is stored in the correct fields in your Outlook folder.

11. Click OK.

12. Click the Finish button to import the data.

Other types of data sources will involve different sequences of steps, but the import process will be similar in all cases. You must choose the type of data, the source file, and how to handle duplicates.

Note   If you import a large number of contact records into Outlook, be sure to review Chapter 15 to learn how to assign categories to your contacts. Assigning categories will make it much easier for you to manage your contact records — especially if you have a lot of people listed in your Contacts folder.

Exporting information from Outlook

Just as you can import data into Outlook from several different formats, you can also export Outlook data into a number of formats. Sometimes, though, the way that Outlook exports data may leave something to be desired. Fortunately, there are alternatives that may work better in some cases.

To export data from Outlook, follow these steps:

1. Select File ➪ Import and Export to display the Import and Export Wizard. If you have the Microsoft Outlook Business Contact Manager installed, you will need to select File ➪ Import and Export ➪ Outlook.

2. Select Export to a file option.

3. Click Next to continue.

4. Choose the type of file you want to create, as shown in Figure 19-17. Most of the format options are best suited for exporting contact information.

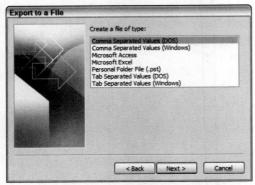

Figure 19-17: Choose the file format for the exported data.

5. Click Next to continue. If this is the first time that you have exported data to a particular format, you may need to insert your Outlook CD-ROM so that the correct export filter can be installed.

6. Select the folder that you want to export, as shown in Figure 19-18. If you choose a folder other than Contacts, you may not be pleased with the results — especially if you hope to save messages. See "Saving Outlook messages" later in this chapter for a better way to save your message text.

Figure 19-18: Choose the folder to export.

7. Click Next to continue.

8. Specify a name for the exported data file.

9. Click Next to continue.

10. Verify the actions to be performed, as shown in Figure 19-19, and then click the Finish button to export the data.

Figure 19-19: Verify that Outlook will export the information that you expect to export.

Note   Be sure to open the exported data file to verify the contents before you delete the data within Outlook. You may discover that the exported data is incomplete or unusable, and it is far better to determine this while you can still recover the information in Outlook.

Saving Outlook messages

If you look at data that you've exported from Outlook, you may be somewhat less than thrilled with the results. The reason for this is that data you export is generally saved in a database type of format, and this may not be what you intended — especially if you were trying to save a message for use in another program.

When you want to save a message, there's another way to do so that will generally produce better results than exporting the message. Follow these steps to save a message as a text file:

1. Select the message that you want to save.

2. Select File ➪ Save As to display the Save As dialog box, shown in Figure 19-20.

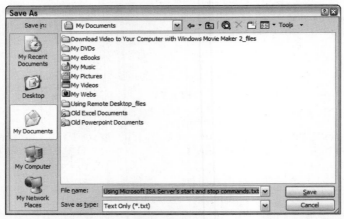

Figure 19-20: Save a message rather than exporting it if you want the message text to appear in a file.

3. Choose the destination for the file.

4. Enter a filename for the message. By default, Outlook will use the message subject as the filename.

5. Click Save to save the file.

When you save a message as a text file, Outlook includes the message header information at the top of the text file. This makes it easy for you to see the information such as who sent the message, the message date, the recipients, and the subject line. Following all of this, you'll see the message text.

Tip Saving a message as text does not save any message attachments. Be sure to save any important attachments separately.

Summary

Outlook is a capable program, but that doesn't mean you have to use it in isolation. As you learned in this chapter, Outlook works well with other programs. You saw that Outlook integrates with the other programs in Microsoft Office. You also learned how to use Outlook's Contacts list to produce form letters using mail merge. You saw that sending e-mail from within other applications is sometimes easier than switching back to Outlook, and you learned how to share data between Outlook and other programs.

✦ ✦ ✦

Delegating Tasks to an Assistant

In This Chapter

Understanding delegates

Assigning delegation

Granting folder access

Acting as an assistant

Not everyone can have administrative assistants do work for them; however, Outlook can delegate Outlook tasks to other users, such as members of a product team, consultants, and even managers. You can, for instance, allow other users to manage your Inbox, edit contacts in your Contacts folder, and create to-do lists in your Tasks folder. To set up Outlook to delegate tasks, your copy of Outlook must be part of a Microsoft Exchange Server 5.5 or higher organization. This allows you to select users from the Global Address List as delegates to access your shared Outlook folders.

Understanding Delegation

Outlook enables you to delegate other users to access all your Outlook folders: Calendar, Tasks, Inbox, Contacts, Notes, and Journal folders. This might be necessary because you may want an assistant to track your Calendar to keep you on schedule. In this case, you can work in your calendar (adding appointments and events, for example), but your assistant can see your Calendar folder as well. That way your assistant can reference your calendar while setting up other appointments and meetings on your behalf.

Similarly, if you delegate a person to have access to your Inbox, they can keep an eye on your incoming messages while you're out of the office in case important business-related messages are sent to you. If you do not have a chance to read your e-mail on the road, an important message does not go unanswered while you're gone.

As a way of illustrating how delegation works, the following permissions can be set for each delegate who has access to another user's Tasks folder. Other folders have the same delegation rights.

None. Does not allow a delegate to view, create, or modify your tasks in your Tasks folder. Use this option if you set up permissions for a delegate to access your other folders (such as your Calendar folder), but you do not want the delegate to access your Tasks folder.

Reviewer (can read items). Allows delegates to see and read tasks in your Tasks folder.

Author (can read and create items). Allows delegates to read and create new tasks in your Tasks folder.

Editor (can read, create, and modify items). Allows full access to your folder, including read, create, and modify rights.

If you assign the Editor permission to a delegate, be aware that the delegate can rename, modify, or delete your Tasks. Use this permission only for those users you trust.

Assigning Delegates

To assign delegates to a task, you must grant permission to those users who you want to send items on your behalf. The following steps show how to set up these assignments:

1. Choose Tools ➪ Options and then click the Delegates tab, as shown in Figure 20-1.

Figure 20-1: Use the Delegates tab to assign delegates to your Outlook tasks.

2. Click the Add button to display the Add Users dialog box, as shown in Figure 20-2.

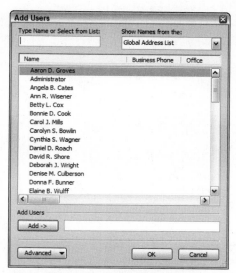

Figure 20-2: Use the Add Users dialog box to add users to be delegated.

3. Double-click the users you want to add as delegates. You can also click a name and then click the Add button.

4. Click OK to display the Delegate Permissions dialog box, as shown in Figure 20-3. If you select a single delegate, that person's name appears in the title bar of the dialog box; however, if you select more than one delegate, the phrase Multiple delegates appears in the title bar. The permissions you set in the following steps apply to all the selected delegates.

Tip

If you want to assign different permissions to different delegates, select each delegate separately in step 3; then assign permissions to each delegate separately.

5. In each of the drop-down lists, select the type of permissions (if any) you want to assign for each user. For example, if you want a user to have full control over your calendar, select Editor (can read, create, and modify items) from the Calendar drop-down list.

6. If you want to send a message to the delegates informing them of their permissions, select the Automatically send a message to delegates summarizing these permissions option. This is a good idea so your delegates know they have permission to access your folders. The e-mail message also informs them of the permissions you've granted them, and instructs them on how to open your folders.

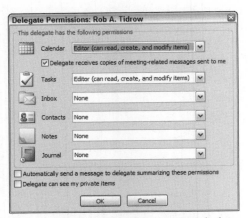

Figure 20-3: Use the Delegate Permissions dialog box to assign permissions to each delegate.

7. If you want delegates to see your private items (such as your private calendar items), select Delegate can see my private items.

8. Click OK to return to the Options dialog box.

9. If you want to add more delegates, click the Add button and return to step 3 above; otherwise go to step 10.

10. Click OK again on the Options dialog box.

If you selected the option to send a message to your delegates containing information about the delegation, Outlook automatically creates the message and then sends it. An example of this notification e-mail is shown in Figure 20-4.

If you have items you want to keep private and do not want others to see, click the Private check box when you are creating the item. For example, if you have an appointment you want to make sure that you can see on your calendar but you do not want delegates to see, select Private at the lower right corner of the New Appointment dialog box; then, in step 7 of the previous exercise, make sure you DO NOT select the Delegate can see my private items check box. If you need to modify this setting, choose Tools ➪ Options ➪ Delegates, select a delegate in the Delegates list, and click Permissions. Deselect Delegate can see my private items and then click OK. If you need to modify other delegates' permissions, do so now. If not, click OK to save your settings.

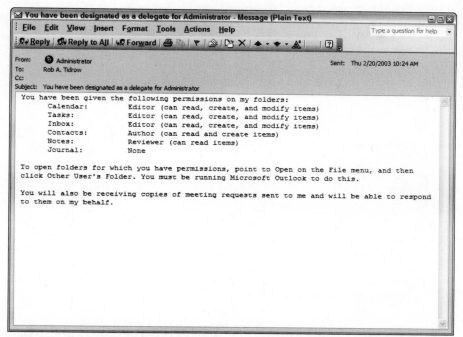

Figure 20-4: Your delegates will receive an e-mail similar to this one notifying them of their delegation permissions.

Granting Folder Access

Another way to allow other users access to your Outlook information is to share your Outlook folders. This is handy if you have subfolders within your Inbox, Calendar, or other "main" Outlook folder. Again, you must have a connection to an Exchange Server to share Outlook folders.

To share folders, use the following steps:

1. In the Navigation Pane pane, right-click a folder you want to share.

2. Choose Sharing to display the Properties dialog box.

3. Click the Permissions tab (if it's not already showing), as shown in Figure 20-5.

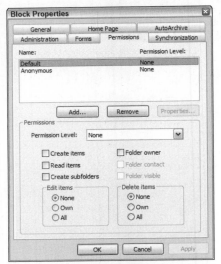

Figure 20-5: Use the Permissions tab to set Outlook folder sharing rights.

4. Click the Add button to display the Add Users dialog box (Figure 20-2).

5. Double-click the names of the users who you want to have share permissions to your folder.

6. Click OK.

7. From the Permission Level drop-down list, select the role of the permission, such as Owner. Table 20-1 explains each role.

	Table 20-1
	Permission Roles

Role Name	Description
Owner	Create, read, modify, and delete all items and files and create subfolders. As the folder owner, you can change the permission levels others have for the folder.
Publishing Editor subfolders.	Create, read, modify, and delete all items and files and create
Editor	Create, read, modify, and delete all items and files.
Publishing Author	Create and read items and files, create subfolders, and modify and delete items and files you create.
Author	Create and read items and files, and modify and delete items and files you create.

Role Name	Description
Nonediting Author	Create and read items and files.
Reviewer	Read items and files only.
Contributor	Create items and files only. The contents of the folder are not shown.
None	No permission. Cannot open the folder.

8. Click OK.

The user who was granted permission can now open the shared folder.

Acting as an Assistant

Take a look at delegation from the other angle — as an assistant or someone who has been granted permission to access someone else's Outlook folders. When a user grants you permission and that user selects the option to send you a message informing you that you have been granted delegate permissions, you receive a message similar to the one shown in Figure 20-4.

To view another person's folders, you must open that user's folder. To do so, follow these steps:

1. Choose File ➪ Open ➪ Other User's Folder to display the Open Other User's Folder dialog box, shown in Figure 20-6.

Figure 20-6: Specify the user and the folder you want to open.

Tip

After you opened a user' folder, those folders appear at the bottom of the Other User's Folder menu. Click one of them to quickly open the folder, bypassing the following steps.

2. Click the Name button and then select a user's name from the Select Name dialog box (see Figure 20-7). You must have been granted delegate permission for the user you specify to open that user's folder.

Figure 20-7: Select a user's name from the Select Name dialog box.

3. Click OK.

4. From the Folder type drop-down list, select the folder you want to open, such as Calendar, to see the selected user's Calendar folder.

5. Click OK to open that user's folder, as shown in Figure 20-8.

Notice in Figure 20-8 that the TaskPad shown on the Calendar of the user named Administrator is not that user's TaskPad. It is the TaskPad of the local user—the assistant. To see the tasks for another user, you must select the Tasks folder from the Open Other User's Folder dialog box (see step 1 in preceding steps). Of course, you must have delegate permission to open this folder.

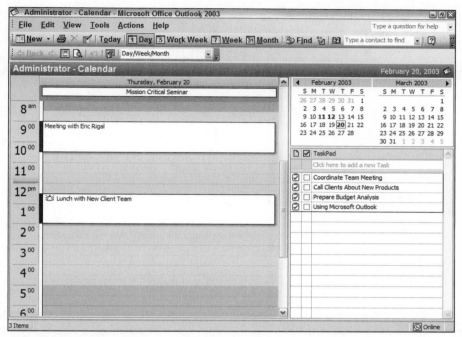

Figure 20-8: Viewing the calendar of another user

Send E-mail on Behalf of Someone Else

Outlook enables you to receive and send e-mail on behalf of someone else. This enables an assistant to send e-mail messages for a busy manager, or one who is away from the office a great deal of time. To do this, you must be granted delegate permission for that user's e-mail. Then use the following steps to access that user's e-mail:

1. Choose File ➪ Open ➪ Other User's Folder to display the Open Other User's Folder dialog box as shown in Figure 20-6.

2. Click the Name to display in the Select Name dialog box as shown in Figure 20-7.

3. Select a user's name that has granted you permission to access his or her e-mail folders.

4. Click OK.

5. From the Folder Type drop-down list, select Inbox.

6. Click OK to display the selected user's Inbox folder as shown in Figure 20-9.

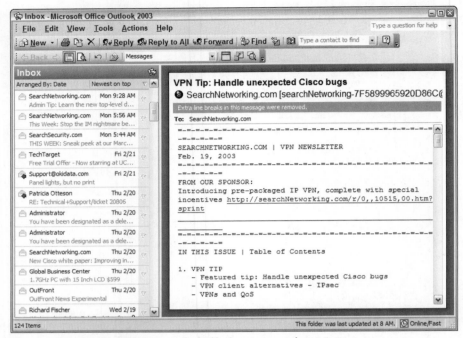

Figure 20-9: View the Inbox on behalf of someone else.

7. Select a message from the Inbox and then click the Reply or Reply To All toolbar button on the Standard toolbar. A reply to message box opens. In the From field, you can see the name of the user you are sending e-mail on behalf of.

8. Type your response, and click Send to send the message.

Manage Another Person's Calendar

After you are granted permission to access another person's calendar, you can view and manage that person's schedule. If you are granted Editor permission, you can read, create, and modify calendar items. This is the highest permission you can be given. The lowest, Review permission, allows you to only read someone else's items. In the middle is the Author permission, which grants you read and create permissions. In most situations, unless you are fully responsible for another person's schedule and need rights to modify (including deleting) items, Author permission is probably the best because it lets you read and create, but not modify calendar items.

The following shows how to manage another person's calendar:

1. Choose File ⇨ Open ⇨ Other User's Folder to display the Open Other User's Folder dialog box, as shown in Figure 20-6.

2. Click the Name to display the Select Name dialog box, as shown in Figure 20-7.

3. Select a user's name that has granted you permission to access their e-mail folders.

4. Click OK.

5. From the Folder Type drop-down list, select Calendar as shown in Figure 20-10.

Figure 20-10: You must choose Calendar from the Folder Type drop-down list to open the selected person's calendar.

6. Click OK to display the other person's calendar.

7. Perform Calendar tasks based on the permissions you are granted, such as adding new meetings, events, or appointments, moving items to different dates or times, or deleting items. Figure 20-11 shows an open calendar and a new appointment being added.

When you modify another person's calendar, that modification appears on the other person's calendar immediately or the next time that person opens Outlook.

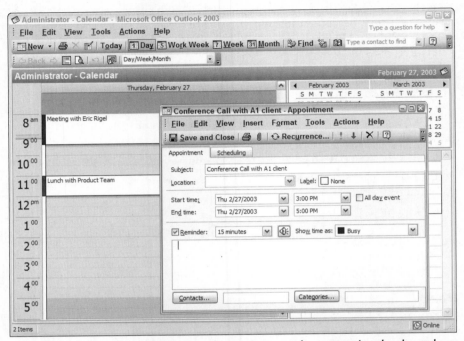

Figure 20-11: You can add new appointments to another person's calendar as long as you have Author or Editor permission.

Summary

Outlook enables you to delegate tasks to other users by letting them access your Outlook folders. When you set up delegates, you can specify which folders they can access and what types of access permissions they have. Delegation of tasks in this way is a powerful tool for any business that is running Microsoft Exchange Server and Outlook in their organization.

In the next chapter, you learn about using Microsoft SharePoint Team services to manage users, viewing data, and posting and sharing information.

✦　　✦　　✦

Using Windows SharePoint Services

Microsoft Windows SharePoint Services is essentially a way of placing information from Microsoft Office 2003 applications into a Web site for collaboration, thus creating a *portal*. A portal is a central Web-based location where you can access various types of data. Microsoft actually has two portal applications. Windows SharePoint Services is an *ad-hoc* portal used for creating small collaboration sites for sharing information within a team or group. SharePoint Portal Server is used to create a portal on an organizational scale. SharePoint Portal Server has far more functionality than Windows SharePoint Services, such as document versioning and check-in and check-out, but it is also much more difficult to implement and requires extensive Web programming and customization. Only Windows SharePoint Services is covered in this chapter; there are entire books available on SharePoint Portal Server.

Understanding Windows SharePoint Services

Windows SharePoint Services (WSS) allows you to share your Microsoft Office 2003 content with other members of your team. Almost any type of content can be shared, including Microsoft Office documents and Outlook data such as calendars. The main advantage of WSS is that it can be installed easily through a few simple automated steps and can be used with a minimum amount of user training. Adding, removing, and editing content on the WSS site is done through either a Web browser or Office 2003 applications. This simple interaction makes WSS more appealing for non-IT teams because a high level of technical knowledge is not required. Figure 21-1 shows the Windows SharePoint Services home page.

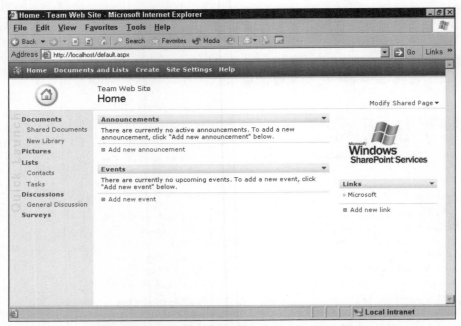

Figure 21-1: An example of the Windows SharePoint Services home page.

WSS can run on a server running Microsoft Windows Server 2003. In addition to collaboration using Office 2003 data such as shared calendars and task lists, WSS also provides a document library. A document library is similar to a shared folder on a file server or Exchange Server because it can contain any type of document or file. The difference, though, is that WSS document libraries are accessed through a Web browser for both file placement and retrieval. In addition, document libraries can be assigned templates that control the type of files that they can contain. Allowing only certain document types in a document library enables you to keep the library in order rather than having different types of files, as can happen with a shared folder on a file server. Finally, WSS document libraries have text searching functionality that can be used to find specific information within the library.

Setting up a WSS Site

There are several steps to setting up an WSS site that your users can use to share their data. You must first install the WSS prerequisites; then install WSS, and create an WSS virtual site.

Installing WSS prerequisites

Windows SharePoint Services requires both a Web server and a database server to be installed on the system that will host WSS. The Web server must be Microsoft Internet Information Services (IIS), included with Windows Server 2003 . The database server can be either Microsoft SQL Server, or Microsoft SQL Server Desktop Engine. SQL Server Desktop Engine is included with WSS and is installed during the WSS install. You don't need to use SQL Server unless your WSS site is going to be very large or needs special data access.

Windows Server 2003, unlike earlier Windows Server operating systems, does not install Internet Information Services by default during installation. To install IIS:

1. Open the Control Panel from the Start menu.

2. Open Add or Remove Programs and click Add/Remove Windows Components to open the Windows Components Wizard as shown in Figure 21-2.

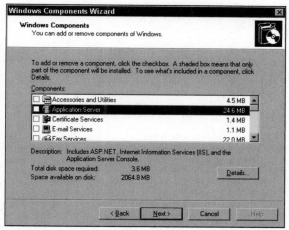

Figure 21-2: The Windows Components Wizard is used to add and remove optional Microsoft Windows components.

3. Highlight Application Server without clicking the check box in the Windows Components Wizard and click the Details button to open the Application Server dialog box.

4. Highlight Internet Information Services (IIS) without clicking the check box in the Windows Components Wizard, and click the Details button to open the Internet Information Services (IIS) dialog box.

5. Ensure the World Wide Web Service check box is selected as shown in Figure 21-3. If it is unchecked and you click the World Wide Web Service check box, a number of other required services are automatically added.

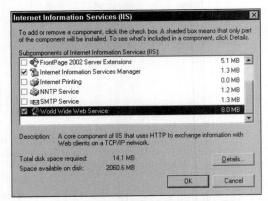

Figure 21-3: The World Wide Web Service must be selected in the Internet Information Services (IIS) dialog.

6. Click OK to close the IIS dialog box.

7. Select the ASP.NET check box in the Application Server dialog box.

8. Click OK to close the Application Server dialog box.

9. If the World Wide Web Service was selected when you opened the IIS dialog, click Cancel; otherwise, click Next in the Windows Components Wizard.

The World Wide Web Service and the other associated components are now added. You might be prompted for your Windows CD so you should have it handy. After the process is complete, click Finish to close the Windows Components Wizard. Close the Add or Remove Programs utility.

Installing WSS

Now that IIS is installed, you can begin installing WSS. WSS is located on either the FrontPage 2003 CD or the Office 2003 Developer Edition CD in a directory called SHAREPT.

1. Locate and open this folder and then double-click the setup program.

2. The first step in the Microsoft Windows SharePoint Services 2.0 Setup wizard is to review the license agreement. Select the box to accept the agreement and then click Next to continue.

3. Next, accept the default setting of Typical Installation and click Next.

4. You can review the options being installed by WSS, and click Install to begin the installation.

Once WSS is installed, your default web site in IIS is *extended* with the WSS site. The installation process will automatically open Internet Explorer to your new WSS site.

Managing users and site groups

Windows SharePoint Services requires the definition of users and their site group memberships for the WSS site. These users are assigned specific access to the site such as the ability to view, add, edit, or remove content. Users are managed through the Site Settings page in the WSS site. Open the WSS site you created in the first section in your Web browser. Enter the address `http://localhost`. Click the Site Settings link at the top of the WSS home page to open the Site Settings page; then click Manage Users in the Web Administration section of the Site Settings page to open the Manage Users page as shown in Figure 21-4.

Note   You must have the administrator role to work with WSS site settings. By default, the user who installed WSS is the only user with this role.

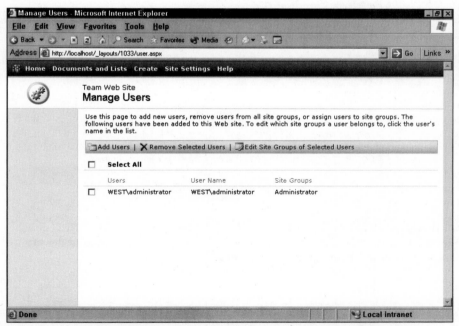

Figure 21-4: The Manage Users page is used to add users and edit site group memberships for the WSS site.

Adding a user

The Manage Users page is used to add and remove users or edit user site groups. To add a user, click the Add Users link on the Manage Users page to open the Add Users page as shown in Figure 21-5. From this page you can add users who can access the WSS site. Specify the user name to add in the users box in the proper form `domain\username` or `system\username` or enter the user's e-mail addresses. Adding users based on the `domain\username` or `system\username` convention will add users who already exist in the domain or locally on the system. If you enter an e-mail address, you can assign a user name in the next step. You can add multiple users in the Users box if you separate them with semicolons. Add both an existing user and an e-mail address to the Users box, separated by semicolons, for the sake of example.

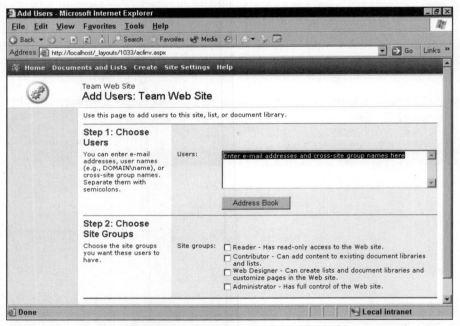

Figure 21-5: The Add Users page of the WSS site is used to add a user to the site and specify his or her site group membership.

WSS mail settings

Invitations are sent automatically by default when users are added to the site. Before you can send invitations from WSS you must configure the mail settings for WSS. To do this you must know the IP address of your SMTP server, the From: address, and the Reply-to: addresses for your messages.

1. On the server running WSS, select Start, All Programs, Administrative Tools, SharePoint Central Administration. The SharePoint Central Administration page allows you to configure the back end of your SharePoint site.

2. In the Server Configuration section, click Configure default e-mail server settings.

3. The Configure E-mail Server Settings page, shown below, is used to configure the default mail server address and e-mail message From and Reply-to addresses. Enter the IP address for the SMTP server.

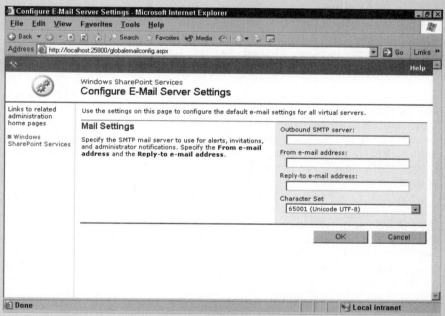

The Configure E-mail Server Settings page is used to set the mail settings for sending invitations.

4. Enter the From: address that will be displayed in the e-mail sent to the invited user.

5. Enter the Reply-to: address that defines the address to which replies to the invitation will be sent.

6. You can also change the character set for the e-mails, but this is optional.

7. After you have configured the mail settings, click the OK button at the bottom of the page and your changes are saved.

8. Close the current browser window.

In addition to specifying the user name you want to add, you must also select to which *site groups* the user belongs. There are a few site groups available for WSS users:

Reader. A reader has only read access to the WSS site, and cannot add or change any content.

Contributor. A user in the contributor site group can view all documents and discussions, and contribute to discussions but not add or change documents or other content.

Web Designer. A user in this site group role can add, remove, and change content as well as templates and layouts for the WSS site.

Administrator. A user in the administrator site group has full control of the WSS site and can add, remove, or change any information as well as set site groups for other users.

Select the appropriate site groups for the user you want to add. It is possible to select more than one site group for the user, but in most cases this is not necessary with WSS. After you have specified the users to add and selected the appropriate site group for the user, click the Next button at the bottom of the page.

The next step in the user addition process, shown in Figure 21-6 requires you to confirm the user information and allows you to send an e-mail notification to the user. In this example two users have been specified for addition, one by user account (west\blair) and one by e-mail address (blair@domain.tld). When you specify users to add by e-mail address a user account must first be created as it is not added automatically. The first user in the Confirm Users section that was specified by user account should have an e-mail address and display name specified. The display name is the name used to identify posts and other entries in the WSS site.

The second user, specified by e-mail address needs a user name and display name specified. The user name is the user account that was created for the user. You can also enter an e-mail messasge to send to the users you are creating, welcoming them to the WSS site. Once you have finished specifying the user information, click the Finish button to add the users.

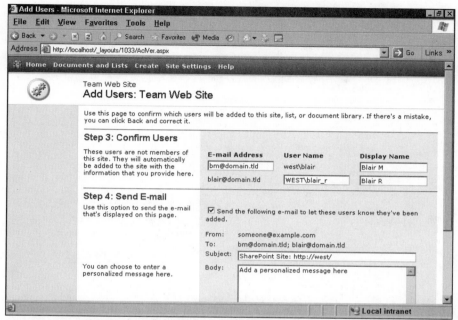

Figure 21-6: The second part of the WSS user addition process requires you to set user account information and allows you to send a welcome e-mail to the new users.

Removing users and changing site group membership for existing users

The Manage Users page can also be used to remove users from the WSS site and change the site group membership of existing users in the site in addition to creating new users. To remove a user, check the box next to the user name, and click Remove selected users. You are then prompted to verify the user deletion. After you click OK, the user is removed. To edit an existing user's site group membership in the WSS site, click the user name to open the Edit Site Group Membership page shown in Figure 21-7. This page displays the user's site group membership. You can select and deselect site group memberships as needed, click the OK button, and your changes are submitted. The user is given the new memberships immediately.

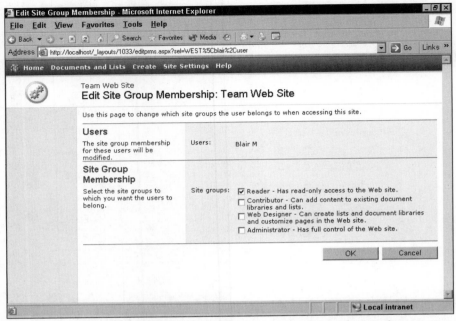

Figure 21-7: The Edit Site Group Membership page is used to change site group memberships for a user.

Tip   By default the user who installs WSS is given the Administrator site group membership in the site. You may not want this user to have the Administrator membership if he or she is not part of your team. You can either remove his or her user account from WSS completely, or change his or her site group membership to a lower level.

Advanced user and site group membership management

To access the more advanced site management features for WSS, open the WSS site in a Web browser and then click the Site Settings link at the top. Click the Go to Site Administration link in the Web Administration section of the Site Settings page. The Site Administration page, shown in Figure 21-8, is used for more advanced WSS site administration tasks. These advanced tasks include enabling and disabling advanced features such as usage analysis, configuring server health settings, and enabling version control.

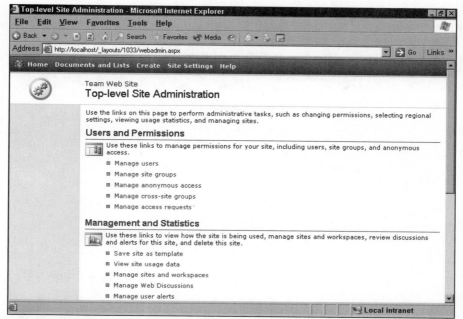

Figure 21-8: The Site Administration page contains links to pages that allow you to perform advanced site administration tasks.

Configure anonymous access

The first important part of the Site Administration page is anonymous browsing. Anonymous access is disabled for the WSS site by default. You can change this setting by clicking the Manage anonymous access settings link. From the Change Anonymous Access Settings page shown in Figure 21-9, select Entire Web site or Lists and libraries to enable anonymous access to those site areas. You can also set the "Allow all authenticated users to access this site?" setting to yes to allow all users authenticated to the system or domain to access the WSS site regardless of whether they have been configured in the Manage Users page. You can then set the site group membership setting for the authenticated users which is set to Reader by default.

Tip Before you enable anonymous access to your WSS site you must have enabled anonymous access to the Web site in IIS in which WSS is installed, the Default Web Site by default. This is outside the scope of this book but can be done from the Directory Security tab of the Web site Properties dialog.

To set anonymous access, select the access level and then click OK. Your changes will be commited.

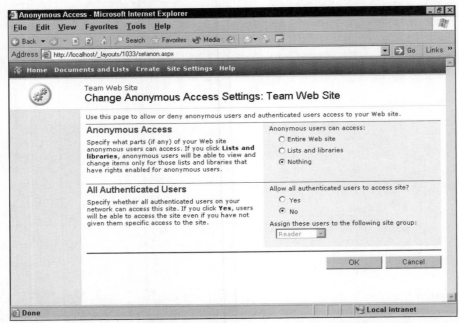

Figure 21-9: The Change Anonymous Access Settings page is used to configure anonymous access to your WSS site, if any.

Advanced site group configuration

The other advanced configuration option is site group configuration. While there are a number of pre-set site groups available, you can also add your own custom site groups or change the permissions of the existing site groups.

Tip You can think of a site group as a group of permissions. When you assign a user membership in a site group, the entire group of permissions associated with that site group is assigned to the user. This makes permission management easier, especially when a certain group of permissions is commonly given to a number of users.

From the Site Administration page (the Site Administration page was discussed at the beginning of the "Advanced user and site group management" section earlier in this chapter), click the Manage site groups link to open the Manage Site Groups page shown in Figure 21-10. The Mange Site Groups page is similar to the Manage Users page in that it can be used to add and remove site groups as well as changing the permissions associated with an existing site group. You will rarely need to change the pre-configured site groups except when you have requirements for special permissions for specific users.

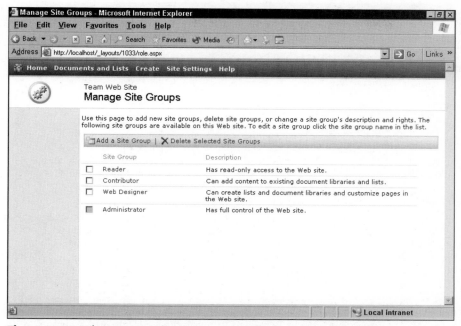

Figure 21-10: The Manage Site Groups page allows you to add, remove, and configure site groups for the site.

To add a site group, click Add a Site Group in the Manage Site Groups page to open the Add a Site Group page shown in Figure 21-11. Specify a name and description for the new site group. After you have named the group, you can begin to select permissions for the new group. The effects of all permissions cannot be documented here, but they are well described in the descriptions on the Web page. Note that selecting certain permissions will also select others that are mutually inclusive. You cannot, for example, select the Add Items permission without the View Items permission being selected automatically. Selecting the Select All button will give this site group the same rights as the default Administrator site group. This can be useful if you want to give a site group almost all of the rights as the Administrator site group, but not all. Click Select all and then deselect the permissions you don't want the site group to have rather then selecting each one individually. After you have finished selecting the permissions for the site group, click the Create Site Group button at the bottom of the page and the site group will be added.

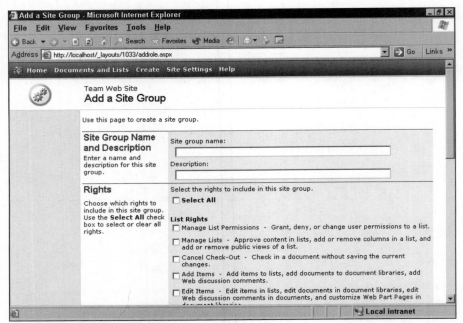

Figure 21-11: The Add a Role page is used to name the new role and assign its permissions.

Removing site groups is as simple as selecting the check box next to a site group in the Manage Site Groups page and clicking Delete Selected Site Groups. You are prompted to verify the deletion; then click OK to continue. You can also edit the permissions assigned to an existing site group by clicking the site group name in the Manage Site Groups page then clicking Edit Site Group Permissions. The Edit Site Group username page is similar to the Add a Site Group page. You can edit the site group description, and select and deselect site group permissions as needed. After you have made changes, you can click the Submit button. You can also use the Edit Site Group username page to copy an existing site group, which is useful if you want another site group with similar permissions but only small changes. Click the Copy Site Group button at the bottom of the Edit Site Group username page to go to the Copy the Site Group username page. This page is identical to the Add a Site Group page except the permissions assigned to the copied site group are selected automatically. Make the required changes, assign a name and description to the site group, and click the Create Site Group button.

Viewing Data in the WSS Site

Viewing data in the WSS site is the simplest part of using WSS. As long as you are logged in as a user with at least the Browser role or anonymous access to the site is enabled, you can view the WSS site in a Web browser. Open the WSS home page by going to the virtual site in which WSS is installed. In the case of this example, the WSS site is installed in the default Web site on a server called `west`. The link to the WSS site is `http://west`. You may need to provide a fully qualified domain name (`http://west.domain.tld`) depending on your DNS settings.

Tip Your security policy on your Windows Server 2003 system will apply to your WSS site as well. For example if the "Limit local account use of blank passwords to console login only" policy is enabled as is the default, users with blank passwords will not be allowed to log in to the WSS site either from a remote system or from the local system using the computer name (i.e., `http://west`) but `http://localhost` will still work. If you are having access problems, remember to check your security policies.

After you are at the WSS home page, you can view the data in the site. There are essentially five classes in an WSS site:

Documents. The documents section of the WSS site contains shared documents. Any WSS user with at least the Author role can place documents on the WSS site for other users to view.

Picture Libraries. Picture libraries simply contain pictures. You can use the picture libraries in WSS as photo galleries for sharing pictures with your team.

Lists. Lists contain information such as contacts, tasks, or links. They are used for sharing specific information rather than the documents section of the site, which only stores general documents.

Discussion Boards. Discussion boards are used for having threaded conversations. Using discussion boards makes team conversations easier than using e-mail because the threaded display makes the information easier to read and is easier for team members to contribute.

Surveys. Surveys give you the ability to build custom polls for your team. Once team members have completed the survey you can then collect the results. This is useful in projects, for example, for conducting post-project satisfaction surveys.

Viewing documents

To view documents in the WSS site, click Documents on the left side of the WSS home page to go to a list of the Document Libraries shown in Figure 21-12. The site shown in the example has only one document library: Shared Documents. Shared Documents is the default document library and is created when WSS is installed.

Click a document library to open it, as shown in Figure 21-13. Here you find a list of documents contained in the library. The list shows the document type as an icon, the filename, the last modified time, and the last user to modify the document. You can also change the document title and filename by hovering your cursor over the filename, clicking the arrow button that appears, and selecting Edit Properties from the menu that appears. You can view the document by clicking the file, and download the document by right-clicking the filename and selecting Save Target As.

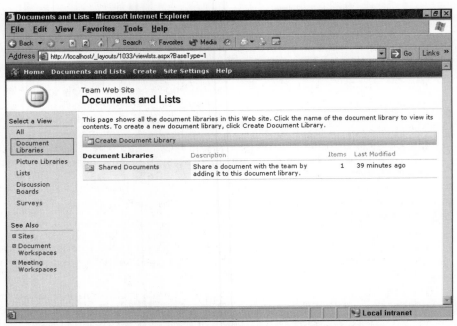

Figure 21-12: Documents are stored in WSS in Document Libraries.

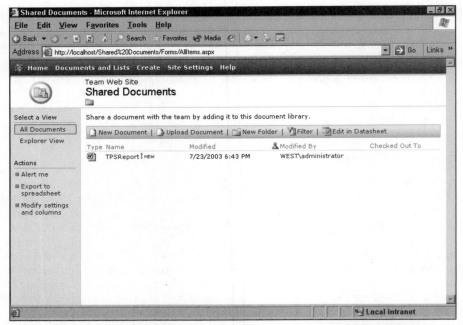

Figure 21-13: The Shared Documents page shows the contents of the library.

In addition, you can check the document out of the library for editing. Hover over the file name again, click the arrow button, and select Check Out. While a document is checked out by one user, no other users can make changes to it. This is a version control feature that prevents multiple versions of the same document from being created. Once you're done editing the document, open the menu again and select Check In to be taken to the Check In page shown in Figure 21-14. When checking a document in you have three options. You can check the document in, check in changes to the document while keeping the document checked out, or undo the check out operation and discard any changes made. You can also add comments then click the OK button to complete the check in operation.

There are two other options within a document library. Click the Filter link to enable filters for the library. With filters enabled you can filter documents from a specific date or user by selecting from the appropriate drop-down box. When filters are enabled, you can click the Hide Filter Choices, and the filter drop-down boxes will disappear.

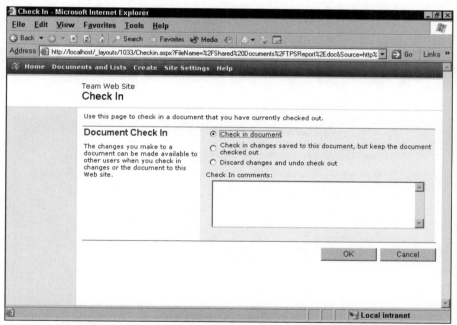

Figure 21-14: The Check In page is used to check in documents that have been checked out of the library for editing.

The other option is the Alert Me option. Hover over the file name, click the arrow that appears, and select Alert Me from the menu to open the New Alert page shown in Figure 21-15. Setting a new alert for a document causes you to be notified when changes are made to the document. By default, you are alerted about all changes to the document. You can also select Changed Items or Web Discussion Updates to be alerted only for those changes. Select the notification interval, each time the item changes, a daily summary, or a weekly summary. Click the OK button to set the alert.

Viewing discussion boards

To view discussion boards, click Discussions on the left side of the WSS page to view the list of boards. Only the General Discussion board exists by default. Click the name of a board to view the discussions. Figure 21-16 shows the discussions within the General Discussion board.

Clicking the plus symbol next to a discussion subject opens the first message in the thread and shows threaded replies below. Clicking the plus symbol next to each reply opens the reply. Using these features you can then browse through the entire discussion in a coherent manner. You can also use the Filter and Alert Me options as discussed in the "Viewing documents" section earlier in this chapter.

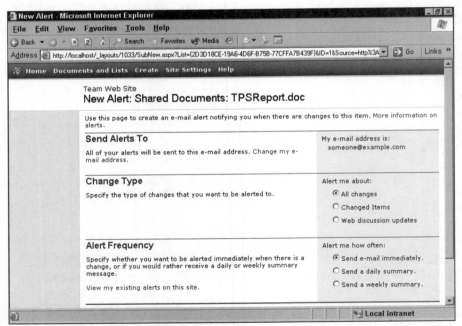

Figure 21-15: The New Alert page is used to configure e-mail alerts when content in the site is changed.

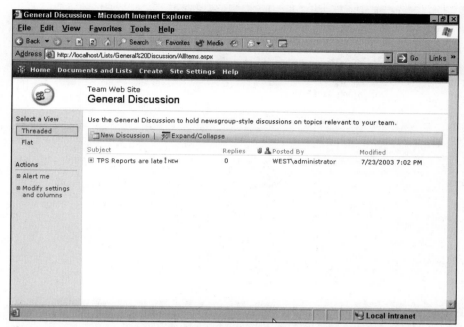

Figure 21-16: A list of discussions is shown within a discussion board.

Viewing lists

To view lists, click Lists on the left side of the WSS home page to open the Lists page as shown in Figure 21-17. Lists are different from the other content in WSS because they contain a specific type of data. The following default lists are shown in the figure:

Announcements. Contains note items and is used for making announcements to the team members. Announcements can be set to expire.

Contacts. Contains contact items and is used to hold contacts that the entire team can use.

Events. Contains calendar items. Important events for the team are contained here.

Links. Contains Web links. Use the Links list to hold commonly accessed Internet sites.

Tasks. Contains task items. Tasks for the team as a whole can be placed here.

It is possible to also have other custom lists. To view the contents of a list, click the list name. Figure 21-18 shows an example of list content. In the example of link items, click the link name to go to that link. The other lists work in a similar fashion. You can also use the Filter and Alert Me options as discussed in the "Viewing documents" section earlier in this chapter.

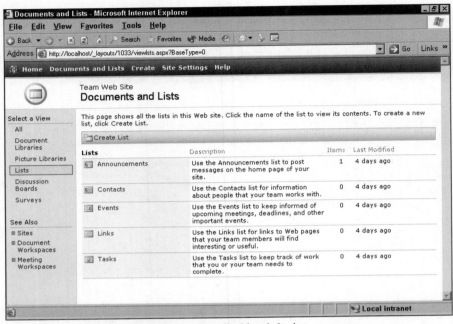

Figure 21-17: A number of lists are installed by default.

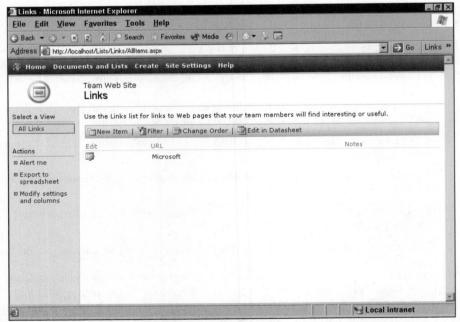

Figure 21-18: An example of the contents of a list.

Adding Data to an WSS Site

Adding data to an WSS site is almost as simple as viewing existing data. You can add data to any of the same WSS areas as discussed in the previous section, "Viewing Data in the WSS Site."

Adding documents

To add a document to a document library, click the Documents link on the left side of the WSS home page to display a list of document libraries. You can also jump directly to a specific library by clicking the library name. You can add a document to an existing library by clicking the library name, or create a new document library by clicking the Create Document Library link then clicking Document Library in the Create Page page. This opens the New Document Library page shown in Figure 21-19. Enter a name and description for the document library, select whether or not to display the library on the quick launch bar (on the left side of the WSS home page), select whether or not to enable versioning, then select a document template for the library. The template defines the type of data that can be stored in the library. Click Create, the new library is created, and you are taken to the new library.

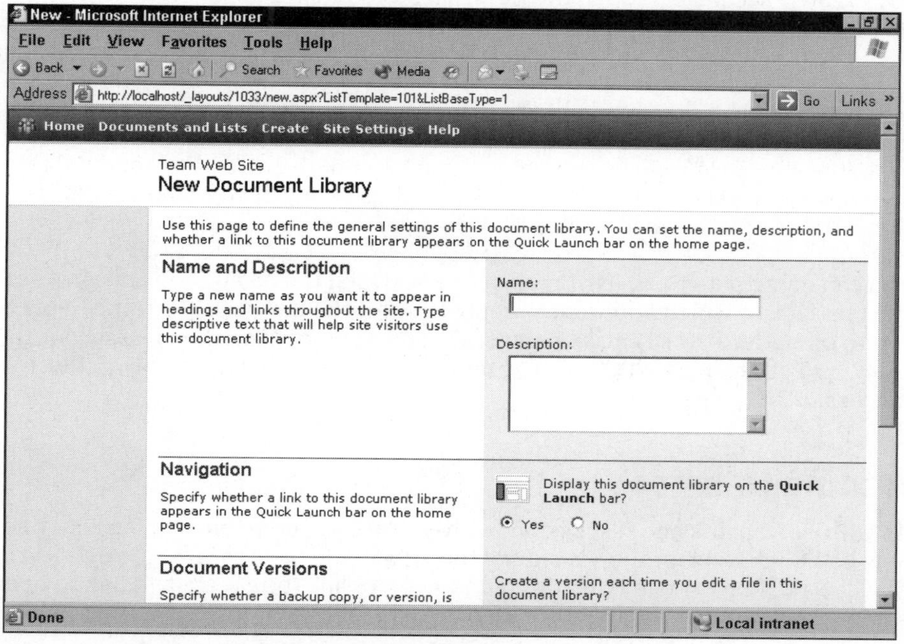

Figure 21-19: You can create a new document library.

After you are in a document library, you can add documents to the library by clicking the New Document link or the Upload Document link. The New Document link opens the appropriate program for creating a document with the existing template type. If this library is set with a Microsoft Word template, for example, clicking New Document launches Microsoft Word. Save the new document, and it will be added to the document library.

You can upload existing documents by clicking the Upload Document link to open the Upload Document page. Select whether or not to overwrite an existing document with the same name by selecting or deselecting the check box and specify the file name by typing it in the box or using the Browse button to locate it on the local system. To upload the document, click the Save and Close link; the document is added to the library.

Adding to discussions

Discussions are more complex than documents because you can add new discussion boards, new discussions, or reply to existing discussions. Click Discussions on the left side of the WSS home page to open the list of discussion boards. Contribute to an existing discussion board by clicking the board name, or add a discussion board by clicking the Create Discussion Board link then click Discussion Board in the Create Page page to open the New Discussion Board page. Give the new board a name and description, and select if you want it displayed in the Quick Launch bar; then click the Create button. The new board is created and you are taken to it.

When you are in a discussion board, you can add a new discussion (thread) by clicking the New Discussion link. This creates the root post of a new discussion. From the New Discussion page, enter the subject of the discussion and the text for the message and then click Save and Close. This subject is used as the discussion title when it is shown in the list.

You can contribute to an existing discussion. Open the discussion and then select the message to which you want to reply to show the message. Click the Reply button to open the New Discussion page, enter the subject and the message for the reply, and click Save and Close. The new message is added as a reply in the discussion.

Adding to lists

As with documents and discussion boards, you can add to an existing list or add a new list. Click Lists on the left side of the WSS home page to view the existing lists. Click an existing list name to add to that list, or click the Create List link to open the Create Page page shown in Figure 21-20.

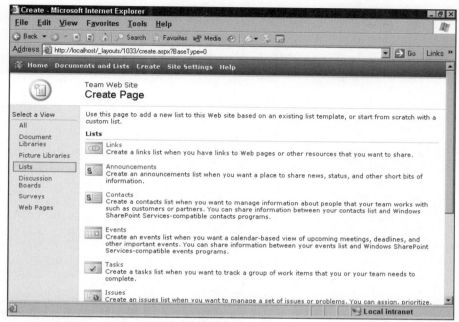

Figure 21-20: A new list can be added.

To add a new list you must first select a list type from the Create Page page. A number of custom list types are available as well as the Custom List, Custom List in Datasheet View and Import Spreadsheet list types, which are used for special lists where the predefined list types are not sufficient. Select a list type; then, in the next page, assign the list a name and description, select if it should appear in the Quick Launch bar, and click the Create button to add the new list. You are taken to the new list.

After you are in a list, creating new list items is simple. Click the New Item link to open the New Item page. Fill out the New Item page with the appropriate information for the list, which varies depending on the list type. Click Save and Close to add the list item.

Summary

In this chapter you learned about Windows SharePoint Services (WSS). WSS is an extensive Web-based collaboration tool allowing you to share information with your team members or colleagues from a Web browser. WSS requires Windows Server 2003 and Microsoft Internet Information Services and is installed from the Microsoft FrontPage 2003 CD or the Microsoft Office 2003 Developer Edition CD. WSS configuration was covered as well as using and adding data to an WSS site.

✦   ✦   ✦

Managing Outlook Users

P A R T

V

♦ ♦ ♦ ♦

In This Part

Chapter 22
Supporting Roaming Users

Chapter 23
Managing Security and Performance

Chapter 24
Controlling Outlook (and Office) with Group and System Policies

Chapter 25
Backing Up and Recovering User Data

Chapter 26
Managing Exchange Server for Outlook Users

♦ ♦ ♦ ♦

Supporting Roaming Users

I t's inevitable in today's computing environment that users will use multiple computing devices. It's not uncommon for a user to have a desktop, a laptop, and a handheld such as a PocketPC device; however, one thing that remains consistent throughout the use of all these machines is the need for a single set of contacts, a single calendar from which to manage appointments, and a single set of tasks to accomplish.

In other words, a roaming user, in the contest of this Outlook discussion here, refers to a user who needs access to a central repository of collaborative information made up of email messages, calendar items, contacts, tasks, and even documents, news, journal items, etc., consistent across multiple compatible devices. This chapter looks at how to make this possible.

That's because Outlook 2003 supports roaming users, which lets users access a single set of information. No matter what the Windows-based computing device, Outlook provides a consistent set of information, and the user is always working with the most recent changes in data.

In this chapter, we'll take a look at some of particulars of which you need to be aware when working with roaming users. We'll examine how to configure multiple user profiles and then look at some of the mechanisms involved when roaming from an Exchange Server installation.

In This Chapter

What are roaming users?

Folder redirection and PST location

Applying policies

Roaming with different versions of Outlook

Roaming issues for Exchange Server users

What Are Roaming Users?

A roaming user, as the name suggests, is someone who uses more than one computer on a regular basis often from different locations. They may travel with portable devices needing access to centrally located information. There are roaming users that frequent a corporate office and those that almost never see "home base." They often require multiple configurations of the same application to afford them this access. Obviously Outlook is equipped to meet these needs. As they do this, access to Outlook data such as the Calendar, Contacts, and e-mail account settings remains constant. It's as if the installation of Outlook travels with you wherever you go.

So how is this feat accomplished? The rest of the chapter examines how.

Using and configuring Outlook profiles

You are probably already familiar with the concept of profiles, especially if you share a Windows-based computer with another person. In the Windows XP operating system, for example, a profile contains nearly everything that defines the end user experience. Further, this end-user experience can be configured one way for one user, while another user has a completely different look and feel, mapped drives, printer connections, and so forth. This is because a user profile keeps all these items separate.

Likewise, Outlook uses profiles to store all information germane to a particular user's experience with the application. This includes information about a person's e-mail server(s), location of their .pst file (remember that Outlook user information might be kept on an Exchange server), and other various options that define how Outlook behaves for a particular user.

Default Outlook profiles

The first time Outlook 2003 is run after a new installation, the Outlook Profile Wizard launches. The wizard then walks a user through the process of creating a profile for their first use of Outlook. This profile is then used every time Outlook starts until additional profiles are created. If, however, a user is upgrading from a previous version of Outlook, Outlook 2003 detects the profile already present, and will use the existing profile on the user's computer and simply upgrade that profile for use in Outlook 2003 instead of using the Outlook Profile Wizard.

Outlook profile configuration is critical in sending and receiving e-mail messages.

Selecting a profile to use when Outlook starts

When Outlook starts, and if no other profiles have been created, the existing profile is used for configuration of Outlook settings. If more than one profile is configured, you can tell Outlook which one to use at startup time, or have Outlook prompt you for the profile to use. This might be a configuration you select if you are sharing the computer — and the installation of Outlook — with multiple users.

To tell Outlook how to behave with configured profiles at startup time, follow these steps:

1. Open the Control Panel and then double-click the Mail icon.

2. In the Mail Setup dialog box, click the Show Profiles button.

3. Do one of the following:

- If you want the same profile used every time you start Microsoft Outlook, click Always use this profile; then, in the drop-down list, choose the desired profile.

- If you want Outlook to prompt for a user profile to use, click the Prompt for a profile to be used radio button.

Now that you know that multiple identities can be used when implementing an installation of Outlook 2003, how do you go about configuring the program for these differing profiles? There are a couple of ways, each explored in the following sections.

 Tip   You can also access the Mail Setup dialog box by right-clicking the Outlook icon placed on the desktop after a default installation and choosing Properties.

Adding and removing a user profile manually

The process of configuring additional Outlook 2003 profiles is done from the same place you manipulated startup behavior; that is, you start by opening the Control Panel. After you have opened up the Control panel if you want to add a profile, do the following:

1. Double-click the Mail icon; then click the Show Profiles button.

2. Click Add.

3. Type a name for the profile and then click OK.

You are walked through the E-mail Accounts Wizard, as shown in Figure 22-1, which guides you through the process of setting up the e-mail settings for use in this new profile. Follow the directions onscreen to complete the profile creation.

 Tip   When you open Outlook and you are prompted for a profile, you can start the new profile creation from that prompt as well

Imagine now that you want to get rid of that pesky profile. You've gotten the big promotion, a new computer with the flat screen monitor, the subsequent corner office, and even one of those annoying Dell Interns at your every beck and call. And because you've got the new rig, you'll no longer be sharing the computer with anyone else. To remove a user profile, follow these steps:

1. Open the Control Panel and click the Mail icon, as you did in the previous steps.

2. Click Show Profiles, and select the profile you want; then click Remove.

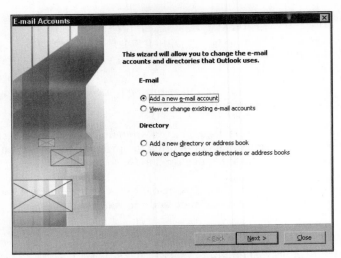

Figure 22-1: The E-mail Accounts Wizard welcome page.

Automating Outlook profiles using the Custom Installation Wizard

Because profiles are so important in defining the end user experience with Outlook (that is, Outlook won't retrieve any of the users' e-mail until the profile has been set up properly), you might prefer to automate profile creation instead of allowing users to create their own profiles using the Outlook Profile Wizard. You can use the Office Custom Installation Wizard to create profiles automatically for your users during installation. Both of these tools are available in the Office 2000 and 2003 Resource Kits.

All Outlook profile information entered in the Custom Installation Wizard is stored in the transform (MST file) that the wizard creates. When you install Office 11, this information is written to the HKEY_LOCAL_MACHINE\Software\Microsoft\Newprof subkey on the target computer. When Outlook 2003 starts for the first time, it performs a check to determine if any Outlook profiles already exist in this subkey on the computer. If no existing profiles are discovered, Outlook reads the customized information from the registry to create a new Outlook profile.

Tip   You can force Outlook to create a new Outlook profile even if a user already has an existing profile by using the Newprof.exe file, as explored later in this chapter.

The Custom Outlook Installation Options panel in the Office XP Custom Installation Wizard provides a simplified interface for creating Outlook profiles.

To create automated user profiles, follow these steps using the Outlook Custom Installation Wizard:

1. Launch the Office 2003 Custom Installation Wizard. (This will vary slightly if you're using the Office 2000 Resource Kit; the end result should be the same.) Click Customize Outlook profile and account information from the Custom Outlook Installation Panel, as shown in Figure 22-2.

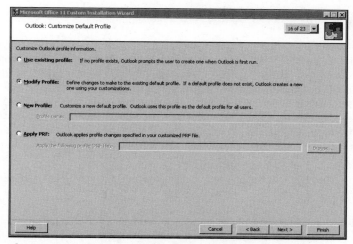

Figure 22-2: The Customize Outlook profile dialog box.

2. In the Configuration type box, select the configuration you want to use— Corporate, Workgroup Settings, or Internet Only Settings.

3. Click a setting in the left pane and then enter the corresponding option you want to use in the right pane.

This is just part of what the Office Profile Wizard can do. When you run the Office Profile Wizard to create a user profile, the end result will be an Office profile settings file (OPS file), which Office Setup uses to apply default settings when Office 11 is installed.

By design, the Profile Wizard excludes some settings, including user-specific information such as the user name and Most Recently Used file list (File menu). For example, the Profile Wizard does not capture the following Microsoft Outlook 2003 settings:

✦ Profile settings, including mail server configuration

✦ Storage settings, such as default delivery location and personal folder files (PST files)

✦ E-mail accounts and directories (Tools ⎪ Options ⎪ Mail Setup ⎪ E-mail Accounts)

✦ Send/Receive groups (Tools ⎪ Options ⎪ Mail Setup ⎪ Send/Receive)

✦ Customized views; for example, the fields displayed in the Inbox or another folder

✦ Outlook Bar shortcuts

✦ Auto-archive options set for a particular folder, which you set by right-clicking the folder, clicking Properties, and choosing options in the AutoArchive tab

✦ Delegate options (Tools | Options | Delegates)

Now, if you're using the Office 2000 Resource Kit, bear in mind that profiles used to be delineated in to two different categories: Corporate or Workgroup settings, and Internet Only settings. Outlook 2003, like Outlook 2002, uses a unified mode and no longer supports these different modes. But since we're dealing with previous versions of Outlook in this chapter, it's worth mentioning here. You won't see this, however, when configuring a profile with the Office 2003 Resource Kit, but if you're using the 2000 Resource Kit, it's an important distinction, as discussed next.

Configuring Corporate or Workgroup settings

If you're configuring the Corporate or Workgroup settings using the Office 2000 Resource Kit, keep in mind the following items:

✦ The General settings under Corporate or Workgroup Settings include an Enter Profile Name box. For the profile to be created, type a profile name in this box.

✦ After you choose the services in the Services List section, configure options for each service as appropriate.

✦ When you configure an Internet e-mail service, enter information in both the Internet E-mail Settings and POP3 Account Settings sections. Make sure you type exactly the same account name in both of these dialog boxes.

✦ When you configure an Internet E-mail service, type Internet E-mail — before the account name in the Enter long account name box in the Internet E-mail Settings section. For example, if the account name is BoycePersonal, you would enter the long account name as Internet e-mail — BoycePersonal.

Configuring Internet Only settings

When you configure the Internet Only settings, keep in mind that after you select the accounts you want to create in the General section, configure options for the account as appropriate.

Creating an Outlook profile automatically by using Newprof.exe

You have other options at your disposal besides the Outlook Profile Wizard or the Custom Installation Wizard. Newprof.exe is yet another tool Outlook uses to create user profiles. Usually, Outlook uses Newprof.exe only to create a new Outlook profile when no Outlook profile exists. If you want to create a new Outlook profile regardless of whether a profile already exists, you can use the Custom Installation Wizard to include Newprof.exe as an application to run after installation.

When you include Newprof.exe as a standalone application, you must also include a reference to a .prf file, a text file that contains Outlook profile settings information. You learn more about the use of the .prf file a little later in this chapter.

Tip   The Office Resource Kit includes a sample .prf file, called Outlook.prf This file contains both an example and instructions for modifying the file to create various Outlook profiles. For further information about profile creation using Outlook.prf, consult the Office 11 Resource Kit Toolbox.

After you have created or modified a .prf file, you are ready to include Newprof.exe as part of the customized Office 11 installation.

To add Newprof.exe to an Office installation, follow these steps:

1. From the Office 2003 Resource Kit's Custom Installation Wizard, click Add in the Add Installations and Run Programs panel to launch the Custom Installation Wizard, shown in Figure 22-3.

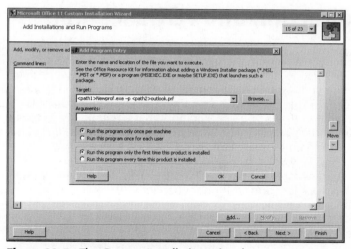

Figure 22-3: The Custom Installation Wizard.

2. In the Command line box, type **<path1>Newprof.exe –p <path2>outlook.prf**. path1 and path2 specify the path to Newprof.exe and Outlook.prf, respectively.

Now you've added Newprof to the Office installation.

Creating an Outlook profile using environment variables

Both the Custom Outlook Installation Options panel in the Custom Installation Wizard and the .prf file now support user environment variables. This support means you can streamline the use of one set of Outlook 2003 profile settings for the configuration of many unique profiles for many different users.

If you have been administering Windows computers for any length of time, you are probably already aware of the use of system variables. Further, you might be aware that through the use of logon scripts or batch files, you can set user environment variables on users' computers. You can then refer to these variables in the Outlook profile settings as `%variable%`. Here's one example: On computers running Windows NT, Windows 2000, and Windows XP, a user's logon name is stored as the default user environment variable %USERNAME%. You can use this variable when configuring Outlook profile settings in several ways. Here are a few:

> **Name of the profile.** ProfileName = Microsoft - %USERNAME%
>
> **Exchange mailbox name.** MailboxName = %USERNAME%
>
> **Name of a Personal Folders file.** PathToPersonalFolders = C:\%USERNAME%.pst

Folder Redirection and PST Location

As discussed earlier in this book, Outlook stores critical user data in a .pst file when using a standalone installation. By default, it is stored on the local machine's hard drive. And while this file is the heart and soul of Outlook use, you can nevertheless store it anywhere you want. In fact, you might want to store it in a different location, especially if you are a roaming user. If you are, you might want that .pst file available from all the places you use a computer. It could be correctly summarized that at the core of the roaming user issue when using Outlook 2003 is the access to a single .pst file from multiple locations.

You can store it anywhere that has read/write access and decent connectivity. A CD-ROM or a network location with poor connectivity would be two choices that would not work, for example.

If you use one computer frequently and want to store .pst files on a network server, and you want all this to take place automatically, consider redirecting the location of your .pst file.

One strategy you could undertake to redirect the Outlook file is to store the Outlook .pst file in you're my Documents folder, and then redirect this folder to a network location. The My Documents location is probably the most easily redirected folder a user has access to. And , because it's a part of a user profile, its usually available no matter where the user goes.

Unless your only computer access is through the office and the administrator at said office has put the kibosh on folder redirection (through a Group Policy, discussed later in this chapter), you should have free reign on where you store the contents of the My Documents folder.

To redirect the My Documents, right-click on the folder from the desktop and then choose Properties, as shown in Figure 22-4.

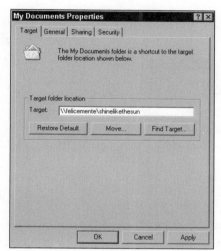

Figure 22-4: You can redirect the My Documents folder from this dialog box.

Redirecting the .pst file

Now that you've go the My Documents folder stored in a different location, your next task is to instruct Outlook where to store your .pst file. You could configure Outlook to store the .pst file in the My Documents folder, or any other location for that matter. That way, you ensure that the .pst data is always available to you as long as you have access to that location.

As you begin to take the steps necessary to change the default location of the .pst file, there are a couple of preliminary tasks you must complete. These steps will apply no matter where you decide to relocate the .pst file, whether in the redirected My Documents Folder or not.

First you need to locate your existing .pst file name and location. You've no doubt seen this by now if you're reading the book in sequence, but it doesn't hurt to review:

1. Open Outlook, and from the Tools menu, choose Options.

2. Click the Mail Setup tab, and then the Data Files button.

3. Now make note of the path and file name for of your .pst file as shown in Figure 22-5. This will differ depending on what operating system you are using. On a Windows 2000 machine using a standalone installation, the default location is here:

```
C:\Documents and Settings\%username%\Local Settings\
Application Settings\Data\Microsoft\Outlook
```

4. Close the Outlook Data Files dialog box, and then click OK.

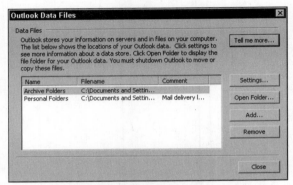

Figure 22-5: The Data File Management dialog box.

You'll need to know the location of the .pst file before you set about relocating it. Once you know the .pst location, you will make a copy of the file to a location that will be consistently available. In the example, I'll show you how to copy to a network server, which wil be the most commonly used instance of .pst file relocation. Here are the steps to follow:

1. Quit all programs, especially Outlook, as it will be accessing the .pst file.

2. Use Windows Explorer to navigate to the .pst file location on your hard drive, and then copy the file to an available network server. Make note of the new location; you'll need it later when reconfiguring Outlook.

Tip   Don't forget to ensure you have the proper permissions to access this network share, or the preceding point will be moot when accessing the .pst folder from a roaming location. And also don't forget to close Outlook so that the .pst file isn't already in use when you try to access it from another location.

That's really all there is to it. A simple copy and paste operation you can easily accomplish with a drag and drop. Now all that's left is to reconfigure Outlook to use the new file. Here's what's necessary to instruct Outlook to use the .pst file on the server:

1. As you did when identifying the local .pst location, start Outlook, and from the Tools menu, choose Options. From the Options dialog box, select the Mail Setup tab.

2. Click the E-mail accounts button, launching the E-mail accounts Wizard.

3. Click the View or change existing e-mail accounts radio button, and then click Next.

4. From the Email Accounts dialog box, choose the New Outlook Data File button at the bottom.

5. This brings up the New Outlook Data File dialog box, where you'll select the Personal Folders file (.pst), choice. Click OK.

6. In the Create or Open Outlook Data File dialog box, browse for or type the network path to the copied .pst file on the network server. Then Click OK twice.

7. Now, from the Deliver new e-mail to the following location option, choose the .pst file located on the network server in the drop down box, and then click Finish.

Note   If the change just made affects the default mail delivery location, and usually it does, receive this message:

"You have changed the default deliver location for your e-mail. This will change the location of your Inbox, Calendar, and other folders. These changes will take effect the next time you start Outlook."

8. Click OK, and then from the Mail Setup tab, click the Data Files button.

9. From the Outlook Data Files dialog box, select the original, local .pst file you identified earlier as the default location, and then choose Remove to remove that local .pst file from your Outlook profile.

10. Click Close, and then OK to close all dialog boxes.

Once you're done changing the directory location of the .pst file, restart Outlook. Assuming the new (copied) .pst is your default delivery location, you will now see a message telling you that all Outlook shortcuts will be recreated. This is necessary because the existing shortcuts point to the old .pst location.

Click Yes to have Outlook revise the Outlook shortcuts so that they direct the way to the network location. There will be no more required input on your part. Once this step is completed, your Outlook profile will now point to a network server location, one that is presumable always available. Thus will your Outlook data always be available.

Furthermore, to enable easier roaming to the .pst file with consistently, you might also want to make a persistent connection a part of your user profile. To do so, you should establish a mapped network drive to the network server storing your .pst file. Here's how:

1. Open Windows Explorer. You could do so through the Start menu or by right-clicking on the My Computer desktop icon (if available) and choosing Explore.

2. In Windows Explorer, from the Tools menu, choose Map Network Drive.

3. Select an available drive letter, then either Browse for or type the path to the shared location of the .pst file, and select the Reconnect At Logon check box to make the connection persistent. Click OK when you're done.

Applying Group Policies

As you may know, the central component of Windows 2000 and beyond administration is group policies. With a group policy, you can accomplish almost every conceivable administrative task, be it deploying an installation of Office, as has been discussed earlier in this book, or removing the ability for certain users, such as the ones who inspire those CDW commercials, to access the Control Panel. As touched on in Chapter 2, the Group Policy settings you create are contained in a Group Policy object (GPO). By associating a GPO with an Active Directory container object — sites, domains, and organizational units (OUs) — you apply these saved settings to the users and computers in those Active Directory containers.

What does that have to do with roaming in Outlook? One of the settings configurable with a group policy is the capability to redirect a folder.

Tip   Configuration of Folder Redirection settings in a Group Policy Object won't work unless your account is in an Active Directory domain. If you are configuring a local GPO, you won't see the Folder Redirection node in the Group Policy editor, as the assumption is (I'm assuming) that local GPO's are used to manage only those computers in a workgroup.

By configuring the GPO settings, you can redirect four common user data folders: Application Data, Desktop, My Documents, and Start Menu. For each one you configure, you have three options that will further affect behavior of the redirected items. These include:

No administrative policy specified. This leaves the user folder at the default location. In the case of non-roaming users, the folder remains on the user's local computer. For roaming users, the folder resides in the roaming profile and is copied across the network to the user's workstation at logon.

Basic – Redirect everyone's folder to the same location. At first glance this setting appears to redirect all users to the same folder. While you can do that, which is handy when you want all users to share a single folder for applications or desktop, you can also redirect users to their own folders. For example, you might configure this setting to point the users' folders to \\server\share\ %username%, which would cause each user to be directed to their own home folder. The key concept is that you're specifying redirection regardless of security group membership.

Advanced – Specify locations for various user groups. This setting lets you specify redirection based on group membership, and provides much more flexibility for folder redirection settings. Rather than specify a single location for all users for which the policy applies, you add groups to a list and specify which folder location each group receives. As with the Basic option, you can redirect a group to a single folder by specifying an absolute path, or redirect each member of a group to his own folder by using the %username% variable.

Again, the procedure here for access of .pst data is nearly identical to the method described in the preceding section. After you've specified your folder redirection behaviors with Group Policy Objects, you should then configure Outlook, through the Data File Management dialog box (File Menu | Data Management) to keep your .pst file in the appropriate redirected location. If you do, you should find data access remains unhindered no matter where you are.

Roaming With Different Versions of Outlook

You should be aware that Outlook 2002 stores data in a different location in the HKEY_CURRENT_USER registry key. Because of this difference, several settings do not roam when you switch between Outlook 2002 and a previous version of Outlook.

User profiles

To use multiple computers, the Outlook user profile name must be the same on every computer that the user logs on to. Using the profile owner's name or e-mail alias as the profile name is a good way to obtain this consistency.

First Run

If you use a computer where Outlook 2003 has been installed but has never been through the First Run step, the Profile Wizard starts even though you have a profile on the server. (Remember that the Outlook Profile Wizard is what Outlook launches the first time it is opened so that a Outlook profile can be configured.) To set the Mail Support registry entry for Outlook, you must follow the wizard through the First Run process. This setting is on a per-machine basis rather than a per-user basis.

Roaming with Personal Folders (.pst) files and Personal Address Books (.pab)

As you have already seen, Outlook 2003, along with previous versions of Outlook, doesn't necessarily use the same location for the .pst file as is the case with

Outlook 2003. The default storage location for Outlook pst files is in the following directory:

```
<Installation drive>:\<Installation directory>\<Profile
Name>\Local Settings\Application Data\Microsoft\Outlook
```

However, this Outlook 2003 behavior may be a departure from previous installations, especially if those earlier versions of Outlook were installed on Windows 9x computers. Windows 9x computers store their profile folders in different locations than do Windows 2000 and Windows XP systems. If you are using Outlook on a 9x system, you may find the .pst file in this location instead:

```
<Installation drive>:\<Installation
directory>\Profiles\<Profile Name> \Application
Data\Microsoft\Outlook
```

Roaming becomes problematic when moving from Outlook 2003 to earlier versions on earlier operating systems and visa versa. To overcome this behavior, make sure to configure the computers on the network to use a static mapped network drive (mapped with the same drive letter on each computer) that is used to store user's data files. In other words, you want the drives referenced in the same way. For example, if one computer maps the X: drive to the shared location of the .pst folder, the other computer should use the X: drive as well, not the H: drive. That way, no matter what version of Outlook is installed, or what Windows operating system is running it, the application will always look to the X: drive to load the .pst file.

Using Windows NT security settings (if the shared location resides on an file server with an NTFS-formatted drive), you're able to configure the roaming storage locations so that each user can access only their specific folders. After you've done this, place the .pst files and .pab files in these folders.

Tip   If you use Outlook 2003 with a personal folder (.pst) file that contains a single folder of 16,000 or more items, you encounter a loss of data when accessing this .pst file from an installation of Microsoft Outlook 97 build 8.02 or earlier. This is because Microsoft Outlook 8.02 or earlier does cannot access data in a .pst file with over 10,000 items. To alleviate this issue, you should either upgrade your version of Outlook to 8.03 or later (what else?), or reduce the number of entries in all individual folders to less than 10,000. Note also that this issue applies to messages archived or AutoArchived to a .pst by Microsoft Outlook 2003 and accessed from Outlook version earlier than 8.03.

After this is accomplished, it's time to configure the Outlook profiles to access the shared .pst files from the server. When you log on to a different computer, the Outlook profile can locate the .pst and .pab files because they have the same path associated with them on any computer that you use. (This is also why time was spent at the beginning of this chapter discussing in great detail the significance of the profile, even if you've encountered this before.)

Be aware that any local .pst files, including AutoArchive files and Personal Address Book files, are inaccessible when you roam.

How to use offline storage (.ost) files

Outlook 2003, as well as Outlook versions 2002 and 2000, is designed to roam while you use an offline storage (.ost) file. Microsoft Outlook 98, however, is not. When you use an .ost file and roam between different computers with one using Outlook 2003 and another using an earlier version of Outlook prior to 2000, you may receive the following error message:

'Unable to open your default mail folders. The Exchange Server has detected that you are using an old copy of your OST file. Please delete the file . . . '

In addition to accessing a consistent set of data from other installations of Outlook when using different machines, you might also expect other customized settings to travel with you as well. This may or may not be the case, as discussed in the following section.

Outlook Bar shortcuts

Outlook Bar shortcuts, as a rule, do not function as expected when using previous versions of Outlook. As you have seen earlier in this book, you can place shortcuts to executable (.exe) files and URL's in the Outlook Bar; however, these shortcuts do not function when used in earlier versions of Outlook 2000 and earlier and generate an error message. Note that the Outlook Bar file (<profile name>.fav) can be overwritten when you log off the computer.

Other profile-specific items you should know about when roaming include:

Quick Launch Icon. The Outlook 2003 icon that is placed in the Quick Launch Bar does not function on a computer running earlier versions of Outlook.

Rules Wizard Rules. Outlook 2003 includes improvements in the Rules Wizard. When you create a rule by using a feature that is only available with Outlook 2003, you receive the following warning: "You are creating a rule that will be incompatible with versions of Outlook earlier than Outlook 2003. If you create this rule, you cannot use your rules with Outlook 98 and earlier versions. For more information, search for help on 'Upgrading Rules'. Are you sure you want to create this rule?" Rules that do not contain Outlook 2003-specific features roam. Rules that contain Outlook 2003-specific features do not roam.

Folder Home Pages. Outlook 2003 offers home pages for folders. Prior to Outlook version 2000, this feature was not available, and you cannot access these home pages with those earlier versions.

Toolbars and Menus. Modifications that you made to the Outlook toolbars with Outlook 2003only roam if the feature or action was available with earlier versions. When you roam from Outlook 2003 to an earlier version, you can expect the following behavior:

- Macros are not advertised if they were added to the toolbar.
- Features new and specific to Outlook 2002 are not advertised when they are viewed on an earlier version.
- The Web toolbar is not available when you use an earlier version.
- The Recently Used feature is not available on an earlier version.

Electronic Forms Designer (EFD) Forms and Custom Forms. Furthermore, there's a chance you will receive the following error message when you roam between computers that use the NT File System (NTFS) and computers that use the File Allocation Table (FAT) file system: "The custom form could not be opened. Outlook will use an Outlook form instead."

Why is this? It has to do with the file name length. NTFS uses long file names, while FAT uses the MS-DOS 8.3 file names. To resolve this behavior, rename the Frmcache.dat file on the 2nd (FAT) computer and then re-download the forms.

Contact Distribution Lists. Distribution lists that you created in the Outlook 2003 Contacts folder are not displayed in earlier versions.

Contact Linking. The Contact Linking feature of available since Outlook 2000 is not available with earlier versions.

Contact Name Format Settings. Changes that you make to the default Full Name format and the default File As order in Contacts options do not roam.

Settings and options that do not roam

Several Outlook items have been discussed whose behaviors are modified when roaming from one computer to another. While modifications can show up in certain features when roaming, there are yet others that simply will not roam. These include the following, with instructions on how to access these features.

The Close original message on reply or forward, and **Display a notification message when new mail arrives option.** To access these settings, on the Tools menu, click Options. Then, on the Preferences tab, choose the E-mail Options.

The Advanced E-mail option. Click Options on the Tools menu to access these settings. On the Preferences tab, click E-mail Options and then click Advanced E-mail Options.

The Tracking Options option. Click Options on the Tools menu to access these settings. On the Preferences tab, click E-mail Options and then click Tracking Options.

The Message Format Options setting. Click Options on the Tools menu as before. Then, from the Mail Format tab, in Message Format section, is the option to Use Microsoft Word to edit e-mail messages.

The General Options section. From the Tools menu, click Options. There, click on the Spelling tab. The top section lists Outlook 2003's General Options.

Startup in Outlook Today. The launching of Outlook into Outlook Today is not a feature that roams with previous versions.

Roaming Issues for Exchange Server Users

Using the Custom Installation Wizard, you can specify Microsoft Exchange Server settings for use in a customized installation of Outlook 2003. You can also use this procedure whether you are installing Outlook 2003 as a standalone product or as part of the entire Office 11 suite.

Specify exchange settings for Outlook user profiles in the Custom Installation Wizard

You have several options for configuring Microsoft Exchange Server connections for users (including the option of not configuring connection information). You can make configuration changes for new Exchange users and for existing users.

For users for whom an Exchange Server connection is not configured, you can specify a user name and server name, as well as offline settings.

For users who have an existing Exchange Server connection, you can keep that connection or replace the current Exchange Server configuration with a new one.

Follow this procedure to define Exchange settings for Outlook user profiles:

1. Click Configure an Exchange Server connection in the Custom Installation Wizard, on the Outlook: Specify Exchange Settings page.

   Tip If you chose New Profile on the previous page, this configuration applies to all Outlook users.

2. Use the default %username% variable setting for the user's logon name.

3. Type the name of an Exchange Server on your network. This name will be replaced with the specific Exchange Server for each individual user when Outlook first starts.

   Tip If you prefer, you can use another system variable name. For example, you can use another system variable name if you have a separate user name specifically for Outlook access. You must specify the Exchange Server name. If this variable is not set on user computers, the Windows NT domain logon name will be used here (if %username% is specified for the logon name in this dialog box).

4. Click More Settings to configure offline settings and then click OK.

5. Select the Overwrite existing Exchange settings if an Exchange connection exists that can use the Exchange Server connection that you defined for all users. Note that this step only applies when you modify a profile. If you are going about defining new default profiles, the profile that you define will be used for all users.

6. Click Next to proceed with the Custom Installation Wizard.

Creating and Migrating Office Profiles

Now that the importance of profiles have been discussed, this section covers additional issues such as moving Outlook profiles with you as your Outlook installation moves from device to device.

To understand this process, you must be sure you fully understand the importance of the Outlook Profile File. Briefly explained, the Profile File is a text file generated using a syntax that Microsoft Outlook then uses to generate a profile. This profile file (.prf) allows you to create MAPI profiles for Outlook users. To create an Outlook .prf file, you can configure profile settings in the Custom Installation Wizard and then export the settings to a .prf file. When you do this, you create a new Outlook .prf file with your specifications.

Creating a .prf file using the Custom Installation Wizard

Using a .prf file, you can set up new profiles for users or modify existing profiles without affecting other aspects of your Outlook (or Microsoft Office) installation. In addition, you can manually edit a .prf file to customize Outlook to your own tastes. This might include editing a profile for the inclusion of services not present in the Custom Installation Wizard user interface.

The most straightforward way to create a .prf file with Outlook profile settings is to customize the settings in the Custom Installation Wizard and then to export the settings to a .prf file.

To create a .prf file in the Custom Installation Wizard, follow these steps:

1. From the Outlook: Customize Default User Profile page, the Wizard will help you select how you want to customize profiles for your users. To specify settings to be included in a .prf file, select Modify Profile or New Profile and then click Next.

2. Using the next three dialog boxes, you are able to customize the profile information. Such customizations might include the configuration of Exchange server connections, and the addition of e-mail accounts.

3. On the Outlook: Remove Accounts and Export Settings page, click Export Profile Settings. When you are prompted, type (or browse to) a filename and location.

Tip You may already have a .prf file from an earlier version of Outlook that you want to update for use Outlook 2003. If this is the case, you should be able to use this .prf file. You can import an Outlook 98 or Outlook 2000 .prf file that includes "Corporate or Workgroup settings only" into the Custom Installation Wizard to specify the profile settings for your transform.

Making changes the Outlook .prf file

It's also possible that your organization requires specialized .prf files to configure behaviors beyond what is included in the Custom Installation Wizard. In this case, it's possible to edit the .prf file created by the Installation Wizard to accommodate these changes. To do so, you will first open the .prf file with any standard text editor like Notepad, make changes, and then save the file. But before you go hacking through the .prf file, it's essential to understand what yo're editing.

There are three main functional sections of an Outlook 2003 .prf file. They are:

1. One section describing specific behaviors for the profile, such as the creation of a new profile, the modification of existing profiles, and whether profiles should be overwritten,

2. A section tailored for organization-specific customizations. These can include names of servers and names of deployed configurations, and

3. The final section includes information that maps certain .prf file instructions to keys within the Windows Registry.

Furthermore, each section of a .prf file contains supplementary information about each section. These comments are there for the aid of humans working with the .prf file, and include detailed descriptions of existing settings. Also included in these sections are instructions for making modifications of the .prf file with desired updates. These .prf file description sections fall under the following eight categories:

✦ Profile defaults

✦ MAPI services to be added

✦ Internet accounts that will be created

✦ Default values for available services

✦ Internet Account settings

✦ Profile properties mappings

✦ Internet account properties mappings

✦ Any MAPI services that will be removed from the profile

Services definitions can also be customized individually by creating separate headings for all of the available services. This allows you to use the same set of values for many different services, as long as the values are unique to the service heading section in the file.

Under normal circumstances, though, you won't change the settings in either the Profile properties mappings or the Internet account properties mappings. This is because these sections contain mappings to registry key settings for information that is defined elsewhere in the file. However, if you are defining new services that will be customized in the edited .prf file, you will need to add requisite mappings for those services in these two sections.

Table 22-1 gives you a quick reference point for the potential accounts specified by a customized .prf file. This table also classifies whether or not the accounts are unique. The table's third section identifies the method Outlook uses to determine if account types of the same type can be added. Certain account types, such as the POP mail account, can be added more than once to a profile (because it's not uncommon, after all, to have one user check mail from several different locations). But as explained below, Outlook makes certain that unique services, such as the Outlook Address book information, are not added more than once when creating the profile from the contents of the .prf file. Expect for the exceptions in the table below, most MAPI services can be added only once to a profile.

Table 22-1
Accounts used by the .prf file

Account	Unique?	Method
POP	No	Account name
IMAP	No	Account name
Hotmail/HTTP	No	Account name
PST	No	Full path to PST (including file name)
Outlook Address Book	Yes	Existence of account
Personal Address Book	Yes	Existence of account
LDAP	No	Account name
Exchange	Yes	Existence of provider

Before processing the .prf file in order to generate the profile, Outlook performs a check of all services to be added to verify whether any should be unique. If any are detected, they will not be added a second time. Additionally, Outlook will verify that any services which are unable to be duplicated have a unique account name

Summary

In this chapter, you looked at some of the ways Outlook 2003 can be made a portable application. It is no surprise that users want to take Outlook organizational data with them, and there are many features that allow for this.

This chapter looked at the importance of a profile, and at the key file (the .prf file)used to create that profile. Additionally, you re-examined the central role the Personal Folders file (.pst) plays in Outlook, and how that file could be made centrally available no matter what device you are using to access the data. You also examined some of the considerations that must be taken into account when using different versions of Outlook to access the same data.

In the following chapter, you'll take this knowledge of how to make sure data is available and focus on how to keep that data safe. You'll examine ways you can govern what enters through the Outlook gateway, and what happens after it gets there.

✦　　✦　　✦

Managing Security and Performance

◆ ◆ ◆ ◆

In This Chapter

Managing virus
settings and
attachment blocking

Backing up and
restoring user
certificates

Blocking spam

◆ ◆ ◆ ◆

None of us want our data corrupted and or missing. This especially applies to the contact and scheduling information Outlook manages. The right virus loose in our system (or is it the wrong virus?) can wreak havoc on our Outlook data, not to mention all of the other files on the system. Outlook represents a prime thoroughfare through which new files are introduced into our computers, and not all of those files have the best of intentions.

This chapter will examine some of the defenses built into the latest version of Outlook to help prevent some of these ill-tempered files from causing harm.

Another security measure that can be used when communicating is the use of digital certificates. These certificates can be used to 'sign' outgoing email so the recipient can reliably verify that the email really is from you. This chapter will look at the steps needed to backup and restore any certificates associated with Outlook.

Additionally, this chapter will explore ways to improve performance of Outlook by dealing with junk email, more colloquially referred to as spam. Spam is an unfortunate fact of life (as those with aol.com, yahoo.com, or hotmail.com accounts can certainly testify) when communicating with email. Outlook 2003 does, however, include some updated features to help us deal with the deluge.

Managing Virus Settings and Attachment Blocking

You know already that e-mail viruses abound, and many of these are directed specifically to Outlook users. This is not because there's anything inherently wrong with Outlook, although certainly security holes have been found and exploited by some computer hackers. Outlook is a good piece of software — easy to use for millions upon millions. And therein lies the problem: Outlook is omnipresent, so if you're writing a computer virus and you want it to spread (and which computer virus makers do so only for their own amusement?), you want that virus to propagate in Outlook mailboxes worldwide. Can anything be done to combat this?

Fortunately, yes. There are several things you can do to stop the spread of viruses in Outlook. One of these is to use a regularly updated antivirus program such as the ones from Symantac, McAffee, or Trend Micro. Other methods are included with each additional release of Outlook, and sometimes these security updates alone can provide an excellent cost/benefit argument for the upgrade to the latest version of Outlook.

Other actions you can perform to protect yourself in a networked computing environment include:

✦ Do not open any attachments unless you know from whom they've been sent.

✦ Educate yourself about which files can do harm to your computer. Opening up a .jpeg or .mp3 file won't cause any harm unless the content is unsavory and your boss is standing over your shoulder. Other files, such as .exe, .bat, or .vbs files give commands to your operating system, and these instructions can lead to a negative computing experience.

✦ Keep macro security set to High or Medium to ensure that macro viruses in documents sent by users you trust do not infect your copy of Word. On the High setting, all unrecognized macros are automatically disabled. On Medium, you receive an alert that allows you to make the choice before enabling a macro. To set the macro security options, choose Macro from the Tools menu and then choose the Security option. (We'll discuss macro security in a more detail later in the chapter.)

✦ Beware of HTML-formatted mail; it might be your best bet to turn off HTML-formatted mail unless absolutely necessary. This is because scripts and ActiveX controls can be embedded in HTML code that tells your system to act wonky. To ensure you aren't affected by such viruses, edit the Secure Content settings in the Security tab of the Options dialog box (Which you can access by choosing Tools | Options). You should leave your Secure content settings on Restricted Sites, which in turn prevents scripts and controls from running in HTML formatted email messages.

Outlook offers several optional features that you can install or not, regardless of the type of installation you perform. See the following section for a discussion of the Outlook features you can add or remove during Office installation. The section "Wide-Scale and Automated Outlook Deployment" explains how to control which of these options is installed during automated and push deployments.

You may not be aware of it, but Outlook does have a built-in level of security when it comes to files. Outlook examines any incoming e-mail messages for an attachment and then evaluates the kind of file attached, dividing attached files into one of two categories — Level 1 and Level 2. If the file meets certain criteria — criteria that places it in the Level 1 category — it is blocked automatically. You are prompted regarding Level 2 files. Note further that Outlook's access to Level 1 files is blocked and can't be changed.

As with most other Outlook behaviors, this can be configured differently if you use Microsoft Exchange Server. Because Exchange Server provides this front line of file examination security, your administrator has the power to add and remove file types for both levels of e-mail security. If a file type is added to both levels, by the way, the Level 1 security will be trump — that is, it will be blocked.

And just so you know what files Outlook 2003 treats as Level 1, Table 23-1 spells it out. These files, when sent as attachments, are blocked unless your Exchange administrator has set a different security level.

Table 23-1
Files Treated as Level 1 in Outlook 2003

File extension	File type
.ade	Microsoft Access project extension
.adp	Microsoft Access project
.asx	Microsoft Windows Media audio/video shortcut
.bas	Microsoft Visual Basic class module
.bat	Batch file
.chm	Compiled HTML Help file
.cmd	Microsoft Windows NT Command Script
.com	Microsoft MS-DOS program
.cpl	Control Panel extension
.crt	Security certificate
.exe	Program

Continued

Table 23-1 *(continued)*

File extension	File type
.hlp	Help file
.hta	HTML program
.inf	Setup information
.ins	Internet Naming Service
.isp	Internet Communication settings
.js	JScript file
.jse	Jscript Encoded Script file
.lnk	Shortcut
.mda	Microsoft Access add-in program
.mdb	Microsoft Access database
.mde	Microsoft Access MDE database
.mdt	Microsoft Access add-in data
.mdw	Microsoft Access workgroup information
.mdz	Microsoft Access Wizard program
.msc	Microsoft Common Console document
.msi	Microsoft Windows Installer package
.msp	Windows Installer patch
.mst	Visual Test source files
.pcd	Photo CD image or Microsoft Visual Test compiled script
.pif	Shortcut to MS-DOS program
.prf	Outlook profile information (msrating.dll)
.reg	Registration entries
.scf	Microsoft Windows Explorer command
.scr	Screensaver
.sct	Windows Script component
.shb	Shortcut into a document
.shs	Shell Scrap Object
.url	Internet shortcut
.vb	VBScript file

File extension	File type
.vbe	VBScript Encoded Script file
.vbs	VBScript file
.wsc	Windows Script component
.wsf	Windows Script file
.wsh	Windows Script Host Settings file

Notice in Table 23-1 that most of the files blocked, such as .bat or .vbs files, are scripting files. In other words, they make your computer perform actions, such as deleting files, making edits to the registry, or otherwise running malicious scripts when opened. Unfortunately, this makes file sharing less convenient for many people, but security must take precedence.

Tip

Sometimes, you may want Level 1 files to be sent back and forth, such as when receiving an Access database file from a colleague. There are a couple of ways to get around this blocking behavior. One, the Exchange administrator can chance Security settings. Two, almost any file can be zipped (compressed with a .zip file extension), and .zip files are Level 2 files. Third, the .mdb file can be placed on a file server and shared on the network.

So what's a Level 2 file? Virtually anything else, such as .jpeg's .mp3's, as well as any of the Microsoft Office file types most commonly used and sent between people, such as .doc, .xls, and .ppt files. These are not blocked, as you may have already encountered.

Keep in mind however, that just because you configure Outlook not to render the attachment data, it is still stored on whatever storage media is being used for your Outlook data file. Access to this data through methods other than Outlook might still allow a virus in an attachment to propagate.

Macro virus security

There are other virus types aside from the ill-tempered code in a batch file or executable. A macro virus is a type of computer virus that's stored in a macro within a file, template, or add-in. If you have never heard of a macro, they are essentially a series of saved keystrokes or menu commands. A macro virus is a menu command that you don't want run when working with the particular application.

To reduce the risk of macro infection in Office files, set the macro security level to High or Medium, and use digital signatures. Note, however, that this is not the be-all and end-all of macro protection. Even Microsoft recommends for the best protection against macro viruses, you should purchase and install specialized antivirus software.

The following are different levels of security configurable to reduce macro virus infection. Set the level of Outlook macro security by clicking the Tools ⇨ Macro ⇨ Security to open the Security dialog box shown in Figure 23-1.

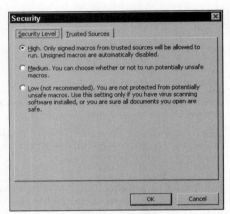

Figure 23-1: Setting the macro security levels with the Security dialog box.

High. You can run only macros that have been digitally signed, and that you confirm are from a trusted source. Before trusting a source, you should confirm that the source is responsible and uses a virus scanner before signing macros. Unsigned macros are automatically disabled, and the file is opened without any warning.

Medium. A warning is displayed whenever a macro is encountered from a source that is not on your list of trusted sources (described in the following section). You can choose whether to enable or disable the macros when you open a file. If the file might contain a virus, you should choose to disable macros.

Low. If you are sure that all the files and add-ins you open are safe, you can select this option to turn off macro virus protection. At this security level, macros are always enabled when you open files.

Outlook sets the default security level is to High. If the security level is set to Medium or High, you can maintain a list of trusted macro sources. When you open a file or load an add-in that contains macros developed by any of these sources, the macros are automatically enabled.

Tip   Outlook can't scan your floppy disks, hard disks, or network drives to find and remove macro viruses, like a good antivirus program can. Outlook security only is applicable when opening files.

Adding a trusted source

How do you maintain a list of trusted sources? You build the list when opening files and then maintain it with the Security dialog box.

Follow these steps to add a macro developer as a trusted source:

1. Open the file, or load the add-in that contains macros from the source you want trust, and thus want to add to the list.

2. In the Security Warning dialog box when the macro tries to load, select the Always trust macros from this source check box.

The creator of the macro should appear in the Trusted Sources tab; you now manage this list by removing macro trusted sources as you want.

Tip   There is one caveat regarding digital signatures. If the Security Warning dialog box does not display the Always trust macros from this source check box, the macros are not digitally signed. You cannot add this macro developer to the list of trusted sources if the macros are not digitally signed.

Backing Up and Restoring User Certificates

You can create a backup file of your digital ID and secure the file with a password. Backup files for Microsoft Exchange digital IDs have an .epf extension. Backup files for Internet e-mail digital IDs have a .pfx extension. To create a backup file, follow these steps:

1. Click Tools | Options and then click the Security tab.

2. In the Digital ID's section at the bottom of this tab, click Import/Export.

3. The Import/Export Digital ID dialog box displays, as shown in Figure 23-2. Click the Export your Digital ID to a file radio button.

4. Click Select, click the digital ID you want to back up, and click OK. The certificate appears in the Digital ID box.

5. In the Filename box, type a name and path for the backup file you want to create, or click Browse.

6. Create a password for the backup file and then confirm your password in the appropriate box. Click OK to finish the procedure.

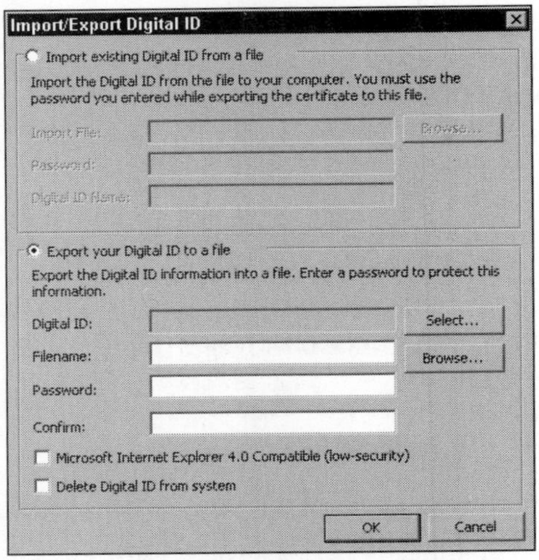

Figure 23-2: The Import/Export Digital ID dialog box.

The restoration of a digital certificate (you can also use this procedure to move a certificate from one computer to another) is the reverse of this process.

1. Perform step 1 from the previous steps.

2. Select the 'Import existing digital ID from a file' option.

3. In the Import File box, specify the name and location of the backup file you created. Click Browse to locate the file.

4. Type the password you created for the backup file; then in the Digital ID name box, type your friendly name. This is usually your mailbox name. Click OK to finish the Import.

Blocking Spam

Unless you've just laid eyes on a computer for the first time, you've probably received e-mail soliciting home mortgage refinancing, vacation giveaways, prescription medication. Similar to phones and snailmail we have all become dumping grounds for direct mail and telemarketers. And now e-mail addresses are seen by some as free advertising channels through which to send solicitations. Getting spam, unwanted e-mail, is an unfortunate side effect of Internet life. Outlook 2003 offers ways to deal with this deluge.

Rules and filters

One method of cutting down on spam is the use of rules and filters. With a rule in place, Outlook can automatically move junk messages from your Inbox to your Deleted Items folder, or to any other folder you specify.

Earlier in this chapter, you learned why macros might potentially be harmful if received from an untrusted source. But you probably use macros all the time from sources you trust to help you get work done more efficiently. An e-mail rule has essentially the same effect as an often-used macro. In effect, an email handling rule is just another macro that's triggered by a specified set of conditions. The macro then tells Outlook what to do with a message that meets those conditions.

Use the Rules Wizard to set up a rule to handle suspected junk mail. Earlier in this tome, you saw how to use this wizard. (Choose Tools ∣ Rules and Alerts, then select New Rule fromteh Rules and Alerts dialog box.) The available rules are as shown in Figure 23-3.

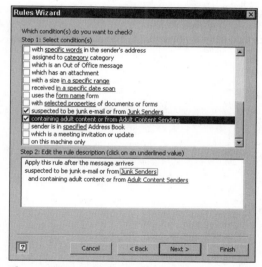

Figure 23-3: Specific rules to help keep spam under control.

Using the New Junk E-Mail Filter

There's a new way interface in Outlook 2003 for handling junk e-mail. It's called the Junk E-mail Filter, and it replaces the rules-based filtering system used with previous versions of Outlook. In previous versions, defining what was and what was not Junk email was a sometimes arduous process, most of which was configured manually.

Now, however, much of the e-mail filtering is automated. You no longer have to enable the Junk E-mail rules; the Junk E-mail Filter is installed and enabled with a default installation of Outlook 2003. There are four levels of Junk E-mail handling, which are set from the Junk Email Options dialog box, which is accessed from the Actions menu by clicking on Junk E-mail options. As shown in Figure 23-4, these filter options are:

✦ **Low:** this setting is designed to catch the most obvious junk e-mail messages, and moves these messages to the Junk E-mail folder.

✦ **High:** which catches most Junk E-mail, but also throws E-mail not considered junk into the Junk E-mail folder.

✦ **Safe Lists Only:** Filters out everything except for those messages from senders on your Safe Recipients List. This is the most secure setting and is my personal favorite.

✦ **No Protection:** This option turns off Junk E-mail filtering, and all messages will be delivered to your Inbox.

Also, there is a check box at the bottom of this dialog box that will delete suspected Junk E-mail instead of moving it to the Junk E-mail folder. This can be a bit risky when using one of the higher Junk E-mail filtering levels, as regular E-mail sometimes gets designated as junk.

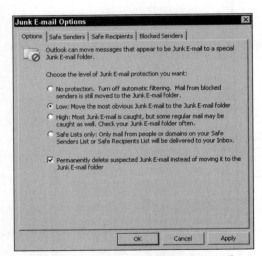

Figure 23-4: Configuring the Junk E-mail options

If this option is turned off, any message that is caught by the filter is then moved to a special Junk E-mail folder, where you can retrieve or review it at a later time. The Microsoft Junk E-mail Filter works by examining the content of a piece of E-mail, and also uses an analysis of how the message is structured. Based on these two factors, it then makes a determination about probability that the massage is from a spammer.

The Microsoft filter does not single out any particular sender or type of content. You can, though, by adding senders to either your Safe Senders List, or to your Blocked Senders list.

Tip   If a name or E-mail address appears on both the Safe Senders List and the Blocked Senders list, the Safe Senders List is trump, and the message from that sender will be delivered to the Inbox.

If you find that a regular E-mail has been sent to the Junk E-mail folder against your wishes, you can add that sender or domain to the Safe Senders list. To add a sender to this list, open the Junk E-mail options dialog box, and choose the Safe Senders tab. Click the Add button, and then type the email address or the domain of the sender. Note also that by default, any senders who are also in your Contacts folder will be considered Safe Senders.

Adding a sender to the Blocked Senders list

If at any time you change your mind about the bill consolidation offers you receive, you can review the Junk Senders list and then add and remove e-mail addresses from it. To do so, follow these steps:

1. Choose Actions | Junk E-mail | Junk E-mail Options to open the Junk E-mail Options dialog box.

2. Select the Blocked Senders tab, then click Add to add a Senders email or domain name to the list. Any future email from that email or domain will be automatically moved to the Junk E-mail folder..

3. Alternatively, you can right-click on a message in your Inbox, and from the context menu, select the Junk E-Mail menu item. This will open a submenu which will allow you to quickly add another user to your Junk Senders list, as shown in Figure 23-5.

Note   Purveyors of spam, unfortunately, seem to always be a step ahead of whatever technologies exits to combat it. The above steps will prove futile against junk senders who address email messages with random, varied, and/or non-existent addressing, that can furthermore be new and different each time

For maximum E-mail protection, and to combat against such one-upmanship as is practiced by spammers, Microsoft recommends that you set the protection level of the Junk E-mail Filter to Safe Lists Only and enable the check box that will "permanently delete all messages suspected of being junk e-mail messages." As mentioned, this is my preferred method, except that I recommend moving messages to the Junk E-mail folder rather that just deleting them, because, hey, you never know. Don't want to miss any really *important* herbal Viagra solicitations.

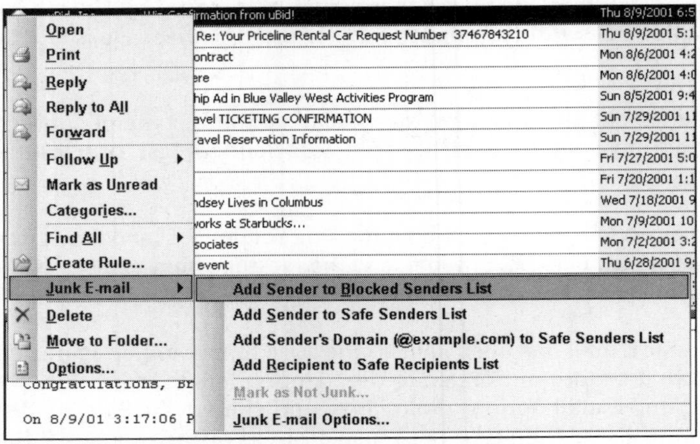

Figure 23-5: Edit the junk e-mail senders with this list.

Blocking external content (Web beacons) from Junk mail senders

It's not unusual to receive content formatted in HyperText Markup Language (HTML). HTML messages can include links to external content, such as pictures or sounds. These links are not the kind that are underlined (hot) and you click on, though. They are references in the HTML source code to an external location on the Internet, and when opening or even previewing the message, Outlook downloads the external content so that the picture can be displayed or the sound played. The idea is that it allows someone to send you an HTML message while reducing overall file size, thus avoiding a log jam in the Inbox. However, as with many advances in technology, it can be a double-edged sword. In the hands of professional spammers, senders use the downloading of external content by your computer to verify your e-mail address as "live." After they know there is a real person associated with your address, you can then become the target of more junk mailings. External content used to identify you in this way is called a Web Beacon. In the case of pictures, they might only be one pixel wide; they have no other use than to see if you're there checking your mail. Whether or not you actually see the picture and think it's the next coming of DaVinci is immaterial.

Outlook 2003 includes a remedy for this. As a measure against Web Beacons, Outlook is configured by default to block external pictures from being downloaded into all HTML email. For example, areas in the message that should have a picture will appear as a red x placeholder instead.

To change this behavior, or to ensure that this feature is in effect for all HTML messages, do the following:

1. From the Tools menu, choose Options, and then navigate to the Security tab.

2. In the Download Pictures section, click the Change Automatic Download Settings button.

3. From the Automatic Pictures Download Settings dialog box, clear the checkbox titled Don't download pictures or other content automatically in HTML e-mail, as shown in Figure 23-6. This will change the default behavior, which is set to prevent against the aforementioned web beacons.

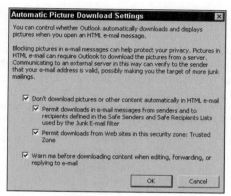

Figure 23-6: Protecting against Web Beacons.

Tip

If there's external content from a legitimate mail you want to receive such as a newsletter to which you've subscribed, you can unblock the external content on a per message basis using the InfoBar menu, or by right-clicking on the blocked item and choosing Download Pictures.

If the message is from a sender or a domain you trust, you can add them to the Safe Senders List by right-clicking the blocked item from an opened message and choosing Add Sender to Safe Senders List. Doing so will then allow all content in that sender's email to be downloaded from now on.

You can also choose View in Internet Zone from the View menu of the open message. This unblocks any content that Outlook blocked. Make sure when you take this step that the message is from someone you trust and from whom you expected e-mail. When you open a message in the Internet Zone, all content is displayed and any scripts in the message run, subject to the configured Internet Zone settings in Internet Explorer. If you subsequently open the message without viewing it in the Internet Zone, whatever content was blocked by Outlook will continue to be blocked.

When you edit, forward, or reply to a message that references external content, your computer will again try to download the content. Outlook, by default, is configured to display a warning.

Summary

In this chapter, you looked at some of the ways available to control what enters your Inbox, and what to do with those things after they are there. You also examined how you can use Outlook's built in features to reduce on the amount of spam you receive daily.

In addition, you learned techniques for dealing with attachments, and learned about how Outlook 2003 blocks most all attachments by default that have the highest potential for mayhem on your system. It is worth restating, however, that these methods are not good replacements for a thorough virus scanning program.

The next chapter examines how to control further aspects of Outlook behavior through the management and application of group and system policies.

✦   ✦   ✦

Controlling Outlook (and Office) with Group and System Policies

✦ ✦ ✦ ✦

In This Chapter

Understanding group policies

Adding Office administrative templates for group policy

Deploying Outlook group policies

Understanding system policies

Adding Office administrative templates for system policies

Deploying Outlook system policies

✦ ✦ ✦ ✦

As an administrator, you are often times asked to govern the behavior of an operating system or a particular application. These computer policies often stem from written corporate policies: management wants the applications to be used in a certain way, and it's your job to make those desires a computing reality. To do so, you need a means for defining the laws of a specific computing environment; then, more importantly, have a lever with which to enforce your legislative will. Fortunately, an administrator has many such levers at his disposal.

One of these tools is the system policy. System policies have been around for a while, and are still the tool needed to control the user environment on Windows NT and 9x computers. System policies are processed at the time of logon for these computers. Windows 2000 systems and beyond, however, make use of group policy.

Another more powerful tool is the Group Policy Object (GPO). GPO's allow both powerful and flexible control over the management of the operating system and software, and have been mentioned from time to time throughout this book. This chapter examines the GPO in greater detail, and specifically concentrates on the settings in group policy that can be tailored to configure how Outlook behaves.

Understanding Group Policies

As mentioned, Group Policy Objects are collections of administrative settings that enable you to control almost every conceivable aspect of the Windows computing environment. Which ones you decide to configure depends on your individual situation and how they impact your users and systems. The following list categorizes the range of major issues that can be controlled through the proper implementation of group policy.

✦ **Hardware changes.** You can use group policies to prevent users from changing existing hardware settings such as display resolution, drive settings, and so on. You can prevent them from changing drivers or installing additional drivers, which helps protect against systems going down because of faulty drivers.

✦ **Application installation and changes.** Use change control to prevent users from installing applications or changing existing installations. This helps control problems caused by buggy applications and/or viruses and Trojan horses introduced through shareware or freeware (not unheard of but less common with commercial applications).

✦ **Security needs.** You can also configure group policies to define whether or not users can use encryption, IPSec, and other security features. In part, this helps keep users out of trouble and helps protect against situations such as a user encrypting his documents and then leaving the company after deleting his certificates. Although you can recover the encrypted data, it can be a protracted process and at best, an annoyance.

✦ **Network requirements and settings.** These settings allow you to prevent users from making changes to their network settings, or installing additional network clients or services.

✦ **Access to services.** You can control users' ability to access and add, remove, change, or control services.

✦ **Local and network resource access.** You can define the actions that users can take in connecting to and using local and network resources.

✦ **Environment settings.** By managing environment settings, you can govern a wide variety of settings that control the user's desktop experience, including the desktop, mapped drives, printers, and so on. Group policies give you an exceptional level of control over the user's environment, and therefore the types of tasks the user can and can't perform.

When thinking about group policies, it can be helpful to use the lever analogy. The lever is a tool to help you implement your will; you want something to move, you use a lever. Likewise, if you want your computer systems — or in this case, your installation of Outlook — to behave in a certain way, a GPO will serve as your lever.

Some of the functions and benefits of group policies are self-evident, while others might take you by surprise. For example, you've no doubt surmised by this point that group policies enable you to enforce the administrative rules of conduct over a wide variety of items. One such feature, as mentioned in Chapter 22, is the group policy that lets you redirect folders. Additionally, they also allow for management of Internet Explorer settings, application of traditional logon and logoff scripts, and much, much more.

One significant aspect about a GPO is that it's a free-floating software object. Any GPO can be linked to multiple sites, domains, or Organizational Units (OU's), and a given container can have multiple GPOs linked to it. In other words, if you've got a painstakingly engineered GPO that you've set up for one OU, you don't have to reinvent the proverbial wheel to use the GPO again. All you do is point it to another Active Directory Object.

When multiple GPOs link to the same Active Directory container, the GPOs in effect are merged, although you can set the order of precedence to define how the GPOs are applied, creating a policy hierarchy. Where policies conflict, the hierarchy resolves the conflict. This is explained in further detail later in this chapter.

You can link a GPO to almost any of the Active Directory container objects: sites, domains, and OUs. By doing so, you have the ability to implement management control over users an applications in the network with an unprecedented degree of flexibility. GPO's, in other words, can be used to manage just a few objects in your organization, or the entire enterprise. To illustrate, consider the following scenarios where GPS are linked to Active Directory container objects:

✦ To manage all users and, more specifically, all computers in a site, link a GPO to an Active Directory site. This can be very useful when software distribution, including application of service packs, is concerned. This usually results in less heavy use of a slow WAN link.

✦ A GPO linked to a domain generally has the broadest impact on domain users, as all user objects reside created in Active Directory in a domain. Additionally, all Organizational Units and their child Organizational units are, by default, affected by the domain wide GPO

✦ To narrow the scope of GPO applicability, consider linking a GPO to an Organizational Unit. Only Active Directory objects in that OU and it's child OU's will be affected.

Creating a Group Policy Object

Now that you know a little more about group policies, you're ready to start creating Group Policy Objects. In fact, you have probably already done this several times already, even if it was just following along with some of the examples in this book.

To quickly review, let's take the example of GPO creation for an OU. To create the GPO for an OU in the domain:

1. Open Active Directory Users and Computers console.

2. Expand the domain container and then select the OU of your choice. Right-click on the OU and choose Properties.

3. Click the Group Policy tab and then click New to create the GPO. Enter the name for your test GPO, and press Enter.

4. The GPO is created automatically with the name you choose. It has no capabilities for management for now, but it's ready to configure. Click Close.

Viewing, modifying, and managing GPOs

You modify GPOs through the Group Policy Editor, a Microsoft Management Console (MMC) console snap-in. You can open the Group Policy snap-in directly through the MMC, or access it through the properties for the Active Directory container to which you want to link the GPO or whose existing GPO you want to modify.

Take the previous example and modify the GPO you just created for the OU. To do so, follow these steps:

1. Open Active Directory User and Computers, and expand the domain container. Find the OU for which you just created a GPO, right-click, and choose Properties.

2. Click the Group Policy tab. You'll see all the existing GPOs linked to that OU, including the one you just set up. Select this GPO and then click Edit.

3. The Group Policy Editor opens, enabling you to edit the selected GPO.

If you open the Group Policy Editor console from the Properties dialog box of a particular object, the console is automatically set to edit that object. (Note that in Windows Server 2003 the Group Policy editor is called the Group Policy Object Editor; it does the same thing, though.) If, however, you want to edit several GPO's via a single console, you should use the Group Policy snap-in added to a customizable MMC.

To illustrate this, say you need to manage a GPO that is linked to a domain, one site GPO, and two OU GPOs. The easiest way to get to all of those is to combine all of them into a single, custom MMC console. Here's how:

1. Click Start ⇨ Run, and type **MMC**.

2. Choose Console ⇨ (it will be the File menu from a Windows XP or Windows Server 2003 machine) Add/Remove Snap-In, and click Add.

3. Select Group Policy and then click Add.

4. In the Select Group Policy Object dialog box, click Browse.

5. In the Browse for a Group Policy Object dialog box, click the level at which you want to select the GPO, or click the All tab to view all GPOs.

6. Select the GPO you want to add to the console and then click OK.

7. Click Finish; then repeat steps 3 through 7 to add the other GPO snap-ins to the custom console.

8. Close the Add/Remove Snap-In dialog box, and save the console.

Note

Unless you user account has been delegated administrative control over a domain or organizational unit, you need domain administrator rights in order to perform the above procedures.

After you've got the Group Policy Editor open, making changes to the Group Policy settings is a fairly straightforward task. The trick is to know what setting affect what aspects of behavior, and how these settings will combine should a user log on with more than one GPO applied to the logon.

While a full understanding of the settings of GPO's is a tall order, actually defining policies is, for the most part, easy. Expand the branch where the policy setting is located, double-click the policy, and select Define This Policy Setting. The Group Policy console enables the associated policy setting, which varies from one to another. In some cases, you select either Enabled or Disabled. Other policy settings require other data that varies according to policy's function. (They're not all like this, but most are — especially the ones in the Administrative Templates subset, which are the ones that have the most direct effect on Microsoft Office behavior.)

Explaining every branch in the Group Policy Editor, and every policy setting, would not be relevant to the scope of this book. In fact, there are several other books dedicated to little else other than going over each of these settings. The focus of this book however is on the settings configurable with Office, and more specifically with Outlook. For now, just understand that the Group Policy Editor enables you to define group policies, and that you can access the Group Policy console through the properties sheets for an Active Directory container where a given GPO is linked, or through a custom MMC console to which you've added the Group Policy snap-in.

Note

For complete information on Group Policy Objects, please see any of these titles available from Wiley Press: The Active Directory Bible, Active Directory for Dummies, or Active Directory Planning and Design.

Adding Office Administrative Templates for Group Policy

As you have seen, in Group Policy, the Administrative Templates allow for tight control over the end-user experience as it pertains to the Windows desktop. Additional Administrative Templates can be added to manage the look and functionality of Office applications. These Office-specific templates are available in the Office Resource kit, and give you additional layers of management of the way Outlook 2003 works.

Adding an Office Administrative Template

Not all of the administrative templates available will suit your needs when configuring a GPO for use with Outlook 2003. Fortunately, other administrative templates with settings more specific to Office command and control are available, but they have to be acquired from the Office Resource Kit and then added to the Group Policy Editor console.

Here's the general procedure for adding supplementary administrative templates to the Group Policy editor when operating in a Windows 2000 or Server 2003 Active Directory domain:

1. Open the Group Policy Object Editor using any of the available means. (You could add the Group Policy snap-in to an MMC console, or access the Group Policy tab from the Properties dialog box of an Active Directory Object.)

2. Expand User Configuration; then expand Administrative Templates.

3. Right-click on the Administrative Templates folder, and choose Add/Remove Templates from the context menu to display the Add/Remove Templates dialog box, as shown in Figure 24-1

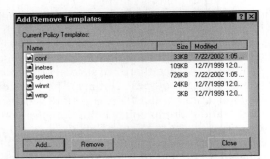

Figure 24-1: Add an administrative template using the Add/Remove Templates dialog box.

4. Click Add; then select the .adm file you want to add to the administrative templates.

Controlling with other administrative templates

As discussed in the overview of group policies, Windows 2000 and Windows XP both support management via application of a GPO. These GPO settings provide hundreds of policies you can use to control system and profile configuration; however, you probably noticed that most of these policies target the system in general, along with a few select applications such as Internet Explorer, Media Player- whoops- did I say applications? I meant other parts of the operating system, as these former apps are now part and parcel of both of these flavors of Windows, no matter what a circuit court judge might say.

But for you, these default settings might not be adequate. You might want to configure other settings that are more specific to Office management, settings that might help Office users work more efficiently with less down time and lost data.

Towards this objective, the Office XP Resource Kit includes a set of Group Policy templates you can use to control Office XP applications in exactly the same way you control Windows and all of its component applications. The Office 2003 Resource Kit, which should be available by the time you're reading this, will also include the Group Policy templates. To use these policies you must first add them to your Group Policy Editor. To do so, follow these steps:

1. Run Gpedit.msc from a command line, or open the properties for an OU in the Active Directory Users and Computers console. Click the Group Policy tab, and edit or create a new policy object (which opens the policy editor).

2. Expand either the Computer Configuration or User Configuration, depending on where you want to apply the policies.

3. Right-click the Administrative Templates container and then choose Add/Remove Templates to open the Add/Remove Templates dialog box.

4. Click Add, and browse to the `\%systemroot%\Inf` folder (it will likely be opened by default) on a computer where the Resource Kit is installed.

5. Select the Office10.adm (or Office11.adm, Outllk11.adm, etc.) file if you want to control policies that apply to Office in general, or select one of the application-specific ADM files. Click Open to open the template; then click Close to close the Add/Remove Templates dialog box.

After completed, you are able to use your new Office Templates just as you to the other templates that manage Start Menu, Desktop, and Control Panel behavior, to name a few.

Now that you've added the application-specific administrative templates, take a stroll through newly added `Administrative Templates\Microsoft Office XP` branch in the Group Policy Editor. Your new editor should look similar to the example in Figure 24-2. To get a feel for what settings control what behavior, begin experimenting and applying some of the settings you've just enabled. If you don't see any new policies, try adding the template to the other configuration container. The policies appear only if they apply to the specified configuration container.

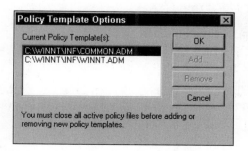

Figure 24-2: Configuring additional Office-specific Group Policy settings

As you begin to explore the policies you just added, notice they contain a wealth of settings that control many aspects of Microsoft Office. Microsoft Office is the most widely used suite of productivity software in use today, so it's a good bet that gaining control over its applications through policies will have a major impact on your user support efforts.

Deploying Outlook Group Policies

As you plan for group policy deployment, you have to know of the order in which GPOs are processed. Windows 2000 adheres to a few rules at processing time, and knowing these rules is not optional if you want to successfully troubleshoot any group policy deployment. Group policies are applied in a specific order. Too, group policies are cumulative, meaning that, by default, the last instance of a particular policy applied overwrites any previous instances of that policy.

Here's the order Group Policy Objects are applied when logging on to an Active Directory domain from a Windows 2000 or XP Professional system:

1. Local group policies

2. GPOs linked to sites

3. GPOs linked to domains

4. GPOs linked to OUs, with parent OUs processed first followed by child OUs.

If you consider the order in which Windows 2000 applies group policies, you'll also understand the group policy hierarchy. The local group policy resides at the bottom of the hierarchy, and has least significance because policies assigned after it through the upper levels of the hierarchy take precedence. The site is at the next level; then the domain and then OU. By allowing policies in higher levels to overwrite policies in lower levels, Windows 2000 provides for inheritance of policies from higher layers. This inheritance behavior means that you have a method of distributing policies enterprise-wide without having to micromanage policies.

However, there are exceptions to the processing order. For example, say you're a domain administrator and you want a certain policy in place no matter what. You don't want someone trumping your carefully planned software distribution scheme. To do this, GPO's provide for a setting so that your policy won't get overridden (it's called No Override), thus accomplishing your task.

Tip   For further information on group policies and the exceptions to the processing hierarchy, see one of Jim Boyce's books such as Windows 2000 Server Bible from Wiley press.

If Group Policies are so great, why are there a few more pages until the end of the chapter? Why bother with anything else when a group policy will let me manage everything in I could possibly think of?Because you might have clients running

Windows 98, that's why. There isn't much to find fault with when it comes to group policies, but one point that stands head and shoulders above the rest is their inability to hold any sway over computers running Windows NT 4 or 9x. This is not so much a drawback with group policies per se, but rather an example of how different the code base is from the 9x/NT 4 generation of Windows operating systems to the Windows 2000 systems and beyond.

It's worth stating again: You can't use a group policy on computers other than Windows 2000 and up. To exert administrative will over these earlier operating systems, you will need to use a system policy.

Understanding System Policies

As mentioned in the previous section, the main drawback of the use of group policies is that they can't be used on every machine in the enterprise unless all machines are running Windows 2000 or above. If you want to exert control over earlier machines, you have to use older technology. Enter the system policy.

Before group policies, Windows offered two ways to manage the desktop environment: through profiles, and through system policies. As anyone with a cursory knowledge of profiles understands, a profile is not true desktop management. Profiles, even mandatory ones, can be changed. To enforce desktop settings, such as the ability to use the Control Panel, Windows administrators used a system policy.

Similar to a group policy, though, a system Policy is a collection of settings that defines the computer environment available to an individual or to a group of users. They are not nearly as robust as GPO's, however. For example, while you can manage the contents of the Start menu, you can't deploy software through a system policy. System policies can be implemented for specific users, groups, computers, or for all users, and you create system policies with the System Policy Editor (poledit.exe).

The System Policy Editor is a graphical tool provided with Windows NT Server 4 that allows administrators to update registry settings for client computers, specific to a particular user, a system, or a group of users. To achieve this, the System Policy Editor creates a file that contains registry settings which are then written to the user or local machine portion of the registry database. User settings that are specific to a user who logs on to a given workstation or server are written to the registry under HKEY_CURRENT_USER. Meanwhile, machine-specific settings are written under HKEY_LOCAL_MACHINE.

The System Policy Editor has been carried forward to the Windows 2000 environment, letting an Active Directory administrator still manage desktop settings for downlevel Windows clients.

One important consideration when working with system policies is that they will always have an effect on the client machine's registry. When you apply a system policy, the new policy overwrites the existing registry settings, and any registry settings that you have reconfigured, whether these are machine-specific changes or changes specific to the user, are modified before the user receives control of the desktop.

Another important difference between Windows NT system policies and Windows 2000 group policies is the ability that users have to change or bypass system policies, limiting their security and effectiveness. To change the settings imposed by a carefully constructed system policy, all a knowledgeable user has to do is open the Registry Editor and change the registry settings that have been defined by the system policy. This would wipe out the effect of the system policy or at least that portion of the policy that related to the modified registry setting.

Windows NT system policies also can cause problems when a user's group membership changes because elements of the system policy might conflict with the user's new needs and responsibilities. Overcoming the problem requires directly modifying the user's registry, or applying a different system policy through the user's profile, both of which require manual intervention either by the user or an administrator.

 Tip Unlike many settings of group policies, system policy changes are not dynamic. In other words, there is no refresh; if you make a change to the policy, affected users must log off and log back on so that the new policy can be downloaded and applied.

By contrast, Windows 2000 group policies can be applied based on site, domain, and OU, and can be further controlled through security group membership. This means that Windows 2000 group policies apply automatically and, moreover, follow the user automatically as long as that user remains in the Active Directory enterprise. If the user moves to a different security group or other container in the AD, the group policies that apply to that group or container automatically apply to the user at next logon. Restrictions and other policy settings defined by the user's old group membership are replaced automatically by the new policies.

With a properly implemented policy, you can customize the user's environment to your specifications, despite the user's preferences and regardless of where he or she logs on. Now take a look at how this customization can be suited to the Outlook 2003 environment.

Adding Office Administrative Templates for System Policies

Just as you can add functionality to group policies, you can do the same for system policies for the purpose of further Outlook management on installations running on

Windows 9x or NT systems. And, similar to when using a GPO, you'll do this by adding a template of additional settings. To do so, follow these steps:

1. From a Windows 2000 Server domain controller, open the System Policy Editor by clicking Start ⇨ Run, and entering **poledit** into the Run dialog box, and then press Enter.

2. The System Policy Editor launches. Choose File ⇨ New Policy to open a blank, unconfigured system policy.

Tip

The Default Computer icon and the Default User icon are displayed in the System Policy Editor window. System Policy settings 'tattoo' the client computer's registry.

For example, when you create persistent changes to the client computer registry, you may inadvertently block access to a client computer for all users (including the administrator). For this reason, Microsoft recommends that you leave the Default Computer and Default User System Policy settings unchanged. Instead, create new policies based on either group membership or individual client computers.

3. Keeping the previous tip in mind, you might want to create a system policy for a single user or group. To create for a group, choose Add Group from the Edit menu; then use the subsequent dialog box to locate the group you want.

4. To add a new administrative template, click Options ⇨ Policy Template to open the Policy Template Options dialog box, as shown in Figure 24-3.

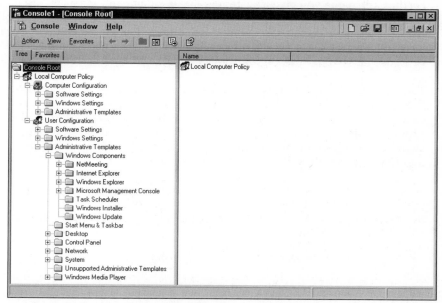

Figure 24-3: Add system policy templates from here.

5. If you have other templates that will work with system policies, you can add them by clicking Add; then browse for the .adm file, and select it just as when working with a GPO.

Via the previous procedure, you've just radically increased your ability to dictate what goes on when the users in your enterprise use Outlook. But before you go and get all Napoleonic, keep in mind that your newly created system policies do you no good until they are actually deployed.

Deploying Outlook System Policies

Although they were put on this earth to accomplish roughly the same administrative objectives, system policies are deployed differently from group policy. Group policies, as mentioned earlier in this chapter, are stored in the Active Directory database and then applied when users are validated against this database. (With the exception of a local group policy, which is stored in the local computer's directory database.)

System policies, on the other hand, are deployed much like logon scripts. In fact, about the only difference between deploying scripts and system policies are the file extensions used. Script files use extensions such as .bat or .vbs, whereas system policies use the extension of .pol.

Further, the name you give a system policy is significant. after you create a system policy, you can save it for deployment. If you intend to deploy to a Windows NT Workstation, give the file the name of NTConfig.pol. If your system policy is meant for Windows 9x clients, on the other hand, you use the name Config.pol. Don't forget these last two points, or your policy efforts will have gone to waste.

The other key thing to remember when deploying system policies is where to store them. When a user of a Windows computer logs on to a domain, that computer establishes a communication channel to the NETLOGON share. It uses this communication pipeline to submit a logon request. The client computer also checks this share for the presence of any logon scripts, and, if found, runs any logon scripts that have been assigned to either the user or computer..

So, where do you save the system policy file(s)? In the folder that's being shared out as NETLOGON. This varies depending on what operating system is running on the computer serving as a domain controller. On a Windows 2000 Server, the NETLOGON folder is this one:

```
\%systemroot%\SYSVOL\SYSVOL\DomainName\Scripts
```

where *%systemroot%* is the variable referencing the Windows installation drive and directory, and *domain name* is the name of your domain. For example, if your Windows installation was stored in a directory called \WINDOWS on the C: drive, the %systemroot% varialble would equate to C:\WINDOWS. You could also use the Shared Folders MMC snap-in to quickly locate the NETLOGON share

Meanwhile, the path on Windows NT 4 domain controllers is different. The NETLOGON share on these systems is the Scripts directory found here:

```
%SystemRoot%\System32\Repl\Import\Scripts
```

Any Windows 9x client that finds a config.pol file in either of these two directories (remember that it's the NETLOGON share to the client, so to technically there's no difference for them) processes that files and applies appropriate registry changes.

Likewise, a Windows NT 4 client connects to the NETLOGON share at either domain controller and process any files called Ntconfig.pol, applying any registry changes stored therein.

The idea, where Outlook is concerned, is to include settings in your policy files(s) that affect the operation of the application from downlevel clients. Remember the function of system policies and how to extend their functionality through the use of administrative templates, and you'll be on your way.

Summary

This chapter explained ways you can externally manage the behavior of an Outlook installation through the application of group policies and through system policies. You looked at how these policies are configured and deployed on different Windows operating system platforms, and some of the considerations to keep in mind when deploying.

In the upcoming chapter, you will turn your attention from managing user data to ensuring that data is never lost. Chapter 25 looks at the critical issues of backup and recovery.

✦   ✦   ✦

Backing Up and Recovering User Data

✦ ✦ ✦ ✦

In This Chapter

Backing up and restoring PSTs

Exchange Server mailbox backup and restore

Backing up rules and other data

Setting retention policies

Configuring and using automatic archival

✦ ✦ ✦ ✦

One of the most fundamental administrative tasks is the backup of vital data. In the case of Outlook, the administrator responsible for this task is oftentimes you; therefore, backup and recovery knowledge is essential in the event the information you manage in Outlook is ever lost, stolen, or damaged.

This chapter takes a look at some of the essential backup and recovery tasks you'll likely encounter during your experience with Outlook 2003. Additionally, you'll examine some of the steps necessary to back up user data even if Outlook does not directly store the information; that is, when Outlook is the front-end application for an Exchange Server solution.

You may be relieved to know, and may have already experienced with previous versions of Outlook, that much of your data file management is done through a process called AutoArchive. During an Archive, Outlook takes data that you've either specified or that has met AutoArchive criteria and moves it to another .pst file. The Archive mechanism then cleans archived data from the current folder. This chapter reviews and explains this process, and leads you through some important configuration parameters of the AutoArchive feature.

Backing Up and Restoring PSTs

Earlier in this book, the importance of the Personal Folders (PST) files was discussed, as well as what kinds of information are stored therein. Remember that if you are not using an

Exchange Server, all Outlook information, including the contents of your e-mail, is stored in one of these PST files. Therefore, backing up and restoring the PST file becomes essential knowledge if you care about the information Outlook keeps — and I assume, for the sake of argument, that you consider your business and personal Contacts as well as the appointments and birthday reminders kept in the Calendar to be important.

The purpose of backing up Outlook data is self-evident: Just as any other backup, an Outlook backup allows you to easily restore the data if it's ever lost or damaged due to a hardware failure or other computer disaster. Moreover, a backup serves another purpose: It also allows you to move or transfer your Outlook information a different location. This other location can be another hard disk on the same computer, a disk on a different computer, or sometimes a removable media source for transport of vital personal organizational information in your coat pocket.

Note   Remember that in the computer world, the term disaster is defined as an event that causes a loss of data. Disasters can be caused by flood, fire, theft, accident, or hacking, to name a few.

Tip   Backing up your Exchange Server mailbox to a PST is a good way to keep a personal backup, even if the Exchange Server administrator backs up the mailbox at the server.

Quick and easy PST file backup

For the belt-and-suspenders approach to safekeeping of personal Outlook data, here are the steps necessary to quickly back up the entire contents of the personal folders (PST) file.

1. Close any message-related programs that might be currently accessing this PST file, such as Outlook, Microsoft Exchange, or Windows Messaging.

2. Choose Start ➪ Settings ➪ Control Panel; then click the Mail icon.

3. Click the Show Profiles button, choose the appropriate profile, and click Properties to open the Properties dialog box.

4. Click the Outlook Data Files button to open the Data Files dialog box, as shown in Figure 25-1. (Alternatively, while Outlook is open, you can open the Folder List in the Outlook bar and click the Data File Mgmt link, or click File ❘ Data File Mgmt.)

5. Click the Personal Folders Service that you want to back up. By default, this service is called Personal Folders; you may have renamed it.

Tip   You may have more than one Outlook Data files location in your profile. If this is true, make certain that you back up each set of personal folders in a separate procedure.

6. Click Settings, and note the path and filename that is listed.

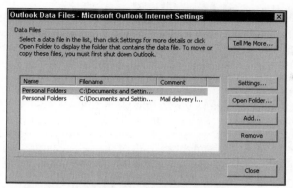

Figure 25-1: The Outlook Data Files dialog box.

7. Close all of the Properties windows.

8. Make a copy of the file you noted in step 5 by using Windows Explorer or My Computer.

A couple of additional notes on the backup of your Personal Folders file.

✦ Because the PST file contains all Outlook data, this file can quickly attain a size too large to place on a 1.44MB floppy disk. If this is the case, you can use any other file storage option: the music industry's bane, the CDRW drive, a zip drive, portable USB storage, DVD-RW, or a SyQuest drive all work brilliantly. Also, remember that you can reduce the size of a PST file when you click Compact Now (which you find from the Outlook Data Files dialog box, and then examining the Properties of the Data file) which compresses the PST file to a size that might possibly fit on a floppy disk after all.

✦ If there are not any Outlook Data files in your profile, and you have been able to store the information you'd expect to store in Outlook, such as messages, contacts, or appointments, your information is most likely being stored in a mailbox on an Exchange Server. Backing up Outlook information when that information is kept on an Exchange Server is discussed later in this chapter.

✦ If you don't see any PST files in the list of services and you know you're not storing information in an Exchange Server mailbox, you can only use Outlook to browse files, and the features in Outlook that store data cannot be used. In other words, there is no data to back up.

I mentioned earlier that you can perform the backup of your PST file to a removable media, such as a floppy disk drive, a zip drive, a CD-ROM re-writeable drive. You may want to consider this step to further safeguard Outlook data, even when you have another backup routine in place. Off-site backups are often recommended and sometimes required with sensitive or critical data, and the removable media allows you to do just this. To do so, copy the backup copy of the file that you just created from the storage media back to the computer hard disk.

Exporting Personal Folders file data

You don't have to use the Mail interface in the Control Panel to make a duplicate of your Personal Folders file. You can also perform this task from within Outlook. This is also an effective technique for sending Outlook information from one computer to another, sometimes via a network server.

Furthermore, there are instances where you might want to take a certain folder from your Outlook information store and either back it up or transport it. The Export feature is perfect for just this occasion because it supports folder-by-folder backup and restore operations. This might be one of those occasions where a floppy might come in handy for transporting Outlook information.

The following steps are necessary to export an individual folder, such as the Contacts folder or a Calendar folder to another location. The example uses the Calendar folder.

1. With Outlook open, choose File ⇨ Import And Export to launch the Import and Export Wizard, shown in Figure 25-2.

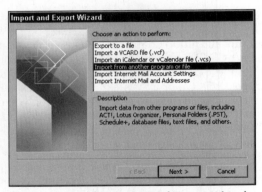

Figure: 25-2: The Import and Export Wizard.

2. Select "Export to a file" and then click Next.

3. Click Personal Folder File (PST) and then click Next.

4. Choose the Calendar folder for export and then click Next. The checkbox near the bottom of this dialog box also lets you specify whether or not to include subfolders.

5. Click the Browse button and then select the location to save the file.

6. In the File Name box, type a descriptive file name and then click OK. Click Finish, and then you will see the Create Microsoft Personal Folders dialog box. You can password protect the backup file, and also set Encryption levers here.

Importing PST file data

Importing is essentially a reverse of the export process, and is fairly intuitive if you have performed an export. You use the procedure to restore or move saved Outlook information, and can even use it to extract a single folder from a previous backup.

The following steps are used to import a previously created PST file into Outlook.

1. Choose File ⇨ Import And Export to launch the Import and Export Wizard.
2. Click Import from another program or file and then click Next.
3. Find the file you want to restore by clicking first on the selection for a Personal Folder File (.pst), and then click Next.
4. Either Browse or type the path and the name of the PST file you want to import, and click Next.
5. Select the folder you want to import, or select the top of the hierarchy to import everything. Click Finish, and the import will commence.

Tip   Another way to accomplish this same task is to choose File | Open | Outlook Data File, and then select the .pst file you want to open. The folder(and subfolder) contents will now appear in your folder list, where you can just drag and drop the content you want from the backed up folder locations to a current one.

Exchange Server Mailbox Backup and Restore

You might not have a Outlook Data file to backup. If this is the case, you are likely using an installation of Outlook that's serving as a front-end application while an Exchange Server stores and manages our Outlook data in an Exchange mailbox. In that event, the Outlook data you're working with is still being saved; it's not being saved on your system, but rather on the machine with the installation of Exchange.

Backing up data on a Microsoft Exchange Server

When Outlook information is stored on an Exchange Server, it is typically backed up at the server. If this accurately describes your working environment, your administrator has a couple of options: He can have Outlook store information on the Exchange Server, or in a set of Personal Folders (PST) files on your hard disk, as in the case of a standalone installation. To figure out where your Outlook data is being kept, follow these steps:

1. Choose Tools ⇨ E-mail Accounts.
2. Click View or Change Existing Email Accounts and then click Next.

3. Look at the Deliver new mail to the following location: option. If the option contains the word "Mailbox" followed by an e-mail name, Outlook stores data in folders on the Exchange Server. If the field contains the words "Personal Folder or another name of a set of personal folders (PST) file," Outlook stores new messages, contacts, appointments, and so on in the Personal Folders (PST) file on your hard disk.

Note

You should also check for Exchange Server in the Account List. Although it's not recommended, you can have a PST in a profile with an Exchange Server mailbox, and even deliver your Exchange Server mail to that PST.

Backing up Personal Address Books

You have other options besides the Outlook Contacts folder for keeping track of names and addresses. One such option is the Personal Address Book (PAB) file.

The Outlook Address Book is created automatically and contains the addresses in your Contacts folder, which it displays in the Address Book dialog box when you click Contacts in the Show names from the list. If Outlook is your only messaging option, you shouldn't need this PAB file. When you update the contents of your Contacts folder, the Outlook Address Book is updated as well. You usually import the contents of the Personal Address Book to your Contacts folder and that will be that; however, it still might be good practice to make sure that this address book is backed up. To do so, you must include any files with the .pab extension in your backup process.

From a system running Microsoft Windows 2000 or Windows Millennium Edition (Me), click Start ➪ Search ➪ For Files or Folders. This procedure might differ slightly from other operating systems such as Windows 98 or XP, but you're trying to open the Search dialog box either way. After Search is open, follow these steps:

1. Type *.pab, click My Computer in the Look In box, and click Find Now. Note the location of the .pab file, and include it in your backup. If you need to restore this address book either to the same computer or a different computer, continue with the remaining steps.

2. Close any message-related programs such as Outlook, Microsoft Exchange, or Windows Messaging.

3. Click Start ➪ Settings ➪ Control Panel ➪ Mail icon to open the Mail Setup dialog box.

4. Click the Show Profiles button, choose the appropriate profile, and click Properties.

5. Click the Email Accounts button.

6. Click Add a New Directory or Address Book, and click Next

7. Click Additional Address Books and then click Next.

8. Click Personal Address Book and then click Next.

9. Type the path and name of the Personal Address Book file that you want to restore, click Apply, and click OK.

10. Click Close, and click OK.

Tip   You can also do this with Outlook open. If so, you will just have to restart Outlook for it to take effect.

Backing up Outlook settings files

There are other files Outlook uses for configuring itself. Aside from the information Outlook accesses, you might also want the look and feel of Outlook to be the same when moving form one computer to another. In this event, you need to be aware to the other files Outlook uses to define how the program behaves.

When moving an installation of Outlook from one setting to another, you may want to include the following files in your back up to keep customized settings intact. These files would be included in addition to the crucial backup of the Personal Folders (PST) file:

Outcmd.dat. This file stores toolbar and menu settings.

***Profile Name*.fav.** This is your Favorites file that includes the settings for the Outlook bar.

***Profile Name*.nk2.** This file stores the nicknames for AutoComplete.

Tip   If you use Microsoft Word as your e-mail editor, signatures are stored in the Normal.dot file as Autotext entries. You should also back up this file. Custom views are integrated to the folders on which they were created. If you export items from one Personal Folders (PST) file to another, your custom views are not maintained.

Backing up a customized signature

If you have created customized signatures that you want to transport to another computer running Outlook, be aware of the custom signature files used. They are located, by default, in the following folder:

```
X:\Documents and Settings\Username\Application Data\Microsoft\
Signatures
```

where *X:* represents the drive where Outlook was installed, and *Username* represents the username used during the Outlook installation. Further, each individual signature has its own file and uses the same name as the signature you used when you created it. For example, if you created a signature named BriansSig, the following files are created in the Signatures folder:

BriansSig.htm. This file stores the Hypertext Markup Language (HTML) autosignature.

BriansSig.rtf. This file stores the Microsoft Outlook Rich Text Format (RTF) Autosignature.

BriansSig.txt. This file stores the plain text format Autosignature.

If you do not want the hassle of creating new signatures, you need to make sure these files are backed up as well.

Backing Up Rules and Other Data

Earlier in this book, the significance of rules were examined and how they are used to help Outlook make decisions about how to handle e-mail and other information. As an Outlook administrator, you might go to a great deal of administrative trouble to design and implement those rules. Shouldn't you be able to back them up to save time and trouble if Outlook need to be transferred or recovered?

Note   If you're not using Exchange Server, the rules are actually stored in a PST file. If using an Exchange Server, then the rules are stored in the mailbox. Therefore, backing up is still a good idea in case you lose your mail store and/or want to move rules to other computers.

You can. The Rules and Alerts dialog box lets you easily backup and restore your rules just as you can your Personal Folders file. When you export rules, they are saved in a file with an .rwz extension. When you import, they are added to the end of the list in the Rules and Alerts dialog box.

Also note that if you upgrade from a version of Outlook prior to Outlook 2003, there may be a .rwz file that can be safely deleted.

To export a set of rules, do the following:

1. From the Navigation Pane, select your Inbox.
2. Choose Tools ⇨ Rules And Alerts to open the Rules and Alerts dialog box.
3. Click the Options button, as shown in Figure 25-3.
4. Click Export Rules.
5. In the Filename box, type the path and filename for the set of rules you want to export.

Note   If you want to export rules for use with a version of Outlook prior to version 2003, you can do so. To perform this operation, look in the Save as type list, select Outlook 2000 compatible Rules Wizard rules or Outlook 98 compatible Rules Wizard rules, and save the rules.

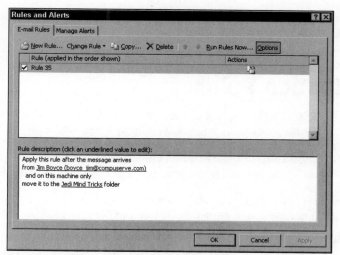

Figure 25-3: The Rules and Alerts dialog box.

The reverse of this procedure shouldn't prove too difficult after you have performed an Export. To Import an existing rule, follow these steps:

1. Perform steps 1 through 3 as described in the previous exercise.

2. Click Import Rules.

3. In the File name box, type the path and filename for the set of rules you want to import.

4. If you want to import a file that contains rules other than Rules Wizard rules, click the file type in the Files of type list.

Note   You can import only one set of rules at a time using this procedure.

You can also backup other types of data Outlook uses, such as the custom dictionary (.txt), send/receive settings (.srs), and custom Outlook templates (.oft). To back these files up, however, you need to resort to the old-fashioned method of navigating to them in the folder hierarchy; there is no graphical interface Outlook provides for backing up these files.

Most of the files are stored under the profile folders of the user. This profile location will vary from computer to computer, depending on the operating system in use. On Windows 2000 machines, for example, the location of end/receive settings is *X:*\Documents and Settings*username*\\Application Data\\Microsoft\\Outlook, where *X:* is the drive where Outlook is installed, and *username* is the name of the current user.

To get familiar with the default storage locations for these other file types, please refer to the Outlook help files and perform a search for Outlook file locations.

Setting Retention Policies

Another added benefit of a Exchange installation is the ability to use a retention policy for deleted user accounts. If you mistakenly delete a mail-enabled user account, you can recreate that user object and, by default, reconnect that mailbox for a period of 30 days. This is because when you select a user, Exchange retains a user's mailbox for a predetermined number of days, set by default to 30 days.

Note   This feature is new to Exchange 2000, and was not available in Exchange 5.5. Exchange 2003 is expected to keep this default retention duration as well.

You set the Exchange retention policy settings in the same way you specify how many days Exchange retains mail that a user deletes. You configure a deleted mailbox retention period at the mailbox store object level.

To configure a deleted mailbox retention period, follow these steps:

1. In Exchange System Manager, navigate to the mailbox store group for which you want to configure a retention policy.

2. Right-click the mailbox store, and click Properties.

3. On the Limits tab, type the number of days you want Exchange to retain deleted mailboxes in Keep deleted mailboxes for and click OK when you're done.

If you delete a user account, the user's mailbox is not automatically deleted until the deleted mailbox retention policy period expires. If you want to reconnect a user to a previously deleted mailbox and are within the threshold of the retention policy number of days, follow these steps:

1. From Active Directory Users and Computers, create a new user object.

Tip   When you create the new user object, clear the Create an Exchange Mailbox check box. Because you are connecting the new user to an existing mailbox, you do not want a mailbox created when you set up the account, as shown in Figure 25-4.

2. From the Exchange System Manager, navigate to the mailbox store location where the mailbox for this new user will use be kept.

3. In the Details pane, locate the mailbox desired for the new user.

Tip   Verify that the mailbox icon appears with a red X. Mailboxes that display with a red X are mailboxes that have been deleted but will be retained in the mailbox store until the deleted mailbox retention period expires.

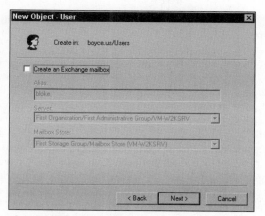

Figure 25-4: Do not create a mailbox for this new user if you intend to connect to a retained mailbox.

4. Right-click the mailbox for the new user and then click Reconnect.

5. In the New User for this Mailbox, select the new user object you created for the new user, and click OK.

Configuring and Using Automatic Archival

You've just seen how to manually export and archive Outlook folders to ensure against data loss, or to quickly transfer Outlook data from one place to another. Now look at how this is all automated through a process called AutoArchive. The AutoArchive feature is not new to this latest version of Outlook, but it is still important to understand how this feature works as well as the ways you can manipulate what and how often AutoArchive backs up critical information. But first, an important question needs to be addressed.

What is the Archive?

You can draw analogies between Outlook and non-computer office technologies such between the Inbox that Outlook uses and the paper-based In Box that might be sitting on your office desk. Microsoft makes these analogies all the time with computer concepts, starting with what you see on the screen when you logon to your computer. Microsoft calls it a desktop, but really it's just a folder of shortcuts and settings.

The analogy Microsoft uses for the AutoArchive is no different: it's roots lie in a paper based office environment. When a piece of mail or a message is delivered to your desk, where is it placed? The In Box. Similarly, Outlook takes incoming messages and delivers them, at first to the Inbox.

Eventually, however, as the messages and the mail kept piling up, that In Box on your desk would become too full to effectively manage. It would need to be cleaned out so that you could retrieve and review important messages more easily, and in doing so you would be faced with decisions about whether or not to save less important messages, or just throw them away.

If you understand these concepts from a paper-based desktop model, you have a basic understanding of the Archive feature in Outlook. The archive lets you occasionally shuffle through your email and other Outlook documents and store those that are important but not frequently used, while simultaneously sending documents that are less important, such as newspapers and magazines, to the trash can. In other words, Outlook's Archive is your filing cabinet and shredder.

You can manually transfer old items to a storage file by clicking File ⇨ Archive, or, as discussed in the next section, you can have old items automatically transferred by using AutoArchive. Outlook can archive all types of items, but it can locate only files that are stored in an e-mail folder, such as a Microsoft Excel spreadsheet or Word document attached to an e-mail message. A file that is not stored in an e-mail folder cannot be archived.

Using AutoArchive

At any time, you can Archive information manually using the methods described above, but there is a background process that helps take care of the Archive process even if you don't remember to do it. This feature is the AutoArchive, which allows you to have old items automatically transferred to an archive file without user interaction.

By default, several Outlook folders are set up with AutoArchive turned on. And to answer the question, "What's old?", the answer is, "Whatever you say is old." As Einstein says, everything is relative, so what's old is a matter of personal preference; however, your starting point of reference is Outlook's default settings. These folders and their default aging periods are:

>   **Calendar**. 6 months
>
>   **Inbox.** 6 months
>
>   **Tasks**. 6 months
>
>   **Journal**. 6 months
>
>   **Sent Items**. 2 months
>
>   **Deleted Items**. 2 months
>
>   **Notes and Drafts**. 6 months

Note   You cannot AutoArchive your Contacts.

The AutoArchive process is a two-step process. You first enable AutoArchive. To do so, follow these steps:

1. With Outlook open, choose Tools ⇨ Options to open the Options dialog box.

2. Click the Other tab.

3. Click the AutoArchive button to open the AutoArchive dialog box.

4. From the AutoArchive dialog box, you can set the AutoArchive options to best suit your needs, including, as shown in Figure 25-5:

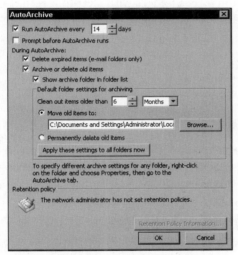

Figure 25-5: The AutoArchive options.

Run AutoArchive every x Days. This option enables AutoArchiving. You then select the number of days you want between AutoArchive intervals. Note that you must first have this option selected before any of the other options become available.

Prompt Before AutoArchive Runs. If you want Outlook to give you a friendly reminder before performing an AutoArchive, check this option.

Delete Expired Items When AutoArchiving (Email folders only). Only mail items with expiration dates are affected by this option. During an AutoArchive, messages with expiration dates that have passed are moved to the Deleted Items folder.

Clean Out Items Older Than. Use this to indicate the aging criteria for the archiving of Outlook items.

Move Old Items To. You can change this default location, if you desire, by clicking on the Browse button. This in turn opens the Find Personal Folders dialog box where you can select a different archive file, or, alternatively, create a new one. If you share you r computer with other Outlook users, this is probably a good idea; otherwise the default file called archive.lis can be used by everyone on the computer. Everyone's archived information is tossed into one file, making restore a more difficult chore.

Permanently Delete Old Items. If you don't want Outlook keeping copies of your old information, including old e-mail, you can have AutoArchive move all items that meet aging criteria into the Deleted Items folder.

Apply These Settings to All Folders Now. This is not as self-explanatory as the name might imply. Rather than actually applying the selected settings to all folders, clicking this button forces folders with a custom settings to use the default settings. Folders that don't have AutoArchive set are not affected.

Retention Policy Information. Click this button to see what settings have been configured for retention of the deleted items, as well as any other policies the administrator has decreed in effect on the Exchange Server. If you don't have Outlook working as the front-end of an exchange Server solution, this button will be grayed out.

The second part of the process takes place when you set the AutoArchive properties for each folder you want to participate in AutoArchive. At the folder level, you can determine which items are archived and how often they are archived. You have the options to automatically archive individual folders, groups of folders, or every single Outlook folder.

AutoArchiving for individual folders

Outlook can AutoArchive all items in all folders except those in the Contacts folder. The items Outlook AutoArchives are those that, like so many cartons of milk forgotten in the back of my fridge, have expired. You get to specify the expiration date for all items Outlook AutoArchives, but it is important to be aware of the defaults.

To turn AutoArchiving on or off for a folder, follow the steps:

1. In the Outlook Bar, depending on your view settings, right-click either the folder name in the Folder List or the shortcut icon in the Outlook Bar for each folder you want to AutoArchive.

2. From the context menu, select Properties to display the folders' Properties dialog box, as shown in Figure 25-6.

3. Select the AutoArchive tab, and ensure that either the Archive this folder using these settings or Archive items in this folder using the default settings is selected.

4. In the other selections of the dialog box, you can set how the Archive conducts itself, and where archive files are created.

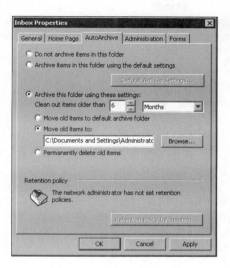

Figure 25-6: Individual folder AutoArchive options.

Excluding individual items from AutoArchiving

The default behavior of AutoArchive is that the properties you define for a folder get applies all child items of that folder; however, this is behavior that can be modified.

To exclude items from the AutoArchiving dragnet, follow these steps:

1. Open the target item in the folder set for AutoArchiving that you want to have excluded.

2. Access the item's Properties dialog box. In the case of a particular e-mail message, choose File ➪ Properties to open the dialog box shown in Figure 25-7.

Figure 25-7: Excluding an item from the AutoArchive process.

3. From the item's General tab, check the Do not AutoArchive this item box, which, for those without the capacity for deductive thinking, excludes the item from either manual or AutoArchive behavior.

Determining when AutoArchive runs

The AutoArchive process runs automatically each time you start Outlook. The AutoArchive properties of each folder are checked by date, and old items are moved to your archive file as appropriate for your AutoArchive policy. Additionally, items in the Deleted Items folder are deleted permanently.

Tip

Many computers are left on all the time, and on some of these computers, Outlook is running minimized. If this is the case with your computer, note that Outlook checks whether or not it should AutoArchive anything whenever it starts. If Outlook never closes and reopens, it will never perform an AutoArchive. For this reason, it is a good idea to close Outlook when leaving work for the day and then reopen when you return. Alternatively, you could configure a Scheduled Task to automatically stop and starts Outlook every evening. To configure a Scheduled Task, choose Start ➪ Programs ➪ Accessories ➪ System Tools. The Scheduled Task program will be listed as one of the System Tools. It's fairly straightforward to use.

Archiving v. Exporting

Archiving and exporting are not the same things, and that's why there is a menu choice for each on the File menu. The main difference between the two is what happens to the originals when the operation is performed, and that difference is significant in terms of your overall backup procedures. When you archive, the original items are copied to the archive file and then removed from the current folder. When you export, the original items are copied to the export file, but are not removed from the current folder. In other words, when you choose to Archive, there isn't a backup copy made of the files being moved, but rather space and clutter in the selected folder is cleaned up. When you export, you end up with a backup copy of your information.

Furthermore, you can only archive one file type, a .pst file, but you can export many file types. Exporting Outlook information to other file types is particularly useful if you want to take your Outlook information to another program. This is because not all programs cooperate with Microsoft's .pst files. For example, if you wanted to store a list of contacts in a database that keeps track of a company's customers, that database can likely be populated by a comma separated value (.csv) file.

When you archive, however, your existing folder structure is maintained in your new archive file. If there is a parent folder above the folder you chose to archive, the parent folder is created in the archive file, but items within the parent folder are not archived. In this way, an identical folder structure exists between the archive file and your mailbox. Folders are left in place after being archived, even if they are empty.

If you're using Outlook as a front-end client for Microsoft's Exchange Server, you can keep your Outlook information neatly tucked away there, and let the Exchange administrator worry about the backing up and Archiving routines. Alternatively, you can store the same information in a Personal Folders file on your local machine. In fact, if you're not using an Exchange server to store and manage your Outlook data, you have no choice other than to use a PST file. Normally, this file will be stored on your local hard drive. Outlook's settings — the information that really isn't of concern to end users but is of fundamental importance to Outlook — are stored in several files across multiple local directories wherever Outlook in installed.

Backing up Outlook involves making a copy of the important messages, settings, calendar entries, and other information you consider crucial., such as the items you bought Outlook to manage in the first place, to an alternative location. You do this for a couple of reasons:

✦ Reduce the amount of space taken by Outlook information on your computer's hard drive

✦ Providing redundancy on the event of a loss of data

If you get many messages delivered to your Inbox every day, your Personal Folders store can get quite large.

Summary

It's inevitable during your computer use that your will someday lose data. The best way to prepare for that day is to familiarize ourselves with the backup and Archive procedures, looked at the differences between the two, and learned about the files used by Outlook to store our valuable information.

This chapter explained the backup procedure by looking at the methods for exporting data from Outlook 2003. We examined the steps necessary to export all of your Outlook Date, or just selected folders of information.

The chapter also explained the Archive and the AutoArchive procedures, where data is moved to make space in our current working folders. It's important to note that the Archive feature, whether done manually or automatically, is not a backup, but rather a move procedure.

✦　　✦　　✦

Managing Exchange Server for Outlook Users

✦ ✦ ✦ ✦

In This Chapter

Managing mailboxes

Creating external addresses (mail-enabled contacts)

Distribution lists in Exchange

Configuring Exchange Instant Messaging

✦ ✦ ✦ ✦

Microsoft Exchange is a powerful tool for enabling Microsoft Outlook. While Outlook by itself provides e-mail, calendar, and other functionality, Microsoft Exchange allows you to connect Outlook clients in a collaborative workgroup environment. While the collaboration features of Exchange are its main selling point, it also allows you to store user data on a central server rather than on the client desktop system.

With an Exchange Server, you gain workgroup messaging, where messages from one local user to another do not have to pass through Internet SMTP mail servers; rather, they are delivered instantly to the recipient's Exchange mailbox. The recipient does not need to check his or her mail in the sense of an Internet message because Exchange uses a "push" protocol to make the new message appear in the recipient's Outlook client instantly with no interaction.

In addition to messaging capabilities, Microsoft Exchange adds other groupware features as well, such as calendar sharing and shared folders. A shared folder is similar to a shared directory on a network file server except it contains a specific type of item (such as messages or calendar items) rather than just files. Shared folders can hold files, too, though.

Managing Mailboxes

Microsoft Exchange has been tightly integrated with Active Directory (in Windows 2000 and newer) since Exchange 2000 was released, and that integration carries over into Exchange Server 2003. Previously in Exchange 5.5 and earlier, mailboxes and a directory of mailbox users were contained in Microsoft Exchange while user accounts were contained in the Microsoft Windows NT domain controllers. With this layout, mailboxes were associated with user accounts for login purposes, but no other information was shared between Exchange and Windows.

Note　Although there are some differences in features between Exchange 2000 Server and Exchange Server 2003, many of the management tasks are the same. This chapter focuses on Exchange 2000 Server as the server platform. You'll find the tasks and methods essentially the same in Exchange Server 2003.

In the more recent versions of Exchange (2000 and up) and Microsoft Windows (2000 and up), the separation between a mailbox and a user account has been removed. Mailbox features in a user account are a result of extensions made to the Active Directory (AD) *schema* by Exchange during installation. The Active Directory schema defines the structure of the information stored in AD. Exchange data is still stored in Exchange, but the actual mailbox definitions are stored in AD as user attributes.

Adding a mailbox automatically

Adding an Exchange mailbox for an Outlook user is simple because it is done automatically when the user is added to Active Directory. Begin by opening the Active Directory Users and Computers snap-in by choosing Start ➪ Programs ➪ Administrative Tools. In the left pane of the snap-in, locate the Users container under the domain in which to add the user. Right-click the Users container; then select New ➪ User to open the New Object–User dialog box. Enter the name information for the new user in the first step, and click Next to continue.

Tip　The addition of a user to Active Directory is not covered in detail here because there is more involved than can be covered within the scope of this book. Only the parts of adding a user relevant to Exchange are discussed here. For more information on adding users to Active Directory, consult the *Windows Server 2003 Bible* or *Windows 2000 Server Bible*.

In the second step of the New Object–User dialog box, enter password information. Set a password for the user, set the applicable parameters, and click Next to continue. The next step, shown in Figure 26-1, is where the Exchange mailbox settings are configured.

Note　If Microsoft Exchange is not installed in this Active Directory deployment, this step in the dialog box will not appear.

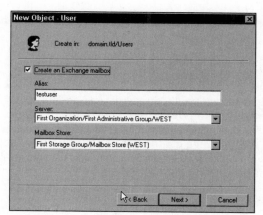

Figure 26-1: An Exchange mailbox is created by default for each new user added to the domain.

An Exchange mailbox is created by default. If you do not want to create a mailbox for the new user, you can deselect the Create an Exchange mailbox check box. You may not want mailboxes for accounts used as service accounts (accounts that are used only by applications) or for other accounts based on your policies. The dialog box contains three configuration options for the user's Exchange mailbox. The alias is a descriptor used by Exchange to identify the mailbox. Each mailbox must have a unique alias and the alias is the same as the user's login name by default. Using the login name is typical practice at most organizations. The second option allows you to specify the server on which the account resides. It is common practice in environments with multiple Exchange Servers to place the user's mailbox on the Exchange Server nearest the user, which is normally on the local network.

In Microsoft Exchange a Mailbox Store is the database containing all data for a group of users. In older versions of Exchange, only one store was available on each server. In newer versions however, you can have multiple mailbox stores. Using multiple mailbox stores is advantageous in large environments where a single store would be very large. Due to the database engine used by Exchange, large mailbox stores become inefficient. Using multiple mailbox stores allows greater scalability when using a single large Exchange Server to serve a single location in a large organization.

Note You can only have one Mailbox Store on a server when using Standard Edition and it is limited to 16GB in size. When using Enterprise Edition, these limits are removed.

If you have more than one mailbox store on the selected Exchange Server, you can select the store in which the mailbox resides in the Mailbox Store drop-down box. After you have selected the correct options in this step of the New Object–User dialog box, click Next to continue; then, click Finish to create the user.

Tip When you delete a user who has an Exchange mailbox, the mailbox is deleted by default along with the user account.

Adding, removing, and moving mailboxes manually

While mailboxes are typically added and removed along with user accounts in Active Directory, it is also possible to add and remove mailboxes separately from the user add and delete processes. This is especially useful if you created a user account and deselected the Create an Exchange mailbox option during the process. If you change your mind later on, it is still possible to add a mailbox for the user. Similarly, you can remove a user's mailbox if it is not required.

Adding a mailbox manually

Both adding and removing mailboxes are done from the Active Directory Users and Computers snap-in. Open the snap-in by selecting Start ➪ Programs ➪ Administrative Tools and then choosing the snap-in. Locate the user account to manage, which is typically in the Users container, and select the container under the domain in the left pane of the snap-in. Right-click the user object in the right pane of the snap-in, and select Exchange Tasks to open the Exchange Task Wizard. The first page in the wizard is typically a Welcome page. You can disable the Welcome page by selecting the Do not show this Welcome page again check box. Click Next to continue. Figure 26-2 shows the next page in the Exchange Task Wizard for a user account that does not already have an Exchange mailbox.

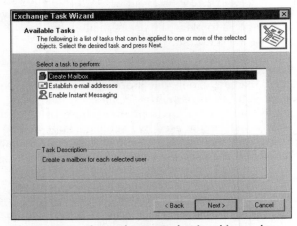

Figure 26-2: The Exchange Task Wizard is used to add a mailbox to a user account.

The first step in the Exchange Task Wizard is to select the task you want to perform. Ensure Create Mailbox is selected and then click Next to continue. The next step is identical to that shown in Figure 26-1. Specify the alias for the mailbox (a unique identifier typically the same as the user's login name) and the Server and Mailbox Store where the mailbox will reside as described in the previous section, "Adding a mailbox automatically." Click Next to continue. The mailbox is created and a summary page is shown with details and the results of the mailbox creation. Click Finish to close the Exchange Task Wizard.

Removing a mailbox manually

Just as with creating a mailbox manually, you may change your mind about a user account's requirement for a mailbox and want to remove it without removing the entire account. Locate the account to manage as discussed in the previous section, "Adding a mailbox manually," right-click, and select Exchange Tasks to open the Exchange Task Wizard. If the Welcome page is shown, click Next to continue. The first step in the Exchange Task Wizard is shown in Figure 26-3.

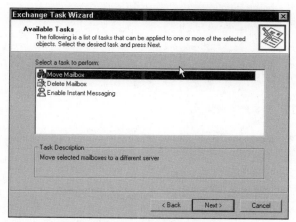

Figure 26-3: The Exchange Task Wizard can be used to manually remove a mailbox from a user account.

Select Delete Mailbox from the list of tasks and then click Next to continue. The Exchange Task Wizard now prompts you to ensure you want to delete the mailbox. If you are sure, click Next to continue. The mailbox is deleted and a summary page is shown. Click Finish to close the Exchange Task Wizard.

Tip

When you delete a mailbox, all of the mailbox contents are deleted including any messages, calendar items, and anything else in the mailbox. Mailboxes can be recovered using deleted mailbox retention. It is helpful, however, to export all items from the mailbox to a PST file using Outlook before deleting the mailbox. This way if you need an item from the deleted mailbox you can simply open the PST file in Outlook rather than restoring the deleted mailbox.

Moving a mailbox

The final manual task that the Exchange Task Wizard can be used for is moving a mailbox. Mailboxes can be moved from one mailbox store to another or from one server to another. As explained in the section "Adding a mailbox manually," locate the user account with the mailbox to be moved in the Active Directory Users and Computers snap-in. Right-click the user object and select Exchange Tasks to start the Exchange Task Wizard. If the Welcome page is displayed, click Next to continue. Choose Move Mailbox from the list, and click Next to continue to the Move Mailbox page as shown in Figure 26-4.

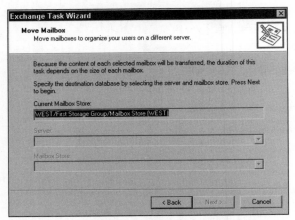

Figure 26-4: The Move Mailbox page in the Exchange Task Wizard is used to move a mailbox to a different server or mailbox store.

Note in Figure 26-4 how both the Server and Mailbox Store drop-down boxes are unavailable. This is because there are no other servers or mailbox stores available. The mailbox resides in an environment with only one server and one mailbox store (due to the limitations on Exchange 2000 Standard Edition). If you have more than one server or mailbox store, select the server and mailbox store from the drop-down boxes and click Next to continue. The mailbox is moved and a summary page is displayed. Click Finish to close the Exchange Task Wizard.

Configuring global mailbox options

There are two ways to configure mailbox options with Exchange: globally, so changes affect all mailboxes, and on a per mailbox basis, where only one mailbox is affected. A few settings are also configurable on a per-mailbox store basis, such as size limits. Configuring on a per mailbox basis is discussed in the next section, "Configuring mailbox-specific options." This section covers mailbox configuration on a global basis but does not delve into Exchange Server configuration because it is beyond the scope of this book.

Message delivery options

Global mailbox options are configured in the Exchange System Manager snap-in. Open the snap-in by selecting Start ➪ Programs ➪ Microsoft Exchange ➪ System Manager. There are a few locations within the Exchange System Manager where mailbox configuration is set, the first being the Global Settings container. Open the Global Settings container in the left pane of the snap-in, right-click Message Delivery, and select Properties. Click the Defaults tab as shown in Figure 26-5.

Figure 26-5: The Defaults tab in the Message Delivery Properties dialog box is used to set default message options.

There are three settings in this tab: Outgoing message size, Incoming message size, and Recipient limits. Outgoing and Incoming message sizes, set to No limit by default, control the maximum size of outgoing and incoming messages. If you have limited bandwidth to your organization, you may want to set these limits. The Recipient limit controls the maximum number of recipients any message may have. This is set to 5000 by default, but you may want to raise or lower it as your organization requires. Having a recipient limit controls both possible spam from users of your Exchange Server as well as message storms caused by users inadvertently sending a message to all users in your address book, though this is a problem only in very large organizations.

Mailbox size and deleted item options

The second set of options controls storage limits for mailboxes on a global basis across a message store. In most cases you will have only one message store per server to configure unless you are using Microsoft Exchange Enterprise Edition. In the Exchange System Manager snap-in, expand the Servers container, expand the server to configure, then expand the storage group in which the mailbox store to configure resides. By default, the first storage group in a server is called First Storage Group. Right-click the Mailbox Store object, select Properties, and click the Limits tab as shown in Figure 26-6.

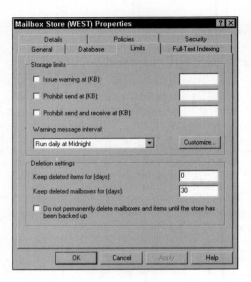

Figure 26-6: The Limits tab in the Mailbox Store Properties dialog box is used to configure mailbox size limits and deleted item retention.

The Limits tab has two sections: the upper section being mailbox storage limits. It is a well-known fact that many users like to keep messages in their mailbox for eternity. The problem with this from an administrative perspective is that these messages consume valuable disk space. Disk space may continue to get cheaper, but there is still overhead and cost involved with large amounts of disk storage, including administration, backup and restore procedures, and performance issues. Mailbox storage limits allow you to restrict how large each user's mailbox may be, though this can be overridden in the mailbox-specific options discussed in the next section.

There are three limits that can be set for mailbox size:

Issue warning. When a user's mailbox reaches this limit a message is sent from Exchange notifying the user that the mailbox is over its limit.

Prohibit send at. When a user's mailbox reaches the limit, no new messages can be sent through Exchange. The user can still receive messages, as to not impede communication from other users, but the mailbox must be cleaned up to get the number of messages below the limit before the user can send messages again.

Prohibit send and receive at. This is seldom used in practice. If this limit is set and a user's mailbox reaches it, he or she can no longer send or receive messages. Messages sent to this user are bounced with a notification to the sender that the mailbox is over its size limit. The reason it is not commonly used is that it impedes communication with the user, which is often unacceptable in a corporate environment. The Warning message interval option is used to specify when the warnings are sent to users over the Issue warning limit. Warnings are sent daily at midnight by default.

The lower section of the Limits tab allows you to configure what's commonly known as deleted item retention. Deleted item retention is an incredibly useful feature for an administrator. A common occurrence is a user permanently deleting an e-mail (emptying the deleted items or using shift-delete) and then realizing that he or she needed the item. Without deleted item retention you would need to restore the message from a tape backup, assuming it was in the mailbox at the time of the last good backup. Deleted item retention provides an Administrative Deleted Items folder from which you can recover deleted items. The main problem with this is that deleted item retention uses space in your mailbox store because deleted items are kept for a period of time.

To configure deleted item retention you must specify a number of days to keep items in the Limits tab. Items are not retained by default. The number of days should be high enough to give users enough time to remember that they needed the old e-mail they deleted, but low enough to not use too much space on your server. A few days should be enough, depending on your environment. You may find it should be higher or lower because you may have users who often need deleted items from further in the past.

In addition to setting deleted item retention for mailbox items, when you delete an entire mailbox, it is retained for 30 days by default. With entire mailboxes, you don't need to consider the space implications of retention because it's rare that you delete a mailbox. Thirty days is a good value, but you may have a policy requirement to keep them longer. You may also find it unnecessary to retain deleted mailboxes for such a long period and change it to a shorter value — or even zero. A value of zero causes the mailbox to be permanently deleted with no retention.

The final option on the Limits page is Do not permanently delete mailboxes and items until the store has been backed up. Selecting this option causes deleted item retention to be in effect until the next mailbox store backup. When the backup occurs, the deleted items are flushed. This feature is useful so that you don't need a long deleted item retention period, but you can be sure that deleted items are not lost and can be recovered from your backups.

Configuring mailbox-specific options

After a user account has a mailbox, there are several options that can be configured on a per-mailbox basis. Mailbox options are set using the Active Directory Users and Computers snap-in. Open the snap-in by choosing Start ➪ Programs ➪ Administrative Tools. Locate the user account to configure (typically in the Users container), right-click the user object, and select Properties to open the user's Properties dialog box. There are four tabs in the Properties dialog box relevant to Microsoft Exchange Server:

> **E-mail Addresses.** The E-mail Addresses tab is used to configure the e-mail addresses associated with the mailbox. A mailbox can have several e-mail addresses, and these addresses do not need to be the same type. You may have SMTP addresses for Internet mail and Lotus Notes or Novell GroupWise addresses for users if you are in a mixed environment.

Exchange Features. The Exchange Features tab is used to enable, disable, and configure any additional Exchange features installed on the server for this mailbox. By default, only the Instant Messaging feature is installed and is disabled by default.

Exchange General. The Exchange General tab contains the majority of the mailbox-specific options for Microsoft Exchange. You can set mailbox delivery and storage restrictions as well as set delegation and forwarding options.

Exchange Advanced. The Exchange Advanced tab is shown only if Advanced Features is selected in the View menu within Active Directory Users and Computers. This tab is rarely used except in very special cases and is not covered here.

Click the E-mail Addresses tab as shown in Figure 26-7.

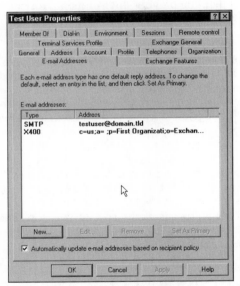

Figure 26-7: E-mail Addresses tab

The E-mail Addresses tab in the user's Properties dialog box is used to set up the addresses associated with the mailbox. By default, e-mail addresses are created based on the Recipient Policy in Exchange System Manager. The Recipient Policy is responsible for creating a default set of e-mail addresses for all users in Exchange. This automatic behavior can be disabled by deselecting the Automatically update e-mail addresses based on recipient policy check box.

In the E-mail Addresses tab you can also add, remove, and edit addresses for the user. You may, for example, have a user with a commonly misspelled name and want to assign two e-mail addresses so that the misspelled name also reaches him or her. This can be done by following these steps:

1. Click the Add button.

2. Select the address type from the list and click OK.

3. Enter the address and click OK. The address appears in the list.

4. Select an address and click the Remove button to remove it, or click the Edit button to change the address.

5. If there is more than one e-mail address of the same type for a user, select an address and click the Set As Primary button to set that address as the one that appears in the From field of messages from the user.

The Exchange Features tab, shown in Figure 26-8, is used to enable, disable, and configure additional Exchange features. By default, the only additional feature installed is Instant Messaging, discussed later in this chapter. Working with features is simple — select the feature from the list and then click the Enable or Disable buttons. With some features you can also click the Properties button to set the configuration options if the feature is enabled.

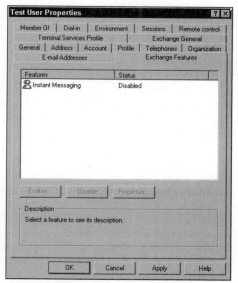

Figure 26-8: Extra Exchange features can be enabled, disabled, and configured in the Exchange Features tab.

The final tab is the Exchange General tab, shown in Figure 26-9. This tab shows two pieces of information — the server, and mailbox store in which the mailbox resides — and contains three buttons that launch configuration dialog boxes.

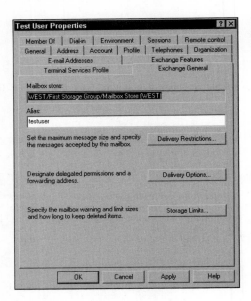

Figure 26-9: The Exchange General tab is used to configure most of the mailbox-specific settings.

Click the Delivery Restrictions button to open the Delivery Restrictions dialog box shown in Figure 26-10. From the Delivery Restrictions dialog box, you can set the maximum size for incoming and outgoing messages, as was covered in the previous section, "Configuring global mailbox options." These control the largest message this user can send and receive. These values overwrite the default and override global settings if they are set, which is useful if you have a few users who need to send or receive larger messages than the default.

The Delivery Restrictions dialog box contains the message restrictions section. By default a mailbox can receive messages from anyone, but you may want to restrict the mailbox so that it can only receive messages from specific users or to reject messages from certain users (in the case of abuse). This restriction must use recipients from the Exchange address list. In order to allow or deny Internet users from sending to this mailbox you must create a mail-enabled contact as discussed in the next section "Creating External Addresses (Mail-Enabled Contacts)." To set message restrictions, select either Only from or From everyone except, and click the Add button; then select a recipient from the list. You can remove a recipient from the list by selecting the recipient and then clicking the Remove button.

Figure 26-10: The Delivery Restrictions dialog box is used to set restrictions on sending and receiving messages.

Figure 26-11 shows the Delivery Options dialog box, opened by clicking the Delivery Options button in the Exchange General tab of the user's Properties dialog box. You can set three configuration items from this dialog box.

Send on behalf. By clicking the Add button and selecting a recipient, that recipient will be able to send e-mails "on behalf" of this user. This is useful for executives with assistants because when the assistant is added to the "Send on behalf" box, he or she can send e-mails with the executive's name, though the e-mail will say "on behalf of" the assistant. Select a recipient from the list and click the Remove button to remove the Send on behalf permission.

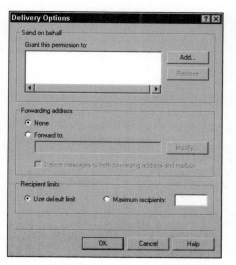

Figure 26-11: The Delivery Options dialog box is used to set delegates, forwarding, and recipient limits.

Forward address. This option allows you to forward all messages to this mailbox to another account. Select Forward to and click the Modify button to select a recipient from the Exchange directory. Messages sent to this mailbox are forwarded automatically to that recipient. You can also select the Deliver messages to both forwarding address and mailbox check box to have messages both forwarded to the specified recipient and placed in the mailbox; otherwise, they are forwarded and not delivered to the original destination mailbox.

Recipient limits. You can set the maximum number of recipients that a message sent from this user may have. The global version of this option was covered in the previous section and that value is used by default. You can select Maximum recipients and specify a number if you want this user to be able to send to a number of recipients other than the default.

The final button in the Exchange General tab is Storage Limits. Storage limits were discussed in the previous section because they pertain to the entire mailbox store, but you can also set limits on individual mailboxes. This is useful when you have users with specific needs. Figure 26-12 shows the Storage Limits dialog box, which is divided into two sections.

Storage limits. This section defines mailbox-specific size limits. By deselecting Use mailbox store defaults and then selecting and specifying values for Issue warning at, Prohibit send at, or Prohibit send and receive at, those actions are taken when the user's mailbox exceeds the specified size.

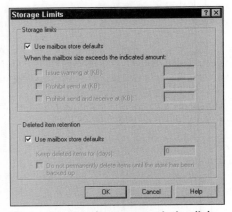

Figure 26-12: The Storage Limits dialog box is used to set mailbox size limits and deleted item retention.

Deleted item retention. This section allows you to set the deleted item retention setting for this specific mailbox, which overrides the global deleted item retention policy. Deselect the Use mailbox store defaults check box and specify the number of days to keep deleted items. You can also select the Do not permanently delete items until the mailbox store has been backed up check box if you want to retain deleted items until the next mailbox store backup.

Creating External Addresses (Mail-Enabled Contacts)

By default, when using Microsoft Outlook with Microsoft Exchange, addresses are kept in the Global Address List ⏤m a list of all recipients in the Exchange environment. You can also send e-mail easily to contacts you have stored in Outlook. There are cases, however, where you may want to share an external contact with all users in your Exchange organization. You can do this by creating what's known as a mail-enabled contact in Active Directory.

To create a mail-enabled contact, follow these steps:

1. Open the Active Directory Users and Computers snap-in by choosing Start ➪ Programs ➪ Administrative Tools.

Note   The key at this point is to decide where your mail-enabled contacts will reside. By default there is no container in Active Directory specifically for contacts. You may want to add a container for contacts if you have a number of them, but that is beyond the scope of this book. See *Windows 2000 Server Bible* or *Windows Server 2003 Bible* for more information on adding containers to AD.

2. For the sake of this example, you can add the contact to the Users container. Right-click the Users container in the Active Directory Users and Computers snap-in located under the domain name in the left pane and select New ➪ Contact.

3. The first page in the New Object–Contact dialog box requires you to enter the name information for the contact. Entering the first and last names and middle initial will cause the Full name field to be populated automatically. You can also specify a value for Display name if you want the contact to be displayed in address lists under a different name. Click Next to continue.

4. Figure 26-13 shows the next page in the dialog box, which is the critical step for creating a mail-enabled contact and is only shown if Exchange is installed in the Active Directory environment. Contacts are mail-enabled by default as shown in the figure. If you do not want the contact to be mail-enabled, deselect the Create an Exchange e-mail address box.

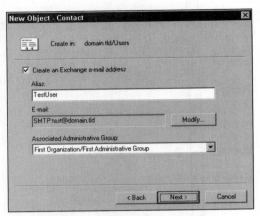

Figure 26-13: Set the mail options for a
mail-enabled contact.

In this page you must set two options for the mail enabled contact. The first is the actual e-mail address that is associated with the contact. Click the Modify button to display the New E-mail Address dialog box, as shown in Figure 26-14. Select an address type from the list, and click OK. In most cases, choose SMTP Address for an Internet e-mail account.

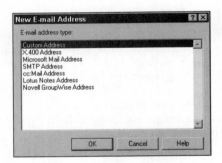

Figure 26-14: Select the e-mail address type
when creating a mail-enabled contact.

After you select the address type and click OK, the Properties dialog box for that address type is displayed. Depending on the type of address chosen, this dialog box may have one or two tabs. Enter the address on the first tab. If there is a second tab for the selected address type, it is typically the Advanced tab. Figure 26-15 shows the Advanced tab for the most typical address type, SMTP. This tab allows you to override the default settings in the Internet Mail Service for this particular contact. If you want to set these options, select the Override Internet Mail Service settings for this recipient and change the settings to your liking. After you have entered the e-mail address and set any advanced options, click OK in the address Properties dialog box. The address is assigned to the contact.

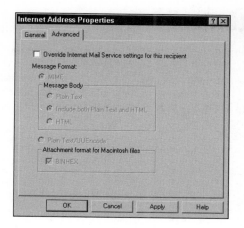

Figure 26-15: The Advanced tab is used to set advanced options for the e-mail address.

The final option for the e-mail address portion of the mail-enabled contact is the administrative group. This setting defines into which administrative group the contact falls and thus which policies are applied to the contact. The default policies for the selected administrative group apply. In most cases you have only one administrative group. Click Next to continue and then click Finish in the final page of the New Object–Contact dialog box to create the contact. The contact appears in the container in Active Directory Users and Computers in which it was created as well as in the Global Address List (GAL). Figure 26-16 shows the contact in the GAL. The globe icon beside the new contact indicates that the address is external.

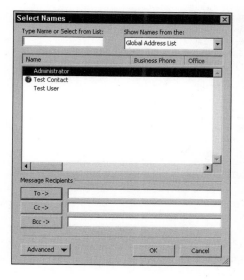

Figure 26-16: External (mail-enabled) contacts are shown with a globe icon in the Global Address List.

Distribution Groups with Exchange

While it is possible to create distribution lists in Microsoft Outlook, these lists are used only on your local copy of Outlook and not shared with other users. It is common to require distribution lists that all users can access. There are many uses for this type of distribution group, such as grouping users in specific departments or geographic sites. While distribution lists in earlier versions of Exchange were stored in Exchange itself, Exchange has utilized Active Directory groups as distribution groups since Exchange 2000.

Creating a group

To create a new group as a distribution list:

1. Open the Active Directory Users and Computers snap-in by choosing Start ⇨ Programs ⇨ Administrative Tools.

2. You must decide on a location for groups. If you have a number of groups, it is best to create a container specifically for them; if you have only a few, you can place them in another container such as the Users container. Right-click the Users container under the domain in which to create the group and select New ⇨ Group. The New Object–Group dialog box is displayed as shown in Figure 26-17.

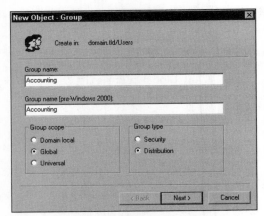

Figure 26-17: Use the New Object–Group dialog box to create both security and distribution groups.

3. Assign a name to the group. The pre-Windows 2000 group name is automatically generated. In this case, you are creating a distribution group, so select Distribution rather than the default of Security for the Group type.

4. The most difficult part of the process is deciding what the scope of the group should be:

   Domain local. A local group can contain members from only within the domain and is shared only within the domain.

   Global. A global group can also contain only members from within the domain, but is shared to all domains in the domain forest.

   Universal. A universal group can contain members from anywhere in the domain forest, and is shared to the entire forest of domains.

5. After you have selected a scope based on who will be in the group and who should be able to see the group, click Next to continue.

6. The next step is shown in Figure 26-18. Check the Create an Exchange e-mail address check box to make the group mail-enabled and make the group a distribution list. The group requires an alias (a unique name) for Exchange, which is generated automatically and must be placed in an administrative group. If you have more than one administrative group, the group inherits the policies of the selected group. This page also includes a warning about group scope and replication. Consult an Exchange reference for more information on the effects of group scope on replication and mail delivery. Click Next to continue.

7. Click Finish in the next page of the New Object–Group dialog box to create the group.

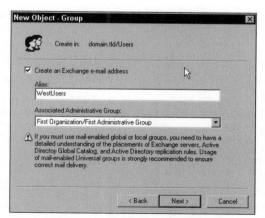

Figure 26-18: You must mail-enable the group in order for it to act as a distribution list.

Adding group members

After the group has been created, you can begin adding group members. Right-click the group you created, and select Properties. Click the Members tab as shown in Figure 26-19 to see the existing group members.

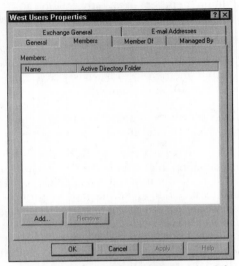

Figure 26-19: Use the Members tab of the group's Properties dialog box to configure which users are members of the group.

To add group members:

1. Click the Add button to display the Select Users, Contacts, Computers, or Groups dialog box.

2. You can now choose who to add as a group member. For a distribution list, you can add users with Exchange mailboxes, mail-enabled contacts, and other mail-enabled groups. Being able to *nest* groups within other groups allows you to create a group containing all users in a region, for example, by adding all of the individual site groups (assuming they have been created) within the region to that group rather than adding a number of users.

3. After you select the object to add as a group member, click Add within the Select Users, Contacts, Computers, or Groups dialog box and it is placed in the lower portion of the dialog box.

4. Add as many objects as you want; then click OK to close the Select Users, Contacts, Computers, or Groups box and add the users to the group.

Removing a group member is as simple as selecting that name from the Members tab of the group Properties dialog box and clicking the Remove button.

Delegating send on behalf permission to a group

It is possible to delegate send on behalf permission to a group rather than a user. This is useful for a number of reasons. It is possible to have a single mailbox for your customer service group, for example, and allow all customer service representatives to be able to read and send messages from this mailbox. Both the user mailbox and the group must be created before you begin.

1. The first step is to log in as the user and open Microsoft Outlook. Select Tools ⇨ Options, and click the Delegates tab as shown in Figure 26-20. Any existing delegates are shown in this tab.

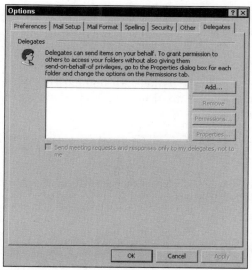

Figure 26-20: Use the Delegates tab to define users or groups who can access this mailbox.

2. To add a delegate, click the Add button to display the Add Users dialog box.

3. Select the distribution group from the list, click the Add button, and click OK. The Delegate Permissions dialog box displays, as shown in Figure 26-21.

You must now specify what permissions are delegated to the distribution group. In this case you want the distribution group to be able to send messages on behalf of this user, so the Inbox setting should be set to Author if you don't want the delegates to be able to delete and change items (only read and send), or Editor if you want the delegates to be able to delete and change items. You can also select Reviewer if you only want the delegates to be able to read items in this mailbox. You can set the other permissions to None or other settings, as required.

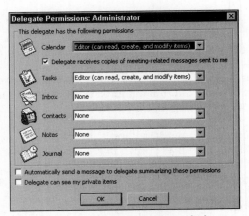

Figure 26-21: You must set permissions for the new delegate.

If you select Automatically send a message to delegate summarizing these permissions, a message will be sent to the entire distribution group informing them of the new delegate permissions they have.

After you have set the permissions, click OK. The delegate distribution list appears in the Delegates tab of the Options dialog box.

Click OK to close the Options dialog box, and any member of the distribution list is now able to send items on behalf of this user.

Configuring Exchange Instant Messaging

Exchange 2000 includes an instant messaging server. This is similar to the MSN Messenger service except is local to your environment and not shared across the Internet. The first key step to configuring Instant Messaging is to ensure it was installed when Microsoft Exchange was first installed. Check in Exchange System Manager (Start ➪ Programs ➪ Microsoft Exchange) by clicking Global Settings under the organization in the left pane, and ensuring that the Instant Messaging Settings object exists in the right pane. If it does not exist (it is not typically installed by default), use the Add/Remove Programs control panel to add the component to Microsoft Exchange 2003.

Instant Messaging configuration

There isn't much to configuring Instant Messaging in Microsoft Exchange. The first step is to set your firewall configuration, although this may be unnecessary if you are not behind a firewall or all users who will use the server are behind the firewall. Open Exchange System Manager by choosing Start ⇨ Programs ⇨ Microsoft Exchange. Under the Organization in Exchange System Manager, expand the Global Settings container, right-click Instant Messaging Settings, and select Properties. Click the Firewall Topology tab in the displayed Instant Messaging Settings Properties dialog box as shown in Figure 26-22.

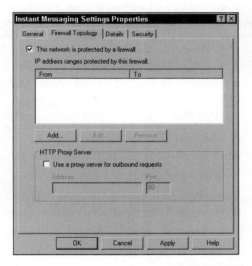

Figure 26-22: Use the Firewall Topology tab to configure Instant Messaging if your server is behind a firewall.

If you are behind a firewall, the This network is protected by a firewall box should be checked. You must then specify the IP address ranges of the systems behind your firewall, which can be obtained from whoever is in charge of your network. To add a range of IP addresses, click the Add button; then enter the beginning and ending addresses for the range and click OK. The range is added to the list. Add each IP address range inside your firewall. At this point, you can also specify an HTTP proxy server. If you are running a proxy server on your network, check the Use a proxy server for outbound requests box and enter the IP address and port for the HTTP proxy. Click OK to save your changes in the Instant Messaging Settings Properties dialog box.

Creating an Instant Messaging virtual server

You now need to create an Instant Messaging Home Server. This is the virtual server to which all IM clients on your network will connect. To begin:

1. Open Exchange System Manager.

2. Under the organization in the left pane, expand Servers, your server, and Protocols.

3. Right-click Instant Messaging (RVP) and select New, Instant Messaging Virtual Server to open the New Instant Messaging Virtual Server Wizard.

4. Click next to continue past the Welcome page.

5. Enter a display name for your virtual IM server and then click Next. The display name is simply used to identify the virtual server in Exchange System Manager.

6. In the next step of the wizard you must select an Internet Information Server Web site to use for IM. This must be an existing Web site. If you are hosting Web sites on your server, you need to create a custom virtual server for IM, but if you are just using this server for IM and Exchange, you can typically use the default Web site. Click Next to continue.

7. Figure 26-23 shows the next step in the wizard where you must assign a DNS name to the IM virtual server. This takes the DNS name of the local system by default, but you may want to switch this to something clearer, such as im.domain.tld (for Instant Messaging). You can make this value anything you want, but it is the name that IM users use to connect to the virtual server. The port value is taken automatically from the IIS site you chose in the last step. Click Next to continue.

Tip   You can use _SRV records in DNS to have clients automatically connect to the IM virtual server. This way they do not need to know its DNS name, but this is beyond the scope of this book.

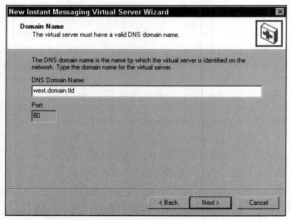

Figure 26-23: Specify a DNS name that IM clients use to connect to this virtual server.

8. The final step shown in Figure 26-24 enables this IM virtual server to host user accounts. If you do not select this option, the IM virtual server can be used only for routing instant messages and will not host user accounts. You must select this check box if this is the only IM server on your network. Click Next to continue.

9. The IM virtual server is created and appears under Instant Messaging (RVP) in the Protocols container in Exchange System Manager. Click Finish to close the wizard.

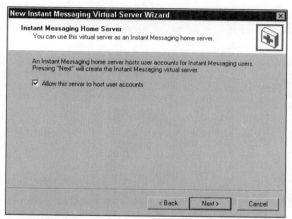

Figure 26-24: Check the box to allow the IM virtual server to host user accounts.

Enabling Instant Messaging for user accounts

The final step is to configure the user accounts to be able to use Instant Messaging.

1. Open the Active Directory Users and Computers snap-in by choosing Start ➪ Programs ➪ Administrative Tools.

2. Locate the user account for which to enable Instant Messaging in the snap-in, typically in the Users container, right-click and then select Exchange Tasks. You can also select multiple users by selecting the first user, then holding the Ctrl key and selecting more users. Right click any of the selected users and select Exchange Tasks.

3. The Welcome page for the Exchange Task Wizard may be shown. Click Next to continue.

4. The first step is to select the task to perform. Select Enable Instant Messaging and then click Next to continue.

5. Figure 26-25 shows the next step in enabling Instant Messaging. You must select an IM server and domain name that the account can use. To select the server, click the Browse button, select the IM server from the list, and click OK. The IM server name appears in the Instant Messaging Home Server box.

6. Select the Instant Messaging Domain Name from the drop-down box. This domain name is used if a DNS SRV record has not been created for the IM server. Click Next to continue.

7. Instant messaging is now enabled for the user or users and they are able to log in to the IM server you created. Click Finish to close the wizard.

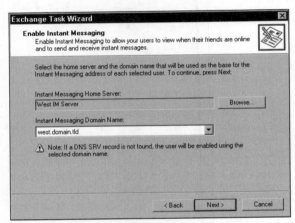

Figure 26-25: Select the IM server and domain name that the user will use.

Summary

In this chapter you learned how Microsoft Exchange is used as a back-end server for Microsoft Outlook. You learned how to add, remove, and move mailboxes as well as how to configure the available mailbox options. We also covered the creation of mail-enabled contacts for adding external e-mail addresses to the directory, the creation of distribution groups, and the configuration of instant messaging in Exchange. The next chapter covers the type of applications that can be custom built for Microsoft Outlook.

✦   ✦   ✦

Basics of Microsoft Outlook 2003

P A R T

VI

◆   ◆   ◆   ◆

In This Part

Chapter 27
Outlook 2003
Application Types

Chapter 28
Creating a Simple
Outlook Form

Chapter 29
Control in Outlook
Forms

Chapter 30
Utilizing Custom
Fields

Chapter 31
Adding Functionality
to Outlook Forms

◆   ◆   ◆   ◆

Outlook 2003 Application Types

◆ ◆ ◆ ◆

In This Chapter

Outlook 2003 client applications

Outlook 2003 Forms Designer

Message forms

Post forms

Built-in forms

Outlook 2003 Office applications

Outlook 2003 Web applications

Building your own Outlook Today

◆ ◆ ◆ ◆

So that you may grasp the full potential of Outlook 2003 application programming, this chapter provides you with an understanding of the different types of applications you can create. You learn about the various Outlook 2003 client applications, Outlook 2003 Office applications, Outlook 2003 Web applications, and LOBjects (Line of Business Objects), which consist of various third-party solutions that utilize these same technologies.

Outlook 2003 Client Applications

The most common Outlook application can be categorized as an Outlook client application. The client applications consist mainly of forms that provide the user interface, and postings routed between folders that provide the content. Although the degree of customization is vast, forms are available for the following functions:

- ✦ Message
- ✦ Post
- ✦ Appointment
- ✦ Contact
- ✦ Journal Entry
- ✦ Task

There are also two additional forms that are both hidden, meaning that they cannot be modified and then distributed independent of Outlook itself. Interestingly enough, both of the following forms can be entirely replicated as a custom form, but that would be unnecessarily redundant. These forms are:

✦ Meeting Request

✦ Task Request

Outlook 2003 Forms Designer

The Outlook 2003 Forms Designer (OFD) is the tool that programmers use to customize the different types of forms. After the forms have been customized, the OFD publishes the form so that it may be used within Outlook. All the buttons, drop-down menus, tabs, fields, and other elements that make up a form are created with this tool. To get a general understanding of each different form type, this section shows you the elements of the forms as seen within the Outlook 2003 Forms Designer.

Although little has changed both inside and outside of the Outlook forms development environment in the past few versions of Outlook, there are some differences. Of immediate note is that there are no longer forms that are termed built-in forms. Of course, all of the forms have always been built-in, so that needless separation has been removed. Not so obvious, though, is the addition of XML to a large portion of the application. These next chapters filter out the XML and focus on the forms design. Note, however, that XML should play a strong role in your application development, and will likely play a much greater role in the future of Office than previously expected.

This chapter provides a general overview of the Outlook 2003 Forms Designer, and Chapter 28 provides detailed insight into the tool by demonstrating specifics on customizing forms.

The Outlook 2003 Forms Designer can be accessed by selecting Tools ➪ Forms ➪ Design a Form. This opens the Design Form dialog box, as shown in Figure 27-1.

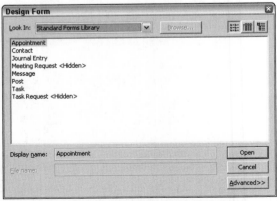

Figure 27-1: The Outlook 2003 Design Form dialog box

The forms you see displayed in the Design Form dialog box are part of the Standard Forms Library, as you can see in the Look In drop-down menu. The Look-In drop-down menu enables you to access both personal and public folders.

Tip When opening a form in Design view within the Outlook 2003 Forms Designer, it's a good idea to get in the habit of holding the Shift key down as you open the form (that is, as you click the Open button). By holding the Shift key down, you prevent the running of any code that is supposed to be triggered as the form opens.

Message forms

Begin by taking a look at the Message form. The Message form is used when composing an e-mail message. This form can be opened via the Design Form menu box by selecting the message form, as described previously in this chapter.

Alternatively, this form can be opened in the Outlook 2003 Forms Designer by opening a standard e-mail message from the Inbox and then selecting Tools ⇨ Forms ⇨ Design This Form.

An example of the Message form opened in the Outlook 2003 Forms Designer is shown in Figure 27-2.

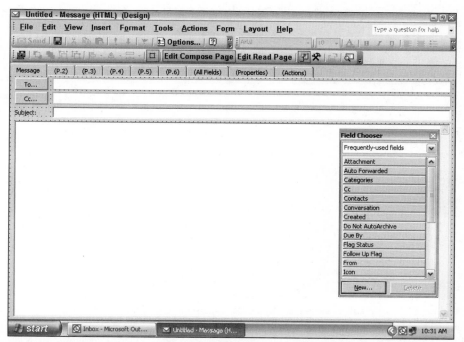

Figure 27-2: This Message form appears in Edit Compose Page mode, as viewed in Outlook 2003 Forms Designer.

Note that the Edit Compose Page button on the toolbar is selected. This means the form appears in this particular format when a user is composing an e-mail message. In addition to the Compose mode, the Message form can also appear in a different mode—Read mode. Figure 27-3 shows the same form in Edit Read Page mode; note how the form has changed to reflect what a user will see when reading an e-mail message. Also note that the addressing fields are disabled in Edit Read Page mode.

As you can see in Figure 27-3, the body of the Message form includes nine different tabs in Design view; however, none of these tabs appear to the end user when the form is being used to compose or read a message. This is because the contents of all the tabs, other than Message, are not configured to display after the form has been published. Details on how to configure the appearance of a tab are covered in Chapter 28.

A characteristic common to all forms is that the first seven tabs (from the left) have the capability to appear in a published form, but only the first six tabs provide you with the ability to customize the form's interface. Figure 27-4 demonstrates how tabs (P.2) through (P.6) are blank to allow for additional functionality on a single form.

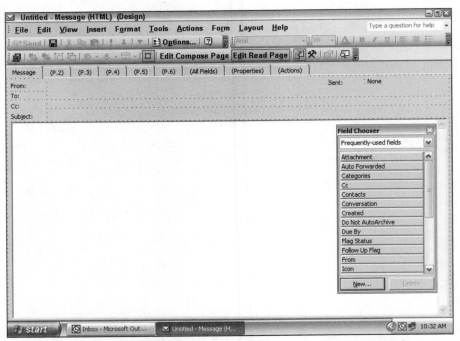

Figure 27-3: The same Message form as it appears in Edit Read Page mode.

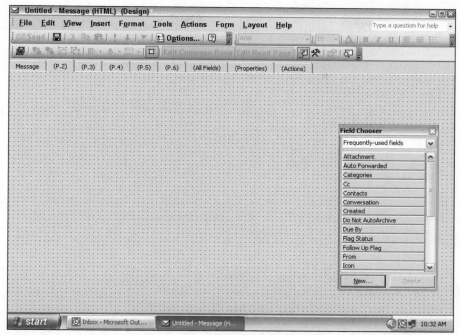

Figure 27-4: Blank tabs are designed to support additional form functionality.

The (All Fields) tab, shown in Figure 27-5, provides a listing of fields supported within the form. The drop-down menu at the top of the tab allows you to show only the fields that you want to see. The New button at the bottom of the window for this tab allows you to add user-defined fields. A user-defined field is a category of data that you define to allow for the storage of data that is not already defined by Outlook 2003.

The (Properties) tab, shown in Figure 27-6, is also common to all form types and is used to specify attributes for a particular form. In addition, the (Properties) tab displays information regarding relationships with Contacts and Categories, as well as additional relational information.

Cross-Reference The (Properties) tab is discussed in greater detail in Chapter 23.

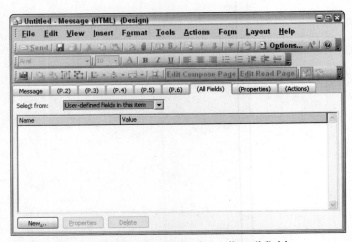

Figure 27-5: The All Fields tab displays all mail fields.

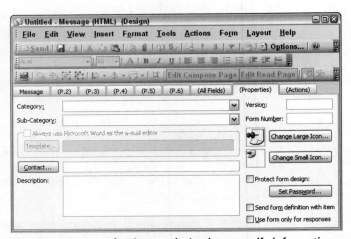

Figure 27-6: Use the (Properties) tab to specify information for a particular form.

The (Actions) tab, shown in Figure 27-7, displays information regarding the behavior of the form. Specifically, this tab identifies the various options regarding how the data behind the form is stored and/or transmitted.

Post forms

Post forms are another type of form used within the Outlook 2003 Forms Designer. Post forms are used to post information to a specified folder, such as publishing comments or documents to a public folder on an Exchange Server. An example of a Post form, as viewed in the Outlook 2003 Forms Designer in Edit Compose Page mode, is shown in Figure 27-8.

Note that the Post form is similar to the message form touched on earlier. The major differences between the two forms are in the addressing sections. Whereas the message requires an e-mail address for its destination, the Post form requires a folder name. You access the Post forms the same way you do Message forms.

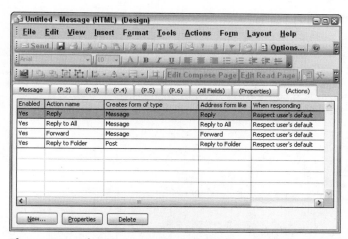

Figure 27-7: The (Actions) tab shows options for how the form data is stored and/or transmitted.

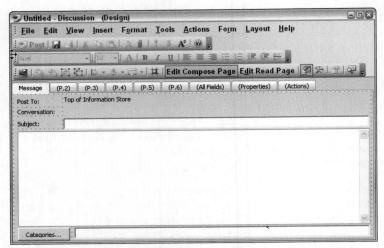

Figure 27-8: This Post form appears in Edit Compose Page mode.

Figure 27-9 shows the Post form in Edit Read Page mode. As with the message form, the only difference between the Post form in Edit Compose Page mode and in Edit Read Page mode is in the addressing section. The remaining tabs of the Post form — that is, (P.2), (Properties), and so on — are similar to the corresponding tabs in the Message form and serve the same purposes.

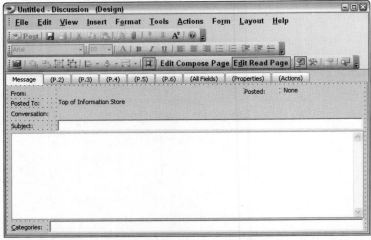

Figure 27-9: The same Post form as it appears in Edit Read Page mode.

More built-in forms

The other forms that make up a portion Outlook 2003's user interface comprise the remaining built-in forms. For example, the Contact form that opens when you add a person in the Contacts section of Outlook 2003 (see Figure 27-10) is another form available for modification.

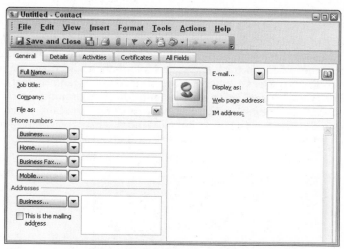

Figure 27-10: The Contact form is an example of another available form.

Other examples of available forms include the following:

✦ Appointment form

✦ Journal Entry form

✦ Task form

> **Tip** You can open these forms and others, located in the Standard Forms Library, in Design view. However, although Outlook 2003 will allow you to open a form in Design view, some forms do not have the option of being published under a different name after you customize them. For example, the Task Request form may not be customized and used within your application. In addition, Outlook 2003 Office Document forms, which are covered later in this chapter, may be opened within the Outlook 2003 Form Designer, but the form containing the Office document may not be customized.

Examine the Contact form in the Outlook 2003 Forms Designer, as shown in Figure 27-11, and notice many of the same characteristics found in the other form types.

Some of the differences worth noting on the Contact form are the additional tabs (Details, Activities, and Certificates) and the Full Name button functionality. Specifically, sub-windows providing additional details open when the Full Name button is selected. Similar features, such as the Address and Call Now features, are scattered throughout the form. These additional features appear when you use the form, not in Design mode.

Note   The main purpose of providing programmers access to the built-in forms within Outlook 2003 is to save them time in developing their own forms. For example, suppose a programmer needs to track tax-related information for an accounting firm. In addition to the taxpayer's tax ID, number of dependents, and marital status, the application would likely need to store other personal information, such as the home address, spouse's name, and profession. Because much of this information is already stored in the Contact form, it makes more sense to customize the Contact form rather than start from scratch with a standard Post form.

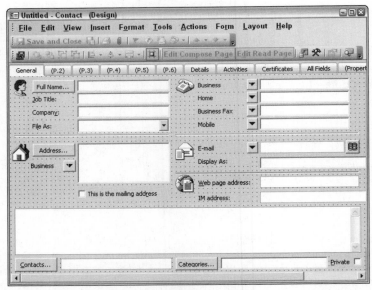

Figure 27-11: Contact form as it appears in Design view within Outlook 2003 Forms Designer

Outlook 2003 Office Applications

The applications within Office 2003 have been designed to be tightly integrated. As a result, Office applications within Internet Explorer 6.0, Word 2003, Excel 2003, and PowerPoint 2003 provide their own functionality within Outlook 2003.

For example, you can forward a Web application from within Internet Explorer by accessing the URL for the application and then selecting Send Page from the Mail button menu, as shown in Figure 27-12.

As you can see in Figure 27-13, address information is inserted above the application so it can be forwarded via e-mail.

This same functionality is also inherent in Word 2003, in Excel 2003, and PowerPoint 2003. Outlook is accessed within these applications by selecting Send To ➪ Mail Recipient from the File menu. In Access 2003, choose File ➪ Send To ➪ Mail Recipient (As Attachment).

In addition to sending Office 2003 documents as the text of an e-mail message, documents may be posted to a personal or public folder within Outlook 2003. To post a document to a folder, select File ➪ Send To ➪ Exchange Folder and then specify the folder to which you would like to post the document. This type of functionality could be appropriate in a document-tracking application, for example.

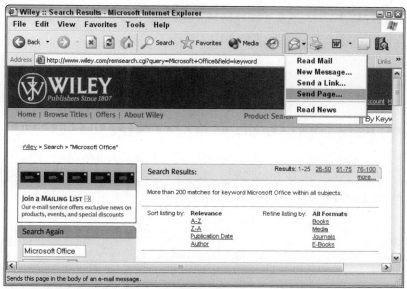

Figure 27-12: Use Outlook 2003 from within Internet Explorer 6.0 to forward an application.

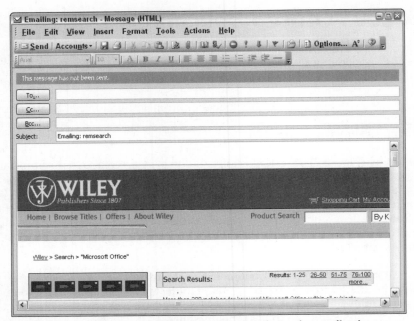

Figure 27-13: Address information is inserted above the application.

Outlook 2003 Web Applications

As Outlook continues to mature, it and the applications with which it integrates become more and more closely tied to the Internet. As a result, Outlook 2003 utilizes and functions with a wide range of Internet technologies. As the Internet matures, Outlook 2003 continues to utilize the technology wherever it can.

Building your own Outlook Today page

In addition to the customization you can implement directly in the Outlook Today interface installed with Outlook 2003, you can build your own Outlook Today page. Because Outlook Today utilizes HTML, any functionality that can be built into a HTML document, Active Server page, XML page, or Dynamic HTML document can be utilized in your own Outlook Today page.

For example, many people choose to customize their Outlook Today to house information of interest to them. Through the same functionality contained within other Web sites, your Outlook Today page can display current weather forecasts, stock prices, or news headlines.

Other examples include Outlook Today pages designed specifically for a company or department. These pages enable companies to disseminate specific information to various divisions without having to fall back on an unhelpful, static, company-wide page. The example presented in this chapter could be modified to provide a wide range of functionality.

Note The CD distributed with this book contains the sample files used in the demonstration that follows. You may modify these files to customize your Outlook Today page, or you can create your own code. In addition, if you have problems accessing the HTML code using any of the methods described in the following text, use the OutTBib.htm file provided in the Chapter 27 folder on the CD-ROM. See Appendix A for details.

Begin by creating the following folder to store your custom Outlook Today files:

```
C:\OutlookToday\
```

Close Outlook 2003 and open Internet Explorer. In the address section, enter the following path:

```
res://C:\Program%20Files\Microsoft%20Office\Office11\1033\outlwvw.dll/outlook3.htm
```

If you have the Microsoft Script Debugger installed, you may be prompted to debug the file, but select No if prompted. The error is a result of the page not being opened from within Outlook 2003. Depending on how your machine is configured, you may not receive an error message at all.

Note Although Internet Explorer 6.0 is an integral part of Office 2003, you have the option to not install version 6.0 and use an older version in its place. You may, however, lose functionality in other areas within Office 2003.

Right-click in the body of the document, and select View Source. Alternatively, you may select View ⇨ Source (see Figure 27-14).

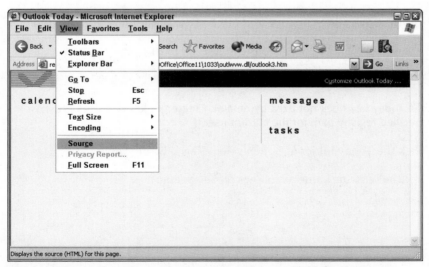

Figure 27-14: Select View ⇨ Source to view the source of the document.

The source code for the document displays in Notepad. From the Search menu in Notepad, select Find, and click Find Next to search for the following text:

```
display:none
```

Change the text you find to read as follows:

```
display:
```

Click Find Next again and make the same change. You should find three instances of display:none, all of which need to be changed to display:.

Save your changes in Notepad as follows:

```
C:\OutlookToday\OutTBib.htm
```

Close Notepad and Internet Explorer.

Tip   When saving an HTML document in Notepad, make sure you display all file types (*.*) in the common dialog box, rather than the text file type (*.txt); then, when you type in the filename, type the .htm file extension as well. If you fail to do so, the file will be saved as a text file, and it will not display properly in a Web browser.

Edit the Registry to instruct Outlook 2003 to display your custom Outlook Today file. To edit the Registry, select Start ➪ Run, enter **regedit** in the text box, and click OK.

Note   Because Windows uses the Registry to store specific information regarding the behavior of applications, you should use extreme care when viewing and/or editing this information. The authors of this book assume no responsibility for any problems that may arise on your PC, so edit the Registry at your own risk.

Figure 27-15 shows the HKEY_CURRENT_USER key within the Registry Editor.

Under the HKEY_CURRENT_USER Registry key, go to the following path:

```
HKEY_CURRENT_USER/Software/Microsoft/Office/11.0/Outlook/Today/
```

Note   The Today key does not exist by default. Create the key if it does not exist in the specified registry path for the current user.

Right-click the Today folder and then select New ➪ String Value.

Name your new string value as follows (case-specific):

```
Url
```

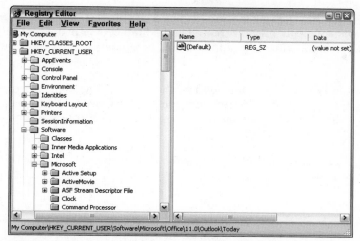

Figure 27-15: `HKEY_CURRENT_USER` key as it appears within the Registry Editor.

After the string value is created, right-click `Url` and then select Modify. The Edit String dialog box opens, as shown in Figure 27-16. Enter the path `file://C:\OutlookToday\OutTBib.htm` in the dialog box, and click OK.

Figure 27-16: Enter the path in the Value data field of the Edit String dialog box.

Close the Registry by selecting Registry ➪ Exit.

To verify the changes, follow these steps:

1. Open Outlook 2003 and select Outlook Today.

2. Right-click the Outlook Today icon and select Properties to open the configuration for Outlook 2003.

3. In the Address section of the Home Page tab, you should see a path pointing to your custom Outlook Today file. Click OK or Cancel to close the dialog box.

Now that you've configured Outlook 2003 to display a specified HTML file, you may customize as you want. The file may be created and edited in Notepad, FrontPage 2000, Visual InterDev, other Office 2000 applications, or whatever other tool you choose.

The sample Outlook Today HTML file included on the CD is displayed in Figure 27-17. This example displays user-specific information, such as the Calendar, Messages, and Tasks, as well as integrates streaming media posted on the corporate intranet to inform employees of corporate news.

Other examples of information that may work well within a custom Outlook Today interface include the following:

✦ 401(k) stock quotes

✦ Weather forecasts

✦ Scrolling news announcements

✦ Hyperlinks to departmental intranet Web folders

✦ Pictures of new employees

✦ Corporate calendar

✦ Financial forecasts

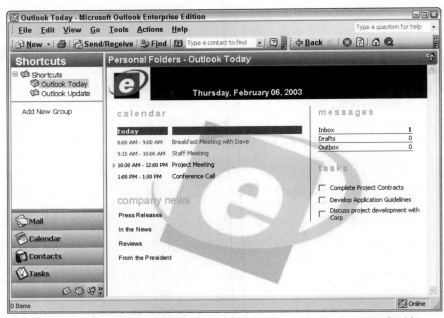

Figure 27-17: This customized Outlook Today page has been integrated with a corporate intranet.

As you can see, the possibilities are nearly endless. Also, the faster your local network and more powerful your workstations, the more advanced tools you can add to benefit your workforce. Of course, such decisions must be tempered with caution. Many businesses still operate much older computers, which will give you an opportunity to create customized Today pages for each target system class.

Summary

In this chapter, you learned of the various types of applications that can be developed or integrated with Outlook 2003. Because Outlook 2003 offers a great deal of functionality that is common among a wide range of applications, the application is a practical tool to integrate into other applications, especially given the ease of integration.

Three main groups of applications exist in Outlook 2003: Outlook 2003 client applications, Outlook 2003 Office applications, and Outlook 2003 Web applications. Three types of forms are available in the Outlook 2003 client application group: Message forms, Post forms, and Built-in forms. Forms are customized within the Outlook 2003 Forms Designer.

Outlook 2003, Word 2003, Excel 2003, PowerPoint 2003, and Internet Explorer can all host applications within Outlook 2003 forms. These applications are described as Outlook 2003 Office applications. Outlook 2003 Web applications integrate with the Internet as well as corporate intranets/extranets.

Finally, Outlook Today can be customized to fit a wide range of individual needs by leveraging the Internet and the latest technologies utilized in Internet Explorer.

✦　　✦　　✦

Creating a Simple Outlook Form

In This Chapter

Accessing the Outlook Forms Designer (OFD)

Manipulating forms

Adding controls

Using the Properties window

Adding fields to a form

Using the Script Editor

Publishing the form

Most Outlook 2003 custom applications utilize custom forms. Perhaps you have a business problem concerning the capture of a very specific and unique set of data. Custom forms enable you to capture only the data you need, and control how the data is presented and where it is transmitted. But that's just the tip of the iceberg. You quickly learn that what you can do with Outlook forms is limited only by your imagination.

Accessing the Outlook Forms Designer

As mentioned in the previous chapter, the Outlook Forms Designer (OFD) is the tool used by application developers to create custom Outlook forms. There are several basic types of form, but only two are commonly used by Outlook users:

✦ Message and Post forms

✦ Appointment forms

All custom Outlook forms are similar to these types of forms. A Message form is suitable for forms that are sent or routed among e-mail recipients. Post forms are used to write information to either a Personal Folder or Private Folder for the purposes of storing information. Typically, data is posted to a Public Folder, so the information may be shared. Use Outlook's Appointment and other forms when you need the functionality in Outlook; rather than re-invent the wheel, it sometimes makes sense to expand on or add to existing functionality in these forms.

Choosing a form

To design a custom form, you need to open one of the basic types of forms in Design view with the Outlook Forms Designer (OFD). To do so, select Tools ➪ Forms ➪ Design a Form.

After the command is selected, the Design Form dialog box opens, as shown in Figure 28-1. From here, you can select the form you want to edit from the Standard Forms Library. In addition, the dialog box enables you to browse through the Personal and Public Folders, Personal Forms Library, user templates in the file system, or any other Outlook module to find the form for which you're looking.

Note   Not all forms displayed in the Design Form dialog box may be edited. Specifically, those forms with the word "<Hidden>" after the title, as shown in Figure 28-1, may not be edited.

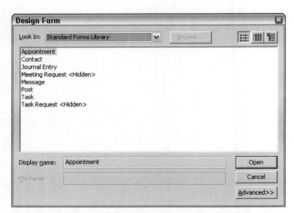

Figure 28-1: <Hidden> forms cannot be edited.

The following sections take you through the various steps of how to modify the Message form. To open the Message form, select Message and then click the Open button. The Message form is displayed in Design view, as shown in Figure 28-2.

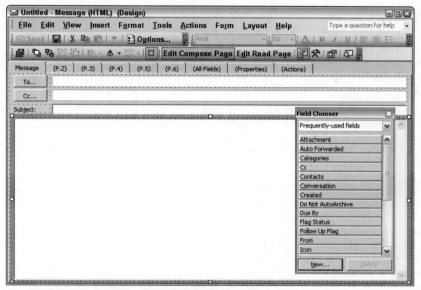

Figure 28-2: The Message form as it appears in Design view.

Manipulating the Form in the Design Window

After you have the form opened in the Outlook Forms Designer, you're ready to make changes to it. You may want to acquaint yourself with the OFD by clicking the different objects within the form. When an object is selected, notice that you can move the object to a different location on the form. In addition, you can resize the object to the desired dimension. The objects shown in Figure 28-3, such as the text boxes, tabs, labels, and other objects, may all be manipulated. The term manipulated refers to how the size, color, border, and other attributes of the form components can be modified to portray a desired look and feel.

Note

Because Outlook forms are often used to replace paper processes, it may make sense to format your Outlook form in a layout similar to the old paper form that it replaces. This softens the transition from paper to the electronic version for those users who have become accustomed to the paper form.

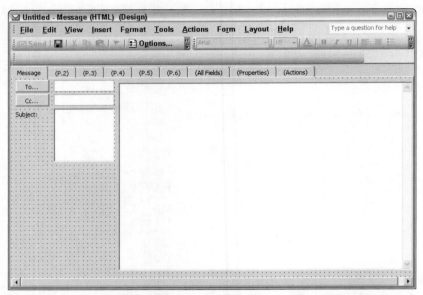

Figure 28-3: Objects shown on the form may be manipulated within the Outlook Forms Designer.

When the Message form is in Design view, notice that you have the option of displaying as many as six pages on one form. When replacing paper forms, Outlook form pages can provide substitutes for each page of a multipage paper form. Again, this softens the transition from the paper process. Before a page appears as part of the completed form, you must configure the page to be active. To do so, follow these steps:

1. Select the tab you want to make active.

2. Select Form ⇨ _Display This Page. Notice that the parentheses are removed from the tab label.

3. Select Form ⇨ Rename Page and then type in the new label for the tab, as shown in Figure 28-4.

Figure 28-4: Activate a page within a form and use the Rename Page dialog box to rename it.

After the form is published, the first two pages of this form appear. (Form publishing is discussed later in this chapter.) At this time, notice that the second page of the form (the P.2 tab), renamed Message Details, does not have any content. Why would you want a page with no content? Well, you wouldn't. That's why you're going to add some controls.

Adding Controls with the Toolbox

You add controls to a form within the OFD by using the Toolbox. The Toolbox is one of the most important tools within the OFD because it is what you use to actually build the user interface. For this reason, it's important to learn each aspect of the Toolbox, which is covered in greater detail in the next chapter. For now, it is important to understand just the general purpose behind the Toolbox. The Toolbox is shown in Figure 28-5.

Figure 28-5: The Toolbox is used to build the user interface.

The Toolbox may or may not appear when you open your form in the OFD. If it doesn't, select Form ⇨ Control Toolbox. Alternatively, you may access the Toolbox by clicking the Toolbox menu icon. (It's the one with the crossed hammer and wrench.)

For the sake of simplicity, go through the steps for how to add the most basic control to a form ⏤m a label. Labels provide descriptions for other controls. Without a label, you would have no idea what the purpose of a control is.

Note   The CD-ROM distributed with this book contains the sample file used in the demonstration discussed in this chapter. If you have problems with any of the steps described in the following text, use the file provided in the Chapter 28 folder on the CD-ROM. The name of the file is SimpleForm.oft. See the Appendix for details.

To add a label, do the following:

1. Click the label button on the Toolbox. The label button is the button with the letter A on it. Your cursor changes to a letter A with a cross next to it.

2. Click the form in a location you would like to create your label, hold the mouse button down, and draw a rectangle in the desired size.

3. Select the Label 1 text, which automatically appears in the label box, and type your description, as shown in Figure 28-6.

Tip   You can also simply drag the label icon onto the form, which creates a label of the default size. This method allows you to define elements on the form that are always the same dimensions, reducing the amount of time you must spend "cleaning up" your work.

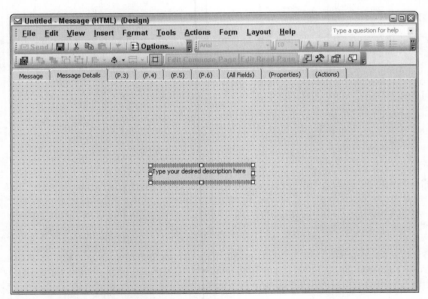

Figure 28-6: Type the desired description.

Using the Properties Window

The Properties window is used to modify how a control appears, define what data fields are accessed with the control, and specify any necessary validation. Using the example form, the following steps demonstrate changing the font of the label through the Properties window.

1. To modify the appearance of a label, right-click the label and then select Properties from the shortcut menu.

2. After the Properties dialog box opens, choose from the various options on the Display tab to modify the appearance of the label, as shown in Figure 28-7.

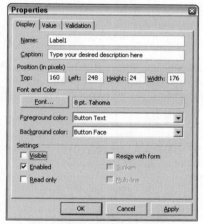

Figure 28-7: Modify the label's appearance through the various options on the Display tab of the Properties dialog box.

3. Change the font by clicking the Font button to open the Font dialog box. Make different font selections and then click Apply to see changes in the label text. Click OK to return to the Properties dialog box.

Experiment with the other choices on the Display tab to get a feel for what each choice does. The Value and Validation tabs do not apply now, but are covered in Chapter 30.

Adding Fields to the Form

As you probably already know, a field represents a piece of information that is used within Outlook 2003. For example, in a Message form, the message recipient, the subject, and the message body data are all stored in separate fields. In addition to these fields, you have the option of including additional standard fields or custom fields on your form. Although not the only method of adding a field, the easiest way to add a field to a form is through the Field Chooser window. The Field Chooser window displays a list of available fields to add to the form.

Although the Field Chooser may display by default when you open the Outlook Forms Designer, you can open the Field Chooser window by selecting Form ➪ Field Chooser if the window is not displayed.

To add a field to the form via the Field Chooser window, perform the following steps:

1. Choose a field category from the drop-down menu at the top of the Field Chooser window, as shown in Figure 28-8. Notice how the list of fields in the window changes as the field category changes. For this example, use the All Mail fields category.

Figure 28-8: The Field category drop-down menu lists fields that correspond to a particular category, such as the All Mail fields.

2. To add a field to the form, click the field on the Field Chooser window you want to add, hold down the mouse button, and drag the field onto the form. For this example, the Importance field was chosen, as shown in Figure 28-9.

3. If you click the drop-down arrow of the ComboBox, you'll notice that the Importance field has three possible choices specified — Low, Normal, and High (see Figure 28-10). You can preset the option for the form by simply selecting the importance level from the drop-down list.

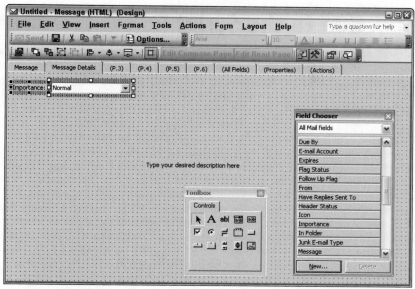

Figure 28-9: The Importance field is added to the form from the Field Chooser window.

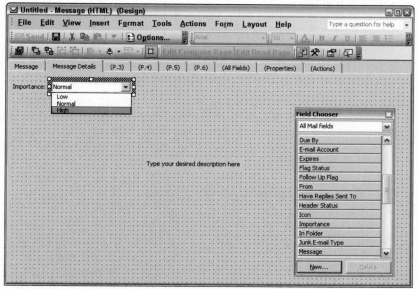

Figure 28-10: Drop-down menu choices are specified in the ComboBox.

Introduction to the Script Editor

The Script Editor is used to add functionality to the form through the use of VBScript. VBScript is a slimmer version of the Visual Basic programming language, hence the VB in VBScript. By creating VBScript functions and/or subroutines in the Script Editor, you specify certain pieces of code to execute when certain events occur.

An example of when you may want to use VBScript and the Script Editor is when you need to integrate a form with a database. Suppose you're creating a scheduling application that records the hours to be billed to your clients. For the billing application to function properly, it needs a client number; however, nobody knows the client numbers that correspond to the client without looking up the number. Through VBScript, you could program a drop-down list box to look up and display client names as they appear in the accounting system database. In addition, you could write code to look up the corresponding client number behind the scenes, and provide the proper client number to the billing application. Any functionality you can provide with VBScript can be implemented in an Outlook form.

Using VBScript with a command button

To demonstrate a simple subroutine within the Script Editor, the following steps show how to create a command button that will display a message when clicked:

1. Select Form ➪ View Code to open the Script Editor.

2. Make the Outlook Forms Designer window active, click the CommandButton control within the Toolbox, and create a command button on the form in the same manner the label was created earlier in the chapter.

3. By default, the command button should be named CommandButton1; however, you can confirm this from the Display tab on the Properties window. Right-click the command button, select Properties from the menu, and verify that the Name text box on the Display tab displays CommandButton1, as shown in Figure 28-11.

4. You're now ready to enter some code. Make the Script Editor active, and type the following code (exactly as shown here):

```
Sub CommandButton1_Click

MsgBox "This is a test."

End Sub
```

5. Close the Script Editor.

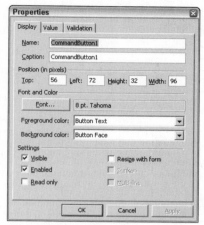

Figure 28-11: Name the command button CommandButton1.

Your code is saved along with the form, even if you close the Script Editor. If you want to save your code, you can do so by saving the form as you normally do. To test the code, run the form. To do so, select Form ➪ Run This Form. The form opens in Normal mode. Select the Message Details tab and then click the CommandButton1 command button. A message appears, as shown in Figure 28-12. Click OK to close the message box and then switch back to the Message form design window.

Figure 28-12: Clicking the command button to get the message generated by the code.

Publishing the Form

At this point, there's only one more step involved in creating a simple form, and that is to publish it. To publish the form, select Tools ➪ Forms ➪ Publish Form.

As illustrated in Figure 28-13, you have the option of saving your form in your choice of folders. In this example, the form is published to the Personal Forms Library. If you intend to send your form to others, select Yes when a dialog appears that prompts you to determine whether to save the form definition with the item.

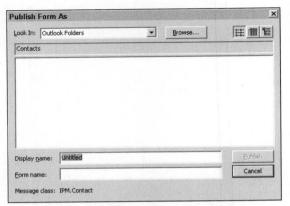

Figure 28-13: Specify publishing options in the Publish Form As dialog box.

This method of publishing a form works fine in a single-user environment; however, when distributing an Outlook 2003 form to multiple users, there are other factors to consider. These details are covered in Chapter 31.

Summary

In this chapter, you learned how to create a simple form in Outlook 2003. The chapter covered the Outlook Forms Designer (OFD), which is used to design forms in Outlook 2003. You may select a standard form from which to develop a customized version, or choose to manipulate the current form you are viewing.

This chapter also covered several aspects of the Forms Designer. When a form is in Design view within the Outlook Forms Designer, the form may be manipulated in a number of ways to suit your individual needs. The Controls Toolbox assists developers in providing additional functionality within a form. The Properties window is used to further customize and configure the controls on a form. The Field Chooser window enables developers to easily add fields with standard configurations to a form.

The Script Editor, which you access from the Forms Designer, utilizes VBScript to provide additional functionality, which includes, but is not limited to, integration with external databases. You add code to your forms with the Script Editor.

In a single-user environment, forms may be easily published to a number of folders; however, much more complexity is involved with distributing a form. This chapter also explored forms publishing.

The following chapter builds on the topics covered in this chapter, explaining how to add various types of controls to your forms.

✦   ✦   ✦

Controls in Outlook Forms

In This Chapter

Labels

Text boxes, check boxes, combo boxes, and list boxes

Frames

Option buttons, spin buttons, and command buttons

Messages

MultiPage and TabStrip controls

Image controls

This chapter covers the details behind each of the controls used in Outlook 2003 application development. Although we do not cover every detail for every control, we do highlight the important ones. Because these controls define the look and feel of your user interface, it's important to use the best control for the job. The success of your application is often a result of how easy it is to use. If an application is too difficult to use, the tasks it performs, no matter how sophisticated, are irrelevant. By familiarizing yourself with these controls and understanding when they're appropriate, you'll have the tools and knowledge you need to design a great application.

Labels

Although the Label control was mentioned in the last chapter, you might want to review the basics of this control as well as dig a little deeper into its properties. For the examples in this chapter, begin with the Contact form opened in Design view within the Outlook 2003 Forms Designer.

1. Open the Contact form in Design view by selecting Tools ➪ Forms ➪ Design This Form.

2. If the Toolbox is not already shown, select Forms ➪ Control Toolbox. Alternatively, you may click the crossed tools icon on the toolbar to access the Toolbox.

After you have completed the preceding steps, your screen should appear similar to the one shown in Figure 29-1.

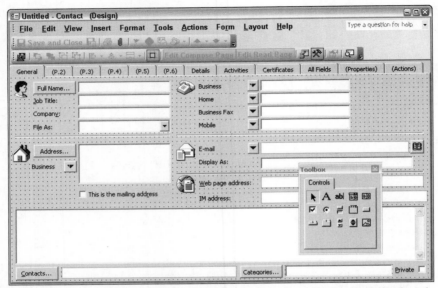

Figure 29-1: Contact form as it appears in Design view with Toolbox displayed.

You want your example to expand the basic capabilities of the Contact form, so the controls added to the form appear on a separate tab.

1. Rename and display the (P.2) page by selecting Form ➪ Rename Page. In the example, we used "1040 Details" for our description (Figure 29-3).

2. Click the Label button (featuring an icon with the letter A) in the Toolbox, and draw a label onto the form page.

3. Right-click the label and then select Properties from the pop-up menu.

4. In the Caption box, change the description of the label to whatever you want, such as "Taxpayer Information" as shown in Figure 29-2.

5. Select a font and font size with the Font button; then select foreground and background colors using the Foreground color and Background color list boxes, and click OK. When complete, your label should look similar to the one in Figure 29-3.

6. In addition to the standard properties, you may want to utilize some of the functionality available to you through the Advanced Properties dialog box. To access the Advanced Properties dialog box, right-click the label and then select Advanced Properties from the pop-up menu. The Advanced Properties dialog box is also displayed in Figure 29-3.

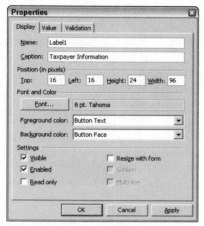

Figure 29-2: Changing the label caption from the Properties window

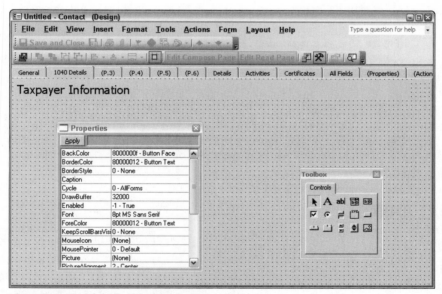

Figure 29-3: A label added to the form

7. To specify an advanced property, select the property you want to configure, edit the property in the field to the right of the Apply button, and click Apply. For example, Figure 29-4 shows the ControlTipText property being modified. This property defines what control tip is displayed when the pointer hovers over the label (that is, the little yellow box that describes the control). Control tips add clarity to each part of the user interface.

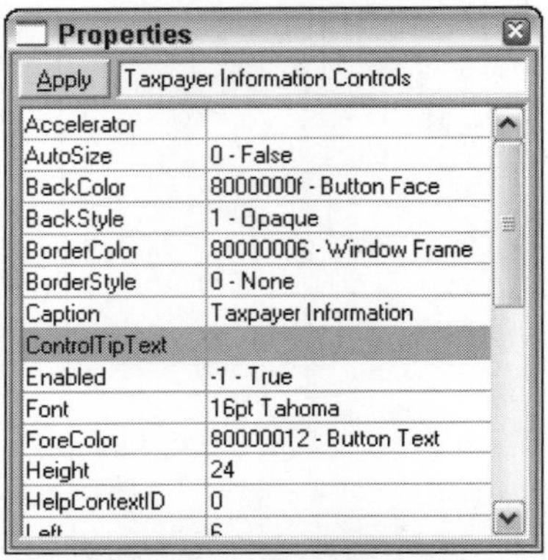

Figure 29-4: Configure the ControlTipText Advanced Property.

The best method of familiarizing yourself with the various options in the Advanced Properties dialog box is to simply play around with them. In other words, go through each one of the properties therein and see what it does. Note, however, that the majority of the properties of the Label control relate to formatting, so you already know 90 percent of the Label control.

Text Boxes

Text boxes are the fields that display the data. In addition to displaying the data, they enable you to input and edit data.

✦ The easiest way to create a text box is to drag and drop from the Field Chooser, similar to the way the Label field is created. If the Field Chooser is not displayed, you can select Form ➪ Field Chooser. Alternatively, you can click the Field Chooser icon on the toolbar. In the example shown later in Figure 29-5, the Job Title field was dragged onto the form from the Field Chooser. Alternatively, you can click the TextBox button on the Toolbox (the icon with "ab|" on it) and manually draw your field onto the form. If you decide to go this route, you need to specify which field your text box refers to by selecting from the list under the Choose Field button on the Value tab of the Properties dialog box. Keep in mind that if you manually draw a text box, you need to manually draw its label. If you use the field selector, both are created at the same time.

As with the Label control, there are a number of different advanced properties you can configure to change the look and feel of your text box.

Frames

Frames (also called *groups*) refer to the etched lines you sometimes see on forms. In addition to enhancing the aesthetics of the form, frames help organize information on the form by grouping fields. How they are grouped is up to the designer, but fields are typically chosen to populate a frame because they share a common function or group of functions. To create a frame, do the following:

1. Click the Frame button in the Toolbox (the icon depicting a box with "XYZ" at the top) and then draw your frame onto the form (see Figure 29-5).

2. Right-click the frame, select Properties from the pop-up menu, and enter your description in the Caption field.

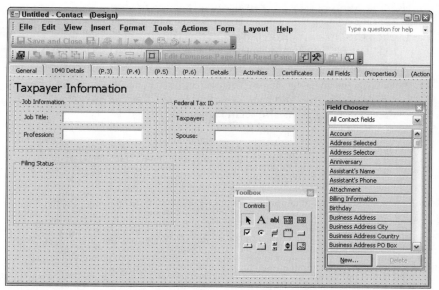

Figure 29-5: Use the Frame tool in the Toolbox to create a frame, and enter a caption for it in the Properties dialog box.

Tip You may notice that the controls you drag into the frame do not appear if they were created before the frame. To alleviate this problem, right-click the control, choose select Order, and select Bring Forward on the pop-up menu. This moves the control "to the top" so that when you drag the control into the frame, it shows up!

Option Buttons

Option buttons enable the user to specify certain information without having to type it in, and they are appropriate when you want to present a limited number of choices to the user. For example, when you want users to specify their 1040 filing status, it makes sense to provide a list of the only four choices available. If users typed the filing status into a text box, variation in the data entered is inevitable. For example, a user with married filing jointly status could type in "Married filing jointly", "married – jointly", "JOINTLY", or any other variation of the same. Running a query against data such as this would be a nightmare!

The main purpose of frames is to organize options and segregate them from the rest of the form. Placing the options in a frame makes them function as a group, so frames not only provide a visual separation for controls, but also provide logical and functional separation.

To add an option button to your form, follow these steps:

1. Click the OptionButton button in the Toolbox and then draw your radio button. The OptionButton button sports an icon of a circle with a black dot in the middle.

2. As with the other controls, the option button can be configured by right-clicking the drawn button and then selecting Properties (or Advanced Properties) from the pop-up menu, as shown in Figure 29-6.

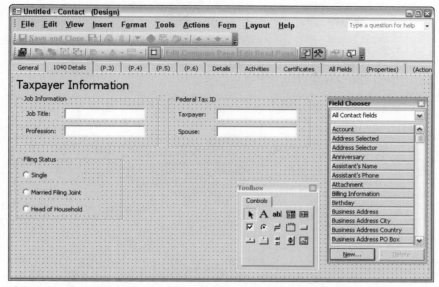

Figure 29-6: Use the OptionButton tool to create and configure option buttons.

Check Boxes

As you can imagine, check boxes are similar to option buttons, except they're square. The only difference relates to the types of data that each displays. Option buttons are often part of option groups, which means that more than one option button can be tied to one field, but only one option button may be selected at any time. Check boxes are typically one box per field, so the data stored in the field is typically of a yes/no nature. To add a check box to your form, follow these steps:

1. Click the CheckBox button in the Toolbox, and draw your check box. The CheckBox icon is a small box with a check in the middle.

2. As with objects created by the other controls, the check box can be configured by right-clicking the drawn check box and selecting Properties (or Advanced Properties) from the pop-up menu, as shown in Figure 29-7.

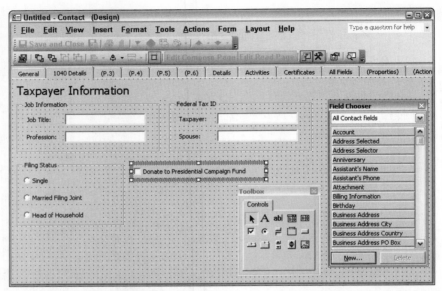

Figure 29-7: The CheckBox tool enables you to create and configure check boxes.

Combo Boxes

Combo boxes look similar to text boxes, but have an arrow on the far right that drops down a list of choices from which the user may select. As with the option buttons, combo boxes are appropriate when you want to provide the user with a list of choices. The advantage a combo box has over option buttons is that you can specify far more choices in a small area. The disadvantage is that the choices are not displayed, except when the user makes a selection. To create a combo box, follow these steps:

1. Select the ComboBox button from the Toolbox, and draw the control onto the form. The ComboBox icon, located to the right of the TextBox icon, shows a miniature version of a combo box and its drop-down menu (Figure 29-7).

2. As with the other controls, configure the combo box through either the Properties or Advanced Properties dialog box.

To demonstrate how to fill the combo box with possible values, look at how to create a custom field called Residency:

1. Select the combo box drawn on the form, right-click, and select Properties from the pop-up menu.

2. On the Value tab, click the New button to the right of the Choose Field button.

3. Type **Residency** in the Name field of the New Field dialog box and then click OK.

4. In the Possible values field on the Value tab, enter Alabama; Alaska; Arizona, as shown in Figure 29-8, and click OK.

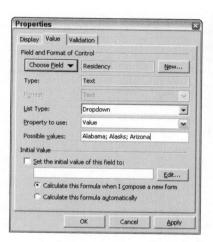

Figure 29-8: Specify possible values for a custom field combo box in the Properties dialog box.

List Boxes

List boxes are similar to combo boxes in that you specify the choices from which the user can choose. One difference is that a list box is larger. In addition, the user scrolls through the choices and selects the one he or she wants, rather than selecting from a drop-down list. The advantage over a combo box is that the choices are displayed, even after selection; however, the size could be a disadvantage. To create a list box, follow these steps:

1. Select the ListBox button from the Toolbox, and draw the control on the form. The ListBox icon looks similar to the ComboBox icon, but only shows two "items" for selection (Figure 29-7).

2. You define the selection choices in the same manner as the combo box, as shown in Figure 29-9. See the section "Combo Boxes" earlier in this chapter for assistance.

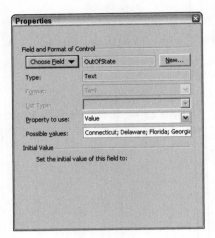

Figure 29-9: Specify possible values for a custom field list box in the Properties dialog box.

Multiple Pages

Multiple pages are useful when you need to squeeze a lot of information into a small area. In fact, you've already been exposed to multiple pages throughout this chapter. The example form has multiple pages — General, 1040 Details, Details, and so on. When referring to the MultiPage control, this means smaller pages being displayed on top of a larger one. To create multiple pages on your form, follow these steps:

1. Click the MultiPage button in the Toolbox and draw the control on the form. The MultiPage icon is the larger of the two icons that resemble a form with two tabs. (The smaller icon is for the TabStrip tool, discussed later in the section, "Tab Strips".)

2. After the pages are created, you may rename the page description by right-clicking the tab of the page to be renamed and selecting Rename from the pop-up menu, which brings up the Rename dialog box, as shown in Figure 29-10.

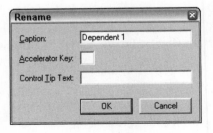

Figure 29-10: Rename a page on a MultiPage control by opening the Rename dialog box.

3. To add or delete a page from the MultiPage control, right-click the page tab and then select Insert or Delete, respectively.

4. You can rearrange the order of your pages by right-clicking the page tab and selecting Move from the resulting pop-up menu. Then, choose a page from the Page Order dialog box and choose Move Up or Move Down to change the order (see Figure 29-11).

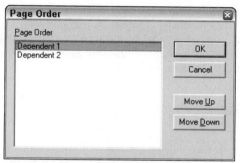

Figure 29-11: You can adjust the page order on a MultiPage control.

5. After you have your new pages configured, you can add controls on top of the MultiPage control, just as you would on any other area of the form. For example, Figure 29-12 shows text boxes added to the first page.

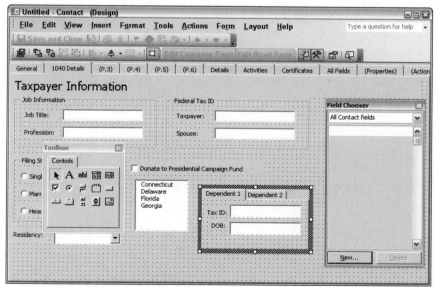

Figure 29-12: Specific controls can appear on each page of a MultiPage control.

Tab Strips

The TabStrip control is similar to the MultiPage control; however, there is one slight difference—the TabStrip control is designed to display the same controls on each tab, whereas the MultiPage control is designed to display different controls on each page. Although you may gain a small degree of performance by using the TabStrip control, the MultiPage control seems easier to use.

To use the TabStrip control, follow the same steps as described in the previous section for the MultiPage control. The TabStrip icon looks like the MultiPage icon, except that it is smaller. Note that you need to add a VBScript subroutine or function if you want the control source of your controls to change when the tabs do. VBScript is covered in more detail in Chapter 34.

Image Controls

Image controls do exactly what their name implies—they display images. As you would expect, the control supports all popular image formats. To add an image to your form, follow these steps:

Tip   Although images can often bring excitement to an otherwise dull form, they also tax computer performance. The number and/or size of the images you include can drastically affect how quickly your form responds to user interaction.

1. Click the Image button, and draw a box where you want your image to be displayed.

2. Right-click the box you've just drawn and then select Advanced Properties from the pop-up menu.

3. Select the Picture property on the Advanced Properties dialog box and click the "..." button in the top-right corner of the form. Point to the image file you want to display in your form and click OK. An example showing a solid image bar beside the Taxpayer Information title appears in Figure 29-13.

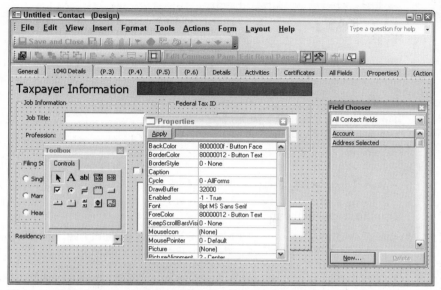

Figure 29-13: Creation and configuration of an Image control

Spin Buttons

Spin buttons usually work in conjunction with a text box. In such a case, the text box typically stores a numeric value, and the spin buttons are used to scroll through a set of numbers. Spin buttons are meant to be a convenience for the user because they enable the user to manipulate the data by a click of the mouse. Some users, however, still prefer to have the option of typing a number into the text box.

Note   Before you create the SpinButton control, create the text box that stores your values. Attaching a custom field to the text box, create the field by using the TextBox tool in the Toolbox, rather than dragging and dropping a field from the Field Chooser. See the section "Text Boxes," earlier in this chapter, for details on creating a text box.

1. After your text box has been created, select it, right-click, and select Properties from the pop-up menu. Using the New button on the Value tab, create a new field called Exemptions, with Integer as the field type (see Figure 29-14), and click OK to return to the Value dialog box.

2. Select the Calculate this formula automatically option button, and click OK.

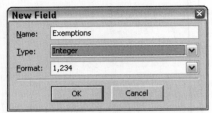

Figure 29-14: Create a custom field text box to which to attach the SpinButton control.

3. Click the SpinButton button in the Toolbox menu and draw the control onto the form. Right-click the control you've just drawn and then select Properties from the pop-up menu.

4. Click the Choose Field button on the Value tab, select Exemptions from the menu under the option User-defined fields in folder, and click OK.

Tip   You can verify that your form is functioning properly by selecting Run This Form from the Form menu.

Command Buttons

Command buttons are controls that require underlying VBScript to function. You could think of the command button as being similar to a key that starts a car engine, with the engine being, of course, the underlying VBScript function or subroutine. Although VBScript is discussed briefly, VBScript is not the focus of this chapter. VBScript is covered later in the book.

The first step is to actually create the command button. To do so, follow these steps:

1. Click the CommandButton button in the Toolbox and then draw a button on the form. Right-click the drawn button and select Properties from the pop-up menu. On the Display tab, verify that the name of the control is CommandButton1, change the caption to read Test, and click OK.

2. You must access the Script Editor to write your VBScript, so select View Code from the Form menu.

3. In the Script Editor, type the following lines of code, as shown in Figure 29-15:

```
Sub CommandButton1_Click

    Dim varDate

    varDate = Date()

    MsgBox "The current date is "& varDate & "."

End Sub
```

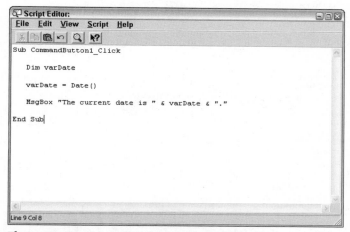

Figure 29-15: Enter VBScript into the Script Editor.

4. Close the Script Editor window and select Form ⇨ Run This Form. When you click the Test button, you should get a VBScript message informing you of the current date, as shown in Figure 29-16.

Figure 29-16: Click the Test button to see this message displaying current date.

Toggle Buttons

Toggle buttons are similar to command buttons, but can be less complex. Although you may define VBScript functions and subroutines behind toggle buttons, you may also treat toggle buttons as yes/no responses. Yes/no responses are feasible because a toggle button has two states — pushed in or not pushed in; therefore, a toggle button could be described as a command button that does pop back when clicked. Oftentimes, toggle buttons appear in pairs, so when one toggle button is pressed, the other is not, as in Figure 29-17. To add a toggle button, simply drag the ToggleButton icon from the Toolbox window to the form; then set the properties for the button as you have learned to do for other control types.

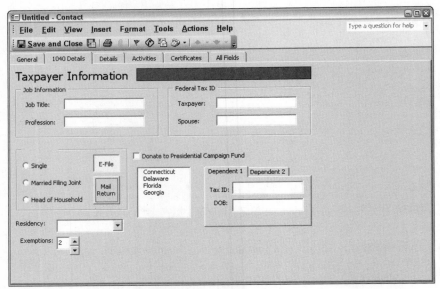

Figure 29-17: An example of toggle buttons.

Summary

In this chapter, you learned about the various controls used within the Outlook 2003 Forms Designer. For example, labels are used to describe the data employed by other controls. In other words, labels give meaning to the information stored within other controls. For example, "Price: $1.50" has much more meaning than just "$1.50". (In this case, "Price:" is the label.)

Text boxes are probably the most commonly used control. In addition to displaying data, text boxes enable the user to enter new data, edit existing data, and delete unwanted data. Frames are the etched boxes you often see around groups of similar data. In addition to enhancing the appearance of the form, frames also aid in the organization of similar data controls. Option buttons are the radio-style buttons used to limit the number of choices to the user. Typically, multiple option buttons will be attached to a single field in what's called an option group. Check boxes are similar to option buttons, but are square and usually apply to yes/no type replies.

Combo boxes contain a list of values from which the user can choose. This offers an advantage over option buttons in that more options can be made available while taking up less space. List boxes also contain a list of values from which the user can choose. List boxes require a bit more space on the form, but can display optional values even after the user has made a selection.

Multiple pages offer the flexibility of overlapping space; pages are accessed by their tabs and can contain different controls. Tab strips are similar to pages, but utilize the same set of controls on all tabs.

Image controls display images and can require significant resources. This control should be used sparingly. Spin buttons provide an interface for scrolling through values in a text box. Command buttons launch VBScript functions or subroutines. The code behind command buttons is created in the Script Editor. Toggle buttons are similar to command buttons, but may interface with yes/no type data as well as VBScript code.

The following chapter delves deeper into a topic touched on briefly in this chapter — using custom fields. With custom fields you can define additional data in a form that is not part of the default set of fields offered by Outlook.

✦   ✦   ✦

Utilizing Custom Fields

Although a wide variety of fields already exist in Outlook 2003, chances are you may still need to add a few fields to your form to suit your individual needs. Adding custom fields to your form accommodates the processes and information unique to your organization. After all, isn't that what custom applications are all about?

◆ ◆ ◆ ◆

In This Chapter

Creating custom form fields

Working with fields

Differentiating shared, combination, and formula fields

Validating and restricting user input

Specifying default values

◆ ◆ ◆ ◆

Custom Form Fields

Before you jump right in and start adding a bunch of new fields to your form, it's a good idea to spend some time planning just what fields to add. In many cases, you will add custom form fields to your forms in addition to the built-in fields provided by Outlook. Custom form fields define information not provided by the built-in fields. For example, you might use custom color fields in an order form to ask the user to choose the color of a shirt she is ordering.

Planning your custom fields

To get an idea of how you should plan for your application, you need to do some analysis. Here are some good questions to ask before creating a form with multiple custom fields:

 ◆ What are the data elements that need to be captured in my form?

 ◆ Which of these fields already exist?

 ◆ How will my form interact with other Outlook 2003 folders, such as the Contacts folder?

 ◆ Can any of my custom data be grouped together?

 ◆ Will the custom data fields continue to accommodate business needs as the organization grows?

The time you spend planning up front will save you time down the road. Applications designed without a great deal of planning often need to be completely rewritten later because the application no longer fulfills the business need. Although you cannot predict the future, you can design your application with the flexibility to grow with the organization.

For example, say you're developing a t-shirt order form that, among other attributes, enables a customer to specify a color. Because Outlook 2003 does not inherently contain fields for color attributes, you need to create custom fields. One approach would be to create three custom fields — a red field, a blue field, and a black field. This approach, however, would make it difficult to expand the options in the future. These fields could be created as part of an option group (explained in Chapter 29), as shown in Figure 30-1.

Suppose you designed your form as shown in Figure 30-1. Now suppose that your company decides to offer 20 different colors, and your form needs to accommodate the change. Does it make sense to add 17 more custom fields to your application? Nope.

If the application were designed with one field — color — the application could easily accommodate a change in colors offered. Figure 30-2 demonstrates this method of accomplishing the same task.

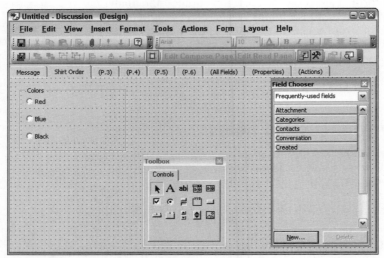

Figure 30-1: These custom fields are designed in a fashion that limits future growth.

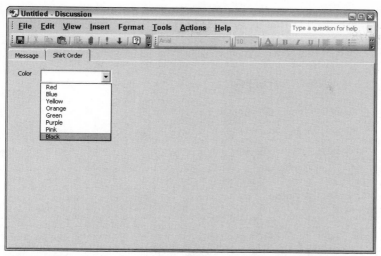

Figure 30-2: This custom field is designed with the flexibility to accommodate future needs.

By spending the time to plan the custom fields, you considered the possibility of more colors being added in the future. Rather than add 17 additional fields to this form, as well as 17 additional radio buttons and labels, you needed to add only the new choices to your combo box.

Creating custom fields

Custom fields can be tied to any control that interacts with data. In addition, custom fields are typically created while you are configuring your control.

Cross-Reference   For information on creating and configuring controls, see Chapter 29.

To create a custom field, complete the following steps:

1. Make sure your form is in design mode within the Outlook 2003 Forms Designer.

2. Create a new control from your Toolbox menu, but make sure it is a control that enables you to interact with data. For this example, use the ComboBox tool.

3. Right-click the control and then select Properties from the pop-up menu.

4. Select the Value tab.

5. Rather than choosing from the Choose Field drop-down menu to assign a field, click the New button in the upper right corner of the Properties window.

6. Enter the name of your new custom field, as shown in Figure 30-3.

Figure 30-3: Enter the name of your new custom field.

At this point, you should choose the appropriate type and format for your custom field. The Type menu specifies the type of data to be stored within the field. Because the field in this example will be storing words, the Text data type is appropriate. If you wanted to store a dollar amount, however, the Currency data type is appropriate; if you wanted to store a date, the Date/Time data type is appropriate, and so on.

For this example, select Text as the type and Text as the format; then click OK to close the New Field dialog box.

The Format menu specifies how the data is presented within the field. When using the Text data type, you have the option of only using the Text format; however, certain data types, such as the Date/Time data type, enable you to choose from a number of formatting options. One value, stored as a Date/Time data type, could be displayed in a number of ways. Figure 30-4 gives you an idea of the numerous choices available in the format field.

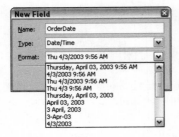

Figure 30-4: The Date/Time data type allows for numerous formatting choices.

Note Be sure to match the appropriate data type to the type of data you will be storing in your field. If you fail to do so, you may run into problems when calculating formulas or coding against the data. For example, currency formatted using the Text option will not function within a formula to calculate sales tax.

Experiment with the data types and the formats that each supports. You'll find there's a great deal of flexibility when displaying your data.

Working with Fields

Now that you are familiar with how to create a custom field, you're ready to learn how to effectively develop fields. This section will not only deal with custom fields, but also relate to the fields already existing in Outlook 2003.

Working with shared fields

Shared fields are fields that are utilized on both the Compose page and the Read page of a form. The Compose page of a form is used when creating a message, as shown in Figure 30-5.

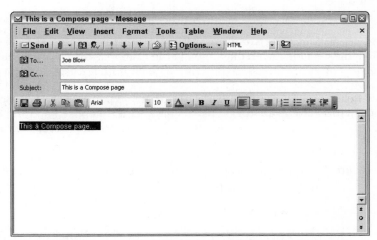

Figure 30-5: The Compose page of a standard message form is used when creating a message.

The Read page of a form is used when reading a message, as shown in Figure 30-6. To avoid confusion, I use the terms *compose page* and *read page* when the form is in Design mode (because it's the same form). When not in Design mode, however, it seems as though two different forms are being used instead of one, so I use the terms *compose form* and *read form* when referring to a form outside Design mode.

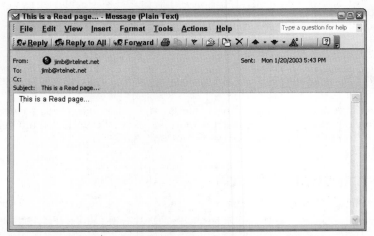

Figure 30-6: The Read page of a standard message form is used when reading a message.

Notice the difference between the two forms. Although both forms have the To, Cc, and Subject fields, these fields are enabled only in the Compose form. These are shared fields because they are linked to the same data on both forms.

To create shared fields, you first need to know how to move between the Compose and Read views of a form. To do so, toggle between the Edit Compose Page and Edit Read Page buttons on the toolbar at the top of the page. Follow these steps to create a shared field:

1. Create the control and then link it to a field in the Compose view as shown in Figure 30-7.

Cross-Reference   Chapter 29 details the steps involved in creating controls.

2. Switch to the Read view, add the control, and link it to the same field you linked to in the Compose view.

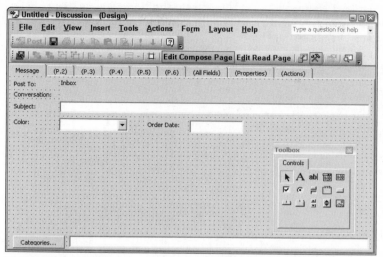

Figure 30-7: In the Compose view, create the control and link it to the required field.

Note If your form includes a reply form, your shared field will not automatically appear on the reply form. You must manually add the control and link it to the shared field in the same manner as explained in the preceding steps.

Using combination fields

A combination field is a type of custom field used to combine two or more fields into one. For example, you may want to display a contact's name in the format Last name, First name. The following example walks you through creating a combination field.

1. While in Design view in the Outlook 2003 Forms Designer, create a new label from the Toolbox menu on your sample form.

2. Right-click the label and select Properties from the pop-up menu.

3. On the Value tab of the Properties window, click New to create a new custom field.

4. Give the custom field a name and then select Type ⇨ Combination.

5. To define the contents of the field, click the Edit button to the right of the Formula field to bring up the Combination Formula Field.

6. After the Combination Formula Field window opens, click the Field button in the lower right corner to begin the process of choosing the fields you want to display.

7. Select Last Name and First Name from the Name Fields menu, accessible from the Field button menu, and type in a comma and a space to the right of "[Last Name]", as shown in Figure 30-8.

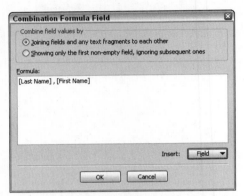

Figure 30-8: Configure the formula for the combination field in the Combination Formula Field window.

8. Click OK to close the Combination Formula Field window, click OK to create the field, and click OK again to close the Properties window.

The end result is a field with the combined information of two fields, as shown in Figure 30-9.

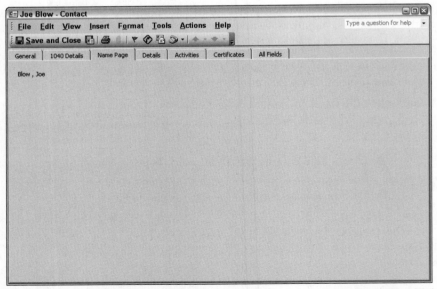

Figure 30-9: The resulting combination field displays the information of two fields.

Using formula fields

Formula fields are similar to combination fields, but rather than fuse fields together, formula fields perform calculations. An example of why you may want to utilize a formula field would be to calculate income tax. The following describes this process:

1. While in Design view in the Outlook 2003 Forms Designer, add two text boxes to the form.

2. Right-click the first text box, choose Properties, and, on the Value tab, click New.

3. In the Name field, type **TaxableIncome**.

4. Select Type ➪ Number and click OK.

5. Right-click the second text box, choose Properties, and on the Value tab, click New.

6. In the Name field, type **TaxRate**, select Type ➪ Number, and click OK.

7. Create a new label from the Toolbox menu.

8. Right-click the label and select Properties from the pop-up menu.

9. On the Value tab of the Properties window, click New to create a new custom field.

10. Give the custom field a name (such as Taxes) and then select Type ➪ Formula.

11. To define the contents of the field, start by clicking the Edit button to the right of the Formula field.

12. After the Formula Field window opens, click the Field button, select User-Defined Fields, and select TaxableIncome.

13. Type ***** to the right of "[TaxableIncome]", then select Field ➪ User-Defined Fields, and choose TaxRate to create the formula shown in Figure 30-10.

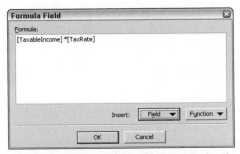

Figure 30-10: Configure the formula for the formula field in the Formula Field window.

14. Additionally, you can select a function to use from the menu accessible through the Function button in the lower right corner.

15. Click OK to close the Formula Field window, click OK to create the field, and click OK again to close to the Properties window.

The end result is a field with the calculated information, as shown in Figure 30-11.

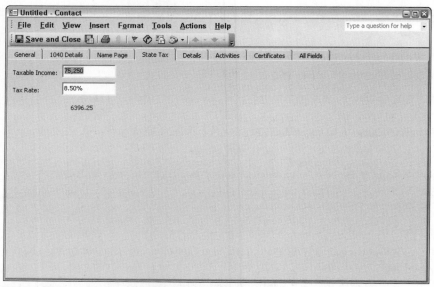

Figure 30-11: This formula field displays the calculated information.

Validating user input

To maintain the integrity of your data, you may need to validate the information the user enters. To accomplish this task, you can configure the Validation tab of the Properties window. For example, the following steps demonstrate how to verify that taxable income is not entered as a negative number.

1. Select the TaxableIncome text box, right-click the control, and select Properties from the pop-up menu.

2. Select the Validation tab, and click in the Validation Formula field.

3. Enter **>=0**, as shown in Figure 30-12. (Note that you can also select fields and functions in this window by clicking Edit and accessing the Field and Function button menus in the lower right corner of the Validation Formula dialog box.)

4. Click in the field Display this message if the validation fails.

5. Enter your validation message, and. click OK again to close the Properties window.

Figure 30-12: Configure validation in the Validation window.

Because you may select multiple fields from the Field menu, you can also compare the values of fields against others. For example, if your form has a due date field, you could verify that the due date is greater than the date created. With the extensive list functions, the possibilities are endless.

Specifying default values for fields

The Value tab of the Properties window allows you to specify default values for your controls, so the value that you specify is automatically placed when the user opens the form; however, the user may still have the ability to change the value. Default values are appropriate in fields that frequently hold a particular value. For example, in the United States, a country field may typically store the value "USA." To specify a default value, do the following:

1. Select the control, right-click the control, and select Properties from the pop-up menu.

2. Select the Value tab, and type a default value in the Initial Value section of the tab. In addition, select the Set the initial value of this field to check box and the Calculate this formula automatically option box. The example shown in Figure 30-13 uses the current date as the default value, as indicated by "Date()".

Alternatively, you may use the Edit button to specify a default value. As you might guess, this window is similar to the other formula configuration windows.

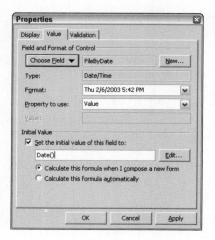

Figure 30-13: Specifying a default value for a text box.

Summary

In this chapter, you learned how to work with custom fields within Outlook 2003. The time you spend planning for your custom fields in the initial stages of development can save you time later. When planning your custom fields, consider how your business needs may change in the future. Try to develop your application in a manner that easily accommodates such changes.

Custom fields are created on the Value tab of the Properties window. A custom field may be created from any control that interfaces with data. Shared fields are the fields used on both the Compose and Read pages of a form. To share a field, configure one control on the Compose page and one control on the Read page to point to the same field.

Combination fields fuse the data from two different fields into one. For example, a First Name field and a Last Name field may be fused together into a LastFirst combination field, which displays the last name followed by the first name.

Formula fields are used to perform calculations. In addition to standard mathematical operations, an extensive list of functions is built into the formula edit tool.

User input may be validated to protect data integrity. The capability of including more than one field in the validation enables you to compare fields against one another.

Default values may be specified for a field on the Value tab of the Properties window. Default values are appropriate when the same information is frequently entered into a field.

The following chapter takes forms a bit further with an explanation of how to add more function to forms by changing form properties and adding code.

✦   ✦   ✦

Adding Functionality to Outlook Forms

✦ ✦ ✦ ✦

In This Chapter

Compose versus
Read modes

Additional form
pages

Form properties

Actions page

Addressing the form

Adjusting tab order

Testing applications

Deploying
applications

✦ ✦ ✦ ✦

So far, this book has covered everything you need to know about creating a basic application in Outlook 2003. This chapter gets a bit more specific and covers some of the elements of more complex applications. For example, some forms have different modes. The Message form is a good example — it provides a Compose mode for composing a message and a Read mode for reading a message.

In this chapter you learn to switch between form modes, add other form pages, and set the properties of forms to control how they appear. This chapter also explains how to restrict actions on a form and how to publish the forms to make them available for use.

Compose versus Read: Changing Form Appearance

The interface used to provide users with messaging information within a Windows environment is typically known as a *form*. In terms of Outlook 2003, users typically design forms within the Outlook 2003 Forms Designer (OFD). From your experience in sending e-mail to your friends, family, and coworkers, you probably understand the basic elements of an e-mail message. Typically, an e-mail message consists of a recipient, a sender, a subject, and a body. The manner in which a user interfaces with these elements, however, is dependent on whether the user is a sender or a recipient. in other words, the user interface seen by the composer of the e-mail message is different from the interface seen by the recipient of the e-mail message. Does this mean you need two forms for one e-mail message? To a certain extent, yes — but not really. A standard e-mail message actually uses the same form for both the composer and recipient; however, there are two modes to a standard e-mail message — a Compose mode and a Read mode.

The Compose mode in a standard message form is exactly what it sounds like — it's the mode used for composing an e-mail message. In a standard message, notice how all text boxes in the form are enabled.

In contrast, the page the recipient reads does not enable all text boxes. In addition, text boxes displaying who the message is from and when the message was received are characteristics of a standard message form in Read mode.

Switching between Compose and Read Mode

So how do you customize your form's appearance in Compose and Read mode? You do so from within the Outlook 2003Forms Designer (OFD), of course. When you view the standard message form in Design view, notice the two toggle buttons on the design menu, as shown in Figure 31-1. Because the Edit Compose Page toggle button is selected, the form is displayed in the Compose mode.

After the Edit Read Page toggle button is selected, the form is shifted to Read mode, as shown in Figure 31-2.

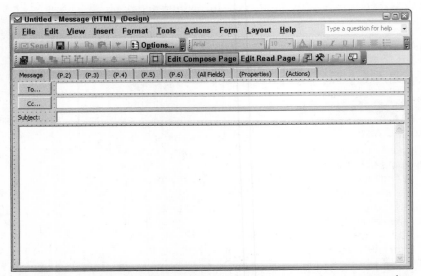

Figure 31-1: The standard message form as it appears in Compose mode in the Outlook Form Designer.

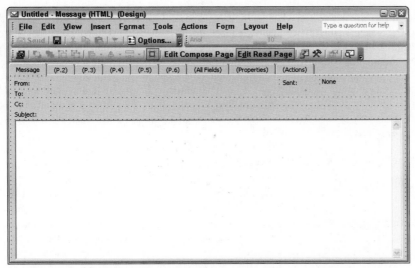

Figure 31-2: The standard message form as it appears in Read mode in the Outlook Form Designer.

Although the Compose and Read modes of a form can be handy when differentiating between how the author and viewer interact with information, these modes can also be a curse. When developing a form of this nature, it's a good idea to double-check that the appropriate fields are present in both Compose and Read modes.

> **Note**   Although the Compose/Read mode forms are appropriate when the viewer needs to interact differently with data than the author, Compose/Read mode forms are not appropriate when the viewer and author interact with the data in the same manner. In fact, if you designed a Compose/Read mode form that displayed information in the same manner for both the author and viewer, you would basically have to do the same work twice. For this reason, the Compose/Read modes may be disabled by deselecting the Separate Read Layout option from the Form menu. However, you should be careful when taking this action. If you disable the Compose/Read mode on a form, any changes you've made to the Read mode portion of the form will be lost.

Adding Form Pages

Form pages are the tabs seen on multiple tab forms, such as the Contacts form. In the context of software applications, *tab* commonly refers to the tab on the top of a form, as well as the page associated with it. Note, however, that in Outlook, the tab-and-page combo is commonly referred to as a *page*. Forms without multiple tabs have simply one page.

Pages are most appropriate when a form utilizes a large number fields or controls that require a large amount of space. Pages enable fields and controls to be categorized and/or temporarily kept behind the scenes, thereby allowing the user interface to accommodate a wide range of information without overcrowding the form.

For example, one page may contain all information relating to the shipping address. Another page may relate to specific billing information. Multiple pages allow for both shipping and billing information to be incorporated into a single form in an organized and uncrowded manner.

To add a new page, follow these steps:

1. While your form is in Design view within the Outlook 2003Forms Designer (OFD), select the page you want to display.

2. Choose Form ➪ Display This Page to mark the page as visible. This action has no visible effect in Design view. However, the selected page will be available when the user opens the form.

Note   After the page is displayed, the parentheses surrounding the page title on the tab disappear.

3. To change the title of the page, select Rename Page to open the Rename Page dialog box. Enter the new title, and click OK, as shown in Figure 31-3.

Figure 31-3: Use the Rename Page dialog box to rename the newly created page.

Using Form Properties

The form's Properties page is the second-to-last page displayed on a form in Design view within the OFD. The Properties page is used to configure certain characteristics (or properties) of the form as a whole. The Properties page can be thought of as a catchall for form properties that are not specified in any other location. In addition, the Properties page may store information to assist the developer in the management of Outlook forms, such as a description of the form, version control, and so on. An example of a properties page is shown in Figure 31-4.

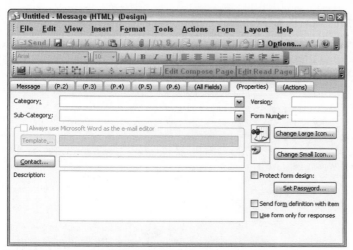

Figure 31-4: A properties page

Certain elements of a properties page are self-explanatory. The Category and Sub-Category fields simply assign category classifications. An example of a category could be Sales, and one subcategory could be Midwest. The Description text box provides a free-form area for adding any necessary comments and/or documentation for the form.

Version control

The Version and Form Number fields assist the developer in tracking what changes, fixes, or enhancements have been made to the form. An example of when a version number comes in handy is when a user comments that she does not have a new feature in her form. The developer can investigate the form the user is currently using and determine whether it is the most current by checking the version number.

Note　Because the difference in forms may be buried in a bunch of VBScript code, utilizing version numbers can save the developer time and energy.

Icons and Word templates

The Change Large Icon and Change Small Icon buttons specify which icons are displayed in Outlook 2003. The Always use Microsoft Word as the e-mail editor check box integrates MS Word with the composition area. In addition, if the check box is selected, the Template button enables you to associate an MS Word template with the composition area of your form.

Linking a form to a contact

The Contact button enables the developer to associate the Outlook form with a Contact record within Outlook. Click the Contact button to open the Address Book and then select the Contact record you want to link to, as shown in Figure 31-5.

Figure 31-5: Use the Select Contact dialog box to link a form to a contact.

Protecting your form

If you are using your form in a multi-user environment, you may want to protect your form with a password. This prevents users from viewing your underlying code, as well as protects the form from tampering or accidental changes. To protect your form with a password, check the Protect form design check box and set the password in the Password dialog box that opens (Figure 31-6). You may change the password using the Set Password button, as shown in Figure 31-4.

Figure 31-6: Protect your form with a password.

Including form definition

If you need to send your form outside your organization, or if your form is not published to the Organizational Forms Library, you may include a definition in your form. To do so, select the Send form definition with item check box. The definition enables the recipient to view your form in the way you intended the form to appear. For users to protect themselves from potential malicious scripts, they are prompted to either enable or disable the code within the custom form with a dialog box when the form loads. However, if you publish the form to the Organizational Forms Library by an Exchange Administrator, users are not prompted. In such a case, it is the responsibility of the Exchange Administrator to verify the integrity of the form.

Limiting to a response

Perhaps you want to send a survey to a number of your coworkers. In addition, you would like to limit the responses of the survey to focus the survey on a specific topic. In this case, you would want to configure your form to be utilized only when your coworkers are returning the results of your survey (that is, when your coworkers are responding to the survey). To do so, select the Use form only for responses check box.

Modifying Behavior with the Actions Page

The Actions page is located to the far right of a form displayed in Design view within the Outlook 2003 OFD. The Actions page defines the type of routing for a form. For example, the Actions page defines whether or not a form has the following capabilities:

✦ Post to a folder

✦ Reply to sender

✦ Reply to all recipients and sender

✦ Forward to another user

An example of how an Actions page may appear is shown in Figure 31-7. The first line represents a standard reply. A standard message form is created, the message is addressed using whatever the user has defined as the default, and the subject line is preceded by RE:. The second line accomplishes the same task, only the message is addressed to all recipients of the original message. The third line forwards the message and precedes the subject line with FW:. The fourth line posts the message to a folder and does not add anything to the subject line.

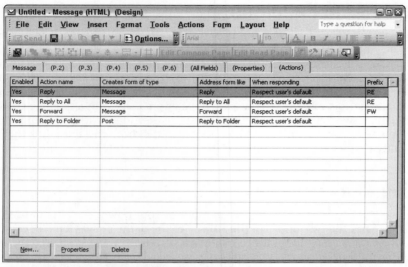

Figure 31-7: Example of a typical Actions page

To manipulate any of these attributes, double-click the attribute you want to change to open the Form Action Properties dialog box, shown in Figure 31-8.

Figure 31-8: Make changes to the attributes of the Actions page using the Form Action Properties dialog box.

New actions may be created with the New button in the lower left corner of the form (Figure 31-7), and actions may be deleted using the Delete button. The Form Action Properties dialog box may also be accessed by clicking the Properties button.

As shown in Figure 31-8, an action can be enabled by selecting the Enabled check box, and form type and characteristics can be assigned as well. Additional behavior characteristics are assigned with the radio buttons under This action will. In addition, a prefix may be added to the subject field.

After the actions have been configured to your specifications, they become a part of the toolbar of the form to which the actions are associated. In the case of the Reply action in a message form, a Reply button appears in the toolbar of a form in Read mode.

Changing the Tab Order

When designing a form, it's a good idea to keep a certain amount of usability in mind. Part of maintaining proper usability involves setting the tab order on your forms. Tab order refers to the order in which the control focus changes as the user presses the Tab key—not to be confused with changing the order of pages in a form. Tab order is especially important to those users who prefer to use their keyboard over their mouse.

To better understand tab order, think of when you're composing a message, and you enter the recipient's e-mail address. After entering the recipient's e-mail address, you press the Tab key. Which field becomes activated? The answer is the Cc: field, located below the To: field. If the user presses Tab again, the focus moves to the Subject field, and so on. It's the tab order that specifies the order in which these fields receive the focus.

To change the tab order of a form in Design view, do the following:

1. Right-click the first control to receive focus and then select Advanced Properties from the pop-up menu.

2. Move to and select the TabIndex property in the Advanced Properties list, click in the text field beside the Apply button, and enter 0. This value of 0 signifies the first control to receive focus.

3. If necessary, set the TabStop property to -1 ↲n True. This property identifies the control as being included in the group of controls that receive focus when the Tab key is pressed.

Note   Certain controls such as labels do not typically participate in the tab order; however, the controls that enable the user to manipulate data typically do.

An example of how your tab properties appear is shown in Figure 31-9.

Figure 31-9: Make changes to the tab properties in the Advanced Properties form.

4. After you have the first control configured, move to the next control that you would like to receive focus.

5. Enter 1 for the TabIndex property. The 1 places the control next in line.

6. Verify that the TabStop property is set to "-1 – True". If it is not, change it to "-1 – True".

7. Proceed to the other controls and increase the numeric value of the TabIndex property by one for each subsequent control.

Caution | Keep in mind that your tab order is affected every time you add a new control to your form. By default, the new control is last in line to receive focus.

Testing Design-Time Form Applications

While designing your applications, you'll probably want to test your forms as you develop them. This allows you to catch a problem in its infancy, rather than catching the problem after other functions have been based on the faulty part of the form. If other functions are based on the problem part, the other functions may have to be changed as well. Testing throughout makes more sense than developing the entire application and then testing all functionality after you publish the application.

To quickly test your form while in the middle of development in the OFD, you can select Form ➪ Run This Form.

A copy of the form is opened in runtime.

Installation and Deployment of OFD Applications

After you have completed your development and tested your application using the methods described earlier in this chapter, you are ready to publish your application. Before you publish your application, however, there are a few questions you need to ask yourself:

✦ Does this application need to be accessed by everyone in the organization?

✦ Should this application have offline capabilities?

✦ Will this application be sent to individuals outside the organization?

Although these questions address how your application should be distributed, they also relate to where the forms should be stored. The forms can be stored in these places:

✦ Personal Forms Library

✦ Organizational Forms Library

✦ Subfolder of an existing Outlook folder, such as Inbox

In the following sections, you learn how to publish a form; then you get a chance to explore some other options relating to publishing forms.

Publishing a form

To publish a form from the Outlook 2003 OFD, complete the following steps:

1. With the form open, select Forms ⇨ Publish Form from the Tools menu. Alternatively, if you choose to use the Form Design toolbar, click the Publish Form icon (the one with a floppy disk and triangle) to open the Publish Form As dialog box shown in Figure 31-10.

2. From the Look In box, select the location where you would like to publish your application. For this example, the form is published to the Personal Forms Library.

Note   The Personal Forms Library is exactly as it sounds — a place (or library) to store your personal forms. In this case, personal means only you can see the forms.

3. Enter the display name of the form and a name for the form in the appropriate text boxes.

4. Click Publish to publish your form.

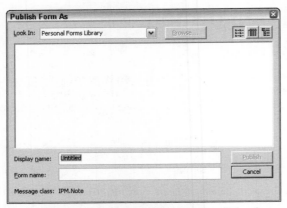

Figure 31-10: Use the Publish Form As dialog box to specify options for publishing your form.

Publishing to Public Folders

Publishing to a Public Folder involves the same steps as described in the preceding section, but you would select a Public Folder from the Look In box rather than the Personal Forms Library. There are a few points of which you need to be aware, however, when publishing to a Public Folder:

✦ As indicated by the word *public*, everybody with access to the folder will have access to the form.

✦ Even though you may have access to a Public Folder, only owners of Public Folders have the sufficient rights to publish a form.

✦ You should typically remove the check mark from the Send form definition with item check box when publishing to a Public Folder because it's not needed and would require additional resources. An exception would be if the form is to be sent outside the organization.

Note   The Organizational Forms Library is similar to the Personal Forms Library, but is shared by the entire organization. Only an Exchange Administrator has sufficient rights to publish a form to the Organizational Forms Library.

Publishing to a Personal Folder file

A Personal Folder file (one with the extension .pst) is a file located on your local machine in which you can store Outlook items, such as custom forms. Because the file is stored locally, you have the ability to access the contents of the form when you're offline. It's not always convenient to dial into a server, so offline capabilities can be handy.

The steps involved with publishing to a Personal Folder file are the same as previously mentioned in the section "Publishing a form," but you select your Personal Folder file from the Look In menu. You may need to create a Personal Folder file to store your application if you don't already have one. If so, follow these steps:

1. Select File menu ⇨ New ⇨ Outlook Data File to open the New Outlook Data File dialog box, as shown in Figure 31-11.

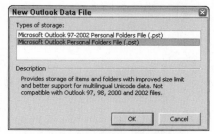

Figure 31-11: Create a Personal Folder file using this dialog box.

2. Choose the type of PST to create (Outlook 2003 or one compatible with previous versions) and then click OK.

3. Select a location for the file, enter a name for your file in the File name field, and click OK.

4. Specify a different name for the folders, if desired, and click OK.

Note   The .pst files created for Personal Folders may be distributed to other users.

Summary

In this chapter, you learned how to add functionality to Outlook 2003 custom forms. For example, some forms have two modes — Compose and Read. The Compose mode sets forth layout and functionality for the author; the Read mode is designed for the recipient.

Form pages are similar to tabs in a tab control. Additional form pages can be added to a form to organize information and provide the flexibility to include a greater number of fields and controls. In addition, a form's Properties page can be used to configure various properties relating to the form as a whole, and the Actions page plays a significant role in the routing capabilities of a form.

When considering how to deploy an application, you should address such issues as who will be using the application, whether or not the users are within the organization, and whether or not offline capabilities are necessary.

The following chapter explores application folders, their types, how to manage their properties, and how to use different folder views.

✦   ✦   ✦

Advanced Messaging Development

♦ ♦ ♦ ♦

In This Part

Chapter 32
Working with
Application Folders

Chapter 33
Collaborative
Messaging Basics

Chapter 34
Using the Outlook
2003 Object Model

♦ ♦ ♦ ♦

Working with Application Folders

✦ ✦ ✦ ✦

In This Chapter

Built-in module
folders

Discussion folders

Tracking folders

Managing folder
properties

✦ ✦ ✦ ✦

From this point on, this book focuses on issues you may face when developing advanced messaging applications. An entire book could be written on the subject of messaging, so the focus here is only on issues often faced by developers — particularly those that relate to Outlook 2003.

This chapter looks at application folders. Application folders are the folders that house Outlook 2003 applications. Here you have the opportunity to explore how to create different types of folders and learn when each type is appropriate.

Application Folder Types

To accommodate the functionality difference between applications, Outlook makes available different types of folders. These folder types can be classified in three categories:

- ✦ Discussion folders
- ✦ Tracking folders
- ✦ Built-in module folders

To get a better idea of each folder type, examine each one individually.

Discussion folders

In basic terms, discussion folders provide a way for people to discuss whatever topics they choose. Discussion folders provide an excellent means for collaboration. Collaboration refers to the sharing of ideas and information with the intent of accomplishing a specific task.

Cross-
Reference   Chapter 33 discusses collaboration in greater detail.

For all discussion participants to be able to see the discussion folder, the folder must be set up as a Public Folder. To set up a discussion folder, follow these steps:

1. If your folder list is not displayed, click Folder List in the Navigation Pane.

2. Go to the Public Folders section in the folder list.

3. Right-click All Public Folders and then select New Folder.

4. Type a name for the new discussion folder. For this example, enter **Discussion Group**.

5. Because discussion postings act in the same manner as e-mail messages, select Mail and Post Items in the Folder Contains field and then click OK.

The folder should appear as a new Public Folder under All Public Folders.

To see for yourself how a discussion folder works, post a new item in the folder. To do so, click the New button in the upper left corner, as if you were creating a new e-mail message. A post message form should appear, as shown in Figure 32-1.

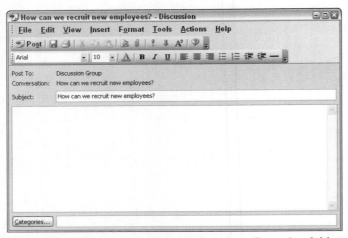

Figure 32-1: When you post a new item in a discussion folder, a post message form with a new subject/conversation defined appears.

Notice how the discussion topic "How can we recruit new employees?" is displayed on both the Subject and Conversation lines. This is because the Conversation line is based on what is entered as the subject. The Conversation line defines the discussion topic; however, when responding to a posted message, the Conversation line of the conversation to which you're responding will remain the same, but you will have the opportunity to enter new text into the Subject line. The specifics behind this are discussed later in the chapter.

If you take a look in the Discussion Group folder, you can see that your message has been posted (see Figure 32-2).

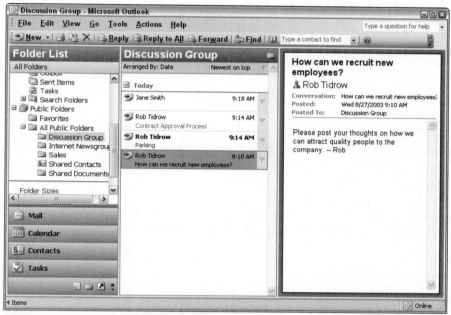

Figure 32-2: A message has been posted to the Discussion Group Public Folder.

By double-clicking the message, any user with access to the Public Folder may view the message. In addition, by clicking the Post Reply button on the message, the user can respond to the initial posting.

The user's response will appear in the Discussion Group Public Folder; however, it may be difficult to differentiate between conversations unless you organize your view of your discussion folders. To group the messages with the conversation to which they apply, select Arrange By ➪ Conversation Topic from the View menu.

Note   The details behind folder views and their capabilities are discussed later in this chapter.

Now that the current view is grouped by conversation, you can add as many conversation topics as you choose. Because the topics may be either expanded or collapsed, you can easily manage a large number of conversation topics and message postings, as you can see in the example in Figure 32-3.

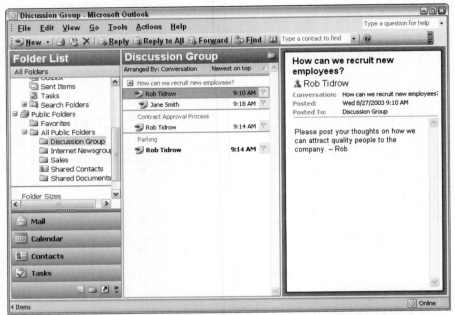

Figure 32-3: Multiple conversation topics and message postings can easily be managed once you've grouped messages by conversation.

Tracking folders

As you may have guessed, tracking folders track specific information, usually relating to some kind of business process. Because the information may be constantly updated, the Compose and Read pages of the form are often the same. In other words, there is typically not a separate Read form.

Tracking information

For example, Figure 32-4 shows a lead-tracking form that keeps track of potential client leads.

Cross-Reference Chapters 28 and 29 discuss the details involved in creating the form in Figure 32-4.

Unlike a discussion post form, this form does not include reply functionality. A reply actually creates a new message, whereas simply editing the content does not. The original message is preserved, but the content stored within the message changes. Therefore, any changes to the data are merely saved.

As with discussion folders, tracking folders are based on mail item folders. The lead-tracking form used in the example features a custom view that groups the service disciplines and potential/existing clients together.

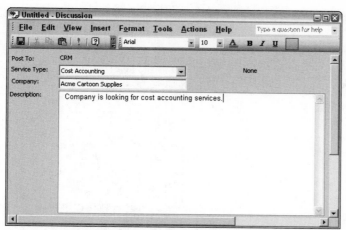

Figure 32-4: This custom lead-tracking form is used in conjunction with a tracking folder.

Note   Custom views are created by right-clicking the headings and adjusting the Group by This Field and Group by Box items. Additional information on custom views can be found later in this chapter.

Tracking documents

In addition, tracking folders can assist in the management of Office 2003 documents. For instance, suppose you want to keep track of company-wide contacts, all information pertaining to those contacts, and all correspondence and documents relating to those contacts. To do so, create a Public Folder named Documents. As you recall, you can create a Public Folder by right-clicking the All Public Folders folder and then selecting New Folder. (You can create a Mail and Post Items folder for this purpose.) Within this folder, you can store Office documents, as shown in Figure 32-5.

To post a document to a Public Folder, you can use one of the following three methods:

✦ From your office application, such as Microsoft Word, select Send To ➪ Exchange Folder from the File menu. Next, select the folder you wish to post to.

✦ From Outlook 2003, select Office Document from the drop-down menu of the New button in the upper left corner. Select the option Post the Document in this Folder.

✦ Drag a document from Windows Explorer into the folder.

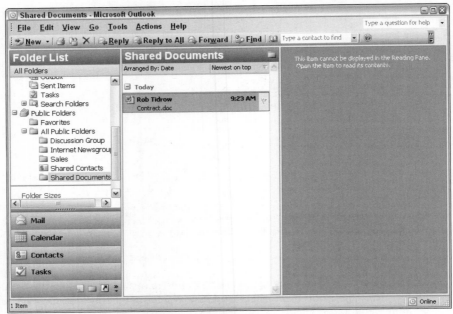

Figure 32-5: Office 2003 documents can be stored within a Public Folder.

To open the document, simply double-click the item.

To tie a document to a contact stored within a Public Folder, imagine you have a custom folder for business contacts called the Corporate Contacts Public Folder and then do the following.

1. Right-click the header associated with the document you wish to assign and select Options from the pop-up menu. The Message Options dialog box opens, as shown in Figure 32-6.

2. Click the Contacts button, and assign the document to the contact of your choice.

After the document has been assigned, the document is associated with that particular contact. The document may then be accessed through the Activities tab of the Contact form, as shown in Figure 32-7, as well as from the Documents folder.

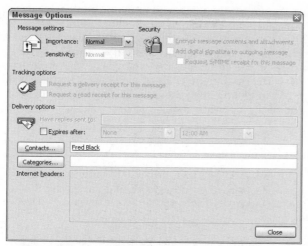

Figure 32-6: Use the Message Options dialog box to tie a document to a contact.

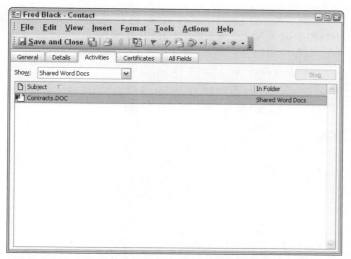

Figure 32-7: Accessing the document through the Activities tab of a Contact form

Note

For the Activities tab to display the document, it must be pointed to the Public Folder containing the appropriate documents (in this case, the Document Public Folder). This may be done on the Activities tab in the Properties dialog box for the Public Folder containing the contacts (the Corporate Contacts folder in our example) and is explained in greater detail later in this chapter.

In fact, there are third-party manufacturers, such as Eastman Kodak, who design document-tracking applications through the use of messaging technologies. Not only do the applications help manage your documents, but they also assist in version control by enforcing a check-out policy. In other words, an employee must check out a document before he or she can make any changes. While the document is checked out, others may view the document, but not make any changes. If the document is checked out for too long, an e-mail message is generated and sent to the employee with notification of the overdue check-in date.

Built-in module folders

Built-in module folders are folders based on an Outlook 2003 built-in module. For instance, if you wanted to create a Corporate Contacts Public Folder similar to the one in the preceding example, an easy way to do so would be to base the folder on the standard Contacts folder.

To create the Corporate Contacts Public Folder, follow the same steps as for the Discussion Groups Public Folder example earlier, but select Contacts Items instead of Mail Items from the Folder Contains field. To enable the folder to view a contact's associated documents, you must add the Public Folder containing the documents (in this example, the Shared Word Docs folder) to the Activities tab of the Properties dialog box. To add the Shared Word Docs Public Folder to the Activities tab, select New, and select the Shared Word Docs folder (see Figure 32-8).

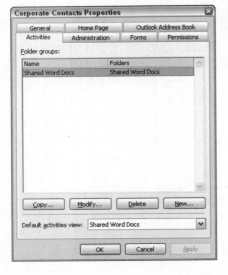

Figure 32-8: Point the Activities tab to the Shared Word Docs Public Folder.

In addition to Contacts, built-in module folders can be configured to act as a Calendar, Tasks List, or other Outlook 2003 built-in module. Calendar Public Folders are good for corporate calendars, whereas public task lists may assist in identifying and tracking corporate goals.

Keep in mind that these types of folders are only based on built-in folders. They may be customized to suit your individual needs.

Managing Folder Properties

Although this chapter has touched on folder properties earlier in this chapter, it hasn't gone into the specifics behind folder properties. As you'll recall, folder properties may be accessed by right-clicking the folder you want to configure and then selecting Properties from the pop-up menu.

Depending on the type of folder you are working with, the Properties dialog box will be different. The differences are organized as tabs in the Properties dialog box. Because many of these property settings are covered in earlier chapters, this chapter focuses only on those properties that greatly affect the applications you program in Outlook 2003.

Specifying a default form

Because most Outlook 2003 applications use custom forms, you most likely want to assign a particular form as the default form to the folder that houses your application. To do so, perform the following steps:

1. Select the Forms tab of the Properties dialog box, as shown in Figure 32-9.

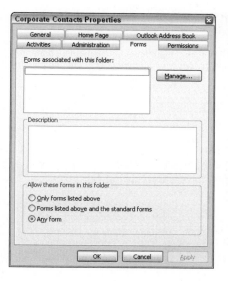

Figure 32-9: Select the Forms tab of the Properties dialog box.

2. Click the Manage button to open the Forms Manager dialog box.

3. Click the Set button, select your form, and click OK.

4. Select the form name and then click the Copy button, as shown in Figure 32-10. This copies the form to a location where it can be used by the folder.

5. Click the Close button to close the Forms Manager dialog box.

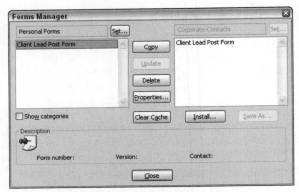

Figure 32-10: Copy the form via the Forms Manager dialog box.

At this point, the form is available to be used within the folder; however, if you want to force the users to use only the form you designed, make sure you select Only forms listed above in the Properties dialog box. The other two options, of course, do not limit which forms are used within the folder.

Defining permissions

Security almost always plays an important role when building applications within Outlook 2003. For this reason, be sure to review and test the permissions assigned to your application folder.

Cross-Reference   Chapter 26 discusses the details of defining folder permissions.

Caution   Be especially careful about assigning the role of Owner to users. Your application is more likely to "break" if the users have too many rights.

Using rules

Traditionally, rules are used to forward e-mail messages to another account; however, rules can be useful for applications that require certain actions when particular information enters a folder. These actions can be defined within the Edit Rule dialog box, shown in Figure 32-11.

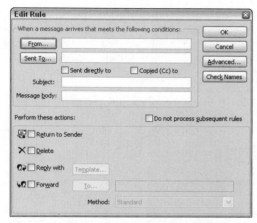

Figure 32-11: Use the Edit Rule window to define what actions occur when certain information enters the folder.

Under the Administration tab of the Properties dialog box, the rules pertaining to the folder can be defined by clicking the Folder Assistant button. This will, of course, open the Folder Assistant window. By clicking the Add Rule button, rules may be created.

Note   Before creating rules using the method just explained, it's recommended that you initially attempt to define your rule using the Rules Wizard. The Rules Wizard is one of the best new features of Outlook 2003 and is easy to use. To access the Rules Wizard, select the folder for which you wish to define the rule, and then select Rules Wizard from the Tools menu.

Using Views

Views are important when it comes to application development. Folder views not only organize information by providing structure, but can also provide a friendly interface for interaction. The remainder of the chapter will demonstrate why views play such an important role in developing Outlook 2003 applications.

Customizing versus defining a view

To manipulate the view of a folder, you first select the folder, and then select View ⇨ Arrange By ⇨ Current View. From that point, another menu opens and displays a number of predefined views. Because the focus here is on application development, you don't need to be particularly concerned with the predefined views; however, you should be concerned with two of the choices: Customize Current View and Define Views.

The Customize Current View choice enables the user to modify the folder view on his or her computer; however, the Define Views choice enables the user to name and define views for the folder. When designing the view for an application, you want to use the Define Views choice.

Figure 32-12 illustrates the Customize Current View dialog box. Note the descriptions to the right of each button.

Figure 32-12: Customize Current View window

Figure 32-13 illustrates the Define Views choice. On the lower half of the dialog box, you can see that the Icon, Categories, From, and Received fields are defined in the current view. The information is grouped in ascending order by the Service and Categories fields. The information is sorted by the PotentialClient field and is not filtered.

Although the dialog boxes look different in comparison, the Modify button of the Define Views dialog box opens a dialog box that looks exactly like the Customize Current View window. Therefore, the only important thing to know is when one or the other is appropriate. Just remember, a customized view in this case pertains only to the view the user that performs the customization sees; a defined view is associated with the folder itself. Therefore, all users of a particular folder can see the view that has been defined for that folder.

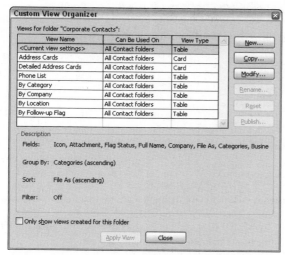

Figure 32-13: Custom View Organizer dialog box.

Manipulating field headings

By selecting the Fields button of the View Summary dialog box, you may define which fields appear in the view. To define which fields appear in the view, select the field you want to include on the left and then click the Add button, as shown in Figure 32-14. You also have the flexibility to add, remove, move up, or move down any field in the view.

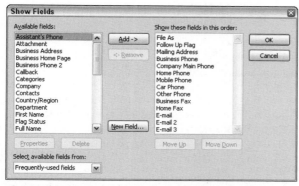

Figure 32-14: Use the Show Fields dialog box to manipulate the field headings of a view.

Note   Outside of the customize/define view dialog boxes, the column headings may also be modified (for the current view) by right-clicking the column header, selecting Field Chooser from the pop-up menu, and then dragging and dropping the fields onto the header.

Grouping information

Grouping information is one of the best ways to organize your items within a folder. By grouping items together, the items suddenly have meaning and are easy to browse. Up to four levels of grouping may be used, giving the view a hierarchical structure.

Grouping may be defined by selecting Group By from the View Summary dialog box. As you recall, the View Summary dialog box may be accessed either through Custom Current View or Define Views from the View/Current View menu, or by right-clicking within a view. The Group By dialog box is displayed in Figure 32-15. As you can see, defining the groups is as simple as selecting a field.

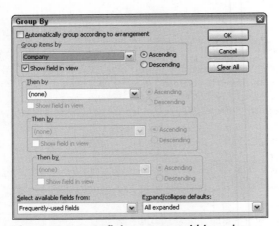

Figure 32-15: Defining groups within a view

Note   Grouping (for the current view) may also be controlled by right-clicking the column header and then selecting Group By Box from the pop-up menu.

Sorting and filtering

Sorting and filtering configuration is also accessed through the View Summary dialog box. Sorting is used to present information in an ascending or descending order, whereas filtering presents only the information specified by your criteria. The sorting dialog box defines which field the information will be sorted by within each group. Figure 32-16 shows the Sort dialog box.

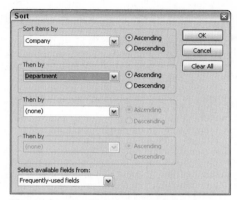

Figure 32-16: Use the Sort dialog box to sort information when defining a view.

The Filter dialog box, shown in Figure 32-17, filters according to the information you specify. This dialog box varies slightly depending on the type of folder selected.

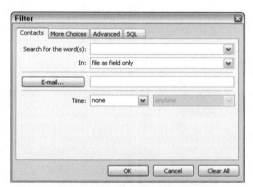

Figure 32-17: Use the Filter dialog box to filter information when defining a view.

Other view settings

The remaining view settings, which you access by clicking Other Settings, represent various font formatting options. Figure 32-18 shows what font formatting options are available.

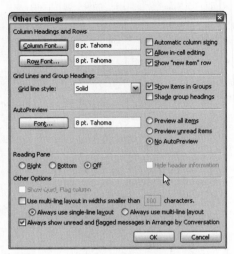

Figure 32-18: The Other Settings dialog box enables you to specify font options when defining a view.

Outlook also provides automatic formatting for a view. Click Automatic Formatting to open the Automatic Formatting dialog box shown in Figure 32-19. These options enable you to specify special formatting for items in the folder that meet certain conditions. For example, you might configure an Inbox view to show messages from a particular person or distribution group in a particular color.

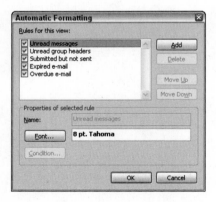

Figure 32-19: The Automatic Formatting dialog box enables format choices to be implemented on selected items when you define a view.

Summary

In this chapter, you learned how to work with folders when designing applications in Outlook 2003. You learned that application folder types can be classified in three categories: discussion folders, tracking folders, and built-in module folders. You also learned that discussion folders are designed to assist in collaboration by providing a convenient means for discussing a topic, and that tracking folders can be used to house information in a central location in an organized manner. The information can be in the form of text or documents.

You also have control over folder properties. Built-in module folders borrow from the characteristics inherent in Outlook 2003 built-in folders. Also, folder properties vary depending on the type of folder you are maintaining.

This chapter also explained that when designing a custom application in Outlook 2003, you need to keep in mind certain key considerations in terms of folder management. These considerations partially consist of specifying a default form, defining permissions, and defining rules.

Finally, you learned that views are an important aspect of Outlook 2003 development. Careful choice of fields, grouping, sorting, and filtering are what define a friendly and effective folder interface.

The following chapter looks at collaboration and how you can create custom forms to support collaborative efforts among your staff.

✦　　✦　　✦

Collaborative Messaging Basics

◆　◆　◆　◆

In This Chapter

Understanding the lingo

Collaboration

Messaging

Collaborative solutions

Workflow applications

MAPI

Outlook 2003 forms

E-forms

◆　◆　◆　◆

In Part VI and Chapter 32, you learned how to configure, utilize, customize, and integrate the key elements of Outlook 2003. Now you're going to shift gears and get a bit more technical and a bit more theoretical. But don't worry — this chapter keeps the theory to a minimum. In this chapter, you learn basic methodologies that surround collaborative messaging applications. These methodologies are the backbone to the solutions that save companies fat cash! In addition, you get a chance to look at some sample applications and learn what makes them so powerful so you can apply the same concepts to your custom solutions.

Understanding the Lingo

Word of warning: We sometimes feel like we have to be MCASs (Microsoft Certified Acronym Specialists) to understand what Microsoft is talking about. (Just kidding, there's no such certification.) However, when developing in Outlook 2003, it's important to understand collaboration and messaging, as well as how they relate to collaborative solutions. It's important for you to know that collaborative messaging has a meaning similar to the dictionary definition, but varies somewhat when addressing the topic at hand.

Collaboration

In general terms, collaboration describes the sharing of information among a group of individuals who intend to accomplish a common goal. Examples include brainstorming, group discussions, and simple teamwork. When implemented within an organization, large or small, collaboration can accomplish the following:

✦ Establishes a shared location for related information

✦ Organizes the information in an understandable and easily accessible manner

✦ Enables people to work as a team without being hassled by continuous meetings

✦ Allows people to be more productive, which saves money

A collaborative solution that utilizes Outlook 2003 (especially when used with Exchange Server) has the capability to accomplish each of these goals. The central location could be a Public Folder, and the organization could be accomplished through a hierarchy of folders within the Public Folder. Because the information is available through a common, shared application (that is, Outlook 2003), the information is easily accessible via a familiar interface. Sharing information in this manner would enable people who are located in different cities to participate on the same project team without the need for traveling between cities. That saves time, makes people more productive, and, of course, saves money.

Collaborative solution

Common elements of a collaborative solution include the integration of multiple sources of information. For instance, Figure 33-1 demonstrates a collaborative solution that integrates SAP (an enterprise-level accounting system used by large corporations that integrates all aspects of business), multiple SQL Server 7.0 databases, Exchange Server, an Outlook 2003 custom form, Internet Information Server, and a custom e-form developed in Visual Basic. Although the individual functions of each piece of the solution are explained later in the chapter, it's important to understand that the integration of applications and communication among people with various business roles are what classify the example as a collaborative solution.

Note   The custom e-form (developed in Visual Basic) and the Outlook 2003 custom form are interfaces that display information specific to a custom application. Both e-forms and Outlook 2003 custom forms have the capability of being transmitted as an e-mail message. Both e-forms and Outlook 2003 custom forms are discussed in detail later in this chapter.

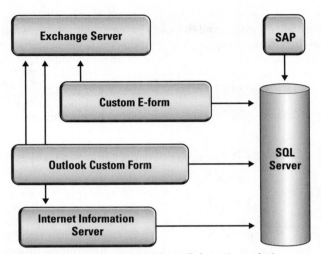

Figure 33-1: An example of a collaborative solution.

The flow of this scenario would be as follows:

1. Data from SAP is stored within SQL Server along with other databases.

2. The custom e-form, the Outlook 2003 custom form, and the Internet Information Server (IIS) Web server all pull data from the SQL Server databases.

3. The custom e-form and Outlook form are routed to various individuals within the organization through Exchange Server. As the forms are routed to each individual, the data contained within the forms is manipulated.

4. After the changes to the data within the forms are complete, the data is synchronized with a SQL Server database.

Collaborative messaging

Collaborative messaging refers to the elements of a collaborative solution that involve the transmission of data through an e-mail message. For example, when a user clicks the Send button on an e-mail message asking a friend in Cincinnati what he's doing New Year's Eve, it's messaging that transmits the question from that user's Windows XP machine over the Internet to the friend's iMac. Even though the machines utilize two different operating systems, they are still able to communicate with one another. If the e-mail message was transmitted as part of a team effort to accomplish a common goal, such as to coordinate a trip to New York's Times

Square on New Year's Eve, the entire process could be considered a collaborative messaging solution. Figure 33-2 identifies the elements of the collaborative solution example that relate to collaborative messaging — in other words, the elements of the solution that involve the transmission of data through an e-mail message. The grayed-out elements in Figure 33-2 represent the elements that do not involve the transmission of data through an e-mail message.

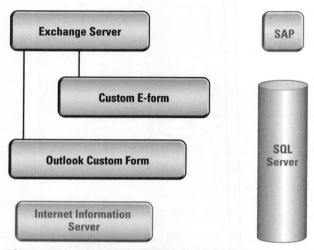

Figure 33-2: Elements relating to collaborative messaging

Workflow applications

Oftentimes, collaborative messaging processes replace business processes that formerly involved a great deal of paper and manual manipulation. For example, a coworker of mine designed an Outlook application that scheduled boys' and girls' sports teams to appropriate athletic facilities. Before the application, the scheduling was performed manually. A workflow application replaces these paper and manual processes by accomplishing the flow of the business process through the use of collaborative messaging. For instance, the Outlook 2003 custom form that is part of Figure 33-2 could represent an office supply request form.

The office supply request form would be considered a workflow application. An example of an office supply request process is represented in Figure 33-3. Keep in mind that the request is routed to the various individuals through the use of collaborative messaging.

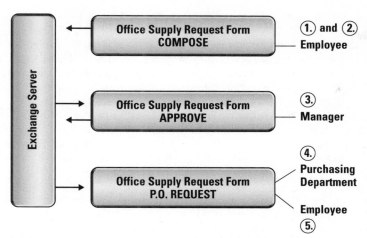

Figure 33-3: Office supply request processes through collaborative messaging.

The office supply request form process is as follows:

1. An employee who needs a new calculator initiates a request by opening the office supply request form from within Outlook 2003.

2. The employee enters the proper information into the form and then clicks the Send button.

3. The form is sent to a manager who is in charge of office supply approval. When the manager opens the form, she has the option of either approving or rejecting the request. In this case, the manager clicks the Approve button.

4. The form is sent to the purchasing department for processing. When a member of the purchasing department views the form, all the relevant information relating to the request is displayed.

5. A copy of the approved request is also sent to the employee so he or she knows that the request has been approved.

6. If the manager had rejected the request, the purchasing department would not have received the form; however, the employee would receive the form stating the request had been rejected.

Before collaborative messaging, this process would probably have involved a carbon copy form completed by the employee and then manually routed to the manager and purchasing department. If any one individual required a record of the request, a paper copy would be made and filed. There's no question that the automated collaborative messaging process is much more efficient.

Messaging application programming interface

Outlook 2003 uses messaging to provide its underlying functionality. Specifically, messaging refers to the messaging application program interface (MAPI). MAPI is the interface that enables different e-mail systems to speak to one another. Because system-based messaging APIs (application programming interfaces) are integrated with many different operating systems (including Windows and the Apple Macintosh OS), cross-platform messaging is possible, assuming the API provides simple messaging functions. Whew! What does this all mean? It means that a Windows XP machine can talk to any Macintosh, which can also talk to a mainframe computer that can talk to your Windows XP machine. Everybody can talk to everybody.

If there were no messaging standard available to different e-mail applications, each software vendor would be forced to write code to accommodate the specific e-mail application interfaces of other vendors. Nobody wants to do that, so MAPI has a lot of supporters. Through MAPI, vendors need to support only one specific standard. Figure 33-4 demonstrates how an application utilizing MAPI is able to communicate among multiple environments. In other words, MAPI acts as the pipeline between the various platforms.

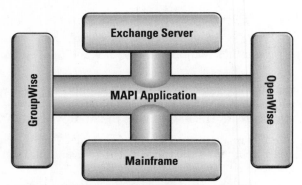

Figure 33-4: Cross-messaging system support with MAPI application

Today, many applications use MAPI to communicate with other applications in a manner more sophisticated than traditional e-mail. Specifically, MAPI can be used to initiate actions in other applications based on the commands transmitted; however, due to the complexity of MAPI, this type of application development can require a great deal of technical expertise.

Outlook 2003 Custom Forms

Outlook 2003 provides an environment for developers to utilize MAPI technologies without the headache of traditional MAPI programming. Outlook 2003 includes an extensive object model that provides a simplified method of using a complex interface.

The majority of the Outlook 2003 user interface consists of Outlook forms. The forms provide a friendly means of accessing the underlying code. These forms can be customized to accommodate specific business needs. The forms are created within the Outlook Forms Designer, as shown in Figure 33-5.

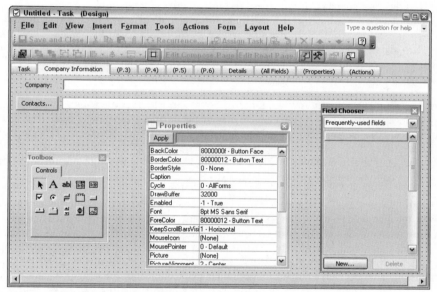

Figure 33-5: Outlook Forms Designer

As you may recall, the details of the Outlook Forms Designer and how to design Outlook 2003 custom forms were explained in Chapters 28 through 32. It's important to understand that these forms can be customized to suit specific needs and that they provide an interface to the underlying messaging system.

E-form Basics

The name *e-form* is a short name for electronic forms. The term electronic form came from the idea of creating an electronic version of an existing paper form; however, e-forms are more than just a replacement for a paper form. Typically, e-forms are key components of workflow applications. In addition to replacing the paper form, the e-form accomplishes the underlying business process that surrounded the paper form. By embedding the business logic into the e-form, the process can be automated. All the user needs to do is enter the information, submit the form, and let it do its thing.

For example, suppose your company surveys employees in each department about the performance of their supervisor. Each employee receives the same survey. Each department head is only interested in the surveys of employees in his or her department when evaluating the performance of the supervisor. In a traditional paper-process model, each employee would complete a form by giving his or her name, the supervisor's name, and responses to the questions. Under this scenario, the surveys would have to be printed, distributed, completed, returned, sorted, and tabulated.

By embedding the survey into an e-form, however, the survey does not have to be printed. In addition, the e-form can be distributed, completed, and returned to the proper department head via business rules embedded into the form. The department head may then view an automated report based on the results of the survey. By implementing the e-form solution, you can replace the slow, inefficient, paper-intensive process with a fast, efficient, automated process.

Although Outlook 2003 custom forms can often accomplish these same goals, e-forms enable you to do more things for a greater degree of functionality. For instance, e-forms can be written to fully exploit the full capabilities of Visual Basic and ActiveX controls to provide a more robust, high-performance application with a complex user interface. Outlook 2003 custom forms use VBScript to perform tasks, whereas e-forms can be created in Visual Basic, Visual Basic for Applications, Visual C++, or Visual J++. Because these development platforms offer a greater degree of functionality, it sometimes makes sense to develop forms in the more flexible environment these platforms provide.

Summary

In this chapter, you learned about the basic methodologies that surround collaborative solution development. In addition, you learned how Outlook 2003 and collaborative messaging can play an important role in providing an overall solution.

Collaboration describes the sharing of information among a group of individuals with the intention of accomplishing a common goal. It can establish shared sources of information, organize the information in a logical and easily accessible manner, assist in working with teams, and make people more productive.

Collaborative solutions typically integrate many different applications containing a wide range of information. Collaborative messaging is an element of a collaborative solution that transmits information through the Exchange Server, Outlook 2003 custom forms, custom e-forms, or any application that utilizes MAPI.

Workflow applications resemble business processes by routing information through the use of collaborative messaging. Workflow applications often replace paper-based manual business processes.

The messaging application programming interface (MAPI) is the interface that allows different e-mail systems to speak to one another.

Outlook 2003 custom forms are created within the Outlook Forms Designer and can accommodate specific individual needs. Applications that require greater flexibility and a high degree of functionality are developed as e-forms, as opposed to Outlook 2003 custom forms.

The following chapter delves deeper into Outlook form development by explaining the Outlook 2003 object model, how to use the Script Editor to add program code to turn forms into applications, and how to debug your custom applications.

✦　　✦　　✦

Using the Outlook 2003 Object Model

In This Chapter

Understanding an object model

Using the OFD Script Editor

Defining the Immediate window

Outlook 2003 Application Object Model

To fully exploit the capabilities of Outlook 2003 and integrate with other applications, you need to understand the Outlook 2003 Application Object Model. By understanding the model, you can manipulate your applications into performing the same complex tasks inherent in Outlook 2003, but without having to understand the minute details of the messaging application programming interface (MAPI).

 Cross-Reference   For more information on MAPI, see Chapter 33.

Understanding an Object Model

An object model can be thought of as the blueprint of a component-based application. When I refer to component-based applications, I am stating that the application is broken down into individual objects and fits into Microsoft's component software model know as the Component Object Model (COM). An object model is a diagram of all the individual components working together to form an application. To give you an idea of what an object model looks like, Figure 34-1 displays the object model for the Office Assistant, which is referred to as the Assistant Object from a programming standpoint.

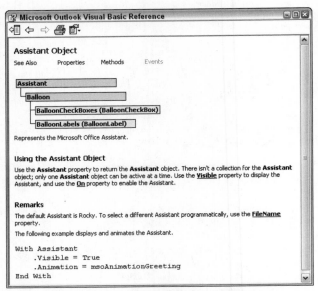

Figure 34-1: Object model for the Assistant Object

Component Object Model (COM)

Applications designed using COM can be broken down into individual components known as objects. Depending on the specifics, these objects go by a number of names, such as COM-object, ActiveX.dll, ActiveX control, ActiveX component, component, or simply just object, but all refer to the same basic concept.

So why are applications designed under the COM software model? There are a number of reasons why it's a good idea to build component-based applications, and here are a few of them:

Reusability. Because the functionality of component-based applications is divided into objects, the functionality can be borrowed for use in another application.

Integration. Because the components can be shared between two different applications, the applications can easily be integrated.

Language independence. Components built as ActiveX components can be shared among programming languages that support ActiveX, such as Visual Basic, Visual C++, and Visual J++. An ActiveX component built in Java can just as easily be used in a Visual Basic or Visual C++ application as it can in a Visual J++ application.

Scalability. By utilizing certain application architectures and the Distributed Component Object Model (DCOM), applications can be scalable. Scalability touches on how easily the application can be distributed to users, and how well the application responds to a large number of users.

Outlook 2003 Application Object Model

As explained earlier in this chapter, an object model can be thought of as the blueprint of an application; therefore, the Outlook 2003 Application Object Model can be thought of as the blueprint for Outlook 2003. To view the Outlook 2003 Application Object Model, select Microsoft Outlook Object Library Help from the Help menu with the Script Editor open. A diagram of the object model should open, as displayed in Figure 34-2. The diagram is interactive—you can click an object to view additional information.

Tip

To open the Script Editor, choose Form ➪ View Code with a form open in Design mode.

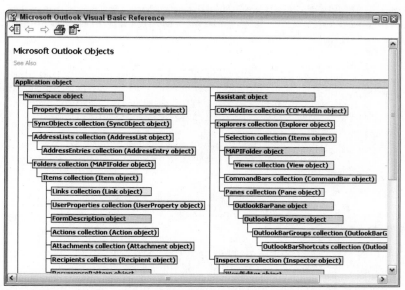

Figure 34-2: Outlook 2003 Application Object Model interactive diagram

The items in yellow represent the object and collection; the items in blue represent an object only. Collections refer to objects that have a set of related objects associated with them. For example, the Folders collection has all the individual folders associated with the object.

Methods versus properties

To understand how to work with an object model, it's important to understand the methods and properties of an object. In simple terms, a method is described as an action associated with an object; a property can be described as a characteristic of the object. To get a better understanding, look at the following code:

```
Function Item_Open()

    Dim strFolder
    Set myNameSpace = Application.GetNameSpace("MAPI")
    Set myFolder = myNameSpace.GetDefaultFolder(olFoldersTasks)
    strFolder = myFolder.Name
    msgbox strFolder

End Function
```

This example uses the GetNameSpace method of the Application object to assign the name space to MyNameSpace. It next uses the GetDefaultFolder method of the NameSpace object to assign the Tasks folder to myFolder. Finally, it assigns the string to the name property of the folder object. The methods completed the actions of obtaining the objects you need, and the property stored the name characteristic you need. The end result is a message, generated by the msbgox statement, that states "Tasks" when the form opens.

To relate this example back to the explanation of the Object Browser, Figure 34-3 shows how you could have used the Object Browser to find the GetDefaultFolder method of the NameSpace object.

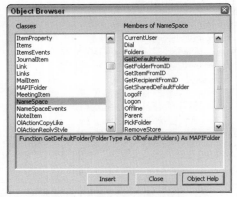

Figure 34-3: Using the Object Browser to obtain the GetDefaultFolder method of the NameSpace object

Using the OFD Script Editor

As discussed in Chapter 28, the Outlook 2003 Forms Designer (OFD) Script Editor is the tool to use to program your VBScript functions and subroutines within Outlook 2003. To access the Script Editor from within the OFD, select Form ➪ View Code.

The function is designed to display a message box when the form is closed. To accomplish this task, use the Item_Close event. You learn more about events in the next section.

Cross-Reference For details on creating a simple function or subroutine, see the introduction to the Script Editor in Chapter 28.

Event handlers

Events are user actions that trigger the execution of any code associated with that particular event. Without events, your code would never be executed. In other words, when an event occurs, such as an On_Click event, the code specified underneath the event will be executed. To assist with programming against events, the Script Editor has a built-in event handler. To access the Event Handler dialog box, select Event Handler from the Script menu. The Insert Event Handler dialog box appears, as shown in Figure 34-4.

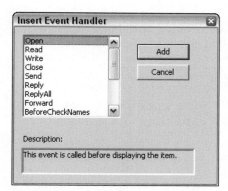

Figure 34-4: An option on the Script menu brings up the Insert Event Handler dialog box.

The list box contains a list of all the possible events. A description of when each event occurs is indicated at the bottom of the Insert Event Handler dialog box. To view a description, select the event. To insert an event into the Script Editor, select the event and then click the Add button. Alternatively, you can double-click the event. A function with the specified event is automatically created in the Script Editor.

Object Browser

The Object Browser is another component of the Script Editor that aids the programmer in development. The Object Browser is a quick reference for determining the members of the selected object. To access the Object Browser from the Script Editor, select Object Browser from the Script menu, or press F2. Figure 34-5 gives you an idea how the Object Browser looks.

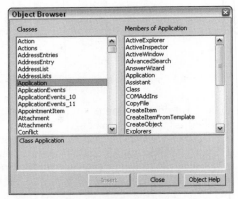

Figure 34-5: Object Browser window

The list on the left provides a list of classes, including the objects, and the list on the right provides a list of the corresponding members. By selecting a member and then clicking the Insert button, the Object Browser inserts the member text into the Script Editor, as shown in Figure 34-6.

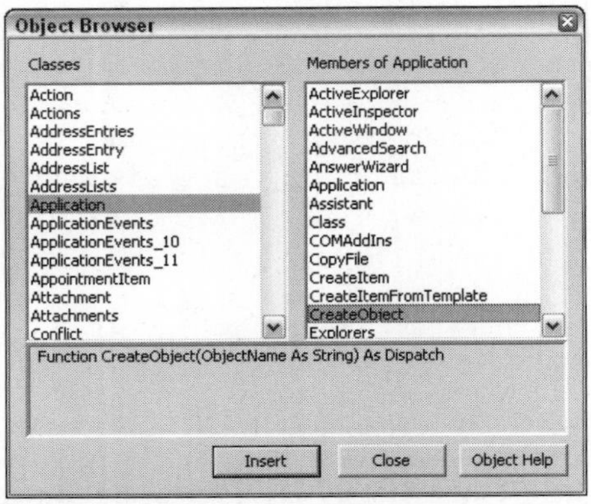

Figure 34-6: Insert member text into the Script Editor by using the Insert button in the Object Browser.

Click the Object Help button from within the Object Browser to open the Help file for that particular object, as shown in Figure 34-7. The Outlook 2003 Object Model Help files are helpful in giving you an understanding of how to work with an object. In addition, the actual models are set up as links to help on the piece of the model you click.

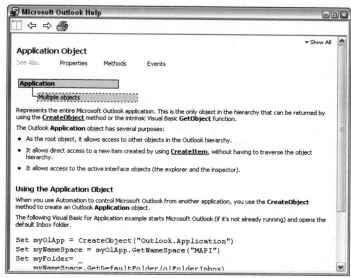

Figure 34-7: Interactive Help file for Outlook 2003 Application Object Model

Debugging Your Code

After you get started writing your own code, chances are your code will not always work on your first try. Don't feel bad — you'll be no different than any other programmer in the world. Thankfully, there are tools to assist in finding where the problems lie within your code. For Outlook 2003, that tool is known as the Script Debugger. The Script Debugger released with Office 2003 has vast improvements over older versions. The new version provides more feedback when debugging, and the break mode support is especially helpful.

To access the Script Debugger, you must first be running your form:

1. To run your form from the OFD, select Form ➪ Run This Form.
2. Open the Script Debugger by selecting Tools ➪ Forms ➪ Script Debugger.

The Script Debugger is empty at this point.

Break mode

When code is executed in break mode, there is a pause before each line of code. By analyzing the behavior of your application as it relates to each line of code, you can determine in which lines problems exist. To see how the Script Debugger can step though code, set the Script Debugger to run the application in break mode by doing the following:

1. Select Debug ➪ Break All, or press Ctrl+Alt+Break.

2. Because the Script Debugger will not step through code until an event is fired, close your form to fire off the Close event.

Figure 34-8 shows the Script Debugger stepping through the code.

Note   The form used for this example displays a "Thank You" message when the form is closed. If there was no code written for this event, the Script Debugger would not have any code to step through.

By selecting Debug ➪ Step Into or pressing the F11 key, you can step though each line of code.

In Figure 34-9, the code for the Close event has changed to utilize a string value to represent the text of the message box. As you step through the example code with the F11 key, the string strThanks is assigned the value "Thank You." As you can see, when the mouse is hovered over strThanks, the value of the string can be viewed in the form of a tip (strThanks = "Thank You").

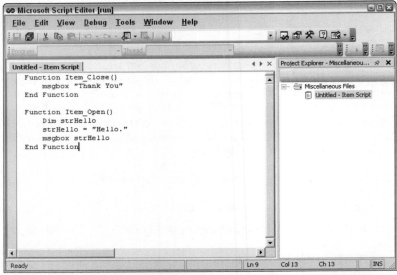

Figure 34-8: Script Debugger steps through the code in break mode.

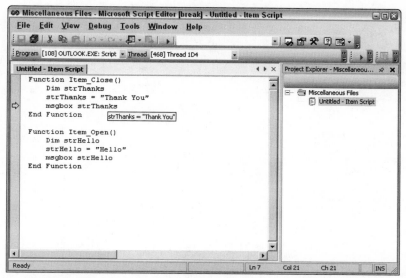

Figure 34-9: View the value of a string by hovering the mouse over the string (strThanks = "Thank You").

Setting break points

Break points enable you to pause your code at a specified point, but without stepping though several lines of code. This is particularly useful when you have several lines of code. To set a break point, do the following:

1. Run your form.

2. Open the Script Debugger by selecting Tools ⇨ Forms ⇨ Script Debugger.

3. Set the Script Debugger to run the code in break mode by selecting Debug ⇨ Break. Another approach is to put your cursor where you want to add your breakpoint in the code window and then choose Debug ⇨ Insert Breakpoint.

4. Set your break point on the desired line by clicking in the left margin.

5. Select Debug ⇨ Continue or press F5.

The code should stop at the break point you specified, as shown in Figure 34-10.

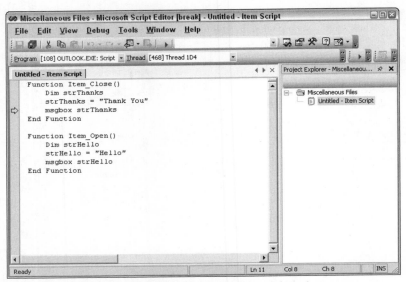

Figure 34-10: Code stops at the break point for debugging.

Summary

In this chapter, you learned some of the basics behind object models, COM, and, specifically, the Outlook 2003 Application Object Model.

Object models are the blueprints of applications. The Component Object Model (COM) is Microsoft's component software model, upon which the Outlook 2003 Application Object Model is based.

There are many reasons to develop component-based applications, but some of the main reasons touch on sharing components, integrating with other applications, language independence, and scalability.

Outlook 2003 provides tools to help you quickly build and debug form code. The Insert Event Handler window can assist in identifying events within the OFD Script Editor. The Object Browser can aid in navigating through the Outlook 2003 Application Object Model. The Script Debugger has a number of features to assist you in troubleshooting your code. Running the Script Debugger in break mode enables you to step through each line of your code individually. Setting break points enables you to pause your code at designated points. There are a number of additional debug windows designed to provide information regarding the current state of the form. Documentation for the Outlook 2003 Application Object Model can be accessed through the Help menu of the Script Editor.

The following chapter expands on this chapter's discussion of programming by exploring COM add-ins for Outlook. The chapter explains the function of a COM add-in, how to create them, and how to use them in Office applications.

✦   ✦   ✦

Advanced Outlook Administration

P A R T

VIII

◆   ◆   ◆   ◆

In This Part

Chapter 35
Using Business
Contact Manager

Chapter 36
Using Outlook Web
Access

Chapter 37
Optimizing Outlook
Installations

◆   ◆   ◆   ◆

Using Business Contact Manager

◆ ◆ ◆ ◆

In This Chapter

What is the Business
Contact Manager?

Installing Business
Contact Manager

Understanding
Business Contact
Manager accounts

Adding a new
account

Managing business
contact information

Tracking sales
opportunities

Linking items to
records

Integrating Business
Contact Manager
with Office 2003
applications

◆ ◆ ◆ ◆

New in Outlook 2003 is the Business Contact Manager, an add-on designed to work with small businesses of up to 25 employees. It enables these employees to better manage relationships with their customers. This includes tracking customer contacts, sales opportunities, and e-mail messaging with their clients. Business Contact Manager can also be used with other Microsoft Office applications to help businesses integrate data from Outlook with other Office data.

What Is the Business Contact Manager?

Whether you have one customer or thousands, managing customer relationships is vital to the long-term success of any business. In fact, maintaining a healthy and productive relationship with your key customers is almost as important as the products and services businesses produce. With Outlook 2003 and the Business Contact Manager, small businesses can step into the growing and important field of Customer Relationship Management (or CRM for short) without a large overhead involved. CRM software is designed to help businesses automate many of their customer relationship tasks such as tracking sales, locating important documents related to a customer, and maintaining a list of projected actions that need to be taken. With Business Contact Manager you can perform several of these tasks on your own computer.

Many businesses are familiar Customer Relationship Management software. This type of software lets businesses track opportunities, assign task priorities, initiate phone calls, and so on. CRM software is usually designed to be deployed in a client/server situation, with the raw data being stored on network servers and the filtered information being available to the clients. CRM information can be shared easily in these installations.

With Outlook Business Contact Manager, some of the same information can be stored and used by businesses; however, the data is stored locally on each computer — it cannot be shared as in a client/server installation. That is why Business Contact Manager is designed for small businesses with up to 25 people. It is believed that these small businesses want some type of business relationship software without the expense and overhead of a full-fledged CRM package. Business Contact Manager can help small business owners and salespeople who need a simple tool to stay connected to business contacts, and to manage business relationships more efficiently and effectively.

Note Microsoft has announced that a CRM solution will be available sometime in 2003-2004. You can learn more about it by visiting www.microsoft.com/BusinessSolutions/default.mspx.

With Business Contact Manager, users can:

✦ Track business relationships

✦ Track every business opportunity to maximize sales results

✦ Send marketing e-mail targeted to business contacts

✦ Run customer data reports

✦ Quickly locate important documents

Figure 35-1 shows the Business Contact Manager add-in.

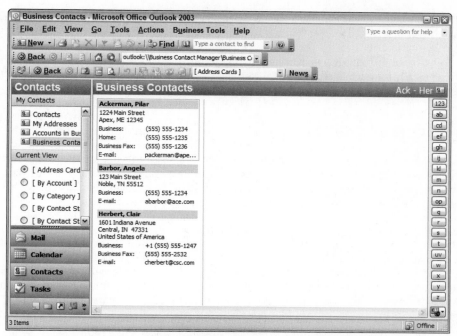

Figure 35-1: Microsoft Business Contact Manager helps you manage your business information and contacts.

Installing Business Contact Manager

Microsoft Business Contact Manager comes as an add-on tool with Microsoft Outlook 2003. It currently comes as an additional CD-ROM disc with its own setup application. To install it, use the following steps:

1. Install Microsoft Outlook and ensure it works properly.

2. Exit Microsoft Outlook.

3. Insert the Business Contact Manager CD-ROM into your CD-ROM drive. The autosetup feature should start automatically. If not, open My Computer, double-click the CD-ROM drive icon in which the Business Contact Manager CD-ROM is inserted, and double-click Setup.Exe.

4. Proceed through the Business Contact Manager Setup Wizard.

5. Restart Microsoft Outlook.

The Business Contact Manager folder displays in the Navigation pane with your other folders.

Note   Do not install Business Contact Manager on a network server. It must be installed locally for each client.

Adding a New Account

Business Contact Manager uses the term *Account record* to describe an item that holds information about the companies, organizations, or business entities with whom you deal. Within your Account records, you can store business contact records that store information about individual business contacts.

When you start using Business Contact Manager, you can add a new account. Business Contact Manager lets you add information about an account in a default form. Account information can be linked to Business Contact and Opportunity records, as well as appear in a list of History items. Note: Many times a group of accounts are assigned to you by a supervisor, manager, or other Business Contact Manager user. These accounts have been preconfigured for you before you first start using Business Contact Manager by your organization.

To add an account, you can fill out the Account form or import an account.

Filling out the Account form

To use the Account form to create a new account, follow these steps:

1. From the Standard toolbar, click the New button.

2. Click New Account to display the Account form, as shown in Figure 35-2.

3. On the General tab of the Account form, fill out information about your account, including Account Name, Primary Contact, and so forth. When filling out the Primary Contact information, you can click the ... button to pick contacts from your Business Contacts folder. How to create Business Contacts is shown later. Also, you must choose File | Save to save your new Account before you can click the ... button.

4. Click the Details tab as shown in Figure 35-3 and fill it out with additional information about your new account. For example, you can set the type of business the account is (Public Company, Partnership, and so on), territory, source of lead, and so on. If you don't know this information now, you can come back to this form later and update it.

5. Click Save and Close.

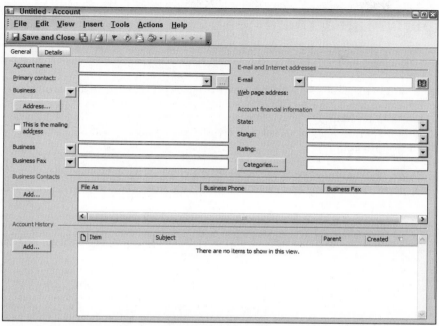

Figure 35-2: Fill out the Account form to set up an account in the Business Contact Manager.

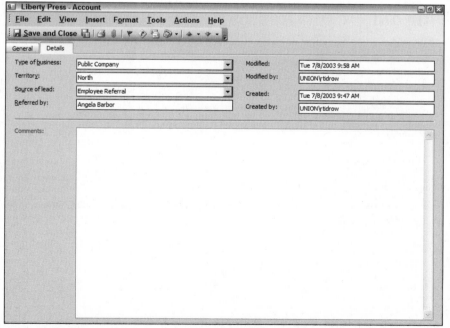

Figure 35-3: You can fill out the Details tab when setting up a new account.

Importing an account

To create a new account by importing another Business Contact Manager account, follow these steps.

Note: To import Business Contact Manager data, you must have a .bcm file with exported accounts available, such as from another user who has exported his/her Business Contact Manager accounts. To learn more about exporting Business Contact Manager data, see the section called "Exporting Business Contact Manager data" later in this chapter.

1. From the File menu, choose Import/Export and then Business Contact Manager (see Figure 35-4) to display the Business Data Import/Export Wizard as shown in Figure 35-5.

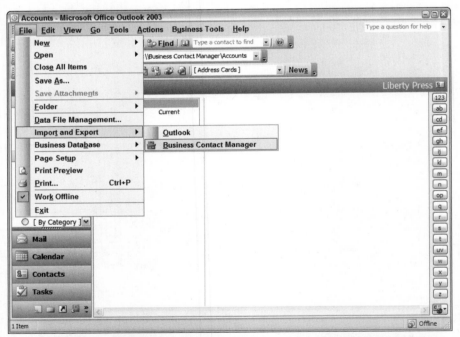

Figure 35-4: Use the Business Contact Manager option to start the Business Data Import/Export Wizard.

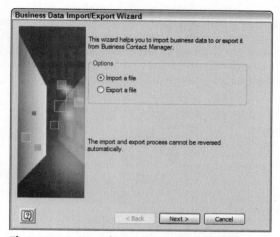

Figure 35-5: Use the Business Contact Manager Import/Export Wizard to import a new Business Contact Manager account.

2. Choose Import a File.

3. Click Next.

4. Select Business Contact Manager data (see Figure 35-6) and click Next.

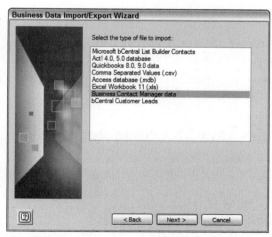

Figure 35-6: Choose to import Business Contact Manager data.

5. In the File to import box, as shown in Figure 35-7, type the path to the file to import. You also can click the Browse button and locate the file in the Open dialog box. Specify if you want Outlook to import duplicate data or not. If you choose to import duplicate data, you can always go back and delete those Business Contact Manager items you no longer need.

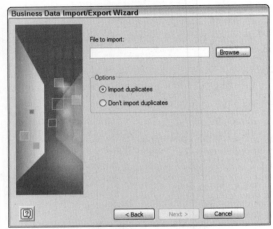

Figure 35-7: Specify the Business Contact Manager file you want to import.

6. Click Next.

7. Click Next to start the import process. This may take several minutes depending on the size of the Business Contact Manager data file you specified.

8. When finished, click Close. The imported Business Contact Manager data is available in the Accounts folder.

Viewing Business Contact Manager Accounts

Outlook displays your Business Contact Manager Accounts in folders much like the folders you use to view regular contacts. To view your account data, do the following:

1. Choose the Business Tools menu.

2. Click the Accounts command, as shown Figure 35-8.

Figure 35-8: Choose Accounts to view your Business Contact Manager Accounts.

3. To open a Business Contact Manager Account, double-click it. This displays the Account in an Account window, as shown in Figure 35-9.

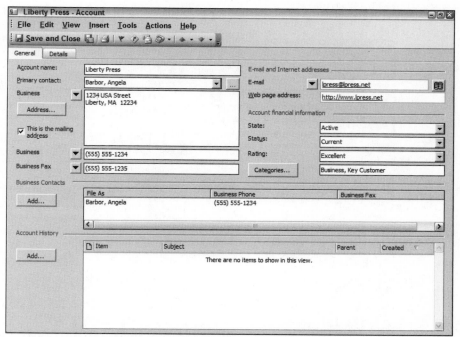

Figure 35-9: You can view Account information in an Account window.

Managing Business Contact Information

A business contact is the person with whom you interact with at a company or organization. Business Contact Manager enables you to create your business contacts in three ways. You can use the Business Contact form, move a contact from another Outlook folder (providing it's a Contacts folder) to the Business Contacts folder, or import a business contact from another source, such as from a database.

Filling out the Business Contact form

Use the following instructions to help you fill out the Business Contact form:

1. On the Standard toolbar, click New.

2. Click Business Contact to display the Business Contact form, as shown in Figure 35-10.

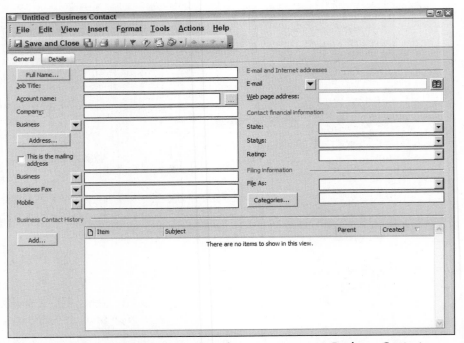

Figure 35-10: Use the Business Contact form to set up new Business Contact Manager contact.

3. Click Full Name to display the Check Full Name dialog box, as shown in Figure 35-11.

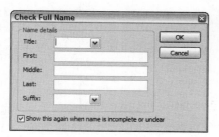

Figure 35-11: Use the Check Full Name dialog box to enter your new contacts' name.

4. Enter name information about the contact you are setting up.

5. Click OK.

6. Assign this contact to an account by clicking the ... button next to the Account name field and choose Add Existing Account or Create New Account. If you have an account for this contact already, choose Add Existing Account and select the account from the Accounts dialog box, as shown in Figure 35-12. Click OK. Otherwise, click Create New Account and enter a new account name in the Create an Account dialog box, as shown in Figure 35-13. Click OK.

Note

When you create a new account name here, Business Contact Manager adds the account name to the Accounts folder. After you finish creating the new business account, you can open the Accounts folder, double-click the new account name, and fill in the rest of the account information.

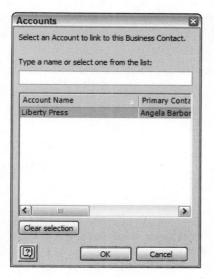

Figure 35-12: You can associate a new business contact with an existing account.

Figure 35-13: Or you can create a new account with which to associate a new business contact.

7. Fill out the rest of the contact information you want to keep with this contact.

8. Click Save and Close to save this contact information. If you want to create a new contact after saving this one, click Save and New.

Moving a contact from the Outlook Contacts folder

If you want to set up a new business contact by moving an existing contact from another Outlook Contacts folder to a Business Contact folder, do the following:

1. Click the Contacts icon on the Outlook Bar.

2. Under My Contacts, select the Contact folder storing the contact you want to move.

3. Drag a contact from the Contacts folder to the Business Contacts in Business Contact Manager folder

4. Repeat as necessary.

Importing a business contact

To import a contact into a Business Contact folder, do the following:

1. From the File menu, click Import and Export.

2. Click Business Contact Manager to display the Business Data Import/Export Wizard.

3. Click Next.

4. Select Business Contact Manager Data.

5. Click Next.

6. In the File to import field, as shown in Figure 35-14, specify the .bcm file that includes exported Business Contacts.

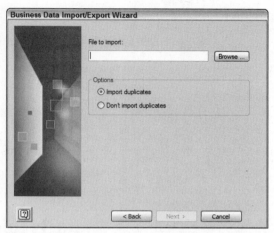

Figure 35-14: Specify the .bcm file that includes exported Business Contacts.

7. Click Next.

8. Click Next again to start the import process.

9. Click Close when the import process completes.

Exporting Business Contact Manager data

To share Business Contact Manager data, you can export Business Contact Manager Accounts or Business Contact Manager Contacts.

Exporting Business Contact Manager Accounts

To export a Business Contact Manager Account, do the following steps:

1. From the File menu, select Import and Export.

2. Click Business Contact Manager to display the Business Data Import/Export Wizard.

3. Select Export a file.

4. Click Next.

5. Select Business Contact Manager Data, as shown in Figure 35-15.

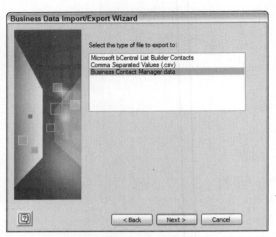

Figure 35-15: Select to export Business Contact Manager Data.

6. Click Next.

7. Type a path and file name in the File to export field. By default, files are stored in you're My Documents folder. Both exported accounts and exported business contacts share the .bcm file extension.

8. Select Accounts, as shown in Figure 35-16.

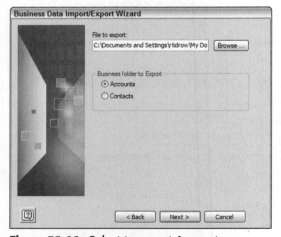

Figure 35-16: Select to export Accounts.

9. Click Next.

10. Click Next again to start the export process.

11. When the export process finishes, click Close.

Exporting Business Contact Manager Contacts

To export a Business Contact Manager Contact, do the following steps:

1. From the File menu, select Import and Export.

2. Click Business Contact Manager to display the Business Data Import/Export Wizard.

3. Select Export a file.

4. Click Next.

5. Select Business Contact Manager Data, as shown in Figure 35-15.

6. Click Next.

7. Type a path and file name in the File to export field. By default, files are stored in you're My Documents folder. Both exported accounts and exported business contacts share the .bcm file extension.

8. Select Contacts, as shown in Figure 35-17.

Figure 35-17: Select to export Contacts.

9. Click Next.

10. Click Next again to start the export process.

11. When the export process finishes, click Close.

Tracking Sales Opportunities

Business Contact Manager lets you easily track sales opportunities you might have with your customers. Business Contact Manager reports created with Crystal Reports help you track your opportunities. Crystal Reports is a third-party product that analyzes and creates data to create customized reports for you to view on-screen, print as hard copy, or embed as objects in other documents. You can enter the details of these opportunities in an Opportunity record. After an opportunity is entered as a record, you can link it to a Business Contact or Account record so you can view the opportunity from different places in the Business Contact Manager, including within an Account History, a report, or the Opportunity record itself.

To create an opportunity, do the following:

1. Click the down arrow next to New on the Standard toolbar to display the New context menu of choices.

2. Click Opportunity, as shown in Figure 35-18.

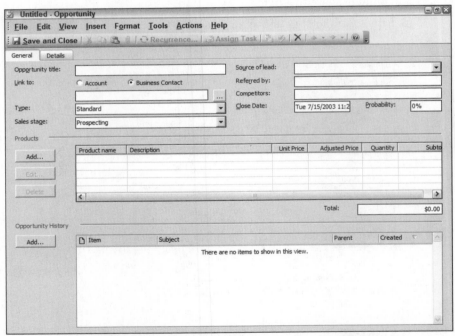

Figure 35-18: Select Opportunity to start creating a new opportunity.

3. Enter information about the opportunity on the General tab of the Opportunity form . You must link the opportunity to an Account or Business Contact. To do this, select Account or Business Contact and then specify an account or contact in the field underneath the Account and Business Contact options. Click the ... button to select Add Existing Account (or Add Existing Contact) or to select Create New Account (or Create New Contact).

4. Click the Details tab, as shown in Figure 35-19. You can edit the Comments field on this tab. The other fields are updated automatically when you save the form.

5. Click Save and Close.

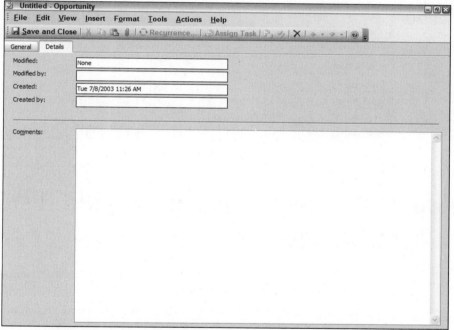

Figure 35-19: Use the Details tab to write comments about the opportunity.

To view your existing opportunities, do the following:

1. Choose the Business Tools menu.

2. Click the Opportunities command, open the Opportunities folder, as shown in Figure 35-20.

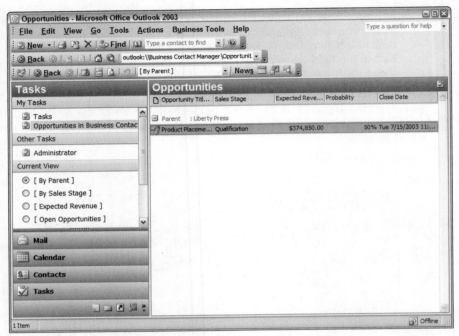

Figure 35-20: View your opportunities here.

Adding Business Notes to a Record History

Business Contact Manager enables you to create business notes to a record history. To do so, follow these steps:

1. Click the down arrow next to the New button on the Standard toolbar to display the New context menu of choices.

2. Click Business Note to display the Business Note form, as shown in Figure 35-21.

3. Enter the information you want to save about the record.

4. Click the down arrow next to the Link to History list to display the Link to History context menu of choices, as shown in Figure 35-22.

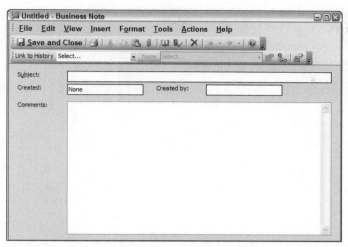

Figure 35-21: Use the Business Note form to add a Business Note to a record history.

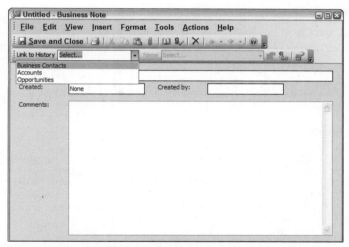

Figure 35-22: Select the type of record to which you want to link your Business Note.

5. Click Business Contacts, Accounts, or Opportunities.

6. Click the down arrow next to the Name list to display the Name list of choices, as shown in Figure 35-23.

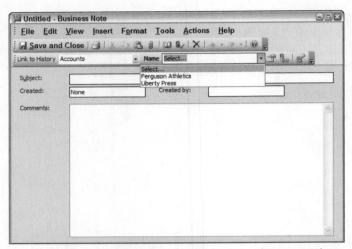

Figure 35-23: The Name list becomes active when you select an item from the Link to History drop-down list..

7. Select the name on the record to which you want to link.

8. Click Save and Close.

Adding Phone Logs to a Record History

Business Contact Manager enables you to add a phone logs to a record history. To do so, follow these steps:

1. Click the down arrow next to the New button on the Standard toolbar.

2. Click Phone Log to display the Business Phone Log form, as shown in Figure 35-24.

3. Enter the information you want to save for the phone call.

4. Click the down arrow next to the Link to History list.

5. Click Business Contacts, Accounts, or Opportunities.

6. Click the down arrow next to the Name list.

7. Select the name on the record to which you want to link.

8. Click the Start Timer button to start recording the time spent on a phone call.

9. Click Pause Timer when the phone call is finished.

10. Click Save and Close.

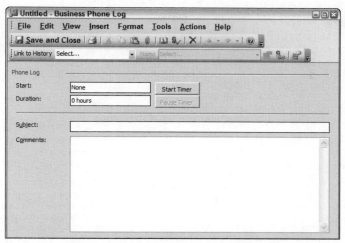

Figure 35-24: Use the Business Phone Log form to add a phone call to a record history.

Linking an Item to a Record

Business Contact Manager enables you to keep your communications and other interactions with customers in one place. You can add items to a Business Contact, Account, or Opportunity record. You can do the same with potential or target customers as well.

Linking an item to a Business Contact record

Use the following steps to link an item to a Business Contact record:

1. Click Contacts on the Outlook bar to open the Contacts folder.

2. Click Business Contacts in Business Contact Manager to open the Business Contact Manager folder.

3. Double-click a business contact to open it, as shown in Figure 35-25.

4. Click Add on the Business Contact form, as shown in Figure 35-26.

5. Select an item, such as Business Note, Mail Message, Opportunity, Task, Appointment, Phone Log, and File.

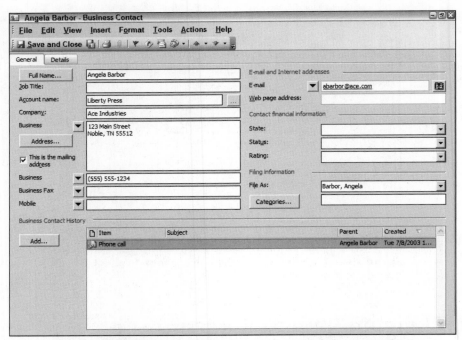

Figure 35-25: An example of a contact opened in Business Contact Manager.

Figure 35-26: Select a Business Contact Manager item to link to a business contact.

6. Enter information about the item you selected, such as filling in information about an opportunity you want to link to a contact, as shown in Figure 35-27. Click Save and Close when finished and to return to the business contact form.

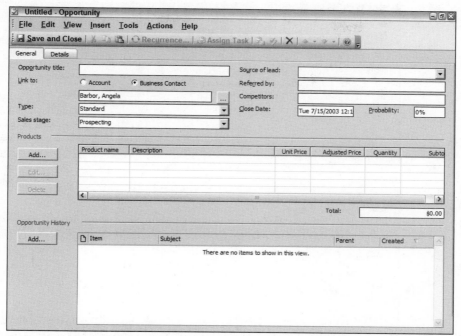

Figure 35-27: Enter information about the item you want to link to a Business Contact record.

7. When finished with the contact form, click Save and Close.

Linking an item to an Account record

Use the following steps to link an item to an Account record:

1. Click Contacts on the Outlook bar.

2. Click Accounts in Business Contact Manager.

3. Double-click the account you want to open, as shown in Figure 35-28.

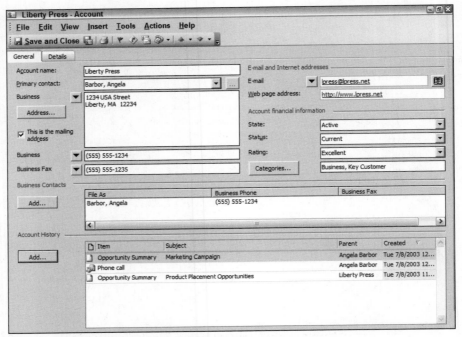

Figure 35-28: You can link business items to Accounts.

4. Click Add on the Account form.

5. Select an item, such as Business Note, Mail Message, Opportunity, Task, Appointment, Phone Log, and File.

6. Enter information about the item you selected and click Save and Close to return to the Account form.

7. When finished filling out the Account information, click Save and Close.

Linking an item to an Opportunity record

Use the following steps to link an item to an Opportunity record:

1. Click Tasks on the Outlook Bar to open the Tasks folder.

2. Click Opportunities in Business Contact Manager.

3. Double-click the opportunity you want to open, as shown in Figure 35-29.

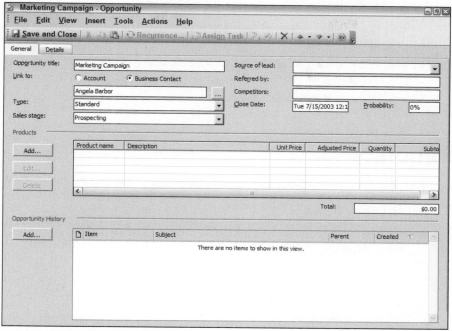

Figure 35-29: Open an opportunity.

4. Click Add on the Opportunity form.

5. Select an item, such as Business Note, Task, Appointment, Phone Log, or File.

6. Enter information about the item you selected. Click Save and Close when finished and to return to the Opportunity form..

7. When finished editing the Opportunity form, click Save and Close.

Working with Other Office 2003 Applications

The Business Contact Manager is designed to work as a stand-alone add-on to Outlook 2003, or to integrate with other Microsoft Office applications. The following are some Business Contact Manager tasks you can do with other Office programs, such as:

✦ Link Office System documents to your contacts so you can quickly and easily locate them

✦ Export reports on your customers and sales opportunities into Excel and Word

✦ Use Business Contact Manager to open and view Office

✦ Create business-related newsletters using Word and Microsoft Publisher 2003 templates

✦ Send personalized professional-looking e-mail messages and newsletters to your mailing lists and Mail Merge tasks

✦ Sort and organize business contacts the way you like

Summary

The Business Contact Manager is an Outlook add-on designed to work with small businesses. You can track and create reports pertaining to your customers and opportunities. Business Contact Manager can also be used with other Microsoft Office applications to let businesses integrate data from Outlook with other Office data. In the next chapter you find out how Microsoft Exchange Server can be optimized for Outlook users.

✦   ✦   ✦

Using Outlook Web Access

✦ ✦ ✦ ✦

In This Chapter

What is Outlook
Web Access?

Preparing To Use
Outlook Web Access

Using Outlook Web
Access

Logging off Outlook
Web Access

✦ ✦ ✦ ✦

Microsoft Exchange Server includes a feature that
enables users to access their Outlook folders from
a remote location using Microsoft Internet Explorer Web
browser. E-mail users can download, read, and reply to e-mail
messages, manage their folders, and perform several other
Outlook-related tasks from a remote location. This feature is
called Microsoft Outlook Web Access and is available only if
your organization has Microsoft Exchange Server 5.0 or
greater running as a mail server. This chapter shows how to
use Outlook Web Access to access Outlook resources from a
remote location.

What is Outlook Web Access?

It's almost impossible not to find a place to hook into the
Internet today. Many homes, businesses, and hotels have
access to the Internet. In fact, McDonald's is starting to offer
wireless (Wi-Fi) connections from within their restaurants.
With this capability users can access Web pages, FTP folders,
and Web-based e-mail. If you are part of an organization or
work for a business that uses Microsoft Exchange Server as
your e-mail server and Microsoft Outlook as your standard
e-mail client, you can use a feature introduced in Exchange 5.0
Server called Outlook Web Access, or OWA for short.

OWA is a Web-based e-mail service. An example of the interface is shown in Figure 36-1. With OWA you can use any
Internet connection and Microsoft Internet Explorer to access
your mail. This is similar to many Internet Service Providers
(such as MyVine.com), Internet portals (such as Yahoo!), and
Web sites that provide e-mail services via the Web.

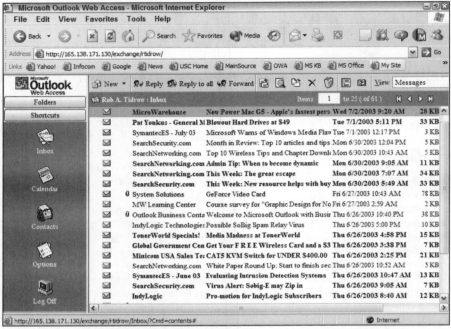

Figure 36-1: You can use Outlook Web Access to send and receive e-mail from your Microsoft Outlook folders.

Preparing To Use Outlook Web Access

To use Outlook Web Access you must have the following set up on your remote system (for example, your home computer):

✦ A connection to the Internet, such as a dial-up connection with a modem or a direct connection using a cable or DSL modem.

✦ Microsoft Internet Explorer 5.5 or higher. To determine if you have 5.5 or higher, start Internet Explorer, choose the Help menu, and click About Internet Explorer. The About Internet Explorer window opens, in which the version number appears. If your version is 5.0 or lower, visit www.microsoft.com/ie to download a more current version.

✦ A valid username and password for your company's or organization's e-mail server.

✦ Microsoft Exchange Server 5.5 or higher.

✦ Your organization's Uniform Resource Location (URL) or Internet Protocol (IP) address for the Exchange Server server. Ask your e-mail administrator for this address.

✦ Your organization's domain name. This is usually different than the Internet domain name your company uses. Again, contact your e-mail administrator for this address.

The speed at which you connect to the Internet determines how quickly you can log in and access your Outlook information. For example, if you have a dial-up connection to the Internet, your connection and download times will be fairly slow. Connecting with a cable modem, ISDN, or DSL solution, however, will greatly increase your download speeds.

Using Outlook Web Access

Connecting to your Outlook information is easy. Although the steps shown here are the basics, your organization may have different ones if your organization has modified connection settings, added runtime scripts, and so forth. Contact your e-mail administrator if these steps do not work for you.

 Note The screen shots of Outlook Web Access shown in this chapter use the most recent version of Exchange, Exchange 2000 Server, SP 2. If your organization uses a different version of Exchange, your displays may look different.

If you meet the preceding setup criteria, perform the following steps to access your Outlook folders from a remote location using Outlook Web Access:

1. Connect to the Internet.

2. Start Internet Explorer.

3. In the Address box, type the URL or IP address of your organization's e-mail server. A URL is similar to `www.mycompany.com`. An IP address looks like `http://123.456.789.123`.

4. In the Address box at the end of the URL or IP address, type **/exchange** to indicate you want to connect to your Exchange Server server.

5. After /exchange, enter your valid network username in the form of /your_user_name. `http://123.456.789.123/exchange/john_doe` is an example of what the final address may look like (see Figure 36-2).

Figure 36-2: Type the URL or IP address of your Microsoft Exchange Server server.

6. Press Enter. A login screen similar to the one shown in Figure 36-3 appears. Your screen may look different and be called something besides Enter Network Password depending on the version of Windows you are using. This screen is from a computer running Windows XP Professional.

7. In the login screen, fill in the following information:

- User Name. Type your authorized user name.

- Password. Type a valid password for the username supplied above.

- Domain. Type your organization's domain name.

8. Press Enter or click OK to log in and start downloading Outlook information to your computer.

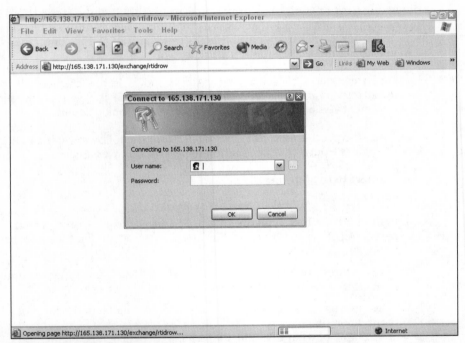

Figure 36-3: Use the login screen to log in to your OWA account.

Figure 36-4 shows an example of OWA information displayed in Internet Explorer.

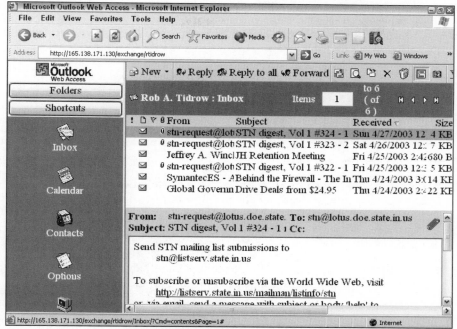

Figure 36-4: An example of e-mail message headers displayed in Outlook Web Access.

9. After the Microsoft Outlook Web Access window appears, you may need to click the Inbox link on the left side of the window to see your messages. Any new mail in your Inbox appears in boldface, similar to your regular Outlook Inbox.

Tip
You can access OWA even if you are logged in locally to your network. For example, if you are working at your office desk and you want to use OWA instead of Outlook to access your e-mail and other Outlook objects, replace the URL or IP address in the address box with your server's name. If your server's name is Nevada, for example, type **http://nevada/exchange/your_user_name** and press Enter.

Performing Outlook Tasks in OWA

Many of the same tasks you perform in Outlook can be performed using OWA. Some of these tasks include the following:

✦ Download, read, reply to, send, and delete e-mail messages

✦ View and manage your Calendar

✦ Create, view, and manage your Contacts

✦ Access Public folders

Many of these tasks are accomplished similarly to the way you do them inside Outlook; however, remember that you are actually viewing your Outlook content inside Internet Explorer, so you will not have access to Outlook's extensive menus and commands, or its toolbars.

The following sections show how to perform the basic tasks in OWA.

Using e-mail in OWA

After you log in to your Outlook account via OWA, you can view, create, or delete e-mail messages. To do so, follow these steps:

1. Click the Shortcuts button on the left side of the browser screen. This are is analogous to the Navigation Pane in Outlook, but it looks more similar to the previous versions of Outlook than Outlook 2003. Figure 36-5 shows this button.

2. Click the Inbox icon on the left side of the browser screen to see your Outlook Inbox.

3. To read an e-mail message, double-click the message in your Inbox to open the message inside its own message window, as shown in Figure 36-6.

4. Click the close button if you want to close the message. If you want to reply to the message, click the Reply button, type your reply text, and click the Send button. Figure 36-7 shows the window you use to create your reply message.

Figure 36-5: Click the Shortcuts button to see your Outlook icons.

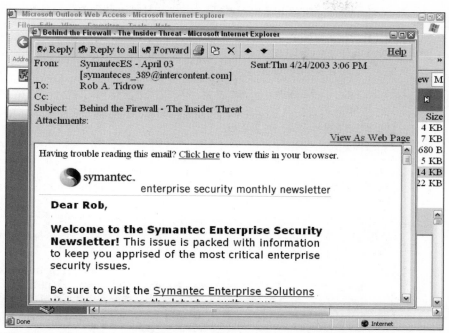

Figure 36-6: Read an e-mail message inside its own window using OWA.

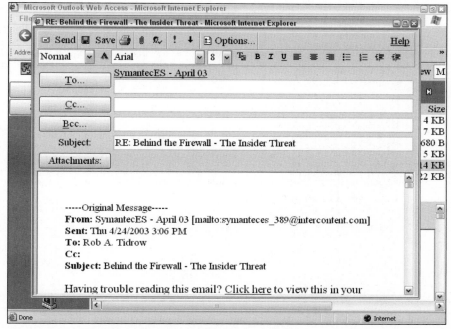

Figure 36-7: You can reply to messages using OWA.

To delete messages in your Inbox using OWA, do the following:

1. Inside the Inbox, click the message you want to delete.

2. Press the Delete button. Notice that the message is deleted immediately, the same way it would be deleted in Outlook.

3. To retrieve the deleted message, click the Folders button on the left side of the screen.

4. Click the Deleted Items folder.

5. Click the item to undelete.

6. Click the Recover Deleted Items button on the OWA toolbar, as shown in Figure 36-8.

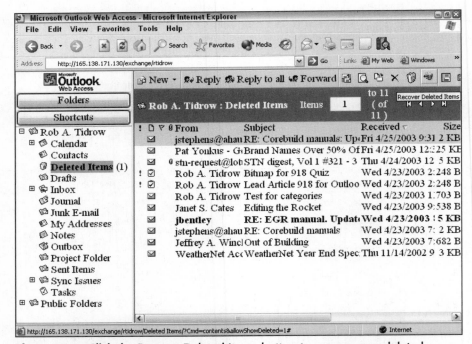

Figure 36-8: Click the Recover Deleted Items button to recover your deleted messages and other Outlook items.

To move e-mail messages to different folders, do the following:

1. Click the Folders icon on the left side of the OWA screen.

2. Click the Inbox or any other mail folder to expand any subfolders you may have listed under them.

3. Click the folder in which the message you want to move currently resides.

4. Drag the message to another folder.

To create a new e-mail message, do the following:

1. Click the Inbox icon or Inbox folder on the left side of the screen.

2. Click the New button on the OWA toolbar to display a blank e-mail window, as shown in Figure 36-9.

3. Fill in the To, Subject, and body text areas of the message.

4. Click the Send button to send your message.

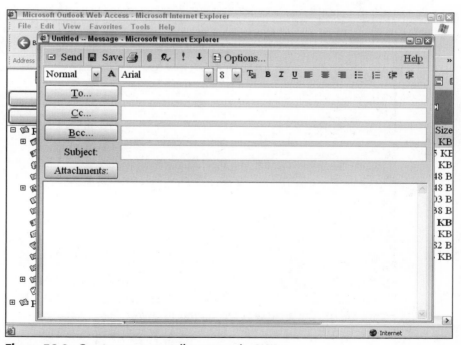

Figure 36-9: Create a new e-mail message in OWA.

Using the Outlook Calendar in OWA

Some of the same Calendar tasks you perform in Outlook can also be done in OWA, such as view your Outlook Calendar in daily, weekly, or monthly views. There are, however, several Calendar features not enabled in OWA. For example, you cannot customize views, see the TaskPad, or change the colors of your Calendar or Calendar items.

To create a new appointment in Calendar, do the following:

1. Click the Shortcuts button on the left side of the OWA screen.

2. Click the Calendar icon.

3. Double-click a time slot for the new appointment, or click the New button the OWA toolbar. This opens a blank appointment window as shown in Figure 36-10.

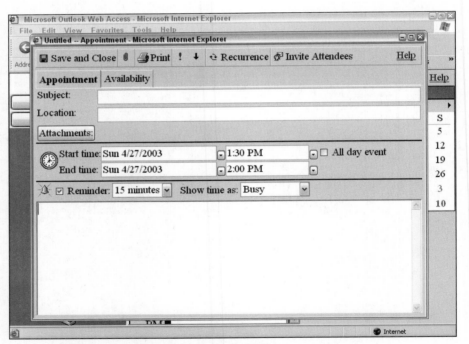

Figure 36-10: Create new appointments in OWA.

4. Enter your appointment information. You can set reminders, availability options, and duration of the appointment. To make the item an event, click the All day event option.

5. Click the Save and Close button.

To view a Calendar item in more detail, make sure the Calendar is showing. Then double-click an appointment, meeting, or event. The item displays in its own window.

OWA also enables you to set up or modify recurring events and meetings. To do this, follow these steps:

1. Create a new meeting or event, or open an existing meeting or event.

2. Click the Recurrence button to open the Recurrence pattern –Web Page Dialog dialog box, as shown in Figure 36-11.

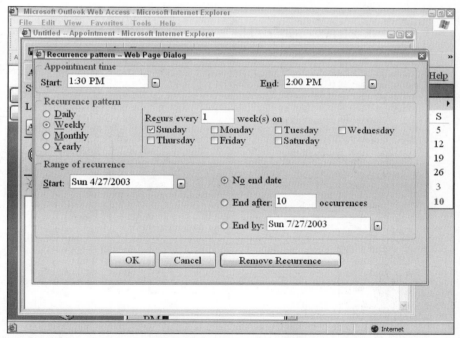

Figure 36-11: Set recurrence schedules using this dialog box.

3. Set or modify the recurrence schedule. If you want to remove the recurrence schedule for this item, click Remove Recurrence.

4. Click OK.

If you open an event or meeting that is part of a recurrence schedule, you are prompted to open only the single event or meeting, or to open the entire recurrence schedule. At this time, you must decide what to do. For example, to modify the time of just one instance of a recurring meeting (the meeting time for that particular event has changed for one week), select Open this occurrence and then click OK; otherwise, select Open the series to edit the entire series schedule.

To display different views of your calendar, click Switch to Daily View (shown as the **1** toolbar button), as shown in Figure 36-12.

You can also switch to Weekly view, as seen in Figure 36-13, by clicking Switch to Weekly View, (shown as the **7** toolbar button).

Another option is to display your Calendar in Monthly view by clicking Switch to Monthly View (shown as the **31** toolbar button), as seen in Figure 36-14.

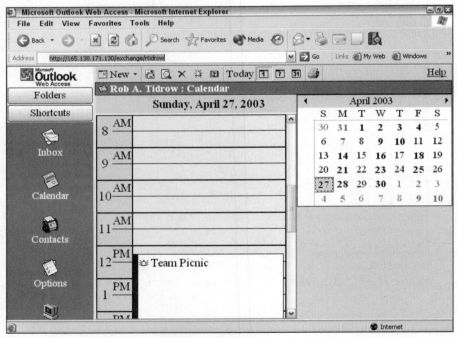

Figure 36-12: Display your calendar in Daily view.

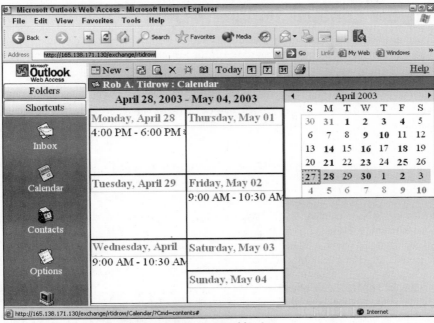

Figure 36-13: Display your calendar in Weekly view.

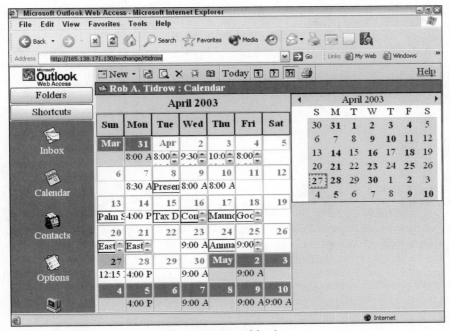

Figure 36-14: Display your calendar in Monthly view.

Using the Contacts feature in OWA

You can view, manage, and create contacts while using OWA. To see your default Contacts folder, click the Contacts icon under Shortcuts on the left side of the OWA screen.

To open a contact, double-click the contact. The contact opens in a window showing the details of the contact. You can edit, view, or print the contact from this window. You can also create a new e-mail message directly from a contact's open address card.

The following shows how to create a new contact in OWA:

1. Click the Contacts icon on the left side of the OWA screen.

2. Click the New button on the OWA toolbar to open a blank new contact card, as shown in Figure 36-15.

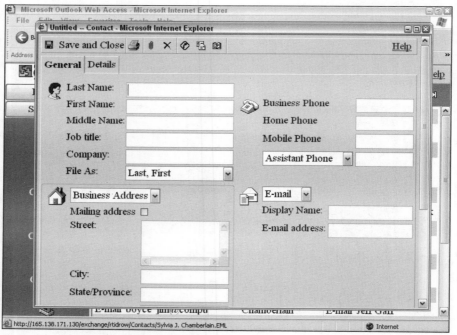

Figure 36-15: Create a new contact with the OWA.

3. Fill out the contact card with you contact's information.

4. Click Save and Close to save the contact to your Contacts folder.

To create a message from a contact, do the following:

1. Double-click a contact in your Contacts folder to display the details of your contact.

2. Click the Send mail to contact button on the Contact Card toolbar to display a new message window with the contact person's e-mail address added to the To: line, as shown in Figure 36-16.

3. Fill out the Subject and message body areas.

4. Click the Send button to send your message.

5. If you no longer need the contact card open, click the Close button.

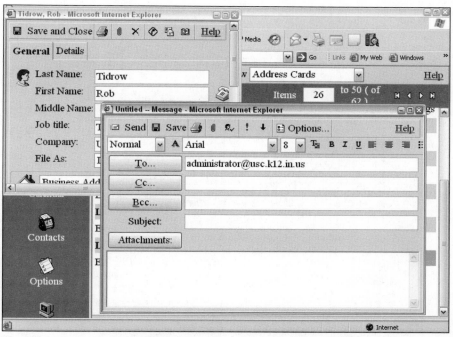

Figure 36-16: You can send a message to a selected contact in OWA.

OWA also lets you perform basic management tasks with your contacts. The following list shows how:

✦ To delete a contact, select the contact and press Delete.

✦ To move a contact to a different contact folder, display your contacts and select one; then drag and drop it to a different folder.

✦ To edit a contact listing, double-click the contact, make your edits, and click Save and Close.

Working with reminders in OWA

When accessing Outlook content using OWA, you will receive reminders — audio and visual — similar to when working in Outlook. If you set a reminder for a meeting when working in Outlook, for example, the reminder displays at its scheduled time, whether you are working in OWA or Outlook at the time the reminder goes off.

When a reminder displays, as shown in Figure 36-17, do one of the following:

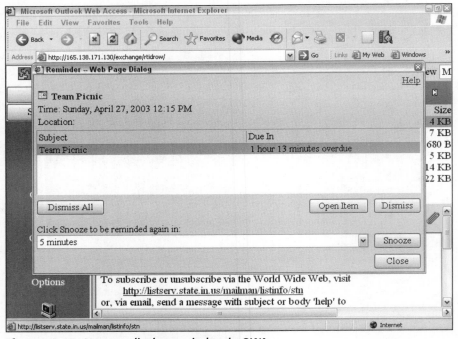

Figure 36-17: You can display reminders in OWA.

✦ Click the Snooze button to shut off the reminder for five minutes, which is the default snooze time. To shut it off for a longer interval, click the down arrow on the Click Snooze to be reminded in drop-down list, and select a different time; then click Snooze.

✦ Click Close to close the reminder.

✦ Click Dismiss to turn off the reminder.

✦ Click Dismiss All if more than one reminder displays and you want to turn all of them off.

✦ Click Open Item to open the selected reminder item. You can view or modify the contents of the item. Click Save and Close to save your settings.

Working with Public Folders

OWA enables you to work with Public Folders set up on your Exchange Server network. Public Folders are folders available to all users of your Exchange network. To open a Public Folder in OWA, do the following:

1. Click the Folders button on the left side of the OWA screen.

2. Click the plus sign (+) next to Public Folders in your folders list. This expands the list of Public Folders available in your organization.

3. Click the name of the Public Folder you want to view. The contents of the folder displays in the OWA window, as shown in Figure 36-18.

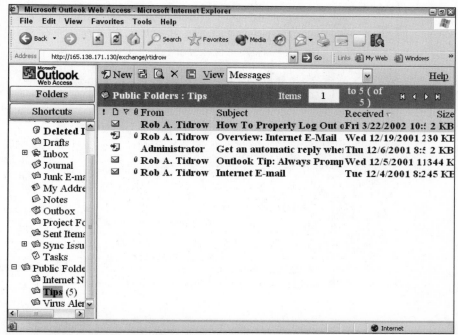

Figure 36-18: You can view the contents of your organization's public folders in OWA.

To post a new message to a public folder, do the following:

1. Open a public folder.

2. Click the New button on the OWA toolbar.

3. Fill out the new, blank message window.

4. Click the Post button.

Managing OWA

OWA includes an Options button that allows you to change some of the OWA configurations. To change OWA settings, do the following:

1. Click the Shortcuts button on the left side of the OWA window.

2. Click the Options button to display the OWA Options window, as shown in Figure 36-19.

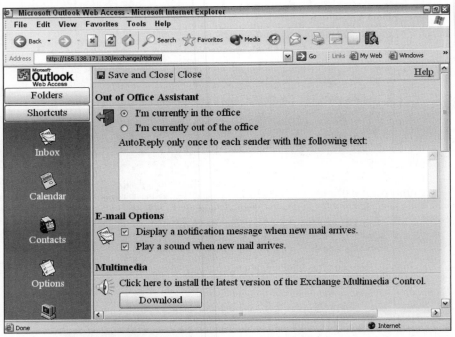

Figure 36-19: Modify your OWA settings using this window.

3. The following lists the items you can modify on this screen:

Out of Office Assistant: You can use this setting when you are out of the office and include a message stating you're gone that is sent automatically to users who send you messages.

E-Mail Options: You can set OWA to notify you when a new message arrives. You can also have OWA play a sound when a message arrives.

Multimedia: To install Exchange Multimedia Control, click the Download button.

Date and Time Formats: Set your date and time styles here. You can also change your time zone setting, if necessary.

Calendar Options: Set the way you want OWA to display your work week, what time your work day begins and ends, and how you want your first week of the year to display.

Reminder Options: Set if reminders should display for Calendar items and if reminders should play a sound.

Contact Options: When sending messages, you can set OWA to check names against the Global Address List or the Contacts folder.

Password: Click the Change Password button to change your login password.

Recover Deleted Items: Click View Items to view and recover your deleted items.

Logging Off OWA

When you are ready to close down Outlook Web Access, you must log off correctly. If you do not, the next person using the computer can read, delete, and send messages as if they were you using Outlook Web Access. This is important if you are using a computer other than your own personal computer, such as a friend's computer, public library computer, hotel computer, and so on.

To log off OWA, do the following:

1. Click the Folders button on the left side of the OWA screen.

2. Click the Log Off button to display the Microsoft Outlook Web Access Logoff window, as shown in Figure 36-20.

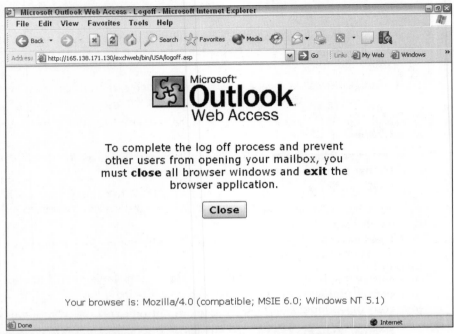

Figure 36-20: Use the Logoff window to completely log off from OWA.

3. Click Close to display a message asking if it's OK to close the Internet Explorer window.

4. Click Yes to complete your logoff process.

Summary

This chapter showed how you can access your messaging information if you are away from the office and your company uses Microsoft Exchange Server 5.5 or above to store Outlook data. You learned how to use an Internet connection and Internet Explorer to use Outlook Web Access to view, create, edit, and manage your Outlook e-mail, Calendar items, and Contacts.

In the next chapter, you learn ways that Exchange administrators can manage and optimize the organization's Microsoft Exchange 2000 Server.

✦   ✦   ✦

Optimizing Outlook Installations

In This Chapter

Improving Outlook performance

Securing Outlook

In many cases, Microsoft Outlook runs fine once it is configured for your messaging service (such as Microsoft Exchange Server). There are, however, some ways you can optimize your Outlook installation to make the most of it. This chapter focuses on performance issues that involve setting your connection type, reviewing and optimizing rules, and compacting offline folder files. You also learn how to secure your copy of Outlook on your desktop.

Improving Outlook Performance

One of the quickest ways to increase your Outlook performance is to increase your connection speed to the network on which you receive messages. For example, if you use Outlook to access your corporate e-mail, public folders, and so on, your company network backbone should have enough bandwidth to handle your requests and those of other users on the network. Users who access e-mail through a dial-up connection should consider upgrading to a faster connection, such as a DSL or cable modem.

Another factor to consider when improving Outlook performance is *latency.* This is the amount of time a request, such as sending a message from your computer to another, takes to be processed by the network and network server(s). Latency issues are paramount to any network administrator responsible for e-mail, Internet connections, file server requests, and other network traffic. If your company's Exchange Server is overwhelmed by requests, you may find it can take longer and longer to log on to Outlook and receive your new messages.

Without proper maintenance on the server and client (Outlook) — that is, removing old messages, disabling inactive users, compacting messages, and so on — you may grow frustrated just trying to access your Outlook information.

Work offline

There are several ways to improve your performance when faced with speed problems. The first is to work offline when your connection speeds are limited. To do this, choose File ⇨ Work Offline as shown in Figure 37-1.

You now can read messages downloaded to your Inbox or other mail folders, create new messages, or manage your messages. You also can work in other Outlook folders, such as Calendar, Contacts, Tasks, Journal, and so on, while offline. Although you must go online to send and receive any new messages, you have better control when you want Outlook to access the network.

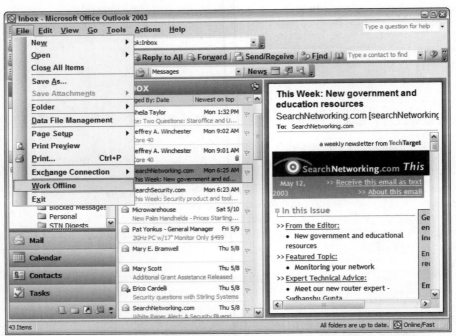

Figure 37-1: Choose to work offline if your network connection is slow.

Prompt for connection type

Your Outlook profile can be configured to ask which connection type — online or offline — Outlook should use at startup. This option is handy for users with laptop systems because they usually change connection types frequently. For example, a laptop user may connect to the Exchange Server via a local area network while in the company office, but connect with a dial-up option while on the road or at home. By enabling this option, you can choose at logon time which connection type is best to give you flexibility with your Outlook installation.

Users who are not mobile can also benefit from selecting connection settings at startup. This is especially true if the connection to your Exchange Server or Internet mail is slow, or if your primary e-mail server has a tendency to be down a lot. You can choose to go offline during those times you know the server is not functioning, and still get other work done while offline.

To set Outlook to prompt you for a connection, do the following:

1. Choose Tools ⇨ E-Mail Accounts to open the E-Mail Accounts Wizard as shown in Figure 37-2.

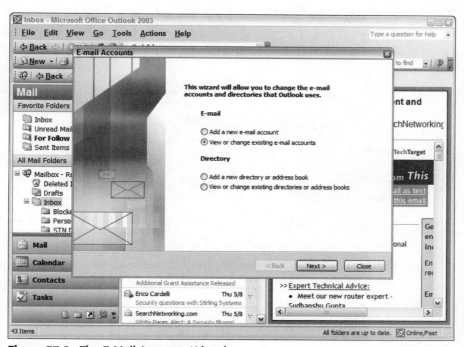

Figure 37-2: The E-Mail Accounts Wizard.

2. Select View or change existing e-mail accounts.

3. Click Next to display the second page of the wizard, as shown in Figure 37-3.

4. Select your Exchange Server account by clicking the Change button to display the next E-Mail Account Wizard page with Exchange Server settings available.

5. Click the More Settings button to display the Microsoft Exchange Server dialog box, as shown in Figure 37-4.

6. Select Manually control connection type when starting.

7. Click OK.

8. Click Next.

9. Click Finish.

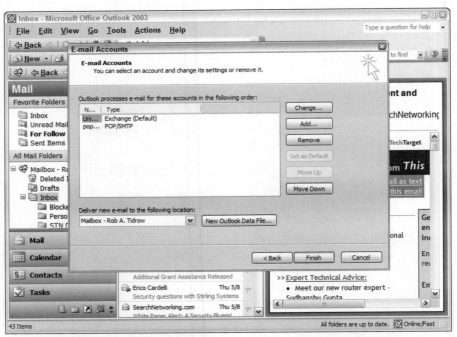

Figure 37-3: You can choose the e-mail account you want to modify here.

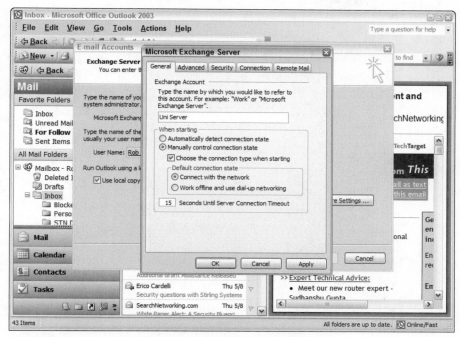

Figure 37-4: Set your logon connection type settings here.

Now shut down and restart Outlook. Upon restarting, Outlook displays a message asking which connection type you want to use. Click Offline to work offline, or click Connect to connect to your network connection.

Optimize rules

Another way to squeeze the most out of Outlook is to optimize Outlook rules. This may mean editing each rule you've created to get the most out of them, or simply creating new ones to handle your incoming and outgoing messages better. To see your rules, do the following:

1. Choose Tools ➪ Rules and Alerts to display the Rules and Alerts dialog box as shown in Figure 37-5.

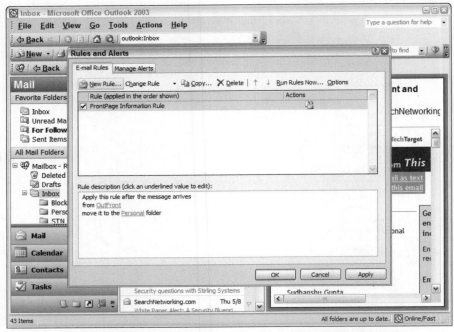

Figure 37-5: Make sure your rules are optimized to get the most out of them.

2. Select a rule.

3. Select Edit Rule Settings from the Change Rule drop-down list.

4. From the Rules Wizard dialog box, as shown in Figure 37-6, make changes to your rule as necessary.

5. Click Finish to save your changes.

6. Click OK.

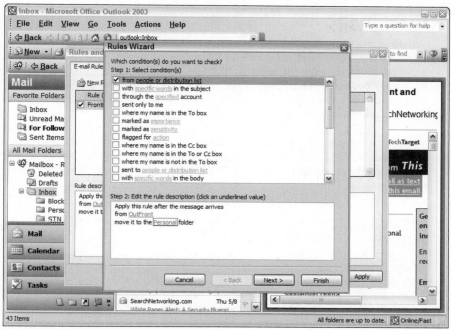

Figure 37-6: The Rules Wizard dialog box.

Some of the changes you might want to make include the following:

✦ Click the Stop processing more rules action at the end of the list of actions for that rule. This way all your rules will not run on a particular message that has already been processed. For example, if you have a rule that sends a message to a Product Info folder, your other rules will continue to run on that message, slowing down your subsequent downloads.

✦ Delete any unnecessary rules. For each rule that runs, Outlook slows down.

✦ If accessing remotely, create rules that move unimportant messages from the Inbox to another client-based folder. This lessens the load put on your Inbox and how much data needs to be downloaded when you access your Inbox.

✦ Reconsider the necessity of the junk mail rule. Because it sits on the client (your computer), the downloading of messages is slowed down when the junk mail rule is used.

Disable the Reading pane

The Reading pane is a great part of Outlook, but it consumes resources and requires that the entire message be downloaded before you can preview it. When working online over a connection that is slow, such as a modem connection or busy Exchange Server network, turn off the Reading pane. To do this, choose View ➪ Reading Pane ➪ Off. Figure 37-7 shows the Reading pane on the right side of the Outlook window before turning it off.

If you want to preview part of your message, use AutoPreview. This view requires only the first 254 bytes of any e-mail be downloaded. Choose View ➪ AutoPreview to turn it on, as shown in Figure 37-8. See Chapter 5 for more information on previewing messages.

Figure 37-7: Turn off the Reading pane to increase performance over a slow connection.

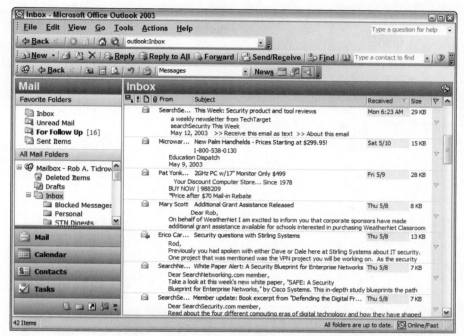

Figure 37-8: Use AutoPreview instead of the Reading pane if you really need to preview your messages.

Compact Your OST file

Over time, your OST file continues to get larger, even if you delete files from it. You should optimize your Offline Folder file occasionally, particularly if you recently deleted a large quantity of messages from it. Do this by compacting the OST file. When you delete an item from Outlook, items still on the server are not deleted; just those on your client. Use the following procedure:

1. Choose Tools ➪ E-Mail Accounts.

2. Click View or change existing e-mail accounts.

3. Click Next.

4. Select your Microsoft Exchange Server account.

5. Click Change.

6. Click More Settings.

7. Click the Advanced tab, as shown in Figure 37-9.

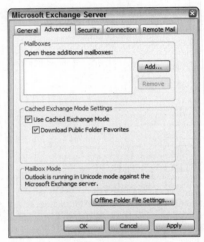

Figure 37-9: The Advanced tab

8. Click Offline Folder File Settings to display the Offline Folder File Settings dialog box, as shown in Figure 37-10.

9. Click Compact Now.

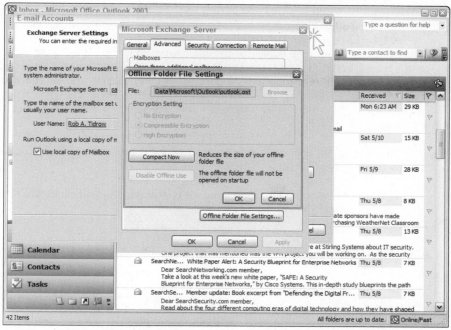

Figure 37-10: Compact your OST file here.

Securing Outlook

If you are like most business and casual users, the information you store in Outlook is not highly sensitive government data; however, most businesses and organizations require some type of procedure to guard against private confidential information leaking out into the public. This might include internal corporate announcements sent via e-mail, profit and loss data, client contact information, and so on. In some cases, calendar information and schedules include sensitive information (not all CEOs, for example, want the public or competitors to know their whereabouts at all times) that the general public or internal staff should not be privy to.

Outlook on a corporate network might use Microsoft Exchange Server. In this case, a username and password authentication is required to access the server. Usually, you enter your login credentials when you initially log on to a Windows domain. In this case, your login information is already submitted when you start Outlook.

If you want to add a layer of protection to Outlook, consider using a password-protected screen saver on your desktop. This stops users from entering your office or desk area and easily gaining access to your Outlook information. To set this, right-click the Windows desktop, choose Properties, click the Screen Saver tab, and select a screen saver. Click the Password Protect option, and set a time interval to activate. The screen saver displays after your system is idle for the allotted time. Press Ctrl+Alt+Delete, or move the mouse pointer or press a key to display the login screen, where you type your username and password to regain entrance to your desktop.

Another way to secure Outlook is to password-protect your PST file. To do this, follow these steps:

1. Choose File ⇨ Data File Management to display the Outlook Data Files dialog box, as shown in Figure 37-11.

2. Select the file you want to protect.

3. Click Settings to display the Personal Folders dialog box, as shown in Figure 37-12.

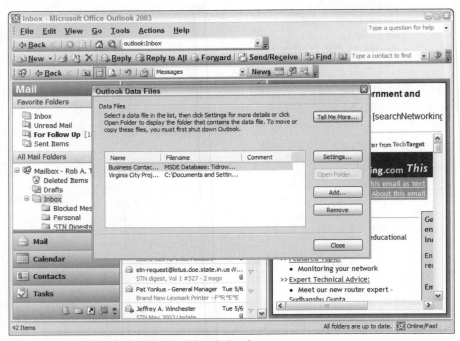

Figure 37-11: The Outlook Data Files dialog box

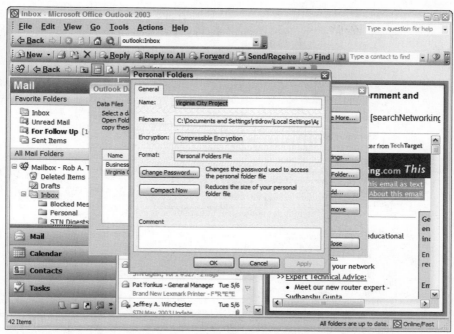

Figure 37-12: The Personal Folders dialog box

4. Click Change Password to display the Change Password dialog box, as shown in Figure 37-13.

5. Fill in the Old password box with your old password, or leave blank if you did not have a password.

6. Fill in the New password and Verify password boxes with your new password.

7. Click OK twice and then click Close.

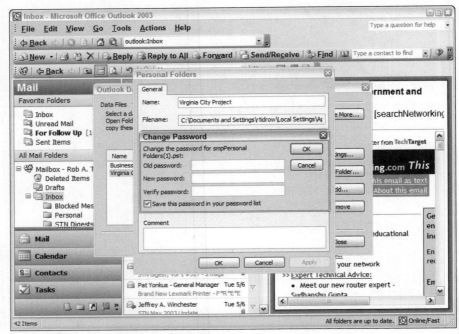

Figure 37-13: Set a password to protect your PST file.

Summary

The performance of your Outlook client is often dependent on the computer where Outlook resides, the connection you have to your e-mail and network, and the speed of your e-mail server. There are settings you can adjust in your Outlook client to get the most from it. This chapter showed you ways you can optimize and secure your installation of Outlook 2003.

✦   ✦   ✦

What's on the CD-ROM

This appendix provides you with information on the contents of the CD that accompanies this book. For the latest and greatest information, refer to the ReadMe file located at the root of the CD.

This appendix provides information on the following topics:

+ System Requirements
+ Using the CD
+ Files and software on the CD
+ Troubleshooting

System Requirements

Make sure that your computer meets the minimum system requirements listed in this section. If your computer doesn't meet most of these requirements, you may have a problem using the contents of the CD.

For Windows 9x, Me, XP, Windows 2000, Windows NT4 (with SP 4 or later):

+ PC with a Pentium processor running at 120 Mhz or faster
+ At least 32MB of total RAM installed on your computer; for best performance, we recommend at least 64MB
+ Ethernet network interface card (NIC) or modem with a speed of at least 28,800 bps
+ A CD-ROM drive

Office 2003 Specific Requirements:

+ PC with Pentium 133 MHz or higher processor; Pentium III recommended
+ Microsoft Windows 2000 with Service Pack 3 or Windows XP or later operating system
+ Minimum of 245MB of hard disk space
+ Minimum of 64MB RAM (128MB RAM Recommended)

Using the CD

To install the items from the CD to your hard drive, follow these steps:

1. Insert the CD into your computer's CD-ROM drive.

2. A window appears displaying the License Agreement. Press Accept to continue. Another window appears with the following buttons (which are explained in greater detail in the next section):

Outlook 2003 Bible: Click this button to view an eBook version of the book as well as any author-created content specific to the book, such as templates and sample files.

Super Bible: Click this button to view an electronic version of the *Office 2003 Super Bible*, along with any author-created materials from the Super Bible, such as templates and sample files.

Bonus Software: Click this button to view the list and install the supplied third-party software.

Related Links: Click this button to open a hyperlinked page of Web sites.

Other Resources: Click this button to access other Office-related products that you might find useful.

Files and Software on the CD

The following sections provide a summary of the software and other materials available on the CD.

eBook version of *Outlook 2003 Bible*

The complete text of the book you hold in your hands is provided on the CD in Adobe's Portable Document Format (PDF). You can read and quickly search the content of this PDF file by using Adobe's Acrobat Reader, also included on the CD.

eBook version of the *Office 2003 Super Bible*

The *Super Bible* is an eBook PDF file made up of select chapters pulled from the individual Office 2003 *Bible* titles. This eBook also includes some original and exclusive content found only in this *Super Bible*. The products that make up the Microsoft Office 2003 suite have been created to work hand-in-hand. Consequently, Wiley has created this *Super Bible* to help you master some of the most common features of each of the component products and to learn about some of their interoperability features as well. This *Super Bible* consists of over 500 pages of content to showcase how Microsoft Office 2003 components work together.

Bonus software

The CD contains software distributed in various forms: shareware, freeware, GNU software, trials, demos, and evaluation versions. The following list explains how these software versions differ:

✦ **Shareware programs:** Fully functional, trial versions of copyrighted programs. If you enjoy particular programs, you can register with their authors for a nominal fee and receive licenses, enhanced versions, and technical support.

✦ **Freeware programs:** Copyrighted games, applications, and utilities that are free for personal use. Unlike shareware, these programs do not require a fee or provide technical support.

✦ **GNU software:** Software governed by its own license, which is included inside the folder of the GNU product. See the GNU license for more details.

✦ **Trial, demo, or evaluation versions:** Software usually limited either by time or functionality, such as not permitting you to save projects. Some trial versions are very sensitive to system date changes. If you alter your computer's date, the programs may "time out" and will no longer be functional.

Highlights of Outlook 2003 software included on the CD

Here are descriptions of just a few of the programs available on the CD:

✦ *NewsGator v1.0*: From Reinacker & Associates, Inc., is a news aggregator that runs in Outlook 2003. NewsGator pulls news, weblogs, and other information from Web sites and news feeds and displays them right in Outlook.

✦ *ExLife v1.53*: From Ornic USA LLC, extends Outlook's rules to provide enhanced message processing, including additional conditions and actions for rules, support for virtual folders, and filters.

✦ **Fax4Outlook:** From 4Team Corporation, adds a key missing ingredient to Outlook 2003 — integration with the Windows Fax service. Fax4Outlook helps you quickly and easily send and organize faxes, receive incoming faxes to your Outlook Inbox, and store outgoing faxes in the Sent Items folder. Fax4Outlook lets you handle faxes in the same way you handle e-mail.

Comprehensive list of software on the CD

The following is a list of all the products available on the CD. For more information and a description of each product, see the ReadMe or Trial Software sections of the CD.

3D Charts for Excel	Acc Compact	AccessBooks
Access Form Resizer	Access Image Albums	Access Property Editor
Access to VB Object Converter	AccessViewer	ACDSee
Acrobat Reader	ActiveConverter Component	Advanced Disk Catalog
Advanced Office Password Recovery	All-in-1 Personal Organizer	Analyse-It
Attach for Outlook	Attachment Options	AutoSpell for Microsoft Office
BadBlue Prsnl Ed	Barcode ActiveX Control & DLL	BlackICE PC Protection
Business Card Creator	c:JAM	CaBook
Camtasia Studio	Capture Express	CD Case & Label Creator
CD Player	Change Management System	Charset Decoding
Classify for Outlook with VBA	ClipMate	Code 128 Fonts demo
Code Critter	Collage Complete	Colored Toolbar Icons
COM Explorer	CompareDataWiz 2002	CompareWiz 2002
CONTACT Sage	Crossword Compiler	CSE HTML Validator
CSE HTML Validator Pro	Data Analysis	Database Browser Plus
Database Password Sniffer	DataDict	Datahouse
DataMoxie	DataWiz 2002	Debt Anaylzer
DeskTop.VBA	Dialgo Personal Call Center App	DinkIT Listbar AX
Document Management	Dubit	El Scripto
Eliminate Spam!	eNavigator Suite	Excel Import Assistant
Excel Link	ExLife	ExSign
EZDetach	Fax4Outlook	FileBox eXtender

Filter Builder	Fort Knox	Fundraising Mentor
Gantt Chart Builder (Access)	Gantt Chart Builder (Excel)	GFI MailSecurity for Exchange
GFI MailSecurity for SMTP	Gif Movie Gear	GraphicsButton
GuruNet	HiddenFileDetector_addin	HtmlIndex
HyperCam	HyperSnap-DX	IdiomaX Office Translator
IP*Works! ASP Edition	IP*Works! WebMail	IT Commander
JustAddCommerce	Keyboard Express	Lark
LiveMath Maker and LiveMath Plug-in	Macro Express	Macro Magic
Mail Administrator	Maillist Deluxe	MailWasher Pro
Math Easy for Excel	Mathematical Summary Utility	Mdb2txt
Milori Training Tools	Mouse Over Effects	MultiNetwork Manager
NewsGator	OfficeBalloonX	OfficeRecovery Enterprise
OutBooks	Outcome XP	OutlookConnect
OutlookSpy	PDF Plain Text Extractor	PERT Chart EXPERT
PlanMagic Business	PlanMagic Finance Pro	PlanMagic Marketing
PlanMagic WebQuest	PocketKnife	Polar Crypto Component
Polar Spellchecker Component	Polar Zip Component	Power Utility Pak
PowerPoint Backgrounds	PrintDirect Anywhere	PrintDirect Utility
PROMODAG StoreLog	Recover My Files	Registry Crawler
ReplaceWiz 2002	Responsive Time Logger	RFFlow
RnR PPTools Starter Set	Scan to Outlook	Schedule XP
Screen Capture	Secrets Keeper	SetClock
SetFileDate	ShortKeys	ShrinkerStretcher
SimpleRegistry Control	Smart Login	Smart Online templates
SmartBoardXP	SmartDraw	SnagIt
Soft Graphics Buttons	Splitter for Access	Spreadsheet Assistant
StoreBot 2002 Stnd Ed	Style Builder	Style XP
Summary Wizard	SuperFax	TelePort Pro
TeraPod File Transfer for Messenger	Toolbar Doubler	TPH Office Batch Printer
Turbo Browser	TX Text Control	UltraPdf

Continued

UnTools	VBAcodePrint	VBToolBox
WBS Chart Pro	WebCompiler	WebMerge
WebSpice Animation sampler	WebSpice Objects	WinACE
WinFax Pro Automator	WinRAR	WinZIP
Word Link	Wordware 2002	Wordware PIM
WordWeb	WorkgroupMail	WS_FTP Pro
WS_Ping Propack	X2Net WebCompiler	Xbooks
ZIP Disk Jewel Case and Label Creator	Zip Express	Zip Repair
ZipOut		

Related Links

Check out this page for links to all the third-party software vendors included on the CD, plus links to other vendors and resources that can help you work more productively with Office 2003.

Other Resources

This page provides you with some additional handy Office-related products.

ReadMe file

The ReadMe contains the complete descriptions of every piece of bonus software on the CD, as well as other important information about the CD.

Troubleshooting

If you have difficulty installing or using any of the materials on the companion CD, try the following solutions:

✦ **Turn off any anti-virus software that you may have running.** Installers sometimes mimic virus activity and can make your computer incorrectly believe that it is being infected by a virus. (Be sure to turn the anti-virus software back on later.)

✦ **Close all running programs.** The more programs you're running, the less memory is available to other programs. Installers also typically update files and programs; if you keep other programs running, installation may not work properly.

✦ **Reference the ReadMe:** Refer to the ReadMe file located at the root of the CD-ROM for the latest product information at the time of publication.

If you still have trouble with the CD, call the Wiley Product Technical Support phone number: (800) 762-2974. Outside the United States, call (317) 572-3994. You can also contact Technical Support on our website at www.wiley.com/techsupport. Wiley Publishing, Inc. provides technical support only for installation and other general quality control items; for technical support on the applications themselves, consult the program's vendor or author. To place additional orders or to request information about other Wiley product, please call (800) 225-5945 or visit www.wiley.com.

✦   ✦   ✦

Index

SYMBOLS AND NUMERICS

@ (at sign) in e-mail addresses, 117
> (greater-than symbol) as e-mail prefix, 107, 126–127
- (minus sign)
    by Calendar recurrence categories, 232
    by Journal types, 288
    by newsgroup messages, 349
101 Languages of the World software (Transparent Language), 133
128-bit encryption, 159
+ (plus sign)
    by Calendar recurrence categories, 232
    for Journal entry types, 9, 81
    by Journal types, 288
    by mouse pointer, 398
    by newsgroup messages, 349
/ (slash) in Setup switches, 50–53

A

/a Setup switch, 50
Access (Microsoft), databases and Outlook folders, 385
Account form (Business Contact Manager), 680–681
Account records (Business Contact Manager)
    adding a new account with Account form, 680–681
    adding business notes to record history, 694–696
    adding phone logs to record history, 696–697
    exporting accounts, 689–691
    importing an account, 682–684
    linking items to, 699–700
    viewing accounts, 684–685
Account window (Business Contact Manager), 685
Accounts folder (Business Contact Manager), 687
Actions menu
    Call Contact command, 219, 220
    Forward as vCard command, 146
    Junk E-mail submenu, 373, 497
    New Contact from Same Company command, 211
    New Mail Message command, 116
    New Mail Message Using submenu, 116, 132
        Microsoft Office submenu, 136, 138
        overriding default format, 116, 132
        Plain Text command, 132
    Recall This Message command, 157
    Resend This Message command, 78
    Send Web Page by E-mail command, 375
Actions page of forms, 627–629
activating a form page, 582–583

Active Appointments command (View menu), 232
Active Appointments view (Calendar), 232–233
Active Directory
    integration with Exchange Server, 534
    linking GPOs to container objects, 503
Active Directory Users and Computers snap-in
    adding a mailbox automatically, 534–535
    adding a mailbox manually, 536–537
    configuring mailbox-specific options, 541
    creating distribution groups, 550
    creating mail-enabled contacts, 547
    enabling IM for user accounts, 557
    modifying GPOs using, 504
    opening, 534
    reconnecting a deleted mailbox, 524–525
Active Directory Users and Groups console
    described, 43
    finding OU for group policies, 43
ActiveX controls and e-mail security, 175
Add a Group Policy Object Link dialog box, 49
Add a Site Group page (WSS), 451
Add Holidays to Calendar dialog box, 381
Add Users dialog box, 429, 553
Add/Remove Snap-In dialog box, 504, 505
Add/Remove Templates dialog box, 506, 507
Address Book Control component, 25
Address Book (Windows), 194, 209
addresses. *See also* Contacts list; e-mail addresses
    Contact form options, 199–200
    mailing address for contacts, 200
    viewing address maps, 218–219
administrative share, 31, 32
administrative templates
    adding for group policies, 506–508
    adding for system policies, 510–512
    overview, 505
administrator role (WSS), 443, 448
administrator site group (WSS), 446
Advanced E-mail Options dialog box, 108
Advanced Find command (Tools menu), 217
Advanced Find tool, 217–218
Advanced Options dialog box, 310–311, 361
Advanced Properties dialog box
    changing tab order of forms, 629–630
    for check boxes, 597–598
    for combo boxes, 598–599

Continued

Advanced Properties dialog box *(continued)*
    for image controls, 602
    for Label control, 592, 594
    for option buttons, 596–597
Advanced published or assigned option (Deploy
        Software dialog box), 44
aging period for folders, 526–527
alerts, setting for WSS documents, 456
aligning text
    RTF format for, 135
    signatures, 143
animating menus, 363
announcements (WSS), 457. *See also* lists (WSS)
Annual Events command (View menu), 233
Annual Events view (Calendar), 233–235
anonymous access (WSS), 449–450
application folders
    built-in module folders, 644–645
    defining permissions, 646
    discussion folders, 637–640
    managing properties, 645–647
    rules for applications, 647
    specifying a default form, 645–646
    tracking folders, 640–644
    using views, 647–652
Application Object Model, 667–668, 671
Apply News Rules Now dialog box, 346
Apply PRF option (Custom Installation Wizard), 40
applying newsgroup message rules, 346
Appointment dialog box, 318
Appointment form, 251–252
Appointment Recurrence dialog box, 261–262
appointments. *See also* Calendar; meetings
    Active Appointments view, 232–233
    adding to Calendar, 74
    changing date for, 254, 255
    changing time for, 252
    creating, 250–255
    creating using OWA, 712–713
    defined, 224, 249
    meetings versus, 249
    recurring appointments defined, 235
    Recurring Appointments view, 235
    reminders, 251–252
    specifying recurring activities, 261–262
Archive command (File menu), 526
archiving
    AutoArchive feature, 78, 515, 525–531
    automatic, for mail folders, 128
    deleting old messages from Sent Items folder, 78
    exporting versus, 530–531
    manually, 526

Arrange By submenu (View menu)
    Current View submenu, 63
        Active Appointments command, 232
        Annual Events command, 233
        By Category command, 236, 290, 314, 323
        By Color command, 315
        By Contact command, 289
        By Type command, 288
        customizing Calendar view, 74, 237
        customizing Contacts list view, 63
        customizing folders, 392
        customizing Last Seven Days Journal view, 293
        customizing versus defining views, 648–649
        defining Calendar views, 237
        Entry List command, 292
        Icons command, 311
        Last Seven Days command, 293, 313
        Notes List command, 311
        Phone Calls command, 294
        Recurring Appointments command, 235
        selecting Calendar view, 226
        Tasks list views, 267
        ...View With Autopreview commands, 231–232
    mail folder options, 64
Assigned option (Deploy Software dialog box), 44
assigning
    applications, 31
    categories to Outlook items, 320–322, 324–325
    delegates, 428–431
    GPO to other OUs and domains, 49
    home page for folder, 375–377
    tasks to people, 273–275
Assistant Object object model, 665–666
assistants. *See* delegating tasks
at sign (@) in e-mail addresses, 117
attachments to e-mail
    attaching files while composing messages, 149–150
    blocking for virus protection, 489–491
    checking size of, 149
    ease of sending, 4
    Insert File button for, 79
    Level 1 category files, 489–491
    Level 2 category files, 489, 491
    multiple files, 149
    overview, 148–149
    removing attachments while retaining messages,
        403–404
    saving messages as text files and, 425
    sending using Office, 150–152
    size limits, 148–149
    uncertainty of delivery, 132, 148–149
    UUENCODE format for, 110
    vCards, 145–146

authentication, 92, 95
Author permission for delegates, 428, 432–433, 437
AutoArchive dialog box, 527–528
AutoArchive feature
    archiving versus exporting, 530–531
    default aging period, 526
    deleting old messages automatically, 78
    enabling, 527–528
    excluding items from, 529–530
    overview, 515, 525–526
    schedule for running, 527, 530
AutoComplete nicknames, backing up, 521
Autodate feature, 253, 268
AutoDialer feature, 219–221
automated and unattended setup
    INI files for, 49–50
    Setup switches, 50–53
Automatic Formatting dialog box, 240–241, 652
Automatic Picture Download Settings dialog box, 499
automating tasks
    Outlook capabilities for, 15, 16
    profile creation with Custom Installation Wizard,
        468–470
    profile creation with Newprof.exe, 470–471
    responding to messages, 183–184
AutoPreview command (View menu), 730
AutoPreview view
    Calendar, 231–232
    e-mail, 730–731

B

backing up
    archiving versus exporting, 530–531
    certificates, 493–494
    Exchange mailbox data, 519–522
    importance of, 516
    other Outlook settings and data, 523–524
    Outlook settings files from Exchange Server, 521
    Personal Address Books, 520–521
    PST files, 515–518
    removable media for, 517
    rules for handling messages, 184–185
    signatures from Exchange Server, 521–522
    signatures from Word, 521
Bcc (blind carbon copy) text box (e-mail), 116–117
Bcc Field command (View menu), 117
.bcm files. See also Business Contact Manager
    exporting accounts, 689–691
    exporting contacts, 691
    importing accounts, 682–684
    importing contacts, 688–689
blind carbon copy (Bcc) text box (e-mail), 116–117

Block Sender command (Message menu), 347
Blocked Senders List command (Tools menu), 348
blocking
    adding blocked senders, 497–498
    external HTML content, 174, 498–499
    newsgroup senders, 347
    removing senders from blocked senders list, 348
    Web beacons to reduce spam, 20–21, 498–499
bold type
    for folders in Folder List, 59
    for unread messages in Inbox, 75, 124–125
break points, setting, 673–674
Browse for a Group Policy dialog box, 504–505
built-in module folders, 644–645
bullets
    RTF format for, 135
    for signatures, 143
business cards, electronic. See vCards
Business Contact form, 686–688
Business Contact Manager
    adding a new account with Account form, 680–681
    adding business notes to a record history, 694–696
    adding phone logs to a record history, 696–697
    Business Contact form, 686–688
    as CRM software, 677, 678
    Crystal Reports with, 692
    exporting accounts, 689–691
    exporting contacts, 691
    exporting Outlook information and, 422
    importing a business contact, 688–689
    importing an account, 682–684
    installing, 679–680
    linking an item to a Business Contact record,
        697–699
    linking an item to an Account record, 699–700
    linking an item to an Opportunity record, 700–701
    moving a contact from the Contacts folder, 688
    overview, 677–679
    tracking sales opportunities, 692–694
    uses for, 678
    viewing accounts, 684–685
    working with other Office applications, 701–702
Business Contact Manager Setup Wizard, 679
Business Contact records (Business Contact Manager)
    adding business notes to record history, 694–696
    adding phone logs to record history, 696–697
    Business Contact form for, 686–688
    exporting contacts, 691
    importing a contact, 688–689
    linking items to, 697–699
    moving a contact from the Contacts folder, 688

Business Data Import/Export Wizard
    exporting accounts, 689–691
    exporting contacts, 691
    importing a contact, 688–689
    importing an account, 682–684
Business Note form, 694–696
Business Phone Log form, 696–697
business solutions, 14
Button Bar (Navigation Pane), 70–71, 365–366
buttons. *See also* controls for forms
    adding or removing toolbar buttons, 61
    menus versus, 60
By Category command (View menu), 236, 290, 314, 323
By Category view
    assigning categories, 324–325
    Calendar, 236, 323–324
    Journal, 290–292
    Notes folder, 314
    overview, 323–325
    printing category items, 325–327
By Color command (View menu), 315
By Color view (Notes), 315
By Contact command (View menu), 289
By Contact view (Journal), 289–290
By Type command (View menu), 288
By Type view (Journal), 288–289

C

CA (Certificate Authority), 160–161
Cached Exchange Mode. *See* CEM
caching. *See also* CEM (Cached Exchange Mode)
    offline mailbox cache, 90–91
    passwords for POP3 or IMAP e-mail accounts, 95
Calendar. *See also* scheduling
    Active Appointments view, 232–233
    adding appointments, 74
    adding holidays, 381
    Annual Events view, 233–235
    Autodate feature, 253
    AutoPreview view, 231–232
    By Category view, 236, 323–324
    changing date displayed, 73–74
    colors for business and non-business hours, 228
    complexity of calculating dates, 223
    creating appointments, 250–255
    creating meetings, 255–261
    customizing views, 74, 229, 237–242
    Day view, 227–228
    default aging period, 526
    Events view, 233, 234
    filtering activities, 239–240
    folders, 387

    linking contact birthdays or anniversaries, 202
    managing another person's, 436–438
    Month view, 230–231
    multiple calendars, 22
    navigating views, 228, 229, 230
    new features in Outlook 2003, 22, 225
    offline access to information, 22
    Outlook Today folder link to, 67
    overview, 7–8
    in OWA, 712–715
    paper calendars versus, 224
    Private check box, 248
    recurrence categories, 232, 233
    Recurring Appointments view, 235
    reminders, 8
    saving as a Web page, 246–248
    selecting range of days displayed, 73
    selecting view to customize, 237–238
    selecting view to display, 61–62, 226–227
    sharing calendars, 225, 243–246
    sorting fields, 239
    specifying recurring activities, 261–262
    tasks and, 265
    terminology, 224
    turning off small calendar and TaskPad, 230
    uses for, 225
    using, 73–74
    viewing another user's, 433–435
    views in OWA, 714–715
    Week view, 229–230
    Work Week view, 228–229
Calendar Options command (Tools menu), 243, 244
Calendar Options dialog box, 381
Call Contact command (Actions menu), 219, 220
canceling. *See also* removing or deleting
    messages in Outbox, 76, 122
    recalling Exchanger Server messages, 77, 122–123
captions
    for frame buttons, 595
    for labels, 592, 593
carbon copy (Cc) text box (e-mail), 116
case-sensitivity, e-mail addresses and, 117
catalogs mail merge type, 412
categories
    adding new categories, 319
    assigning to Outlook items, 320–322, 324–325
    By Category view, 236, 290–292, 314, 323–327
    Calendar recurrence categories, 232, 233
    for contacts, 202
    creating in Journal, 291–292
    deleting, 322
    for distribution lists, 166

installing Outlook and, 46, 48
linking messages to, 124
Master Category List dialog box, 291, 318–319, 322–323
for Notes, 306–307
Organize feature, 368–369, 370
personalizing your list, 319
printing category items (Memo Style), 325–326
printing category items (Table Style), 326–327
resetting the Master Category List, 322–323
sharing using e-mail, 327–329
sharing using the Registry, 329–331
for tasks, 272
uses for, 317
Categories command (Edit menu), 320
Categories dialog box
adding categories, 319
assigning categories to Outlook items, 320–322
deleting categories, 322
Master Category List button, 318, 319
shared categories in, 329
sharing categories using e-mail, 327–329
specifying categories for Notes, 306–307
Cc (carbon copy) text box (e-mail), 116
CD with this book
eBooks included, 738–739
highlights of software included, 739–740
installing items, 738
list of software included, 740–742
Other Resources page, 742
Outlook Today page example, 576
ReadMe file, 742, 743
Related Links page, 742
system requirements, 737–738
troubleshooting, 742–743
types of software, 739
CEM (Cached Exchange Mode)
configuring e-mail accounts for, 154, 155
non-cached mode versus, 23–24
OST file location, 90–91
overview, 21, 23–24
status line information, 59
using, 154
Certificate Authority (CA), 160–161
Certificate Services, 160
certificates. See also digital signatures
backing up, 493–494
configuring a server as a CA, 160
Contact form Certificates tab, 205–206
costs, 160
defined, 159
installing, 160

obtaining a digital ID, 160–161
restoring, 494
sharing between computer systems, 161
Change Anonymous Access Settings page (WSS), 449
Change Password dialog box, 735–736
Change Security Settings dialog box, 161
Check Address dialog box, 199–200
check boxes for forms, 597–598
Check Full Name dialog box, 198, 687
Check Names dialog box, 118–119
/checkupdates Setup switch, 50
client applications. See also specific forms
Contact form, 569, 570
defined, 561
forms available for, 561–562
Message form, 563–567
other built-in forms, 569–570
Outlook 2003 Forms Designer, 562–563
Post form, 567–568
closing
Personal folder file, 396
setting preferences for e-mail, 106
collaboration. See also scheduling; sharing information; WSS (Windows Sharepoint Services)
business solutions, 14
collaborative messaging, 657–658
collaborative solutions defined, 12, 656
custom forms, 656, 661
defined, 655–656
difficulties of, 12
e-forms, 656, 662
messaging application programming interface, 660
need for, 12
overview, 662–663
scenario for collaborative solution, 657
scheduling meetings for, 12–14
workflow applications, 658–659
Collaboration Data Objects, 25
colors
for business and non-business hours (Calendar), 228
for flags, 20, 139
for newsgroup message headings, 350
for Notes, 66, 82, 305–306, 315
Organize feature, 369, 371
planning custom fields and, 610–611
COM (Component Object Model), 666–667
Combination command (Type menu), 615
combination fields of forms, 615–616
combo boxes for forms, 598–599
command buttons for forms, 588–589, 604–605

command line, running Group Policy Editor from, 507

compacting
OST file, 731–733
Personal folders, 77

company name in Contact form, 197, 198

Complete Install option, 27

Component Object Model (COM), 666–667

Compose mode of forms
defined, 622
Message form, 563–564
Post form, 567, 568
shared fields and, 613–615
toggling with Read mode, 614, 622–623

composing e-mail messages
addressing messages, 116–120
attaching files, 149–150
from contacts, 213–215
entering a subject, 120–121
entering message text, 121–122
inserting documents as text, 150
keeping messages short, 115
overview, 115
in OWA, 711
replying to messages, 126–127
starting a new message, 116
using stationery, 147–148

Confidential sensitivity setting, 140

Configure E-mail Server Settings page (WSS), 445

configuring Outlook 2003
adding PST files for e-mail accounts, 100–102
creating and managing profiles, 102–105
ease of, 85
E-mail Accounts Wizard overview, 86–87
e-mail preferences, 106–109
Exchange Server e-mail accounts, 87–94
HTTP e-mail accounts, 99–100
IMAP e-mail accounts, 94–98
mail format options, 109–110
message delivery options, 105–106
newsgroup setup, 335–338
for Outlook Today page, 573–575
POP3 e-mail accounts, 94–98
security zones, 175–176

connection
Exchange Server e-mail account settings, 92–93
IMAP e-mail account settings, 96
for OWA, 704, 705–707
performance and connection speed, 723
persistent, for roaming users, 475–476
POP3 e-mail account settings, 96
prompt for connection type, 725–727
reconnecting a deleted mailbox, 524–525
status line information, 59

Contact form. See also Contacts list
Activities tab, 204–205
Add Picture button, 200–201
address options, 199–200
All Fields tab, 206–208
Categories text box, 202
Certificates tab, 205–206
creating contacts manually, 211–212
creating new fields, 207–208
Design mode versus using, 570
Details tab, 202–204
Display as text box, 201
e-mail address options, 201
General tab, 196–202
IM address text box, 202
Internet Free-Busy item, 204
Label control for, 591–594
name options, 196–198
NetMeeting-related items, 202–203
notes text box, 202
in OFD, 569, 570
phone number options, 198–199
Private check box, 202
Web page address text box, 201

Contact or Actions submenu (File menu), 211

contacts (Business Contact Manager). See also
Business Contact Manager
Business Contact form, 686–688
exporting, 691
importing, 688–689
moving from the Contacts folder, 688

Contacts folder. See Contacts list

Contacts for Note dialog box, 308

Contacts list. See also Contact form
Address Book (Windows) versus, 209
Address Cards view, 195
address options, 199–200
Advanced Find tool, 217–218
AutoDialer feature, 219–221
By Contact view (Journal), 289–290
categories for contacts, 202
certificates and, 205–206
composing e-mail messages from contacts, 213–215
contacts defined, 194
contacts overview, 193–195
creating contacts from e-mail messages, 212–213
creating contacts in OWA, 716–717
creating contacts manually, 211–212
creating messages from (OWA), 717
creating new fields, 207–208
creating vCards from records, 145
displaying contact cards, 74
displaying records for e-mail addresses, 119

down arrows in, 74
e-mail address options, 201
entering e-mail addresses from, 118
exporting contacts, 422–424
Find tool, 216–217
folders, 387
getting started using, 193
IM address stored with contacts, 195, 202
importing contacts, 208–210, 422
integration with other Office applications, 11–12
Internet Free-Busy feature, 204
linking birthdays or anniversaries to Calendar, 202
linking contacts, 202
linking forms to contacts, 626
linking Notes to contacts, 307–308
linking tasks to contacts, 272
mail merge using, 410–415
managing in OWA, 718
moving contacts to Business Contact Manager, 688
multiple lists, 194
name display and file format, 197
name options, 196–198
NetMeeting and, 202–204
New Contact button, 211
new features in Outlook 2003, 22, 195
notes about contacts, 202
offline access to information, 22
overview, 8–9, 62, 74
in OWA, 716–718
phone number options, 198–199
picture display on contacts page, 195, 200–201
preventing sharing for records, 202
QuickFind feature, 216
roaming users and, 480
searching contacts, 215–218
sharing information with vCards, 8
sorting names in, 62–63
Speed Dial list, 221
using, 74–75
viewing address maps, 218–219
views, 62–63
Windows objects and, 195
contacts (WSS), 457. See also lists (WSS)
Contributor permission for delegates, 433
contributor site group (WSS), 446
Control Panel
    Add or Remove Programs applet, 441
    Mail applet, 86, 103, 466, 516
Control Toolbox command (Form menu), 583, 591
controls for forms
    adding with Toolbox, 583–584
    check boxes, 597–598
    combination fields, 615–616

    combo boxes, 598–599
    command buttons, 604–605
    custom fields, 609–613
    formula fields, 617–618
    frames (groups), 595–596
    image, 602–603
    Label, 584–585, 591–594
    list boxes, 599–600
    MultiPage, 600–601
    option buttons, 596–597
    shared fields, 613–615
    specifying default values for fields, 619–620
    spin buttons, 603–604
    TabStrip, 602
    text boxes, 594–595
    toggle buttons, 606
    on top of MultiPage control, 601
    validating user input, 618–619
Copy command (Edit menu), 399, 408
Copy the Site Group page (WSS), 452
copying
    Copy and Paste commands for, 399
    by dragging items, 398
    Excel charts to e-mail messages, 408–409
    profiles, 104
    rules for handling messages, 183
    sending copies of e-mail messages, 116
    site groups (WSS), 452
    text from Notes, 304
Corporate Workgroup (CW) mode, 85
Create an Account dialog box, 687–688
Create Microsoft Personal Folders dialog box, 394–395
Create New Folder dialog box, 386, 389–390
Create New Signature dialog box, 141–142, 143
Create Page page (WSS), 459, 460, 461
Create Signature dialog box, 141, 142, 146
CRM (Customer Relationship Management), 677, 678.
    See also Business Contact Manager
Crystal Reports with Business Contact Manager, 692
Current View area (Navigation Pane), 365
Current View submenu (View menu)
    Active Appointments command, 232
    Annual Events command, 233
    By Category command, 236, 290, 314, 323
    By Color command, 315
    By Contact command, 289
    By Type command, 288
    Customize Current View command
        customizing Calendar view, 74, 237
        customizing Contacts list view, 63
        customizing Last Seven Days Journal view, 293
        defining Calendar views, 237

Continued

Current View submenu (View menu) *(continued)*
   customizing folders, 392
   customizing versus defining views, 648–649
   Entry List command, 292
   Icons command, 311
   Last Seven Days command, 293, 313
   Notes List command, 311
   Phone Calls command, 294
   Recurring Appointments command, 235
   selecting Calendar view, 226
   Tasks list views, 267
   ...View With Autopreview commands, 231–232
custom form fields
   creating, 611–613
   flexibility for, 610–611
   planning, 609–611
custom forms. *See* forms
Custom Install option, 27
Custom Installation Wizard
   Add, Modify, or Remove Shortcuts page, 38
   adding Newprof.exe to Office installation, 471
   Add/Remove Files page, 36
   Add/Remove Registry Entries page, 37
   Apply PRF option, 40
   automating profile creation using, 468–470
   Change Office User Settings page, 36, 37
   creating .prf files using, 482–483
   Customize Default Application Settings page, 34–35, 36
   Default Setup behavior option, 33, 34
   Disable Installed on First Use option, 36
   Disable Run from Network option, 36
   Do Not Migrate Previous Installation State option, 36
   Exchange settings for profiles, 481–482
   Identify Additional Servers page, 38
   Installed on First Use option, 27
   Modify Profile option, 40
   Modify Setup Properties page, 42
   MSI file path specification, 33
   naming the MST file, 33
   New Profile option, 40
   Not Available, Hidden, Locked option, 35
   Not Available option, 27
   Open the MST File page, 33
   Outlook: Add Accounts page, 41
   Outlook: Customize Default Profile page, 39–40, 482–483
   Outlook: Customize Default Settings page, 42
   Outlook: Remove Accounts and Export Settings page, 41–42, 483
   Outlook: Specify Exchange Settings page, 40–41
   Remove Previous Versions page, 33–34
   Run all from My Computer option, 27

   Run from My Computer option, 35
   Select the MST File to Save page, 33, 34
   Set Feature Installation States page, 36
   Specify Office Security Settings page, 38–39
   specifying components to install, 34–35
   Use existing profile option, 39
Custom Outlook profile dialog box, 469
Custom View Organizer dialog box, 237–238, 242, 648–649
Customer Relationship Management (CRM), 677, 678.
      See also Business Contact Manager
Customize command
   Tools menu, 60, 362
   View menu, 61, 336, 358
Customize Current View command (View menu)
   customizing Calendar view, 74, 237
   customizing Contacts list view, 63
   customizing Last Seven Days Journal view, 293
   customizing versus defining views, 648–649
   defining Calendar views, 237
Customize dialog box
   Always show full menus check box, 60, 362
   customizing menus, 362–363
   Options tab, 60, 362
Customize Outlook Today button, 67, 359
Customize Outlook Today window, 359–361
Customize View dialog box
   Automatic Formatting button, 240
   Fields button, 238
   Filter button, 239
   Format Columns button, 241
   Group By button, 238
   Other Settings button, 240
   Sort button, 239
Customize View: Messages dialog box, 390
customizing
   adding holidays to Calendar, 381
   Calendar views, 74, 229, 237–242
   category list, 319
   Contacts list view, 63
   folder opened at startup, 69
   folders, 390–393
   forms, 15
   forms not allowing, 569
   macros for repetitive tasks, 382–383
   menu display, 60
   menus, 362–363
   Navigation Pane, 70, 71, 365–366
   Outlook Today folder, 67–69, 358–361
   security, 366–368
   TaskPad, 377–380
   toolbars, 61, 336, 363–365
   views, defining versus, 648–649

Cut command (Edit menu), 399
CW (Corporate Workgroup) mode, 85

D

Data File Management command (File menu), 77, 734
data types and field formats, 612–613
date. *See also* Calendar; time
    Autodate feature, 254
    changing for appointments, 254, 255
    setting for appointments, 251
Day command (View menu), 62, 227
Day view (Calendar), 227–228, 714
Day View With AutoPreview command (View menu),
    231–232
debugging code
    accessing the Script Debugger, 671
    break mode for, 672–673
    setting break points, 673–674
DECM (Directory-Enabled Client Management), 30–31.
    See also group policies
defaults. *See also* resetting
    aging period for folders, 526
    Default Computer icon, 511
    Default User icon, 511
    folder to open with Outlook, 361
    fonts for e-mail, 110
    Journal view, 288
    mail editor, 110
    mail folders, 128–129
    Note options, 309–310
    profiles, 466
    specifying a default form, 645–646
    specifying default values for fields, 619–620
    stationery, 110
    WSS lists, 457
Delegate Permissions dialog box, 429–430, 553–554
delegating tasks
    acting as an assistant, 433–435
    assigning delegates, 428–431
    granting folder access, 431–433
    managing another person's Calendar, 436–438
    overview, 427–428
    permissions for delegates, 427–428, 429–430,
        432–433
    send on behalf permission for distribution groups,
        553–554
    sending e-mail on behalf of someone else,
        435–436, 545
Deleted Items folder. *See also* mail folders
    default aging period, 526
    deleting items from, 77, 402–404
    described, 129

    emptying (purging deleted items), 77, 129, 404–406
    overview, 402
    undeleting messages using OWA, 710
    using, 77
deleting. *See* removing or deleting
Delivery Options dialog box, 545–546
delivery receipt, 109, 123
Delivery Restrictions dialog box, 544–545
demo versions of software, 739. *See also* CD with
    this book
Deploy Software dialog box, 44
deploying
    Cached Exchange Mode versus non-cached mode
        for, 23–24
    OFD applications, 631–633
    Outlook group policies, 508
    Outlook system policies, 512–513
deploying Office with group policies
    adding the package to the server, 32
    administrative templates for GPOs, 507
    assigning the GPO to other OUs and domains, 49
    changing the deployment method, 47
    controlling Office applications with group
        policies, 49
    creating transform files, 32–42
    DECM and, 30–31
    defining group policies, 42–47
    setting global package properties, 47–48
    testing the package, 48
Design a Form command (Tools menu), 562, 580
Design Form dialog box, 562, 563, 580. *See also* OFD
    (Outlook 2003 Forms Designer)
Design This Form command (Tools menu), 563, 591
desktop systems, sharing information with laptop
    systems, 393
developing for Outlook, 15–17
dial-up connection, 93, 168
digital signatures. *See also* certificates
    backing up and restoring certificates, 493–494
    icon for digitally signed messages, 162
    for macros, 493
    obtaining a digital ID, 160–161
    Outlook capability for, 21
    overview, 159
    sending a digitally signed message, 161–163
    trusted sources and, 493
Directory-Enabled Client Management (DECM), 30–31.
    See also group policies
Disable Installed on First Use option (Custom
    Installation Wizard), 36
Disable Run from Network option (Custom Installation
    Wizard), 36

disabling. *See also* enabling; toggling on/off
    group policy settings, 505
    Reading (Preview) pane, 730–731
    rules for filtering newsgroup messages, 346
discussion boards (WSS), 453–454, 460
discussion folders
    overview, 637
    posting messages, 638–639
    setting up, 638
    viewing messages, 639–640
Display This Page command (Form menu), 582, 624
displaying. *See* viewing; views
distribution groups (Exchange). *See also* distribution
            lists
    adding members, 552
    creating, 550–551
    delegating send on behalf permission to, 553–554
    removing members, 552
    scope of groups, 551
    uses for, 550
Distribution List command (File menu), 165
Distribution List dialog box, 165–166
distribution lists. *See also* distribution groups
            (Exchange)
    creating, 164–166
    defined, 164
    mail merge and, 413
    roaming users and, 480
    uses for, 164
    using, 166–167
Do Not Forward flag, 139
Do Not Migrate Previous Installation State option
            (Custom Installation Wizard), 36
Document Libraries (WSS)
    adding documents, 459–460
    editing documents, 455
    filtering documents, 455
    opening, 453
    overview, 453
    setting alerts for documents, 456
    viewing documents, 453–454
document tracking. *See* Journal
documents. *See also* Document Libraries (WSS)
    ease of sending with e-mail, 4
    Journal tracking for, 9, 288–289
    sending to folders, 571
    tracking with tracking folders, 641–644
Download Headers command (Tools menu), 169
downloading
    headers using Remote Mail, 168–169
    messages using Remote Mail, 170–171
    newsgroup message headers, 342

Drafts folder, 78, 129, 526. *See also* mail folders
dragging
    attachments to e-mail, 149
    e-mail to folders, 153
    moving versus copying, 398
    toolbars, 60–61
due date for tasks, 66, 266, 270

E

Easy Translator software (Transparent Language), 132
eBooks included on CD with this book, 738–739
Edit Compose Page mode. *See* Compose mode of
            forms
Edit menu
    Categories command, 320
    Copy command, 399, 408
    Cut command, 399
    Mark as Read command, 125
    Mark as Unread command, 125
    Paste command, 399
    Paste Special command, 408
Edit Read Page mode. *See* Read mode of forms
Edit Rule dialog box, 189–190, 647
Edit Signature dialog box, 142–143
Edit Site Group page (WSS), 452
editing
    appointments, 252, 254, 255
    changing Calendar date, 73–74
    changing meeting time, 260
    GPOs, 504, 505
    Notes, 304–305
    .prf files, 483–485
    Registry to share categories, 329–331
    rules for filtering newsgroup messages, 346
    rules for handling e-mail messages, 182–183
    signatures in e-mails, 144
    tasks, 273
    WSS documents, 455
Editor permission for delegates, 428, 432, 436
e-forms, 656, 662
electronic business cards. *See* vCards
e-mail. *See also* e-mail account configuration; mail
            folders; mailboxes (Exchange); OWA
            (Outlook Web Access)
    account for newsgroups, 334
    addressing messages, 116–120
    attachments, 4, 79, 148–152
    automatic response, 183–184
    AutoPreview view, 730–731
    Bcc text box, 116–117
    Cc text box, 116
    Check Names dialog box, 118–119

checking for new mail, 60
communication changed by, 4
composing messages, 115–122, 147–148, 213–215, 711
conventions for message text, 121
creating contacts from e-mail messages, 212–213
creating messages, 79
digitally signed messages, 21, 161–163
distribution lists, 164–167
encrypting messages, 21, 163–164
entering a subject, 120–121
entering message text, 121–122
example of completed message, 121–122
filtering junk and adult content mail, 185–187
flagging messages, 139
forwarding messages, 107, 126, 139
free accounts, 334
From text box, 116
incorrect addresses for, 117–118
inserting Excel charts in messages, 408–409
keeping messages short, 115
mail merge for messages, 11
managing mail folders, 127–129
message format options, 131–138
NDRs (Non-Delivery Receipts), 118
new features in Outlook 2003, 17–22
newsgroups versus, 335
organizing messages, 152–153
Out of Office Assistant, 187–190
in OWA, 708–711
popularity of, 3
printing messages, 77, 79, 125
printing selected text from messages, 125
reading messages, 79, 124–125, 435–436, 708, 709
receipt request options, 109
Remote Mail, 167–171
removing attachments while retaining messages, 403–404
replying to messages, 107, 126–127, 708, 709
resending messages, 78
retention policy for deleted user accounts, 524
rules for handling messages, 75, 176–187
Safe Senders list, 497
saving drafts, 78
saving messages as files, 424–425
securing against HTML content, 173–176
Select Names dialog box, 119–120
sending from other applications, 415–418
sending messages, 79, 122–124, 159–169
sending Office documents as, 416–418
sending on behalf of someone else, 435–436, 545, 553–554

server copies of e-mail messages, 168
setting message importance and sensitivity, 139–140
sharing categories using, 327–329
sharing information using, 6
signatures, 21, 110, 140–144, 521–522
starting a new message, 116
stationery for, 147–148
status line information, 59
To text box, 116, 167, 201
using, 78–80
using CEM, 154
views for mail folder, 64
viruses and HTML-formatted mail, 488
voting feature, 123, 154–156
Web pages with messages, 375, 376
e-mail account configuration. *See also* profiles
adding PST files, 100–102
for CEM, 154, 155
changing the account order, 105
Exchange Server accounts, 87–94
format options, 109–110
HTTP accounts, 99–100
IMAP accounts, 94–98
message delivery options, 105–106
POP3 accounts, 94–98
preferences, 106–109
E-mail Accounts command (Tools menu), 86, 154, 519, 725, 731
Email Accounts dialog box, 475
E-mail Accounts Wizard
adding profiles, 467
Advanced page, 96–98
CEM configuration, 154, 155
compacting OST file, 731–733
configuring Exchange Server accounts, 87–94
configuring HTTP accounts, 99–100
configuring IMAP accounts, 94–98
configuring POP3 accounts, 94–98
creating profiles, 104
Exchange Server Settings page, 87–88, 154, 155
Internet E-mail Settings page, 95–96, 99
opening, 86
removing profiles, 467
setting prompt for connection type, 725–727
specifying incoming mail store, 106
welcome page, 468
e-mail addresses
addressing messages, 116–120
Bcc text box, 116–117
Cc text box, 116

Continued

e-mail addresses *(continued)*
Check Names dialog box, 118–119
configuring for Exchange mailboxes, 541, 542–543
Contact form options, 201
from Contacts list, 118, 213–215
creating external addresses (mail-enabled contacts), 547–549
displaying contact records for, 119
distribution lists, 164–167
entering in address text boxes, 118
From text box, 116
for HTTP e-mail accounts, 99
for IMAP e-mail accounts, 95
importance of correct addresses, 117–118
NDRs (Non-Delivery Receipts), 118
for POP3 e-mail accounts, 95
rules for, 117
Select Names dialog box, 119–120
standard format for, 117
To text box, 116, 167, 201
E-mail Options dialog box, 106–108
emoticons, 121
Empty "Deleted Items" Folder command (Tools menu), 404
emptying Deleted Items folder, 77, 129, 404–406
enabling. *See also* disabling; toggling on/off
activating a form page, 582–583
AutoArchive feature, 527–528
group policy settings, 505
IM for user accounts, 557–558
encryption
encrypting messages, 163–164
Exchange Server e-mail account, 92
icon for encrypted messages, 164
128-bit, 159
Outlook capability for, 21
for Personal folders, 395
for PSTs, 102
U.S. regulations for exporting, 159
End-User License Agreement (EULA), 26, 32
Entry List command (View menu), 292
Entry List view (Journal), 286, 292–293
envelopes mail merge type, 412
environment settings, 502
environment variables, 472
erasing. *See* removing or deleting
EULA (End-User License Agreement), 26, 32
evaluation versions of software, 739. *See also* CD with this book
event handlers, 669
events. *See also* appointments; Calendar; lists (WSS); meetings
Annual Events view (Calendar), 233–235
defined, 224, 669

Events view (Calendar), 233, 234
handlers, 669
modifying in OWA, 713–714
WSS lists, 457
Events view (Calendar), 233, 234
Excel (Microsoft) charts, inserting in an e-mail message, 408–409
Exchange Conferencing (Microsoft), 262–264
Exchange Folder command (File menu), 417, 571
Exchange (Microsoft). *See also* Exchange Server; mailboxes (Exchange)
Active Directory integration with, 534
Mailbox Store, 535
Outlook enabled by, 533
overview, 533
Exchange Server. *See also* CEM (Cached Exchange Mode)
Active Directory integration with, 534
adding a mailbox automatically, 534–536
adding a mailbox manually, 536–537
backing up Outlook settings files, 521
backing up Personal Address Books, 520–521
cached local mode, 87, 90
configuring e-mail accounts, 87–94, 154, 155
configuring global mailbox options, 538–541
configuring Instant Messaging, 554–558
configuring mailbox-specific options, 541–547
creating external addresses (mail-enabled contacts), 547–549
distribution groups with Exchange, 550–554
locating Outlook data, 519–520
Mailbox Store, 535
moving a mailbox, 538
newsfeeds using, 6
Out of Office Assistant and, 188–189
Outlook folder access and, 6
OWA requirement, 704
removing a mailbox manually, 537
roaming user issues, 481–482
settings for profiles, 481–482
unsend feature, 77, 122–123, 156–157
voting feature, 123, 154–156
Exchange System Manager
checking IM installation, 554
configuring IM, 555
creating an IM virtual server, 556–557
Global Settings container, 539
reconnecting a deleted mailbox, 524–525
setting deleted mailbox retention period, 524
Exchange Task Wizard
adding a mailbox manually, 536–537
enabling IM for user accounts, 557–558
moving a mailbox, 538
removing a mailbox manually, 537

ExLife program (Ornic USA), 739
Expedia Web site (Microsoft), 218–219
Export command (File menu), 330
Export Registry File command (Registry menu), 330
Export to vCard file command (File menu), 145
exporters, 24
exporting
  archiving versus, 530–531
  Business Contact Manager accounts, 689–691
  Business Contact Manager contacts, 691
  certificates, 493–494
  checking data after, 424
  contacts, 422–424
  finding common formats for, 418
  information from Outlook, 418, 422–424
  Personal folder data, 518
  rules for handling e-mail messages, 522
  rules for handling messages, 184–185
External Content Settings dialog box, 174

F

/f Setup switch, 50–51
Favorites file, backing up, 521
Fax Service command (File menu), 417
faxes, sending Office documents as, 417
Fax4Outlook program (4Team), 740
Field Chooser command (Form menu), 586, 594
Field Chooser window, 586–587, 594–595
fields. See also controls for forms; specific fields
  adding to forms, 586–587
  combination fields, 615–616
  creating custom fields, 611–613
  custom field mappings for importing, 421
  formula fields, 617–618
  manipulating headings in views, 649–650
  planning custom fields, 609–611
  selecting for mail merge, 412
  shared, 613–615
  sorting Calendar fields, 239
  specifying default values, 619–620
  validating user input, 618–619
  values for combo boxes, 598–599
File command (Insert menu), 149
File Destination Path dialog box, 36
File menu
  Archive command, 526
  Data File Management command, 77, 734
  Export command, 330
  Export to vCard file command, 145
  Import and Export command, 209, 419, 422, 518, 519
  New submenu
    Appointment command, 251
    Contact or Actions submenu, 211
    Distribution List command, 165
    Folder command, 72
    Journal Entry command, 297
    Mail Message command, 116
    Meeting Request command, 251
    Notes command, 303
    Outlook Data File command, 394, 633
  Open submenu
    Other User's Folder command, 433, 435, 437
    Outlook Data File command, 396, 401, 519
  Print command, 125
  Properties command, 529
  Save As command, 399, 424
  Save as Web Page command, 246
  Save command, 78
  Send To submenu
    Exchange Folder command, 417, 571
    Mail Recipient command, 151, 416, 417
    options available, 417
    overview, 151
  Work Offline command, 724
files. See also attachments to e-mail; backing up; CD
        with this book; specific kinds
  exporting information to, 422–424
  importing, 419–422
  inserting as text in e-mails, 150
  Level 1 category files, 489–491
  Level 2 category files, 489, 491
  for mail merge, 412
  Outlook folder file, 385
  Personal folders for project files, 388
  saving Outlook messages as, 424–425
  sending using Office, 150–152
  viruses and file types, 488, 489–491
Filter dialog box, 239–240, 651
filtering
  Calendar activities, 239–240
  documents (WSS), 455
  junk and adult content mail, 185–187, 494–499
  newsgroup messages, 343–348
  views, 650–651
Find submenu (Tools menu), 217
Find tool, 216–217
finding
  common formats for importing and exporting, 418
  OU for group policies, 43
  Outlook data on Exchange Server, 519–520
  PST file location, 473–474
  searching contacts, 215–218
  WSS installation files, 442
Flag for Follow Up dialog box, 139
flagging, 20, 139
flames (newsgroup insults), 334
floating toolbars, 60
Folder command (File menu), 72

Folder Contents pane
    changing the view, 61–67
    creating more room for, 60
    overview, 59
Folder List, 59, 72–73
folders. *See also specific kinds*
    Access databases and, 385
    assigning home page for, 375–377
    browsing methods for, 60
    built-in module folders, 644–645
    categories of, 387–388
    compacting Personal folders, 77
    creating, 386, 388–390
    customizing, 390–393
    default aging period, 526
    default to open with Outlook, 361
    discussion folders, 637–640
    Folder List access to, 59
    managing properties, 645–647
    moving e-mail messages using OWA, 711
    moving items, 397–399
    Navigation Pane access to, 59, 365
    opened at startup, 69
    opening another user's folder, 433–435, 437
    Organize feature, 368–374
    organizing by categories, 368–369, 370
    organizing by colors, 369, 371
    organizing using rules, 372–373
    in Outlook Today Messages section, 69
    overview, 385–386
    project folders, 388
    redirecting, 472–476
    restrictions on items in, 69–70
    saving items as text files, 399–400
    sending documents to, 571
    sending Office documents to, 417
    setting aging period, 527
    sharing, 386, 400–402
    status line information, 59
    tracking folders, 640–644
    turning AutoArchiving on/off, 528–529
    types of, 387
    uses for, 386
    view settings for, 60
    viewing entire tree in Navigation Pane, 387
    Windows Explorer versus Outlook, 69–70, 127–128
    for WSS installation files, 442
Follow Up Flag field, 390–392
following newsgroup message threads, 349–350
Font dialog box, 143
fonts
    for Label control, 592
    RTF format for, 135

    setting defaults for e-mail, 110
    for signatures, 143
foreign languages
    characters in plain text messages, 133
    translation software for, 132
Form Action Properties dialog box, 628–629
form letters mail merge type, 412
Form menu
    Control Toolbox command, 583, 591
    Display This Page command, 582, 624
    Field Chooser command, 586, 594
    Publish Form command, 631
    Rename Page command, 582, 592
    Run This Form command, 589, 605, 671
    View Code command, 588, 667, 669
Format Columns dialog box, 241–242, 392–393
Format menu
    field data presentation and, 612–613
    Plain Text command, 132
formatting
    HTML format for e-mail messages, 135–136, 137
    plain text for e-mail messages, 131–132
    removing from received e-mail, 107
    RTF format for e-mail messages, 133–134
    setting mail editor options, 110
    setting mail format options, 109–110
forms. *See also* OFD (Outlook 2003 Forms Designer);
            specific forms
    activating a page, 582–583
    adding controls with the Toolbox, 583–584
    adding fields, 586–587
    adding new pages, 623–624
    associating Word templates with, 625
    as business solutions, 14
    changing icons, 625
    changing tab order, 629–630
    check boxes, 597–598
    client applications, 561–562
    combination fields, 615–616
    combo boxes, 598–599
    command buttons, 604–605
    commonly used forms, 579–580
    creating a command button, 588–589
    creating custom fields, 611–613
    custom forms using MAPI technologies, 656, 661
    customizing, 15
    defined, 4, 621
    e-forms, 656, 662
    formula fields, 617–618
    frames (groups), 595–596
    hidden, 562, 580
    image controls, 602–603
    including definition with, 627

labels, 584–585, 591–594
limiting responses, 627
linking to contacts, 626
list boxes, 599–600
MultiPage control, 600–601
OFD Actions page for, 627–629
OFD Properties page for, 624–627
option buttons, 596–597
Outlook 2003 Forms Designer, 562–563
overview, 4
paper forms layout and, 581
Personal Forms Library, 589
planning custom fields, 609–611
Properties dialog box, 585
protecting, 626
publishing, 589–590, 631–633
renaming, 582, 592, 624
running, 589, 605, 671
Script Editor, 588–589
shared fields, 613–615
specifying a default form, 645–646
specifying default values for fields, 619–620
spin buttons, 603–604
Standard Forms Library, 563, 569
switching between Compose and Read mode, 614, 622–623
TabStrip control, 602
testing, 630
text boxes, 594–595
toggle buttons, 606
validating user input, 618–619
version control, 625
Forms editor, 15–16
Forms Manager dialog box, 646
Forms submenu (Tools menu)
Design a Form command, 562, 580
Design This Form command, 563, 591
Script Debugger command, 671, 673
formula fields of forms, 617–618
Forward as VCard command (Actions menu), 146
forwarding e-mail messages, 107, 126, 139
4Team's Fax4Outlook program, 740
frames (groups) for forms, 595–596
Free/Busy Information command (Tools menu), 245
Free/Busy Options dialog box, 243–245
freeware programs, 739. *See also* CD with this book
From text box (e-mail), 116

G

GAL (Global Address List), 549
global distribution groups (Exchange), 551
global package properties, setting, 47–48
GNU software, 739. *See also* CD with this book

Go menu
Go to Date command, 253
Go To submenu, 230
Journal command, 287
Go to Date command (Go menu), 230, 253
Go To Date dialog box, 230, 231, 253
Go To submenu (Go menu), 230
Gpedit.msc. *See* Group Policy Editor
GPOs (group policy objects). *See also* group policies
adding, 43
assigning to other OUs and domains, 49
configuring for roaming users, 476–477
creating, 503–504
deploying, 508
Folder Redirection settings, 476–477
lever analogy for, 502–503
linking to Active Directory container objects, 503
managing, 504–505
modifying, 504, 505
multiple GPOs linked to same container, 503
overview, 501–503
reusing, 503
uses for, 503
graphics. *See* images
greater-than symbol (>) as e-mail prefix, 107, 126–127
Group By dialog box, 238–239, 282, 650
group policies. *See also* GPOs (group policy objects)
adding administrative templates for, 505–508
adding GPOs, 43
assigning applications, 31
change control using, 30
controlling Office applications with, 49
controlling with administrative templates, 506–508
DECM and, 30–31
defining, 42–47
deploying Office with group policies, 31–49
deploying Outlook group policies, 508
described, 30
enabling and disabling settings, 505
issues controlled by, 502
levels for application of, 30, 42
lever analogy for, 502–503
at the OU level, 30–31, 42–43
OU Properties dialog box, 43
overview, 501–503
package property sheet, 44–47
publishing applications, 31
for redirecting folders, 476–477
for roaming users, 476–477
software policies, 43–44
system policies versus, 509–510
Windows 98 and, 508–509
Group Policy Editor, 44, 504, 506–508

group policy objects. *See* GPOs
grouping information in views, 650
groups (frames) for forms, 595–596

H

hardware, preventing users from changing, 502
headers (e-mail)
    downloading, 168–169
    marking and processing, 170–171
Help included in Typical Install, 24
hidden forms, 562, 580
hiding. *See* toggling on/off; viewing
holidays, adding to Calendar, 381
home page, 375–377, 479
Home Server for IM, 555–557
Hotmail accounts, 99, 334
HTML
    blocking external content, 173–176, 498–499
    configuring security zones, 175–176
    conversion of Office documents into, 138
    overview, 135–136
    sending e-mail messages as, 135–136, 137
    setting defaults for e-mail, 110
    virus dangers and e-mail, 488
HTTP, 93, 99–100

I

/i Setup switch, 51
icons
    adding or removing from Navigation Pane, 71
    changing for forms, 625
    Default Computer icon, 511
    Default User icon, 511
    for digitally signed messages, 162
    for encrypted messages, 164
    menus versus, 60
    Notes views, 311, 312
    paperclip icon in Journal, 292
    viewing Navigation Pane icon options, 71
Icons command (View menu), 311
IIS (Internet Information Services), installing, 441–442
IM (Instant Messaging)
    address stored with contacts, 195, 202
    checking whether installed or not, 554
    configuring Exchange IM, 555
    creating a virtual server, 555–557
    enabling for user accounts, 557–558
    Exchange versus MSN Messenger, 554
    Home Server, 555–557
    overview, 22
images. *See also* attachments to e-mail
    on contacts page, 195, 200–201
    ease of sending with e-mail, 4

file formats supported for Contacts list, 200–201
    image controls for forms, 602–603
IMAP (Internet Mail Access Protocol)
    connection settings, 96
    e-mail account configuration, 94–98
    e-mail message storage, 98
    incoming server settings, 97–98
    as online protocol, 94
    outgoing server settings, 96, 97–98
    POP3 versus, 94
    PST files for accounts, 98, 100–102
    Root Folder Path setting, 98
    security, 94
IMO (Internet Mail Only) mode, 85
Import and Export command (File menu), 209, 419,
    422, 518, 519
Import and Export Wizard
    exporting information from Outlook, 422–424
    exporting Personal folders data, 518
    importing Contacts list data, 209–210
    importing information into Outlook, 419–422
    importing PST file data, 519
importance of e-mail messages, setting, 139–140
importers, 24
Import/Export Digital ID dialog box, 493–494
importing
    Business Contact Manager account, 682–684
    business contacts into Business Contact Manager,
        688–689
    certificates, 494
    contacts, 208–210, 422
    custom field mappings for, 421
    finding common formats for, 418
    information into Outlook, 418–422
    .prf files from previous Outlook versions, 483
    PST file data, 519
    rules for handling e-mail messages, 523
    rules for handling messages, 185
    steps for, 419–422
    types of information supported, 419
Inbox. *See also* mail folders; reading e-mail messages
    AutoArchive feature, 526
    bold type for unread messages, 75, 124–125
    default aging period, 526
    managing old messages, 75
    marking messages as read or unread, 125
    opening messages, 75
    Outlook Today folder link to, 67
    overview, 75, 128
    rules for handling messages, 75
    sorting messages in, 76, 80
    using, 75–76
    viewing another user's, 435–436

INI files for automated installation, 49–50
Insert Event Handler dialog box, 669
Insert File dialog box, 149, 150
Insert menu
    File command, 149
    Item command, 149
Insert Merge Field dialog box, 413
Installed on First Use option, 27
installing
    Business Contact Manager, 679–680
    certificates, 160
    group policies to prevent user installations, 502
    IIS, 441–442
    items from CD with this book, 738
    OFD applications, 631–633
    WSS, 442–443
    WSS prerequisites, 441–442
installing Outlook 2003. *See also* optimizing Outlook
        installations
    adding features, 28
    automated and unattended setup, 49–53
    Cached Exchange Mode versus non-cached
        mode, 23–24
    Complete Install option, 27
    components installed in Typical option, 24–25
    creating Office profiles, 54
    Custom Install option, 27
    deploying Office with group policies, 31–49
    deploying with SMS and DECM, 30–31
    deployment options, 23–24
    End-User License Agreement (EULA), 26, 32
    just-in-time (JIT) installation, 27, 31, 57
    Minimal Install option, 27
    Not Available option, 27
    reinstalling, 29
    removing features, 28
    repairing, 29
    Setup Wizard, 26–28
    standalone and one-by-one installations, 24–28
    Typical Install option, 24–25
    uninstalling, 29
    updating Office, 29
    wide-scale deployment, 30–49
Instant Messaging. *See* IM
Instant Messaging Settings Properties dialog box, 555
integration
    Business Contact Manager with Office, 701–702
    Exchange Server with Active Directory, 534
    with Microsoft Exchange Conferencing, 262–264
    with NetMeeting, 262–264
    with Office applications, 11–12, 407–410
    with the Web, 374–377
    with Windows Media Services, 262–264

IntelliMirror (DECM), 30–31. *See also* group policies
interface (Outlook)
    changing the view, 60–67
    overview, 58–60
Internet Address Properties dialog box, 548–549
Internet Connection Wizard, 336–338
Internet Explorer (Microsoft), 175, 704
Internet Free/Busy Service (Microsoft), 204, 243–246
Internet Information Services (IIS), installing, 441–442
Internet Mail Access Protocol. *See* IMAP
Internet Mail Only (IMO) mode, 85
Internet Only settings, profiles and, 470
Internet resources. *See also* URLs
    address maps (Expedia), 218–219
    CRM solution from Microsoft, 678
    Hotmail site, 334
    integrating Outlook with the Web, 374–377
    for Office updates, 29
    translation software for foreign languages, 133
    Transparent Language Web site, 133
    U.S. encryption export regulations, 159
    for Wiley products, 743
Item command (Insert menu), 149

J
JIT (just-in-time) installation, 27, 31, 57
/j*option* Setup switch, 51
Journal
    adding entries manually, 297–299
    By Category view, 290–292
    By Contact view, 289–290
    By Type view, 288–289
    category tracking, 290–292
    contact tracking, 289–290
    creating categories, 291–292
    creating entries, 81
    default aging period, 526
    document tracking by type, 288–289
    entries, 286
    Entry List view, 286, 292–293
    folders, 387
    Last Seven Days view, 293–294
    limiting data to be tracked, 296–297
    linking entries to files, 298
    links to documents in, 287
    navigating entries, 9, 81
    overview, 9–10, 65, 285–287
    phone call tracking, 219, 220, 286, 294–295
    Phone Calls view, 294–295
    plus sign (+) for entry types, 9, 81
    sharing information, 299
    timing entries, 298

Continued

Journal *(continued)*
    turning on, 287–288
    viewing entry details, 81
    views, 65
Journal command (Go menu), 287
Journal Entry command (File menu), 297
Journal Entry form, 297–299
Journal Options dialog box, 287–288, 296–297
Junk E-mail components, 25
Junk E-mail Filter, 495–497
Junk E-mail folder, 496
Junk E-mail Options command (Actions menu), 373, 497
Junk E-mail Options dialog box, 186–187, 373, 496–497
Junk E-mail submenu (Actions menu), 373, 497
junk mail. *See* spam
just-in-time (JIT) installation, 27, 31, 57

K

Kerberos-based authentication, 92

L

/l Setup switch, 51, 52
labels for forms
    adding to forms with Toolbox, 592
    adding with Toolbox, 584
    Advanced Properties dialog box, 592, 594
    changing the caption, 592, 593
    for Contact form, 591–594
    control tip for, 594
    font size for, 592
    Properties dialog box, 585, 592–593
LAN (Local Area Network). *See* networks
laptop systems, sharing information with desktop
        systems, 393
Large Icons view (Notes), 311
Last Seven Days command (View menu), 293, 313
Last Seven Days view, 293–294, 313
launching. *See* opening; running
Layout command (View menu), 341
letterhead forms, 14
Level 1 category files, 489–491
Level 2 category files, 489, 491
License Agreement for CD with this book, 738
line break preferences for e-mail, 107
linking
    contact birthdays or anniversaries to Calendar, 202
    contacts to each other, 202
    e-mail messages to categories, 124
    Excel charts to e-mail messages, 408–409
    forms to contacts, 626
    GPOs to Active Directory container objects, 503
    item to a Business Contact record, 697–699

    item to Business Contact Manager Account record, 699–700
    item to Business Contact Manager Opportunity record, 700–701
    Journal entries to files, 298
    Journal links to documents, 287
    Notes to contacts, 307–308
    Outlook Today folder to Calendar and Tasks list, 67
    roaming users and, 480
    tasks to contacts, 272
links (WSS), 457. *See also* lists (WSS)
list boxes for forms, 599–600
List view (Notes), 311
lists (WSS)
    adding, 460–461
    default lists, 457
    defined, 453
    viewing, 457–458
local area networks. *See* networks
local distribution groups (Exchange), 551
locating. *See* finding
logging
    meeting request responses, 13
    phone logs (Business Contact Manager), 696–697
logging off OWA, 721–722
logging on to OWA, 705–707

M

Macro submenu (Tools menu)
    Macros command, 382
    Security command, 367, 492
macros
    adding a trusted source, 493
    adding for repetitive tasks, 382–383
    digital signatures for, 493
    not recordable in Outlook, 15
    virus security, 488, 491–493
Macros command (Tools menu), 382
Macros dialog box, 382
Mail dialog box, 103–105
mail editor, 110
mail folders. *See also* Personal folders (PST files);
        specific folders
    archived files for, 128
    creating new folders, 128, 152–153
    deletion of expired items by AutoArchive, 527
    folders created by default, 128–129
    managing, 127–129
    overview, 64, 387
    restrictions on items in, 69–70
    toggling off Reading (Preview) pane, 33
    using, 75–78

views, 64
Windows Explorer folders versus, 127–128
mail merge
checking before sending, 415
data source's effect on, 410
destination for, 412
distribution lists and, 413
for e-mail messages, 11
permanent file for, 412
selecting records and fields for, 412
types of, 412
using Contacts list records, 411–415
Mail Merge command (Tools menu), 411
Mail Merge Contacts dialog box, 411–414
Mail Message command (File menu), 116
Mail Recipient (as Attachment) command
(File menu), 417
Mail Recipient command (File menu), 151, 416, 417
Mail Recipient (for Review) command (File menu), 417
Mail Setup — Outlook dialog box, 86, 103–104
Mailbox Store (Exchange), 535
Mailbox Store Properties dialog box, 539–541
mailboxes (Exchange)
adding automatically, 534–536
adding manually, 536–537
configuring global options, 538–541
configuring mailbox-specific options, 541–547
deleted item retention, 541, 547
deleting users having Exchange mailboxes, 536
global versus per-mailbox options, 538
Mailbox Store, 535
message delivery options, 539
moving, 538
recovering deleted mailboxes, 537
removing manually, 537
restricting messages, 544–545
retention policy for deleted items, 541, 547
size limits, 539, 540–541, 546
mail-enabled contacts, creating, 547–549
mailing labels mail merge type, 412
Manage Site Groups page (WSS), 451–452
Manage Users page (WSS)
adding users, 444, 446–447
changing site group membership, 447–448
opening, 443
removing users, 447
MAPI (messaging application programming interface),
660–661
mapping network drives, 476
maps, viewing for contact addresses, 218–219
Mark as Read command (Edit menu), 125
Mark as Unread command (Edit menu), 125

marking messages, 125, 170
marking tasks as completed, 269, 279
Master Category List dialog box
adding categories, 291, 319
categories missing from, 323
overview, 318–319
resetting the list, 322–323
Meeting form
Appointment tab, 256, 257, 263–264
Scheduling tab, 257, 258, 260–261
Meeting Request command (File menu), 251
meetings. *See also* appointments
adding additional attendees, 260–261
appointments versus, 249
changing time for, 260
creating, 255–261
defined, 224, 249
dry run for scheduling, 13
integrating with NetMeeting, Windows Media
Services, and Microsoft Exchange
Conferencing, 262–264
logging responses to requests, 13
modifying in OWA, 713–714
Outlook advantages for scheduling, 13
overview of scheduling, 6, 12–14
requesting, 13, 256–259
selecting attendees, 257–259
setting time for, 257
specifying recurring activities, 261–262
viewing attendee availability, 259–260
Memo Style for printing category items, 325–326
menus. *See also specific menus*
animating, 363
backing up settings, 521
buttons or icons versus, 60
customizing, 362–363
menu bar overview, 58
resetting to original options, 363
roaming users and, 480
viewing all commands, 60, 362
Merge to New Document dialog box, 414
message delivery options, 105, 106, 539
Message Delivery Properties dialog box, 539
Message form
(Actions) tab, 567
activating a page, 582–583
adding controls with the Toolbox, 583–584
adding fields, 586
(All Fields) tab, 565, 566
Compose mode, 563–564
manipulating in Design window, 581–583
Continued

Message form *(continued)*
  opening, 563, 580–581
  (Properties) tab, 565, 566
  Read mode, 564
  tabs in Design view, 564
  Tracking tab, 156, 157
Message menu
  Block Sender command, 347
  Watch Conversation command, 350
Message Options dialog box
  Categories button, 124, 327, 328
  Contacts button, 124
  Do not deliver before check box, 124
  Expires after check box, 124
  Have replies sent to check box, 124
  receipt request options, 123–124
  Save sent message check box, 124
  Security Settings button, 162, 164
  Use Voting Buttons option, 123, 155
Message Rules dialog box, 344–346, 348
Message Rules submenu (Tools menu)
  Blocked Senders List command, 348
  News command, 343
messages. *See* e-mail; newsgroups
messaging application programming interface (MAPI),
    660–661
methods versus properties, 668
Microsoft. *See also specific programs*
  Access databases and Outlook folders, 385
  Excel charts in e-mail messages, 408–409
  Exchange Conferencing, 262–264
  Expedia Web site, 218–219
  Internet Explorer, 175, 704
  Internet Free/Busy Service, 204, 243–246
  Management Console (MMC), 504
  NetMeeting, 202–204, 262–264
  Visual Basic Editor, 15, 382, 383
  Visual Studio .NET, 16–17
Microsoft Exchange Server property sheet
  Advanced page, 89–90, 732
  Automatically Detect Connection State setting, 89
  Choose the Connection Type When Starting
    setting, 89
  compacting OST file, 732
  Connect Using Internet Explorer's 3rd Party Dialer
    setting, 93
  Connect Using My Local Area Network setting, 92
  Connect Using My Phone Line setting, 93
  Connect with the Network setting, 89
  Connection page, 92–93
  Download Full Items setting, 90

Download Headers Followed by the Full Item
    setting, 90
Download Only Headers setting, 90
Encrypt Information setting, 92
Exchange Account setting, 88
General page, 88–89
Logon Network Security setting, 92
Manually Control Connection State setting, 89
Name and Password setting, 92
opening, 87
OST file location, 90–91
Remote Mail page, 93–94
Seconds Until Server Connection Timeout
    setting, 89
Security page, 91–92
Use Local Copy of Mailbox setting, 90, 91
Work Offline and Use Dial-Up Networking
    setting, 89
Microsoft Installer (MSI), 33, 50
Microsoft Office submenu (Actions menu), 136, 138
Microsoft Outlook Business Contact Manager, 422
Minimal Install option, 27
minus sign (-)
  by Calendar recurrence categories, 232
  by Journal types, 288
  by newsgroup messages, 349
MMC (Microsoft Management Console), 504
Modify Profile option (Custom Installation Wizard), 40
Month command (View menu), 62
Month view (Calendar), 230–231, 714, 715
Month View With AutoPreview command (View menu),
    231–232
Move to Folder command, 399
moving around. *See* navigating
moving items
  contacts to Business Contact Manager, 688
  Cut and Paste commands for, 399
  e-mail messages using OWA, 711
  Exchange mailbox, 538
  folder items, 397–399
  to mail folders, 153
  Move to Folder command for, 399
  setting preferences for e-mail, 106
  toolbars, 60–61, 363
MSI (Microsoft Installer), 33, 50
MSN accounts, 99
MST files. *See* transform files
MultiPage control for forms, 600–601
My Documents folder, 472–473

N

names
bold type in Folder List, 33
Contact form options, 196–198
Contacts list file format and, 197
distribution list, 165
Exchange Server e-mail account, 87, 88
finding contacts, 216
form, 582, 592, 600, 624
HTTP e-mail account, 99
IMAP e-mail account, 95
MST file, 33
MultiPage control, 600
multiple computers and profile names, 477
Personal folder, 395
POP3 e-mail account, 95
PST, 101
rules for filtering newsgroup messages, 344
signature, 141
sorting Contacts list names, 62–63
system policies, 512
titles or suffixes for contacts, 197, 198
transform files, 33
using for e-mail addresses, 118
vCard, 145
navigating
Calendar views, 228, 229, 230
Journal entries, 9, 81
Navigation Pane command (View menu), 358
Navigation Pane Options dialog box, 70, 71
Navigation Pane (Outlook Bar)
adding or removing items, 70, 71
Button Bar, 70, 365–366
Current View area, 365
customizing, 70, 71, 365–366
new features in Outlook 2003, 19, 70
overview, 59
resetting to defaults, 70
shortcuts and roaming users, 479–480
toggling on/off, 60, 70, 358, 365
using, 70–72
viewing entire folder tree, 387
viewing options for icons, 71
NDRs (Non-Delivery Receipts), 118
.NET Passport account, 243–244
NetMeeting (Microsoft), 202–204, 262–264
networks. See also sharing information
Disable Run from Network option, 36
Exchange Server e-mail account connection, 92
group policies for, 502
installing administrative share in network share, 32

mapping network drives, 476
new features in Outlook 2003, 21
property settings, 89, 92
New Alert page (WSS), 456
New Appointment command (File menu), 251
New Call dialog box, 220–221
New Contact command (File menu), 211
New Contact from Same Company command (Actions menu), 211
New Discussion Board page (WSS), 460
New Document Library page (WSS), 459–460
New E-mail Address dialog box, 548
new features in Outlook 2003. See also specific features
Cached Exchange Mode, 21
Calendar and Contact sharing and access, 22
instant messaging (IM), 22
Navigation Pane, 19
network/offline improvements, 21
quick flagging, 20
Reading Pane, 19–20
search folders, 17–18
security improvements, 21
SharePoint Team Services (STS), 21–22
Web beacon blocking, 20–21
New Field dialog box, 207–208, 612
New Instant Messaging Virtual Server Wizard, 556–557
New Item page (WSS), 461
New Mail Message command (Actions menu), 116
New Mail Message Using submenu (Actions menu)
Microsoft Office submenu, 136, 138
overriding default format, 116, 132
Plain Text command, 132
New Message form, 353–354
New News Rule dialog box, 343–344
New Object — User dialog box
adding a mailbox automatically, 534–535
creating distribution groups, 550–551
creating mail-enabled contacts, 547–548, 549
New Outlook Data File dialog box, 394, 475, 633
New Profile dialog box, 103
New Profile option (Custom Installation Wizard), 40
New submenu (File menu)
Appointment command, 251
Contact or Actions submenu, 211
Distribution List command, 165
Folder command, 72
Journal Entry command, 297
Mail Message command, 116
Meeting Request command, 251
Notes command, 303
Outlook Data File command, 394, 633

Newprof.exe, 470–471

News command (Tools menu), 343

NewsGator program (Reinacker & Associates), 739

Newsgroup Subscriptions dialog box, 339–340, 351

newsgroups

    accuracy of information from, 333

    blocking senders, 347

    cautions for using, 334, 354

    colors for message headings, 350

    defined, 333

    downloading message headers, 342

    e-mail account for, 334

    e-mail versus, 335

    filtering messages, 343–348

    following message threads, 349–350

    messages in Public Folders, 6

    moderated versus unmoderated, 334

    newbie etiquette, 352

    overview, 333–335

    posting messages, 352–354

    preparing to use, 335

    setting up, 335–338

    size of messages, 342

    subscribing, 338–340

    synchronizing messages, 351–352

    uses for, 334–335

    viewing new messages, 350–351

    viewing selected messages, 341–343

Newsreader. *See* Outlook Newsreader

.nk2 files, backing up, 521

No Response Necessary flag, 139

/nocache Setup switch, 52

/nocheckupdates Setup switch, 52

Non-Delivery Receipts (NDRs), 118

None permission for delegates, 428, 433

Nonediting Author permission for delegates, 433

/noreboot Setup switch, 52–53

Normal sensitivity setting, 140

Not Available, Hidden, Locked option (Custom Installation Wizard), 35

Not Available option, 27

Notes command (File menu), 303

Notes folder

    categories for Notes, 306–307

    copying text from Notes, 304

    creating Notes, 303–304

    default aging period, 526

    default options, 309–310

    editing Notes, 304–305

    linking Notes to contacts, 307–308

    opening, 303

    overview, 65–66, 388

    paper notes versus Outlook Notes, 301–302

    specifying colors for Notes, 305–306

    timestamp options, 310–311

    typical Note, 302

    viewing Notes by color, 66, 82, 315

    views, 65–66, 311–315

    Windows treatment of Notes, 304

Notes List command (View menu), 311

Notes List view (Notes), 311–312

Notes Options dialog box, 309–310

notifying

    permissions notification for delegates, 429, 431

    users (WSS), 446

NTLM Password Authentication, 92

Number command (Type menu), 617

O

Object Browser, 670–671

object model

    Application Object Model, 667–668, 671

    Assistant Object example, 665–666

    Component Object Model (COM), 666–667

    defined, 665

    methods versus properties, 668

OFD (Outlook 2003 Forms Designer). *See also* forms; Script Editor

    Actions page, 627–629

    activating a form page, 582–583

    adding controls with the Toolbox, 583–584

    adding fields to forms, 586–587

    adding form pages, 624

    changing tab order, 629–630

    commonly used forms, 579–580

    Contact form in, 569, 570

    hidden forms, 562, 580

    installing and deploying applications, 631–633

    manipulating forms in Design window, 581–583

    Message form in, 563–567, 580–583

    opening, 562

    overview, 562–563, 661

    Post form in, 567–568

    Properties page, 624–627

    Properties window, 585

    publishing forms, 589–590

    running forms, 589

    Script Editor, 588–589

    selecting a form, 580–581

Off command (View menu), 730

Office (Microsoft)

    Business Contact Manager integration with, 701–702

    changing the view, 60–67

    controlling applications with group policies, 49

group policies for, 507
Internet Free/Busy Service, 204, 243–246
Journal tracking for documents, 9–10
Outlook applications, 571–572
Outlook integration with other applications, 11–12, 407–410
percent of time spent in Outlook, 3
programming interface, 16
sending documents (other options), 417
sending documents to e-mail recipients, 416–418
sending e-mail messages as documents, 136–138
sending files using, 150–152
updating, 29
Office Profile Wizard. *See* Profile Wizard
office supply request form, 658–659
Office 2003 Super Bible on the CD, 738, 739
offline access, 21–22, 724
Offline Folder Settings dialog box, 732–733
offline folders, 387
offline store (OST) file, 90–91, 479, 731–733
101 Languages of the World software (Transparent Language), 133
128-bit encryption, 159
Online Meeting Participant command (File menu), 417
Open Other User's Folder dialog box, 433–434, 435, 437
Open Outlook Data File dialog box, 396, 401–402
Open submenu (File menu)
    Other User's Folder command, 433, 435, 437
    Outlook Data File command, 396, 401, 519
opening. *See also* running; viewing
    Active Directory Users and Computers snap-in, 534
    another user's folder, 433–435, 437
    built-in forms from Standard Forms Library, 569
    CD files, 738
    Design Form dialog box, 562
    Document Libraries (WSS), 453
    documents in tracking folders, 642–643
    E-mail Accounts Wizard, 86
    E-mail Options dialog box, 106
    Field Chooser window, 586, 594
    Group Policy Editor, 504
    Manage Users page (WSS), 443
    Message form, 563
    Message Options dialog box, 123
    messages in Inbox, 75
    Microsoft Exchange Server property sheet, 87
    New News Rule dialog box, 343
    Notes folder, 303
    OFD, 562
    Outlook with Outlook Today folder opened, 360
    Personal folder file, 396
    Personal folders on another computer, 401–402

    Personal folders on your computer, 396
    Rules and Alerts dialog box, 177
    Rules Wizard, 177
    Script Debugger, 671
    Script Editor, 588, 667, 669
    selecting profile when Outlook starts, 103, 466–467
    Site Administration page (WSS), 448
    Site Settings page (WSS), 443, 448
    starting a new e-mail message, 116
    System Policy Editor, 511
    Task form, 270
    Toolbox (OFD), 583, 591
OPF files, 54
Opportunity records (Business Contact Manager)
    adding business notes to record history, 694–696
    adding phone logs to record history, 696–697
    linking items to, 700–701
    tracking sales opportunities, 692–694
OPS (profile settings) file, 469
optimizing Outlook installations
    compacting your OST file, 731–733
    disabling Reading pane, 730–731
    improving performance, 723–733
    prompt for connection type, 725–727
    rules for handling e-mail messages, 727–729
    security, 733–736
    working offline, 724
option buttons for forms, 596–597
Options command. *See also* Options dialog box
    Tools menu, 141
    View menu, 123
Options dialog box
    Advanced Options button, 310
    AutoArchive button, 527
    blocking external HTML content, 174, 498–499
    Calendar Options button, 381
    Data Files button, 473
    default Outlook folder, 361
    Delegates tab, 428–429, 430, 553
    Download Pictures section, 498–499
    E-mail accounts button, 475
    E-mail Options button, 106
    Empty Deleted Items folder check box, 77
    Empty the Deleted Items folder upon exiting check box, 404–406
    encryption settings, 161
    Export Rules button, 184, 185, 522
    Get a Digital ID button, 160
    Import Rules button, 185, 523
    including vCard with signature file, 145–146
    Journal Options button, 296

Continued

Options dialog box *(continued)*
  Junk E-mail button, 186, 187
  Mail Format tab, 141, 145–146
  Mail Setup tab, 473, 475
  Note Options button, 309
  Other tab, 77, 310, 361, 404, 527
  Preferences tab, 106, 309, 381
  Security tab, 160, 161, 174, 488, 498
  settings and options that do not roam, 480–481
  Signature for New Messages list box, 143
  Signatures button, 141
Options submenu (Tools menu), 243, 244
order. *See* prioritizing
ordering Wiley products, 743
organizational unit (OU), 30–31, 42–43
Organize command (Tools menu), 369
Organize feature
  categories option, 368–369, 370
  colors option, 369, 371
  folders option, 369, 372–373
  overview, 368–369
  using, 369–374
  views option, 369, 373–374
organizing. *See also* scheduling; *specific tools*
  Calendar features for, 7–8
  Contacts list features for, 8–9
  e-mail in Personal folders, 152–153
  Journal features for, 9–10
  Tasks list features for, 10–11
Ornic USA's ExLife program, 739
OST (offline store) file, 90–91, 479, 731–733
Other Settings dialog box
  Calendar, 240
  TaskPad, 283–284
  views, 651–652
Other User's Folder command (File menu), 433, 435, 437
OU (organizational unit), 30–31, 42–43
Out of Office Assistant, 187–190
Out of Office Assistant dialog box, 188, 189–190
Outbox, 76–77, 122, 129. *See also* mail folders; sending e-mail messages
Outcmd.dat file, backing up, 521
Outlook Bar. *See* Navigation Pane (Outlook Bar)
Outlook Business Contact Manager (Microsoft), 422
Outlook Data File command (File menu)
  New submenu, 394, 633
  Open submenu, 396, 401, 519
Outlook Data Files dialog box
  backing up PST files, 516–517
  compacting Personal folders, 77
  noting PST file location, 473–474
  password-protecting PST files, 734–736

Outlook Messaging Components, 25
Outlook Newsreader
  adding toolbar button for, 336
  filtering messages, 343–348
  following message threads, 349–350
  posting to newsgroups, 352–354
  setting up, 336–338
  subscribing to newsgroups, 338–340
  viewing new messages, 351–352
  viewing selected messages, 341–343
Outlook Profile Wizard, 466
Outlook Today folder
  customizing, 67–69, 358–361, 572–577
  overview, 67–68
Outlook Today page
  building your own, 572–577
  configuring Outlook for, 573–575
  creating folder for, 573
  example on CD, 576
  information for, 576–577
  path in Internet Explorer, 573
  Registry changes for, 574–575
  source code for `display`, 574
Outlook 2003 Bible on the CD, 738–739
Outlook 2003 Forms Designer. *See* OFD
Outlook 2003 (Microsoft). *See also* configuring Outlook 2003; installing Outlook 2003; *specific features*
  client applications, 561–570
  integrating with the Web, 374–377
  integration with other Office applications, 11–12
  interface overview, 58–60
  new features, 17–22
  object model, 665–674
  Office applications, 571–572
  setting as default mail editor, 110
  starting with Outlook Today folder opened, 360
  Web applications, 572–577
Outlook.pst file, 385
OWA (Outlook Web Access)
  Calendar in, 712–715
  changing configurations, 720–721
  Contacts list in, 716–718
  e-mail in, 708–711
  logging off, 721–722
  overview, 703–704
  preparing to use, 704–705
  Public Folders and, 719–720
  reminders in, 718–719
  tasks available in, 707–708
  using (logging on), 705–707
Owner permission for delegates, 432

P

/p Setup switch, 53
PAB (Personal Address Book) files, 477–479, 520–521
package deployment method, changing, 47
package property sheet, 44–47
Page Order dialog box, 601
paperclip icon in Journal, 292
Paragraph dialog box, 143
Password dialog box, 626
passwords
    authentication methods for, 92
    for backing up and restoring certificates, 493, 494
    caching by Outlook, 95
    Exchange Server e-mail account, 92
    for forms, 626
    for IMAP e-mail accounts, 95, 99
    for OWA, 704, 706
    for Personal folders, 395
    for POP3 e-mail accounts, 95, 99
    for PSTs, 102, 734–736
Paste command (Edit menu), 399
Paste Special command (Edit menu), 408
Paste Special dialog box, 408–409
pathname for Personal folders, 394
performance improvements
    compacting your OST file, 731–733
    connection speed and, 723
    disabling Reading pane, 730–731
    latency and, 723–724
    prompt for connection type, 725–727
    rules for handling e-mail messages and, 727–729
    working offline, 724
permissions for applications, 646
permissions for delegates
    Calendar permissions, 436–437
    Delegate Permissions dialog box, 429–430, 553–554
    granting folder access, 431–433
    notifying delegates, 429, 431
    permission roles, 432–433
    send on behalf permission for distribution groups, 553–554
    types of, 427–428
Personal Address Books, 477–479, 520–521
Personal folder file, 394–396
Personal folders (PST files). *See also* mail folders
    adding to profile, 100–102
    backing up, 515–518
    compacting, 77
    compatibility with previous Outlook versions, 101
    creating, 128, 152–153, 393–397
    different versions of Outlook and, 477–479
    encryption for, 102

    exporting data, 518
    for IMAP accounts, 98, 100
    importing data, 519
    importing files from, 420
    naming, 101
    noting location of, 473–474
    opening, 396, 401–402
    organizing e-mail in, 152–153
    overview, 387
    passwords for, 102, 734–736
    pathname for, 394
    for POP3 accounts, 98, 100
    for project files, 388
    publishing forms to, 632–633
    redirecting, 473–476
    sharing, 400–402
    size of PST files, 517
    storing in My Documents folder, 472
    uses for, 393
Personal Forms Library, 589
Personal sensitivity setting, 140
personalizing. *See* customizing
Phone Calls command (View menu), 294
Phone Calls view (Journal), 294–295
phone logs, 696–697
phone numbers. *See also* Contacts list
    AutoDialer feature, 219–221
    Contact form options, 198–199
    multiple, for contacts, 199
    Speed Dial list, 221
    Wiley Product Technical Support numbers, 743
picture libraries (WSS), 453
pictures. *See* images
Plain Text command
    Actions menu, 132
    Format menu, 132
plain text format, 107, 131–133
plus sign (+)
    by Calendar recurrence categories, 232
    for Journal entry types, 9, 81
    by Journal types, 288
    by mouse pointer, 398
    by newsgroup messages, 349
policies. *See* group policies; system policies
Policy Template Options dialog box, 511–512
POP3 (Post Office Protocol 3)
    connection settings, 96
    delivery options, 98
    e-mail account configuration, 94–98
    e-mail message storage, 98
    IMAP versus, 94

Continued

POP3 (Post Office Protocol 3) *(continued)*
    incoming server settings, 97–98
    as offline protocol, 94
    outgoing server settings, 96, 97–98
    PST files for accounts, 98, 100–102
    security, 94
    sending a test message, 96
portals, 439. *See also* WSS (Windows Sharepoint
      Services)
Post form, 567–568
Post Office Protocol. *See* POP3
posting
    documents to tracking folders, 641–642
    messages to discussion folders, 638–639
    messages to newsgroups, 352–354
    messages to Public Folders (OWA), 720
Preview pane. *See* Reading (Preview) pane
.prf files
    accounts used by, 484
    creating with Custom Installation Wizard, 482–483
    importing from previous Outlook versions, 483
    modifying, 483–485
    sections of, 483
Print command (File menu), 125
Print dialog box, 125
printing
    category items, 325–327
    messages before sending, 79
    messages in Inbox, 125
    messages in Outbox, 77
    selected message text, 125
    task details, 273
prioritizing
    e-mail accounts, 105
    rules for filtering newsgroup messages, 344–345
    rules for handling messages, 181
    tasks, 271
Private check box
    Calendar, 248
    Contact form, 202
    delegating tasks and, 430
    tasks, 272
Private sensitivity setting, 140
Process Marked Headers command (Tools menu), 170
productivity. *See also* performance improvements
    Outlook advantages for, 5
    sharing information and, 6–7
profile settings file (OPS), 469
Profile Wizard, 54, 469–470, 477
profiles. *See also* e-mail account configuration
    adding manually, 467
    adding Personal folders to, 100–102
    automating with Custom Installation Wizard,
      468–470
    automating with Newprof.exe, 470–471
    backing up data and settings, 523–524
    changing the account order, 105
    copying, 104
    Corporate or Workgroup settings and, 470
    creating, 103–104
    creating using environment variables, 472
    default Outlook profiles, 466
    defined, 102
    Exchange Server name in, 88
    Exchange settings for, 481–482
    First Run step and, 477
    Internet Only settings, 470
    multiple computers and names of, 477
    multiple, Outlook handling of, 103–104
    Outlook versus other Windows profiles, 103
    overview, 102–103, 466
    removing manually, 467
    for roaming users, 466–472
    selecting when Outlook starts, 103, 466–467
    switching between, 105
    types of information stored in, 103
projects, 388, 393
prompt for connection type, 725–727
`Pro.msi` file location, 33
Properties command (File menu), 529
Properties dialog box
    AutoArchive settings for folders, 528–530
    for check boxes, 597–598
    for combo boxes, 598–599
    for controls of forms, 585
    for distribution groups, 552
    for frame buttons, 595
    for Label control, 585, 592–593
    for list boxes, 599–600
    managing folder properties, 645–647
    for option buttons, 596–597
    for OU, 43
    specifying default values for fields, 619–620
Properties dialog box for Exchange Server
    E-mail Addresses tab, 541, 542–543
    Exchange Advanced tab, 542
    Exchange Features tab, 542, 543
    Exchange General tab, 542, 544–547
Properties page for forms, 624–627
properties versus methods, 668
`property=value` Setup parameter, 53
PST files. *See* Personal folders
Public Folders
    built-in module folders, 644–645
    as business solutions, 14

collaboration using, 14
discussion folders, 637–640
overview, 6, 7, 387
OWA and, 719–720
posting documents to, 641
posting messages using OWA, 720
publishing forms to, 632
tracking folders, 640–644
viewing documents in, 642–643
Publish Form As dialog box, 590, 631–632
Publish Form command (Form menu), 631
Published option (Deploy Software dialog box), 44
publishing
    applications, 31
    forms, 589–590
Publishing Author permission for delegates, 432
Publishing Editor permission for delegates, 432
purging (emptying) Deleted Items folder, 77, 129,
    404–406

Q

/q Setup switch, 51, 53
Quick Launch icon, 479
QuickFind feature, 216

R

Read mode of forms
    defined, 622
    Message form, 564
    Post form, 568
    shared fields and, 613–614
    toggling with Compose mode, 614, 622–623
read receipt, 109, 124
reader site group (WSS), 446
reading e-mail messages
    on behalf of someone else, 435–436
    creating contacts from e-mail messages, 212–213
    marking messages as read or unread, 125
    overview, 79, 124–125
    in OWA, 708, 709
    preferences for formatting, 107
    preferences for receiving messages, 108
    printing messages, 125
    Remote Mail, 167–171
Reading Pane submenu (View menu), 730
Reading (Preview) pane
    disabling, 730–731
    new features in Outlook 2003, 19–20
    overview, 59
    toggling on/off, 60, 64
ReadMe file on CD with this book, 742, 743
Recall This Message command (Actions menu), 157

Recall This Message dialog box, 157
recalling Exchanger Server messages, 77, 122–123,
    156–157
receipt request, 109, 123, 124
record history (Business Contact Manager)
    adding business notes, 694–696
    adding phone logs, 696–697
recurring activities
    appointments, 235, 261–262
    meetings, 261–262
    tasks, 275–279
Recurring Appointments command (View menu), 235
Recurring Appointments view (Calendar), 235
redirecting
    data folders, 476–477
    GPO settings for, 476–477
    My Documents folder, 472–473
    PST files, 473–476
REGEDIT (Registry editor), 330–331, 574–575
Registry
    cautions about editing, 329
    key for machine-specific settings, 509
    key for user settings, 509
    Outlook Today page configuration, 574–575
    sharing categories using, 329–331
    subkey for profile information, 468
Registry menu, 330
Reinacker & Associates' NewsGator program, 739
reinstalling Outlook 2003, 29
Reminder Sound dialog box, 251–252, 272
reminders
    Calendar, 8, 251–252
    in OWA, 718–719
    sounds for, 251–252, 271–272
    task, 271–272
Remote Installation Services (RIS), 30, 31
Remote Item Header dialog box, 170
Remote Mail
    connecting and downloading headers, 168–169
    defined, 93
    Exchange Server e-mail account settings, 93–94
    marking items for action, 170–171
    overview, 167–168
    uses for, 168
removing or deleting. See also disabling; toggling
        on/off
    attachments while retaining messages, 403–404
    by AutoArchive, 527, 528
    canceling messages in Outbox, 76, 122
    categories, 322
    Deleted Items folder items, 77, 402–404

Continued

removing or deleting *(continued)*
    distribution group members, 552
    e-mail messages using OWA, 710
    emptying Deleted Items folder, 77, 129, 404–406
    Exchange mailbox manually, 537
    filters for newsgroup messages, 347
    items from folders, 386
    Navigation Pane items, 70, 71
    old messages from Sent Items folder
        automatically, 78
    Outlook features, 28
    page from MultiPage control, 601
    profiles manually, 467
    reconnecting a deleted mailbox, 524–525
    recovering deleted Exchange mailboxes, 537
    retention policy for deleted Exchange
        mailboxes, 541
    retention policy for deleted items, 528, 541, 547
    retention policy for deleted user accounts, 524
    senders from blocked senders list, 348
    setting preferences for e-mail, 106
    site groups (WSS), 452
    toolbar buttons, 61, 363
    undeleting e-mail messages using OWA, 710
    unnecessary rules, 729
    unsending Exchanger Server messages, 77,
        122–123, 156–157
    users having Exchange mailboxes, 536
    users (WSS), 447
Rename dialog box, 600
Rename Page command (Form menu), 582, 592
Rename Page dialog box, 582, 624
repairing Outlook 2003, 29
replying to e-mail messages
    automatic response, 183–184
    composing your reply, 126–127
    Forward button, 126
    including original message in reply, 107, 126–127
    No Response Necessary flag, 139
    in OWA, 708, 709
    POP3 or IMAP account settings, 96
    preferences, 107
    Reply to All button, 126
    Reply to Sender button, 126
    sending your reply, 127
    voting feature for, 123, 154–156
requesting meetings, 13, 256–259
Resend This Message command (Actions menu), 78
resending e-mail messages, 78
reserving resources, 224, 249. *See also* Calendar

resetting. *See also* defaults
    Master Category List, 322–323
    menus to original options, 363
    Navigation Pane to defaults, 70
    toolbars to defaults, 363
resizing. *See* size
restoring. *See also* importing
    certificates, 494
    PST file data, 519
    recovering deleted Exchange mailboxes, 537
Restricted Sites security zone, 175–176
retention policy
    for deleted Exchange mailboxes, 541
    for deleted items, 528, 541, 547
    for deleted user accounts, setting, 524
Reviewer permission for delegates, 428, 433, 436–437
rich text format (RTF), 110, 133–135
RIS (Remote Installation Services), 30, 31
roaming users
    adding a profile manually, 467
    applying group policies, 476–477
    automating profiles with Custom Installation
        Wizard, 468–470
    automating profiles with Newprof.exe, 470–471
    Corporate or Workgroup settings, 470
    creating profiles using environment variables, 472
    default Outlook profiles, 466
    defined, 465–466
    different versions of Outlook and, 477–481
    Exchange Server user issues, 481–482
    Internet Only settings, 470
    OST files and, 479
    persistent connection for, 475–476
    Personal Address Books and, 477–479
    .prf files for, 482–485
    profiles overview, 466
    redirecting My Documents folder, 472–473
    redirecting the PST file, 473–476
    removing a profile manually, 467
    selecting profile when Outlook starts, 466–467
    settings and options that do not roam, 480–481
Routing Recipient command (File menu), 417
RTF (rich text format), 110, 133–135
Rules and Alerts command (Tools menu), 177, 184,
        185, 522, 727
Rules and Alerts dialog box
    Change Rule button, 182–183
    Copy button, 183
    New Rule button, 177
    optimizing rules, 727–729
    Options button, 184, 185, 522
    Run Rules Now button, 182

rules and filters for blocking spam
    Blocked Senders list, 497–498
    blocking external HTML content (Web beacons),
        498–499
    Junk E-mail filter, 495–497
rules for applications, 647
rules for filtering newsgroup messages
    actions, 344
    applying, 346
    conditions, 344
    creating, 343–346
    disabling, 346
    effectiveness of, 343
    existing messages and, 347
    modifying, 346
    prioritizing, 345
    removing filters, 347
rules for handling e-mail messages
    automatic response to messages, 183–184
    backing up (exporting), 184–185, 522–524
    controlling processing order, 181
    copying rules, 183
    defined, 176
    filtering junk and adult content mail, 185–187
    importing, 185, 523
    modifying rules, 182–183
    optimizing, 727–729
    by Out of Office Assistant, 189–190
    overview, 75, 176
    performance and, 727–729
    Personal folders and, 397
    Rules Wizard for, 176–181, 184
    running manually, 182
    templates, 177
rules for organizing folders, 372–373
Rules Wizard
    creating rules, 176–181
    handling junk mail, 495
    responding automatically to messages, 184
    roaming users and, 479
Run all from My Computer option, 27
Run from My Computer option, 27, 35
Run Rules Now dialog box, 182
Run This Form command (Form menu), 589, 605, 671
running. See also opening
    E-mail Accounts Wizard, 86
    forms, 589, 605, 671
    Group Policy Editor from the command line, 507
    MMC, 504
    REGEDIT, 330, 574
    rules manually, 182
.rwz file extension, 522

S
Safe Senders list, 497
sales opportunities tracking, 692–694
Save As command (File menu), 399, 424
Save As dialog box, 399–400, 424
Save as Web Page command (File menu), 246
Save as Web Page dialog box, 246–247
Save command (File menu), 78
Save Exported Rules As dialog box, 184
Save My Settings Wizard, 54
saving
    Calendar as a Web page, 246–248
    exporting rules for handling messages, 184–185
    folder items as text files, 399–400
    installation snapshot, 54
    messages as drafts, 78
    Outlook messages as files, 424–425
    sent e-mail messages, 124
    setting preferences for e-mail, 107, 108
    system policy files, 512–513
Schedule Plus, 25
scheduling. See also appointments; Calendar;
        meetings; tasks
    Calendar features for, 7–8
    creating appointments, 250–255
    defined, 250
    integrating with NetMeeting, Windows Media
        Services, and Microsoft Exchange
        Conferencing, 262–264
    managing another person's Calendar, 436–438
    meetings, 6, 12–14, 256–261
    in OWA, 712–715
    reserving resources, 224, 249
    Tasks list features for, 10–11
Script Debugger
    break mode, 672–673
    opening, 671
    setting break points, 673–674
Script Debugger command (Tools menu), 671, 673
Script Editor
    creating VBScript for command buttons, 588–589,
        604–605
    debugging your code, 671–674
    event handlers, 669
    Object Browser, 670–671
    opening, 588, 667, 669
    overview, 588
    testing the command button, 605
scripts, e-mail security and, 175
search folders, 17–18
searching. See finding
Secure Password Authentication (SPA), 95, 96

security. *See also* encryption; passwords; spam
   actions to protect against viruses, 488
   adding a trusted source, 493
   attachment blocking, 489–491
   blocking external HTML content, 174, 498–499
   certificates, 159–161
   configuring security zones, 175–176
   customizing, 366–368
   digital signatures, 21, 159–163
   encryption, 21
   Exchange Server e-mail account settings, 90–91
   group policies for, 502
   IMAP versus POP3, 94
   Level 1 category files, 489–491
   Level 2 category files, 489, 491
   macro virus security, 488, 491–493
   new features in Outlook 2003, 21
   optimizing, 733–736
   setting the level for Outlook, 367–368
   virus protection, 366–368, 487–493
Security command (Tools menu), 367, 492
Security dialog box, 175–176, 367–368
Security Properties dialog box, 162, 163, 164
Select Attendees and Resources dialog box, 257–259
Select Contact dialog box (forms), 626
Select Contacts dialog box (Notes), 308
Select Group Policy dialog box, 504
Select Members dialog box, 165
Select Name dialog box
   for another user's folder, 434, 435, 437
   for Contact form, 201
Select Names dialog box (e-mail), 119–120, 167, 215
Select Task Recipient dialog box, 273
Send To submenu (File menu)
   Exchange Folder command, 417, 571
   Mail Recipient command, 151, 416, 417
   options available, 417
   overview, 151
Send Web Page by E-mail command (Actions menu), 375
sending e-mail messages. *See also* attachments to
       e-mail; forwarding e-mail messages; replying
       to e-mail messages
   automatic response, 183–184
   on behalf of someone else, 435–436, 545, 553–554
   copies to multiple recipients, 116
   digitally signed messages, 161–163
   Do not deliver before option, 124
   encrypting messages, 163–164
   Expires after option, 124
   flagging messages, 139
   having replies sent to someone else, 124
   in HTML format, 135–136, 137

   immediately after creating, 122–123
   linking messages to categories, 124
   as Office documents, 136–138
   from other applications, 415–418
   Out of Office Assistant for, 187–190
   overview, 79
   permissions notification for delegates, 429, 431
   as plain text, 131–133
   preferences, 108
   recalling Exchanger Server messages, 77, 122–123,
      156–157
   receipt request, 109, 123–124
   resending, 78
   in RTF format, 133–135
   saving sent messages, 124
   setting message importance and sensitivity,
      139–140
   setting options for, 123–124
   test message for POP3 account, 96
   using distribution lists, 164–167
   vCards with, 145–146
   for voting, 155
   Web pages with, 375, 376
   WSS user notification, 445, 446
sending Office documents to e-mail recipients, 416–418
Send/Receive submenu (Tools menu)
   Free/Busy Information command, 245
   selecting account, 60
   Work with Headers submenu
      Download Headers command, 169
      Process Marked Headers command, 170
sensitivity of e-mail messages, setting, 139–140
Sent Items folder. *See also* mail folders
   default aging period, 526
   deleting old messages automatically, 78
   described, 129
   resending messages, 78
   saving sent messages in, 124
   using, 78
services, group policies for, 502
/settings Setup switch, 51, 53
Setup INI Customization Wizard, 49–50
Setup switches, 50–53
Setup Wizard
   Add or Remove Features option, 28
   Choose advanced customization... option, 27
   Complete Install option, 27
   Custom Install option, 27
   End-User License Agreement (EULA), 26
   Installed on first use option, 27
   Installed on First Use option, 27
   Minimal Install option, 27

Not Available option, 27
Reinstall or Repair option, 29
Run all from My Computer option, 27
Run from My Computer option, 27
running, 24–25
Uninstall option, 29
shared fields of forms, 613–615
SharePoint Central Administration page (WSS), 445
SharePoint Portal Server, 439
SharePoint Team Services (STS), 21–22. *See also* WSS
(Windows Sharepoint Services)
SHAREPT directory, 442
shareware programs, 739. *See also* CD with this book
sharing information. *See also* collaboration;
newsgroups
calendars, 225, 243–246
categories, 327–331
folders, 386, 400–402
Journal, 299
between laptop and desktop systems, 393
non-Outlook users and, 6
overview, 6–7
preventing sharing for contact records, 202
preventing sharing for tasks, 272
vCards for, 8
Show Fields dialog box
Calendar, 238
customizing folders, 390–392
manipulating field headings in views, 649–650
TaskPad, 280, 281
showing. *See* toggling on/off; viewing
signatures, digital. *See* digital signatures
signatures (e-mail). *See also* digital signatures
automatically appended to messages, 143–144
backing up from Exchange Server, 521–522
backing up from Word, 521
company disclaimers and, 144
creating an auto signature, 140–144
creating in Word, 143
defined, 140
editing in messages, 144
length recommendations, 144
new features in Outlook 2003, 21
separate signature for each account, 21
specifying, 110
vCard with, 145–146
Site Administration page (WSS), 448
site groups (WSS), 446–448, 451–452
Site Settings page (WSS)
configuring anonymous access, 449–450
opening, 443, 448
opening Manage Users page from, 443
site group configuration, 450–452

size
checking size of attachments, 149
Exchange mailbox limits, 539, 540–541, 546
Exchange mailbox message delivery options, 539
icons for Notes, 311
keeping e-mail messages short, 115
limits for attachments, 148–149
of newsgroup messages, 342
of PST files, 517
resizing Button Bar (Navigation Pane), 71
signature length, 144
sizing. *See* resizing
slash (/) in Setup switches, 50–53
Small Icons view (Notes), 311
SMS (System Management Server), 30
Software Installation Properties property sheet, 47–48
software on the CD with this book
highlights of software included, 739–740
installing, 738
list of, 740–742
system requirements, 737–738
troubleshooting, 742–743
types of, 739
software policies, 43–44
Sort By dialog box, 282–283
Sort dialog box, 239, 651
sorting
Calendar fields, 239
Contact form Activities tab, 204
Contacts list names, 62–63
Inbox messages, 76, 80
tasks, 267
tasks in Outlook Today, 360
views, 650–651
sounds for reminders, 251–252, 271–272
Source command (View menu), 573
SPA (Secure Password Authentication), 95, 96
spaces in e-mail addresses, 117
spam
blocking external HTML content, 174, 498–499
defined, 173
filtering junk and adult content mail, 185–187
Junk E-mail components, 25
performance and rules for, 729
prevalence of, 494
protecting against, 373
rules and filters for, 495–499
Safe Senders list, 497
sharing e-mail address in newsgroups and, 334
unsubscribe requests and, 173
Web beacon blocking for reducing, 20–21, 498–499
spammers, 173
speed. *See* performance improvements

Speed Dial list, 221

spin buttons for forms, 603–604

Standard Forms Library, 563, 569

starting. *See* opening; running

stationery, 24, 110, 147–148

Status Bar command (View menu), 359

status line, 59

Storage Limits dialog box, 546–547

STS (SharePoint Team Services), 21–22. *See also* WSS (Windows Sharepoint Services)

styles for Outlook Today, 69, 360

subject text box (e-mail), 120–121, 183

subscribing to newsgroups, 338–340

surveys (WSS), 453

switching between profiles, 105

synchronization
    newsgroup messages, 351–352
    OST file and, 90
    status line information, 59

System Management Server (SMS), 30

system policies
    adding administrative templates for, 510–512
    deploying, 512–513
    group membership changes and, 510
    group policies versus, 509–510
    naming, 512
    need for, 508–509
    overview, 501, 509–510
    saving, 512–513
    users' ability to bypass or change, 510

System Policy Editor, 509, 511–512

system requirements for CD with this book, 737–738

T

/t Setup switch, 51

Table Style for printing category items, 326–327

TabStrip control for forms, 602

tallying votes, 156, 157

Task form
    assigning tasks to people, 273–275
    Details tab, 272–273
    opening, 270
    setting task options, 270–273
    Task tab, 270–272

Task Recurrence dialog box
    daily recurrence pattern options, 276
    monthly recurrence pattern options, 276–278
    opening, 275
    weekly recurrence pattern options, 276, 277
    yearly recurrence pattern options, 278, 279

Task Request form, 569

TaskPad
    changing properties for, 378–380
    customizing look of, 280–284
    described, 267, 279
    displaying, 279
    marking tasks as completed, 279
    toggling on/off, 377–378
    turning off in Calendar, 230

TaskPad command (View menu), 267, 269, 378

tasks. *See also* delegating tasks; lists (WSS)
    adding macros for repetitive tasks, 382–383
    assigning to people, 273–275
    Autodate feature, 268
    categories, 272
    creating, 80, 268–269
    details information, 272–273
    difficulties scheduling, 265–266
    due date, 66, 266, 270
    editing, 273
    linking to contacts, 272
    marking as completed, 269, 279
    notes for, 272
    open-ended, 266
    in Outlook Today, 69, 360
    overview, 265–267
    printing details of open task, 273
    prioritizing, 271
    Private check box, 272
    recurring, 275–279
    reminders, 271–272
    setting options for, 270–273
    sorting, 267
    status information, 271
    uses for recurring tasks, 278
    WSS lists, 457

Tasks folder. *See also* tasks; Tasks list
    default aging period, 526
    overview, 66, 388
    permissions for delegates, 427–428, 432–433
    Tasks list in, 10
    views, 66–67

Tasks list. *See also* tasks
    creating tasks, 80, 268–269
    marking tasks as completed, 269
    open-ended tasks in, 266
    Outlook Today folder link to, 67
    overview, 10–11
    preventing sharing, 272
    TaskPad view, 267, 279–284
    views and, 267

teams. *See* sharing information

templates, 4–5, 25, 177
testing
    command buttons for forms, 605
    forms, 630
    package during deployment, 48
testing the package, 48
text boxes for forms, 594–595, 603–604
text files, saving, 399–400, 424–425
time. *See also* Calendar; date
    changing for appointments, 252
    changing for meetings, 260
    Note timestamp options, 310–311
    setting for appointments, 251
    setting for meetings, 257
    timeline in Journal views, 288, 289, 290
    timing Journal entries, 298
time zones, e-mail and change in, 4
title bar, 58
To text box (e-mail), 116, 167, 201
toggle buttons for forms, 606
toggling on/off. *See also* disabling; enabling; viewing
    AutoArchive for a folder, 528–529
    Navigation Pane, 60, 70, 358, 365
    Reading (Preview) pane, 60, 64
    small calendar and TaskPad (Calendar), 230
    status bar display, 359
    TaskPad, 377–378
toolbars
    adding or removing buttons, 61, 363
    backing up settings, 521
    creating a custom toolbar, 364–365
    customizing, 61, 336, 363–365
    floating, 60
    moving, 60–61, 363
    Outlook Newsreader button, 336
    overview, 59, 60
    Remote Mail, 169
    resetting to defaults, 363
    roaming users and, 480
    viewing, 59, 60, 358
    Web toolbar, 374
Toolbars submenu (View menu)
    Customize command, 61, 336, 358, 364
    displaying toolbars, 59, 60, 358, 363
    Web command, 374
Toolbox (OFD)
    adding controls with, 583–584
    CheckBox button, 597
    ComboBox button, 598
    CommandButton button, 604
    Image button, 602–603
    Label button, 584, 592

    ListBox button, 599
    MultiPage button, 600
    opening, 583, 591
    OptionButton button, 596
    SpinButton button, 604
    TabStrip button, 602
    ToggleButton icon, 606
Tools menu. *See also* Options dialog box
    Customize command, 60, 362
    E-mail Accounts command, 86, 154, 519, 725, 731
    Empty "Deleted Items" Folder command, 404
    Find submenu, 217
    Forms submenu
        Design a Form command, 562, 580
        Design This Form command, 563, 591
        Script Debugger command, 671, 673
    Macro submenu
        Macros command, 382
        Security command, 367, 492
    Mail Merge command, 411
    Message Rules submenu
        Blocked Senders List command, 348
        News command, 343
    Options command, 77
    Options submenu, 243, 244
    Organize command, 369
    Rules and Alerts command, 177, 184, 185, 522, 727
    Send/Receive submenu
        Free/Busy Information command, 245
        selecting account, 60
        Work with Headers submenu, 169, 170
tracking. *See also* Journal; tasks
    documents using tracking folders, 641–644
    information using tracking folders, 640–641
    receipt request for e-mail, 109, 123–124
    sales opportunities, 692–694
    tallying votes, 156, 157
tracking folders
    overview, 640
    tracking documents, 641–644
    tracking information, 640–641
Tracking Options dialog box, 109
transform files. *See also* Custom Installation Wizard
    creating manually, 32
    creating with Custom Installation Wizard, 32–42
    described, 32
    naming, 33
    profile information stored in, 468
translation software for foreign languages, 132
Transparent Language
    Easy Translator software, 132
    101 Languages of the World software, 133

trial versions of software, 739. *See also* CD with this book
troubleshooting software on the CD, 742–743
Trusted Sites security zone, 175–176
trusted sources, adding, 493
turning on/off. *See* toggling on/off
Type menu
    Combination command, 615
    Number command, 617
Typical Install option, 24–25

U

unattended installation. *See* automated and unattended setup
undeleting e-mail messages using OWA, 710
uninstalling Outlook 2003, 29
universal distribution groups (Exchange), 551
unsending Exchanger Server messages, 77, 122–123, 156–157
updating Office, 29
Upload Document page (WSS), 460
URLs
    entering in Contact form, 201
    for Hotmail accounts, 99
    for MSN accounts, 99
    for OWA, 704, 705
Use existing profile option (Custom Installation Wizard), 39
users, roaming. *See* roaming users
users (WSS)
    adding, 444, 446–447
    configuring anonymous access, 449–450
    notifying, 445, 446
    removing, 447
    selecting site groups for, 446
    site groups available, 446
UUENCODE format for attachments, 110

V

VBScript
    for command buttons, 588–589, 604–605
    overview, 588
    for TabStrip control, 602
    for toggle buttons, 606
vCards
    attaching to messages, 145–146
    creating from Contact records, 145
    described, 8
    importing contacts from, 209
    including with signatures, 146
    overview, 144–145

View Code command (Form menu), 588, 667, 669
View in Internet Zone command (View menu), 499
View menu. *See also* Current View submenu
    Arrange By submenu
        customizing Calendar view, 74, 237
        customizing Contacts list view, 63
        customizing folders, 392
        customizing Last Seven Days Journal view, 293
        customizing versus defining views, 648–649
        defining Calendar views, 237
        mail folder options, 64
        selecting Calendar views, 226, 231–232, 233, 235, 236
        selecting Journal views, 288, 289, 290, 292, 293, 294
        selecting Notes views, 311, 313, 314, 315
        selecting Tasks list views, 267
    AutoPreview command, 730
    Bcc Field command, 117
    Day command, 62, 227
    Layout command, 341
    Month command, 62
    Navigation Pane command, 358
    Options command, 123
    Reading Pane submenu, 730
    Source command, 573
    Status Bar command, 359
    TaskPad command, 267, 269, 378
    Toolbars submenu
        Customize command, 61, 336, 358, 364
        displaying toolbars, 59, 60, 358, 363
        Web command, 374
    View in Internet Zone command, 499
    Week command, 62
    Work Week command, 62
View Summary dialog box, 238, 649, 650
...View With Autopreview commands (View menu), 231–232
viewing. *See also* opening; toggling on/off
    address maps, 218–219
    all commands on menus, 60, 362
    another user's folder, 433–435
    attendee availability for meetings, 259–260
    Bcc text box, 117
    browsing folders, 60
    Business Contact Manager accounts, 684–685
    changing the view, 60–67
    contact cards, 74
    contact records for e-mail addresses, 119
    discussion boards (WSS), 456–457
    discussion folder messages, 639–640

documents (WSS), 453–454
flags by color, 20
Journal entry details, 81
lists (WSS), 457–458
Navigation Pane icon options, 71
newsgroup messages, 341–343, 350–351
Notes by color, 66, 82, 315
TaskPad, 279
toolbars, 59, 60, 358
Web toolbar, 374
WSS site data, 452–458
views. *See also* Calendar
    application folders and, 647–652
    Contacts list, 62–63, 195–196
    customizing versus defining, 648–649
    filtering, 650–651
    for folders, 60
    grouping information, 650
    Journal, 65, 288–295
    mail folder, 64
    manipulating field headings, 649–650
    Notes folder, 65–66, 311–315
    Organize feature, 369, 373–374
    Other Settings dialog box, 651–652
    sorting, 650–651
    Tasks folder, 66–67
    Tasks list, 267
virtual server for IM, 555–557
viruses. *See also* security
    actions to protect against, 488
    adding a trusted source, 493
    attachment blocking, 489–491
    dangers of, 487
    macro virus security, 488, 491–493
    Outlook targeted due to popularity, 488
    overview, 366–367
    protecting against, 367–368
Visual Basic Editor (Microsoft), 15, 382, 383
Visual Basic Scripting Support, 25
Visual Studio .NET (Microsoft), 16–17
voting feature, 123, 154–157

W

Watch Conversation command (Message menu), 350
Web applications, 572–577
Web beacons, blocking, 20–21, 498–499
Web command (View menu), 374
Web designer site group (WSS), 446
Web pages. *See also* Internet resources; URLs
    assigning home page for folder, 375–377
    displaying Web toolbar, 374

    integrating Outlook with the Web, 374–377
    saving Calendar as, 246–248
    sending with e-mail messages, 375, 376
Web toolbar, 374
Web-based e-mail. *See* OWA (Outlook Web Access)
Week command (View menu), 62
Week view (Calendar), 229–230, 714, 715
Week View With AutoPreview command (View menu),
    231–232
Wiley Product Technical Support, 743
Window Layout Properties dialog box, 341
Windows Components Wizard, 441–442
Windows Explorer folders versus Outlook folders,
    69–70, 127–128
Windows Media Services, 262–264
Windows 98 (Microsoft)
    group policies and, 508–509
    system policies for, 501, 508–513
Windows Server 2000 Bible, 547
Windows Server 2003 Bible, 547
Winter style (Outlook Today), 360
Word (Microsoft)
    associating templates with forms, 625
    creating signatures in, 143
    integration with Outlook, 11–12
    mail merge using Contacts list, 410–415
    setting as default mail editor, 110
Work Offline command (File menu), 724
Work Week command (View menu), 62
Work Week view (Calendar), 228–229
Work with Headers submenu (Tools menu)
    Download Headers command, 169
    Process Marked Headers command, 170
workflow applications, 658–659
workgroups. *See* sharing information
WSS (Windows Sharepoint Services), 460–461
    adding a user, 444, 446–447
    adding documents, 459–460
    adding site groups, 451–452
    adding to discussions, 460
    adding to lists, 460–461
    administrator role for, 443, 448
    advanced site group configuration, 450–452
    advanced user and site group management,
        448–452
    changing site group membership, 447–448
    configuring anonymous access, 449–450
    editing documents, 455
    filtering documents, 455
    installing prerequisites, 441–442

Continued

WSS (Windows Sharepoint Services) *(continued)*
    installing WSS, 442–443
    locating the installation files, 442
    mail settings, 445
    managing users and site groups, 443
    overview, 439–440
    removing site groups, 452
    removing users, 447–448
    setting alerts for documents, 456
    setting up a site, 440–452
    viewing data (overview), 452–453
    viewing discussion boards, 456–457
    viewing documents, 453–454
    viewing lists, 457–458

X

/x Setup switch, 53

Wiley Publishing, Inc.
End-User License Agreement

READ THIS. You should carefully read these terms and conditions before opening the software packet(s) included with this book "Book". This is a license agreement "Agreement" between you and Wiley Publishing, Inc. "WPI". By opening the accompanying software packet(s), you acknowledge that you have read and accept the following terms and conditions. If you do not agree and do not want to be bound by such terms and conditions, promptly return the Book and the unopened software packet(s) to the place you obtained them for a full refund.

1. **License Grant.** WPI grants to you (either an individual or entity) a nonexclusive license to use one copy of the enclosed software program(s) (collectively, the "Software," solely for your own personal or business purposes on a single computer (whether a standard computer or a workstation component of a multi-user network). The Software is in use on a computer when it is loaded into temporary memory (RAM) or installed into permanent memory (hard disk, CD-ROM, or other storage device). WPI reserves all rights not expressly granted herein.

2. **Ownership.** WPI is the owner of all right, title, and interest, including copyright, in and to the compilation of the Software recorded on the disk(s) or CD-ROM "Software Media". Copyright to the individual programs recorded on the Software Media is owned by the author or other authorized copyright owner of each program. Ownership of the Software and all proprietary rights relating thereto remain with WPI and its licensers.

3. **Restrictions On Use and Transfer.**

   (a) You may only (i) make one copy of the Software for backup or archival purposes, or (ii) transfer the Software to a single hard disk, provided that you keep the original for backup or archival purposes. You may not (i) rent or lease the Software, (ii) copy or reproduce the Software through a LAN or other network system or through any computer subscriber system or bulletin-board system, or (iii) modify, adapt, or create derivative works based on the Software.

   (b) You may not reverse engineer, decompile, or disassemble the Software. You may transfer the Software and user documentation on a permanent basis, provided that the transferee agrees to accept the terms and conditions of this Agreement and you retain no copies. If the Software is an update or has been updated, any transfer must include the most recent update and all prior versions.

4. **Restrictions on Use of Individual Programs.** You must follow the individual requirements and restrictions detailed for each individual program in the About the CD-ROM appendix of this Book. These limitations are also contained in the individual license agreements recorded on the Software Media. These limitations may include a requirement that after using the program for a specified period of time, the user must pay a registration fee or discontinue use. By opening the Software packet(s), you will be agreeing to abide by the licenses and restrictions for these individual programs that are detailed in the About the CD-ROM appendix and on the Software Media. None of the material on this Software Media or listed in this Book may ever be redistributed, in original or modified form, for commercial purposes.

5. Limited Warranty.

(a) WPI warrants that the Software and Software Media are free from defects in materials and workmanship under normal use for a period of sixty (60) days from the date of purchase of this Book. If WPI receives notification within the warranty period of defects in materials or workmanship, WPI will replace the defective Software Media.

(b) WPI AND THE AUTHOR OF THE BOOK DISCLAIM ALL OTHER WARRANTIES, EXPRESS OR IMPLIED, INCLUDING WITHOUT LIMITATION IMPLIED WARRANTIES OF MERCHANTABILITY AND FITNESS FOR A PARTICULAR PURPOSE, WITH RESPECT TO THE SOFTWARE, THE PROGRAMS, THE SOURCE CODE CONTAINED THEREIN, AND/OR THE TECHNIQUES DESCRIBED IN THIS BOOK. WPI DOES NOT WARRANT THAT THE FUNCTIONS CONTAINED IN THE SOFTWARE WILL MEET YOUR REQUIREMENTS OR THAT THE OPERATION OF THE SOFTWARE WILL BE ERROR FREE.

(c) This limited warranty gives you specific legal rights, and you may have other rights that vary from jurisdiction to jurisdiction.

6. Remedies.

(a) WPI's entire liability and your exclusive remedy for defects in materials and workmanship shall be limited to replacement of the Software Media, which may be returned to WPI with a copy of your receipt at the following address: Software Media Fulfillment Department, Attn.: OUTLOOK(r) 2003 BIBLE, Wiley Publishing, Inc., 10475 Crosspoint Blvd., Indianapolis, IN 46256, or call 1-800-762-2974. Please allow four to six weeks for delivery. This Limited Warranty is void if failure of the Software Media has resulted from accident, abuse, or misapplication. Any replacement Software Media will be warranted for the remainder of the original warranty period or thirty (30) days, whichever is longer.

(b) In no event shall WPI or the author be liable for any damages whatsoever (including without limitation damages for loss of business profits, business interruption, loss of business information, or any other pecuniary loss) arising from the use of or inability to use the Book or the Software, even if WPI has been advised of the possibility of such damages.

(c) Because some jurisdictions do not allow the exclusion or limitation of liability for consequential or incidental damages, the above limitation or exclusion may not apply to you.

7. U.S. Government Restricted Rights. Use, duplication, or disclosure of the Software for or on behalf of the United States of America, its agencies and/or instrumentalities "U.S. Government" is subject to restrictions as stated in paragraph (c)(1)(ii) of the Rights in Technical Data and Computer Software clause of DFARS 252.227-7013, or subparagraphs (c) (1) and (2) of the Commercial Computer Software - Restricted Rights clause at FAR 52.227-19, and in similar clauses in the NASA FAR supplement, as applicable.

8. General. This Agreement constitutes the entire understanding of the parties and revokes and supersedes all prior agreements, oral or written, between them and may not be modified or amended except in a writing signed by both parties hereto that specifically refers to this Agreement. This Agreement shall take precedence over any other documents that may be in conflict herewith. If any one or more provisions contained in this Agreement are held by any court or tribunal to be invalid, illegal, or otherwise unenforceable, each and every other provision shall remain in full force and effect.